£12·00

FURNITURE IN ENGLAND, FRANCE AND THE NETHERLANDS
FROM THE TWELFTH TO THE FIFTEENTH CENTURY

Furniture in England, France and the Netherlands from the Twelfth to the Fifteenth Century

by
Penelope Eames

The CINOA Award
1977

The Furniture History Society
London 1977

PUBLISHED IN 1977

ISBN 0903335 02 6

*Text set throughout in Monotype
Garamond, series 156*

Printed on Mellotex high white matt

PRINTED IN ENGLAND BY W. S. MANEY AND SON LTD HUDSON ROAD LEEDS LS9 7DL

EDITORIAL NOTE

THE NEED for a major study of medieval furniture which combines the evidence of documentary sources with a knowledge of technical advances in the woodworking trades and an art-historian's vision has long been felt. Few scholars possess both the academic qualifications and versatility of mind to research this formidable subject, but by uniting these approaches and concentrating on securely provenanced furniture, often associated with archives which establish its date and original function, Dr Penelope Eames makes a positive break with antiquarian traditions of the past and has written a modern classic. Of particular interest is the perceptive manner in which the author illuminates the influence of medieval social concepts on furniture design; by underlining the vital importance of courtly conventions Dr Eames sets surviving masterpieces of medieval furniture in a convincing perspective. Her monograph will inspire not only students of furniture but social historians, art historians and all medievalists, in short everyone endowed with cultural curiosity.

Such an ambitious publication could not have been contemplated without generous financial support from well-wishers; the Furniture History Society is overwhelmingly grateful to all who helped to make up the sizeable shortfall. The largest contribution came through Dr Eames from the Confédération Internationale des Negociants en Œuvres d'Art (CINOA) who unanimously voted her their annual award of 5,000 dollars; we are thus deeply indebted to this organization and congratulate Dr Eames on winning the prize. The Paul Mellon Centre for Studies in British Art (London) Limited granted a substantial sum, Liverpool University provided £500, the Baring Foundation also gave welcome support and several personal members came forward with offers of assistance. The financing of this impressive volume, a milestone in the Society's history, is therefore very much the result of collaborative effort and we are profoundly grateful to our benefactors. The monograph has been published simultaneously as the Furniture History Society Journal, Vol. XIII (1977). Dr Eames has most generously agreed to waive any claim to royalties on the sale of the first edition, so in addition to benefiting the Furniture History Society in a variety of subtle ways the profit from this venture will help to finance future publications.

CHRISTOPHER GILBERT

In accordance with the terms of the CINOA prize awarded to Dr Penelope Eames the Furniture History Society is glad to acknowledge the generosity of affiliated associations. The member-countries are listed in alphabetical sequence.

Art and Antique Dealers League of America
Associazione Antiquari d'Italia
British Antique Dealers Association
Bundesgremium des Handels mit Bildern, Antiquitäten und Gegenstanden
Bundesverband der Deutschen Kunst und Antiquitätenhandel
Chambre des Antiquaires de Belgique
Chambre Syndicale de l'Estampe
Dansk Kunst- och Antikvitetshandler Union
Federazione Italiana Mercanti d'Arte
Irish Antique Dealers Association
National Antique Dealers and Art Dealers Association of America
New Zealand Antique Dealers Association
Society of London Art Dealers
South African Antique Dealers Association
Sveriges Kunst- och Antikhandlarförening
Syndicat des Antiquaires et Commerçants d'Art Suisses
Syndicat National des Antiquaires
Vereeniging van Handelaren in Oude kunst in Nederland

PHOTOGRAPHIC ACKNOWLEDGEMENTS

Grateful thanks are due to the owners and custodians of furniture illustrated in this monograph for access to and permission to photograph the items. Most of the photographs were taken by the author, but the following have kindly supplied prints and given permission to reproduce them. Plates 7, 27, Royal Commission on Historical Monuments (England) Crown Copyright; 12, 13A, Arch. Phot. Paris/S. P.A.D.E.M.; 17, 49, Museum van de Bijloke, Ghent; 23, 24, 25, the Dean and Canons of Windsor; 28, 29, 69, Musée des Arts Décoratifs; 34, Musées Royaux d'Art et d'Histoire, Bruxelles; 35, the Museum of London; 38, British Crown Copyright, reproduced with permission of the Controller of Her Britannic Majesty's Stationery Office; 41, Merton College, Oxford; 63, The Metropolitan Museum of Art, Cloisters Collection.

CONTENTS

		PAGE
EDITORIAL NOTE	.. ..	v–vi
LIST OF PLATES	.. ..	x
FOREWORD	.. ..	xi–xii
PREFACE	.. ..	xiii–xiv
INTRODUCTION	.. ..	xv–xxiv
PART 1	.. ..	1–227

SECTION A.   ARMOIRES, BUFFETS AND DRESSOIRS   1–72

TYPE 1   The Locker.   (i) Stone recess with wooden doors   12–17
    Catalogue Raisonné
      Cat. 1.   Pair of lockers at Obazine, N. transept   12–13
      Cat. 2.   Locker at Obazine, W. end   13–14
      Cat. 3–7.   Lockers in the Zouche chapel, York Minster   15–17

    The Locker.   (ii) Locker inserted into original structure.   17–21
      Cat. 8.   St Albans 'Watching Loft'   17–20
      Cat. 9.   Locker in the Exchequer, Vicars Choral, Wells Cathedral ..   20–1

TYPE 2   (a) Freestanding. Single, double or multi-bayed   21–35
    Catalogue Raisonné
      Cat. 10.   Armoire at Obazine..   21–5
      Cat. 11.   Armoire at Bayeux Cathedral   25–7
      Cat. 12.   Armoire at Winchester College, in the Exchequer   27–8
      Cat. 13.   Armoire in the Busleydon Museum, Malines   29–30
      Cat. 14.   Armoire in Westminster Abbey, Muniment Room   30–3
      Cat. 15.   Armoire from the Town Hall, Ghent; Bijloke Museum   33–4
      Cat. 16.   Armoire at Obazine, vestry of the church of St Etienne ..   35

TYPE 2   (b) Freestanding, with enclosed drawers in place of shelves   35–7
    Catalogue Raisonné
      Cat. 17.   Armoire of the Spanish merchants of Bruges   35–7

    (c) Freestanding, multi-drawer without doors   37–44
    Catalogue Raisonné
      Cat. 18.   Armoire of the Vicars Choral, Wells, in the Muniment Room ..   40–1
      Cat. 19.   Armoire of St George's Chapel, Windsor, in the Aerary ..   41–3
      Cat. 20, 21.   Armoires at Winchester College   43–4

ARMOIRES OF UNCERTAIN TYPE   44–54
    Catalogue Raisonné
      Cat. 22.   Armoire in Chester Cathedral   44–6
      Cat. 23.   Armoire traditionally from St Quentin, Somme; Museé des Arts
         Decoratifs, Paris   46–9

Armoires for Hanging Clothes, both Ecclesiastical and Secular   49–52
Catalogue Raisonné
Cat. 24.   Armoire at Aylesbury, Buckinghamshire   50–2
Cat. 25.   Armoire at King's College, Cambridge   52–4

THE BUFFET AND DRESSOIR   55–72
   Buffets   56–62
   Dressoirs   62–5
Catalogue Raisonné
Cat. 26.   Buffet connected with the household of Marguerite of York   ..   65–70
Cat. 27.   Buffet at Plougrescant, Côtes-du-Nord   70–2

SECTION B.   BEDS AND CRADLES   73–107
   Beds   73–93
   Cradles   93–101
Catalogue Raisonné
Cat. 28.   Cradle of 1478/9, made for the birth of Philip the Fair or Margaret
           of Austria; Musées Royaux d'Art et d'Histoire, Brussels, no. 360   101–4
Cat. 29.   Cradle from Newland, Gloucestershire. Known as the Cradle of
           Henry V; H.M. The Queen, on loan to the London Museum   104–7

SECTION C.   CHESTS   108–80
Footed chests   138–62
   Slab-ended chests   138
   Ark chests   138–40
   Hutches (1) and (2)   140–59
Catalogue Raisonné

Cat. 30.   Chest at Climping, Sussex   143–5
Cat. 31.   Chest at York Minster, in the Chapter House   145–8
Cat. 32.   Chest at Westminster Abbey, Chapel of the Pyx   149–50
Cat. 33.   Chest in the Musée des Arts Decoratifs, no. 982   151–2
Cat. 34.   Chest in the Musée Municipal de la ville de Paris (Carnavalet) ..   153–4
Cat. 35.   Chest at Merton College, Oxford   155
Cat. 36.   Chest at Cound, Shropshire   156
Cat. 37.   Chest at Malpas, Cheshire   157–8
Cat. 38.   Chest at Neenton, Shropshire   158–9
Panelled chests   160–2
Catalogue Raisonné

Cat. 39.   Chest at Brasenose College, Oxford   160–2

Unfooted chests   162–80
   Dug-out chests   162
   Box chests   162–72
Catalogue Raisonné

Cat. 40.   Chest at Winchester College, Muniment Room   165–7
Cat. 41.   Chest at Bruges, Gruuthuse museum, no. 597   167–9
Cat. 42 and 43.   Chests at All Souls College, Oxford   169–70
Cat. 44.   Chest at Ghent, Bijloke museum   170–2
Standard chests   172–7

Catalogue Raisonné

Cat. 45.   Chest in Hereford Cathedral, Vicars Choral Library   174–5
Cat. 46.   Chest at Bruges, Gruuthuse museum, no. 558   175–7
Cat. 47.   Chest in Westminster Abbey Library   177
Plinth chests   178–80

Catalogue Raisonné

Cat. 48.   Chest in Romsey Abbey, Hants   178–80

SECTION D.   SEATING   181–214
Seats of authority   181–202
X-seats   182–7
Post and boarded forms   191
Post seats of authority   192–4
Boarded seats of authority   194–7
Chamber seating   198–202
Benches, forms and stools   202–14

Catalogue Raisonné

Cat. 49.   Turned chair at Hereford Cathedral   210–11
Cat. 50.   Chair, boarded type, at Stanford Bishop, Herefordshire   ..   211–13
Cat. 51.   Bench, boarded type, *in situ*, Muchelney Abbey, Somerset   ..   213–14

SECTION E.   TABLES   215–27

PART 2.   STYLE AND TECHNIQUE   228–34

PART 3.   CONCLUSION   235–44

APPENDIX I.   The Obazine armoires (Cat. 1, 2, 10) in the context of the history of the Abbey Church of St Etienne   245–7

APPENDIX II.   The 'Zouche' chapel at York Minster   247–9

APPENDIX III.   Dating evidence concerning the screen and armoire (Cat. 14) in the Muniment Room, Westminster Abbey   249–50

APPENDIX IV.   The suite of adminstrative offices of the Vicars Choral, Wells Cathedral   250–1

APPENDIX V.   *Bonnor's Perspective Itinerary*, London, 1798   251–2

APPENDIX VI.   Part of an account by Georges Chastellain of a feast of the knights of the Order of the Golden Fleece held at The Hague on 2nd May 1456   ..   253

APPENDIX VII (a).   Part of the account by Olivier de la Marche of a feast celebrating the marriage of Charles the Bold and Marguerite of York in 1468 ..   253–5

APPENDIX VII (b).   Extract of an account of a feast at Bruges in July 1468, in celebration of the marriage of Charles the Bold and Marguerite of York   ..   255–6

APPENDIX VIII (a).   Introduction to Alienor de Poitiers's treatise, *Les Honneurs de la Cour*   256–7
          (b).   Extract from Alienor de Poictiers, *Les Honneurs de la Cour*   ..   257–68
          (c).   Free translation and rearrangement of part of Alienor de Poitiers's treatise   268–73

APPENDIX IX.   Panelled Construction   274–6

BIBLIOGRAPHY   277–85

INDEX   287–303

LIST OF PLATES

Plates of items not included in the Catalogue Raisonné

59   Detail of ironwork, Portal of St Anne, Nôtre Dame, Paris.

60A   Reconstruction of a fifteenth-century wardrobe by Viollet-le-Duc. (From E. E. Viollet-le-Duc, *Dictionnaire Raisonné du Mobilier Francais*, 1, Paris, 1858, pl. XVI.)

60B   Narrow buffets. From Henry Shaw, *Specimens of Ancient Furniture*, London, 1866, pl. XXV.

61   Narrow buffet at Antwerp. (Vleehuis museum no. 31.E.23.)

62   Narrow buffet at Antwerp. (Vleehuis museum, no. 31.E.24.)

63A   Detail of *The Last Supper* by Dieric Bouts, *c.* 1468, Louvain.

63B   Extant stools in the Metropolitan Museum of Art, New York. (See *Bulletin of the Metropolitan Museum of Art*, New York, 1947/8, 257.)

64A   Detail, title-page of the 2nd book of the Toison d'Or, *c.* 1473. (Oesterreichisches Nationalbibliothek, Vienna.)

64B ⎫
     ⎬   Extant altar chest at Newport, Essex.
65   ⎭

66A   Detail of iron screen, chantry chapel of Thomas Bekynton, Bishop of Bath and Wells (1443–65), Wells Cathedral.

66B   Door knocker, cold cut iron. House of Jacques Cœur, Bourges, *c.* 1454.

67   Charles V receiving an illuminated bible from Jean de Vaudetar. Miniature by Jean Bandol, 1372. (MS 10B 23, Rijksmuseum, The Hague.)

68   Richard II. Panel painting, *c.* 1395. (Westminster Abbey.)

69   Mutilated bench bearing the defaced arms of Rigaud d'Aurelhe. Musée des Arts Decoratifs, Paris (Peyre collection, 1049).

70   Fixed hall table at Winchester College.

71   Oak window shutters from a demolished house in the Brandstraat, Ghent. (Bijloke museum, Ghent.)

72A   Door in the Hôtel de Ville, Damme. In the NE. corner of the hall.

72B   Laver in the Exchequer, Vicars Choral, Wells Cathedral.

72C   Carved panels incorporating the devices of Jacques Cœur; chapel door, house of Jacques Cœur at Bourges (1443–54).

FOREWORD

THIS STUDY examines the furniture of England, France and the Netherlands between the twelfth and fifteenth centuries. The twelfth century marks the earliest moment in which enough evidence exists to enable us to begin to assess Romanesque furniture in a general way. (Before the twelfth century, extant medieval furniture which is complete rather than fragmentary is almost wholly confined to a handful of thrones, the majority of which are of stone or metal.) The end of the fifteenth century is chosen since it coincides with the demise of pure Gothic art in our area and the arrival of Renaissance motifs grafted upon Gothic forms in the early years of the sixteenth century; and according to one school of thought, it marks the division between what is accounted medieval and modern history.[1]

The furniture which is included covers fixed and movable forms of all materials, but excludes a particularly specialized group now found almost exclusively in churches and cathedrals; stalls, pulpits and altars. It will be noted in this survey that no division can be made between what was domestic and what was ecclesiastical in furniture. This group has been ignored because the surviving examples are so numerous that a separate volume would be needed to do them justice, and there is, in any case, a tradition of separate treatment.

The intention of this study is to examine extant furniture and correlate it with other forms of contemporary evidence, in an attempt to see it in the light of its own time. The evidence utilized falls within the following categories:

1. Extant furniture of impeccable origins which has been examined for this book.

2. Furniture which has been examined and which, though lacking a secure provenance, employs techniques which cannot be reproduced in modern times (e.g. certain forms of iron work).

3. Furniture which lacks a secure provenance but which has been examined in great detail, proving to have few, if any, restorations.

4. Documentary evidence in printed sources, primarily inventories and wills.

5. Household accounts in printed sources.

6. Literary sources, e.g. accounts of festivals, marriages, etc.

7. Household statutes and books of household management and etiquette.

8. Illuminations from MSS, and other visual evidence such as panel paintings and sculptures.

---

[1] This division may be precisely argued: 1485 is no longer accepted as a meaningful date for the dividing line, but it can be argued that the Reformation (1539) provides the most reasonable division between English medieval and modern history. However, in terms of furniture study, a horizon of c.1500, though meaningless for social history, is more realistic and avoids throwing the analysis of the earlier periods out of balance by including the years of degenerate Gothic, together with the mass of evidence available for the early sixteenth century. (The quantity and character of the evidence for the first half of the sixteenth century demands a study on its own.)

Select bibliographies are included at the end of each entry in the Catalogue Raisonné; the criteria used for selection are as follows:

(1) Primary evidence.

(2) Comment *supported by evidence*.

(3) The consensus of opinion at a recent date.

A uniform standard of examination for the furniture in the Catalogue was an ideal, but impractical, aim. Conditions of storage and availability vary widely; factors such as lighting, whether access is possible to all sides of an object and whether the interior can be seen, in the case of storage furniture; whether photographs or drawings are permitted and how much time is allowed for study by the owner or authority concerned. All these factors have a bearing upon the degree of investigation that was possible in each case.

The translation of terms for medieval textiles has been deliberately omitted in many instances; since this is a specialist subject, translations can seldom be made without reference to other evidence and it was felt that such treatment would have over-burdened the text with peripheral material.

PENELOPE EAMES

PREFACE

MY WORK in the field of medieval furniture has spanned many years and has necessitated extensive travel. I am grateful for the help given by the many custodians of ancient objects, too numerous to mention individually, who have patiently answered my enquiries at home and abroad.

My particular gratitude is due to the officers of ecclesiastical foundations, colleges, universities and museums who have made special arrangements on my behalf, often at considerable inconvenience, and have allowed me access to objects not generally on view. I take this opportunity of recording especial thanks to: the Dean and Canons of St George's Chapel, Windsor; the Librarian of the Muniment Room of Westminster Abbey; the Dean and Chapter of York Minster; the Dean and Chapter of Wells Cathedral; the Dean and Chapter of Hereford Cathedral; the Warden and Fellows of All Souls College, Oxford; the Warden and Fellows of Merton College, Oxford; the Principal and Fellows of Brasenose College, Oxford; the Provost and Fellows of King's College, Cambridge; the Warden and Fellows of Winchester College; Dr F. Mathey, directeur of the Musée des Arts Décoratifs, Paris; the ecclesiastical authorities of the Cathedral of Bayeux and the Abbey Church of Obazine; Dr R. de Roo, Conservateur en Chef of the Musées Royaux d'Art et d'Historie, Brussels; Dr M. Bafcop, Archivist-Conservateur of the Musée Busleydon, Malines; Dr A. de Schryver, Conservateur of the Musée de Bijloke, Ghent; and Mrs J. Lambrechts-Douillez of the Museum Vleehuis, Antwerp.

I am deeply obliged to the Leverhulme Trust and the University of Liverpool for the award of Fellowships between 1969–1971.

I have received timely financial assistance over the years, to defray the cost of travel and photography, for which I heartily thank my own university, Liverpool; the Marc Fitch Fund; and the Twenty-Seven Foundation. Without this aid much of the investigation of extant furniture would have moved no further than the planning stage.

I would like to thank my former tutors, Dr H. M. R. E. Mayr-Harting and Professor A. R. Myers for the rigorous approach which they have taught me to emulate; Professor C. N. L. Brooke, for his interest and encouragement from the inception of this work; Dr C. T. Allmand for his expert assistance with the interpretation of medieval French sources; Dr L. O. J. Boynton and Mr Peter Thornton for their kindness and advice with many points of detail; Professeur J. Thirion for helpful suggestions on the ordering of the text; and M. Jean Cailleux for his efforts in obtaining photographs for reproduction. I must also thank the University of Liverpool Library for their patience in obtaining a large number of foreign volumes and articles on loan.

I would like to express my profound appreciation to the Council of the Furniture History Society for offering to publish this work, and I must record a special debt to the Editor, Mr Christopher Gilbert, who has carried the burden of seeing a complicated volume of this nature through the press. I am deeply sensible of the honour done me by the Confération Internationale des Negociants en Œuvres d'Art (CINOA) in awarding the first of their annual prizes to this study.

Finally, I would like to thank my son, Florian, for his assistance in checking documentary sources; and last, but by no means least my husband, for his help with the proofs of the volume, his unfailing encouragement over the years of research, and his companionship on many memorable exploratory forays.

PENELOPE EAMES

Paris, 5.vi.77.

INTRODUCTION

THE SCOPE CHOSEN for this study, covering the furniture of England, France and the Netherlands from the twelfth to the fifteenth centuries, is based upon strong political and social connexions in the first instance, and upon clearly defined movements in artistic expression — Romanesque and Gothic — in the second. It is obviously true that all European countries influenced one another to some extent in the Middle Ages, and even the Scandinavian countries cannot be ignored in this wide context. The subject is a vast one, too large to be treated in other than the most general terms in a single study. Broadly based surveys of medieval furniture have been attempted, but a definitive study of a limited area of central importance is almost entirely lacking.[2] The urgent need for a study in depth, and the choice of France and those countries especially indebted to her civilizing influences — England and the Netherlands — seemed compelling and needs, I trust, no defence. Not only are several aspects of the subject unexplored and therefore singularly rewarding in the context of the Middle Ages, but such a study carried with it implications of a wider nature. The *form* of much that was important in furniture from the sixteenth century to the end of the eighteenth century — the great state bed, for instance — was due to a habit of mind which was consistently expressed in the Middle Ages; an attitude to possessions which re-enforced social realities in terms of the form and decoration of plate, textiles and furniture. Nowhere was the structure of medieval society given a more precise and original expression in the character and use of furnishings than in the courts of France.

The beginning of our period saw the influence of Normandy upon England sharpened through the invasion and conquest of England by Duke William, himself a vassal of the King of France. A shared style of architecture, the Romanesque, had obvious implications in terms of furniture design, and courtly language and manners on both sides of the channel were now French. The sovereign nature of the English possession (a kingdom) and the subservient nature of the Norman (a dukedom) meant a reorientation of interest for William and, more importantly, for his successors. The dukedom of Normandy, re-enforced by marriage alliances, gave English kings an expectancy with regard to French lands and engendered a tension between the two countries which endured for four centuries, reaching a pinnacle of strength for the English in 1420 when, through victory in battle and diplomacy, Henry V saw France declared a dependency of the English crown. This preoccupation of England with France over so long a period ensured that French influence never grew stale but was continually nourished by close, living contact. The influence of France upon England is abundantly clear, but the reciprocal debt of France to England is less easy to define. This sustained contact was reflected not only in style but also in subtler and more fundamental ways, at least in the later Middle Ages when documentary evidence increases and allows us to assess usage, in terms of furniture, with greater precision.

[2] The most recent broadly based survey is Eric Mercer's *Furniture 700–1700*, London, 1969. With regard to the lack of definitive studies, an exception must be noted in respect of H. Kreisel's magnificently illustrated study of extant German furniture, which surveys the material from the art-historical viewpoint (*Die Kunst des Deutschen Möbels*, 1, Munich, 1968).

The contribution of the Netherlands was of a somewhat different character: it was a late phenomenon, providing a gloss to style and technique in furniture which gave surface brilliance to those fundamental forms and usages emanating from France. The highly influential position of Burgundy in the later Middle Ages grew from an act of generosity on the part of King John II of France, a Valois, who in 1363 gave the Duchy of Burgundy (in France) to his son Philip, nicknamed 'the Bold'. Six years later Philip married Margaret, heiress of the counties of Flanders and Franche Comté and of Artois, Nevers and Rethel. Thus the lands of the Duchy of Burgundy in central France were joined by other French lands and were united with Netherlandish possessions, creating a political entity of some importance even though weakened by geographical division. Successive Valois dukes, John the Fearless (1404–1419) and Philip the Good (1419–1467), added to these possessions through marriage alliances, seizures, purchases and political manoeuvring, so that by the mid-fifteenth century the original holding in the Low Countries had been enlarged to include Namur, Brabant, Limburg and Antwerp, the counties of Holland, Hainault, Zeeland and Frisia and the Duchy of Luxembourg; while the French lands were increased by the acquisition of the 'Somme towns' (S. Quentin, Corbie, Amiens, Abbeville and the County of Ponthieu), Boulogne, and the counties of Mâcon and Auxerre together with the castellanies of Peronne, Roye and Montdidier.[3]

The ever-increasing importance of the wool and cloth trades in the later Middle Ages meant growing pressure for political stability between England and the Netherlands. In the early fifteenth century, mutual self interest brought about a political alliance and, in spite of vacillations during the century in which Philip the Good saw advantage in treating with the French and discomforting the English, the forcefulness of the economic bond ensured that Netherlandish influences in art gradually permeated English society. The connexion was cemented in 1468 by the celebrated marriage of Marguerite of York, sister of Edward IV, with Philip the Good's son and successor, Charles the Bold, at Damme near Bruges. During the sixteenth century, the influence of the Netherlands reached its climax in England, dominating style in furniture and deflecting interest away from the purer classicism of the Italian Renaissance. In the fifteenth century, it is certain that the style of Netherlandish (or Burgundian) furniture would never have been so influential if it had not been intimately connected with a court life which formed the model for England,[4] usurping the influence formerly exercised by France.

The territorial aggrandisement of the Valois dukes of Burgundy was reflected in the magnificent style of their courts which outshone their model, France, debilitated by internal dissensions and by the effects of the Hundred Years War with England. The importance of impressive display at court was well understood by medieval princes, and there was nothing new in Burgundian policy in this respect. When social and political power was exercised through continuous contact between the seigneurial lord and his men of every rank, as it was in the feudal societies of the Middle Ages, that power was

---

[3] For the history of these acquisitions, see R. Vaughan, *Philip the Bold*; *John the Fearless*; *Philip the Good*; and *Charles the Bold*, London, 1962, 1966, 1970 and 1975.

[4] Olivier de la Marche's treatise, 'L'etat de la maison du Duc Charles de Bourgogne' was composed at the request of Edward IV, to serve him as a model, J. Huizinga, *The Waning of the Middle Ages*, London, 1968, 40.

sustained, re-enforced and advertised by ceremony. Court ceremonial was structured by elaborate rules of precedence and behaviour in which the position of each individual, in any given situation, was apparent, not only in what he *did*, but by what he *used* in terms of his clothing, his food and his furnishings.[5] Certain forms for furniture, and indeed for furnishings in general, reflected those degrees of honour, or precedence, which were termed *estate*. No single factor was of greater importance in terms of the history of furniture in the later Middle Ages than the underlying principles of estate which might govern use, form, ornament and fabric. But although the character of the courts of Burgundy was traditional and French in origin, their interest is enormously enhanced for us by their flamboyance and by the unprecedented insight into their management which is afforded by the writings of contemporary historiographers and others, in particular Georges Chastellain, Olivier de la Marche and Alienor de Poitiers.[6] Burgundian court life, extravagantly interpreting French rules,[7] served as the model for England and, indeed, the traveller Leo of Rozmital and his entourage, who had already experienced Burgundian ducal hospitality, described the English court of 1465 as if it were no whit inferior to that of Burgundy.[8] The management of the king's household had wide influence in terms of furnishings and their usage for society as a whole, since every level with any pretensions to gentle manners was accorded recognition in the rules of ceremonial.[9]

The example of the courtly magnificence of the dukes of Burgundy was adapted by the rich bourgeois Flemish traders in settled circumstances to produce the beautiful, cool Gothic interiors familiar in the works of the Master of Flémalle, who invented the idea of projecting divine incidents, such as the Annunciation, against a contemporary domestic interior.[10] This Master's example was followed by painters such as Jan van Eyck and Roger van der Weyden, and in paintings of the lives of saints, as well as in portraits of contemporaries, we see the forms of furniture prescribed by court etiquette used in smaller households. (Sufficient architecture and architectural detail, furniture and documentary material survive to demonstrate that these paintings are an accurate mirror of bourgeois life at the time, recreating for us with warmth and immediacy the

---

[5] 'Every estate or rank, if it were not to be lost, was marked by certain possessions or "gear" '. F. R. H. du Boulay, *An Age of Ambition*, London, 1970, 70.

[6] Ed. Le Baron K. de Lettenhove, *Œuvres de Georges Chastellain, III, Chronique 1454–1458*, Brussels, 1864; ed. C-B. Petitot, *Collection Complète des Memoires Relatifs à l'histoire de France. t. ix, x. Les Mémoires de Messire Olivier de la Marche*, Paris, 1825; Alienor de Poitiers, 'Les Honneurs de la Cour', La Curne de Sainte-Palaye, *Mémoires sur l'Ancienne Chevalerie*, II, Paris, 1759, 183–267.

[7] Alienor de Poitiers indicates that a *French* source was consulted at the Burgundian court when doubts concerning appropriate ceremony were experienced, see Appendix VIII (b) and (c), lines 590–6.

[8] We learn that Edward IV's court was 'the most splendid that could be found in all Christendom' and we are treated to a description of the elaborate ceremonial observed at the banquet in celebration of the Queen's safe deliverance of the Princess Elizabeth (born 11 Feb. 1465). Ed. M. Letts, *Travels of Leo of Rozmital*, Cambridge, 1957, 45–7.

[9] A fifteenth-century English book of etiquette sets out in appropriate order a list of persons eligible for consideration in matters concerning precedence; only *poor* artisans, and labourers — in fact the peasant class — are excluded; 'The Boke of Nurture' by John Russell, Marshal and Usher to Humphrey, Duke of Gloucester, who was imprisoned and died suddenly in 1447; ed. F. J. Furnivall, *The Babees Book*, EETS, 1868, 186–7.

[10] E. Panofsky, *Early Netherlandish Painting* [2 vols], Cambridge, Massachusetts, 1964, 204.

B

domestic comfort and amenity enjoyed by the wealthy burghers of such powerful cities as Ghent, Bruges and Ypres.)[11]

Furniture serves the fundamental needs of eating, working and repose (tables, seating and beds) and of storage (boards or shelves, chests and armoires). In the Middle Ages, all these requirements were served not only in furniture which was freestanding and movable, but also in less adaptable built-in furniture which, by its very character, was inalienable from a building. The built-in solution was particularly suited to an age in which seigneurial households moved many times annually to supervise the administration of possessions which were often widely separated one from another.[12] Built-in furniture obviated the need for transporting large quantities of furniture, and was a measure of protection against thieves in unoccupied dwellings, since movable objects were easily stolen. That the peculiar circumstances of this form of life fundamentally affected the role of furniture, whether movable or fixed, can be readily appreciated, for delicately constructed furniture was vulnerable in either context. But a second consideration affecting furniture grew from the social organization of society, and here the implications are less well understood; yet the significance of social influences was arguably of even greater importance, outlasting not only the need for mobility but also the Middle Ages itself, remaining a powerful force in furniture design as late as the eighteenth century.[13]

Throughout the Middle Ages feudal concepts were ingrained in social behaviour, with a chain of power and commitment linking each individual with a master: whether peasant or artisan, the servant of a great household trained at grammar school and university and representing what we should recognize as the professional classes, or a seigneurial lord, holding land of another or of the king. All men acknowledged the power vested in a person or persons who, in some sense, provided their livelihood, controlled their destiny, or established them in their position, a power which found its ultimate expression in the head of state. (The king himself acknowledged God as his lord.) So simple an outline of the social order gives no hint of the complicated pattern which emerged in the later Middle Ages in England and in parts of the Netherlands, when the absolute power exercised by seigneurial lords was eroded. Yet, even though the power and reality of feudal organization had diminished in England and the Netherlands, if not in France, in the fourteenth and fifteenth centuries, its *concepts* still governed the accepted rules of etiquette. Indeed, it could be convincingly argued that the feudal ideal controlled ceremonial, with its emphasis on precedence, more jealously as seigneurial power felt itself threatened. Such matters may appear, at first sight, to be of purely academic interest to the furniture historian, providing peripheral information which is

[11] A particularly good collection of fittings from local fifteenth-century houses (window shutters, etc.) is housed in the Bijloke museum at Ghent, see pl. 71.

[12] Great lords, such as William the Conqueror, sought to avoid handing a large number of contiguous manors to one individual as a reward for services, believing that land holding in large blocks facilitated the organization of rebellion. A haphazard pattern of land-holding was the result of this prudent policy which the complex interaction of marriage alliances, gifts, sequestrations and redistributions over the centuries did little to alter. The religious foundations, which were among the richest land holders, were no exception to this general rule.

[13] For example, the form of the hung bed, invented in the Middle Ages, with a canopy denoting estate. Throughout the eighteenth century, not only in the courts of Europe but also in the country houses of England, important bedrooms were always equipped with *canopied* structures.

of little value in the actual study of furniture. But we shall see that expressions of an attitude of mind are fundamental to an analysis and an appreciation of medieval furniture. A narrow, art-historical approach will only satisfy a small part of our enquiry. We are bound to ask ourselves *why* simplicity in furniture when textiles and plate were outstandingly expensive and elaborate?[14] And we follow up this question with others. Was all furniture unimportant? How does the evidence of documents, literature and art modify the impressions created by surviving furniture? These questions cannot be simply answered, but their examination in subsequent pages will, I trust, prove both fascinating and rewarding.

The social framework of society in which position, or *estate* as it was called, was maintained and strengthened by visual means (the use of the correct 'gear' in any situation being important), meant that certain objects, including certain kinds of furniture, were adjuncts of ceremony, subject to the rules of precedence, expressing in their character and form the degree of estate of a particular individual.[15] The practical application of the rules governing the use of objects of estate was subtle, for the controlling consideration was *precedence* rather than *rank*. Precedence is mutable, changing according to the company of any individual group of persons, whereas rank is a constant factor. A peasant before his own fireside, in the exclusive company of his wife and children, was lord and master, and might occupy a chair,[16] yet such a man sitting in the hall of his seigneurial lord, on the occasion of some festival, would occupy a form or stool at a table below the dais. At court, rules of precedence could nullify considerations of rank in individuals, for we know that in certain circumstances the Steward of Edward IV's household took precedence *over all other persons at court* since he was held to represent his master, and parallel evidence exists for Burgundy.[17]

Every student of the arts of the Middle Ages must ask how far surviving works accurately reflect contemporary priorities. There can be no doubt as to the importance of architecture: a grand total of churches and cathedrals survive to astound us with their technical and intellectual brilliance, even if every contemporary palace has perished, been reduced to ruins, or been transformed so as to be unrecognizable as a medieval structure.[18] And in furnishings, we find that the excellence discernible in the rare and precious survivors from the groups of textiles and plate corroborate an importance which

[14] For an indication of the different values of plate, textiles and furniture in England, see Penelope Eames, *Medieval Domestic Furnishings* (M.A. Thesis, Liverpool University, 1969), i–xxxix. French and Burgundian inventories and accounts show a similar pattern of values between the three groups.

[15] See Penelope Eames, 'Documentary evidence concerning the character and use of domestic furnishings', *Furniture History*, VII, 1971, 41–57.

[16] A misericord in the church at Screveton, Notts., shows a peasant warming himself at a fire seated in a chair with a carved back, see M. W. Barley, *The house and home*, London, 1963, pl. 10.

[17] A. R. Myers, *Household of Edward IV*, Manchester, 1959, 142, §68. Olivier de la Marche's treatise, which served as a model for Edward IV in matters of household management, notes how the First Chamberlain is served at table with the same degree of honour as is the Duke of Burgundy himself (Petitot, II, 489). See also Appendix VIII (c), lines 828–37, 867–73.

[18] Some indication of the size of the loss may be gauged from one example. The inventories and accounts of Philip the Bold note no fewer than 29 ducal châteaux plus 4 hôtels between the years 1363–77. B. Prost, *Inventaires Mobiliers et Extraits des Comptes des Ducs de Bourgogne*, I, Paris, 1902/4, see index.

documentary evidence shows to have been tantamount to obsessive.[19] It has been shown that the open nature of seigneurial households, to which persons of low rank and unpredictable behaviour had access (since they might be the lord's men), meant that valuable and fragile furnishings could only be deployed under supervision. Supervision naturally occurred when the lord, important members of the household, or guests were present in any room or area, and at such times furnishings might take on especial significance as adjuncts of estate. As later investigation will show, this significance was discernible not only in the *quality* of furnishings but also in their *form*. We find, then, that the needs of a mobile household — in the sense of a household continually in transit from one manor to another — were reinforced by the everyday need for adaptability in the use of valuable furnishings. This adaptability was necessary, not only because of the problems of security in an 'open' dwelling, but also because it enabled rooms to serve a number of purposes. If only minimal furnishings were normally in permanent positions, then space could be utilized for a number of activities by bringing out of store furnishings of the required kind.[20] Textiles were perfectly suited to these requirements, being easily taken down and rolled, to be stored under lock and key, or strapped on horses' backs or in baggage carts. Whenever necessary, bare walls and heavy boards or seating could be transformed by the suspension and draping of silks and tapestries, and the impact of quantities of splendidly coloured cloth could be made individually significant by the use of armorial bearings. A further recommendation was the luxurious nature of textiles in an age when bodily comfort was hard won. In furnishings, textiles provided an extension of the high degree of luxury common in clothing.

Precious plate of gold and silver for the table or chapel was classed as jewellery and shared with textiles a position of supreme importance in the equipment of the household. Plate was used as coin, and therefore wealth could be displayed in the form of table and chapel utensils and used as an adjunct of estate, being removed and locked away at the conclusion of the various ceremonies of the day, whether connected with the reception of visitors, with eating or with worship. The use of certain forms in table plate was carefully regulated to reflect degrees of estate, in common with other furnishings.[21]

Before transferring our attention from the general character of furnishings to furniture itself, it is pertinent to note that the matters under discussion were not largely controlled by personal choice, as is the case in more recent times. In the Middle Ages, position was sustained by forms of advertisement in which the example provided by the court served as a model for lesser households. Georges Chastellain (d. 1475), historiographer to Philip the Good and Charles the Bold of Burgundy, explains that 'after the deeds and exploits of war, which are claims to glory, the household is the first thing that strikes

---

[19] For example, textiles: the Bayeux tapestry, an eleventh-century embroidery at Bayeux, and the Lady and Unicorn tapestry panels of *c.*1500, in the Musée Cluny, Paris. Plate: the French gold cup in the British Museum, now mutilated, represents what was once a huge class of precious table-ware often ornamented with jewels and owned by noble and middle-class persons alike.

[20] Eames 1971, 48 ff.

[21] For instance, the *covering* of a piece of plate, whether drinking cup or dish, signified precedence, see Eames 1971, 42.

the eye and which it is therefore most necessary to conduct and arrange well'.[22] This unequivocal statement of the importance of the household enables us to understand why documentary sources show such similarities in the possessions of individuals of similar positions, for it is well-nigh impossible to detect quirks of taste or personality from inventories. Individuals owned the household equipment and personal possessions which reflected their estate whether they were particularly drawn to certain forms of art or not, for, in a sense, these objects and the manner of deploying them *maintained* individuals in that estate. Such a matter was far too important to be subject to whims of fancy.

This survey of medieval furniture will utilize evidence of several kinds, for its purpose is to study extant furniture and to enlarge our understanding of it through a correlation with contemporary sources. The sources available to us are of several categories, *each with its peculiar bias*,[23] and different categories of evidence used in conjunction often act reciprocally as a control upon our conclusions. A single example will illustrate this point. Manuscript illuminations provide a rich source of visual evidence; they capture the imagination with their intensity of colour, and they show instantly and in detail a scene which, in words, might occupy many pages and prove less memorable into the bargain. But in using them as evidence, various questions arise, and two of the most obvious ones may be mentioned here. Is the artist faithfully portraying a scene he saw or had described to him, or is he using the style and forms of a school of painters, not necessarily of his own time and country? If we are not sure of the answers to such questions, the evidence may still be valuable provided that we recognize its limitations. And if we are on certain ground in this respect, able to show from surviving furniture and buildings that the scene depicted is materially accurate (as is the case with a wealth of illuminations and panel paintings produced in the Netherlands in the fourteenth and fifteenth centuries), can we then draw far-reaching conclusions about furniture without cross checking with other forms of evidence such as accounts and inventories, descriptive literature and books of household management and etiquette? It would be most unwise to do so, as the following limited analysis will show. Many of the Netherlandish paintings of the later Middle Ages were commissioned to record great events which culminated in a series of feasts, and here we see the seigneurial lord at table. The fact that there is, perhaps, only one important seat (not necessarily a chair, but distinguished by having a hanging behind and *above* it), the remainder of the seating of the hall consisting of forms and stools, should not be taken as evidence that chairs (or dignified seats) were rare at the time, for, as early as the end of the twelfth and beginning of the thirteenth century a chair is noted as a part of the furniture of every well appointed bed chamber.[24] What the illustrator is showing us is how a *certain* entertainment was conducted. We know from *other forms of evidence* that this entertainment followed a highly stylized, almost ritualistic pattern in which the rules of estate dictated the appropriate

[22] Quoted in Huizinga, 31.

[23] This bias is investigated for English inventories, see Penelope Eames, 'Inventories as sources of evidence for domestic furnishings in the 14th, and 15th centuries', *Furniture History*, IX, 1973, 33–40.

[24] Alexander Neckam (1157–1217), in his *De Naturis Rerum*, speaking of the chamber, recommends that a chair be placed beside the bed ('Juxta lectum cathedra'). Ed. A. Scheler, *Lexicographie Latine du XII et du XIII siècle. Trois Traités de Jean de Garlande, Alexandre Neckam et Adam du Petit-Pont*, Leipzig, 1867, 90.

forms in furnishings. We also know, though we could not gain this knowledge from the painting itself, that the scene does not necessarily represent a permanent arrangement of furnishings but is more probably an assembly of appropriate objects — furniture, textiles and plate — organized specifically for an individual occasion.[25] This digression is, I hope, justified in showing how essential is the use of different forms of evidence to this study, not only in the interests of scholarship, but also as a means of enhancing our appreciation of the visual records of art and archaeology which remain.

Our study is conditioned by what has survived. In terms of actual furniture, chance rather than a meaningful pattern has dictated what remains. The largest single category represented in surviving examples is the chest, and although this was a very common article in the Middle Ages it was by no means the only favoured form for storage furniture. The chest has survived in relatively large numbers chiefly because it was habitually deposited in churches and abbeys for safe keeping,[26] as well as being used by ecclesiastical foundations for their own goods. In these institutions, unlike private dwellings, the destruction of old furniture for reasons of inconvenience or changed standards of taste, has been less drastic over the centuries. In contrast, the armoire, though certainly numerically inferior to the chest as a storage article in the Middle Ages, was nevertheless very common, yet comparatively few survive; and some of the commonest items of all, such as tables and beds, are only represented by a handful of examples. For all forms of furniture, twelfth and thirteenth-century examples are much rarer than examples of the fourteenth and fifteenth centuries. The same general picture applies to the other forms of evidence which are utilized: the earlier, the rarer. Wills, inventories and household accounts survive in greater numbers for the later Middle Ages, as do descriptions of important events which incorporate references to furniture. Household statutes and books of etiquette, though probably always incorporating some earlier material,[27] are chiefly fifteenth-century works. And the utility of representational art, if not its actual incidence, is greatly enhanced for us in the fifteenth century because at this date it often mirrored contemporary usages accurately. Thus, all the available evidence combines to allow us a greater insight into the form, quality, decoration and use of furniture in the fourteenth and fifteenth centuries than is possible for the two earlier centuries included in this study.

Almost all our historical evidence concerns the nobility and middle classes, and we know relatively little concerning the furniture of that enormous class, the poor peasantry. However, peasant furniture is likely to have been rough and crude, in character with peasant dwellings and clothing, and since our interest must lie with those sections of society capable of influencing design, this lack of a substantial body of evidence for the peasantry is unimportant. The furniture historian's first task must be to analyse furniture

---

[25] Eames 1971, 49–53.

[26] The instruction in the will of Richard Welby of Multon, 1465, illustrates this common practice: 'My plate and surplus moneys etc. to be kept in a chest at Croyland Abbey till my children attain full age', A. Gibbons, *Early Lincoln Wills*, Lincoln, 1888, 191.

[27] 'Bishop Grosseteste's Household Statutes' has come down to us in a MS which mentions the nineteenth year of Henry VI (Furnivall, 1868, 328–31); the name, however, indicates a date within the Bishop's lifetime (1175–1253), and the similarity between this and other fifteenth-century treatises on household management strongly suggests that traditional attitudes are incorporated in later material.

in its most sophisticated context; from his findings here, some knowledge of the more slowly evolving styles of the poor may eventually accrue.

There is abundant evidence for the later Middle Ages to show that no distinction should be drawn between ecclesiastical and secular furniture, though for reasons of space stallwork, altars and pulpits are omitted in this study. The common habit of including a chapel in middle-class as well as in noble households in the fourteenth and fifteenth centuries[28] meant that the equipment necessary for Christian worship was present in the dwellings of all the persons falling within our survey. Furthermore, as chapel services (together with audiences and feasting), provided the main framework for conspicuous seigneurial display, chapel appurtenances were among the most important groups of equipment in any seigneurial household.[29] In fact the matter is fundamental, for the Christian faith, its ceremonies, and places of worship were inextricably mixed with everday life in a manner which seems extraordinary to us today.[30] The inventories of the chapels of great households may be compared with those of religious institutions without any differences being apparent between the two groups. Indeed, the evidence of hundreds of wills shows that quantities of vestments and chapel plate used by religious bodies came from seigneurial chapels. The situation with furniture itself was parallel, and although it is true that churches and abbeys had the wealth to pay the highest wages for good carpentry, the same is true of great seigneurial lords.[31] What dictated the degree of elaboration and expense thought appropriate by lords for furniture in household chapels or elsewhere was governed by considerations of estate, so that the lord's chapel seat would have been the most likely object to be accorded special treatment within the chapel, together with the pulpit and altar. If the lord's seat was included in stallwork, rather than being an individual chair, we should expect the whole group to compare favourably with stallwork in churches and cathedrals, and although too little survives for this point to be demonstrated, one such group surviving

[28] In an English royal context, a private chapel was always attached to the king's houses from Henry II's time, see T. H. Turner, *Some Account of Domestic Architecture in England from the Conquest to the end of the thirteenth century* [i], Oxford, 1851, 3–4.

[29] The richness of private chapel equipment was sometimes astonishing. Henry le Scrope of Masham owned more than ninety-two copes when he was executed in 1415; see C. L. Kingsford, 'Two Forfeitures in the Year of Agincourt', *Archaeologia*, LXX, 1918–20 [1920], 77.

[30] du Boulay, 142, draws attention to the inextricable mix of politics and religion highlighted for us in the Paston letters. Sometimes the use of church property for secular purposes was so ostentatiously unsuitable that it became an affront to the clergy, but they were nevertheless incapable of preventing abuses at St Paul's, London, in the fourteenth century. The churchyard was used for games and wrestling matches, and within the church twelve scriveners sat at the west end waiting to be hired by merchants and others who required documents to be drawn up for them, and even stalls were erected by tradesmen. The N.–S. axis of the church was a recognized thoroughfare and porters with merchandise, as well as ordinary pedestrians, continually made use of it. (A. R. Myers, *London in the Age of Chaucer*, Norman, Oklahoma, 1972, 82–3.) The interplay of religion in everyday affairs was not always irreverent, however. From Olivier de la Marche we learn that the Lord's Supper accounted for the precedence given to the officers who carried the bread and wine to the duke of Burgundy's table. Bread led the procession, followed by wine, for these were the precious materials of the sacrament and they were carried in the order in which Christ first gave them to us. M. Canat de Chizy, 'Marguerite de Flandre, Duchesse de Bourgogne. Sa Vie Intime et l'État de sa Maison', *Mémoires de l'Académie Impériale des Sciences, Arts et Belle-Lettres de Dijon*, VII, 1859, 83.

[31] For example, between 1363–1477 the same masters (masons and carpenters) are found employed by the Duke of Burgundy and by towns and churches. M. Canat de Chizy, 'Étude sur la Service des Travaux Publics et Spécialement sur la charge de Maître des Œuvres en Bourgogne', *Bulletins Monumentales*, LXIII, 1898, 366.

in France supports this view.[32] Again, in matters of ornament, the secular and the ecclesiastical are seen as inextricably mixed. In churches and cathedrals, armorial textiles and plate abounded,[33] supporting the worldly character of the carving of many misericords. The subjects decorating the furnishings of the private rooms of the priors of Christchurch, Canterbury, can be cited as typical of the age, reflecting the status of the office of the prior rather than his religious calling,[34] while in secular ownership divine subjects are encountered for bed hangings and other furnishings as well as the more usual armorial devices.[35] A noteworthy survivor in this context is the gold cup in the British Museum,[36] which was made for the table of the king of France in c.1380, and is decorated with scenes in the life of St Agnes.

[32] The Musée des Arts Decoratifs, Paris, possesses stallwork from a seigneurial chapel (PE 1058, dated 1500–1525), in which the lord's seat is given special prominence by being higher from the ground than the seats on either side of it; the height of the back of the stalls is the same for all, a feature which may have been dictated by the height of the chapel ceiling. The quality of the carving is high.

[33] The bequest of armorial textiles and plate by the Black Prince to Canterbury in 1376 is typical in its character, if not in its scale and quality, of many such gifts. J. Nichols, *A Collection of all the Wills . . . of Kings and Queens of England . . . and Every Branch of the Blood Royal*, London, 1780, 69–70.

[34] Inventories of 1331, 1334 and 1339. W. H. St John Hope, 'Inventories of the . . . Priors of the Monastery of Christchurch, Canterbury', *Archaeological Journal*, LIII, 1896, 258–83.

[35] For example, 1405, mirror of the Duchess of Burgundy decorated with the Holy Sepulchre, C. C. A. Dehaisnes, *Documents et Extraits Divers Concernant l'Histoire de l'Art dans la Flandre, l'Artois et le Hainaut*, II, Lille, 1886, 885. 1423, bed of Henry V with cherubim, *Rotuli Parliamentorum*, IV, 235. 1480, bed of the Duchess of Buckingham with the Annunciation, N. H. Nicolas, *Testamenta Vetusta*, I, London, 1826, 356.

[36] O. M. Dalton, *The Royal Gold Cup in the British Museum*, Trustees of the British Museum, London, 1924. See also fn. 19.

Part I

SECTION A

ARMOIRES, BUFFETS AND DRESSOIRS

The medieval armoire (still so-called in France) was the equivalent of the modern cupboard. The term armoire is retained in an English text, not for pedantic reasons, but in order to avoid confusion with the medieval cupboard, or open board for plate.

The armoire was of two basic types.

1. The fixed armoire, contrived in a variety of ways but always forming part of the structure or fittings of a building and inalienable from it. This form of armoire was, by its nature, often excluded from wills and inventories concerned with movables, though it may have occasionally received incidental recognition as a means of describing the location of other objects.[37] Or, in certain circumstances, the provision of fixed armoires may be inferred, as has been pointed out with regard to the inventory of Charles V's possessions at Vincennes which are too numerous to be stored in the chests which are listed.[38] Fixed armoires might be part of the original fabric of a building, being of the same date as the walls and roof, as at York and Wells (Cat. 3–7, 9). Alternatively, they might intrude as fixtures keyed into earlier stonework, as at St Albans (Cat. 8); in the latter circumstances they are likely to be made largely or wholly of wood. Unmutilated examples of this type of armoire are rare, since such armoires were often totally destroyed with buildings, or in the event of the survival of early fabric they tended to disappear as buildings were changed and modernized. While most extant armoires of this type are found in churches or monasteries, this narrow pattern of survival is misleading, for it is clear that fixed armoires were widely used, being common in London, for example, in the thirteenth century.[39]

2. The free-standing armoire, whose form enabled it to be moved without structural alteration to either itself or its surroundings. These armoires were sometimes considered

---

[37] See the heading of the list of textiles in the Garderobe of the Duchess of Burgundy in 1405, pp. 7–8.

[38] C. Hohler, 'Court Life in Peace and War', ed. Joan Evans, *The Flowering of the Middle Ages*, London, 1966, 135–78.

[39] An early Assize containing regulations for settling boundary disputes in the city of London has been shown by T. H. Turner to make reference to the building of armoires in the stone arches of the walls of adjoining properties (see text and commentary, Turner, 17 ff., 276 ff.). Though there are difficulties in interpreting this interesting document in visual terms, certain conclusions are justified. (i) Fixed armoires were not uncommon in twelfth-century London. (The armoires must have been fixed for had they been movable, merely resting against party walls, they would have been irrelevant in boundary disputes.) (ii) The armoires fitted arched recesses, as do many of the surviving cloister armoires, e.g. N. wall of the cloister of Furness Abbey (ruined), *Furness Abbey*, H.M.S.O., 1966, 13; also Obazine, Cat. 1, 2. (iii) The armoires were recessed 1 ft. within the thickness of the wall and if finished flush would have been of this depth; they may, however, have been deeper if a projection into the room was permitted.

The traditional date of this Assize is 1189 and is quoted by Turner, but a recent analysis, which Professor C. N. L. Brooke has kindly brought to my notice, finds that all sections of the document are later, though the portion under discussion is '... incontestably ... earlier than the twelve-seventies' (see ed. H. M. Chew/ W. Kellaway, *London Assize of Nuisance 1301–1431*, London Record Society, 1973, x–xi.)

as movable property,[40] but evidence suggests that they might also on occasion be inalienable from property.[41] Many examples of this type of armoire have survived in original condition, especially from the later Middle Ages.

Whilst a distinction between types 1 and 2 must be noted, it should be observed that the difference is of technical interest only, since there is no reason to suppose that the determining factor responsible for the selection of either a fixed or movable armoire reflected use, form (in the wide rather than the narrow sense), style or date. The choice of type 1 or 2 must often have rested upon planning, or the lack of it, at the construction stages in the history of buildings, so that only if the precise use of areas was foreseen can a fixed armoire have been chosen.

The armoire, whether as fixed locker or as free-standing object, developed in several interesting ways in the later Middle Ages. Its original form — that of simple shelved or unshelved storage space closed by doors — was never lost, but other forms and combinations of forms accrued and tended to carry the same terminology, leading to a confusion of language which was unresolved for several centuries. Late developments were the armoire with doors and drawers behind in place of shelves (Cat. 13); the armoire framed like a grid, having either open pigeon holes[42] or numerous drawers (Cat. 14–17); finally, the armoire which became amalgamated with another form of furniture — the series of open shelves or boards for plate, known as buffet, dressoir or cup board — producing an object which combined closed storage with open shelves (Cat. 23). Short analyses of these developments are given as introductions to the relevant entries in the Catalogue Raisonné.[43]

As with all types of furniture, most references to armoires in inventories, accounts and other sources give few details as to form or use. Nevertheless, they show us how common armoires were both among the nobility and middle classes.

c. 1293   Will of Thomas de Stanes, London merchant:

an 'almariolum'.

(Sharpe, I, 113.)

1321, 1323   Inventories of Eudes de Mareuil, chaplain of Beauvais Cathedral:

'. . . in aumariis . . . quedam armariola.'

---

[40] They occasionally occur in wills: 'all his chests, aumbries, forms, and all other utensils in his shop' (will of John de Stonelee, 1362); R. R. Sharpe, *Calendar of Wills proved & enrolled in the Court of Husting, London*, II, London, 1890, 110–11.

[41] In an inventory of landlord's property, 1485, listed at the entry of a new tenant into a house in Botolf Lane, London, we find: 'a grete, new, standyng almerye with iij levys . . . a greate almarye with ij leves . . .'; H. Littlehales, ed. *The Medieval Records of a London City Church*, I, EETS, 1904, 29. (For a note on the legal aspect of this inventory, see Eames 1969, 37 f.)

[42] 1426, 'La chambre ou madame soloit gésir . . . 45. Item, uns grans armairés ou a plusieurs megans, et dedens yceulx plusieurs choses d'apothecarie . . .' (A. de Barthélemy, 'Inventaire du Château des Baux en 1426', *Révue des Sociétés Savantes*, 6e série VI, 1877, 142, 45.) (At the Château des Baux, in the chamber where Madame La Comtesse d'Avelin was accustomed to lie . . . Item, a large armoire with many pigeon-holes, in which are various medicinal items . . .)

[43] It is possible that other forms developed in our area, but have not as yet been identified. In Spain and Germany, for instance, the drop-front armoire existed which was the ancestor of the bureau. (See O. Wanscher, *The Art of Furniture*, London, 1966, pls. 130–1; Kreisel, pl. 62.)

(V. Le Blond, *Testament & Inventaires des Biens d'Eudes de Mareuil, Chapelain de la Cathédrale de Beauvais; Inventaire du Mobilier de Maître Thomas, Maçon de Voisinlieu-lès-Beauvais*, Beauvais 1913, 33, 44.)

1354   Inventory of the Bishop of Alet:

'. . . parva camera de turri . . . unum armarium fusteum in quo erant duo coffreti parvi de corrio aperti; in uno nichil erat, in alio vero diverse littere . . . unum armarium fusti.'

(J. Guiraud, 'Inventaires Narbonnais du XIVe Siècle', *Bulletin de la Commission Archéologique de Narbonne*, VIII, 1904/5, 207, 231.)

(. . . in a small tower room, a wooden armoire containing 2 small leather-covered boxes, 1 empty and the other containing various papers . . . a wooden armoire.)

1363   Robinet de Foulville rendered 1 'armaire' to the Duke of Burgundy, in payment of tax.

(Prost, I, 8.)

1369   Inventory of goods at Chalon, held by the Duke of Burgundy:

'*1055* . . . 1 viez armaire . . .'

(Prost, I, 190.)

1372   Inventory of a Lyon locksmith:

'duos armayolos de sapino'

(V. de Valous, 'Inventaire des biens d'un Serrurier de Lyon', *Mémoires de la Société Littéraire, Historique et Archéologique de Lyon*, XIII, 1879/81, 40.)

(2 soft wood armoires.)

1376   Inventory of the goods of a Dijon taverner:

'Des grans armaires ferrez, à 4 enchastres, . . . uns autres petis armaires, viez, . . .'

(Prost, I, 476.)

(Large, ironbound armoires with 4 fittings [?divisions] . . . another small, old armoire.)

1376   Inventory of the priest Jean Lemaigre:

'. . . magnum armareolum, . . .'

(L. Lex, 'Inventaire des Biens Meubles et Immeubles de Jean Lemaigre, Curé de Pont-Sainte-Marie, Près de Troyes', *Révue de Champagne et de Brie*, XI, 1881, 223.)

1406   List of goods belonging to John Olyver, a London draper:

1 'almerye'.

(A. H. Thomas, *Calendar of Plea & Memoranda Rolls, 1413–1437*, Cambridge, 1943, 4.)

1426   Inventory of the goods of the Comtesse d'Avelin, Château des Baux:

'Le retrait de la chambre de madame . . . 7. Item, i grand tablier double marqueté par dedens pour jouer aux tables et aux echacs, et plusieurs autres choses de peu de value, en uns grans armairés.'

(Barthélemy, 150. Barthélemy notes, 150, fn. 10, that 'armairé' signifies a built-in structure; the fact that these armoires are only mentioned with reference to their *contents* — movable goods — supports this statement.)

(The inner chamber of Madame's chamber . . . Item, 1 large 2-leaved table worked with marquetry on its inside surfaces for gaming, and several other things of small value, in a large armoire.)

1468   Inventory of the goods of the Comte de Dunois, bastard of the Duke of Orleans:

'. . . unes petites armoires joignans la cheminée de Madamoiselle Katherine, . . .'

(L. Jarry, 'Inventaire de la Bibliothèque et du Mobilier de Jean . . . Comte de Dunois, au Château de Châteaudun', *Mémoires de la Société Archéologique et Historique de l'Orléanais*, XXIII, 1892, 144.)

(. . . a small armoire adjacent to Mlle Katherine's chimney, . . .)

1485   Inventory of inalienable goods in a house in Botolf Lane, London, taken over (with the lease of the property) by an Italian merchant:

'In the Chaumbre by the Sommer parlour . . . a grete, new, standyng almerye with iij levys . . . In the Kechen . . . a greate almarye with ij leves.'

(H. Littlehales, *The Medieval Records of a London City Church*, E.E.T.S., 1904, 29.)

Where evidence is more specific, we learn of the different uses of armoires, e.g.:

(1)   Providing storage for records or books.

1246   The majority of the books belonging to the Abbey of Saint-Sernin de Toulouse were placed 'in armario'; they were considered a part of the Treasury.

(M. J. C. Douais, *Inventaire des Biens, Meubles et Immeubles, de l'Abbaye de Saint-Sernin de Toulouse*, Paris, 1886, 7.)

1334   'Philippe . . . roy de France, à . . . Guy Chevrier . . . commandons . . . que vous aillez a Quatremaires . . . visitez . . . tant en chambres, en edifices, en parois, aumoires . . . pour cause d'aucuns escrips trouver, . . .'

(L. Delisle, *Actes Normands de la Chambre des Comptes sous Philippe de Valois*, Rouen, 1871, 94, 95.)

The use of armoires for papers is implicit in these instructions of Philip of France regarding the search to be instigated by Guy Chevrier and others at the hôtel of the King's sister, Jeanne de Valois, at Quatremaires.

1364/5   '*432.* Pour faire . . . trois grans armaires de bois de chesne, bon et net, fendu à la resse, et icelles enfoncier et revestir de bonnes aiz de noier et de chesne, bien fenées et courroiées, pour mettre en icelles les lettres et chartres qui souloient estre ou Tresor de Talent pour estre là à plux grant seurté et pour les veoir et avoir plux prestement toutes foiz qu'il sera mestier, faictes par maistre Belin et ses aides; . . .'

(Prost, I, 58.)

(For making . . . 3 large armoires, well made and finished, built-in and equipped with good shelves of walnut and oak and well banded with ironwork, for storing the archives . . . of the 'Tresor' [tower] of Talent Castle. The archives to be put in these armoires for greater security and so that they may be viewed and taken out more speedily whenever necessary. The armoires made by Master Belin and his assistants.)[44]

Philip the Bold ordered at least one other group of large built-in armoires for archives (see J-J. Vernier, 'Philippe Le Hardi, Duc de Bourgogne. Sa Vie Intime Pendant Sa Jeunesse. Ses Qualités et ses Défauts; ses Goûts et ses Habitudes.' *Mémoires de la Société Académique du Département de l'Aube*, LXIII, 1899, 48.)

1435   'Item une aumaire de bois de quesne attachée contre une paroire, esquelles avoit plusieurs escriptures, . . .'

(J. Félix, *Inventaire de Pierre Surreau, Receveur Général de Normandie, suivi du Testament de Laurens Surreau et de l'Inventaire de Denise de Foville*, Paris, 1892, 80.)

(Item, an oak armoire fastened to a partition, containing various writings.)

1446   'Item unum Armariolum novum pro Computis conservandis.'

(Inventory of the Prior of Durham. [Ed. J. Raine], 'Wills and Inventories I', *Surtees Society*, 1834/5, 91.)

(1 new armoire for storing accounts.)

1502   'Itm. to William Trende for money by him layed out for the making of a cheste and almorys in the Quenes Counsaille Chambre for to put in the bokes   x s.'

(N. H. Nicolas, *Privy Purse Expenses of Elizabeth of York*, London, 1830, 96.)

(Armoire for the books in the Council Chamber of Henry VII's Queen.)

---

[44] Prost points out that Belin d'Anchenoncourt was a Master Carpenter of Dijon from 1348, and became the Duke of Burgundy's Maître des Œuvres de Charpenterie in 1367; he died in 1395.

(2)   For the storage of jewels (including plate), and coin.

1212   '. . . j. anulum precii xx. solidorum cum toto almererio in quo fuit; . . .'
             (*Curia Regis Rolls of the Reigns of Richard I & John, 1210-1212*, VI, H.M.S.O.,
             1932, 209.)
             (1 ring valued at 20 sol. with the whole armoire in which it was.)

1305   Plea of trespass when 20 persons entered the house of Alice of Ebbegate
             and assaulted her, breaking open her cupboards, 'forcers' and coffers and
             taking away gold and silver jewels.
             (A. H. Thomas, *Calendar of Early Mayors' Court Rolls*, 230–1.)
             (We may conclude from this evidence that plate and jewels were kept in
             Alice Ebbegate's armoires: no other goods are mentioned as stolen.)

1321   'In camera supra . . . Item, in aumariis dicte camera . . .'
             There follows a list of plate, then:
             'plures litteras repositas in pluribus scrinis et bustis.'
             (Le Blond, 33–4.)
             (In the armoires in the higher chamber items of plate, and records stored
             in a number of cases and boxes.)
             This entry belongs to the inventory of goods found in the house of Eudes
             de Mareuil, Chaplain of Beauvais, after his death.

1465/6   An account of the travels of the nobleman, Leo of Rozmital, who left
             Prague with his suite in November, 1465, speaks of visiting Brussels and
             there seeing the Duke of Burgundy's 'treasure and jewels'.
             'It is said that nowhere in the world were such costly treasures, if only
             because of the hundred-thousand pound weight of beaten gold and
             silver gilt vessels which we saw in many cabinets, and which was so
             abundant that we never thought to see the like.'
             (Letts, 28.)

(3)   In wardrobes, for storing clothing, textiles, armour, etc.

1253   'To the Sheriff of Hampshire. *Contrabreve* to make two small cupboards in
             the king's upper wardrobe in his castle at Winchester where his cloths are
             kept, one on each side of the fireplace with 2 loopholes (*archeris*),[45] and a
             partition (*interclusum*) of board across the wardrobe in like manner; . . .'
             (*Calendar of Liberate Rolls IV, 1251–60*, H.M.S.O., 1959, 96.)

1256   'To Godfrey de Lyston [Keeper of the King's manors at Cokham and
             Braye], *Contrabreve* to wainscot the new chapel erected by the new turret
             in the upper bailey of the castle of Windsores, the nurses' chamber in that

---

[45] Although the Editor gives 'loopholes' as the translation here, the articles in question are certainly chests.

bailey, . . . and to make an *almariolum* in the middle of the turret of the upper bailey to keep the queen's clothes . . .'

(*Cal. Lib. R.*, IV, 296.)

1285   'Item pro factura cuiusdam Almarii in garderoba cum serrura et aliis ad idem pertinentibus .iii.s'.iiij.d'.o'.'

(M. S. Giuseppi, 'The Wardrobe and Household Accounts of Bogo de Clare, 1284–6', *Archaeologia*, LXX, 1918–20 [1920], 29.)

(Item, for making a certain armoire in the Wardrobe with lock and other things pertaining to it, 3*s*. 4*d*.)

1304   'Pour faire . . . les aumoires de la taillerie madame.'

(J-M. Richard, *Mahaut, Comtesse d'Artois et Bourgogne (1302–1329)*, Paris, 1887, 266.)

(For making . . . the armoires in Madame's tailors' workroom.)
This workroom appears first in the accounts concerning carpenters at the Comptesse d'Artois' castle of Hesdin in 1304: armoires, *presses* and a bench were installed for the purpose of maintaining the textiles in good repair. A household such as that of Mahaut used quantities of textiles in the form of wall and bed hangings, napery and clothing. In the same account, we learn of the installation of a loom at the castle, though we have no evidence concerning what kind of cloth was woven on it. (Richard, 368–9.)

(See Cat. 24, pl. 30; also pl. 60A.)

1386   '*1500*. Andrieu de Ternay, charpentier, demourant a Arras, donne quittance le 2 Décembre, de 17 fr. à lui dus pour la vendue d'unes aumaires faites de bois et d'aix de chesnes de 14 piez de long, à 4 estaiges, doublée dedens, de toille de canevas, pour mectre les bacinez et le harnoiz de Mgr.; et pour mectre une verge de fer et pour toille pour faire par devant lesd. aumaires une maniere de custodes.'

(B. &. H. Prost, *Inventaires Mobiliers et Extraits des Comptes des Ducs de Bourgogne de la Maison de Valois, II, Philippe le Hardi 1378–1390*, Paris, 1908–13 (4 fascs.), 247–8.

(Andrieu de Ternay, carpenter of Arras, paid 17 fr. for an armoire made of wood and of oak planks, 14' long with 4 shelves lined inside with 'canevas' [a coarse cloth], for storing the Duke's helmets and armour; and for fixing an iron rod and for cloth for hanging in front of the armoire to serve as a dust sheet.)

1405   'Draps de laine et autres choses, estans es armaires de la dite Garde Robbe, . . .'

(Dehaisnes, II, 901.)

(Woollen cloth and other things, which are in armoires in the said Wardrobe.)

This entry occurs in the long inventory of Margaret of Flanders, Duchess of Burgundy.

(4)   For chapel ornaments, vestments, etc.

1256   'To Godfrey de Lyston, [Keeper of the King's manors at Cokham and Braye]. *Contrabreve* to ... make an *almariolum* ... under the altar of the great chapel [at Windsor] for the vestments of the chapel; ...'
(*Cal. Lib. R.*, IV, 296.)

1468   'Unes aumoires fermans à deux guichez, en façon d'un autel, en la chapelle du galetas des galleries.'
(Jarry, 143.)
(An Armoire closed with 2 doors, like an altar, in the *galatas* chapel in the galleries [of Châteaudun].)

1482   '... grant aultel dudit Saint-Anthoine de Mascon ... Item, au costé dextre et dernier, ledit aultel est un petit armère ouquel est le repositoire de *corpus Christi*, ung vayssel d'argent à manière d'une salière et dessus une potence où est *corpus Christi*.'
(H. Batault, 'Inventaire du Mobilier de l'Hopital Sainte-Antoine à Mâçon', *Mémoires de la Société d'Histoire et d'Archéologie de Chalon sur Saône*, VII, 1883–8, 141.)
(... high altar of St Anthony of Maçon, ... Item, at the right side [and behind] the said altar is a small armoire wherein is kept a silver vessel like a salt-cellar and above it, upon a bracket, is kept the Host.)

(5)   For the storage of food and drink and of utensils connected with eating.

1368   'Thomas Kynebell, rector of St. Martin Pomeroy: in the Pantry: ... 2 *almaries*, ...'
(A. H. Thomas, *Calendar of Plea and Memoranda Rolls 1364–1381*, Cambridge, 1929, 92.)

1373   Thomas Mocking, citizen of London, (fishmonger):
'in the *dispensa* (storehouse), 1 aumbry with vats.'
(Thomas, 1929, 155.)

1384/5   The Duke and Duchess of Burgundy: in the *Saucerie* (part of the office of the Kitchen), were stored the dishes and vessels of copper, brass and pewter. They were ranged in orderly fashion in armoires which had doors made like windows, but filled with cloth (for ventilation). The doors had chains and bolts.
(Canat de Chizy, 1859, 115.)

1391   Inventory of the goods of Richard Toky, grocer:
        'Pantry and Buttery. One *ambry*, 40d; one hanging *ambry* . . .'
        (A. H. Thomas, *Calendar of Plea and Memoranda Rolls 1381–1412*,
        Cambridge, 1932, 211.)
        This description of a *hanging* armoire is most unusual for the Middle Ages.

1468   Jean, Comte de Dunois, at Châteaudun:
        'Item, en l'eschansonnerie, unes petites armoires . . .'
        (Jarry, 125.)
        (Item, in the Buttery, a small armoire.)

At least one type of armoire used for food storage has survived from the later Middle
Ages. A form of armoire, one-bay wide, is found associated with Flemish hospitals[46]
and convents (though there is no evidence to suggest that such a form was confined to
such contexts). One such armoire, owned and described by Baron Verhaegen in 1883,
came from the Great Convent at Ghent (now the Bijloke Museum), founded in 1234.[47]
The provenance of this armoire, the existence of a similar one in the Vleehuis Museum
(Antwerp) carved at the base with the name: SUSTER BEEL VA [N] GOER[48] and the
use of tall, ventilated armoires of seventeenth and eighteenth-century date by nuns of
the Ghent convents in their refectories as late as the 1880s, shows convincingly that such
armoires were used for food storage. Although not all the armoires brought within this
group of *begijnenkast* by Pauwels[49] have carving pierced right through a door or doors,
the Verhaegen example has this feature, and provides the first piece of direct evidence
that such pierced carving was sometimes designed to provide ventilation for food.[50]
However, it is certain that pierced carving for ventilation was not exclusively used for
food storage, so that the presence of pierced work does not enable us to define use from
this factor alone without other evidence.[51] Baron Verhaegen's paper describes how the
nuns of his day used individual armoires surviving from the seventeenth and eighteenth
centuries which were ranged side by side in the refectory for the storage of utensils and
certain foods; these armoires had lattice work ventilation in place of pierced carving and
formed, when their doors were open, isolated eating spaces enabling each nun to
consume as much or as little as she chose in relative privacy, within the limits of her
food allowance.

It has been shown that armoires were useful objects, but most of the references to
them tell us little or nothing about the quality of the work involved in individual

[46] See G. Caullet, 'Les Œuvres d'Art de l'Hopital Notre-Dame à Courtrai', *Bulletin du Cercle Historique et
Archéologique de Courtrai*, XI, 1913/14, pl. VII.
[47] 'Armoire de Réfectoire à l'Usage des Béguines', *Révue de l'Art Chrétien*, I, 1883, 225–6.
[48] H. Pauwels, 'De Begijnenkast vorm en Oorsprong', *Bulletin des Musés Royaux d'Art et d'Histoire*, 1960, fig. 6.
[49] Pauwels, 48–62.
[50] In an English context, P. Macquoid/R. Edwards, *Dictionary of English Furniture*, London, 1954, Cupboards
(food), 183–4, note that direct evidence that pierced panels for ventilation is lacking, their use as food cupboards
being inferred. R. W. Symonds, 'Evolution of the Cupboard', *Connoisseur*, CXII, 1943, 92, speaks of ventilated
food cupboards and their fittings but his comments lack references.
[51] '. . . and all the forep[ar]t of the almeries was thorough carved worke (*for to geve ayre to the towels*) . . . in
every almerie cleane towels for the mounkes to drie there hands on when they washed and went to dyn.' [My
italics.] Concerning Durham Abbey before the dissolution, 'Rites of Durham', *Surtees Soc.*, CVII, 1902, 79.

C

armoires. The majority will certainly have been strong and serviceable, showing individuality but lacking special embellishment, in common with the general character of medieval furniture. However, evidence from two sources shows that occasionally armoires ranked as adjuncts of estate, and in these circumstances they warranted the kind of care and financial outlay which was normally expended on furnishings within this category. The first reference demonstrating this point appears uninformative, but Richard has investigated the character of the workforce involved and the result of his research is of outstanding interest to the furniture historian, since it refutes the popular theory that skilled artists never worked on furniture in the Middle Ages.

1299   '. . . faire unes aumaires a mettre les aournemens de la capelle.'
            (Richard, 1887, 307.)
            (. . . to make an armoire for the storage of the chapel ornaments.)

This bald statement in the accounts of Mahaut, Comtesse d'Artois et de Bourgogne, gives no hint of the importance of the armoires. Mahaut was possessed of enormous wealth and was evidently a great builder and improver of existing structures. She undertook elaborate works at Hesdin and Bapaume, her principal châteaux, and also at at least twenty-three other places.[52] These armoires were made for the Château d'Hesdin and at the time Mahaut employed, on a permanent basis, a group of sculptors (*imagiers*) who worked alongside carpenters, giving an artistic quality to whatever was undertaken. The *imagiers* were important craftsmen, paid on a different scale from the carpenters; they were expected to use their talents on such widely differing objects as sacred figures for the chapel, important furniture such as the armoires, various forms of seating and even joke machinery (*engins d'esbattement*), designed to cover persons with water or powder or beat them with sticks.[53] Mahaut's *imagiers* were the equivalent of the great furniture makers of later periods, but the contribution that they made to furniture design must await discussion in Parts 2 and 3. The armoires in question were the work of the *imagier* Guissin, together with Bauduin de Wissoc and Jean de Saint-Omer who were lesser craftsmen.[54] Guissin also worked on a crucifix, altar tables, a statue of St Louis and on the *engins d'esbattement*;[55] he was only one of a number of *imagiers* patronized by the Countess. Although we have no details concerning the armoires, we know that they belonged to the relatively small number of pieces of furniture in the Middle Ages which could be described as works of art.

     The second reference to armoires of special significance concerns a group of elaborate character which reflected commercial, rather than seigneurial power.

1379/80   Account for the town of Bruges.
            'Acheté chez Gilles de Man, clerc, V feuilles d'or battu employées aux armoires qui se trouvent au Ghiselhuus comme pour dorer la corniche des dites armoires et les ogives, chaque cent d'or IIII sol gros.'
            (Dehaisnes, II, 565.)

[52] Richard, 1887, 271–81, 284–5, 288, 291–7, 399.
[53] Richard, 1887, 307, 334.
[54] Richard, 1887, 307.
[55] Richard, 1887, 307, 334.

(Purchased, through Giles de Man, clerk, 5 leaves of pressed gold for the Guildhouse armoires: for gilding the cornice and ogee arches, each 100 of gold 4 sol. gross.)

We notice that the armoires were carved and painted, or painted only, with ogival tracery embellished with gold leaf. As with Mahaut's armoire, it is the work of the *imagiers* — carving and gilding — and not elaborate construction that indicates importance, the significance of which will be discussed in Part 2.[56] (Dehaisnes notes that the Bruges merchants also decorated the Guildhouse chimney in 1389/90, employing Jean Coene to make a lion and the arms of the Duke of Burgundy for this purpose.)[57]

[56] See pp. 230 f., and p. 243.
[57] Dehaisnes, II, 673.

Catalogue Raisonné

ARMOIRES

TYPE 1.   THE LOCKER

(i)   A Stone Recess with Wooden Doors

The remains of numerous lockers have survived as holes in walls, sometimes grooved for a shelf, and sometimes with rebates which show that the doors once lay flush with the wall.[58] Unmutilated survivors, however, are very rare and therefore of outstanding importance; an early group at Obazine in France,[59] and a fifteenth-century group at York are here described (Cat. 1–7).

CATALOGUE No. 1 (PLATES 1–2)

Pair of Armoires, locker type, in the N. Transept, Church of St Etienne, Obazine (Corrèze). See also Appendix I.

Doors of oak, untreated
Right-hand door   w. 2′ 3¼″ h. 4′ 5¾″
Left-hand door   w. 2′ 3″ h. 4′ 4¾″
Thickness of wood 1¾″

Description (September 1973)

The wood is rough and entirely original. The left-hand door is made of a single piece, the right-hand only having one vertical joint near the hinge. The ironwork is strong and is entirely original except for the centrally-placed horizontal closing bar, which is a crude and relatively modern fitting. The original closing fittings have been torn out and the wood left unpatched, so that there is no difficulty in recognizing the original arrangement. Originally, a single movable horizontal bar was fitted with a single hasp which engaged a lock in the right-hand door, extending across to hold the left-hand door shut at the same time. This simple method of closing both doors in a single movement is used on the freestanding armoire in the church (Cat. 10), though in the latter more complicated provision is made (2 hasps and 2 locks in place of one as here).

[58] Only a few examples need be listed. Library of St Swithin's Priory, Winchester (now the Cathedral library); a book store built *c.*1170 with 8 large, arched recesses for book armoires. (W. Oakeshott, 'Winchester College Library before 1750', *Transactions of the Bibliographical Society*, 5th series, IX, 1954, 7, pl. IIIa.) Thirteenth century: Château de Montbard, in the great tower. (E. E. Viollet-le-Duc, *Dictionnaire Raisonné de l'architecture Francais*, 1, Paris, 1867, *Armoires*, 470.) And in the choir of the abbey church of Vezelay (Viollet-le-Duc, 1858, 467). And Westminster Abbey, chapel of St John the Baptist, a square-headed, double locker (*Royal Commission on Historical Monuments, London I (Westminster Abbey)*, London, 1924, pl. 67). Early fourteenth century: Stokesay Castle, Shropshire, in the N. tower, 2nd floor. And Old Soar, Kent, in the principal room (Turner, 175 ff.). Fifteenth century: Lincoln, a house in the Close with square-headed locker and moulded frame with shields ([J. H. Parker], *Some Account of Domestic Architecture in England from Richard II to Henry VIII* [III], Oxford, 1854, facing 73).

[59] Now Aubazine (Corrèze, 18 k. SW. of Tulle). The modern spelling, used on maps etc., is ignored by the Abbey authorities and the small commercial centre in its immediate vicinity. As all the literature concerning the furniture uses the earlier form *Obazine*, I am also adhering to it.

Each door closes within a stone rebate which permits it to lie flush with the wall surface. The doors are hung on two substantial hinges with long straps. A third strap, placed centrally and of decorative rather than functional use, follows the design of the hinge straps. The straps are flat and straight, widened at intervals to describe an arc above and below and finished with fleur-de-lis terminals which are raised or humped, giving a visual interest to an otherwise plain design. The straps are nailed in position and are countersunk. All the central fleurettes have been prised away and some outer fleurettes are also mutilated. The doors bear a series of tiny holes with wider depressions surrounding them; these holes outline each iron strap and trace lines which run beneath the fleur-de-lis finials.

Analysis

This pair of armoires is the only example of those of precisely similar form, surviving in the church and abbey of Obazine, to be equipped with original doors and ironwork. (Parallel examples: church, S. transept; convent, small library in the cloister and W. wall of the refectory, both in ruin.)

The armoires share the same rough character as the church doors which flank them in the N. transept. Their character, and in particular their ironwork, is precisely the same as that found on the armoire at the W. end of the church and it has therefore been concluded that both groups were made at the same time.

The series of tiny holes with indented circles round them are paralleled on the freestanding armoire in the church (Cat. 10). The theory that the marks on the free-standing armoire were occasioned by nails attaching metal strips[60] is untenable when the evidence from these N. transept lockers is considered, for here the lines of holes occupy positions which would imply that the bands collided with the finials of the iron strapping.

It has been shown in Appendix I that this pair of armoires date from the first years of the building of the church and were complete in 1176.

Armoires of this type without doors survive in considerable numbers[61] but examples with their original doors are very rare. We have seen that such fixtures were common in houses and they were certainly incorporated in the building of private chapels, as we learn from a reference concerning the Château de Jonville in 1404.[62]

CATALOGUE NO. 2 (PLATE 3)

Armoire, locker type, in the W. end, Church of St Etienne, Obazine (Corrèze). See also Appendix I.

Doors of oak, untreated
w. across both doors 3' 8½"; max. h. doors 4' 11¾"; thickness of wood c.1½".

Description (September 1973)

The locker is built as a stone box free of the W. wall of the church at sides and front and engaged only at the back. It is domed and has a typically twelfth-century moulding, in lieu of a capital, which is carried the length of the sides. The full depth of the stone

[60] Le Marquis de Fayolle, 'Armoire du XIIe Siècle et Tombeau de Saint Etienne à Obasine (Corrèze), *57e Congrès Archéologique de France* (Société Française Archéologique), 1890, 225–6.
[61] See fn. 58.
[62] 'En la chapelle, en une aumoire de pierre de cousté l'autel, . . .' ([L. de la Trémoille], *Les La Trémoille Pendant Cinq Siècles. I. Guy et Georges, 1343–1346*, Nantes, 1890, 282.)

box is utilized, but the height is only that of the doors; it is, in effect, set on a deep plinth for convenience in use.

The doors are set within rebates in the stonework and lie flush; the left-hand and right doors are themselves rebated in sympathy to allow the right door to lie over the left-hand door when closed. Each door is a single piece of timber and bears three iron straps, the upper and lower being hinge straps and the central being decorative. The straps are all of the same design, being flat and straight, widened at intervals to describe an arc above and below, and finished with fleur-de-lis terminals which are raised or humped, giving a visual interest to an otherwise plain design; they are nailed in position and countersunk. Many of the fleurettes of the terminals are mutilated. The unpatched scars left by the removal of the lock (right door, centre) and bar above it (extending across both doors) indicate the nature of the original locking device: a moving bar, lodged on the right-hand door when the doors were open, had a single hasp designed to engage a square lock plate on the right-hand door and a loop on the left-hand door when the armoire was closed.

Like the doors on the pair of armoires in the N. transept (Cat. 1), these doors also have a series of holes with surrounding circular depressions; no satisfactory explanation for these marks has been suggested.

Analysis

Although the armoire has every appearance of being virtually untouched twelfth-century work, its present position cannot be original and it is now built against an eighteenth-century wall (see Appendix I). It has been concluded by de Fayolle that the armoire was faithfully re-erected, using old materials, in the eighteenth century and I accept this view.[63] The armoire was, presumably, of this unusual form because the object or objects for which it was designed were too large to be accommodated within the thickness of a wall, in the usual locker manner, and it was clearly considered too useful to be dispensed with in the eighteenth century. The armoire is not so much remarkable for its form as for its material, for it would cause no surprise if it were of wood, integrated with a wooden partition. The armoire has the same rough character as the church doors in the N. transept (see Appendix I). The doors and the ironwork of the armoire both closely resemble those found in the pair of lockers in the N. transept of the church (Cat. 1); this comparison indicates that the same smith was involved in both fittings and that they were made at approximately the same time. De Fayolle has shown that the lockers in the N. transept were complete in 1176.[64] The ironwork strapping upon the armoire is of the same design as is found on the freestanding armoire in the church (Cat. 10). All the lockers, however, (W. and N.) are cruder in both woodwork and iron-work than is the case with the freestanding armoire.

Although this armoire has been moved, the evidence set out in Appendix I shows that it was part of the original building of the church and is of *c*.1176; its original position in the church is unknown, but it was presumably somewhere in that part of the W. end which was demolished in the eighteenth century.

[63] de Fayolle, 227.
[64] de Fayolle, 229.

CATALOGUE NOS. 3–7 (PLATES 4–6)

Five Armoires of locker type in the room called the Zouche chapel, York Minster.[65] See also Appendix II.

Oak, now polished

Description (April 1970)

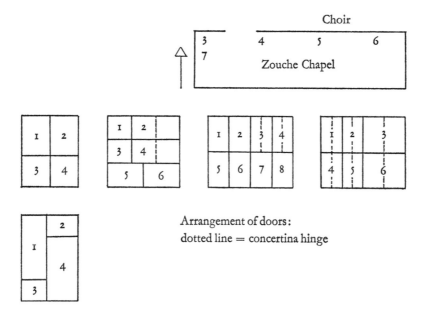

FIG. 1. *Top*: position of armoire in the Zouche chapel
Below: individual armoires — sketch diagrams to show arrangements of doors and hinges

The armoires are accommodated within the thickness of the walls which were built to contain them; room and fittings form a single design unit of the same date. (The architectural details of the room, both internally and externally, are dated to *c*.1500 on stylistic grounds, see Appendix II.) The armoire doors are flush with the walls, with a moulding at the top and sides which projects in front of the stonework. The side mouldings finish in bases, in the manner of a pilaster, though there are no capitals; the top mouldings are surmounted by a crenellated cornice.

The armoires are constructed of vertical boards reinforced with substantial iron hinge straps. Some straps have single hinges (armoires 3, 7), while others with wider doors employ a mixture of single and double hinges enabling the widest doors to be opened concertina fashion, to avoid the inconvenience of a wide and unwieldy door sticking out into the room (armoires 4–6). No two armoires have the same arrangement of doors, but it should be noted that 7 has been altered while the others have remained

[65] A free-standing armoire, with details which correspond with these lockers, also exists in York Minster and must have been made at the same time.

unchanged. (The doors of armoire 7 now slide, instead of opening outwards, and some portion of them has been cut away, so that the original arrangement of this armoire cannot be determined with certainty.)

A variety of forms are found in the ironwork, but all appear to be contemporary. The lock plates are chiefly rectangular with projecting, trefoiled corners; or formed of simple rectangles with slightly concave sides. The strap hinges have finials of two forms, fleur-de-lis and foliated triangular. The straps are interrupted by sex-foil rosettes and are attached to hinge plates of two forms: long, rectangular plates (making a T-form with the strap); and a plate which virtually continues the line of the widest part of the strap itself. Both forms lie partially covered by the applied wooden side mouldings of the armoires. The handles are circular and faceted and depend from the centre of sex-foil plates.

As has already been noted, armoire 7 has been mutilated. The remaining armoires have been skilfully restored in modern times, but this repair work is minor and entirely in sympathy with the original work in wood and iron; there are insignificant modern locks with small oval plates.

The general character of the armoires is robust; the framework is sophisticated; the ironwork is well made. The general effect of the room itself is impressive, owing to the scale of the fittings and the neatness with which they are accommodated.

Analysis

The completeness of the 'Zouche Chapel', in which room and fittings form a single entity, gives these armoires a position of the greatest interest and importance. We can correlate them with a number of documentary references; for example, the group made for the Duke of Burgundy's archives at Talent in 1364/5 and those made for Elizabeth of York's Council Chamber in 1502.[66] The evidence suggests that such fittings were not uncommon in the Middle Ages. However, the survival of so large a group *in situ* is unique within the confines of this study.

We have seen that the room containing these fixtures was built in *c*.1500 (Appendix II), and that the armoires were built within niches designed for them. The character of the woodwork and ironwork of the armoires corroborates the evidence of the stonework of the room.

The crenellated cornice form was much favoured in the fifteenth century and continued in use in the early years of the sixteenth century. We see it on the railing of the 7th Lord Percy's tomb of 1415 in the Fitzalan Chapel of Arundel Castle, and a late example is found on the flamboyant gothic retable of the life of St John the Baptist of *c*.1520.[67] The framework at the sides of the armoires, placed *over* the hinge plates, is paralleled at Westminster (Cat. 14), as are certain features of the ironwork. Rosettes occur in both examples, recalling work ranging from the 1420s or 1430s to the early years of the sixteenth century and examples of rosettes which interrupt the hinge strap, as they do at York, instead of terminating it as they do at Westminster, are found on the

---

[66] See p. 5.
[67] J. Casier/P. Bergmans, *L'Art Ancien dans les Flandres. Mémorial de l'Exposition Retrospective Organisée à Gand en 1913*, Brussels/Paris, 1914, pls. XLIII, XLIV.

Ghent armoire of *c*.1490–1510 (Cat. 15) and on a door of the Town Hall of Damme which was almost certainly part of the work carried out there in 1464 (see pl. 72A).

The concertina doors, present on some of the York armoires, were evidently found convenient for book storage, as is shown in a fourteenth-century Italian miniature in which are seen two armoires with concertina doors folded open exposing shelves of books.[68]

All the evidence of the woodwork and ironwork of the armoires is consistent with a date of *c*. 1500, corresponding with the date of the building of the range of rooms of which the 'Zouche Chapel' is a part.

(ii) Fitted and Enclosed Storage Areas which Project and are often Independent of Original Structure

After the recessed stone locker, the projecting, fitted locker stands next in neatness and permanence. Such fixtures are often entirely of wood and were probably common in wooden buildings throughout the Middle Ages, as well as in buildings of stone; very few lockers survive *in situ* but two are included in the Catalogue (8, 9). In addition, there is a group of mutilated armoires some or all of which may have fallen within this category (Cat. 22–5).

CATALOGUE No. 8 (PLATES 7–8)

Group of Armoires of locker type in St Albans Cathedral. Part of the 'Watching Loft', overlooking the Shrine of St Alban.

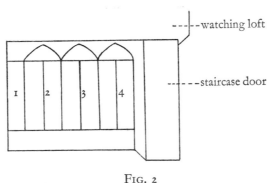

FIG. 2

Oak

Door 1 w. 10¾″

  2 w. left door 14½″; right door 14¾″

  3 w. left door 13¾″; right door 14¼″

  4 w. left door 10¼″; right door 10¾″

  h. of all doors 4′ 2¼″; h. of panel above lockers, at centre of arch 1′ 10¼″.

[68] See R. Hunt, 'The sum of knowledge', ed. Evans, 1966, 191, figs. 33–4 (MS 620 fol. Ir, Bib. Municipale Classée, Cambrai). One armoire is evidently in the author's library and the other in a bookshop.

Description (July 1969; only locker 4 was seen open)

The armoires are incorporated within an elaborate wooden structure which forms a partition blocking off the void created by one stone arch east of the high altar. The partition is of two stages, the lower comprising armoires and staircase door; and the upper, a loft or chamber having a series of open, traceried lights which allow a view of the Shrine of St Alban. The left-hand armoire, no. 1, is single; the others, nos. 2–4, are double. A deep, elaborately moulded plinth runs beneath the armoires and from it rise cluster columns which delineate each armoire. The doors are cut off squarely, level with the capitals of these columns; above each door is an arched panel carved with tracery. Above the capitals of the cluster columns, the ribs fan out to support the overhang of the chamber above, the Watching Loft. The armoire doors are carved with perpendicular tracery, nos. 2–4 matching and no. 1 being slightly different. The plinth beneath no. 1 is scuffed which suggests that this armoire, in addition to being narrower than the others, was used differently, it being necessary here as nowhere else to put a foot on the plinth in order to use the armoire. All the hinge-work for the doors is hidden from the front. Doors to armoire 4 and the staircase door have long, straight hinge straps countersunk on the inner surfaces: two straps to each door. The terminals of the hinge straps are cut with tracery. These countersunk hinges are original on armoire 4 (the only one seen open).

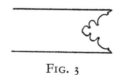

FIG. 3

The right-hand door to armoire 4 has two original bolts on the inner surface to hold the upper and lower edges of the door in place. Both bolts have domed, round-headed nails on stems which act as levers. The upper bolt, of rectangular section, has a long tapering 'tail' of round section ending in a knop.

The locks of all the doors are lost and the wood in the lock area has been repaired, so that a reconstruction of the original arrangement is impossible; the doors are now secured with modern loops and padlocks.

Analysis

St John Hope believed the Watching Loft to be the Feretrar's room referred to in the *Liber Benefactorum*, between two entries dated 1413 and 1429 respectively: that it cost 20*s.* to erect and was the gift of Robert Malton:

'ROBERTUS DE MALTON CLERICUS DE PIPA CONTULIT AD OPUS PRESENTIS ECCLESIE PRO ANIMA RADULPHI KESTERVENE QUON-DAM RECTORIS SANCTI BOTOLPHI EXTRA ALDRICHEGATE LONDON. XXs. ET IDEM ROBERTUS CONTULIT NOVE CAMERE FERETRARII JUXTA MAIUS ALTARE.   XXs.'

St John Hope points out that before the building of Abbot Wallingford's reredos the Watching Loft could fairly be described as standing near the high altar.[69] There would seem to be no reason for contesting this view. The sum of 20s. provided is certainly not excessive for so large a wooden structure, but comparisons for expenditure on wood-work, although easily made, are hazardous since we are not always aware of what precisely was covered in a context of this kind.[70]

The St Albans Watching Loft has been compared with a French fifteenth-century screen now in the Metropolitan Museum of Art, New York, which is fitted with two open shelves and two lockers and was 'probably made for a sacristy or dining hall'.[71] This comparison with a screen which may have been domestic seems highly relevant, for the St Albans screen is dainty and intimate, beautiful in form and execution but ill-attuned to the monumentality of the Abbey as a whole. It destroys the architectural harmony of an area of the church, cutting arbitrarily across the arch which acts as its host. Considered as an isolated structure it is admirable, but in its context it is unsatisfactory.

The hinge straps with their traceried terminals may be compared with a number of pieces of furniture, in particular with those of the armoire of the Spanish merchants of Bruges (Cat. 17).

[69] W. H. St John Hope, 'Of the great Almery for Relics in the Abbey Church of Selby, with Notes on some Other Receptacles for Relics', *Archaeologia*, LX, 1907, 420.

[70] In the great households in the later Middle Ages, and in any context where the upkeep of fabric was a continual concern, evidence suggests that carpenters or joiners, painters and other craftsmen were continually employed on a long term basis. In such cases, where new work was carried out, the accounts might note the cost of materials and carriage only, since the cost of the labour itself was already covered in individual retention arrangements, and would have been entered elsewhere. We find that we cannot attempt an assessment of what individual payments in accounts represent without some indication of the terms under which an individual worked. The Duke of Burgundy's accounts are instructive in this respect. We often find payments *for materials alone* in the case of craftsmen working in the Duke's service:

'*2731*. 15 août Jehan Poncet, charpentier des menues euvres de charpenterie de Mgr touche 3 fr. pour bois acheté par lui pour faire une litiere pour Mme.' (Prost, I, 516.) However, when the Duke pays a craftsman who is not attached to his service (and there are many such craftsmen thus casually employed), the entry may explain that labour is covered in the cost:

'*1438*. 8 août, ordre de payer 86 fis. à Jehan d'Orleans, peintre et varlet de chambre du roy, pour la façon d'un biers pour Jehan monsr.' (Prost, I, 261–2.) Here, we find a very large sum is paid for a cradle of estate for John the Fearless, made by a craftsman attached not to the Duke of Burgundy's service but to that of the King of France. Similarly, the King of England had craftsmen attached to his service. The officer of Joiner (which originated in the office of lance maker in the Tower of London) is not infrequently referred to. Payments are made for taking timber and also for *making* doors, windows, chests and furniture, and the latter payments appear to be low when compared with straightforward valuations for single pieces of furniture. For example, 1446, Bartholomew Halley (holding the office of King's Joiner with premises on Tower Wharf) was paid £3. 5s. 2d. for making: chests for bows and bowstrings, a staff for a pellet gun, and doors, windows and lattices in the Queen's closet at Eltham (R. A. Brown/H. M. Colvin/A. J. Taylor, *History of the King's Works*, I, London, 1963, 224–5). We may compare this with straightforward valuations for chests (valuations which presumably represent approximate resale value) and we find sums which vary between about 4d. and 10s. for one chest in the fourteenth century (Eames, 1969, xxxii–xxxiii). Even here, where we are confronted with simple valuations in which costs of labour and materials must be reflected, the almost total lack of descriptive evidence for wooden furniture in inventories renders comparisons almost meaningless.

If we recall the high quality of work visible in the Watching Loft we shall feel bound to compare it with a chest worth 10s. rather than with a cheaper one. If we do this, I think we must concede that the sum of 20s. for the Watching Loft is only realistic if it represented a payment in circumstances where the full cost of labour and materials was spread out and accounted for in different ways because the workmen involved were attached to the Abbey under some form of contract; such a contract might well have allowed them free board and lodging as well as other benefits.

[71] J. J. Rorimer, 'The Treasury at the Cloisters and Two Ingolstadt Beakers', *Bulletin of the Metropolitan Museum of Art, New York*, 1951, 251.

Reference should here be made to a similar structure (screen composed of armoires) once in the abbey church of Selby and, by appalling mischance, now totally destroyed by fire.[72]

Select Bibliography

J. J. Rorimer, 'The Treasury of the Cloisters and 2 Ingolstadt Beakers', *Bull. M.M.A.*, 1951, 251.

St John Hope, 'Of the Great Almery for Relics in the Abbey Church of Selby, with Some Notes on Some Other Receptacles for Relics', *Archaeologia*, LX, 1907, 418–20.

St Albans Cathedral, H.M.S.O., 1952.

CATALOGUE No. 9 (PLATE 9)

Armoire of locker type formed as part of the screen of a doorway. Exchequer, Vicars Choral, Wells Cathedral. See also Appendix IV.

Oak

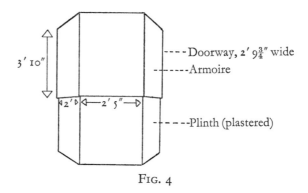

FIG. 4

Description (December 1969)

The exterior woodwork of the armoire is supported upon a plastered brick or stone base, and the whole forms the entrance to the Exchequer. The doorway itself is simply an opening which is reached by a spiral stair from the Refectory below. The doorway has no door (the original arrangement), and was probably closed with a heavy curtain. The armoire utilizes the space within the stairwell which is just above head level as a person climbs or descends the staircase.

The armoire is of robust, panelled construction with a single door giving access to an unshelved interior. It is straightforward, competent work in good preservation and is unaltered except for the loss of the original lock.

[72] See St John Hope 1907, 411–22, pls. XXXVII–XXXVIII. The published photograph shows that these lockers were fine examples of fifteenth-century work, and their unusual manner of opening makes it important to note them here. Each locker was arranged in the form of two vertically placed panels, the upper of which projected over the lower in the manner of a sash window; only the upper panel was decorated. To open the lockers, the upper panel was pulled downwards over the lower panel thus covering it and disclosing the contents of the upper area without the encumbrance of projecting doors. It seems likely that the form of opening was designed so that the lockers might occasionally form display cabinets, for they apparently held relics.

Analysis

This method of incorporating an armoire in a doorway screen is neat and economical and may well have been a common way of making the *speres* (often doorway screens) which are frequently referred to.[73] The most important aspect of the armoire is its context, for it is a very rare survivor of a class of furniture, fitted to the fabric of a building, which was once common. The domestic scale of the Exchequer and its untouched appearance of *c*.1457 with timber ceiling, window, fireplace and laver (pl. 72B), together with the armoire/screen, needs only the addition of a table and seating to make it complete, a comfortable and well-appointed room for work, conversation and, perhaps, private dining.[74] The panelled construction of the armoire, massive rather than delicate, recalls the substantial character of the Brasenose College chest (Cat. 39).

TYPE 2 (a) FREESTANDING: SINGLE, DOUBLE OR MULTI-BAYED

Extant freestanding armoires, largely in their original condition, are far more numerous than complete examples of the locker types, and although early examples are confined to a small and well-known group, many have survived from the later Middle Ages. The lack of early comparative material makes it difficult to form conclusions concerning scope and variety in form and technique. The fuller evidence for armoires belonging to the fourteenth and fifteenth centuries, however, shows that at this period technical and stylistic development was conservative, but that a surprising variety of form was encompassed.[75]

CATALOGUE NO. 10 (PLATES 10–11)

Armoire (freestanding) in the church of St Etienne, Obazine, (Corrèze). See also Appendix I and Cat. 1, 2.

Oak untreated
l. 8′ 1″; h. 7′ 5″; w. 2′ 9½″.

[73] The numerous references to screens, particularly in the Liberate Rolls of Henry III are discussed in [J. H. Parker], *Some Account of Domestic Architecture in England from Edward I to Richard II* [II], Oxford, 1853, 43–4. See also the inventory of the Château de Montbeton (1496) where the entrances of at least four rooms were equipped with panelled screens (E. Forestié, 'Un Mobilier Seigneurial du XVe Siècle. Le Château de Montbeton en 1496', *Bulletin Archéologique et Historique de la Société Archéologique de Tarn-et-Garonne*, XXIII, 1895, 41 *16*; 43 *42, 50*; 46 *151*).
[74] In the king's household a great officer such as the steward might take meals 'in his chamber, or in any other office, as often as hit pleasith hym.' (Myers, 1959, 142 § 68). At Wells, the officers charged with the financial administration of the Vicars Choral, who occupied this suite of rooms, must have been amongst the most influential and powerful men of their College.
[75] Here I am in disagreement with Eric Mercer who suggests the reverse (*Furniture 700–1700*, 104–5). Mercer notes that armoires were neither common nor varied before the sixteenth century. For France, Viollet-le-Duc has shown that armoires were habitually used by rich and poor alike before the fifteenth century and he believed it to be the most important piece of domestic furniture throughout the Middle Ages (Viollet-le-Duc, *Dictionnaire Raisonné du Mobilier Francais*, I, Paris 1858, 13, 18). In an English context, Macquoid/Edwards suggest the same common usage (see 1954, under Aumbry and Bookcase).
The views expressed in both these works are well borne out by documentary evidence, see pp. 2 ff. Although time has dealt severely with medieval armoires, the examples in the Catalogue provide ample corroborative evidence to complement written records and demonstrate, as records seldom do, a surprising variety in *form*.

Description (September 1973)

All the woodwork at the front of the armoire is original; the armoire is now raised off the floor on modern boards.

Front   Three wide uprights are extended to form the feet and are joined laterally (tenon and mortise) by 4 wide boards. The 2 doors are flush with the framing, the right composed of 3 boards and the left of 2 and they encroach upon the 3 uprights which are indented to receive them. The cornice, extending across front and sides, is carved with zigzag motif.

The doors are hung on long straps, countersunk, 2 to each door, which are of the same pattern — though of finer section — as those upon other armoires in the church (lockers, Cat. 1, 2). The straps are flat, widened at intervals along their lengths, and terminate in fleur-de-lis finials which, in contrast to the straps, are raised or humped. All the central fleurettes have been broken off. Two small decorative iron plates are nailed to the central upright between the doors, continuing the horizontal line of the hinge straps. The armoire is fitted with 2 fine locks and a single bar with 2 hasps, which is held horizontally in a series of collars decorated with diagonal hatching. The lock plates are square, attached with conspicuous square-headed nails which provide a decorative, serrated border. The central area of the lock plates is raised in a rectangle to a height approximately the distance between the woodwork and the outside of the bar, thus enabling the hasps to engage in the locks. The bar is a single fitting, moving in its collars, with 2 hasps attached. When the doors are open, the bar is lodged on the right-hand door; it has an elaborate cranked handle at the right end, worked with a grotesque head which grasps a small bar in its teeth which is itself terminated with a grotesque head at each end. At the ends of the hasps are square-headed nails set on stalks, for leverage. All the ironwork so far described is original and unaltered. On the left-hand door, beside the lockplate, is a small circular handle which may be original; certainly, some sort of handle would be needed to pull this door open, whereas on the right-hand door the bolt would serve this purpose. A thin metal strip, with one join, is attached beneath the doors and extends across the front of the armoire; it does not appear to be original, serving neither decorative nor useful purpose and is out of character with the rest of the attachments. There does not appear to be any connexion between this strip and the series of tiny holes with circular depressions round them which can be discovered on the front of the armoire. These holes trace lines across the armoire: (1) the lowest, a horizontal line crossing frame and doors, level with the bolt; (2) a short horizontal line on the centre rail; (3) a line which crosses the frame and curves to follow the outline of the doors; (4) a straight horizontal line crossing the armoire above the doors.

Sides   Though lacking in decorative fittings, the sides are today more elaborate than the front. The 2 uprights, which are extended to form the feet, are each finely worked as a pair of engaged columns, the outermost towards the front of the armoire being worked upon the *corner* and therefore visible from the front as well as from the sides. These engaged columns have tiny bases and round arches springing from the capitals which themselves support an undecorated entablature. Between these uprights with their engaged columns are 4 round-headed arches set in pairs in 2 registers. The 3 columns on each register are worked in the round (turned) and have a slight inward kick to their arches, a local detail found in the arches of the nave of the church. The entablatures of these arcades are flush with the entablature above the engaged columns, the boarding behind the arcading being recessed. The arches have 2 lines of string moulding and there is a line of zigzag carving at the foot of the upper register, matching the carving on the cornice. Ventilation holes cut on both sides are secondary. Some boards behind the arcading are replacements and a number of columns are missing:

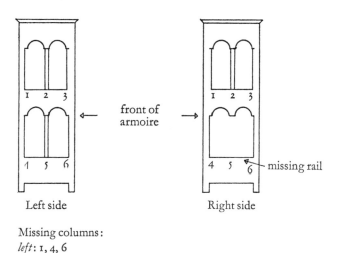

Left side   front of armoire   Right side

Missing columns:
left: 1, 4, 6
right: 4, 5, 6, together with the rail supporting these columns

FIG. 5.   Sides of armoire (traces of red paint remain in the carving of the cornice)

Analysis

From the historian's point of view, this armoire is the most important example of medieval furniture in France. It has been shown that it was made at the time of the building of the abbey church of St Etienne at Obazine, and may be dated to *c.*1176 through a correlation with fixtures in the church (Cat. 1, 2; Appendix I). It is thus an early survivor and stands *in situ*, in excellent preservation, in a context where tight dating is possible. These factors, combined with the armoire's own quality of massive monumentality, make it of outstanding interest. The armoire, like the architecture which surrounds it, is bold and simple in form and of considerable weight, a quality shared by all surviving wooden furniture of pre-fourteenth-century date. But the boldness is never crude; on the contrary, it is accompanied by delicacy in the working on the sides of the armoire, and by subtlety in the design and form of the ironwork. The delicacy of the sides can be thoroughly appreciated only at first hand, but the niceties of the ironwork are more readily discernible verbally and photographically. The raised fleur-de-lis finials on the flat straps are effective at a distance; and the changes in width which the straps undergo is a means of achieving added strength (2 nails are possible on the wide sections in place of 1) on a visually delicate strap, and also of achieving some subtlety in the horizontal rhythms of the design. The lock plates, hasps and bolt are all carefully worked and for that reason rewarding on close inspection, but perhaps most of all one admires the logic of the design of the locks and the directness with which it is implemented. This armoire is opened with 2 keys which indicates that the contents were the responsibility of 2 men.[76] The *single* bar which controls the hasps ensures that both these men must be present if the contents of any part of the armoire were to be made available. The arrangement of these fittings is echoed in the armoire at Malines (Cat. 13), but in the latter, although the appearance is identical in the placing of lock plates and bolt, the bar is not a single fitting as at Obazine.

Opinions have varied concerning small details. Viollet-le-Duc considered that the traces of paint on the cornice indicated that the armoire was originally painted, while de Fayolle believed that the painting was secondary.[77] The tiny holes with surrounding circular depressions, found in many places on the front of the armoire, were thought by Viollet-le-Duc to be handworked,[78] a conclusion de Fayolle refuted. De Fayolle considered that the marks were made by nails which once attached thin metal strips running across the armoire in 4 lines, the lowest of which was level with the bolt.[79] This theory is untenable when considered in a wider context. The marks are also found elsewhere, for similar holes with circular depressions around them outline every iron strap on the pair of armoires of locker type in the N. transept of the church (Cat. 1). On these locker armoires, the lines traced by the marks collide with the fleur-de-lis finials of the ironwork, so that additional metal bands could never have occupied such a position. Viollet-le-Duc's theory is certainly wrong, as anyone who has seen the armoire will realize. But a convincing explanation evades us. The marks are larger than any of the nails used to secure the ironwork and their positions do not suggest attachment pins for leather or linen. (Although running across the doors of the freestanding armoire at bolt height, there are no marks which trace the outline of these doors which would be most necessary.)

The different treatment between front and sides is not uncommon in medieval furniture. It may take the form it takes here, in which sides and front are differently assembled, a characteristic shared by the fifteenth-century armoire in the Vestry at Obazine (Cat. 16). Or it may take the form of contrasting surface treatment upon a form of assembly which is the same throughout, as at Noyon.[80] The fundamental contrast between sides and front at Obazine may have been enhanced by differential painting. The flat surface of the front would allow some elaboration in this respect, as at Bayeux (Cat. 11), which would be impossible on the sides where the delicate turned columns provide an early example of a technique which was common throughout the Middle

---

[76] The sharing of keys was the normal method of safeguarding valuables and guarding the reputations of custodians; see 6 keys held for a common chest at Guildhall, London (Eames, 'An Iron Chest at Guildhall of about 1427', *Furniture History*, x, 1974, 1–4, pl. 1.

[77] Viollet-le-Duc, 1858, 5; de Fayolle, 228.

[78] Viollet-le-Duc, 1858, 5.

[79] de Fayolle, 225–6.

[80] A famous painted armoire, with figure subjects on the front and chevrons on the sides, illustrated by Viollet-le-Duc, 1858, 10. Lamentably, it disappeared in the 1914/18 war (G. Janneau, *Les Meubles*, 1, Paris, 1929, 9).

Ages.[81] However, I am inclined to agree with de Fayolle who believed the surviving paint to be secondary, for it seems unlikely that a brilliantly painted object would have been designed for a church whose architecture is so markedly lacking in decorative detail.

CATALOGUE No. 11 (PLATES 12–13A)

Armoire (freestanding) in Bayeux Cathedral. In the Treasury, 1st floor.

Oak, painted

l. 17' 2¼"; h. without finials 9' 3¼"; w. 2' 11¾".

Description (August 1968)

The armoire has been reduced in length and clumsily re-made with an utter disregard for its original arrangement. It is now composed of 14 compartments in 2 registers, 7 lower and 7 upper. Only the 8 doors at the right-hand end, 4 upper and 4 lower (bracketed), preserve the original scheme.

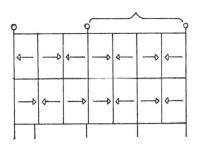

Arrows indicate opening edge of doors

FIG. 6

The doors close flush with a simple flat and narrow framework and are of boards (presumably mortise and tenon joinery). The uprights of the frame are extended in 3 instances to form feet; 3 other feet, which do not correspond with the stiles, also support the armoire, and here again mutilation obscures the original design. The bracket feet are pierced. Three finials surmounting the armoire survive. The spandrels and the finials are the only decorative features worked in the wood; only the finials, however, being faceted and knopped, are designed to be seen in the round.

The ironwork has been little altered, if the rearrangement of the armoire is taken into account, and the original scheme for each bay can be appreciated without difficulty. Each door is suspended by 2 long hinge straps and has a centre brace of complementary form. All strap finials are fleur-de-lis. (Straps and finials are flat and are not countersunk.) The hinge plates on the framework have bifoliated terminals and each plate is arranged to serve 2 hinges except at the ends, giving a neat design well suited to the narrow

---

[81] For example, 1226, columns applied to the tomb chest of William Longespée, Earl of Salisbury, Salisbury Cathedral; thirteenth and fourteenth-century church screens at Sparsholt, Berks., Stanton Harcourt, Oxon., and King's Lynn (see A. Vallance, *English Church Screens*, London, 1936, figs. 65, 54, 67); and fifteenth-century examples in Netherlandish paintings, e.g. the Master of Flémalle (see Panofsky, figs. 211, 203).

D

stiles.[82] The locking arrangements on the 2 right-hand bays indicate that the original scheme was as follows. A single lock to each pair of doors (simple, flat rectangular plate) with a hasp attached to a bolt above it, fixed centrally on the right-hand door, the bolt moving left to close the left-hand door in the locked position. The bolt held with straps having bifoliated terminals. The left-hand door of each pair fitted with a ring handle attached to flat straps in the form of a cross with bifoliated terminals.

The armoire was once entirely painted, and the surfaces of the doors and framework, without mouldings, are clearly designed with this in mind. Although a considerable amount of actual paint survives on the wood, it is no longer possible to follow the decorative scheme as a whole, nor to assess the quality of the work but as gold leaf was employed it is likely to have been high. Two different running motifs were used on rails and stiles respectively, and this ornament can be traced in several places. The painting on the doors, however, has all but disappeared, only a fragment remaining on the far left-hand door, lower register.[83] Four figures, apparently monks, stand or process two by two carrying a long platform on poles which seems to support a reliquary; above them are 2 censing angels. The colours are now much dirtied and worn and cannot be distinguished in the light available in the room.[84]

The armoire is now built against a stone seat which runs behind it along the length of the wall.

Analysis

The Armoire is sadly mutilated:[85] its proper form is lost and its painted decoration — the whole *purpose* which dictated its form — has almost entirely vanished. But in spite of its mutilations, it provides useful evidence of those elaborate pieces of furniture, mentioned in documents and rarely surviving, of which St Edward's Chair and the cradle made for one of the children of Marie of Burgundy and Maximilian of Austria are other examples (Cat. 28). Such furniture was never available for continual display, but was designed for purposes of ceremony and estate, located only in areas where a degree of control over persons was possible. Only in such conditions could delicately painted furniture survive in the Middle Ages; pieces of this kind were of limited use and were rare at the time they were made.[86] This armoire was apparently designed to contain reliquaries,[87] and the elaborate and costly work with which it was once ornamented reflects the importance inherent in its purpose. Placed in the Treasury of the cathedral built between 1230–40,[88] it would only have been seen and used by a limited number of

---

[82] The published drawing of this detail is misleading (Viollet-le-Duc, *Dictionnaire Raisonné du Mobilier Francais*, I, Paris, 1858, 8): the hinge is set too far in, so that the nailed terminals of the plate would lie *on the doors* instead of on the frame, suggesting that the artist never saw the armoire.

[83] Viollet-le-Duc states that the subject of the paintings was the translation of relics, and refers the reader to drawings which show the scenes in some detail (Viollet-le-Duc, 1858, 6–8).

[84] Viollet-le-Duc gives the scheme for the doors as white on red, while the motifs on the rails and stiles employed black as well (Viollet-le-Duc, 1858, 8).

[85] Noted by C. Daly, 'Armoire Peinte du XIIIe Siècle', *Révue Générale de l'Architecture et des Travaux Publics*, X, 1852, 132.

[86] See the discussions concerning furniture of estate, Parts 2 and 3.

[87] See Daly, 132–3. The armoire also enclosed the armour of a knight who held an hereditary office and accompanied the bishop of Bayeux at festivals (Daly, 153–4).

[88] J. Vallery-Radot, *La Cathédrale de Bayeux*, Paris, 1958, 15, 54; the Treasury dates from the building of the Choir.

privileged persons. The armoire has been accepted as a thirteenth-century work, made when the Treasury was first completed, and there is nothing in its character to suggest an alternative view. A date of *c*.1240 seems a reasonable conclusion.

There is so little surviving furniture before the fourteenth century that one inevitably compares the Bayeux armoire with that of Obazine of *c*.1176 (Cat. 10). Because of the mutilation of the Bayeux armoire and the loss of its decoration, the armoire at Obazine now appears to be finer, with a delicacy in its woodworking and a degree of subtlety in the design and attachment of its ironwork. In addition, the Obazine armoire, being complete, is more impressive in form, having a grand monumentality about it. In this case, however, a comparison in matters of form and general appearance is likely to be misleading. It is clear that the woodworking at Bayeux was deliberately reticent in order to provide the maximum of uninterrupted surface for the painting; without this painting, it is impossible to judge the success of the design.

There are some similarities to be noted in the ironwork of the armoires of Obazine and Bayeux: fleur-de-lis finials; rectangular lock plates; and integral bar and hasp form of locking.

Select Bibliography

C. Daly, 'Armoire Peinte du XIIIe Siècle', *Révue Générale de l'Architecture et des Travaux Publics*, x, 1852, 130–4, pl. 8.

F. Roe, *Ancient Coffers and Cupboards*, London, 1902, 31.

J. Vallery-Radot, *Cathédrale de Bayeux*, Paris, 1958, 55, pl. XIX.

J. Viaux, *Le Meuble en France*, Paris, 1962, 34–5.

E. E. Viollet-le-Duc, *Dictionnaire Raisonné du Mobilier Francais*, 1, Paris, 1858, *Armoires*.

CATALOGUE No. 12 (PLATE 13B)

Armoire at Winchester College. In the Exchequer.

Oak, untreated

l. 7′ 7″; h. including floor beam 8′ 4½″; w. *c*. 2′ 1¾″.

Description (July 1973)

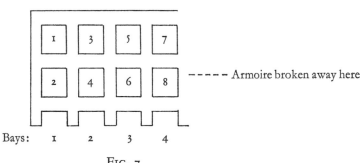

Fig. 7

The armoire is rough and simple, yet strong and serviceable. It has 4 bays with 2 doors to each bay; however, it is mutilated, and there is no indication of how many bays are lost. It has 10 feet which are extensions of the frame, 5 at the front and 5 at the back, and these feet are fixed to beams of corresponding section which are carefully scribed to the uneven floor. The armoire has a back and is fully partitioned between each bay. Originally, the space behind each door had a bottom board and one shelf. Each door is composed of 2 boards and shuts flush with the frame; the join between the boards is strengthened by strap hinges, 2 to each door, placed near the bottom and near the top. The doors open in pairs, 1 and 2 hinged left, 3 and 4 hinged right and so on. This enables the iron straps on the doors of the inner bays to share attachment plates. The hinge straps and plates are unornamented. Doors 4–8 have keyholes which appear to be secondary. There are simple wooden swivel catches arranged to engage a pair of doors which appear to be original. There are two kinds of ?brass handles: doors 1–4, 6 and 8 have mushroom form, and doors 5 and 7 knobs of *c.* 1″ diameter springing from slightly larger plates. Both types must be secondary, yet there are no indications of original attachments.

The only elaboration in this assembly of flat timbers is provided by the robustly moulded cornice.

Analysis

The armoire belongs to the type which is completely straightforward, strong and serviceable but lacks any touches of individual quality to aid stylistic dating. It is the work of ordinary craftsmen working in wood and iron. We notice that the simple T-shaped hinges share plates on the framework, as they do at Malines (Cat. 13) and elsewhere. The cornice moulding is late medieval in character, lacking the balance of forms found in Renaissance work. Both ironwork and cornice moulding suggest the fifteenth century.

The armoire has been correlated by John Harvey with an entry of 1413 in the Winchester College muniments:[89]

> 'Custus domorum cum necessariis' includes payments to 'Johanni Lokiere pro xxij Twistes cum suis Gymeux et clavis ad idem pro nova almaria in domo compotorum pond. lij. lb.'; and also,

> 'In com. Willelmo Ikenham carpentario existenti in Collegio ad faciendum j almariolum pro libris compotorum . . .'

> (To John Lokiere for 22 'Twistes' and their 'Gymeux' and the keys for them for the new armoire in the Exchequer, weight [iron] 52 lbs;

> To William Ikenham, the College carpenter, for making 1 armoire for account books.)

---

[89] WCM 22094.

CATALOGUE NO. 13 (PLATES 14–15)

Armoire (freestanding) from the house of the Aldermen of the city of Malines. Busleydon Museum, Malines. The Museum authorities state that this is the *komme* of the city, used to store the charters.

Oak, untreated
l. including cornice 6' 2½"; h. including cornice 5' 10"; w. 1' 11¾".
Projection of cornice, 2¼".

Description (July 1970)

The armoire combines a businesslike attitude to design with fine workmanship, and although the woodworking techniques are straightforward, the cornice is sophisticated and the whole is made with great attention to detail. The ironwork is of the highest quality and a restrained use of stop chamfering is employed.

The front of the armoire has an outer rectangular framework with a single central stile (presumably there is a central rail rebated and lying behind the doors). The outer stiles are extended to form feet. Four doors of equal size are arranged in pairs, and open outwards from the central stile; the lower edges of the upper doors meet the upper edges of the lower doors without the visual intervention of a rail. The doors are boarded and lie flush with the framework. The sides of the armoire are differently constructed: a simple rectangular framework, with stiles elongated to form feet, encloses a single panel. The whole is surmounted by an elaborately moulded cornice. The simplicity of the woodwork acts as a foil to superb ironwork which is entirely original and in a perfect state of preservation.

The ironwork has an uncommon finish, being bright like steel (?tinned). Each door is hung on 2 long hinge straps which are set near the top and bottom of each door. Thus 2 straps at the centre on either side of the armoire, serving an upper and lower door respectively, are placed close together and can share a single hinge plate on the outer stile. The straps reach to the very edges of the doors. The strap ends are slightly flared to give a graceful line and a greater width to the Gothic tracery with which they are cut. At the hinge end, the straps are slightly stepped to give a wider attachment plate. The hinge plates on the frame are straight sided on the hinge sides and flared on the outer sides and are cut with tracery to match the strap ends. Each door is fitted with a lock plate which lies parallel with that of its neighbour. Each door has a bolt with integral hasp which moves within two keeps attached to the door; in the locked position, the bolts to adjoining doors engage a common keep on the central stile. The keeps have decorative raised annular attachments, some of which are serrated. The hasps are X-scored where they join the bolt and are nicked in so that they lie precisely within the raised guards on the lock plates provided for them; they have large round-headed nails on stalks at their ends which serve as handles. The lock plates are flat and rectangular with slightly concave sides; they are attached with large square-headed nails, of pyramidal form, at each corner. Two locks are provided for within each plate and the keyholes lie on either side of the hasp fitting. Keyholes as well as hasp slots have raised guards which are finished below with shallower decorative tabs cut with tracery. The arrangement of the fittings within the lock plate is symmetrical. Great care has been lavished upon the design and execution of all the ironwork.

Analysis

The well-nigh perfect preservation of the armoire reflects its important use and the efficiency of its custodians, for it has obviously been kept by the aldermen of Malines in conditions of considerable security, for there has never been any attempt to meddle with the closing arrangements.

The fittings show that 2 keys were involved for each of the 4 compartments of the armoire, an arrangement normally contrived to ensure that more than one person was present when compartments were opened and closed. I do not know of anything which closely resembles the remarkable lock plates and hasp fittings, though the principle is familiar and occurs as early as Obazine (Cat. 10), and is illustrated by Dervieu in a ?thirteenth-century context.[90] The stop chamfering used here is most unusual before the sixteenth century; the techniques are found at Windsor (Cat. 19) which is stylistically dated early sixteenth century. The bright finish to the ironwork, which is such an arresting feature of this armoire, is almost certainly the 'white iron' occasionally referred to in documents, e.g.

1435   'Item ung coffre, couvert de cuir, ferré de fer blanc . . . ung autre coffre, couvert de cuir, ferré de fer blanc, à deux serreures, . . .'

            (Félix, 69, 70.)

The boarded doors are common throughout our period, being found, e.g. at Obazine (Cat. 10), *c.*1176, Bayeux (Cat. 11), *c.*1240, and Westminster Abbey (Cat. 14), late fifteenth century. The panelled sides, however, suggest closer dating and their weight and simplicity are much like the Wells example (Cat. 9) of *c.*1457. The elaborate ironwork, although unique in many respects, has the flared traceried terminals to the hinge straps familiar from the armoire of the Spanish merchants of Bruges, dated 1441 (Cat. 17). The cornice moulding is consistent with a fifteenth-century date. The restraint shown in the woodwork and ironwork (although elaborately worked, the ironwork ignores the excesses of flamboyant Gothic) suggests a date well before the end of the fifteenth century and *c.*1470 is suggested on stylistic grounds.

CATALOGUE No. 14 (PLATE 16)

Armoire (freestanding) at Westminster Abbey. In the Muniment Room. See also Appendix III.

Oak

l. 7' 11½"; h. including cornice 8' 4"; w. 1' 11¾".

Description (February 1971)

Armoire of 3 bays and 7 main internal compartments concealed behind individual doors (see Fig. 8). The central horizontal member of the frame is set to lie behind flush,

---

[90] Lt.-Col. Dervieu, 'Serrures, Cadenas et Clefs du Moyen Age', *Bulletins Monumentales*, 1914, 210–11, fig. 10.

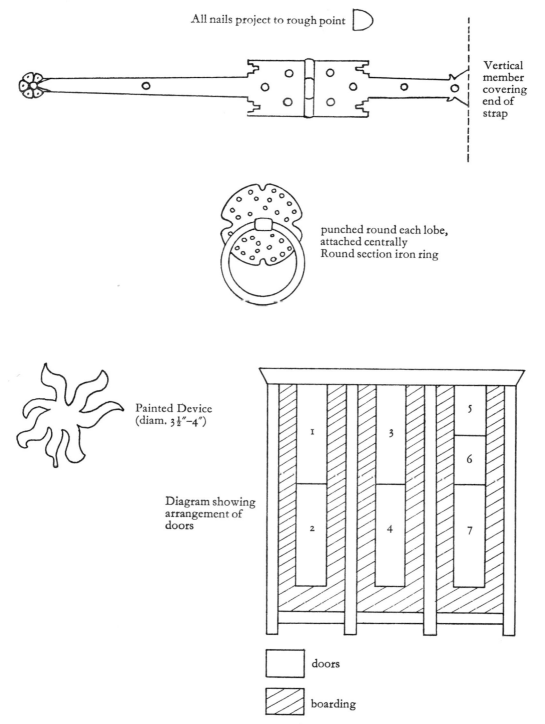

All nails project to rough point

Vertical member covering end of strap

punched round each lobe, attached centrally
Round section iron ring

Painted Device
(diam. 3½″–4″)

Diagram showing arrangement of doors

1
2
3
4
5
6
7

☐ doors

▨ boarding

FIG. 8.   Armoire, Cat. 14.

boarded doors, so that the external appearance stresses *verticals*. The doors and the fixed boards beside them lie within the 4 uprights which are extended to form the feet. The lower horizontal members project to match the vertical framework and the armoire is crowned with a projecting, moulded cornice. The framework is hollow chamfered. The doors, of vertical boarding, are hung on elaborate straps with single hinges and are narrower than the appearance of the armoire suggests for the hinge is set upon a fixed board at a distance from the vertical framework. The woodwork is without alterations.

The original full complement of hinge straps of one pattern survives; the portion of the hinge strap which lies upon a fixed board lies *under* the vertical framework, showing that it must have been attached before the armoire was completely assembled. The lock plates appear to be replacements. The surviving circular handles are original (doors 1–4, 7) though 2 are missing (doors 5 and 6).

The oak is now a rich, dark colour but small areas of painting can be identified, not in terms of colour but showing as of different tone:[91] at the front, the outermost right-hand vertical member of the frame has 3 stars, *c.* $3\frac{1}{2}$–4" in diameter and spaced about 6" apart. Round the corner, at the side of the armoire, the panel within the uprights is also diapered with the same device. The painting corresponds with that upon the lower portion of the partition in the Muniment Room, against which the armoire now stands (see Appendix III).

There is a small break in the cornice on the right-hand side.

Analysis

The armoire is heavy and plain at first sight, but investigation shows it to be a finely made example within the medieval tradition of heavy storage furniture. Now dark with polish, the evidence of the screen against which it stands, and the few traces on the armoire itself, show that it was once painted bright red and powdered with white stars. This kind of treatment throws a different light on the plainness of the woodwork which we appreciate as creating an unobtrusive field for heraldic ornament, for it seems likely that the painting is original rather than secondary. If the painting is original, however, it is interesting to note that an absolutely flat surface, uninterrupted by projections, was not considered an essential background as it was at an earlier date, e.g. Bayeux (Cat. 11).

The armoire is full of individual qualities. The hinge plates are cut with squared-off tracery, in contrast to the commoner rounded forms (see St Albans, Cat. 8), and the hollow chamfer on the framework is unusual. The narrowness of the doors (see Fig. 8) suggests a particular use: it is necessary to put a hand round the corner to utilize the full width of each storage compartment. Such an arrangement rules out the storage of large objects but might prove most convenient for rolls. The boards on either side of the doors would tend to prevent the rolls spilling out on to the floor when the doors were opened, and yet would hardly interfere with ready accessibility.

The definite character of the woodwork and ironwork suggests many parallels, all of which belong to the fifteenth century or later. The ends of the hinge straps are covered

---

[91] With reference to the screen, painted in a similar fashion (see Appendix III), Lethaby reported in 1925 that it was 'painted bright red and powdered with white stars'. (W. R. Lethaby, *Westminster Abbey Re-Examined*, London, 1925, 211.)

by wooden verticals (see Fig. 8), as at York (Cat. 3–7). The flower-shaped terminals to the hinge straps and the quatrefoil plate to the handles belong to a fifteenth and early sixteenth-century style which is again found at York (Cat. 3–7). An early example of the sex-foil plate is seen on the left panel of the Merode Triptych (panel of the donors) by the Master of Flémalle, perhaps Robert Campin (1378/9–1444), painted early in the Master's career.[92] The sex-foil form, but with much flatter petals like those on the handle plates of our armoire, is found on the cradle of state made for one of the children of Marie of Burgundy and Maximilian of Austria in 1478/9 (Cat. 28). And a later example is found on either side of the peytral of the bard belonging to Henry VIII in the Tower of London.[93] It should also be noted that the handle plate at Westminster is studded with nails, very much in the manner of the circular handle plate on the inner side of the door of 1496 in the Aerary, Windsor Castle.[94] The cornice moulding is Medieval in character, rather than Renaissance.

There are strong reasons for believing that the armoire was made at the end of the fifteenth century; although traceried hinge straps and sex-foil forms (if we read the *strap* as a petal, the sex-foil is used at Westminster) occur earlier, the first at St Albans (Cat. 8) of between 1412–29, and the second in the Mérode altar piece of well before 1444, the jagged cutting of the traceried ends at Westminster are likely to be a late aberration. The parallel with the York armoires seems very convincing, and I feel unable to accept the suggested correlation of the Westminster armoire with the entry in the Treasurer's Roll of 1380/1.[95]

Select Bibliography

W. R. Lethaby, *Westminster Abbey Re-Examined*, London, 1925, 289.

RCHM *London I* (*Westminster Abbey*), 1924, 51b, pl. 96.

L. E. Tanner, *The Library and Muniment Room*, Westminster Papers no. 1, Oxford, 1935, 14.

CATALOGUE No. 15 (PLATE 17)

Armoire (freestanding) in the Byloke Museum, Ghent. From the Town Hall, Ghent.

Oak

l. 10′ 1″; w. 1′ 11¼″.

Description (August 1970)

The armoire is panelled front and sides, each panel being carved with an identical linen fold pattern which is surrounded on 3 sides (top and sides) with an elaborately convoluted moulding. The carving is of very high quality.

[92] In the Metropolitan Museum of Art, New York. See Panofsky, pl. 91.
[93] See C. Blair, 'Emperor Maximilian's Gift of Armour to King Henry VIII', *Archaeologia*, XCIX, 1965, 24. Stated to be standard early sixteenth-century form.
[94] The door constructed of overlapping boards; see M. F. Bond, 'The Windsor Aerary', *Archives*, I, no. 4; 1950, 4.
[95] Tanner, 14.

The armoire has a modern cornice, which is probably a faithful reproduction of the original form.

The outermost stiles of the frame at front and back are extended to form 4 short feet. The armoire is divided into 3 bays with doors of full height, each door being composed of 6 panels.

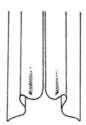

FIG. 9.   Form of linen fold; top folds are identical with lower folds shown in sketch

There are 2 hinge straps to each door, placed to lie along the top and bottom rails, with a very distinctive circular rose half-way along their length pierced with fretwork. These hinges appear to be replacements, but there can be no doubt that they reproduce the original form exactly since the Museum has a series of doors identical to those of the armoire (exhibited on the wall behind the armoire) which bear original ironwork of identical design. These doors, no longer attached to furniture, suggest that the complete armoire was one of a matching group made at the same time.

The sides repeat the design of the front, being filled with 6 panels of linen fold arranged in 3 registers.

Analysis

The two chief features of this armoire are the linen fold panels and the remarkable hinge straps. (Evidence for the dating of linen fold, which appeared in the fifteenth century, is traced in Appendix IX.) The elaborate mouldings on 3 sides of the panels of the Ghent armoire point to a late date, as does the similarity shown between sides and front. The characteristically medieval design adopted different rhythms for front and sides, e.g. Obazine (Cat. 10) of *c*.1176, and Malines (Cat. 13) of *c*.1470, and this lack of three dimensional continuity in design was generally upheld, even at the end of the fifteenth century, e.g. the Plougrescant buffet (Cat. 27). The adoption of *regularity* in design was one of the contributions of the Renaissance. Against this evidence for a sixteenth-century date must be set that of the hinge straps. We find that the same form, with the distinctive circular, fretted rose half-way along the length of the strap, occurs in a painting of 1442 of St Jerome in his study, attributed to Jan van Eyck and Petrus Christus.[96] The lack of close agreement in the stylistic evidence for this armoire suggests that a date between the panel of St Jerome of 1442 and the early sixteenth century is probable, and *c*.1490–1510 is suggested.

[96] Detroit Institute of Arts; see Panofsky, I, 189, fig. 258.

CATALOGUE No. 16 (PLATE 18)

Armoire (freestanding) in the Abbey Church of St Etienne, Obazine (Corrèze). In the Vestry.

Oak, untreated
l. 8′; h. without finials 7′ 1½″; w. 3′ 9½″.

Description (September 1973)

The armoire is massive and simple, with 6 boarded doors at the front arranged in 2 registers. The frame of the armoire has 3 heavy, projecting mouldings: cornice and bottom mouldings and another exactly in the centre, which together provide very definite horizontal stresses to the design. The mouldings are continued round the sides of the armoire which is divided into 6 panels of linen fold, set in 2 registers. The outermost stiles at the front and back of the armoire are elongated to form 4 plain feet. Five finials surmount the cornice, 1 at each corner and 1 at the centre front. The arrangement of the front is asymmetrical with 2 large doors and 1 small above and below the centre moulding. The smaller doors have lost their catches. The 2 large doors on each register share a bolt which is lodged on the right-hand door in each case. The bolts are rectangular and have shell knops and cusped drop handles; they are held in collars on fretted plates which have cable work ribs above and below the bolt housings. The bolt housings on the left-hand doors are missing. The long hinge straps are squarely finished and have simple, traceried ends. A series of secondary ventilation holes have been cut in the front.

Analysis

The heavy horizontal mouldings are the most characteristic quality of this armoire and in this respect, though in no other, it recalls German fifteenth-century work.[97] The Obazine armoire is entirely late Gothic in character: heavy cornice moulding (here accompanied by centre and lower mouldings); broad linen fold panels, like those carved on the Damme door (pl. 72A); and shell knop resembling the fitting on the Gruuthuse chest (Cat. 46). The armoire may be stylistically dated 1450 90.

TYPE 2 (b) FREESTANDING:
WITH ENCLOSED DRAWERS IN PLACE OF SHELVES

CATALOGUE No. 17 (PLATES 19–21)

Armoire of the Guild of the Spanish Merchants at Bruges (1441). Gruuthuse Museum, Bruges, no. 523.

Oak, now polished
max. l. 3′ 7¾″; h. 2′ 0¾″; w. 1′ 8½″.
Shields: upstand ¼–½″.

---

[97] See Kreisel, fig. 123.

Description (August 1970)

The armoire is constructed much like a slab-ended chest with 2 solid sides, rebated to accommodate a pair of flush doors. Inside, the armoire has a central vertical division which separates two pairs of drawers, each pair lying one above the other (2 drawers are now missing). Each door, and the top of the armoire, is ornamented with a single carved wooden shield which lies proud of the surface.

The armoire has its original hinge furniture with slightly concave straps and ogival tracery terminals, 2 to each door. Each hinge strap is bent round the corner of the armoire to extend a short distance along the side. The sides of the armoire are simple boards which lie flat on the ground and have a small nick at the centre.

The sides, back and front of the drawers are made up of single pieces of timber held together with wooden pegs. There is no dust board.[98] The drawers have projecting flanges running their whole length on each side which fit the grooves provided for them in the sides and central vertical partition of the armoire.

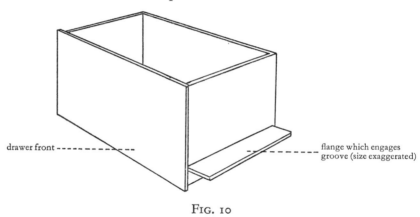

drawer front - - - - - - - - - - - - -   - - - - - - - - flange which engages
                                                   groove (size exaggerated)

Fɪɢ. 10

Three separate locking arrangements can be traced, two of which are documented. The original lock of 1441 (right-hand door) is now hidden beneath a replacement plate; the heavy lock on the left door, which is a double lock, was added in 1547.

The armoire is strong and carefully made.

Analysis

The history of the armoire has been set out by Dr J. Maréchal, chief archivist of Bruges.[99] Dr Maréchal has established that this armoire was the *arca* which, from 23 April 1441, held the privileges and titles belonging to the guild of the Spanish merchants at Bruges. In 1441 six consuls held identical keys to a single lock.[100] In 1547 it was decided to equip the armoire with two more locks allowing the consuls, who now numbered only three, to hold individual keys. At this time the armoire is referred to as

[98] Fixed, horizontal division beneath a drawer.
[99] J. Maréchal, 'L'Armoire aux Privileges et Titres du Consulat de Castille-Leon à Bruges en 1441', *Handlingen Société d'Emulation Bruges*, 1961, 105–9.
[100] Maréchal, 105.

a *cajon*, and we hear of the 4 *cajas*, or drawers, which were marked A–D, and of the particular documents which were within each.[101] The armoire stored the community's most important archives until 1596, when it was replaced by a receptacle of iron. Inventories indicate that while it served its original purpose it was kept in the *comptoir* of the *salle d'audience*.[102] The shields of the armoire are the royal arms of Castille-Leon (top); the arms of Burgos, capital city of Castille-Leon (left door); and a device which is specifically Spanish, the 'bande engoulée de deux têtes de dragon'.[103]

The armoire has a number of interesting aspects. It provides useful evidence for the dating of similar hingework found elsewhere, and allows a precise understanding of the use of an individual piece of furniture. There is nothing Spanish about the workmanship of the armoire, and there is every reason to believe that it was made in Bruges. Above all, the use of drawers in a dated context provides useful evidence for other furniture.

Select Bibliography

J. Maréchal, 'L'Armoire aux Privileges et Titres du Consulat de Castille-Leon à Bruges en 1441', *Handlingen Société d'Emulation Bruges*, 1961, 105–9.

TYPE 2 (c) FREESTANDING: MULTI-DRAWER, WITHOUT DOORS

Efficient administration in medieval times depended upon the keeping of records, as it must do in any highly organized society. A few armoires survive, looking much like card index files, to show that rolls were sometimes stored in a manner which permitted speedy consultation.[104] The superiority of this form of record storage over the chest is obvious, and indeed the advantages of the armoire are specifically referred to in a Burgundian account concerning furniture for the castle of Talent in 1364/5.[105] Although we cannot say with precision when the multi-drawer armoire was introduced, it is probable that the form, like the surviving examples, was a late one, rendered practicable through the acceptance of the sawn, as opposed to the riven, technique in timber working.[106] It is clear, however, that the multi-drawer armoire did not supplant the chest as a form of record storage, but provided an alternative solution. The parallel use of multi-drawer armoire and chest for documents can only be explained if they served different requirements. It would, therefore, seem reasonable to deduce that the multi-drawer armoire implied both permanent administrative quarters, as at Talent, and record storage in a permanent locality, and the chest served the same function in

[101] Maréchal, 105–6.
[102] Maréchal, 106–7.
[103] Maréchal, 107–8.
[104] The finest example, dated 1518, is German and is equipped with 40 drawers (Basle Museum); see Kreisel, pl. 100.
[105] See p. 5.
[106] For a discussion on the use of riven timber throughout the Middle Ages, and also in certain circumstances on into the nineteenth century, see A. L. J. van de Walle, 'Some Technical Analogies between Building and other Crafts in the Use of Split Wood during the Middle Ages', ed. A. J. Taylor, *Château Gaillard*, III, London, 1969, 152–5.

circumstances of impermanence where factors of mobility for records and personnel were a consideration. We may, perhaps, infer that well-equipped exchequer offices in the later Middle Ages utilized both forms of record storage. (Chests and shelved armoires were possibly made more convenient and up to date by using record boxes, a few of which survive.)[107]

The three extant examples of multi-drawer armoires included in the Catalogue are without doors (Cat. 18–21) and it is, perhaps, open to question as to whether they were described as armoires in medieval times. However, as they were evidently a variant of the form of armoire with drawers enclosed by outer doors (Cat. 17; also the sixteenth-century example at Stratford-upon-Avon)[108] their inclusion as armoires seems correct; and other evidence supports this view. At Windsor, an extant multi-drawer armoire (Cat. 19) has drawers marked with the names of the manors whose finances were the concern of St George's Chapel, and although there are difficulties in correlating it with documentary evidence, it is clear from two entries in the accounts that armoires were provided for storage of records:

1367   'in uno novo armariolo facto pro munimentis collegii   xiiis. iiiid.'
and

1422/3   '. . . j. armarioli . . . pro rotulis et evidenciis . . .'[109]

More precise, however, is a French account of 1430, which describes the furniture to be provided for documents as armoires with 'laiettes'. As *escrin* was the normal term for a box, we may say with confidence that drawers and not boxes are indicated here by the word *laiette*. The evidence is as follows.

1430   5942, fol. 23: 'Le 10 jour d'aoust, l'an 1430, furent prins ou coffre du
              trésor 32 l. 13s. 6d. p. pour la mise et despens fais à cause de l'ynventaire
              des chartres et lettres de l'ostel de céans, totallement assortir icelles et
              maistre par laiettes ès aumoires du dit trésor avecques le répartoire sur ce
              fait, icelles mises et despens fais par la manière qui l'ensuit:

              Premièrement, à Jehan le Bailly, escripvain . . . 4 l. 12 s. p.

              Item, à Jehan Mariavalle, escrinner, pour 56 laiettes de bois à 4 s. p. la
              pièce, . . . pour mettre les dites chartres et lettres, . . . 10 l. 16 s. p.

              Item, à Haudry, charpentier, pour la besongne que il faitte tant ès aumoirés
              du tressor, et en la façon des barres qui les cloent, comme de autre
              besongnes par lui faittes . . . 3s. 8d. p. pour jour, vallent: 22 s. p.

              Item, pour le merrain desdites barres: 3s. 8d. p.

              Item, a Jehan Le Charpentier, serreurier, pour ferrer les panneaulx des
              dites aumoires qui ont esté levées pour y faire fenestres, et pour serreures

---

[107] This form of record storage also appears to be late. There are extant record boxes with horn covered labels at Durham University in the care of the Department of Palaeography and Diplomatic; at Winchester College; and there is a fifteenth-century example in the Bijloke Museum at Ghent.

[108] See Macquoid/Edwards, 1927, Cupboards, fig. 3; the armoire is stated to have been made for the Corporation of Stratford-upon-Avon in 1594.

[109] 1367 entry: A. K. B. Roberts, *St. George's Chapel, Windsor Castle, 1348–1416*, Windsor, 1947, 220 (5); 1422/3 entry: Bond, 1950, 3.

à doubles gardes, clefz, crampons, verrous et autres choses pour la dites besongne, par marché fait avec lui: 44 s. p.'

'. . . registre des lettres et tiltres de rente appartenans à l'ostel des Quinze-Vins de Paris, fait l'an mil CCCC et trente, ou mois de juillet, par Messire Jehan de Estivey, Soubz-aumosnier du Roy Nostre Sire, . . . et plusieurs autres du dit hostel, lesquelles ont été mises par ordre en aulmoires, divisées par quartiers en la ville de Paris et environs, en layettes signées par les lettres de A. B. C.'

(L. Le Grand, 'Les Quinze-Vingts depuis leur Fondation jusqu'à leur Translation au Faubourg Saint-Antoine', *Mémoires de la Société de l'Histoire de Paris et de L'Ile-de-France*, XIII, 1886, 109 (2), 110.

(5942, fol. 23: On 10 August, 1430, taken from the chest of the treasury £32. 13s. 6d. for expenses incurred in making the inventory of charters and letters of the 'ostel de céans', for sorting them out completely and putting them on shelves into the armoire of the said treasury, together with the inventory made of them, the costs and expenses being as follows:

Firstly, to John le Bailly, writer, 4 l. 12 s. p.;

Item, to John Mariavalle, box-maker, for 56 wooden drawers at 4s. each, for storing the archives. 10 l. 16 s. p.

Item, to Haudry, carpenter, for the work which he did as much in respect of the armoires of the treasury, and in the making of the bars which close them, as in the other work done by him . . . 3s. 8d. p. per day, total: 22 s.p.

Item, for the ?brass for the said bars: 3s. 8d. p.

Item, to John Le Charpentier, locksmith, for the ironwork on the panels of the said armoires which lift up to make shutters, and for double-guard locks, keys, crampons, bolts and other things for the work done, 44 s. p.

. . . register of letters and entitlements to rents of the house of the fraternity of the Quinze-Vingts of Paris, made in 1430, by John Estivey, sub-almoner of our lord the king, and certain others of this house, which archives have been, by order, placed in armoires, divided into *quartiers* in the city of Paris and suburbs, in drawers marked A, B, C.)

We may state that these armoires for archives took the form of wooden frames which accommodated fifty-six wooden drawers. They were 'closed' with brass bars and secured by means of lift up, presumably unattached shutters (for hinges are not mentioned), held in position by crampons and equipped with bolts and double-guard locks and keys. Possibly the brass bars were used to lock the drawers in the daytime, enabling a whole row to be locked in position in one movement and yet enabling drawers to be made available with minimal trouble. The lift-up shutters would have provided additional security at night. It is instructive to note that three different trades were involved in the production of these armoires: a carpenter for the frames, a box-maker for the drawers, and a locksmith for the ironwork. This division of labour and the separate payments made, is entirely characteristic of the Middle Ages.

CATALOGUE NO. 18 (PLATE 22)

Multi-drawer Armoire of the Vicars Choral, Wells. In the Muniment Room, Vicars Choral, Wells Cathedral. See also Appendix IV.

Oak, untreated

l. 6' 4¾"; h. 5' 2½"; w. 1' 3½".

Description (December 1969)

This armoire occupies almost the whole of the Muniment Room, if one allows space for a standing person using the drawers. (It would appear that the Muniment Room was a storage chamber, rather than a room for work and storage; at Wells, work on the rolls must have been carried out in the adjoining Exchequer.)

The armoire is now mutilated and the original form cannot be reconstructed on visual evidence. We are left with a unit which is divided horizontally into two parts, and the change in the arrangement of the uprights in the upper and lower portions makes it certain that these two parts were indeed differently arranged. The upper part is fitted with 6 rows of small drawers lying in pairs with uprights set between pairs of drawers; many drawers are lost but about fifty-two survive. The lower part of the armoire is now a void and at the bottom is an original board, fixed at floor level. The drawers lie precisely above one another, forming a grid. The bottom board of each drawer is elongated at the centre front to form a finger tab which serves as a simple yet efficient handle; the tabs are smooth with wear. The drawers are assembled with nailed joints. The carpentry is rough but serviceable. There is no decorative detail whatsoever in the woodwork, and there are no iron fittings.

The armoire is no longer used for record storage.

Analysis

In common with the armoire in the adjoining Exchequer (Cat. 9), this multi-drawer armoire owes its chief interest to its position within a suite of rooms begun in *c*.1457; there is a strong probability that it belongs to the initial furnishing of the rooms on occupation. However, unlike the Exchequer armoire which is of locker type, the present armoire is freestanding so that the possibility of its having been made at a later date cannot be ignored. In such a functional object, devoid of decoration in wood or iron, dating is difficult. Guide lines are provided by the documentary evidence to armoires with drawers for records, and by other extant armoires of similar type. We have seen that 1430 is not too early for a multi-drawer armoire in France (pp. 38–9), so that the date of Bishop Bekynton's work for the Vicars Choral would be perfectly possible at Wells. Both the armoires at Windsor and Winchester (Cat. 19–21), though useful as examples of multi-drawer armoires, have characteristics which permit stylistic dating which suggests the end of our period and they do not provide close parallels with the Wells example. We find, then, that there is no evidence which inhibits the acceptance of a date for this armoire which coincides with the completion of the administrative offices of the Vicars Choral. This probability is given greater weight when we recall the circumstances which prompted the Bishop's building programme. The physical improvements initiated in 1457 were designed to facilitate a well regulated system of life for the Vicars, and the system would hardly have been allowed to become weak by a failure to provide storage for accounts and other records. Since we do not yet know when the Exchequer suite was brought into use[110] the armoire should be dated between 1458–70.

CATALOGUE No. 19 (PLATES 23–5)

Multi-drawer Armoire of St George's Chapel, Windsor. In the Aerary (treasury) of St George's Chapel, Windsor Castle; N. wall.

Oak

l. 11'; h. 7'.

Description (November 1969)

The armoire is a simple grid of rails and stiles forming 9 vertical and 7 horizontal rows providing individual pigeon holes for sixty-one drawers which slot into the frame and are not hung. The drawers are of different sizes, the uppermost being the smallest. The armoire is divided into 3 vertical bays with 4 feet at the front. The two outermost bays have 7 rows of 3 drawers; the central bay matches except for the lowest row where one long drawer takes the place of the usual three. The drawers are labelled (names of manors, etc.) in large, free brush strokes. Both frame and drawers are sawn wood. The drawers are very roughly made and are nailed together; the bottom board runs right to the front, showing the rough cross-grain in an ungainly manner.

Although so roughly assembled, the armoire is obviously strong and is intact, in excellent condition and still retains its original function as a piece of storage furniture for rolls.

Each drawer is fitted with a small ring handle of plain round section held in a decorative plate; the fittings, of two similar patterns (A and B), are tinned iron.

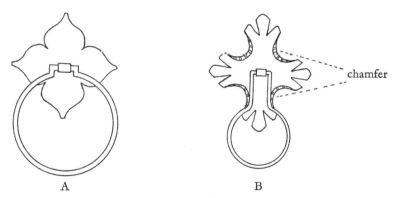

A: Ring handle fits snugly into attachment collar;
B: Ring handle becomes distinctly angled at attachment point.

FIG. 11.   Sketch of handles A and B

[110] Precise evidence may one day come to light in the many rolls at Wells relating to the Vicars Choral which remain uninvestigated.

E

Analysis

The Aerary, from the time it was built in 1353-5, served as the treasury of St George's Chapel and was the repository for plate, coin and documents. We learn that the reeves of St George's manors presented their accounts annually at the Aerary to the treasurer, steward and two associate canons, and that before 1477 (when a new counting house was begun) the room had a table in the centre covered with a chequered cloth, with a number of benches round it.[111] The function of the Aerary as the centre of the financial administration of the St George's Chapel manors and other properties etc. was thus identical with what we understand to have been the function of the exchequer suite at Wells (Cat. 9, 18; Appendix IV).

Some documentary evidence survives for the furnishings of the Aerary, and two particular entries concern the provision of armoires for muniments.[112] The second of these entries, of 1422/3, has been tentatively correlated by St John Hope and later writers with the extant armoire standing against the N. wall:

> 'Et solut. Johanni Horstede operanti circa reposicionem j armarioli in domo computar. Pro rotulis et evidenciis collegij intus custodiendis per duos dies capienti per diem sine scibo   vjd. xijd.'[113]

The problems affecting the acceptance of the date 1422/3 for the armoire may be stated in turn.

(1) One man could not make the entire armoire in two days. However, entries in accounts for work on furniture are often split up, and if we suppose that the drawers were made separately (as was the case with the multi-drawer armoire for the Quinze-Vingts of Paris (see pp. 38-9), then it seems feasible that a man working fast could make the framework in the Aerary in a matter of two days.

(2) The writing on the drawers is unhelpful in this context, but it should be considered. Mr Maurice Bond, Hon. Custodian of the Muniments, kindly informs me that the labelling includes acquisitions falling between 1352-1547; and the first drawer, marked 'Dr. Chamberln' refers to Canon William Chamberlain (1660-1666), so that the labelling could be part of the reorganization of the Aerary at or shortly after the Restoration.

(3) If the armoire were made in 1422/3, it would be the earliest multi-drawer armoire which we can identify, being slightly earlier than that of the Quinze-Vingts account of 1430 (see pp. 38-9).

(4) The most serious objection to the date of 1422/3 concerns the handles; if either of the patterns A or B are original fittings, then the correlation with the account entry cannot stand. However, although there is no visual evidence of other handle attachments, it is just possible that each handle plate conceals the scar of an earlier fitting; or alternatively, that the drawers were pulled out by means of a leather thong or strap nailed beneath the drawers. The evidence for dating the handles is as follows:

---

[111] Much has been written concerning Windsor Castle, but the fullest and most up-to-date account of the Aerary, from which these details are taken, is Bond, 1950, 2-6.

[112] Of 1367 and 1422/3 respectively. For entry of 1367, see p. 38.

[113] W. H. St John Hope, *Windsor Castle*, Parts I-II, London, 1913, 506, 511 (55); Bond, 1950, 3.

Type A

(a)   The door of Bishop Fox's chantry, Winchester Cathedral, of 1528 has plates of the same form attaching the handle to the door.

(b)   A casket in the Gruuthuse Museum, Bruges (no. 1281) has a plate of the same form together with other fittings: a lock plate of the kind of outline which occurs in the sixteenth century in England, and a handle of the same form as that on the casket associated with Charles V and dated 1532 in the museum of Leathercraft (since 1977 at Northampton).

Type B

I know of no exact parallel, but similar work occurs on the drawers of the leather-covered chest belonging to Queen Katherine Parr (crown with K R studded in nails on lid), illustrated by Macquoid.[114] Some of the fittings on this chest are, like Type B, stop chamfered. This refinement is extremely rare in fifteenth-century work in France, the Netherlands and England, though it occurs on the Malines armoire (Cat. 13).

Select Bibliography

M. F. Bond, *The Inventories of St. George's Chapel, Windsor Castle 1384–1667*, Windsor, 1947.

M. F. Bond, 'The Windsor Aerary', *Archives*, I, No. 4, 1950, 2–6.

J. N. Dalton, *Manuscripts of St. George's Chapel, Windsor*, Windsor, 1957.

A. K. B. Roberts, *St. George's Chapel, Windsor Castle, 1348–1416*, Windsor, 1947.

W. H. St John Hope, *Windsor Castle*, I–II, London, 1913.

Catalogue No. 20 (plate 26)

Multi-drawer armoire (8-bay) at Winchester College. Muniment Room, N. wall.

Catalogue No. 21

Multi-drawer armoire (4-bay) at Winchester College. Muniment Room, E. wall.

Both armoires, oak

Description and Analysis (July 1973)

Both these armoires are accepted as well within the sixteenth century,[115] but as they have a close bearing upon the example at Windsor it seems important to include a note on them here. Both armoires are similar and were evidently made at the same time, having drawer fronts carved with linen fold out of the solid wood. The carving is quite delicate, yet the assembly is rough. The arrangement is a simple grid: for Cat. 20, 40 drawers (8 across by 5 down); and for Cat. 21, 20 drawers (4 across by 5 down). The drawers have their original pear-shaped, or cusped, drop handles depending from quatrefoil plates. The armoires still store records. The labelling is modern, but the

---

[114] P. Macquoid, *A History of English Furniture, the Age of Oak*, London, 1938, figs. 54–5.
[115] J. H. Harvey, 'Winchester College Muniments', *Archives*, v, 1961/2, 204 (12).

system of arrangment incorporates estates acquired in 1551. Of particular interest is the fact that the drawers are *hung* within the framework, with a bottom board extending sideways to form a flange on each side which engages in grooves provided in the framework. This form of construction is absent at Windsor (Cat. 19) but occurs in the armoire made for the Spanish merchants of Bruges, 1441 (Cat. 17).

ARMOIRES OF UNCERTAIN TYPE

There are a number of armoires which are mutilated, so that their original type, whether fitted to fabric or freestanding, cannot be precisely determined, and these are grouped together in the pages that follow.

CATALOGUE No. 22 (PLATE 27)

Armoire in Chester Cathedral. In the Chapter House.

Oak

Door 1	h. 4′ 9″	w. 1′ 9½″
2	h. 4′ 9″	w. 1′ 9″
3	h. 2′ 3″	w. 1′ 9″
4	h. 2′ 6½″	w. 1′ 9″

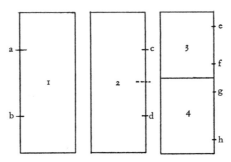

FIG. 12.   Sketch showing disposition of doors and hinges — (a–h) indicate hinges

Description (May 1974)

The armoire has 4 original wooden doors with original wrought iron scrollwork; the doors are set in a later frame of at least two periods, the part below the doors being nineteenth or twentieth century. Since the armoire is a made up piece only the original work — the doors — are considered here.

Each door is a single plank of ?riven oak. Door 4 has a rectangular wooden insertion (to the left, above the horizontal iron member) which may cover the position of an original lock plate. All existing lock plates are secondary. Door 2 has a wooden insertion between the upper and lower hinges which is wedge-shaped, like the surviving hinges (see Fig. 12), suggesting that there were originally 3 and not 2 hinges to this door, but there is no evidence of a 3rd hinge on door 1. It is difficult to be certain about the authenticity of the hinge plates, which are of butterfly form. All have some modern screws, but plates f–h (see Fig. 12) do appear to be ancient and have some original nails. These plates, and the patch on door 2 (wedge-shaped, position indicated as dotted line on sketch), show that the original hinge plates were of butterfly form, and that those that may be replacements copy the original form faithfully. The plates lie rebated, flush with the woodwork, enabling the ironwork to run over them without interruption whenever necessary.

The iron rod used in the scrollwork is of triangular section, though somewhat rounded rather than sharply angled, since it was wrought not cold cut. The small lengths of rod of D section on the armoire noted below are modern restorations.

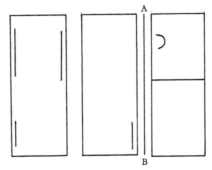

Fig. 13. Sketch indicating restorations to the ironwork: all lines within the doors indicate replacements of D-section rod, together with the line marked A–B on the frame between doors 2 and 3/4

The ironwork is arranged in four different designs, each door being considered separately in terms of design, but whether the position of these doors, *vis-à-vis* one another, is correct cannot be determined. Each design is based on the scroll.

Door 1

Three interconnecting scrolls filling the height of the door, with tendrils shooting from these three circles to occupy the triangular voids.

Door 2

A design on the tree principle with a central vertical stem and a series of 4 almost identical matched scrolls or branches on either side, surmounted by a 5th pair of scrolls of lyre form.

Doors 3 and 4

Each have a pair of scrolls symmetrically arranged on either side of a horizontal stem.

Doors 1 and 2 have a straight vertical rod on each edge with a few inward turning tendrils attached.

The finials of the rods are decorated as follows, the motifs all occuring on each of the doors:

  (i) a 3-lobed leaf form
  (ii) a circular flower form filled with round bosses, and
  (iii) a circular flower form filled with petals.

These finials are stamped on the hot metal with a die, as can be clearly seen from the fact that the iron has often been pushed outwards beyond the die, as happens when a seal is imprinted by hand on wax. Each door has one or more finials which are bent away from the wood, and these might have been designed to serve as handles.

All the attachment nails on the rods are upstanding and prominent, with no attempt made by the smith to add covering leaves.

Analysis

The form of the armoire can no longer be determined, and it is possible that the doors were once attached to stonework or to a frame fitted within the fabric of a building; some form of locker seems likely for the original arrangement, the doors only being re-used when a freestanding armoire replaced the fitted one.

The ironwork is wholly consistent with a date conforming with the documented iron grille of Queen Eleanor's tomb in Westminster Abbey (1294); it may be compared with a magnificent example of the same period which survives in France (Cat. 23).

The Chester work cannot be accepted as the work of the smith Thomas de Leghtone, however, the man responsible for the Eleanor grille, for the Chester designs are composed within a much narrower imaginative compass. Nevertheless, the Chester work is technically skilful and the design is accomplished with its freely flowing scrolls.

Select Bibliography

M. Ayrton/A. Silcock, *Wrought Iron and its Decorative Use*, London, 1929.

P. Macquoid/R. Edwards, *Dictionary of English Furniture*, London, 1953, Aumbry.

CATALOGUE No. 23 (PLATES 28–9)

Armoire (form unknown) traditionally from the Church of St Quentin (Somme). Musée des Arts Décoratifs, Paris, no. 24557; given by Mme A Doucet in 1925. The traditional belief, for which there is no evidence, is that this was the sacristy armoire of the Church.

Medieval wrought iron attached to post-medieval frame.

Left door   w. 1′ 10¼″
Right door   w. 2′ 2⅜″
             h. 5′ 0¾″ (both doors)
Border A–C   w. 2″

Description (September 1973)

The disposition and design of the ironwork suggests that the present arrangement upon later woodwork is reasonably accurate; however, it is clear that insufficient room was allowed for the border which once occupied the lower edge of the design, see D in Fig. 14. No evidence exists for the original form of the framework to the doors.

The armoire is composed of two doors of unequal width set within a border at sides and top (Fig. 14, A–C). A fourth border at the bottom (D) is now missing, but broken ironwork at the lower edges of A and C indicate that the border was originally a complete 4-sided framework attached to the original rails and stiles and not part of the opening area of the armoire. The area indicated by E on the sketch is not part of this border, but lies within door 2.

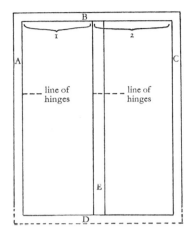

FIG. 14.   Sketch showing arrangement of doors and borders

The ironwork is varied, elaborate and imaginative and is composed of different designs for various areas. The motifs are wholly secular in character. The skeletal work of the designs is formed with D section rod; this rod has, as both finials and overlying elements, floral and animal forms which are pinned in position without any attempt at disguising attachment points. Border A is a scroll of oak leaves; and B–C strawberries with leaves. The design at E (a border which is part of a door) is also a strawberry leaf and fruit scroll and forms an approximately central link between two panels. Each door is composed of a central stem from which spring, on either side, a symmetrical and repetitive series of six inward curving branches. Door 1 has oak leaves (as terminals to scrolls, and overlying the scrolls); door 2 has a similar arrangement using fig leaves. At the base of these tree-like forms door 1 has a series of oak leaves overlaid to form a design in high relief and on either side is a horizontal band of oak leaves inhabited by a group of rootling pigs, three to each side facing inwards towards the oak 'stem'. Door 2 has a base which spreads left and right in a manner which more nearly approximates to a conventional root system but is, in fact, composed of a pair of inward facing mythical beasts, worked in high relief, with tails which become integrated with a horizontal band of fig scroll which runs on either side of the fig 'stem'.

The doors are hinged to open concertina fashion. Door 1 has a hinge along its left edge and door 2 is hinged to door 1 (see Fig. 14). This arrangement is most curious, for the hinge connecting the two leaves is not central, so that the folding back of the doors could never have been entirely neat since door 2 is wider than door 1. The hinges are attached by simple straight straps, countersunk and lying beneath the scrollwork design. It is impossible to say whether these hinge straps, with their coating of paint, are original. What is certain is that doors 1 and 2 must always have been of different widths, for the ironwork patterns do not permit an equal arrangement.

Locking arrangements on door 2 appear to be secondary.

Traces of gilding can be discerned on the ironwork of the upper part of door 2.

The woodwork of the armoire, believed to be seventeenth century, is painted a very dark ?green.

Analysis

The wrought iron, with its decoration of leaf finials and overlying floral and animal motifs makes full use of the invention of the die stamp which is found in work in both England and France in the thirteenth century.[116] The most outstanding documented work of this kind is the grille (1294) of the tomb of Queen Eleanor at Westminster Abbey, made in Leghtone in England by Thomas de Leghtone.[117] In France, the S. door of the W. end (Gate of St Anne) of Nôtre Dame, Paris, attributed to the smith Boulanger (see pl. 59)[118] exploits the technique with a brilliance which is unsurpassed. Numerous examples in humbler contexts are dated with reference to their surrounding architecture. In dealing with early wrought iron, the lack of a corpus of closely dated material of *equal sophistication* means that no precise date can be ascribed to any particular piece on stylistic grounds, but a date of *c.* 1290–1320 would seem appropriate for the ironwork of this armoire.

Maffei compares the St Quentin armoire with the ironwork on the doors of an armoire in the church of St John at Liège, which survives out of its original context.[119]

The St Quentin armoire shares with the Eleanor grille and the doors at Nôtre Dame (pl. 59) that element of fantasy, so familiar from medieval illuminations and textiles (the Bayeux embroidery is the most famous example) in which animal motifs are employed; this characteristic is not invariably employed in ironwork of broadly the same period, however, being absent alike in the design of the doors of Henry III at Windsor[120] and the Chester armoire (Cat. 22). The design on the left door of the St Quentin armoire is particularly intriguing, being devoted to oak leaves and, at the base of the door, to a scroll of oak leaves and pigs with down-turned snouts. Pigs might rootle anywhere, but pigs rootling in oak woods surely suggested — in the Middle Ages as now — the search for truffles (a kind of underground mushroom) which flourish in the vicinity of certain oaks (*chênes-truffiers*) growing in the Périgord region and forming one of the great gourmet dishes of France. This delicacy is recorded as being a favourite with the Duc de Berry in 1370; truffles were obtained for him from the Périgord region and delivered to the Château of Vincennes for Charles V, and to the Duc de Berry's own

[116] See C. Ffoulkes, *Decorative Ironwork, 11–18th Centuries*, London, 1913, 16.
[117] See Ayrton/Silcock, 25.
[118] See H. Havard, *La Serrurerie*, Paris [n.d.], 31.
[119] E. Maffei, *Le Mobilier Civil en Belgique au Moyen Age*, Namur [n.d.], 32.
[120] See St John Hope, 1913, 409.

Paris house.[121] In the Middle Ages, when so much was known about herbs, and pigs were often left to forage for themselves in woodland, there seems every reason to believe that truffles had been discovered well before the Duc de Berry's account of 1370.

In view of the armoire's traditional provenance, the secular character of the designs should be noted, contrasting sharply with the armoire at Bayeux (Cat. 11).

Select Bibliography

M. Faré, 'Les Caractères de Raison du Mobilier Gothique' *Art et Industrie*, 1946, no. 2, pl. p. 53.

E. Maffei, *Le Mobilier Civil en Belgique au Moyen Age*, Namur [n.d.], 32.

J. Viaux, *Le Meuble en France*, Paris, 1962, 34.

ARMOIRES FOR HANGING CLOTHES, WHETHER ECCLESIASTICAL OR SECULAR

We have seen that armoires were commonly used for storing clothes (pp. 6–8). A surviving armoire at Aylesbury, Buckinghamshire (Cat. 24), which may well be unique in our area of study, suggests that this furniture was often equipped with rods or arms to support long robes and vestments. The evidence already quoted for clothes armoires is general in character, but some documentary evidence, as well as an important early literary source, provide closer correlations with the Aylesbury armoire in that rods or arms for hanging clothes are specifically mentioned. Such fittings within armoires probably developed from the habit of fitting rods to walls so that clothing could be aired as well as hung. Alexander Neckam (1157–1217) recommended the use of rods in the chamber for clothing:

> 'In camera . . . Ab alia autem pertica dependeant supara, flamea vel faleola, perizonia, capa, pallium, tunica, thoga, collobium et epitogium.'[122]

> (In the chamber . . . from other rods let there hang — [list of various articles of clothing].)

Other evidence shows that the practice was favoured both in England and France.

> In the Comtesse d'Artois' chamber, near the bed, was the *perche* upon which clothes were hung[123]

In 1370/1, Bishop Geoffroy le Meingre, in his palace at Laon, also hung robes from a rod or rods of some form:

> '4. In camera domini officialis . . . unum gibetum ad superponendum robas.'[124]

> (In a state room of the lord Bishop, a 'gibbet' for hanging clothes.)

---

[121] See Baron de Watteville, 'Un Interieur de Grand Seigneur Francais', *Révue France Moderne*, 1890, 45–6.
[122] Ed. Scheler, 90, 91.
[123] Richard, 1887, 366.
[124] L. Broche, 'Inventaire du Mobilier du Palais Episcopal de Laon, au Dècés de l'Evêque Geoffroy le Meingre, (1370–1371)', *Bulletin Archéologique du Comité des Travaux Historiques et Scientifiques*, 1903, 247.

Similar arrangements were recorded in 1386 concerning Arnaud Andrieu, Apostolic Collector for the province of Narbonne:

> '220. Item quedam pertica ad tenendum vestes . . .'[125]

And in 1402 we learn that the treasury of the Cathedral Church of St Paul in London had rods for copes etc. which were themselves *fitted within two armoires*:

> an *armariolum*, on the west side of the room in which were 24 *perticae*; and near it, a second *armariolum* with 26 *perticae*.[126]

In the evidence which has been set out, two entries are particularly significant in terms of the Aylesbury armoire. The first is the 1370/71 inventory of Geoffroy le Meingre which uses the term 'gibetum' which so neatly describes the form of the Aylesbury clothes rods or arms; and the second is the last entry of 1402 concerning St Paul's, where we find that the rods or arms are fittings within armoires. Geoffroy le Meingre's inventory suggesting that very close parallels to Aylesbury existed in France in the later Middle Ages is further re-enforced by a drawing of Viollet-le-Duc's shown on pl. 60A. Viollet-le-Duc provides a reconstruction of a garderobe in the early fifteenth century, and his text suggests that the evidence came from the medieval woodwork still in position in the garderobes of the Château de Pierrefonds in his own day.[127] We see a chamber with a central area reserved for seamstresses[128] and a series of magnificently large armoires stretching from floor to ceiling lining the walls. The two armoires on the left are closed with curtains, in place of doors, and we see behind them a series of swinging arms over which various kinds of clothing are thrown. The form of the swinging arms drawn by Viollet-le-Duc is precisely the same as those on the Aylesbury armoire (Cat. 24).

CATALOGUE NO. 24 (PLATE 30)

Armoire (original form unknown) in St Mary's Church, Aylesbury, Buckinghamshire.

Oak

l. without cornice   6' 7¾"
h. with cornice   6' 6"

---

[125] Guiraud 1904/5, 360.

[126] W. S. Simpson, 'Two Inventories in the Cathedral Church of St. Paul, London, dated respectively 1245 and 1402', *Archaeologia*, L, 1887, 453.

[127] See Viollet-le-Duc, 1858, pl. XVI and 362 (1). Unfortunately, when Viollet-le-Duc himself remodelled Pierrefonds, all early woodwork was destroyed and appears to have been unrecorded except for the tantalizingly oblique reference in the *Dictionnaire*. Pierrefonds was built by Louis d'Orleans soon after 1390 and was most elaborate and finely equipped; its builder did not enjoy it for long, for Louis was murdered in 1411.

[128] Although the somewhat fanciful appearance of the seamstresses within a railed off area at work in the garderobe suggests a degree of artistic license, it seems very probable that in fact Viollet-le-Duc was using evidence found at Pierrefonds, as seems to have been the case with regard to the reconstruction of the armoires. There is evidence that couturiers undertook dressmaking commissions and carried them out while visiting great households, no doubt using similar facilities to those installed by Mahaut, Comtesse d'Artois in her *taillerie* in 1304 (see p. 7). The Duchess of Burgundy paid for 4 *costuriers* and a *furrier* to work at her château for 3 days making clothes for herself and for her daughter, Mlle Marguerite (born 1373) in 1384/5 (see Canat de Chizy, 1859, 266). And similar practices were followed in England for we learn that in 1480 Edward IV employed tailors to work in the wardrobe, making clothes for himself and lining arras hangings etc. (see Nicolas, 1830, 120).

Opening between rebates: l. 5′ 8½″
                         h. 5′ 5¾″
Front uprights: left   w. 6″
               right   w. 8⅜″

Inside measurements: Floor to top of bar which supports the spring of the arm, 3′ ¾″ (this is the allowance in which clothes could fall freely).
Top bar of swinging arm w. 2¾″ tapering to 1⅝″ at free end. Arms were originally spaced about 4″ apart on the shelf, as is shown by the dowel holes; dowel holes are 1⅛″ diameter.

Description (November 1969)

The armoire has a brass plate attached recording its restoration in the present century.

The armoire has an original moulded cornice extending the full length of the front, standing up slightly higher than the top board; the sides of the cornice are left unfinished and were clearly not meant to be seen, suggesting that the armoire was designed to fit within a particular space.

The armoire was once fully enclosed: it has back, sides, top and at the front the timbers are rebated all round for doors or shutters (now missing).

The armoire is composed of heavy timbers, and presents the same appearance inside and out, looking much like screening or partitioning in a timber-framed house. It has heavy floor beams, forming a plinth, on all four sides into which are set a series of massive uprights grooved vertically up to the centre to hold heavy panels; the uprights have a rough, flat chamfer. (Because the grooves are central in the uprights the outside and inside walls are identical with projecting vertical posts and recessed panels between.) The two sides are different: the left side has a central as well as 2 corner uprights with 2 panels between; the right side has corner uprights with 1 panel. This discrepancy, which appears to leave the right side structurally weaker, is compensated for by the provision of a wider front upright on the right-hand side, and by the existence of a horizontal beam or shelf inside.

The interior of the armoire has a single fitting: a heavy timber shelf at the right, fitted to the corner uprights within the rebate at the front, and cut in to lie flush with the side panel. The shelf supports a series of arms extending the full width of the armoire, which pivot on large pegs or dowels which are accommodated in holes on the shelf and in the roof. There were originally 6 arms, as is indicated by the unstopped dowel holes, but only 3 now remain and these are largely restored. Enough old timber survives, however, to show that the restoration of the arms is accurate. The arms swing outwards, extending beyond the confines of the armoire, and when necessary they are held within the armoire by a catch on the inside at the left, which holds the foremost arm at its free end; once this outermost arm is held, the others are automatically kept in position without the need for individual catches. It is clear that the textiles inside the armoire were envisaged as taking up all the internal space and that they hung down from the arms.

There were evidently once 2 doors or shutters, for there is a groove at the top, left and centre, for a catch and something which corresponds with this in the partly restored floor beam beneath. The method by which the armoire was closed is a mystery, and the suggestion that there may have been doors lying within the rebate seems to be ruled out by the absence of scars for hinges in the usual places on the uprights. (There is a scar where a piece of wood has been cut out on the front left-hand upright, on the centre of its side face, and another nick elsewhere, but these do not appear to have been connected with hinge plates.) It seems therefore likely that the armoire was closed with loose shutters which fitted the 1″ rebate on the front and were held by catches fixed to woodwork which once abutted the armoire, being lifted away when the armoire was in use.

The armoire is assembled by means of woodworking techniques (tongue and groove, and pegs) and there are no nails.

Analysis

The restorations to the armoire are small and carefully implemented: they are easy to distinguish since the modern wood is of a different colour to the original oak. The greatest loss is not, therefore, the minor signs of wear which have been skilfully repaired but the fact that the armoire is now out of context, being no longer in a building containing work of a similar character; the armoire's provenance appears to be unknown.

A second major misfortune is the loss of the shutters, if indeed this is the correct interpretation of the evidence of the rebates and catch grooves. It has been shown that loose shutters, rather than doors, might be used for armoires (see pp. 38–9), though Viollet-le-Duc's restoration of a similar armoire with swinging arms shows curtained fittings (pl. 60A). Notwithstanding the mutilations which the armoire has suffered, however, it is of outstanding interest, being possibly the only survivor of a type which documentary evidence suggests was common enough (see pp. 49–50). There is no ironwork to help in dating, but the chamfered timbers and heavily moulded cornice suggest a late fifteenth-century date, analogous with the Westminster armoire (Cat. 14). The correlations discussed above (pp. 49–50) indicate that the form was used in ecclesiastical and domestic contexts alike; indeed, both heavy vestments and the thick robes worn in the Middle Ages would have benefited equally from being suspended from long and high supports, and the equipment for chapels would have required storage of this nature within substantial households, as much as within ecclesiastical foundations.

Select Bibliography

N. Pevsner, *Buckinghamshire*, London, 1960, 22, 55.

CATALOGUE No. 25 (PLATE 31)

Armoire at King's College, Cambridge. In the SE. Chapel.

Oak

l. 7′ 10″;   h. 5′ 9″;   w. 2′ 6¾″.

Description (August 1970)

The armoire appears to have been built as a locker (type 1 ii) and is now a freestanding, 2-bay armoire. The sides are very rough and were clearly not meant to be seen; there is a small cornice which is fitted only to the front. The armoire may have originally had additional bays.

The armoire has a simple, heavy framework in which 3 uprights at the front are extended to form feet. Two doors close flush with the frame on either side of the central stile. The back and sides are composed of substantial uprights grooved along their centres to hold heavy boards, and except for the chamfer on the inside only, they present the same appearance within as without. (Some additional boarding attached to the outside at a later date masks this character in some areas.)

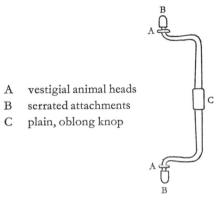

A   vestigial animal heads
B   serrated attachments
C   plain, oblong knop

FIG. 15.   Diagram showing position of decorated areas on the handles fitted to each door

The cornice is original and somewhat roughly shaped; its upper surface is almost flat and it has been abraded.

The interior shelving is now incomplete and some modern pegs have been added.

The 2 doors are heavy wooden boards of double thickness, the outer group placed vertically and the inner horizontally; the 2 sets of boards are held together with a profusion of nails, so that the outer surfaces of the doors are generously studded with iron nail heads. Three heavy hinges support each door with straps which extend the full width of the doors and a single hinge plate on the uprights extending almost to the full height of the doors. This ironwork is massively simple yet handsome, with squared-off ends; it is carefully countersunk. Four substantial locks remain intact and are without keyhole plates, an original arrangement. Inside the doors, iron loops of uncertain use remain. There is a single handle on each door which has a somewhat slight appearance in comparison with the weighty hingework, but is nevertheless entirely strong and serviceable, see Fig. 15.

The whole armoire is very substantial and is handsomer than a photograph suggests.

Analysis

This armoire has been stylistically dated late fifteenth century in the Royal Commission volume;[129] I agree with this finding and would justify this opinion as follows:

---

[129] *RCHM Cambridge*, I, 1959, 116b.

The armoire combines early and late features in a way which we can associate with an antiquarianism characteristic of the fifteenth century. Countersunk hinges are found at Obazine in *c*. 1176 (Cat. 10), Chester, early fourteenth century (Cat. 22), St Quentin, early fourteenth century (Cat. 23) and St Albans, early fifteenth century (Cat. 8). Countersunk hinges are particularly important when a wrought iron decorative design, ignoring hinge straps, is employed and thus they are to be associated with the twelfth and thirteenth centuries, the *floruit* of this particular form of artistry. The serrated loops for the handles are reminiscent of Malines, *c*. 1470 (Cat. 13) though the latter are incomparably finer, and the animal heads on the handles themselves are a degenerate reminder of that interest in the fantastic and the grotesque which is expressed with vigour at Obazine (Cat. 10). This type of English ironwork which uses twelfth and thirteenth-century forms earnestly, yet by comparison inadequately, is a fifteenth-century phenomenon, coinciding with the new cold cut technique employed in sophisticated work.[130] The antiquarian interest in wrought iron is found in blatant guise in the chests at Malpas (Cat. 37), and Icklingham, Suffolk.[131]

The heavy, centrally grooved framework with boards between, resembling partitioning, recalls Aylesbury, late fifteenth century (Cat. 24).

The King's College armoire is designed as a piece of fitted furniture and there is no place in the main chapel, or in the side chapel where it now stands, where it could have been properly accommodated, either in its present 2-bay form or as a larger object made up of additional bays. The stylistic date of the armoire, the fact that it could not be fitted anywhere in the chapel, coupled with the fact that King's College chapel was not completed until 1515 (accounts of stonework only survive), all re-enforce the view that the armoire was introduced into the chapel from elsewhere in the College. Perhaps, during its removal, the cornice was abraded as this large and heavy object was tilted to take it through narrow doorways.

Select Bibliography

RCHM Cambridge, I, 1959, 116b and pl. 192.

---

[130] Cold cut iron had replaced wrought iron in metropolitan contexts; the most remarkable example of the technique in England is the screen of Edward IV in St George's Chapel, Windsor Castle.

[131] It should be stated clearly that these impressive objects are only found wanting when compared with examples of the period which inspired them. For the Icklingham chest, see Macquoid/Edwards, 1927, Chests and Coffers, fig. 6.

THE BUFFET AND THE DRESSOIR

In France, the armoire has kept its term from the Middle Ages to the present day. In England, however, the medieval term *aumbry* is no longer used, *cupboard* having taken its place. In the Middle Ages the cup board was, as is implied, a board or boards for plate. The loss of the medieval term in England, and the adoption of a term belonging to another form of furniture, implies a close association between two forms. This interrelation, which we shall now investigate, prompts me to link this group with armoires, though we shall see that distinct and individual types of furniture were evolved whose appearance differs from that of the armoire. The problems surrounding the objects variously called buffet, dressoir and cup board in the Middle Ages are vexed by the confusion in contemporary terminology, since a few terms, sometimes used indiscriminately in a single document,[132] serve for furniture of several forms and uses. These uses were, indeed, broadly similar as we shall see, but as some of this furniture served as adjuncts of estate and some was humble and utilitarian, there is a wide difference in importance, and this is reflected in form and quality. It is this difference which we shall now analyse.

The important furniture, described variously as buffet, dressoir and cup board,[133] was used in the hall or chamber for displaying plate, and as a form of sideboard for serving wine and other drinks to important persons; whereas the other types comprised the numerous shelves, boards for dressing food and armoires (no doubt assembled in several ways as are the dressers surviving from the seventeenth century and later) belonging to service quarters, and to the service areas of important rooms, and used for readily accessible storage of dishes and utensils, food and drink and for the preparation of meals. As we shall see, the chief reason for the difficulty experienced in the Middle Ages over adopting consistent terms for this furniture was the development of the objects themselves, which changed more rapidly than did the language available for identification. Since there was no medieval system governing the use of dressoir, buffet and cup board which was consistently applied (except in so far as the term cup board was solely English)[134] it is necessary at the outset to adopt one in order to facilitate discussion and analysis, though it must be recognized that such a course is arbitrary.[135] I propose to use *buffet* for the important object used in hall and chamber for display,

[132] See the 1435 inventory of Pierre Surreau: 'En la salle basse . . . ung drecheur on il a deux aumaires fermans à clef . . . En la grant salle . . . ung buffet, à une aumaire fermée à clef . . .' (Félix, 8, 9, 68, 71).

[133] A red herring in the form of the term *crédence* must also be noted in this connexion. In our period, *crédence* meant drinking the lord's beverage as a guard against poison: '. . . Credence is vsed, & tastynge, for drede of poysenynge . . .' (John Russell's *Boke of Nurture*, c. 1460–80 but probably from an earlier source, Furnivall 1868, 196). As a term for furniture in France, England or Burgundy, *crédence* is post medieval; it became a fashionable term for buffet, dressoir or cup board among nineteenth-century furniture historians who followed Viollet-le-Duc. The term should be ignored.

[134] In English documents *cup board* does seem to indicate buffet with some consistency, with *dressoir* or *dresser* indicating the service furniture which I have termed dressoirs; but this is not invariably the case, as is shown in the inventory of Richard Lyons of 1376, where we find *coppeborde* in important chambers such as the hall, but also in the kitchen (*coparde*); (A. R. Myers, 'The Wealth of Richard Lyons', ed. T. A. Sandquist/M. R. Powicke, *Essays in Medieval History Presented to Bertie Wilkinson*, Toronto, 1969, 308, 318).

[135] An attempt to see a medieval distinction in *dressoir* and *buffet* will not bear investigation, as Maffei has pointed out (Maffei, 29).

and for the special service of drink; and *dressoir* for the dressing boards or shelves and other storage furniture forms which were in service quarters, or arranged as food counters and hatches to halls and chambers. The distinction I make, therefore, is primarily one of use, rather than of form, since the latter is impossible to determine adequately in the case of dressoirs, because the character of contemporary records concerning the furniture in service quarters, and the rarity of surviving examples, makes an accurate visual interpretation of the evidence impossible for this group. For buffets, on the other hand, the situation is clearer for not only do numerous examples survive[136] but we also have many manuscript illuminations celebrating important occasions in hall or chamber which can be correlated with the furniture and with written records (see pls. 60B–62; Cat. 26, 27).

Buffets

We have no evidence for an adequate assessment of the form and function of the buffet until the later Middle Ages (though earlier references occur),[137] at which time there is ample material to show that the buffet was, with the chair and the bed, an adjunct of estate, sensitive to degrees of precedence. The buffet developed rapidly in the fourteenth and fifteenth centuries, showing a precocious vitality in an age in which furniture had been slow to respond to changing fashion. The buffet provides one of the most fascinating furniture forms for study, since it is so closely allied to social aspirations and behaviour. Two main forms of buffet existed side by side; both outlasted the Middle Ages, but whereas the first was the most important in the fourteenth and fifteenth centuries, the second was more adaptable and for this reason more significant in terms of furniture history.

(1) In its more important form, the buffet was a simple, stepped structure with a series of open display shelves whose number indicated degrees of estate or honour — the greater the number of shelves or stages, the greater the honour. Allied to this function of an instantly recognizable and precisely regulated symbol of estate or power, was a statement concerning wealth, for the buffet was connected with refreshment and its steps or stages were normally used for plate,[138] a riser providing convenient support for dishes placed on the step below. Except in the matter of *form*, the wooden structure was of small importance for this buffet was always draped with textiles when in use.[139] In most representations the stepped buffet is without back or canopy, but Alienor de Poitiers shows that it might in fact have these additions; in her text, the back and

---

[136] Although considerable numbers survive in continental museums, the great majority are heavily restored.

[137] In the twelfth-century lease of the manor of Ardleigh, Essex, held by St Paul's London, we find: 'In aula fuerunt duo bancha tornatilia, et una mensa dormiens, et unum buffeth; . . .', ed. W. H. Hale, *The Domesday of St. Paul's in the Year MCCXXII*, Camden Society, 1858, 137.

[138] We normally hear of the buffet in the context of the feast; or, in illuminations, we may see it as part of the well-appointed interior; in both these contexts it is resplendent with plate. However, as an adjunct of estate, the buffet had a part to play in the ceremonial connected with mourning, and might then be *draped yet devoid of plate* (Appendix VIII, lines 1149–51).

[139] It is always totally covered in illustrations, e.g.: fifteenth-century MS of Quintus Curtius, Bodleian, see [Parker] 1854, facing 77; also, the Beheading of St John Baptist by the Master of St Severin, late fifteenth century, Boston Museum of Fine Arts, see *Bull. M.M.A.*, 1952/3, 274; also, Italian fifteenth-century panel painting attributed to Apollonio di Giovanni in Hanover, see *Bull. M.M.A.*, 1970, fig. 5. Other evidence makes a point of this characteristic; see Appendix VI, lines 7–9; Appendix VII (a), lines 29–32; and Appendix VIII (b), lines 137–8, 259–61.

canopy are of textiles (see Appendix VIII (b), lines 152–75). The stepped buffet belonged in hall or chamber, but space was required to deploy it, for it was, in effect, like accommodating a staircase in a room and its dimensions might be considerable.[140] It was not invariably quadrangular in plan.[141] It might serve solely as the focal point for an important occasion; or it might be used, plate and certain foods being taken from it as required.[142] No examples of the stepped buffet have survived from the Middle Ages.[143]

The stepped buffet was one of the grandest pieces of furniture it was possible to display and this sense of importance was born of the strict limitations and implications attached to its use and form. Alienor de Poitiers (who speaks only of women) defines this for us with some precision, stating that the queen of France and Marie of Burgundy displayed 5 stages; Isabelle of Portugal, 4; the Countess of Amiens and others of her rank, 3; wives of bannerets, 2; and lesser noble ladies, 1.[144] These buffets, with their precious load, were part of the elaborate and symbolic trappings which supported pageantry at court, and in the management of great occasions the court of Burgundy was pre-eminent. The Feast of the Pheasant, which took place at Lille in 1454, was one of the stupendously extravagant occasions for which the dukes of Burgundy were renowned. The occasion ended with the entrance of a twelve-year-old girl, the Princess of Joy, who rode her horse into the hall where the diners sat, accompanied by three attendants. She dismounted, climbed the steps to the duke's table, knelt and placed a chaplet on his head. A cynosure for all eyes on this occasion was the 6-staged buffet near the high table which was protected with wooden barriers, and only cup bearers were permitted to approach it.[145] In descriptions of great occasions or festivities such as this, the buffets are often lingeringly appraised as one of the great sights of the occasion.[146] Georges Chastellain, writing of the feast of the chevaliers of the Toison d'Or at The Hague in 1456, calls them *dressoirs*.[147] He speaks of three, the grandest of which was reserved *solely for display* and had 5 or 6 stages bearing gold objects set with jewels. The other two buffets, also stepped but of undisclosed height, were used for the service of the chevaliers' table and the other tables, and were decked with silver-gilt and plain silver vessels respectively. Thus, the most gorgeous plate was untouched, forming a display of great power and wealth, both by virtue of its intrinsic worth and because it was superfluous to requirement. (Elsewhere it is noted that Philip the Good

[140] Jean le Fevre de St Remy, first King of Arms of the Order of the Toison d'Or, wrote of the works put in hand by Philip the Good in 1429 at Bruges, for the forthcoming celebrations in connexion with his marriage to Isabelle of Portugal. In a newly constructed festival hall stood buffets of 5 stages, measuring 70′ long × 20′ high, garnished with vessels of gold and silver-gilt, the gold vessels being on the uppermost 3 stages and larger, silver-gilt vessels on the lower 2 stages. (A. van Zuylen van Nyevelt, *Episodes de la Vie des Ducs de Bourgogne à Bruges*, Bruges [n.d.], 256–7.)
[141] One source describes a buffet as triangular (Appendix VII (b), lines 41–52). Round buffets are also mentioned: c. 1350, 'Pour un buffet ront', J-M. Richard, 'Vente Apres Décès des Meubles de Jehan Le Caron dit Caronchel, Bâtard et Usurier à Arras', *Bulletin de la Commission des Antiquités Départementales du Pas-de-Calais*, IV, 1875 [–1878], 94; also 1496, '*209*. Item ung dressado redon', Forestié, 49, *209*.
[142] See Appendix VI, lines 7–24; also Appendix VII (a), lines 55–64.
[143] There is, however, at least one example in a later, German context, see Kreisel, fig. 245.
[144] See Appendix VIII, fig 1.
[145] See O. Cartellieri, *The Court of Burgundy*, London, 1929, 140, 142.
[146] See Appendix VII (a), lines 23–64.
[147] See Appendix VI, line 8.

owned table silver worth over 60,000 marks when he died.[148]) Olivier de la Marche, writing of the festivities in celebration of the marriage of Charles the Bold and Marguerite of York in 1468, speaks of the splendour of the lozenge-shaped buffet (and here and elsewhere in his works *buffet* is the term preferred,[149] in place of dressoir as used by Chastellain). Olivier de la Marche describes the great number of precious objects, including unicorns' horns, on this high buffet without telling us specifically how many stages it had, but an English account describes it as of triangular (as against lozenge) form with 9 stages. Here we have a great rarity, a precise correlation between a Burgundian and an English account and we see that the English term used for the buffet is *copeborde*.[150] (It should, perhaps, be mentioned in passing that the 9 stages of the English version may be an exaggeration, in view of the evidence already quoted regarding the number of stages displayed for a great feast by Philip the Good[151]).

The stepped buffet was too cumbersome an object for many situations, at court as much as elsewhere, and a second form answered the needs created by intimacy and restricted space.

(2) This buffet consisted of display space which was generally arranged as shelves *running the full depth of the structure*, though sometimes very small steps were employed (see pl. 60B).[152] This form allowed the measurement in depth to be as strictly contained as circumstances dictated. Apart from this restriction, the buffet had many forms which developed around the theme of including:

(a) closed storage space (armoires and drawers) with the display areas (see pls. 61 and 62), and

(b) backs, or backs and canopies, which rose up behind and above the uppermost display shelf (see pl. 60B, also Cat. 27).

The narrow buffet occurs frequently in art. Its display shelves were evidently arrayed with plate standing on simple runner cloths and its woodwork was otherwise totally exposed (see pl. 60B). The quality of the woodworking had to convey that richness which, in the stepped buffet, had been created by textiles and for this reason the narrow buffet was often elaborately carved. This highly wrought quality is particularly evident in three surviving examples illustrated here, and each one shows a different combination of storage and display space. The two examples at Antwerp have been skilfully restored but retain their original form (pls. 61 and 62); they are extremely delicate objects, suitable for a private chamber rather than a hall. The Plougrescant buffet (Cat. 27, pl. 33), now mutilated, is conceived on a grand scale and its original importance is underlined by the presence of a canopy.

The narrow buffet was as adaptable as the stepped buffet was intractable in use. Not only was it of accommodating proportions, but its characteristic combination of display areas with enclosed, secure storage space showed that it was never intended solely for

[148] See Appendix VII (a), lines 69–75.
[149] See also his account of the celebrations in Paris at the accession of Louis XI in 1461, Petitot, x, 229.
[150] See Appendix VII (b), line 41.
[151] See p. 57.
[152] Another example is shown by Maffei and is taken from a miniature in the MS 'Histoire du Bon Roi Alexandre'; we see a narrow buffet with back and canopy, board for display near the floor and 3 small *stepped* display shelves. (Maffei, fig. 21.)

display but combined dignity with utility. There is no evidence to indicate whether the number of display boards on the narrow buffet indicated degrees of precedence, but we may safely assume that where a back and canopy were included, as at Plougrescant, a degree of dignity was involved, for the importance of the canopy in furniture is fully understood.[153] However, although the narrow buffet might include storage space it was, first and foremost, an assembly of boards for plate and, as we have seen, this function was imbued with prestige. (This emphasis was slowly reversed in England in the sixteenth and seventeenth centuries, as the courtly habit of displaying plate was abandoned, but we observe that the term *cup board*, with its subtle implication of gentle manners, remained attached to the object when all its space was enclosed, and the relevant medieval term, aumbry, having no such sophisticated overtones, was lost.)[154]

We have seen how the importance of the stepped buffet as an adjunct of estate is established in the writings concerning the Burgundian court and elsewhere. The impression that the narrow buffet might fulfil exactly the same requirement is confirmed in an inventory of the Château d'Angers, held by René of Anjou (King of Sicily and Duke of Aragon) in 1471:

'. . . ung dressouer de parement à ciel, et à armoires à deux guichez fermans à clef . . .'[155]

(A buffet of state with a canopy and with armoires closed with 2 doors secured with keys)

The elaborately carved buffet at Plougrescant is an example of a narrow buffet of estate, with a canopy, and a single display board which is designed solely for display, for the board is placed too high for it to be used for service.

In England, although numerous references to buffets occur in circumstances which show that the article in question was an adjunct of estate,[156] the evidence is generally unspecific as to whether a stepped or narrow buffet is involved. However, there can be no doubt that England followed France and Burgundy in the use of the stepped buffet as a barometer of power. Macquoid/Edwards note that Henry VII displayed 9 or 10 stages at a banquet at Richmond Palace, and clearly here a stepped buffet was involved;[157] and the authors draw attention to the instructions in the late fifteenth-century treatise, 'Ffor to Serve a Lord', which strongly suggest the stepped form.[158] In another fifteenth-century English book of etiquette, we cannot be sure whether the stepped or narrow

---

[153] See Eames 1971, 50 and fn. 58.

[154] I would suggest in this connexion that the English term *court cupboard* of the sixteenth and seventeenth centuries meant 'as at court' and not a short or small cupboard, from the French, as has sometimes been suggested.

[155] V. Godard-Faultrier, 'Le Château d'Angers au Temps de Roi René', *Mémoires de la Société d'Agriculture, Sciences et Arts d'Angers*, IX, 1866, 60.

[156] See the account of the entertainment accorded to the lord Gruuthuse by Edward IV, when he was received at Windsor Castle; C. L. Kingsford, *English Historical Literature in the 15th Century*, Oxford, 1913, 379–88, particularly 387. The buffet is singled out for mention in a description which ignores all furniture which is not an adjunct of ceremony and estate.

[157] Macquoid/Edwards 1954, Dressers, 219.

[158] The procedure at the end of the meal is discussed: 'Thenne uprysyng, servitours muste attende to avoyde tabills, trestellis, formys and stolys, and to redresse bankers and quyssyons. Then the boteler shall avoyde the cupborde, begynnyng at the lowest, procede in rule to the hieste, and bere hit in-to his office . . .'; Furnivall 1868, 373.

buffet is being discussed, but the instructions given suggest that a quantity of plate is involved, for display as much as for use:

> 'Son, when thy souereignes table is drest in thus array, kouer alle other bordes with Saltes; trenchers & cuppes thereon ye lay; than emperialle thy Cuppeborde with Siluer & gild fulle gay, . . .'[159]

The narrow buffet, and also the stepped buffet when it was being serviceable as well as decorative, was used at meal times as a form of side table, and was particularly associated with the ewery and thus with the distribution of wine and ale. We see it portrayed in art, e.g. The Last Supper by Dieric Bouts (pl. 63), c. 1468, where two servers are visible at the dressoir — here a hatch — behind Christ and, to the right, the narrow buffet with canopy, with a servant beside it waiting to attend to those at table. In a sufficiently important household the man waiting to serve at the buffet might himself be a great seigneurial lord.[160] Both books of etiquette cited above give instructions concerning the cloth to be laid on the buffet and make plain the association between the buffet and the Office of the Ewery.[161]

In inventories, wills and accounts we are sometimes able to identify the buffet, as distinct from the humble dressoir, by its location within the house (hall or chamber), together with some indication of importance (phrases such as *buffet* or *dressoir de salle*, or *de parement*, or evidence that the object was used for plate). But evidence of location in hall or chamber alone is inadequate as a means of identifying the buffet, because dressoirs, often no more than boards, were used in important chambers for serving food. The following entries are, therefore, inconclusive, though we may feel that buffets rather than dressoirs are meant.

12th century 'In aula . . . unum buffeth.'

(Lehmann-Brockhaus, 34 (113).)

1348   'unum dressador' describes items 29 and 96 in the inventory of André Frédol, Abbot of Saint-Afrodise at Béziers, and the objects were found in the room where the Abbot slept and in his hall.

(J. Guiraud, 'Inventaires Narbonnais du XIVe Siècle', *Bulletin de la Commission Archéologique de Narbonne*, VII, 1902/3, 222, 225.)

---

[159] The 'Boke of Nurture' by John Russell, Marshal and Usher to Humphrey, Duke of Gloucester; Furnivall 1868, 131.
[160] In 1471 'The King [Edward IV] kept his estate in ye whyt hall, . . . and therl of Wylshyre wayted on the Kinges coberd as chef boteler for yt day . . .'; Kingsford 1913, 383.
[161] Firstly, 'Ffor to Serve a Lord' instructs: 'Ffirst, in servise of all thyngys in pantery and botery, and also for the ewery. ffirst, table-clothis, towelles longe and shorte, covertours and napkyns, be ordeyned clenly, clene and redy accordyng to the tyme. Also basyns, ewers, Trenchours of tre or brede, sponys, salte, and kervyng knyves.
Thenne ayenst tyme of mete, the boteler or the ewer shall brynge forthe clenly dressed and fayre applyed Tabill-clothis, and cubbord-clothe, cowched upon his lefte shulder, laying them upon the tabill ende, close applied unto the tyme that he have firste coverd the cubbord; and thenne cover the syde-tabillis, [along the side of the hall, below the dais], and laste the principall tabill [dais table] with dobell clothe draun, cowched, and spradde unto the degre, as longeth therto in festis.' (Furnivall 1868, 367.)

1373   '*1672*. . . . en sale . . . buffet, 1. . . .
                 1673. En la chambre vert: buffet, 1 . . .
                 1675. En la chambre de parement: buffet, 1 . . .'

                 (Inventory of the Château de Montbard, held by the Duke of Burgundy. Prost, I, 312.)

1493   '. . . my cupbord stondying in my halle, . . .'

                 (Will of William Honyboorn, a dyer of Bury. S. Tymms, 'Wills and Inventories from the Registers of the Commissary of Bury St. Edmund's and the Archdeacon of Sudbury', *Camden Society*, XLIX, 1850, 81.)

In contrast, the obvious importance of the objects in the following entries makes their identification as buffets certain.

1371   '*1417*. A Phelippe Cirasse, charpentier, demorant à Paris, . . . pour un grant dresseour de parement, à mettre en la chambre de Mme, . . .'

                 (Prost, I, 255.)

                 (To Philip Cirasse, carpenter, living in Paris, . . . for a large state buffet for the chamber of the Duchess of Burgundy.)

As this buffet occurs in a list of furnishings required for the birth of a child to the Duchess of Burgundy, the context makes it certain that this was the state buffet for the birth of John the Fearless; Alienor de Poitiers makes it clear that such buffets were an important item in the lavishly equipped chambers set aside for such occasions.[162]

1377   '*2851*. En tout le chastel . . . deux grans dreceours, l'un en la sale et l'autre en la chambre Mgr . . .'

                 (Prost, I, 545. Inventory of the Chateau d'Aisey-le-Duc, held by the Duke of Burgundy.)

1379   'PARTIES DES JOYAULX DU PETIT MESNAGE TROUVEZ OU DRESSOUER ESTANT EN LA CHANBRE DU ROY AUX BOYS. . .'

                 (J. Labarte, *Inventaire du Mobilier de Charles V*, Paris, 1879, 213.)

                 (Some of the jewels [a term which included plate] of the small household found in (or on) the buffet in the king's chamber at the Chateau of Vincennes . . .)

Following this heading in the inventory are over 142 items of household plate; most are plain silver and a few are silver-gilt but none are set with precious stones. They are clearly the items in everyday use, as is implied in the heading. The inventory containing this information is concerned with the plate in this instance and only mentions the buffet as a means of locating it, so that we have no information as to size and form.

1388   '*2726*. Symon de Dommartin recoit le 28 juillet 1,267 fr. 10 s.t. à lui dus pour deux flacons d'argent dorez, haichiez, ciselez de façon de quoquille,

---

[162] See Appendix VIII (b and c), lines 254–61.

pesans 105 marcs 5 onces, à 12 fr. le marc, que Mgr a fait mettre par devers lui pour mectre sur son dreceoir.'

(Prost, II, 432.)

(Symon de Dommartin received on 28th July, 1,267 fr. 10 s.t. owing him for 2 flagons of silver-gilt, cut and chased with shell work, weighing 105 marks, 5 ounces, at 12 fr. the mark, which the Duke of Burgundy had made by him for putting on his buffet.)

Sometimes these sources indicate the form of the buffet and we easily recognize the narrow buffet with enclosed, secure storage compartments. We notice how varied descriptions are as scribes grope for suitable means of identifying a piece of furniture which is transitional, lacking a single contemporary noun for identification.[163]

1378   'a *cuppeborde* called *vesseller*.'

           (Sharpe, II, 207. Will of John Croydon, a London fishmonger.)

1405   'en la sale . . . 1 buffet de bos a serrure . . .'

           (Dehaisnes, II, 912. Inventory of the Duchess of Burgundy.)

           (In the hall . . . a wooden buffet which locks.)

1435   'En la salle basse . . . ung drecheur ou il a deux aumaires fermans à clef . . . En la chambre ou gesoit led. deffunt. Premièrement ung drécheur à deux aumaires . . . ou quel drécheur estoit la vesselle d'argent courant oud. hostel . . . En la grant salle . . . ung buffet, à une aumaire fermée à clef, . . .'

           (Félix, 7, 9, 48–9, 68, 71. Inventory of Pierre Surreau.)

           (In the lower hall . . . a buffet with 2 armoires closed with locks . . . In the chamber where the deceased lay, firstly, a buffet with 2 armoires which held the silver in everyday use in the house . . . In the great hall . . . a buffet with 1 armoire closed with a key.)

1468   '. . . en la chambre du meillieu . . . deux dressouers fermans . . . en la salle desdites galleries, . . . ung dressouer ouvert, . . .'

           (Jarry, 144, 145. Inventory of Jean, Comte du Dunois, bastard of Orleans.)

           (In the central chamber . . . 2 closed buffets . . . in the chamber of the aforesaid galleries, an open buffet.)

Dressoirs

Let us now examine the evidence for the furniture, often confused with buffets, which was used for preparing, serving and storing food and utensils. In the interest of clarity, I shall call this group dressoirs, although it will be recalled that contemporary practice followed no such conveniently consistent rule.[164]

---

[163] Problems of identification continued after our period, as has been noted, see p. 59. The following evidence, taken from Nicolas 1830, 190, speaks for itself: (1) In the list of furniture in Henry VIII's palaces (Harleian MS 1419) we find 'Item. Two cuppbordes, with ambries.'; (2) In J. Palsgrave, *Esclarcissement de la Langue Francoyse*, London, 1530, 'Cupborde of plate, or to sette plate upon, *buffet*; cupborde to putte meate in, *dressover*; coupborde, unes almoires'.

[164] See pp. 55–6.

Dressoirs, being utilitarian and lacking any special significance, were free of the need to conform to those rules which affected furniture which was an adjunct of estate. Whereas the number of shelves on the buffet was adjusted to accord with degrees of honour, the dressoir was shelved according to convenience.

The dressoir itself is of small importance to us. It cannot be satisfactorily studied for a variety of reasons. Ordinary, rough furniture, if it has survived anywhere, has not attracted attention in modern times and is unrecorded; the chances of finding extant examples with a secure provenance are remote. Furthermore, we cannot hope to find much in the way of representations of the kitchen offices of households in the art of the Middle Ages, and in written records the dressoir is normally noted in even more cursory fashion than furniture of the more important halls and chambers. Why, then, do we need to concern ourselves with the dressoir at all? The answer to this lies in our need to understand written records. If we are to enlarge our understanding of the use and importance of the buffet through documentation, the problem of the confusion of contemporary terminology between the buffet and the dressoir has to be tackled so that each can be identified and the dressoir thereafter ignored. (It may also be argued that, in identifying dressoirs, we gain some small peripheral understanding of the management of an important office of the household, namely the kitchen.)

Our chief aid in identifying the buffet and the dressoir in inventories is location. The buffet belonged to hall and chamber. The dressoir, however, though primarily associated with the service quarters, sometimes provided service facilities for meals in halls and chambers, as we shall see in the evidence below.

Most references to dressoirs in service quarters tell us nothing about their form, and the following extracts are typical in this respect.

1323   '. . . item, in dispensa dicte domus, . . . unum buffetum.'

(Le Blond, 45.)

(. . . item, in the spense of the said house, . . . a dressoir.)

1338   'Item, en la haute cuisine, . . . 1 grant dréchouoir.'

(J. Roman, 'Inventaire des Meubles du Château de Rouen', *Bulletin Archéologique*, 1885, 546, *11*.)

(Item, in the upper kitchen, . . . 1 large dressoir.)

1376   'La cusyne . . . 3 petitz copardes.'

(Myers, 1969, 318.)

1440   In the Kitchen, 4 dressers, 3 large and 1 small.

(N. Drinkwater, 'The Old Deanery, Salisbury', *Antiquaries Journal*, XLIV, 1964, 58.)

It is tempting to interpret these descriptions as belonging to pieces of furniture which were substantially like the dressers used in farm houses in France, England and Wales in the seventeenth and eighteenth centuries. Such a view is suggested by the evidence concerning the storage of the copper and pewter ware belonging to the Office of the

Kitchen in the household of Margaret of Flanders, Duchess of Burgundy, which was arranged in orderly fashion upon *dreceurs* which had window-like doors hung with cloth.[165] We should obviously make a firm distinction between the dressoir which was a piece of furniture and the many boards, shelves or hatches used for arranging or 'dressing' food.[166] Although the latter hardly qualify as furniture, they had no special term in medieval times.

1390   '. . . en la cuisine dudit hostel [Priory of St Eloy-de-Paris] de viez ais en
              maniere de dresseours.'
              (L. Pannier, 'Inventaire des Meubles Contenus dans la Maison de la Rue
              des Murs', *Bibliothèque de l'École des Chartes*, XXXIII, 1872, 362.)
              (. . . in the kitchen of the said house, some old boards arranged like dres-
              soirs.)

1471   'En la panneterie . . . troys aes qui servent de dressouers, . . .'
              (Godard-Faultrier, 65.)

1485   'A dressing bord of elmen for the larder of x fote, . . . A dressyng-borde
              of elmen for the Kytchin xij fote long, . . .'
              (C. L. Kingsford, 'On Some London Houses of the Early Tudor Period',
              Archaeologia, LXXI, 1920/1, [1921], 45.)

Sometimes these boards were clearly what we should recognize as a table.

1384/5   Office of the Kitchen at Corbeil.
              'ij pieces de bois à faire ij treteaux pour le dressoir de la sausserie.'
              (Canat de Chizy 1859, 282.)
              (2 pieces of wood to make 2 trestles for the dressoir in the Saucery.)

   The boards used as hatches between service quarters and halls or chambers can still be seen in the screens passage of some Oxford and Cambridge colleges, and we see one portrayed in Dieric Bouts's Last Supper (pl. 63) to the left, with the heads of two servers who stand outside the hall or chamber in order to pass prepared food through to be served to those at table. We clearly recognize such fittings in some documentary references.

1261   To the Sheriff of Dorset. '*Contrabreve* . . . to make a dresser (*stabelliam*) [at
              Gillingham] between the king's hall and kitchen to set out (*dirigendum*) the
              king's food, . . .'
              (*Calendar of the Liberate Rolls V. 1260–1267*, H.M.S.O., 1961, 47.)

The basic simplicity and utility of these fixtures ensured their survival beyond our period *for as long as the order of serving food remained essentially unchanged.*[167] These food counters may be correlated with the *dressour* or *dresser* mentioned in the Household

---

[165] See Canat de Chizy 1859, 115.
[166] See the discussion in Macquoid/Edwards 1954, Dressers.
[167] A Tudor account concerning Windsor Castle enables us to visualize a particular food counter with ease: 1534/5: '. . . as also makyng a new leved Dore and a Wykett in the same ffor the great Kechyn wth a ffoldyng Dresser upon the said wykett to sett mette upon at the serves tyme . . .', St John Hope 1913, 264.

Ordinance of 1318 and in the Black Book of Edward IV; upon them were set meats and other foods *excluding wine*, for wine and other drinks were served by men of superior rank from the buffet, as we have already seen.[168]

1318   Household Ordinance. (Concerning the Hall.)

Le Serieant Surueour du dresour pour la Sale.

Item vn sergeant surueour de dressour pour la sale, qi deit auiser dez luez de lour seruice, solonque ceo qi les gentz de graunde estate et autres serrount assiz en la sale.'

T. F. Tout, *The Place of the Reign of Edward II in English History*, Manchester, 1914, 284.

(Item a sergeant sewer of the dressoir for the hall, who must look to the taking up [of dishes from the dressoir] of that food allowed according to the rules of precedence to each individual when those men of great estate and others are seated in the hall.)

Black Book of Edward IV, §33.

'A sewar for the King . . . shall not abrigge nor withdraw no dishe of seruyse that is delyuered or deuysed by other officers at the dressour, but trewely to sew tham vppon the Kinges table . . .'

(Myers 1959, 112.)

One further piece of evidence must be noted, even though it adds further to the existing confusion over the use of the term dressoir in medieval times. In the mid-fourteenth century, 'Le Dressour' was a *room* where meats were dressed at Windsor Castle.[169]

CATALOGUE No. 26 (PLATE 32)

Buffet of the Household of Marguerite of York in the Busleydon Museum, Malines

Oak

l. 3′ 3¾″; h. to underside of display board, 2′ 5⅛″; w. including restored back, 1′ 1¼″.

Description (July 1970)

    Buffet of panelled construction with corner uprights extended to form legs; these legs are now truncated. Front divided into three sections: a central panel, carved with linen fold and an armoire on either side, each with a single door carved from the solid wood and hinged on the outside edge. The sides of the buffet have a single panel of linen fold. Mouldings frame three sides of the linen fold panels (upper and side edges), with a chamfer on the lower edge. The display board (top) is modern. The back has been strengthened.

---

[168] See p. 60.
[169] In 1362/3 Richard Bledlowe, carpenter, was paid £20 for building this room near the new kitchen; see St John Hope 1913, 186, 189, 193, 207, 208.

The handsome strap hinges and lock and catch plates appear to have been transferred from another piece of furniture of late fifteenth-century date. The legs, now cut down, may have originally been fitted with a display board near the floor; if the buffet was originally of the usual height, something would have been needed lower down as a brace. In spite of mutilation and restoration, the arrangement of the storage area is original and the subject matter of the carving on the two doors makes the buffet of outstanding interest.

The doors are carved with identical devices which are differently grouped on each door; in addition, the right-hand door is carved with the initals C M. The devices are as follows.

(1) the *briquet de Bourgogne*;

(2) the rays, here associated with

(3) the pierres *éclatantes* or *enflambées*, and

(4) a flower, which I believe to be a marguerite, which intertwines the *briquet* on the left door and forms a growing clump on the right door. The carving throughout is vigorous yet crude.

Analysis

Before the buffet was cut down, it is likely that its form resembled the buffet at Antwerp (pl. 61). However, although the latter is of superb quality and is superior in almost every respect to the Malines example, the buffet at Malines is carved with devices which enable us to pinpoint it with some exactness. The devices on this buffet give it an interest which transcends its inadequacies; although it is mutilated and of indifferent workmanship it is, in a sense, an historical document.

The devices (1–3) are associated with Philip the Good and Charles the Bold. In an illumination showing Philip the Good at mass, the hangings of his pavilion are powdered with these devices,[170] and the chronicler, Jean le Fevre, tells us that when Philip married Isabelle of Portugal the hangings of the hall dais at Bruges were ornamented with his device, the 'fusilz à pierres enflambées'.[171] In the case of the buffet, however, the presence of C M makes it certain that the devices are those of Philip the Good's son, Charles the Bold, Duke of Burgundy (1467–1477), the initials standing for Charles and for Marguerite his Duchess (Marguerite of York, married to Charles the Bold in 1468 and died in 1503). There is a wealth of evidence in support of this view. The banners of Charles's army, taken at the battle of Nancy (1477) and preserved in museums and churches in Switzerland, provide irrefutable evidence, as do the illuminated borders of many MSS associated with Charles the Bold and Marguerite of York. From the Nancy standards, see, for example, that which bears Charles's motto 'Je lay enprins', the *briquet*, rays and *pierres éclatantes*, and C M linked with a tasselled cord, noted by Deuchler as standing for 'Carolus-Margarethe'.[172] And, from the possessions of Marguerite of York, see for instance the manuscript illuminated for her in Brussels with margins ornamented

---

[170] From the *Traité sur l'Oraison Dominicale*, Bib. Roy. MS 9092, Brussels; see F. Deuchler, *Die Burgunderbeute*, Bern, 1963, fig. 367.
[171] See van Zuylen van Nyevelt, 257.
[172] Deuchler, 274, fig. 228.

with her device and motto 'Ben en aviengne' together with the initials C M.[173] See also Marguerite of York's marriage crown, together with its case, preserved in the treasury at Aachen. The crown has the initials C M placed at regular intervals around the upper circlet, and the box lid carries C M, the armorial bearings of England and Burgundy, and Marguerite of York's motto 'Bien en avenir'.[174] One of the clearest examples of devices (1–4) combined adorns the borders of the title-page of the second book of the *Toison d'Or* of *c.* 1473 (pl. 64A) which is illuminated and shows Charles the Bold at a chapter of the Order and sets out his full titles below. The borders include:

(1) Coat of arms of the Toison d'Or, held in a collar; used once.
(2) Ribbons with 'Je lay enprins'; used twice.
(3) C M; used thrice.
(4) Marguerites which run and intertwine the link between the initials; used thrice.
(5) *Briquet, pierres éclatantes* and rays; groups used twice.

In this illumination it is noticeable that the most favoured view of the marguerite flower is the side view of the half open flower, and not the circular full-face view of the fully open flower. It is likely that the side view was considered more characteristic, giving a view of calix and petals and an appreciation of the vivid pink tips on the undersides of the petals. The calix was considered important, it seems, for we learn that in 1468 the chamber prepared for Marguerite of York at Bruges was chequered with white, pink and green, 'la couleur de la Margrite'.[175] If we now turn back to the carved doors of the buffet and give due weight to the difference between fine drawings which had the added advantage of colour and a rough, uncoloured carving executed upon coarse grained oak, it will be seen that the flower which intertwines the *briquet* on the left door of the buffet and grows in a low clump on the right could represent the half-open marguerite; taken in conjunction with the evidence of the rest of the carving we are bound to conclude that this flower *is* the marguerite.

We have established that the buffet is connected with Charles the Bold and Marguerite of York; it must, therefore, be dated somewhere between their marriage in 1468 and Marguerite of York's death in 1503. There is interesting circumstantial evidence for a closer date, however, which may now be discussed.

The buffet has always belonged to the Hôtel de Busleydon, now the Musée Communal, as far as its history is known. The Museum occupies the house of the Busleydon family of Malines, who were particularly successful in the fifteenth century when Marguerite of York chose Dr Francis Busleydon, a graduate of the universities of Louvain and Padua, as tutor to Philip the Fair, son of Marie of Burgundy and Maximilian of Austria. Francis Busleydon remained with Philip, eventually becoming chief of his privy council.[176]

The connexion between Marguerite of York and Malines is important; the town was one of the four *villes douaires* which, on the terms of her marriage contract, provided

[173] Bib. Roy. MS 9296, Brussels. See J. Cain, *Le Siècle d'Or de la Miniature Flamande*, Cat. exhibition held at Brussels, Amsterdam and Paris in 1959, 145 and pl. 7.
[174] See Lord Twining, *European Regalia*, London, 1967, 67, 158–9, pls. 31a, 57b.
[175] From the *Memoires* of Jean de Haynin — 'échecquetée, toute de garroles blanc, rouge et vert, la couleur de la Margrite'. See van Zuylen van Nyevelt, 294.
[176] See L. Hommel, *Marguerite d'York où la Duchesse Junon*, Paris, 1959, 175–6.

her with an annual revenue on the death of her husband.[177] After the death of Charles the
Bold at the battle of Nancy, Marguerite of York settled in Malines, buying an old house
in the Rue de l'Empereur in November, 1477 (the hôtel de Cambrai); later, with the
purchase of eight other houses and the help of the architect Antoine Kelderman, she
transformed the group of buildings into a modern palace which was almost complete in
1486 and was named the Hôtel Bourgogne. Here, her household of about one hundred
persons was established — a household which had not been curtailed at the death of
Charles the Bold.[178] Marguerite of York lived in the Hôtel Bourgogne until 1497, when
she retired to a nunnery close by.[179] She died in Malines in 1503.

It is clear that Malines was exceedingly important during the time of Marguerite of
York's widowhood. Hommel suggests that her court became the centre of government.[180] Another authority suggests that the Grand Conseil, established at Malines from
3 January 1474, exercised an exclusively judicial power, which is something rather less
than full government.[181] However, while the detailed administrative arrangement of the
government of Burgundy may be debated, for our purpose it is enough to say that the
existence of the Grand Conseil at Malines, and her own presence there gave Marguerite
of York, who acted as guardian to Philip the Fair, opportunities for influencing affairs
and made it certain that her household retained considerable state and importance.

In considering the buffet once again, the history of Marguerite of York's life at
Malines suggests that the buffet was made between the time she occupied the Hôtel
de Cambrai — presumably early in 1478 (she bought the house in November 1477) and
1497 when she left the Hôtel Bourgogne to enter a nunnery. We may surmise that at
some time Marguerite of York's furniture from the Hôtel Bourgogne was dispersed, the
buffet finding its way into the Busleydon household, possibly through purchase,[182]
for it is inconceivable that such a humble object could have been a gift from Marguerite
of York to Francis Busleydon.[183]

Let us now consder the character, or quality, of the buffet in the context of its ownership. We know very little concerning the quality of the furniture which was considered
appropriate for furnishing the private and state apartments of medieval lords, for
illuminations can only guide us as to their form and tell us nothing of their execution;
occasionally, we discover that the quality of workmanship was very high, as for example
the cradle of state made for one of the children of Marie of Burgundy and Maximilian of
Austria in 1478/9 (Cat. 28). All the evidence suggests, however, that such furniture was
exceptional; it was furniture of estate and was confined to those rooms where seigneurial

[177] See Homel, 324 f.
[178] See Homel, 158, 159, 161.
[179] See Homel, 238–9.
[180] 'C'est à Malines, dans l'hôtel de la douairière, que s'élabore, à partir de 1477, la politique de l'État bour-
guignon, que se prennent les décisions gouvernementales importantes. Par lettres patentes du 28 septembre
1479, Maximilien fait de Malines le siège de ses différents conseils.' Hommel, 155.
[181] See L. Th. Maes, *Le Parlement et le Grand Conseil à Malines*, Malines, 1949, 3 ff. For a discussion of the scope
and functions of the Grands Conseils of the dukes of Burgundy, see F. Brabant, 'Étude sur les Conseils des
Ducs de Bourgogne', *Bull. Com. Roy. Hist.* (5), i, 1891, 90–101.
[182] Occasionally, we learn of the purchase of second-hand furniture, e.g. the bed bought in 1385 from the
executors of James Raygate by Richard de Ravenser, archdeacon of Lincoln; see Gibbons, 68.
[183] Small gifts from persons of exalted rank to servants of a certain standing were always within the categories
of jewellery (which included plate) or textiles (which included furs).

power was displayed—rooms which later came to be called state apartments. There were many offices and chambers throughout a great medieval house which needed furnishings which befitted the standing of the users, but which were not designed to reflect the ultimate seingeurial power in any given context. It seems likely that this buffet belonged to one of these lesser chambers in the Hôtel Bourgogne for the use of one of the officers of the household, whose position allowed him or her to receive the customary evening rations of food and particularly of drink which were dispensed from the buffet. It is possible that most, if not all the furniture which was newly acquired for a great household in the later Middle Ages was rendered as individual to that household as was the livery worn by its servants. There must have been many ordinary objects, like this buffet and the Richard de Bury chest in the Burrell Collection, which were individually marked by means of carving or painting, but which were not necessarily used *personally* by the individuals concerned. What makes the buffet unusual as a survivor in this respect is that the devices upon it enable us to pinpoint the owner with precision, for we have not only family devices but also personal ones. It is the C M and the marguerite flowers which make a precise attribution possible and give the buffet its special interest. Indeed, it seems to have been a habit of the Valois dukes of Burgundy to use personal devices on possessions of various kinds.[184] But it should be emphasized that where we find the heraldic devices of a single family standing alone, unqualified by the addition of personal devices, we have no precise knowledge of the original owners, for we find that the Burgundian ducal devices and the lilies of France were used indiscriminately by loyal subjects as decorations to both furniture and buildings with which the dukes were only very indirectly concerned.[185] In this connexion it should also be noted here that the famous object at Louth, Lincolnshire, which is of somewhat similar form to the Malines buffet, and known as 'Sudbury's Hutch' cannot be accepted as medieval.[186]

Select Bibliography

F. Deuchler, *Die Burgunderbeute*, Bern, 1963.

J. van den Gheyn, 'Contributions a l'Iconographie de Charles le Temeraire et de Marguerite d'York', *Annales de l'Academie Royale d'Archéologie Belgique*, LVI, 1904, 384–405.

[184] During the 1380s, the combination of the marguerite flower and initials, arms and devices was frequently employed for Philip the Bold and his Duchess, Margaret of Flanders, and also with reference to their daughter Marguerite, as the following evidence shows. (i) Marguerite flowers and M embroidered on clothing for Mlle Marguerite (Prost, II, 202); (ii) Marguerite flowers and the Duke's arms embroidered on the Duke's parade horse cloth (Prost, II, 230, *1423*); (iii) Letters and marguerites on the sails and cover of the poop of the Duke's ship (Prost, II, 234–5, *1455*; 240, *1475*); (iv) 60 gold letters, P M on the belt of the Duke's *jaque* (type of doublet), and 69 gold marguerites upon another doublet (Prost, II, 245–6, *1492*); (v) P & M interlaced with the Duke's devices on bed and chamber hangings in 1388 (Prost, II, 431–2, *2721*). We also find, in the Duchess's inventory of 1405, the initials P M on an X-chair, see p. 185.

[185] For example, the chimney of the Guildhouse at Bruges, see pp. 10–11. There are 4 other pieces of furniture extant with the Burgundian devices carved upon them, only 1 of which can be closely dated by heraldic evidence; none can be intimately associated with the persons whose devices they bear. (i) Chest of the Corporation de Chaudronniers (Musée Tournai), with the *briquet* and fleur-de-lis, see Casier/Bergmans, pl. XCVII, fig. 160; (ii) Armoire of the hospital of Notre Dame of Courtrai with *briquet, caillou qui éclate* and fleur-de-lis, see Caullet, 109–13, pl. VII; (iii) Chest with *briquet* in the Musée d'Archéologie (Bijloke), Ghent, see Caullet, 113; (iv) Chest in the hospital at Alost dated to 1477–1482 by the conjunction of the *briquet* and lilies of France (Marie of Burgundy) with the double-headed eagle (Maximilian of Austria), see Casier/Bergmans, pl. XCVI, fig. 158.

[186] See Eames 1969, 225.

J. van den Gheyn, 'Encore l'Iconographie de Charles le Temeraire et de Marguerite d'York' *Ann. Acad. Roy. Arch. Belgique*, LIX, 1907, 275–94.

E. G. Grimme, *Der Aachener Domschatz*, Dusseldorf, 1972, 111–12, pls. 109–10.

L. Hommel, *Marguerite d'York où la Duchesse Junon*, Paris, 1959.

J. Squilbeck, *Marguerite d'York et son Temps*, Brussels, 1967.

Baron A. Stalins, *Origine et Histoire de la Famille Stalins de Flandre, depuis le XIIe Siècle, et un Briquet Heraldique dit de Bourgogne, où Fusil de la Toison d'Or*, Paris/Ghent/Maçon, 1939.

Lord Twining, *European Regalia*, London, 1967, 67, 158–9, pls. 31a, 57b.

Le Siècle d'Or de la Miniature Flamande. Le Mecenat de Philippe le Bon. Exposition organisée à l'occasion du 400ᵉ anniversaire de la foundation de la bibliothèque royale de Philippe II à Bruxelles, le 12 avril, 1559. Preface H. Liebaers/D. C. Roell. Introduction J. Cain, 1959.

CATALOGUE No. 27 (PLATE 33)
Buffet at Plougrescant, Côtes-du-Nord.
Chapelle de St Gonéry, south transept.

?Cedar: a reddish, coarse grained wood; unpolished.

l. 8′ 3″; h. to display board, 6′ 1″; h. above display board to canopy, excluding finials, 2′ 9″; w. 2′ 6″.

Description (July 1969)

Lower front   Panelled construction with side uprights extended to form feet. This simple construction is masked by a plinth at the base and by a central horizontal moulding, both of which are applied to and project from the framework. A series of 8 applied columns divide the front vertically, their bases resting on the plinth and on the central moulding respectively, so that there are 4 to each register. The upper 4 columns stop short above the base and are then resumed higher up to finish in a crocketed finial; the void was designed for a figure, missing in all cases. The lower 4 columns are decorated with spiral and other designs. Between the columns are 3 armoires on each of the 2 registers, 6 in all. The 4 armoires on the left (2 upper and 2 lower) hinge on the left; the remainder hinge on the right. The upper armoire doors are carved with figures, the lower with free, writhing interlaced designs.

Sides   The right side is panelled and divided horizontally to match the front, a single panel of figures in the upper register and 2 panels with ?plant motif on the lower register. The left side has panels of twisted columnar forms.

Upper area, back and canopy   The back preserves the same 3 vertical divisions with ribs which project in the manner of a vault to support the cantilevered canopy. Between the ribs, the back is carved with busts in ogee arches. The canopy has a pierced rail placed within horizontal spiral mouldings and is interrupted by vertical posts designed to carry figures of flying angels below, and to be extended to form finials above. The pierced and fretted rail is continued round the sides of the canopy. Above the rail, between the finial posts, is a pierced and fretted gallery. All finials survive, 4 at the front and 1 at the back corner of each side. There were originally 6 figures of flying angels beneath the rail of the canopy; 4 attached to finail posts, and 3 interspersed at regular intervals between, with a pierced frieze between them. Part of this pierced frieze is broken away, and the second angel from the left is missing.

Much of the carving is mutilated, the features of many of the figures having been deliberately erased. In the lower front, the figure subjects appear to be religious. The carving is very individual in character, accomplished and bold.

All the ironwork, which is confined to the lower front, is original. The hinges match, being long, fretted openwork straps set proud of the wood. The lock plates are rectangular and are all of the same character, though none precisely match. The lower left and lower right plates are missing. The handles are of cusped, drop form.

Analysis

The buffet is remarkable in several respects. It is a large and important piece of furniture, as is indicated by the height of the display board and by the presence of the canopy. This buffet was designed to display plate but not to be used for service, for the display board is at a height which would have enabled it to be seen but not to be touched. It therefore combines a storage space with a display board which had no strictly utilitarian function, unlike most of the narrow buffets which survive or are portrayed in art (see pls. 60B, 61, 62). With a display board designed solely for effect, the Plougrescant buffet shows that narrow buffets might interlock with stepped buffets in this respect, as in others (see pp. 59 ff.). The Plougrescant buffet was a buffet of estate, and may be almost precisely correlated with the entry in the 1471 inventory of the Château d'Angers, except in the number of armoires involved.

'En la chambre de Mademoiselle Margerie . . . ung dressouer de parement à ciel, et à armoires à deux guichez fermans à clef.'[187]

(A buffet of estate with a canopy and with armoires closed with 2 doors shutting with a key.)

The subject matter carved on the Plougrescant buffet is as individual as is the quality of the workmanship itself, and one feels that such an object must have been designed with a particular patron in mind. There is no reason to suppose that it was necessarily made for the chapel where it now stands; it may have equally belonged to a secular or ecclesiastical household. A buffet of similar form from England, though much smaller and totally lacking in the visual surprises characteristic of Plougrescant, is illustrated by Macquoid/Edwards; although much restored, it is stated to have always belonged to the Somerset family.[188]

The overall quality of the carving and of the ironwork of the Plougrescant buffet is high, which makes the mutilations to the figures particularly unfortunate. The wood is

[187] Godard-Faultrier, 60.
[188] 1954, Dressers, fig. 2.

most unusual, being the only example from the medieval period which I have seen. The ornament is late Gothic in all respects and flamboyant tracery is much in evidence. The decoration of the applied columns on the front, lower register, recalls the corner columns on the tomb chest of Marie of Burgundy in the church of Notre Dame, Bruges, made between 1495–1502, and the interruption in the columns on the upper register of the buffet for lost figures is, in Marie of Burgundy's tomb, complete. As the buffet is both elaborate and sophisticated, a date parallel with Marie of Burgundy's superb tomb is suggested.

SECTION B
BEDS AND CRADLES

Beds

All the beds that have survived which fall within the context of this study belong to the fifteenth century and later, so that our conclusions for the earlier centuries are based entirely upon written evidence and upon art. For the twelfth and thirteenth centuries, the evidence of painting, sculpture and allied arts is particularly valuable, since written evidence is meagre compared with the later Middle Ages. However, problems arise in the accuracy with which we can interpret art lacking in true perspective, and further-more, Viollet-le-Duc's warning that the evidence of art cannot always be taken literally for the twelfth and thirteenth centuries must be borne in mind.[189] Before realism came to dominate art in the later Middle Ages, artists were governed by formalized codes of representation in which the objects portrayed were not necessarily those familiar to them in their own country at the time in which they lived. In spite of difficulties, however, the broad basis of development for the twelfth century has been established, first by Viollet-le-Duc[190] and later by Dervieu,[191] and only in matters of detail can any new and useful comment be made.

Twelfth-century pictorial representations suggest that a characteristic form of bed had the four foot posts heightened to stand about fifteen inches above the mattress. The posts might be bobbin turned or faceted, surmounted by knops, and with a low railing on four sides to contain mattress and bedding.[192] The railing might be broken at the centre of one side to make it easier to climb into bed. In a famous example of this form at Chartres, the bed also has a canopy of wood or metal which rises from one of the sides of the bed, rather than having a connexion at the head end as is usual later.[193] An alternative form, found in a mid-twelfth century English MS, is without railing but has both a head and foot board which is pierced with round-headed slits and surmounted at each of the corners by a sphere.[194] In this example, the head area is stressed, a feature discounted by Dervieu in beds of this date.[195] Bedding beneath head and shoulders seems to have given a very unnatural sleeping posture. In all twelfth-century representa-tions, any curtains which are present appear to be part of the chamber rather than the bed, being hung between columns or slung in some similar manner to form a private cubicle in which the bedstead stands unencumbered. In the twelfth century, if a canopy is used as part of a highly decorated bedstead, the evidence from Chartres suggests that it was made in wood or metal (rather than cloth), incorporating the kind of inlay and painting used on the bedstead itself.

[189] Viollet-le-Duc 1858, 174.
[190] Viollet-le-Duc 1858, 171–87.
[191] Lt.-Col. Dervieu, 'Le Lit et le Berceau au Moyen Age', *Bulletins Monumentales*, 1912, 387–415.
[192] See Dervieu 1912, fig. 2; from Moissac Abbey.
[193] See Dervieu 1912, fig. 3; tympanum, west portal. For a photo of this sculpture of the Virgin, see ed. H. Hayward, *World Furniture*, London, 1965, J. Hunt, 'Byzantine and Early Medieval Furniture', fig. 52.
[194] See the 3 miniatures illustrating the nightmares of Henry I, from the Chronicle of John of Worcester; C. Brooke, 'The Structure of Medieval Society', ed. J. Evans 1966, 15, fig. 7.
[195] Dervieu 1912, 395. For the high headboard, see also Viollet-le-Duc's twelfth-century source, 173, 175.

But although the forms were simple, the beds of seigneurial lords were certainly especially elaborate at this time for they existed as important pieces of furniture in their own right, rather than as a framework of modest cost in which all expense and elaboration was directed towards the textiles with which they were hung, a development which was to follow. The belief that elaborate beds of metal and wood, inlaid and painted and resembling contemporary representations were, in fact, in general use among ecclesiastical and secular lords rests upon the evidence of Theophilus, a practical craftsman with a particular interest in metal work living in NW. Germany in the first half of the twelfth century. Theophilus's treatise, *De Diuersis Artibus*,[196] describes how copper sheets were engraved, turned to *émail brun* and scraped and then put in a dish with melted tin so that the scraped parts became white as if they were silver plated. These sheets were then *fitted round painted chairs, stools and beds*.[197] Theophilus discloses that among his patrons were bishops and wealthy laymen.[198] Work of this kind is paralleled in England in the tomb of William de Valence (1296) which is covered with copper plates enriched with Limoges enamels.[199] (This tomb, with its oak effigy, is a unique survivor, all other similar works having had their plates torn off.)

During the thirteenth century, although evidence is still meagre, we can detect a movement away from the simple form of unencumbered bedstead to more sophisticated forms; simple bedsteads continued for different uses, but in important contexts emphasis changed. We have already noticed at Chartres that beds with canopies existed in the twelfth century, though the presence of canopies was evidently not compulsory for important beds in the early part of the century, as is shown by the absence of this feature in the miniature depicting Henry I asleep (see fn. 194). The increase in the importance of the canopy or celour takes place during the thirteenth century, and by the early fourteenth century its presence is established as a necessary adjunct for beds of the seigneurial classes. Throughout the Middle Ages the canopy was called the celour, and 'dossier' or 'tester' signified the area behind the head.[200]

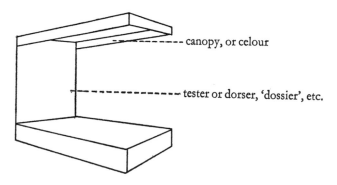

canopy, or celour

tester or dorser, 'dossier', etc.

FIG. 16.

Parts of the important bed

[196] C. R. Dodwell, London, 1961. Dodwell gives the Latin text with a translation.
[197] See Dodwell, 130.
[198] Dodwell, xxxix–xl.
[199] In Westminster Abbey; see RCHM *London*, I, 14, 43, pls. 78–9.
[200] For the evidence for the Middle Ages concerning the meaning of 'celour' and 'tester', see Eames 1971, 57, fn. 10. Difficulties have arisen because, by the seventeenth century, the meaning of the terms had become reversed and celour meant the area behind the head, not above it

It is a pregnant moment in the history of furniture for those countries which took their cue from France, for the supreme importance of the canopy in state beds lasted without a break until the nineteenth century. This new emphasis upon the canopy is first highlighted in England in an entry in the Close Rolls between 1242/7, where we find the earliest record of an English state bed, as Colvin, Brown and Taylor have shown. It was made for Henry III for Westminster Palace and had green posts powdered with gold stars, with a canopy which was painted by Master William for twenty marks.[201] The decoration of gold stars on green was Henry's favourite form of ornament and presumably the bed had a wooden canopy supported by four posts. We have definite knowledge of wooden, curtained beds with posts supporting canopies in an early fourteenth-century context in France, and there is no reason to suppose that this represents the earliest incidence of the type outside England.[202] This evidence of wooden four-posters supporting canopies is interesting for two main reasons. In the first place, it establishes the presence of the canopy as part of the state bed and we are able to trace its presence in similar contexts from this moment. In the second place, the type with four posts *supporting* the canopy proved to be a branch line, not a main line development in the Middle Ages, and did not re-emerge as a significant form until *c.*1500. Emphasis turned away from the exposure of the bedstead in the later Middle Ages and concentrated upon a totally draped form with a *suspended* canopy. (As we shall see, however, exposed bedsteads continued in use in certain circumstances, but they ceased to represent the most influential form of bed.)

After Henry III's state bed of 1242–7, the development of the canopied bed of the Middle Ages is taken a stage further in a manuscript source of the end of the thirteenth century, illustrated by Viollet-le-Duc.[203] This provides a link between the elaborately ornamented, but unencumbered bedstead and the draped, canopied structure which succeeded it as the most important form. The miniature shows a bedstead of familiar twelfth-century type with short posts and railing between, broken on one side to allow easy access as at Chartres, but now standing beneath a textile canopy which is stiffened with iron rods and suspended from the ceiling. In this early example, there is no physical or visual link between bed and canopy, for the curtains are looped up, and the arrangement has every appearance of being transitional. The link between bed and suspended canopy was later achieved in two ways: by using matching textiles on bed and canopy, and by placing a permanently lowered hanging behind the head which extended from canopy to sleeping surface and joined the two elements (the dossier), even when the curtains were raised in the daytime. This miniature indicates, as the four-poster bed does not, the primary lines of development for the state bed within our period, and it is only necessary to convert the bedstead in the drawing into a couch, with frame and supports hidden by bedding, to arrive at the basic form which dominated state beds during the fourteenth and fifteenth centuries, indicated with the greatest clarity in such Netherlandish masterpieces as the Arnolfini marriage in the National

[201] *The Kings Works*, I, 497–8.
[202] Richard 1887, 365.
[203] Viollet-le-Duc 1858, 178; from Bib. Imp. 6767.

Gallery, dated 1434.[204] At the end of the thirteenth century, the description of three beds belonging to Marguerite de Hainaut, Comtesse d'Artois, shows that all interest in state beds now centres around their textiles.

1298   'Premierement, 1 lit des armes le Roy de France, cuete pointe, drap de kevech, couvertoir d'ermine, 111 tapis, XII coussins, une gourdine à chiel de bleu cendal simple.

Item, 1 autre lit, cuete pointe ouvrée de compas, à brodure semée d'escuchons des armes de Haynnau, de Luscembre, de Holande et de Bar, drap de kevech, 111 tapis, 1 couvertoir d'escarlate affinet.

Item, 1 autre lit des armes le Roy d'Alemaigne et le Roy d'Engleterre, cuete pointe, drap de kevech, 111 tapis, gourdine à chiel de vermeill cendal simple, XII coussins, 11 lons coussins et 1 grant coussin pour sen char, 1 vert couvertoir de menu vair.'[205]

(Firstly, a bed with the arms of the king of France, coverlet, cloth of *kevech*, counterpoint of ermine, 3 hangings [curtains], 12 cushions, 1 canopy of blue unlined *cendal*.

Item, 1 other bed, powdered overall with an embroidery of the arms of Hainaut, Luxembourg, Holland and Bar, cloth of *kevech*, 3 hangings [curtains], 1 coverlet of fine scarlet.

Item, 1 other bed of the arms of the king of Germany and the king of England, coverlet, cloth of *kevech*, 3 hangings [curtains], canopy of unlined vermilion *cendal*, 12 cushions, 2 long cushions and 1 large cushion for her chair, 1 green coverlet mounted with miniver.

    The fashion for the hung bed happened to coincide with an enormous increase in the quantity of evidence available to us for study, and because the textiles used were often extremely valuable and were classed as personal property, men tended to keep careful track of them in inventories and wills, in a manner which was unnecessary for either furniture classed as fixtures (real estate) or less valuable and important movable property.[206] Hung beds were often heirlooms and were gifts of princes.[207] Chamber textiles, plate and clothing were the great vehicles of personal display falling within the classification of movables or personal property and they were often recorded in great detail. Increased documentary evidence is paralleled in the greatly enhanced usefulness of art, in terms of furniture history. With the new approach of *reality* in pictorial representation, invented in the Netherlands (see pp. xvii–xviii), the importance of any subject, whether sacred or secular, was enhanced by a detailed setting; the symbolic,

---

[204] See G. T. Faggin, *The Van Eycks*, London, 1970, 94, pl. XXXVII.
[205] Richard 1887, 381.
[206] For an analysis of this evidence in England, see Eames 1973, 33–40.
[207] For example, 1389, will of Ralph Lord Bassett, 'he . . . shall have the use of my great velvet bed for life, but not to be alienated from him who should bear my name and arms', Nicolas 1826, 126. See also the reference to a magnificent bed given by Richard II to the duke of Burgundy, p. 81.

as well as the intrinsic value and beauty of the hung bed made it a favourite element in the composition of interiors.[208]

Thus, on all sides, the volume and utility of the evidence available to us for hung beds combines to provide us with a detailed picture of their character. This character was composed of two main elements: the quality, decoration and disposition of the textiles, and the size of the canopy over the bed. The canopy was a mark of privilege and was used to denote honour in many contexts, in particular in association with seating as well as with beds.[209] For beds, the canopy was either a 'whole celour', extending above the full area of the bed and signifying that a high degree of honour was appropriate; or it was a 'demi celour' or half canopy, which was as broad as the bed but not as long and was used by persons of standing as a mark of deference to those of greater privilege in the same household. Like all furniture of estate, the hung bed responded to rules of precedence rather than rank.[210] While the importance attached to the size of the canopy is easily appreciated, other refinements which denoted shades of privilege are less immediately apparent. It is stated by Alienor de Poitiers, however, and may be deduced by implication from other sources, that nuances of social distinction were also conveyed by such details as the number and position of beds in a suite of rooms and by the type of fur used for the coverlets.[211] This symbolism could be interpreted by those versed in courtly manners, so that by merely glancing at the furnishings of chambers they were aware of the degree of honour due to the occupant, though it is evident that on occasion the degree of honour claimed could disturb spectators.[212] Although extraordinary to us today, the use of the hung bed as a barometer of power became the most tenacious element in its survival and led to a situation in the Middle Ages, which will be treated below, in which a bed had to be displayed *although it was never intended it should be slept in*.

The idea of a bed which represented the correct degree of honour for its occupant on a particular occasion became general, and only certain beds were suitable for servants.

1354   Inventory of the official house of Guillaume, bishop of Alet.

'*753. Item, pro lecto scutifferorum dicti domini officialis, una culcitra . . . 757. Item, pro lecto famulorum, unus matalas . . .*'

(Guiraud 1904/5, 231.)

(753. Item, a feather bed for the bed of the squires of the said lord official. 757. Item, for the bed of the servants, a mattress . . .)

1395   Will of Lady Alice West.

'. . . to Idkyne my chambrer', xx.li. and a bed couenable for her estat.'

---

[208] The superiority of this corpus of material, over earlier MS illuminations, is the control which the artists have achieved over the problems of perspective, enabling us to draw conclusions about form with certainty. A few examples may be listed. Van Eyck's Arnolfini marriage in the National Gallery; the Louvre Annunciation by Roger van der Weyden; and the Annunciation in the Metropolitan Museum of Art, N.Y., possibly by Jan van Eyck.

[209] See Eames 1971, 42–5, 50.

[210] See p. xix.

[211] See Appendix VIII, fig. 35.

[212] Alienor de Poitiers seems to have disapproved when Marie of Burgundy used a degree of honour equal to that used by the queen of France, see Appendix VIII, lines 550–61.

(F. J. Furnivall, *The Fifty Earliest English Wills in the Court of Probate, London*, EETS, 1882, 6.)

1412   Will of Roger Kyrkby, vicar of Gainford.

'. . . unum lectum pro statu suo congruentem, . . .'

(Raine, 1834/5, 55.)

(. . . 1 bed in conformity with his position . . .)

1415   Will of Edward Cheyne, 'Squier' son of Sir John Cheyne, knight.

'. . . item a paire of gentilmennysshetis of the largest assise of iij levys; item a paire of gentilmenysshetis of ij levys and half; . . .'

(E. F. Jacob, *The Register of Henry Chichele, Archbishop of Canterbury 1414–1443, II*, Oxford, 1937, 46.)

1424/5   Will of Roger Flore Esq., of London and Oakham, Rutlandshire.

'. . . 2 servauntes beddys for the 2 said chambers.'

(Furnivall 1882, 56.)

There is much evidence to show that the manners of courts were followed by the wealthy middle class. As has been noted, the Netherlandish painters, in their studies of the Virgin and saints, habitually set them against a background of middle-class amenity and comfort, in which the hung bed is rarely absent; and the Arnolfini marriage portrait shows again that the hung bed was part of the chamber furnishings of the well-to-do. Documents support the evidence of art, showing the use of hung beds by the nobility and middle classes alike in England and the Netherlands, though in France evidence for middle-class ownership is more elusive, perhaps because the manner of listing bedding often makes it uncertain as to what is involved.[213] The following entries have been chosen as a sample to illustrate the various points which have been made: the lavishness of the textiles used by the nobility and the care with which they are enumerated; the presence and size of the celour or canopy (and where no size is given, a *whole* canopy is meant); and the wide ranging ownership of the hung bed. We shall see that the fabrics which are used in various ways to furnish an entire chamber are often listed with the bed and we shall notice that the wooden framework of the bed is seldom mentioned.[214]

1334   Inventory of goods at Quatremares, held by Jeanne de Valois, sister of Philip VI of France and wife of Robert d'Artois.

'Premièrement VIII oreilliers, chascun en petit sac linge blanc, et sont de veluiau vermeil, brodez à cynes à armes atachée à couz de cynes, et sont les dites armez de France, de Valois, de Costentinoble et d'Artois.

---

[213] For example, '. . . item, duos lectos panorum completos' (*c.* 1340, from a will of an inhabitant of Grignan, SE. France; L'Abbé Fillet, 'Le Mobilier au Moyen Age dans le Sud-Est de la France', *Bulletin Archéologique du Comité des Travaux Historiques et Scientifiques*, 1896, 58.

[214] There are two reasons for this: the framework was of relatively low value and was also frequently regarded as a fixture, unlike the textiles with which it was draped, see p. 229.

Item un grant drap d'or, aussi comme à couvrir un grant lit, contenant VI draps d'or, dont il y a un des draps double au bout aussi comme une aune.

Item une penne d'ermine à couvertouer, et semble qu'elle feust pour joindre au dit drap, et a XXV tires de lonc et XLIIII tires de lé.

Item un couvertouer à lit de veluyau vermeil fourré, l'envers de cendal jaune, broudé de cynes d'argent à armoirie de France, de Valois, de Costentinoble et d'Artois, et sont les dites armoiries atachées au couz des cynes, touz semblables des oreilliers dessus diz.

Item un ciel et chevetel de ce mesmes et touz semblables, et a ou ciel ou chevez et ou couvertouer en chascun un drap linge blanc, pour garder qu'il ne frient l'un à l'autre.

Item IX pièces de draps de laine, de semblable couleur et armoirie que les choses precedens.'

(Delisle, 108–8.)

(Firstly, 8 head pillows, each in a small bag of white linen, and the pillows are of vermilion velvet embroidered with swans with arms worked round their necks, the arms being of France, Valois, Constantinople and Artois.

Item, a large length of cloth of gold, suitable for covering a large bed, containing 6 lengths of cloth of gold of which 1 length is folded under by as much as a yard.

Item, a pane of ermine for a counterpoint, made to join with the cloth of gold and of 25 *tires* in length and 44 *tires* in breadth.

Item, a coverlet of vermilion velvet lined with fur with a surround of yellow *cendal*, embroidered with a design of silver swans and arms, being the arms of France, Valois, Constantinople and Artois, and the said arms are round the necks of the swans, matching the pillows listed above.

Item, a celour and tester of the same work, matching in all respects, and where the celour, tester and coverlet touch there is a white linen cloth to make sure that there is no friction between them.

Item, 9 pieces of woollen cloth of the same colour and with the same design of arms as the other items listed above.)

1375   Will of Johanna Dachet, (*d.* 1375).

'a white bed embroidered with hounds *cum testur et demi silur*.'

(Sharpe, II, 201–2.)

1382   Will of Johanna Mitford, widow of John Mitford, draper (d. 1382).

'a bed embroidered with dogs with demi-celure.'

(Sharpe, II, 235.)

1392   Will of Richard, Earl of Arundel.

'. . . le lit rouge et blew de satyn de dymy seele ove touz les apparailles d'icell . . .

mon lit de soy rouge ov entier seele, qu'est acustume d'estre a Reigate, ove tout l'apparaill d'icell . . .'

(Nichols, 132, 133.)

(. . . the bed of red and blue satin with half celour, with all the accessories belonging to it . . .

my red silk bed with whole celour, which is generally kept at Reigate, with all the accessories belonging to it.)

1393/4   Account of hangings for a complete chamber, or suite of chambers, for the Duke of Burgundy; these textiles were purchased in Paris.

'A Colin Bataille, bourgois de Paris, qui dehuz lui estoient pour une chambre de tapisserie blanche toute ovrée a pluseurs ymaiges sur le contenu du romant de la Rose, contenant pluseurs pieces, garnies de cordes et de robans toute preste pour tendre, c'est assavoir le couvertoire du lit contenant LVI alnes quarrées, le ciel contenant XXXVI alnes et demie quarrées, les longiens contenans IX alnes quarrées, le dossier contenant XXX alnes quarrées, le tapis de la couche, contenant XXXII alnes et demie quarrées,

IIII grans tapis a tendre pour faire muraille contenant ensemble VIIIˣˣ XVI alnes quarrées, ung banchier contenant XXIIII alnes quarrées, et XII quarreaulx contenant neuf alnes, qui font pour tout IIIᶜ LXXV alnes, valent au pris chascune alne de XXVs.   IIIIᶜ LXVII fr. demi. Et pour trois cortines de soye d'Arras eschaquetées de blanc et de vert pour ladicte chambre.   XXVIII frs.'

(Dehaisnes, II, 712.)

(To Colin Bataille, bourgeois of Paris . . .

for a chamber [i.e. all the textiles to equip a chamber] of white tapestry worked overall with various scenes illustrating the Romance of the Rose, contained in many lengths of tapestry, complete with cords and ribbons ready for hanging [i.e. from walls, etc.] comprising the coverlet of 56 square yards

the celour of 36½ square yards

the *longiens* [?valances] of 9 square yards

the tester of 30 square yards

the hanging of the couch of 32½ square yards

4 large hangings for suspension round the walls, in total 176 square yards

a banker of 24 square yards and 12 cushions of 9 yards, total 375 yards valued at 25 *s.* per yard, 467½ frs. And for 3 curtains of Arras silk chequered in white and green for the above chamber, 28 frs.)

1404   An inventory of the Duke of Burgundy lists a chamber given by Richard II in 1396.

'Item, une chambre de drap d'or que le Roy Richard d'Angleterre donna a feu mondit seigneur a Calais en aoust mil IIIᶜIIIIxx et XVI garnie de ciel, dossier tenans ensemble de coustepointe et de trois courtines de cendal en graine de bateure de la devise de ladite chambre, de courvertoires d'armines, couste pointe d'armines et ung chevet de lit de deux carreaulx de mesmez, l'un grant et l'autre petit, et de treze tappis de haultelice de ladite devise.'

(Dehaisnes, II, 843.)

(Item, a set of chamber textiles of cloth of gold which King Richard of England gave to the late Duke of Burgundy at Calais in August, 1396, comprising celour, tester and 3 curtains of *cendal* ingrain with beaten foil of the design of the chamber hangings, with ermine coverlet and with a bedhead composed of 2 pillows en suite, one large and one small and 13 hautelisse tapestry hangings worked with the same design.)

1409   Inventory of goods in the Comte de Hainaut's house in Paris.

'Une chambre de tappicerie à un lion, contenant cil, dossier et couverture pour le lit, avecques cincq pièces de tappicerie de mesmes, estant à présent en la chambre de parement dudit hostel . . .
Ung demi-ciel et dossier, à ung homme et femme sauvaiges, avecques la couverture du lit et deux custodes de sarge vermeilles, sans personnage, tendues de présent en la chambre de messire Guy, seigneur de Monceaulz.'

(L. Devillers, *Cartulaire des Comtes de Hainaut de 1337 à 1436*, III, 1886, 415.)

(Chamber textiles of tapestry worked with a lion, comprising celour, tester and counterpoint for a bed, with 5 pieces of matching tapestry, now in the chamber of state of the said house . . . A half-celour and tester, worked with a design of a wild man and woman, with the coverlet of the bed and 2 *custodes* [?loose covers] of vermilion serge without figures, hanging at present in the chamber of Guy, Seigneur of Monceaulz.)

1418   Will of Thomas Tvoky.

'. . . a bed of Lyn wit a hool silour and Couerlet of the same wroght wit mapil leues and fret of iij. foill, & iij. nettes of Silk grene for quirtayns for the same bed
also a bed of red and grene dimi Selour wit iij. quirtayns of worsted; . . .'

(Furnivall, 1882, 36.)

1418   Will of Edmund Stafford, bishop of Exeter.

'. . . unum lectum de serico videlicet coopertum tam cum testura, celura, curtinis et tapeto ac costeris pro camera, . . .'

(Jacob 1937, 156–7.)

(A silk bed comprising counterpoint, tester, celour, curtains and carpet with hangings for the walls of the room.)

1426   Inventory of the Château des Baux

'En la grand chambre de la tour, là ou morut madame . . .

73. Item, le lit, en quoy gisoit ma dicte dame, garni de coussere, traversier, d'une coutrepointe perse, i chiel rouge, i dossier, et le couvertoir a i. devise brodée i. cabrol blanc.

74. Item, iii courtines ou currens d'estamine rouge, i. coutrepointe blanche, i. sarge rouge, et i. flassade dessoulx la coussere, iii. linceulx et iiii orilliers blancs. . .

La Garderobe . . .

29. Item, i. grand chiel de cendal rouge, viel pointée, a les armes des Baux au millieu, et à l'entour d'Orange, doublé de toille que fu rouge.

30. Item, la couverte du lit de la dicte chambre, pointée et armoyée comme le chiel.

31. Item le dossier de ladicte chambre et une pièce de courtine . . .

35. Item, i. chambre de sarge verde vielle a demi chiel, dossier et couverte, a une rose au milieu et iii currens d'estamine . . .

39. Item, i demi chambre de sarge verde, en quoy a demi chiel, dossier et couverte, avec i. pot de broudure plain de fleurs de lis.

40. Item, i. autre demi chambre de sarge verde, vielle, en quoy a demi chiel, dossier et couverte, armoyée des armes de Villars que tiennent ii griffons qui pau val.'

(Barthélemy, 131, 135, 142, 144.)

(In the large chamber in the tower where Madame [Comtesse d'Avelin] died . . .

73. Item, the bed in which my lady lay, equipped with feather bed, bolster, and counterpoint of *perse*, 1 red celour, 1 tester and the coverlet embroidered with the device of 1 white hart.

74. Item, 3 running curtains of red *estamine*, 1 white counterpoint, 1 red serge, and 1 cover beneath the feather bed, 3 sheets and 4 white head pillows.

The Wardrobe . . .

29. Item, 1 large celour of red *cendal* with [?vallance worked with points] decorated in the centre with the arms of Baux and round it the arms of Orange, lined with a red material.

30. Item, the coverlet of this chamber with points [along the edge] and arms to match the celour.

31. Item, the tester of the same chamber and a curtain [of the bed].

35. Item, 1 chamber of old green serge with half-celour, tester and coverlet with a rose in the centre, and 3 running curtains of *estamine* . . .

39. Item, 1 half chamber of green serge, with half-celour, tester, and coverlet embroidered with a vase full of lily flowers.

40. Item, another half chamber of green serge, which is old, having a half-colour, tester and coverlet, with the arms of Villars with 2 griffons; of small value.)

1435   Inventory of Pierre Surreau; once a servant of Charles VI, Surreau rallied to the English cause, becoming Receiver General for Normandy from 1422 and later Treasurer to Henry VI. He lived in some state at Rouen and died in 1435.

'Item ung lit de deux lez, le traversain, ung paire de draps, . . . cottepointe et une couverture verte, . . .

Item le chalit dud. lit, . . .

Item le ciel et dossier de toile blanche, estant sur led. lit, . . .'

(Félix, 80.)

(Item, a bed of 2 *lez* [wide], the bolster, a pair of cloths [?hangings] . . . counterpoint and a green coverlet . . .

Item, the frame of the said bed . . .

Item, the celour and tester of white material, which are on the said bed . . .)

1454   From the Hostillar's rolls, concerning the guest chambers at Durham Abbey.

'*In primis in nova camera vocat. Kyngeschambre* sunt 1 lectus cum tapeto et silour unius secte et ridellez blodei coloris et costours circa totam Cameram eiusdem coloris.'

('Extracts from the Account Rolls of the Abbey of Durham', I, *Surtees Society*, XCIX, 1898, 147.)

(Firstly, in the new chamber called the King's Chamber, 1 bed with ?tester and celour ensuite and blue curtains and hangings round the entire chamber [walls] of the same colour.)

While the rectangular textile celour of two sizes was the commonest form of canopy for the hung bed in the later Middle Ages, another form which was conical, like a bell tent, was also much used and seems to have been particularly favoured in great households in the fifteenth century.[215] This second shape was called a *sparver* or *sperver*,[216] and its function was identical with that of the rectangular canopy in that it indicated privilege. As well as being used suspended over beds and seating (see pl. 67), its form seems to have been particularly suitable for hanging above and around a bath tub (see below). The form is clearly shown suspended over a bed in an illumination of *c.* 1485 in the British Museum,[217] and over Charles V's chair in the miniature by Jean Bandol of 1372 (pl. 67), and above the Virgin's seat in the 'Sacra Conversazione' in the Louvre

[215] Dervieu cites evidence for a sparver bed as early as 1266; also a particularly beautiful example of 1480 which was surmounted by a silver-gilt apple — no references are given for this evidence (Dervieu 1912, 400, fn. 1).
[216] Correlated by Macquoid/Edwards with the bearings of the Upholsterers Company (1954, 69). The arms are of 3 pavilions and are described in the original grant of arms in 1465 as *spervers*, see A. C. Fox-Davies, *Public Arms*, London, 1915, 816–17.
[217] Reproduced by Macquoid/Edwards 1927, Beds, fig. 2.

by the Master of Flémalle (perhaps Robert Campin, *c.* 1375–1444), where we see the Virgin in a comfortable, bourgeois interior.[218] The following written evidence concerning sparvers provides some correlations with representational art.

1371   Account of a purchase made for the Duke of Burgundy from Thomas de Chalons. (Thomas de Chalons was *courtepointier* to Philip VI of France in 1349/50 and later served King John and Charles V.)[219]

'*1420*. '. . . a Thomas de Chaalons, cointepointier et varlet de chambre de Mgr, pour un grant espevrier de cendal vert, de 11 liz de large garni de courtines, un grant paveillon quarrey, de mesmes, à 4 evangelistres, un autre paveillon de toile de Reins et pluseurs autres paveillons et espreviers, ensemble pluseurs carreaulx et autres choses par lui faiz et achettez de lui, du commandement de Mgr, tant pour Mme, pour cause de sa gecine et auxi de ses relevailles, comme pour Jehan mon^r, leur filz.'

(Prost, I, 256.)

(To Thomas of Chalons, counterpoint maker and 'varlet de chambre' to the Duke of Burgundy, for a large sparver of green *cendal*, of 2 widths, complete with curtains; a large square pavilion of the same [cloth], decorated with the 4 evangelists; another pavilion of cloth of Rennes and various other pavilions and sparvers, together with various cushions and other things made by and bought from Thomas de Chalons, by order of the Duke as much as of the Duchess, on account of the Duchess being brought to bed and also leaving her bed due to the birth of *M*. John, their son [John the Fearless].

1379/80   Inventory of Charles V.
34 'paveillons' are listed in the inventory, mostly of silk of some kind.
(Labarte, 389–91.)

1423   Inventory of Henry V.
'Item, 1 Tent bede de drap de Baudekyn d'or, fait pur le gesyne de la Roigne, ovec 11 panes d'escharlet, furrez des Ermyns, ovec tout l'aparaille, pris c li.'
(*Rotuli Parliamentorum*, IV, 229.)

(Item, 1 tent bed of gold brocade, made for the Queen's lying in, with 2 panes of scarlet furred with ermine, and with all the accessories thereto, value £100.)

1468   Inventory of the Château de Chateaudun, held by the Comte de Dunois.
'It. ung autre petit pavillon carré, en facon d'espervyer, de taffetaz vert, avecques son dossier . . .'
(Jarry, 135.)

[218] See Panofsky, pl. 107.
[219] See Prost, I, 256, fn. 2.

(Item, another little square pavilion made in the manner of a sparver, of green taffeta, with its tester.)

This description suggests an unusual form — a cone which became rectangular at the bottom.

1472   Concerning the chambers prepared at Windsor for the entertainment of the lord Gruuthuse by Edward IV.

'. . . In yᵉ ijᵈᵉ chamber was an other of astate, the wᶜʰ was alle whyt. Also in the same chamber was made a couche wᵗ fether beddes, hanged wᵗ a tent knit lyke a nett; and there was yᵉ coberd. Item, in the iijᵈᵉ chamber was ordeined a bayne or ij, wᶜʰ were couered wᵗ tentes of whyt clothe . . .'

(Kingsford, 1913, 387.)

1509   Inventory of the goods of Edmund Dudley, minister of Henry VII, found in his house in Candlewick Street, London.

'In the Gret Chambre . . . A gret coffer with ij lyddes; wherin ys a sparver of purpull velvytt with curteyns of blewe sarsenett.
A sparuer of blewe sarsenett.
A counterpoynt of blewe sarsenett lyned with blewe buckeram.
A sparver of rede sarsenett with a canape of rede sylke knyt, enbrodrid about the skyrttes of the canape with sleydes [raw untwisted silk].
A sperver of crymeson cloth of gold and grene and crymeson saten, fugrie palie . . .'

(Kingsford, 1920/1, 40.)

Viollet-le-Duc has shown conclusively for the fifteenth century that beds in the Chambre de Parade, or State Chamber, were part of the trappings of ceremony and were not used for sleeping;[220] the key evidence for this, which he quotes, comes in Alienor de Poitiers's treatise.[221] The practice can also be inferred in many less specific references to state beds[222] or to state chambers. For instance, the hall at Bruges which was constructed as part of the preparations put in hand in 1429 for the marriage of Philip the Good to Isabelle of Portugal, had a portion of its area fitted as a 'Chambre de Parement', complete with bed measuring 18 ft. long by 12 ft. wide.[223] For the celebrations of the marriage of Charles the Bold and Marguerite of York in 1468, we learn that the Duke's chamber had a 'chambrette' where he slept, and a 'salette de reception' where he held state; the latter room was furnished with 'un lit de parement'.[224] In

[220] Viollet-le-Duc 1858, 184–5.
[221] See appendix VIII (b), lines 248–9.
[222] For example, 1387, inventory of the Duchess of Burgundy's goods in the Château de Germoles (Saône-et-Loire). '1867. ung autre lit à parer, soignié à une fuille d'aubespin, et à une fleur de lix, contenant 5 aunes de long, 1 quartier moins, et 4 aunes et 1 quartier de large, pesant 280 l.' (Another state bed, elaborated with a branch of hawthorn and with 1 lily, being 4¾ yards long and 4¼ yards wide, value 280 l.) Prost, II, 335.
[223] van Zuylen van Nyevelt, 257.
[224] van Zuylen van Nyevelt, 291.

England, the practice of equipping a chamber of state and a chamber for sleeping was certainly followed, as is shown by the arrangements made by Edward IV for the entertainment of the lord Gruuthuse at Windsor in 1472.[225] In the three 'chambres of Pleasance' there was a bed for the lord Gruuthuse himself (cloth of gold with tester and celour), and in the second chamber was another bed of state together with a couch.[226] Although such beds were not slept in, however, they did evidently fill a useful purpose when occasion demanded, quite apart from their important visual functions; they were used as seats,[227] and to lay the baby upon on the day of baptism.[228]

Apart from the bed in the Chambre de Parement, Viollet-le-Duc lists a number of other ceremonial uses for beds, but it is clear that *lit*, as used in the Middle Ages, did not always describe accurately the equipment involved.[229]

Before moving on, we are bound to ask why the hung bed was so successful a piece of furniture. We have seen how it developed in the thirteenth century and dominated fourteenth and fifteenth-century design as we are able to trace it through the evidence of art, literature and documents, throwing into obscurity the other alternative types of bed which were certainly numerically superior. We note how the influence of the hung bed continued in Europe, reaching a second flowering in the extravagant state beds of the seventeenth and eighteenth centuries. We find that there were cogent reasons which accounted for the supremacy of the hung bed. The canopied bed became inseparably associated with prestige, honour, power, wealth and privilege. But important as these associations were, they were by no means the sole factors which determined the success of this particular form of bed in the Middle Ages. Its success then must be seen as a part of the development in the use of chamber textiles which were found to be ideally suited to the needs of the mobile household.[230] Even the expense involved enhanced the appeal of chamber textiles, for seigneurial lords were committed to extravagant display and textiles, together with plate, were a necessary investment for wealth.[231] With mobility as a first consideration within the great household, grand wooden furniture — such as painted and inlaid bedsteads — could not compete with the advantages offered by the hung bed, which allowed the wooden framework of the bed to be solid yet relatively cheap, a fixture[232] which could be left in position when required. To these practical advantages was added one additional virtue which eventually became an overriding consideration. As we have seen, the hung bed was able to express the accepted social

[225] See Kingsford 1913, 386 ff.
[226] See Kingsford 1913, 387.
[227] See the painting of the Virgin receiving the Magi, Joos van Ghent (Metropolitan Museum of Art), Panofsky, pl. 292.
[228] See Appendix VIII (b), lines 794–7.
[229] Viollet-le-Duc 1858, 185–6. The baptismal bed in church, erected in honour of the infant Marie of Burgundy ('un lict de carreaux de drap d'or') was, in fact, 'une table quarrée sur deux trettaux haults comme un lict'; both statements from Alienor de Poitiers. And the 'lit de justice' was possibly always a seat, as it is in Viollet-le-Duc's example, equipped with a canopy.
[230] See pp. xix–xx.
[231] See pp. xx–xxi.
[232] The wooden frame was not invariably a fixture but seems frequently to have been treated as one. See Eames 1973, 34–5. Continental evidence also suggests that the convenience of beds as fixtures was recognized, e.g. the 25 beds in the Paris house of the Comte de Hainaut in 1409 which were 'donnez avecques ledit hostel à mondit Seigneur'. (Devillers, 416.) With this kind of evidence, however, it is seldom possible to know what type of bed is involved.

order in visual terms with greater precision than any alternative form of bed, using varying forms and varying qualities of textiles and furs symbolically; it was this facility, accompanying all its other conveniences, that made the hung bed a uniquely *practical* object for its time, rather than a magnificently wasteful one, as at first sight it might appear to be.

Although the hung bed dominates all forms of evidence in the later Middle Ages, we have some evidence which is concerned with a number of other forms. In the first place, there were the *couchettes* whose presence could indicate privilege; they often shared rooms with hung beds and might themselves be equipped with the trappings of state. Isabel of Bourbon's *couchette* had silk hangings and an ermine covering in 1456,[233] and other sources confirm the use of colours and curtains.

1496   '73. Item lo sobrecel de una coucheta de saya verda, roja e blanca.'

              (Forestié, 44.)

              (Item, the celour of the couch, of green, red and white silk.)

The textiles of the couchette might be carefully matched with those of the more important bed.

1481   'Item, encore plus, ung lict et traversain en queutis royez en eschaquier.

              Item, unc couchette pareillement ouvrée et le traversain sans plus.'

              (L. de la Trémoille, *Archives d'un Serviteur de Louis XI*, Nantes, 1888, 134.)

              (Item, also a bed and bolster . . .

              Item, a *couchette* worked to match and the bolster and nothing else.)

But as *couchette* was a general term, like *lit*, no precise definition is possible. The most that can be said is that the term probably indicated a low bed, and a *couchette* seems to have been of secondary importance when another bed was present.

We have seen that the *couchette* could be an important item, taking its place with beds of state. It could also be an ordinary utilitarian object without any significance or importance, as we understand from the fact that the *charretiers* in the stables at the Château of Chateaudun slept on 'couchetes' in 1468.[234]

Alienor de Poitiers shows that important *couchettes* might be equipped with wheels, resembling those stored under beds,[235] and *couchettes* of this kind occur in inventories.

c. 1459   At Caistor Castle, held by Sir John Fastolf.

              'Item, j rynnyng Bedde with a materas.'

              (T. Amyot, 'Transcript of Two Rolls, containing an Inventory of Effects Formerly Belonging to Sir John Fastolfe', *Archaeologia*, XXI, 1827, 264.)

1468   Inventory of the Comte de Dunois, Château de Chateaudun.

              'It. ung chaslit et une couchete roullonée, . . .

              It. huit membres de chasliz et quatre autres de couchete roullonée.'

---

[233] See Appendix VIII (b), lines 104–29.
[234] See Jarry, 136.
[235] See Appendix VIII (b), lines 38–42. See also the fifteenth-century illumination of such a *couchette*, Furnivall 1868, pl. XV.

(Jarry, 143.)

(Item, a bed frame and a wheeled *couchette* . . .

Item, 8 parts of bed frames and 4 other parts of wheeled *couchettes*.)

1482   Inventory of the hospital of St Antoine at Mâcon.

'Ung lit garny de coulte et de cussin et d'une couvert verte, de nulle ou peu de valeur.

Item . . . une couchete, laquelle se mest dessoubs ledit lit et sert.'

(Batault, 148.)

(A bed complete with feather bed, cushion and green coverlet, of little or no value.

Item, . . . a *couchette* which is put beneath the said bed.)

These wheeled beds were probably akin in some respects to the travelling beds[236] mentioned in documents which accompanied seigneurial lords on their journeys and might have hangings. These travelling beds may have always had folding frames like the ones listed in 1371 and 1481 (below), and some at least must have been elaborate since they were deemed suitable presents for princes, 1471, p. 89.

1302–1329 Richard notes that Mahaut, Comtesse d'Artois, had a travelling bed which was called 'le petit lit madame.'

(Richard 1887, 365.)

1371   Will of Sir Walter Manney.

'. . . all my beds and dossers in my wardrobe excepting my folding bed, paly of blue and red, which I bequeath to my daughter of Pembroke.'

(Nicolas, 1, 1826, 85.)

1398   Will of John of Gaunt.

'. . . mes autres lits faitz pur mon corps, appelles en Engleterre trussyng beddes, ove les tapites et autres appurtenances . . .'

(Sir S. Armitage-Smith, *John of Gaunt*, London, 1904, 426.)

(. . . my other beds made for my personal use, called in England 'trussing beds', with the hangings and other appurtenances.)

1442   Will of Humphrey Stafford of Hoke.

'unum trussyngbed vocatum Ruben Sparver cum costeris eiusdem . . .'

(Jacob 1937, 621.)

(. . . a trussing bed called Ruben Sparver with the hangings belonging to to it . . .)

---

[236] It may not be too fanciful to suppose that in many respects the travelling beds of the Middle Ages resembled the field bed of *c*.1690–1700 in Nordiska Museet, Stockholm; see Wanscher, 191.

1471   Inventory of René of Anjou, King of Sicily and Duke of Aragon. (At the
            Château d'Angers.)

            'Une chambre de boys et ung lit de camp que feu Monsr de Calabre donna
            au roy, . . .'

            (Godard-Faultrier, 53.)

            (A wooden room [?wooden screens in place of textiles] and a camp bed
            which the late duke of Calabria gave to the King . . .)

1481   Inventory of the Seigneur de Craon.

            '. . . ung charlict *qui se ploye* à porter par le pays.'
            [my itals.]

            (de La Trémoille 1888, 131.)

            (. . . a folding bed frame which is for taking when travelling.)

1509   Inventory of Edmund Dudley.

            '. . . a counterpoynt of popynjaye and blonkett, palie, for a trussyng
            bed . . . a trussyng bedstede.'

            (Kingsford 1920/1, 40, 41.)

The wooden bedstead which was intended to stand with its wooden parts showing
was clearly much used in the fourteenth and fifteenth centuries as well as earlier, but in
documents it can be confused with the many references to bed frames.[237] The wooden
bed frames, often for hung beds or *couchettes*, were generally termed bed boards or
charlits.

1376   Inventory of Richard Lyons.

            'Item beddes de bord pur 12 litz, . . .'

            (Myers 1969, 317.)

1435   Inventory of Pierre Surreau.

            'Item ung grant lit de troiz lez, le traversain, ung paire de draps de trois
            toilles, une couttepointe blanche . . . Item unes custodes blanches, dont le
            ciel et dossier sont en forme de cottepointe et les pendans de toile blanche
            . . . Item une grant sarge bleue . . . Item le grant calit.'

            (Félix, 58–9.)

            (Item, a large bed of 3 widths, the bolster,[238] a pair of cloths [?sheets] of
            3 pieces of linen [each], a white counterpoint . . . Item, white hangings[239]

---

[237] We can only guess at the manner in which these frames were made. Possibly the bed was composed of
slats of wood laid horizontally and slotted into wide boards forming a frame, as in the surviving tenth-century
example from the Oseberg ship burial. Possibly leather straps, forming an interlaced hammock, were substituted
for wooden slats.
[238] The *traversains* were also curtains (additional to the bed curtains) in certain state beds, see fig. 37, p. 273.
[239] The term *custodes* used here suggests some form of protective covering, like dust sheets.

of which the celour and tester match the counterpoint and the hangings of white linen . . . Item, a large blue serge.

Item, the large bed frame [of the bed].)

Various forms of wooden bedsteads existed, from low simple forms with headboards, to tall, canopied structures. Most references are unspecific but serve to show how common such bedsteads were.

1253   Concerning the king's bed at Westminster.

            'Jacobo Junur pro panellis ad lectum domini Regis jungendis . . .'

            (Brown/Colvin/Taylor, 224 (14).)

            (James the joiner, for panels for the king's bed . . .)

1302   Inventory of Guillaume as Feives, bourgeois of Paris.

            'Item, due couchie lignee . . .'

            (H. Stein, 'Inventaire du Mobilier de Me Guillaume as Feives', *Bulletin de la Société de l'Histoire de Paris*, 1883, 173.)

            (Item, 2 wooden couches . . .)

1354   Inventory of the bishop of Alet, in the Château de Cournanel.

            '290. Item unum lectum cum pedibus.'

            (Guiraud 1904/5, 202.)

            (Item, a bed with feet.)

1380   Will of Cecilia Rose, widow of a clerk.

            'Her wooden bedstead of *bord*, with curtains etc.'

            (Sharpe, II, 228.)

1392   Will of Richard, Earl of Arundel.

            '. . . un rouge lit estandard appelle Clove, . . .'

            (Nichols, 131.)

1485   Account for work at Coldharbour, London, in preparation for occupation by Lady Margaret Beaufort.

            'ij beddes redy maad, . . .'

            (Kingsford 1920/1, 46 (f. 23b); from the joiner's account.)

The presence of headboards on wooden bedsteads is occasionally indicated.

1356   Appraisement of the goods of Stephen le Northerne.

            '. . . one wooden bedstead, and 2 wooden testers for a bedstead, . . .'

            (H. T. Riley, *Memorials of London and London Life*, London, 1868, 283.)

1468   Inventory of goods of the Comte de Dunois at the Château de Chateaudun.

            '. . . ung chaslit à dossier, . . .'

(Jarry, 145.)

(. . . a bed frame with headboard.)

1485   Fixtures handed over with the lease of a house in Botolf Lane, London.[240]

'. . . a standyng bed, made with estrychborde, with the hed on the same wyse . . .

a standyng bed, corven with estrich borde of beyond see makyng.'

(Littlehales, 28.)

Such beds are also found in paintings and illuminations, see Hugo van Goes's late work, the 'Death of the Virgin' which depicts a bed without curtains with a headboard of linen fold panels, painted between 1467–81;[241] and the fifteenth-century MS showing a bed with side and headboard carved with arcading of Romanesque type.[242]

A number of fifteenth-century German alpine beds survive with tall headboards which continue upwards to form short, angled, cantilevered canopies or half-celours.[243] Whether this precise form was used within our area of study is not clear, but a manuscript source shows that France knew of a much neater solution in the late fourteenth century. In the bible of Charles V, dated 1391, in The Hague[244] we see a bed with a ribbed headboard which rises and curls over to form a half-celour in one, uninterrupted line. The technique may have been borrowed from boat building, and it can still be admired in the restored fifteenth-century ceiling of the Merchant's Gallery in Jacques Coeur's palace at Bourges. The bed depicted in Charles V's bible shows a sophisticated solution to the problem of producing a headboard and half-celour in wood; furthermore, it has delicacy and charm combined with strength, which is a rare combination in medieval structural woodwork.

The last form of bedstead remaining to be discussed is the type with a whole celour or canopy of wood. Henry III's bed of 1242–7, which had green posts powdered with gold stars and a painted canopy, has already been noted, and it will be recalled that Mahaut, Comtesse d'Artois, also had beds with posts between 1302–29.[245] In addition to these sources, the following evidence may be quoted.

1386   Inventory of Arnaud Andrieu, 'Collecteur Apostolique' for the province of Narbonne.

'. . . in camera dicte domus:

1. Item primo unum lectum de postibus novis et alium pro familiaribus, . . .'

(Guiraud 1904/5, 334.)

---

[240] This is a most interesting document, showing that a quantity of wooden furniture, glass windows etc. were classed as fixtures, see Eames 1973, 39, fn. 9.

[241] Hugo van Goes is first heard of in 1467 when he was a free master painter of the guild at Ghent; he died in 1481. For the 'Death of the Virgin', see Panofsky 337, pl. 314.

[242] See M. Faré, 'Les Caractères de Raison du Mobilier Gothique', *Art et Industrie*, 1946, no. 2, 50.

[243] See Mercer, figs. 60, 71; also H. Schmitz, *Encyclopaedia of Furniture*, London, 1956, 74, 75.

[244] Illustration of Christ healing the palsied man: MS 10B, 23, fol. 513v, Mus. Meermanno-Westreenianum (see Panofsky, pl. 7 (20)).

[245] See p. 75 and fn. 202.

(. . . in the chamber of the said house:

1. Item, firstly, a new bed with posts, and another for the servants, . . .)

(It is assumed that beds with posts had whole celours, although this is not stated in the evidence; it seems most unlikely that posts would have been used except as supports for whole celours.) Some idea of the appearance of beds with posts at the end of our period may be deduced from a restored example in the Musée des Arts Decoratifs in Paris.[246] This bed has a delicately worked and unrestored right hand column at the foot of the bed, carved with the arms of Rigault d'Aurelhe, Seigneur of the Château de Villeneuve-Lembron (Auvergne) whence the bed is believed to have come; Rigault d'Aurelhe died in 1517. In England, a four-poster bed which has lost its celour is in the Saffron Walden Museum.[247] The four columns are carved with lozenges, in the manner of the ornament on the tomb of Marie of Burgundy of 1495–1502, and the bronze screen of Henry VII's chapel in Westminster Abbey of 1503–19.[248] The Saffron Walden head-board is carved with linen fold. The bed posts now supporting the gallery at Broughton Church, Chester, however, for which a date of 1446–83 has been advanced, fall well outside our period.[249] The columned bed with whole celour which was open at the sides and ends (though sometimes enclosed with curtains) was evidently accompanied by a more enclosed type.[250] Documentary evidence for boarded beds is continental, though as so much evidence is unspecific we cannot be certain that the type was entirely ignored in England. A bed which was boarded in on two or three sides must have been warm and comfortable in winter, though it was less adaptable than the form which placed greater reliance on curtains as a method of enclosure.

1420   'Item, une grant cousche de bort d'Islande, enchassillée.'

           (Douet d'Arcq, 'Inventaires des Châteaux de Vincennes et de Beauté', *Révue Archéologique*, XI, 1854, 462.)

           (Item, a large couch of riven oak,[251] enclosed round about.) This piece of furniture was found in the highest room in the tower of the Château de Beauté, where Charles V died.

1471   Inventory of René of Anjou, King of Sicily and Duke of Aragon. In the Château d'Angers.

---

[246] (No. PE 968.) This bed was purchased at Touzain in 1895 by the collector M. Peyre; it was presented to the museum in 1905. It is now exhibited in a gallery with much other woodwork from the same donor with reputedly the same provenance.

[247] Bought at an Essex sale by the collector William Tuke and presented to the museum in 1882. Illustrated by Macquoid/Edwards 1954, Beds, fig. 6.

[248] See *RCHM London*, I, pl. 121.

[249] See W. F. J. Timbrell, 'The Medieval Bedposts in Broughton Church, Chester', *Transactions of the Lancashire and Cheshire Historical Society*, LXVI, 1914, 228–44. Timbrell's dating was based on the carved heraldry and accepted by Macquoid/Edwards (1954, Beds, 38), almost certainly on the published evidence alone. However, Timbrell failed to mention that the columns were Corinthian, of forms which would not have been stylistically out of place in the seventeenth century; it is likely that the posts belong to the second half of the sixteenth century.

[250] Probably the ancestors of the highly ornate box beds of the Breton peasantry. See also the restored bed. Peyre Collection, no. 969, Musée des Arts Decoratifs, Paris.

[251] See p. 230.

'Item une couchete de boys toute enchassillée de mesmes sur laquelle a unes armoires de boys pour mectre le harnoys du roy,

Item en ladite couchete a ung rideau de estamine blanche bandé de soye bleue et grise . . .

Item ladite couchete est garnie de couete traversier et couverture perse semée de fleurs de lys,

Item sur ladite couchete a ung tableau de Nostre Dame qui tient son enfant, . . .

Item audevant des armoires où se met le hernoys du roy ung rideau destamine blanche pareil dicelui de la couchete, . . .'

(Godard-Faultrier, 51–2.)

(Item, a wooden *couchette* entirely enclosed with wood, upon which are fitted wooden armoires for storing the King's equipment.

Item, the said *couchette* has a curtain of white *estamine* with bands of blue and grey silk . . .

Item, the said *couchette* is equipped with feather bed, bolster and coverlet of *perse* powdered with lilies.

Item, on the said *couchette* [?in the woodwork surrounding the bed] is a painting of Our Lady holding her child . . .

Item, the armoires for the King's armour are closed by a white *estamine* curtain, matching that used for the *couchette* itself.)

Like the boarded bed in the 1420 entry above, this one in the Château d'Angers was also situated in one of the more private rooms used by René of Anjou, the 'chambre du petit retrait'.

1496   In the Château de Monbeton.

'21. Item ung gran cadalliech enchassilhat.'

(Forestié, 42.)

(Item, a large bed frame, enclosed round about.)

Cradles

Few cradles have survived from the Middle Ages, but there are two famous fifteenth-century examples — one from England and the other from the Netherlands — and both are described in the Catalogue Raisonné (Cat. 28 and 29). Our knowledge of earlier cradles is drawn entirely from the evidence of art, documents and literature.

Before discussing the forms found in representational art, we must look first at written evidence, since this will influence the interpretation we place on the images portrayed in MSS and paintings. Initially, we must look again at Alienor de Poitiers's treatise; we shall see that it is as informative for cradles as it proved to be for beds. The clarity with which Alienor de Poitiers explains the implications of the different textiles, furs and furniture forms in the equipment surrounding the infant at the time of its birth and on the day of its baptism, provides us with an understanding of, and an insight into the significance of earlier evidence from all sources. As with beds, we discover that more than one cradle was necessary where the nobility was concerned. The important cradle was the state cradle which provided a suitable setting in the daytime when the infant might be visited and admired; the second cradle was the night cradle in which the baby slept in a nursery, cared for by a number of special servants.[252] Written evidence which is informative is chiefly concerned with state cradles. (We learn very little about night cradles from documents for, like all pieces of furniture which were of no social significance, they rarely warranted descriptions in inventories.) Alienor de Poitiers shows that the textiles and furs employed for state cradles were key features in measuring appropriate degrees of honour, in parallel with the evidence for beds. For example, we see that a princess's cradle had a counterpoint of ermine which touched the ground, while that of a countess was of miniver and must on no account reach the floor.[253] Let us now look at the relevant portion of Alienor de Poitiers's treatise, freely translated and rearranged.[254]

1484–1491

    Lines

    748–9   Guidance concerning countesses and other noble ladies for the day the infant is baptised.

              The infant must be brought to a chamber from the nursery and in that chamber there must be, as is customary, a high cradle hanging by means

    750–3   of iron rings between 2 wooden uprights. The cradle must be provided with a circular or square pavilion (sparver) matching

    751–4   the form used for the *couchette*; this pavilion must be of silk or *saye*, but of the two, silk is more honourable

    754–6   and splendid.

    774–5   A carpet should be laid before the cradle and the cradle itself should be covered with a counterpoint of miniver,

    762–4   like those used to cover the beds. The covering of the cradle must on no account be larger than the cradle itself; for this to extend $\frac{3}{4}$ of a palm's width past the sides of the cradle is enough, for it must never be allowed to

    764–9   reach the ground.

Turning now to earlier evidence, we should consider it in the context of this portion of Alienor de Poitiers's text and also in the light of her description of all the furnishings in the chambers used after an infant's birth (Appendix VIII (b) and (c)).

c. 1281   1   'Item, la chambre toute couverte par dessus le ciel et toutes parrois aussi couvertes tout de tartaire ou de cendal, tout d'une coulour, semez d'aucune euvre nouvelle.

---

[252] We hear of four such servants in respect of the Comtesse de Rethel's infant in 1403: 'la dame qui gardera l'enfant', 'la berceresse', 'la nourisse', and 'la femme de chambre'. J. Garnier, 'État des Objets d'Habillement de Literie, d'Ameublement et de Vaisselle Achetés à Paris par Ordre de Marguerite de Flandres, Duchesse de Bourgogne, pour les Couches de la Comtesse de Rethel, sa Belle Fille', *Révue des Sociétés Savantes*, 6e série, I, 1875, 604–5.

[253] See Appendix VIII (b), lines 219–20; 762–5; also fig. 36, p. 272.

[254] For text, see Appendix VIII (b).

2 Item, toute la chambre sera couverte parterre de tapis de la coulour dessus dite, et semée de pareille semeure.

3 Item, il faut V oreilliers de broudeure beaus et riches a parer.

4 Item, il faut 1 couvertour de drap d'or, fourré d'ermine pour l'enfant.

5 Item, 1 autre d'escarlate, fourré de vair.

6 Item, 1 autre fourré de gris.

7 Item, une courtine vert de douze toillez.

8 Item, 11 courtines de toilles vert, de huit lez la piece.

9 Item, il faut 11 berceus, 1 pour jour et 1 pour nuit.

10 Item, 11 lieus, l'un broudé des armes de Flandres et de France et sera de jours, l'autre de soie tout plain qui sera de nuit.'

(Dehaisnes, I, 75.)

1 (Item, the chamber to be entirely hung, both the ceiling and all round the walls, with cloth of *tartaire* or *cendal*, all of the same colour and decorated with an up-to-date design.

2 Item, the floors of the entire chamber should be covered with a carpet of a colour and design which matches the wall hangings.

3 Item, there must be 5 head pillows of state covered with splendidly rich embroidery.

4 Item, there must be 1 coverlet of cloth of gold lined with ermine for the infant.

5 Item, another of scarlet lined with miniver.

6 Item, another lined with *gris*.

7 Item, a green curtain of 12 lengths.

8 Item, 2 green curtains of *toilles*, each 8 widths.

9 Item, there must be 2 cradles, 1 for day and 1 for night.

10 Item, 2 *lieus*, 1 for day embroidered with the arms of Flanders and France, and 1 for the night, of plain silk.)

In comparing the *c.* 1281 evidence with the relevant parts of Alienor de Poitiers's treatise, we see that in spite of the passage of some two hundred years there seems little difference in the luxurious nature of the equipment appropriate for great ladies; indeed, the degree of amenity and luxury indicated in both sources is their most striking characteristic. Alienor de Poitiers *implies* that there is more than one cradle, for the infant is brought into a special chamber where a particular kind of cradle is awaiting its arrival and is specially arrayed; this cradle is undoubteldy the cradle of state (lines 750–4). The earlier text *states* that there are two cradles and calls them the day and night cradles (Item 9). Alienor de Poitiers indicates that the state or day cradle had to be of a particular form which was traditional: (a) the cradle was high and (b) it was suspended between uprights. I think we may assume that the state cradle was always high and the night cradle was low, for if there was no difference in height, why should it be mentioned? The high cradle was chosen because it was imposing and answered to a situation in which the infant was viewed by standing persons; but it was inconvenient for any purpose connected with tending the child. The night cradle was presumably much lower to enable the infant to be *seen and nursed from a sitting position*; this would be essential in the medieval situation where the baby was continually tended and not shut away in a room alone. Regarding the suspended form, this was clearly a characteristic of the state cradle in Alienor de Poitiers's time and was, at that time, already traditional.

Let us now look at other written evidence; we shall see that much of it underlines factors which are already established, but that interesting additional information is given.

1371   Duke of Burgundy's accounts.

'8 août, ordre de payer 86 fr. à Jehan d'Orleans, peintre et varlet de chambre du roy . . . , pour la façon d'un biers pour Jehan monsr.'

(Prost, 1, 261–2, *1438*.)

(8th August, order to pay 86 fr. to Jehan d'Orleans, painter and 'varlet de chambre' to Charles VII of France, for work on a cradle for M. Jehan [the infant John the Fearless].)

Although no details are given here, the credentials of the man employed as well as the price charged show that the work was skilful and elaborate.

1403   List of articles ordered in Paris by Margaret of Flanders, Duchess of Burgundy, for the use of her daughter-in-law, the Comtesse de Rethel.

'A Guillaume Sename, de Lucques, marchant, demeurant à Paris . . .

10   . . . pour deux draps de graine, brochez d'or de Chippre, pour mettre tout à l'entour du couvertouer qui sera fait d'ermines, pour le grant bers à parer pour le dit enffant, la pièce quatre vins escus, vaillent   180 frans.

11   A lui, pour quatre aulnes de veluau vermeil cramoisi, pour faire ung saint pour le dit grand bers à parer   40 f demi

12   A Colin Vaubrisset, marchant, demeurant à Paris, pour la vente de douze cens d'ermines, emploiez entièrement en la fourrure du couvertoir du grant bers à parer pour le dit enffant, dont cy devant est faite mencion le cent au pris de trent frans,   vallent 360 frans

13   A lui, pour la vente de cinq milliers de menu vair, dont l'en a fourre les deux couvertouers du lit de ma ditte Damoiselle de Rethel, et trois autres petis couvertoirs pour lever, couvrir et tenir son enffant, le millier au pris de quarante francs, pour ce   200 frans . . .

17   A lui, pour douze cens doz de connis, emploiez entièrement à fourer ung petit couvertoir pour le dit enffant . . .

28   A maistre Jehan Du Liège, charpentier, demourant à Paris, pour l'achat de deux bers, l'un de parement et l'autre pour bercer et nourrir le dit enffant, pour deux berseulx servant à yceulx bers, deux cuves de bois d'Illande à baignier, et deux chapelles à ce appartenant, trente six f, et pour une husche de blanc bois pour mettre dedens le dit bers de parement, pour le porter plus seurement de Paris à Arras, devers ma ditte Damoiselle

de Rethel, tout pour le fait de la ditte gessine, deux frans. Pour ces parties . . . 38 f. . . .

30   A Christofle Besan, paintre et varlet de chambre de mon dit seigneur, pour avoir paint et doré de fin or bruny, aux armes de mon dit Seigneur de Rethel et de ma ditte Damoiselle, le grant bers de parement dont cy devant est faite mencion pour le dit enffant, et une tablette à mettre darrier la teste d'icellui enffant, où est l'image de Notre-Dame . . .   50 f.'

(Garnier, 605, 606, 608, 609.)

(To Guillaume Sename, merchant of Lucca, living in Paris,

10   . . . for 2 lengths of *graine* woven with gold for making a border right round the coverlet of the state cradle, the main part being of ermine, the price of the cloth   180 francs.

11   To the same, for 4 yards of crimson velvet *cramoisi*, for making a small ? sparver for the said cradle of state $40\frac{1}{2}$ francs.

12   To Colin Vaubrisset, merchant, living in Paris, for 1,200 ermine skins, all used for the coverlet of the large state cradle for the said infant (already mentioned), at 30 francs per 100 skins   360 francs.

13   To the same, for 5,000 skins of miniver used for the 2 coverlets of the bed of the said Damoiselle de Rethel, and 3 other small coverlets for picking up, covering and holding her baby, the price 40 francs per 1,000 skins,   200 francs . . .

17   To the same, for 1,200 rabbit skins for entirely covering a little coverlet for the said infant . . .

28   To master Jehan Du Liège, carpenter, living in Paris, for 2 cradles [i.e. the cradle boxes only] 1 of state and the other for rocking and feeding the said infant[255]
and for 2 stands for the said cradles [i.e. so that they could be rocked or swung, according to whichever principle of construction was used]; 2 tubs of riven oak for bathing the infant,
and 2 rounded cases for keeping them in, 36 francs; and for a white wood case for the state cradle in order that it may be carried with greater safety from Paris to Arras and there delivered to the said Damoiselle de Rethel, all made for the birth mentioned above, 2 francs.
For these goods   38 francs . . .

30   To Christofle Besan, painter and 'varlet de chambre' to the Duke of Burgundy, for painting and gilding with fine, burnished gold the large above mentioned state cradle for the said infant with the arms of Seigneur

---

[255] In this account we learn of the two servants with special duties (see also fn. 252): the 'berceresse' and the 'nourisse'. These highly trusted individuals had specific tasks: the 'berceresse' sat with the infant and rocked the cradle and the 'nourisse' was the wet nurse. The luxurious bedding purchased for these servants is listed, see items 5 and 6, Garnier 604–5.

de Rethel and with those of the said Damoiselle de Rethel; and for [painting] a panel with the head of Our Lady to be placed behind the infant's head   50 francs.)

1416   Inventory of goods of Yves de Vieupont, Baron le Neubourg and of Blanche de Harcourt, his wife.

'Item, un bers à bercer enffans . . .
Item, un paveillon que l'en tent sur les enffans de mondit seigneur de Vieupont avec une sarge blanche bien usée.'

(C. de Robillard de Beaurepaire, *Inventaire du Mobilier du Château de Chailloué*, Rouen, 1866, 20, 21.)

(Item, a cradle for rocking a child [i.e. the cradle box and rockers are combined] . . . Item, a pavilion for hanging over the lord of Vieupont's infants, with a serge which is worn.)

1423   Inventory of Henry V.

'Item, 1 Tent bede de drap de Baudekyn d'or, fait pur le gesyne de la Roigne, ovec 11 panes d'escharlet, furrez dez Ermyns, ovec tout l'aparaille, pris c li.'

(*Rot. Parl.*, IV, 238.)

(Item, 1 tent bed (sparver) of gold brocade, made for the Queen's lying in, with 2 panes of scarlet cloth lined with ermine, with all the equipment, price £100.)

Unfortunately, few details are given here, but the splendour of the sparver bed suggests that the equipment (including the cradles) for an English queen was of the same character as that used in France and Burgundy; in this instance it cannot be doubted, for the queen concerned was Catherine of France.

1468   Inventory of Jean, Comte de Dunois, bastard of the Duc d'Orleans.

'. . . ung bers . . . trois grans draps de parement de gésine . . . le petit drap de parement de bers pour l'enfant . . . ung grant berseau, . . .'

(Jarry, 123, 124, 129.)

(. . . a cradle . . . 3 large state hangings for the lying in . . . the little state hanging for the infant's cradle . . . a large frame to support a cradle . . .)

1469   Inventory of Marguerite de Bretagne, first wife of Francois II, Duc de Bretagne.

'100. Item ung couvertouer à mectre sur ung bers, de veloux bleu, garny de taffetas bleu, et par le millieu fourré d'armines . . .
153. Item ung grant bers doré, à quatre pommettes de cuivre, aux armes de ladite damme.

154. Item ung couvertouer d'ermines pour ledit bers, bordé de drap d'or cramoesy et doublé de taffetas violet.'

(A. de La Borderie, 'Inventaire des Meubles et Bijoux de Marguerite de Bretagne', *Bulletin de la Société Archéologique de Nantes et de la Loire-Inferieure*, IV, 1864, 56, 59, 60.)

(100. Item, a coverlet for a cradle of blue velvet trimmed with blue taffeta with the centre part furred with ermine . . .

153. Item, a large gilded cradle, with 4 knops of copper, and with the arms of the said Duchesse.

154. Item, a coverlet of ermine for the said cradle, bordered with cloth of gold *cramoesy* and lined with violet taffeta.)

We see that this accumulation of evidence supports Alienor de Poitiers's statement that great state cradles were a traditional part of the equipment surrounding the births of the infants of the nobility. As in other matters of courtly etiquette, we find that France and Burgundy were one in the later Middle Ages, and although there is less detailed evidence for England the marriages of English kings with foreign princesses served to reinforce continental practices in this respect.[256] Furthermore, the English extant cradle (Cat. 29) shows that the form of state cradle prescribed by Alienor de Poitiers was used in England also.

We find that most of the evidence concerns state cradles (entries dated *c.* 1281, 1371, 1403 and 1469) as we should expect. But two entries mention night cradles: the lists of *c.* 1281 and 1403, where we learn that the night cradle was for the rocking and nursing of the infant. This enables us to connect the night cradle with the duties of the 'berceresse' and of the 'nourisse' mentioned in the 1403 list and to identify this type of cradle when we find it connected with one or both of these tasks in the evidence of 1416. We notice that in the 1416 entry the night cradle was apparently a simple box with attached rockers — 'un bers a bercer enffans', for no stand (berceau) is mentioned; but the cradle with integral rockers was evidently not the only form for the night cradle, for item 28 in the 1403 list shows that *both* state and night cradles in this instance were of two parts, a cradle box and a separate stand. For reasons which will be discussed in the Catalogue entry, I believe we should recognize the surviving English cradle (Cat. 29) as a night cradle, although it is also of two parts like a state cradle.

Alienor de Poitiers's treatise is mainly concerned with descriptions of textiles and furs; she tells us that the state cradle for countesses was high and in two parts (a cradle and a stand in which it is hung)[257] but we are not told whether the state cradle for queens and princesses was of the same form (though we know that the cradle coverings were distinct).[258] This query is pleasingly resolved by the evidence of the surviving state

---

[256] See Macquoid/Edwards 1954, Cradles, 149, quoting evidence for state and night cradles in England.
[257] See p. 94.
[258] In following Alienor de Poitiers's rules in these matters, we need to know something of the ranks which existed within the same title before we can be positive about the degrees of honour assumed by individuals. For example, Alienor de Poitiers's countesses equal to the Vicedamesse d'Amiens might not assume an ermine cradle cover, yet the Comtesse de Rethel had one (see Appendix VIII, fig. 35, and 174–5); since the title of Comtesse might include one of the eight peers of France (e.g. Mahaut, Comtesse d'Artois) we see that the stratification which existed within this rank was of considerable significance.

cradle from the Netherlands (Cat. 28), made in 1478/9 for the birth of Philip the Fair or Marguerite of Austria. This cradle was made for Marie of Burgundy, mother of these children, and we know from Alienor de Poitiers's text that Marie of Burgundy assumed the same degree of honour as the queen of France.[259] The surviving cradle is high and of two parts and we see, therefore, that the *form* of state cradle for queens was the same as that prescribed by Alienor de Poitiers for countesses. (This conforms with the evidence for beds; the rank of queen was distinguished from that of countess by the number and position of state beds and by the quality of their hangings and coverings, but both ranks were entitled to the same *form* of bed: the hung bed with a whole celour.) The surviving cradle of 1478/9 provides a second link with the above evidence, for we find a striking correlation not only in the matter of form but also in that of decoration. We are impressed firstly by the quality of draughtsmanship discernible in the most complete part of the design: the initials M M which are linked with an extraordinarily free, yet disciplined, floral arabesque pattern; and secondly by the evidence of a highly expensive overall decoration in gold leaf. Such evidence is rare and remarkable in the context of medieval furniture and calls for an explanation. We find that explanation in the evidence of 1371 and 1403 which both concern commissions by Philip the Bold and his Duchess, Margaret of Flanders. We discover that state cradles for the Burgundian nobility in the line of succession were decorated by the greatest artists in the land, and we remind ourselves that the surviving cradle was made for Marie of Burgundy, heiress of Charles the Bold. In the case of the cradle for the infant John the Fearless, 1371 (see p. 96), the painter was Painter to the King of France; and in the case of the cradle for the infant born to Margaret of Bavaria and John the Fearless, 1403 (see pp. 96–8), the artist was Painter to the Duke of Burgundy. Where we are given some details, we see that the arms of the infant's mother were incorporated in the design (1403, item 30; 1469, item 153) as found on the surviving cradle; that gold leaf was employed (1403, item 30; 1469, item 153); and that the delicacy of the work necessitated a special case for transport (1403, item 28). We notice that the cradles were very expensive as items of wooden furniture, though their cost was modest compared with textiles and furs (see, e.g., the ermine coverlet, 1403, item 12). In the partial breakdown of the cost of the state cradle of 1403, we see that the carpenter's work was relatively cheap (item 28); it was the painter's work which accounted for most of the cost, though some of this expense will have been due to the use of gold leaf. The extant cradle (Cat. 28) and documentary evidence together provide positive proof that in the rare cases where a piece of wooden furniture was an adjunct of estate, that furniture was executed by the greatest artists who were available.

We have seen that a state cradle formed one small item in the total of new equipment deemed necessary for the birth of an heir or heiress of the Valois dukes of Burgundy (1403 list), the total cost of which was on one occasion over 4,923 francs.[260] We wonder, perhaps, how often this equipment was provided, and why it was so lavish. I believe it is likely that the total equipment was a once-for-all outlay for the first birth of a

[259] See Appendix VIII (b), lines 550–61.
[260] See Garnier, 611.

particular marriage, with replacements to individual items as needed for later babies. The cost seems so great, even for the time, that it is difficult to believe that it can have been repeated for every infant, many of whom died in infancy. Furthermore, we know from royal inventories that there was no stigma attached to the re-use of chamber textiles made for other individuals. It does seem to accord with the evidence, however, that a second or third wife would have her own equipment, so that several sets might have to be purchased in any one generation. If this surmise is correct, the surviving cradle of 1478/9 would have been made for the first-born, Philip the Fair, and re-used by the second infant of the marriage, Marguerite of Austria. As to the lavishness of the total provision for these important births, such extravagance as we see cannot be separated from the overall standard of display which seigneurial lords found it necessary to adopt. There were few things more important than the survival of the line, and the symbolism surrounding the birth of an heir acknowledged this fact. Perhaps, too, we can detect a very faint aura of human concern for the young wives who owed their situation to social and political expediency rather than to personal choice, and who frequently died in childbirth. Why else should the chamber be covered over walls, ceiling and floors with some *new* design, if not to intrigue and delight one of the two major individuals in the drama?[261]

To turn now to the evidence provided by representational art, a sequence was recorded first by Viollet-le-Duc and later by Dervieu.[262] From a twelfth-century MS source, Dervieu illustrates a high cradle framed with turned posts having four knops and attached rockers.[263] Possibly cradles using turned wood were common at this time over a wide area, resembling a cradle which survives in Sweden;[264] indeed, the evidence of the use of turned wood in seat furniture, in particular, suggests that this was so.[265] Dervieu believed that the swung cradle supported between uprights, of which Cat. 28 and 29 are examples, was a fifteenth-century development.[266]

CATALOGUE NO. 28 (PLATE 34)
State Cradle of 1478/9, made for Philip the Fair or Marguerite of Austria. (Called the Cradle of Charles V.) Musées Royaux d'Art et d'Histoire, Brussels, no. 360.
Oak, painted and covered with gold leaf.
1.   4′ 9″
h.   without projection of posts, 2′ 6½″
w.   2′ 5″
l.   spigots (for suspension of cradle on missing stand), 5¼″

Description (July 1970)
The cradle was designed to swing between uprights, which have not survived. It is severely mutilated, having lost parts of its woodwork and much of its decoration. There

[261] Entry of *c.*1281, pp. 94–5, items 1 and 2.
[262] Viollet-le-Duc 1858, *Berceau*; Dervieu 1912, 387–415.
[263] Dervieu 1912, fig. 10.
[264] See W. Holmqvist, *Sveriges Forntid och Medeltid*, Malmö, 1949, fig. 369.
[265] For example, the Hereford Cathedral chair, Cat. 49.
[266] Dervieu 1912, 411–12.

are iron spigots fitted near the top on the outside surface at each end, designed to engage fittings in the missing stand and to hang the cradle and allow it to swing, on the same principle as the English cradle, Cat. 29. Each spigot is set in a circular sex-foil rose with a central domed boss.

The cradle is composed of boards held in a simple frame without mitred corners; elaborate mouldings are attached to the frame. The sides and ends have a horizontal division and there is a railing above the cradle box. The corner posts extend above and below the box, to support the railing above and 2 open tracery panels below. These tracery panels are at the ends only and serve as a decorative sled on which the cradle can rest when not slung between the missing uprights. The corner posts are each carved with a pair of buttresses. The box was originally double walled, presumably to give a particularly good finish to the inside, but the inner skin is almost entirely missing and its character cannot now be assessed.

The entire surface of the cradle was once covered with paintings in colours and gold leaf. The decoration is now largely lost but enough remains to show that the quality of the draughtsmanship and execution was very high; there can be no doubt that the cradle was decorated by an artist who was a master craftsman. The end panels are the most complete, and are decorated with the initials M M intertwined with thistles and ?holly. One side panel has the arms of Maximilian of Austria and Marie of Burgundy, while the decoration on the other side is completely lost. Presumably the four panelled borders at the bottom of the cradle were designed to contain lettering, but only the device of Maximilian remained to be traced and recorded in the nineteenth century:

HALT MAS IN ALLEN DINGEN [moderation in all things]

Analysis

The cradle's history has been set out by Metzdorf and summarized by Destrée;[267] Metzdorf published drawings of the designs which were discernible in his day, and he quotes the entry for the cradle from the catalogue of 1854 in which the collection of antiquities at Brussels was described by M. Schayes, the first Conservateur. Two interlocking statements in this catalogue have tended to remain attached to the cradle. In the first place, the cradle is stated to be that of the Emperor Charles V (born at Ghent); and in the second place it is given a Ghent provenance. The first statement was qualified by the Musées Royaux at a later date to the effect that the cradle was Charles V's but had been made for one of the children of Maximilian of Austria and Marie of Burgundy. As had been noted, the arms on the cradle, the linked initials M M and the motto of Maximilian, demonstrated conclusively that the cradle was indeed made for one of the children of this marriage. Whether it was subsequently used by the next generation in the person of the infant Charles V is immaterial in terms of our study, though such re-use seems to me improbable (see pp. 100–1). Thus the name by which the cradle is known is thoroughly misleading, but it is probably too late to change it, for the cradle is famous

[267] L. Metzdorf, 'Le Berceau de Charles V', *Bulletin Mensuel de Numismatique et d'Archéologie*, II, nos. 2 and 3, 1882, 29–31, pls. II and III. J. Destrée/A. J. Kymeulen/A. Hannotiau, *Les Musées Royaux du Parc du Cinquantenaire et de la Porte de Hal à Bruxelles*, Brussels [n.d.] no. 20 (J. Destrée, 'Berceau dit de Charles Quint').

as the 'Cradle of Charles V'. Turning now to the question of the provenance, M. Schayes stated (1854) that the cradle was brought from Ghent to Brussels before 1560, on the evidence of a passage in Marcus van Vaernewyck's *Historie van Belgie* which tells of a 'simple cradle of painted wood'[268] visible in the Prinzenhof at Ghent. This evidence was accepted by Metzdorf who went on to suggest that the cradle was made at Ghent in 1482 (the year of the death of Marie of Burgundy) when the children went to live there, as a bed for the child Marguerite. (The birth places of these children, Bruges and Brussels respectively, provided unhelpful evidence in forming a hypothesis to explain the Ghent provenance.) Destrée was clearly unconvinced by the evidence for a Ghent provenance, and today it would be hard to make a case for so fragile a correlation. Even in its modern, mutilated condition, the cradle could not be called a simple object, and in the sixteenth century it would have been even more brilliant with gold leaf than it is today.

We are thus left with no more evidence than is provided by the cradle itself; yet this is surely substantial. It has been shown that two cradles were necessary when the birth was to noble parents — a state cradle in which the infant was displayed, and a simpler, lower cradle in which the baby normally lay, the night cradle (see pp. 99–101). The Brussels cradle, covered in gold leaf and painted with arms and devices is certainly a state cradle; furthermore, its form is precisely that prescribed by Alienor de Poitiers in her discussion of the correct procedure to be adopted on the day of baptism where she says there must be a high cradle hanging by iron rings between uprights, as is customary.[269] To turn now to the question of the date of the cradle, the arms and devices of Maximilian of Austria and Marie of Burgundy show that it was made for one of their children: either Philip the Fair, born June 1478, or Marguerite of Austria, born January 1480. (Having disposed of the evidence for a Ghent provenance, we need not consider Metzdorf's theory that the cradle was made in 1482; in any case, a high, swinging cradle would be quite unsuitable, even dangerous, for a child of over two years old, as Marguerite was in that year.) As has been suggested, it seems probable that state cradles were commissioned for the birth of the first-born of a particular marriage and thereafter used by all subsequent children of that marriage, together with all the magnificent equipment used in the chambers devoted to the occasion. If this were indeed the case, the cradle would have been made for Philip the Fair and re-used for Marguerite of Austria, its useful life ending with the infancy of Marguerite, the last child of the marriage. But even if this suggestion is discounted and it is felt that we cannot state for which of the two children the cradle was made, there are only two years in which it could have been produced: 1478 for Philip the Fair (born June) or 1479 for Marguerite of Austria (born *January* 1480).[270]

The quality of the draughtsmanship is one of the surprises of the cradle, for in spite of its worn surfaces, enough remains of the linked M M decoration to show that this

---

[268] 'eenvondige houte geschilderde wieg'.
[269] See Appendix VIII (b), lines 770–3; also p. 94.
[270] A tantalizing footnote to this question may perhaps be added: although Alienor de Poitiers tells us about arrangements on the day of Philip the Fair's christening which she may have witnessed, she does not describe his state cradle.

was the work of a master, rather than an ordinary painter. Documentary evidence has been quoted to show that for certain important commissions the greatest artists were employed to decorate state cradles;[271] we have also seen that such men *decorated* the cradle after it had been *fashioned* by a carpenter.[272] This surviving cradle is of outstanding importance in demonstrating how furniture was treated aesthetically on the rare occasions when it ranked as an adjunct of estate.

Select Bibliography

J. Destrée, 'Berceau dit de Charles Quint', J. Destrée/A. J. Kymeulen/A. Hannotiau, *Les Musées Royaux du Parc du Cinquantenaire et de la Porte de Hal à Bruxelles*, no. 20, Brussels [n.d.]

L. Metzdorf, 'Le Berceau de Charles V', *Bull. Mensuel Num. Archéol.*, II, nos. 2–3, 1882, 29–31; pls. II, III.

CATALOGUE No. 29 (PLATE 35A)

Cradle from Newland, Gloucestershire (the so-called cradle of Henry V). London Museum no. D 48. (Lent by H.M. the Queen.) See also Appendix V.

Oak

Cradle: l.   3' 2"   Stand: l.   3' 10½"
          h.   1' 5"   h.   2' 10"
          w. 1' 6"–1' 8½"   w. 2' 4"

Description (December 1974)

The cradle is of 2 parts: a box and a stand in which it swings. The stand is composed of 2 inverted T-shaped forms with buttresses, linked at ground level with 2 stretchers. The box is somewhat roughly finished and is made of a series of heavy boards worked with deep, horizontal mouldings on their outside surfaces; inside, the boards are plain and smooth. The cradle box is now open at the bottom as well as at the top. Each side is composed of 2 boards joined horizontally; the division is camouflaged by the ribbed surfaces. The top of each side has an inward batter, to allow the hand to glide easily when the cradle is rocked, but the end boards are squarely cut (a batter was unnecessary here as the posts would prevent handling). On the inside of the lowest board on each side is a deep groove about 1" above the bottom, running horizontally the whole length of the box. This groove is not carried round the end boards, and presumably once held the cradle bottom. There is no attempt to form a neat joint at the corners of the box; the boards are abutted against one another, and the sides cover the cross grain of the end boards and are pegged in position. The box has 3 rectangular slots on each side near the top (there are none at the ends), and a series of holes near the bottom, 4 to each side and 2 at each end. Some of the holes are now threaded with cord. The box tapers slightly from head to foot (see width measurements above), and has a substantial hook on the

---

[271] See pp. 96–8, 100.
[272] See the evidence of 1403, items 28 and 30, pp. 96–8.

outside surface of each end which is designed to receive a ring fitted to the inner surface of each post of the stand; this arrangement is original. In addition, there is another ring of uncertain use on the inside surface of each post.

The stand has chamfered posts and each is surmounted by a well carved bird with a long tail and folded wings. The heads of the birds are now much worn and the beaks have gone. The inverted T-angle is buttressed with curved, flat boards which have well carved, stylized flowers on the outer surfaces and a hollow chamfered edge.

The surface of the wood generally is glossy and dark and would appear to have been unpainted, were it not for a small trace of paint film showing as a dark, raised surface below one of the birds.[273] Apart from the wear on the heads of the birds, the condition of the box and stand is excellent and there is only evidence of minor repairs to strengthen the structure (e.g., metal strap at foot of frame).

Analysis

By tradition, the cradle was used by the infant Henry V (born Monmouth Castle, 1388), but it has long been recognized as of late fifteenth-century date;[274] I share this opinion for the following reasons.

The ribbed box is strongly made yet of primitive construction; it resembles the fifteenth-century panelling in the Guildhall porch at Lavenham, Suffolk (perhaps the earliest English wall panelling which survives). At Lavenham, the boards are ribbed from top to bottom, there being no divisions as in later panelling. This correlation is particularly interesting, in view of the comment made by Bonnor in 1798, likening the cradle to old wall panelling (see Appendix V). No doubt when Bonnor wrote, much more of this work survived. The hieratic quality of the birds also suggests a medieval date. The chamfer on the posts and buttresses seems to favour a fifteenth-century date, see Cat. 14. The strongest evidence for a late fifteenth/early sixteenth-century date lies in the carving of the buttresses. Here we find a type of stylized flower, elongated in order to fill the triangular void, which can occur in the seventeenth century and can hardly have been used much before 1500.

The cradle has been given a variety of provenances,[275] while at the same time generally retaining the tradition that it had belonged to Henry V. The facts are as follows. *Bonnor's Perspective Itinerary*, London, 1798, described the cradle with care and insight and printed a drawing made earlier, in 1773 (see Appendix V). The account is of considerable interest; it will be noted that it demolished all credibility in the Caernarvon provenance (see fn. 275, no. 1), showing that the cradle was certainly at the Rectory, Newland, Gloucestershire in 1773, in the possession of the Revd Peregrine Ball.[276] After

[273] I am grateful to Mr John Clark of the London Museum, for pointing out this feature.
[274] See Macquoid/Edwards 1954, Cradles, 149; also *Medieval Catalogue,* London Museum Catalogues, no. 7, H.M.S.O., 1954, 291.
[275] (1) Cradle of the first Prince of Wales from Caernarvon Castle, *London Magazine,* March 1774; (2) Cradle of Henry V, at the Rectory, Newland, Gloucestershire in 1773, and reputedly from Courtfield (5 m. north), where Henry V was nursed. *Bonnor's Copper Plate Perspective Itinerary or Pocket Portfolio,* London, 1798, 34, pl. XI, fig. 3 (see Appendix V); (3) Henry V's cradle from Monmouth Castle. E. E. Barrett, 'The Cradles of the Past', *Connoisseur,* XXXIII, 1912, 94; (4) Chepstow Castle, *Medieval Catalogue,* 291.
[276] Cox's *History of Monmouthshire,* 1800, gives 'Peregrine', Bonnor giving only 'Mr. Ball'.

I

Ball's death in 1794, the cradle passed through a number of hands. In 1908 it was sold at Christies to Edward VII and in 1911 it came to the London Museum from Windsor. No other facts are known, but a number of unfounded statements have gained currency at one time or another (see fn. 275). Let us now look at these statements in turn.

(1)   By the time the cradle reached the London Museum, the provenance of Chepstow Castle had become firmly attached to it, though the reasons for this are entirely mysterious; this provenance was printed in the *Medieval Catalogue*.

(2)   Through confusion with a second extant cradle (also traditionally belonging to Henry V and with a provenance of Monmouth Castle), handed down in the Beaufort family, the present cradle was given a Monmouth Castle provenance by Barrett.

As the above notes demonstrate, the only reliable evidence is Bonnor's of 1798 and we can state with confidence that the cradle, looking exactly as it does today, was at the Rectory at Newland, in the possession of the Revd Peregrine Ball, in 1773. When we look at the developments in the cradle's history since Bonnor wrote, we find little to persuade us of the reliability of verbal tradition. (Between 1789, the year Ball died, and 1911, when the cradle came to the London Museum, it had acquired 2 extra provenances, making 4 in all.) What then should we make of the tradition, mentioned by Bonnor, that the cradle had been handed down in the Ball family by a rocker to Henry V, who carried out her duties at Courtfield and received the cradle as a perquisite? It must be acknowledged, in the first instance, that once the cradle passed out of the hands of the Ball family there was a greater risk of traditions becoming distorted, and it may be conceded that there could be a substance of truth in the Ball family story. The cradle cannot have been made for Henry V, for stylistically it is a hundred years too late. But if we accept the rest of the tradition and the Courtfield provenance as a possibility, it is a reasonable conjecture that the identity of the baby concerned should have become confused, over the centuries, with the one name which gave the manor of Courtfield especial lustre and significance. A point which gives some credence to the Ball tradition is the statement that the cradle was the perquisite of a rocker. It would be difficult to invent such an idea, and it accords well with the lack of documentary references to cradles in English medieval inventories, for if cradles were habitually disposed of by great families in this manner when they were outgrown, the dearth of evidence is explained, since they would seldom have remained in the household until the time when the head of the family died (the major occasion for the taking of inventories as represented by surviving examples). The suggestion raises another interesting point: if the rocker received a cradle as a perquisite, was it the day (state) cradle or the night cradle which was involved? I think it is likely to have been the night cradle because this was the one the rocker used, see the Burgundian evidence, pp. 94, 96 and 99.

The observation of Bonnor's regarding the contrast between the indifferent technique used in the assembly of the cradle as against the competence of the carving (birds and buttresses), which he believed could only be explained by the involvement of at least two craftsmen, should not go by without comment. We have seen how Mahaut, Comtesse d'Artois, employed notable *imagiers* or sculptors who often took over an object when a carpenter had fashioned it, and gave it artistry through carving and painting; and we have noted that this process is recorded respecting the state cradle for the Comtesse de Rethel in 1403.[277] I believe that Bonnor is right, and that this is precisely what happened with regard to the Newland cradle, and it is particularly interesting to note that part or all of it was once painted. However, I do not wish to suggest that the the carver employed on the cradle was anything more than a competent craftsman. The parallel ends with the use of two different men who exercised different skills on the same object.

With regard to the slots near the top at the sides of the cradle, it is likely that these are original and were designed to carry bands which crossed over the bedding to restrain the infant, like the examples shown by Dervieu.[278]

A final point remains to be discussed. Is this a day cradle — a cradle of state — or a night cradle? I believe we can answer this with confidence, on the evidence of the *height* of the cradle. It will be remembered that the state cradle needed to be tall (see pp. 94–5); the present cradle is low. The height of the cradle frame sets the cradle at a comfortable height for a seated person to tend the occupant, and although the form of the cradle agrees with Alienor de Poitiers's prescription for a state cradle, we have seen that night cradles were also made in the same manner, swinging between uprights (see pp. 96–7, item 28; pp. 99–100).

Select Bibliography

E. E. Barrett, 'The Cradles of the Past', *Connoisseur*, XXXIII, 1912, 91–101.

Bonnor's Copper Plate Perspective Itinery or Pocket Portfolio, London, 1798, 34–5, pl. XI, fig. 3. (For 34–5, see Appendix V.)

London Magazine, March 1774.

Macquoid/Edwards, *Dictionary of English Furniture*, 1954, Cradles.

Medieval Catalogue, London Museum Catalogues no. 7, H.M.S.O. 1954, 291, pl. LXXXVI.

---

[277] See pp. 96–8, items 28 and 30, where it is stated that Jehan Du Liége, a carpenter, supplied a cradle of state and a night cradle, together with 2 stands, and Christofle Besan, Painter to the Duke of Burgundy, painted and gilded the state cradle. Regarding the evidence concerning the Comtesse d'Artois, see p. 10.

[278] Dervieu 1912, figs. 10, 12, 14.

SECTION C
CHESTS

In an age in which mobility and security for household possessions were primary considerations, the adaptability of the chest in its various forms made it the most indispensable single article of furniture within our period. The chest was, at one and the same time, a piece of furniture and an article of luggage, as we understand these general terms today. The importance of the chest as a receptacle for all manner of goods has been frequently noted though perhaps inadequately demonstrated, an omission which it is hoped to rectify below.

The survey will concern itself with chests which are sufficiently large to occupy floor space, and cannot, in the interests of conciseness, include small boxes, cases or caskets termed *escrins*, *estuys* and *coffrets* in French sources. (These are often of precious materials and considerable numbers of them survive.) Nor will this survey consider cope chests, for although not necessarily solely confined to ecclesiastical ownership, each surviving example in England is unique as to size and form and warrants individual and extensive study.[279]

As is shown in Fig. 17, a surprising number of variations in the form of chests existed in the Middle Ages. The chief interest in these variations is technical, for they solve the same problems in different ways. However, there are two major divisions in this pattern which concern utility, and they are likely to have been very old ones: as between chests that are footed with lids that are flat and chests that rest directly upon the ground with lids that are domed. Footed chests may be accounted ideal for normal storage, since they preserved their contents from contact with damp floors and other unwholesomeness; but they were unsuitable for travelling purposes, whether by horse, cart or ship without the addition of a protective envelope. For travel, a simple box form, without projections, was the safest and most convenient, and where exposure to weather was a continual hazard, as with travel by horse or cart, a domed or canted lid to throw off water was an advantage.

Evidence for chests is ampler than for any other form of furniture. Relatively large numbers of them survive, even though these only represent a minute fraction of the total in medieval times.[280] This immunity from destruction on the scale which overtook other types of common furniture, such as beds and tables, is partly due to the conservative forces operating in institutions. A large number of chests have survived in institutions; some were needed by those bodies for their own purposes, and some were

---

[279] Secular lords often had as much need of these chests as did religious foundations; e.g., Henry le Scrope of Masham, executed in 1415 for plotting against Henry V, owned 92 copes in the list of his forfeitures, and this represented an incomplete total (see Kingsford 1920, 77).

[280] In 42 chambers and offices listed as part of the complex of the Château Cornillon in 1380, 74 chests are noted, and such a total is by no means unusual for one great seigneurial household (see J-H. Albanès, 'Inventaire du Château Cornillon en 1380', *Revue des Sociétés Savantes*, 7 série, I, 1879, 182–232; and the Duchess of Burgundy had 154 chests in a single room in 1405, see Dehaisnes, II, 915).

FOOTED   UNFOOTED

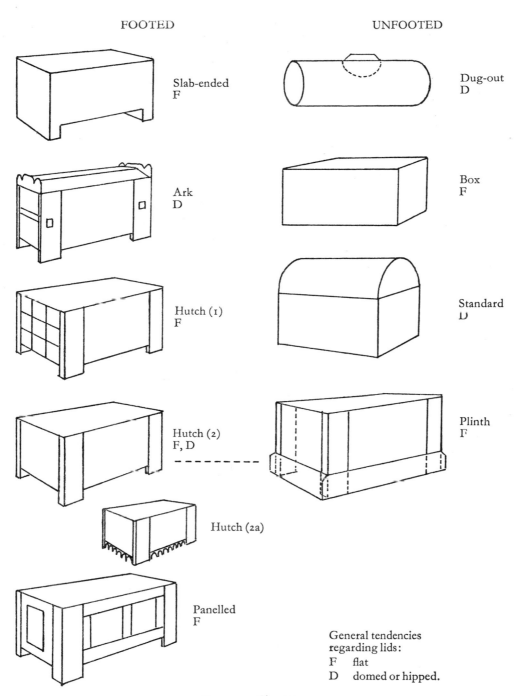

Slab-ended
F

Dug-out
D

Ark
D

Box
F

Hutch (1)
F

Standard
D

Hutch (2)
F, D

Plinth
F

Hutch (2a)

Panelled
F

General tendencies
regarding lids:
F   flat
D   domed or hipped.

FIG. 17.   Chest types

deposited by individuals for safety.[281] Doubtless, some of these 'intrusive' chests were never removed and helped to increase what was already a considerable quantity of such furniture. In domestic contexts, however, old furniture was generally swept away to make room for up-to-date and/or fashionable items, until Horace Walpole's interest in Gothic in the mid-eighteenth century spearheaded a movement in antique furniture collecting.

The evidence of extant chests is supported by a considerable volume of documentary evidence, though it is true that most references lack descriptive material and go no further than noting the existence of a chest, generally as a means of identifying its more valuable contents. (This body of material is extensive because chests and their contents were generally accounted as movables, and most surviving inventories are concerned with personal rather than real estate.[282]) As earlier sections have shown, written evidence provides a framework in which to assess surviving furniture, and notwithstanding its limitations this generalization is also true for chests. Before turning to this evidence in detail, however, something must first be said about the many terms used to describe chests in the Middle Ages, of which *arche, bahut, cista, coffre* and *huche* are the commonest.

Bearing in mind the fundamental division in the form, arising out of function, as between the footed chest and the chest of simple box form, the conclusion is inescapable that some of these French and Latin terms originally described different forms of chest consistently, rather than solely representing linguistic regional habits or conventions, instilled by different kinds of education. Nevertheless, it is a fact which has long been recognized that a consistent use of language to describe different forms and functions of chest was already blurred in the period under discussion.[283] This is not to say that individuals did not distinguish between various forms of chest in the Middle Ages; they did so constantly on every side, for most inventories which list chests use two or more terms to describe them.[284] Rather is it to state that language was constantly changing, so that although we may sometimes interpret terminology with confidence and establish correlations between terms and extant chest forms, straightforward rules tend to be both inadequate and misleading, and each case must often be tested afresh. In order to aid analysis, however, extant chest forms are identified in the text by individual terms which adhere to accepted usage where possible, see Fig. 17.

This is surely not the place to usurp the function of the dictionaries and resort to a tediously extended analysis of terminology; the references given below under the many uses of the chest provide abundant corroborative evidence of the vagaries of medieval usages without the need to underline the difficulties in every case. Suffice it here to take

---

[281] See, for example, 1322, inventory of Robert de Bethune, Comte de Flandres: 'Item, une huge qui est en le tressorie del eglise de Courtray.' (Dehaisnes, I, 245). See also 1361, p. 121. And 1465, will of Richard Welby, 'My plate and surplus money etc. to be kept in a chest at Croyland Abbey till my children attain full age', Gibbons, 190–1.

[282] See Eames 1973, 33–9.

[283] See Viollet-le-Duc 1858, *Bahut*, 23; and more recently, J. Viaux, 'French Domestic Furniture of the Middle Ages', *Connoisseur*, CXXXIII, 1954, 252.

[284] See, for example, 1321, inventories of Eudes de Mareuil, Chaplain of Beauvais Cathedral; here *archam, cista, coffro, huchello*, and *scrinario* are all given (Le Blond, 18, 31, 32, 33). Also 1346, *archarum, coffra* and *huchetorum* are found (H. Furgeot, 'Inventaire du Mobilier du Château de Berzé', *Cabinet Historique*, XXV, 1879, 154, 155). Also 1464, inventory of St Mary's Church, Warwick, 'irebound coofres' and a 'gret olde arke' (C. J. Hart, 'Old Chests', *Transactions of the Birmingham and Midland Institute*, XX, 1894, 65–6.

one function of the chest where our interpretation of terminology may be fairly tested and use it to examine how far a correlation of description and form is justified. With this in mind, let us therefore examine first the chest as a piece of travelling equipment.

1. Chests and baggage

When the seigneurial household moved between manors, large quantities of clothing and chamber textiles were regularly transported, together with plate and personal jewels and many other goods; each office of the household might be allotted a specific number of carts and sumpter horses, and the manner of marking baggage strictly regulated.[285] Household and personal equipment was packed in a variety of ways and the largest items were stowed in covered carts, while other items were either slung beneath carts or packed on the backs of sumpter horses.

Looking at records, we find a bewildering number of items of travelling equipment, some of which need only briefly concern us, since our interest is confined to the chest. On the periphery of our enquiry, it will be seen that we have principally to deal with the *bahut* and the *malle*. It has long been understood that the *bahut* was first and foremost a kind of envelope designed to contain a *coffre* when travelling; Viollet-le-Duc believed that the term lost its distinctiveness in the Middle Ages and might signify not only the envelope, but also the *coffre* itself, a conclusion with which Havard disagreed.[286] The evidence below suggests that while the word *bahut* might occasionally mean *coffre* (as in the 1386 entry), in the great majority of cases it meant the envelope and nothing more. (Indeed, it is noticeable that in the evidence below the term *bahut* does not occur outside a context concerned with travel.) The *bahut* as envelope might surround either a *coffre* (1386) or a *malle* (1368); it might be of tapestry (1386/7) or of some material such as wood or wicker covered with leather (1386). The evidence below shows that the *malle*[287] might be of wood (1386) or leather (1390); it might have locks and other ironwork (1374, 1386, 1390); and it might be attached to a horse's saddle (1391).

The *bahut* and the *malle*, which appear to have been exclusively for travelling, were supported by other specialized equipment such as bags — *bargia, bogie, bouge* (1227, 1374, 1380); and covers: *housse, huscia*, of leather (1229, 1377, 1378), waxed canvas (1238) and greased hides — 'barehides', which might be large enough to cover carts (1446, 1502, 1509). Before moving on to particular references to the chest itself, the common use of the *bahut* as envelope needs some explanation and the suggestion I have to make bears closely upon the whole system of preparing households for travel in the

[285] In 1384/5, when the Duchess of Burgundy travelled from Paris to Arras, the Kitchen required 2 'charettes' drawn by 7 horses, the Sausserie 1 'charette' drawn by 4 horses, the Paneterie 1 'charette' drawn by 5 horses, the Duchess's jewels (which will have included her plate) 1 'charette' drawn by 6 horses, etc. In total, 14 carriages or carts and 73 horses were required, see Canat de Chizy, 1898, 274. Edward IV had 1 'charyet' and 7 horses for the 'Office of Jewelhous', and 1 sumpter horse and 1 sumpter man for his chapel; only the king's own baggage was allowed to be marked 'undir colour of the kinges' (Ordinance of 1445). See Myers 1959, §43, 123; §60, 137; §3, 63.

[286] Havard considered that before the sixteenth century *bahut* described an article of luggage, with a domed lid, see H. Havard, *Dictionnaire d'Ameublement et de la Décoration depuis le XIIIe Siècle Jusqu'à nos Jours*, I, Paris, 1887, 215–16.

[287] Waterer's definition of male as 'probably a kind of limp bale or holdall' is incomplete, since the evidence of 1386 shows that it might be of wood. (J. W. Waterer, 'Leather', ed. C. Singer, *History of Technology*, II, Oxford, 1957, 183.)

Middle Ages. Why were two items necessary (*bahut* plus *coffre*) — and it will be recalled that the *bahut* might be a substantial outer container, complete with ironwork and locks — when one leather-covered box without feet and with a domed lid would have fulfilled requirements more simply? And if extra protection were needed, surely a loose covering of waxed canvas or oiled skins could have been strapped about the box. I believe that the *bahut* was often, though not invariably, designed to accommodate a footed chest, so that important and valuable items such as clothing, chamber textiles and possibly books might be left undisturbed from one journey to another, by simply lifting the whole chest containing them into and out of a *bahut*. Thus packing was simplified and on arrival important goods were already suitably stored in footed chests away from dampness and other forms of infection injurious to their delicate contents. Clearly, this system was expensive and would have involved considerable extra weight in travelling; it would thus have been unsuitable for many requirements and here the unfooted chest with domed lid provided the alternative. We have, then, on the one side, a *bahut* protecting an inner container which was not necessarily designed for travelling, and on the other, a specifically baggage article. The evidence for the latter is firm and incontestable. Sources using French speak of 'coffre . . . a sommeer' (1334), 'coffre de soumier' (1337), and 'somme et coffre' (1395) for those chests which were designed to be strapped to the saddle of the sumpter horse. Sources using both French and English speak of trussing coffres: 'coffr' trussator' (1322); 'coffres a trusser' (1377); 'trussyng-cofrez' (1411); and 'trussyng cofres' (1416). Since to truss meant to pack close, it has always been accepted that the trussing coffer was a specifically baggage article, though whether it was necessarily a sumpter chest is not clear.

The term 'standard', however, is confined to English and, when applied to a chest,[288] is associated with the transportation of large quantities of goods (1467 entry below).[289] The term is accepted as describing the box form with domed lid, found in Cat. nos. 45–7. The correlation of the term with the box form (without feet) is confirmed in the 1395 entry, where we also learn that these particular standards were carried in a cart. Though normally described simply as a 'standard', 'cofrstandard' also occurs (1423), probably to avoid any confusion with another form of furniture, such as a bed.[290] Continental chests of standard form have survived and clearly the type was common enough; Havard believed that the French term was *bahut*.[291]

The evidence discussed so far has been neat and consistent and has enabled us to gain a fair picture of the different sorts of receptacles used for travelling. One or two descriptions, however, seem eccentric and it is perhaps instructive to note them here:

1240	*cista* not *coffre*
1312	*huche de bois* not *coffre*
1374 (2)	*coffre d'ozier couvers de cuir* not *bahut*
1380	*coffino in modum bogie* not *bogie*
1471	'long cofyns' not coffers.

[288] It could also mean other things, e.g. 1415: 'vn graunt poot de brass appell vn Standard', Kingsford 1918–20, 89.
[289] See Murray's *New English Dictionary*, 1888, *standard*.
[290] See evidence of 1392, p. 90.
[291] Havard, I, 214–15.

In view of attempts to discover a consistent and meaningful separation in the French terms *coffre* and *huche*, and the English terms coffer and chest the entries of 1240 and 1312 are of particular interest.[292]

The evidence of the English Cofferers' Ordinance of 1517, upon which Symonds based many of his conclusions regarding all forms of chest[293] is useful in acquainting us with the number of individual receptacles used for travel and storage, for without this Ordinance we might suspect duplications in terms which, in fact, did not exist.[294] However, this kind of evidence is disappointing for the Middle Ages, if we expect it to reflect precise demarcations between trades.

Liberate Rolls of Henry III:

1227 'Liberate to Godfrey Spigurnel 29s. 11d. to acquit certain new coffers (*cofras*) for the king's chapel, and new saddle-bags (*bargias*) for the saddle of the sumpter-horse (*summar'*) of the chapel, . . .'

1229 'Liberate to Thomas Spigurnel, sergeant of the king's chapel, 17s. 3d. to pay for the new equipment (*hernesium*) bought for the chapel, to wit a saddle for the sumpter-horse (*sumer'*), 6s., and for a chest (*barhut*), 6s., and for a housing (*huscia*), ? ?d., . . .'

1238 'Liberate to Godfrey Spygurnel, serjeant of the king's chapel, 17s. 5d. to pay for the new harness (*harnesium*) bought for the sumpter-horse (*summerium*) of the chapel, to wit for a sumpter-saddle (*summaricia sella*) 6s., for a chest (*barhut*) half a mark, . . .'
      [Items concerned with horse harness follow.]

1238 'Liberate to William de Eyswy . . . 12s. 3½d. for a sack and a [housing] (*huscia*) and waxed canvas (*canavacio incerato*) and other canvas (*et alio*) for trussing and packing (*trussianda et inponenda*) the things aforesaid.'

1240 'Liberate to Edward [son of Odo] . . . 5s. for a leather box (*cista*) made by the king's order to carry the image of St. Edward with the king in his wardrobe; . . .'

      (*Cal. Liberate Rolls, Henry III, I, 1226–1240*, London, 1916, 45, 144, 306, 356, 478.)

---

[292] See P. Ansart, 'Le Bahut, Meuble Essentiel du Moyen Age, *La Vie à La Campagne*, 1911, 243, where the simple correlation *bahut* = chest without feet, *huche* = footed chest is given. And R. W. Symonds, 'The Chest and Coffer: Their Difference in Function and Design', *Connoisseur*, CVII, 1941, 15–21, where a more complex set of requirements for each term is suggested: chest = wooden, footed, handle-less, flat lidded, the product of the woodworker; coffer = box form, leather covered, domed lid, with handles, the product of the leather worker.

[293] See fn. 292. But the flexible use of terms in the Middle Ages, together with the wide variety of forms and fittings for chests generally which is demonstrated in the references below, as well as in the Catalogue Raisonné, show that the rigidity suggested by Symonds is unrealistic.

[294] From it we learn that 'baggys, powches, malys, bowgettes, cloth sakkes, barhidys for covering carts, standardes and trussing coffreres' were all individual items; it is particularly relevant to note that the *malle*, standard and trussing coffer were all different.

1242   'Contrabreve to cause W. de Haverhull the treasurer to have eight good strong carts to carry the king's treasure to Winchester, and the men taking it to have a sure and safe escort for that journey.'

(Cal. Liberate Rolls, Henry III, II, 1240–1245, London, 1930, 150.)

1312   Account of the hôtel d'Artois.

'Pour 1 huche de bois, ou fu mise la tombe pour apporter a Pontoise 16s.'

(Dehaisnes, I, 206.)

(For a wooden huche for packing the tomb for transportation to Pontoise 16s.)

1322   Inventory of Roger de Mortimer.

'Garderobe domine . . . ij. coffr' trussator, . . .'

(A. B. Larking, 'Inventory of the Effects of Roger de Mortimer at Wigmore Castle and Abbey, Herefordshire', Archaeological Journal, xv, 1858, 361.)

1334   Inventory of goods of the Comtesse d'Artois.

'Item . . . un coffre viez de aes et de cuir noire à sommeer cloué, . . .'

(Delisle, 110.)

(An old chest for a sumpter horse of wooden boards with black leather attached with nails.)

1337   Inventory of goods of the Sire de Naste.

'Item, deus coffres de soumier vers a escus, prisiés   xxxs.'

(Dehaisnes, I, 320.)

(Item, 2 sumpter chests for strapping near the rider, value   30s.)

Duke of Burgundy's accounts.

1368   '. . . 2 grans males, garnies de bahuz, pour mettres ses robes, . . .'

(. . . 2 large malles complete with bahuts for them, for packing the duke's clothing . . .)

1374 (1)   '2013. . . . Pierre Du Fou, coffirier, . . . pour 3 males garnies de baüz et de courroyes, et pour une paires de bouges pour forge, et pour unes petites bouges à marreschaut, tout fermante à clerf, et pour une male de cerf, ferment à clerf, achetées de lui.'

(. . . Pierre Du Fou, coffrer, for 3 malles fitted with bahuts and with straps, and for a pair of bags for the forge, and for small bags for the farriery, all lockable with keys, and for a deerskin malle, lockable with a key, bought from him.)

1374 (2)   '2049. ... 11 fr. dus à Pierre Du Fou, coffrier, demeurant à Paris ...,
            pour 1 coffre d'ozier, couvers de cuir, ferrez, lesquelz il a faiz pour Mme.'

            (...11 fr. owed to Pierre Du Fou, coffrer, living in Paris ..., for a
            wicker chest covered with leather, with iron fittings, which he made for
            the Duchess of Burgundy.)

            (Prost, I, 159–60 (914); 374; 385.)

1376   Inventory of goods of the magnate Richard Lyons, in the wardrobe of his
            London house.

            'Item 1 clotheseke et 2 males oue 2 bosages, ...'

            (Myers 1969, 313.)

1377   Duke of Burgundy's accounts.

            '3143. 24 juin, la duchesse, à Rouvres, mandate 2 fr. à Jehan de Sainte-
            Menehost, sellier, de Dijon ..., pour une houce de cur qu'il avoit faite
            pour le coffre aus joiaux de Jehan monsr. et pour rencorner dos les 4
            cornez aud. coffre.'

            (Prost, I, 592.)

            (24th June, the Duchess of Burgundy, being at Rouvres, ordered payment
            of 2 fr. to Jehan de Sainte-Menehost, saddle-maker of Dijon ..., for a
            leather cover which he made for M. Jehan's jewel chest, and for putting
            corner peices of horn on the 4 corners of the said chest.

1377   A list headed:

            'Ceux sont lez joiaulx que Mons' Gwichard Dangle, counte de Huntyn-
            don, perdist a Osprenge.   Primerment, ces cofres a trusser, ...'

            (W. Paley Baildon, 'Three Inventories: (1) The Earl of Huntingdon,
            1377; (2) Brother John Randolf, 1419; (3) Sir John de Boys, 1426',
            Archaeologia, Second Series, XI, 1908, 164.)

            (These are the jewels which M. Guichard d'Angle, Earl of Huntingdon,
            lost at Ospringe.   Firstly, his trussing chests ...)

1378   Duke of Burgundy's accounts.

            '265. 6 novembre, ordonnancement par la duchesse, alors à Gand, à
            Jehan Le Lormier de Gand, pour une housse de cuir de vaiche, ... pour
            couvrir un grant coffre que ledit mons. le comte [de Flandres] donna a
            Mme, ...'

            (Prost, II, 40.)

            (6th November, commissioned by the Duchess, at present at Ghent, from
            Jehan Le Lorimier of Ghent, for a cover of cow hide ... for covering a
            large chest which the count gave to the Duchess of Burgundy.)

1380   Inventory of goods at the Château Cornillon.

'144. In tertio estagio turris . . . In primo coffino, qui est in modum bogie [lists textiles and plate].'

(Albanès, 209.)

(In the 3rd floor of the tower, in the first chest which is in the form of a saddle bag.)

1384   Will of John de Coggeshale of London.

'. . . a pair of *Trussyng-kofrers*.'

(Sharpe, II, 250.)

1386   Duke of Burgundy's accounts.

'1417. 17 Sept., 63 fr. à Pierre Du Fou, coffrier, demourant à Paris, c'est assavoir: pour 8 coffres garniz de behuz pour la chappelle de Mgr., dont il en a 2 paires à porter sur somme, et a en chascune paire de somme un autel à chanter, à 10 fr. la piece, 20 fr.; pour une paire de sommes à porter à sommier, 8 fr.; pour 3 grans coffres pour les aornemens de lad. chapelle, à 6 fr. l'un, 18 fr.; pour une male et 1 bahu fermant à clef, 7 fr.; pour un grant coffre long à mectre torches 4 fr. et pour les 3 bahuz 6 fr.'

(Prost, II, 229.)

(. . . to Pierre Du Fou, coffrer, living in Paris, for 8 chests fitted with their individual *bahuts*, for the Duke of Burgundy's chapel, of which 2 pairs are for carrying on a sumpter pack, and for each of these a portable altar, at 10 frs. each, total 20 frs.; for a pair of sumpter packs for carrying on a sumpter horse, 8 frs.; for 3 large chests for the ornaments of the said chapel, at 6 fr. each, 18 frs.; for a *malle* and 1 *bahut*, lockable with a key, 7 fr.; for a large, long chest for holding torches, 4 fr., and for the 3 *bahuts*, 6 fr.)

1386   Inventory of the goods of Arnaud Andrieu, Collecteur Apostolique for Narbonne province.

'360. Primo tres bahuti cum uno copertorio de corio. . .
361. Item allii duo et quedam bogie de corio nigro. . .
362. Item una mala de fusta . . .'

(Guiraud 1904/5, 373.)

(360. Firstly, 3 bahuts with 1 leather cover. . .
361. Item, the other 2 [coverings] and a curtain saddle bag of black leather.
362. Item, a *malle* of wood. . .)

Duke of Burgundy's accounts.

1386/7   'A Jehan Cosset, bourgoiz d'Arras, varlet de chambre de monseigneur, pour la vendue et delivrance de XII bahuz, ouvrez de tappisserie des armes de monseigneur d'euvre d'Arras, pour mettre sur les sommiers des offices de l'ostel de monseigneur, chascun d'iceulx bahuz tenant XII aulnes.   CVIII frans.'295

(To Jehan Cosset, bourgeois of Arras and 'Varlet de Chambre' to the Duke of Burgundy, for selling and delivering [to the duke] 12 *bahuts*, made of Arras tapestry and worked with the duke's arms, for putting on the sumpter horses of the offices of the duke's household, each of these *bahuts* being of 12 yards.   108 francs.)

1388   '2594. . . . à Pierre Du Fou, . . . pour . . . une paire de coffres couvers de *bahu*, garnis de courroies, à y mectre ses joyaux . . .'

(. . . to Pierre Du Fou . . . for . . . a pair of chests covered with *bahuts* and complete with straps, for holding the Duke of Burgundy's jewels.)

1389   '3235. . . . a Jehan Le Heron, coffrier, . . . 1 somme à mectre sur 1 sommier qui porta 2 coffres apres luy, esquelz avoit pluiseurs draps de soye . . .'

(To Jehan Le Heron, coffrer, 1 sumpter pack for putting on a sumpter horse which carries 2 chests behind [the saddle] in which are several lengths of silk.)

1390   '3598. 11 fr. audit coffrier [Jehan Le Heron of Paris] pour 2 coffrez fermans à cleif pour y mectre et porter les joiaulx de mons. le conte de Nevers . . . 1 bahu de cuir pour les couvrir . . . pour la chainete et ferrure d'une male a mectre son linge . . .'

(11 frs. to the said coffrer for 2 chests, lockable by means of keys, for holding and carrying the jewels of the Comte de Nevers . . . 1 leather *bahut* for covering them and for the small chain and ironwork of a *malle* for his linen . . .)

(Dehaisnes, II, 637; Prost, II, 398; 503–4; 606.)

1391   Inventory of the goods of Richard Toky.

'one *malesadell*, 2s. 8d.'

(Thomas 1932, 213.)

1395   Will of Lady Alice West.

'. . . a chariot [cart] with twey standardes heled with lether, which that serueth for myn harneys . . .'

(Furnivall 1882, 5.)

1395   Accounts of Guy, Seigneur de La Trémoille de Suly et de Craon.

'A Guillaume Roussel, voiturier . . . pour le salaire de lui et d'un cheval, pour avoir mené de Paris à Dijon, en un bahu, plusieurs robes brodées, une cotte d'armes et autres choses . . .'

295 See also 1389: 4 armorial tapestry *bahuts* for the Comte de Nevers (Prost, II, 550 (3381)); and 1391–2: 18 armorial tapestry *bahuts* for sumpter horses, each of 5 square yards of tapestry made in Paris (Dehaisnes, II, 687).

'A Robin Garnier, coffrier, . . . pour une somme et uns coffres ferrés et fermans à clef, es quelx fu portée la finance de Monseigneur à Dijon pour son voyaige de Hongrie . . .'

(La Trémoille 1890, 31, 35.)

(To Guillaume Roussel, carrier, for the hire of himself and a horse for having brought from Paris to Dijon, various embroidered clothes, in a *bahut* . . .

To Robin Garnier, coffrer, for a sumpter pack and an iron bound chest, lockable by key, to be used for carrying Monseigneur's money to Dijon for his journey to Hungary.)

1411   Will of Margaret de Cortenay.

'To Alice Donnyll, . . . my 'cofres' called 'Trussyngcofrez' and all my napery . . .'

(F. W. Weaver, 'Somerset Medieval Wills 1383–1500', *Somerset Record Society*, XVI, 1901, 51.)

1416   Action for debt concerning Bonaverus of Bologna and Peter Alfons of Portugal.

'1 pair of *trussyngcofres.*'

(Thomas 1943, 49.)

1423   Inventory of goods of Henry V.

'Item, III cofrstandard' liez de ferr', en la Garderobe du Prince, pris en toutz   XL s.'

(*Rot. Parl.*, IV, 239.)

(Item 3 standard chests bound with iron in the Prince's wardrobe, total value   40*s.*)

1446   Inventory of the Prior of Durham Abbey.

'Garderoba . . . Item ij Barehidez.'

(Raine 1834/5, 93.)

1466   Inventory of goods of the Duchess of Suffolk.

'Stuff brought from Wingefeld to Ewelme in a Standard [contents, chapel textiles, etc.].'

(*Historical MSS Commission, Appendix to 8th Report*, 1881, 628.)

c. 1471   Black Book of Edward IV.

'§90. OFFICE OF CHAUNDELERY: . . .

All other necessarijs, as . . . long cofyrs . . . Here hath byn vsed a sompter man and hors for the king and chambre and hall to carry the long cofyns, with grete and smale lightes redy at nede . . .'

(Myers 1959, 190–1.)

1502   Privy Purse expenses of Queen Elizabeth of York.

'Itm . . . to John Hertley for the amending of the barehide belonging to the close carre of the wardrobe of the robys   vs. . . .
Itm a grete trussing basket   vjd. . .
Itm . . . for a barrell of greese . . . for lycoryng of the Quenes barehydes xij s.'

(Nicolas 1830, 16, 19, 37.)

1509   Inventory of the goods of Edmund Dudley.

'. . . a coueryng of lether for a cart . . .'

(Kingsford 1920/1, 42.)

A form of travelling chest which was clearly distinct from chests used on sumpter horses or in carts was the chest for taking on board ship.

1322   Inventory of goods of Robert de Bethune, Comte de Flandres, at Courtrai.

'Item, un coffre de mer qui fu Huon le Jouene, ou quel il a lettres . . .'

(Dehaisnes, I, 245.)

(Item, a ship chest made by Huon the joiner, containing papers.)

c. 1350   Debts of Jehan d'Annechin, bourgeois of Tournai.

'Pour I coffre de mer ou il y a pluseurs joiaus,   xls.'

(Dehaisnes, I, 370.)

(For I ship chest containing various jewels.)

1388   Inventory of goods at the Chastel de Rupplemonde, held by the Duke of Burgundy.

'2110. Un coffre de mer de 4 piez ou environ, ferré et à sarrure et bougon, ouquel l'en met les ornemens de la chapelle.'

(Prost, II, 350.)

(A ship chest of about 4 ft. long, iron bound and lockable ?with fitted pockets, used for keeping chapel ornaments.)

1415   Will of Edward Cheyne.

'a shipchest att London with yren . . .'

(Jacob 1937, 47.)

1417   Will of William Hugham.

'Unam cistam vocatam shipcofre et j arcum; . . .'

(Jacob 1937, 105.)

(A chest called a ship chest and I ark [chest].)

1426   Inventory of goods in the Château des Baux.

             '31. Item, i arche de marine de nouguier en quoy ma dicte dame soloit
             tenir ses meilheurs lettres de son trésor, . . .'

             (Barthélemy, 141.)

             (Item, 1 ship chest of walnut, in which my lady was accustomed to keep
             the most important papers of her treasury . . .)

1477   Will of Alice Colyn.

             '. . . a *ship chest*.'

             (Sharpe, II, 576.)

We see from these references that the ship chest was characterized by at least one of the
principles common to all chests designed for travel in that it had a domed lid (an ark —
see 1426); yet though like an ark chest it was not precisely the same (see 1417, 1426);
it might be of walnut (1426); and it might be strapped with iron (1388, 1415) and fitted
with locks and ?pockets (1388).

   We have examined baggage articles at some length in order to appreciate the diversity
of the equipment which served the needs of travelling households and to note in some
detail the problems regarding terminology. Let us now look at other evidence concerning the uses of chests in different contexts.

2.   Chests storing coin

1238   Henry III.

             'To John de Lexinton and William de Peretot and his fellows, appointed
             receive the thirtieth of Noting [ham]. *Contrabreve* to buy chests and canvas
             (*archas* et *canevaz*) to place the thirtieth in.'

             (*Cal. Lib.* R., *Henry III*, 1, 314.)

1321   Inventory of goods of Eudes de Mareuil.

             'In magna cista debent esse quinquaginta libre in parvis parisiensibus in
             quodam saculo . . .'

             (Le Blond, 18.)

             (In a great chest there ought to be 50 livres (Paris) in small coin in a
             certain bag.)

1331   Inventory of the goods of Jean Haut-de-Cœur.

             'CC ij lb iiij s. parisis en XVI.ˣˣXVII royaus dor de XII. s. parisis le pieche
             trouve en le huge dudit Jehan. XXIIj lb. VIs. VIII d. p. XL. aigniaus dor
             de xj s. VIIJ. d. parisis trouves en celi huge.'

             (F. Brassard, 'Inventaire, après décès, de Jean Haut-de-Cœur', *Mémoires
             de la Société Impériale d'Agriculture, Sciences et Arts, séant à Douai*, 2 série II,
             1852/3, 273.)

(202 lb. 4s. Paris in 337 gold 'royals' of 12s. Paris the piece, found in the chest of the said Jehan; 23 lb. 6s. 8d. Paris, 40 gold 'lambs' of 11s. 18d. Paris, found in this chest.)

1361   Will of Michael de Northburgh, Bishop of London.

'. . . he leaves one thousand marks, to be placed in a chest to stand in the treasury of St. Paul's, for advancing loans, . . .'

(Sharpe, ii, 62.)

1426   Will of Thomas Beaufort, Duke of Exeter.

'. . . lego & assigno c li. ad deponend' in secura cista infra collegium Regine in universitate Oxon', . . .'

(Nichols, 255.)

(I leave £100 to be deposited in a strong chest in Queen's College at Oxford university.)

c. 1471   Black Book of Edward IV.

'§14 . . . Item the King offerithe or sendithe to the shryne of Seint Thomas of Canterbury . . . iiij florynes of golde, fro his priuy cofers yerely.'

'§73. COFFERER of the kinges housholld, wych takyth in charge all the receytes for the thesaurer of houshold, as of money . . .'
(Myers 1959, 91, 150.)

3.   Chests storing plate and personal jewels

1200   '. . . et post intravit in cameram suam et fregit archas suas et cepit coclearia sua argentea et aurum et argentum et pannos uxoris sue et anulos et firmacula sua et proprios anulos extraxit de digitis . . .'

(*Curia Regis Rolls of the Reigns of Richard I & John I, 1196–1201*, H.M.S.O., 1922, 255.)

(. . . and after he had entered his room he broke his chests and took out his silver spoons and his gold and silver and his wife's cloth and her rings and brooches, and taking his own rings from his fingers . . .)

1321   Inventory of goods at the Château d'Hesdin.

'. . . en une autre huche . . . [lists plate]'

(Dehaisnes, i, 235.)

1379   Duke of Burgundy's accounts.

'351. . . . au Put Hoste, dud. Chastillon pour le fust et facon d'un coffre qu'il a fait pour mettre la vaisselle d'argent de mad. damoiselle et 20 s.t. à Huguenin Le Serrurier pour ferrer led. coffre.'

(Prost, ii, 56–7.)

K

(. . . to Put Hoste, living at Chastillon, for the wood and the making of a chest, made by Put Hoste for holding the silver plate of the said Damoiselle, and 20 s.t. to Huguenin the Locksmith for the ironwork on the said chest.)

1384   Inventory of goods of Jeanne La Boiteuse, Duchesse de Bretagne.

'Item un coffre ferré couvert de cuir . . . [lists plate]'

(A. de La Borderie, 'Inventaire des Meubles de Jeanne La Boiteuse, Duchesse de Bretagne', *Révue des Provinces de l'Ouest*, I, 1854, 207.)

(Item an iron bound chest, covered with leather.)

1393/4   'Item in j parva cofre empta pro jocalibus domini trussandis, xiij d.'

(W. Paley Baildon, 'A Wardrobe Account of 16/17 Richard II 1393–4', *Archaeologia*, 2nd Series, XII, 1911, 510.)

(Item, 1 small chest bought for trussing the lord's jewels, 13*d*.)

1426   Inventory of goods at the Château des Baux.

'. . . en la grand chambre de la tour, là ou mourut madame . . . ung autre coffre qui s'appelle *des joyaux*, ront ferré . . .' [contained jewels]

(Barthélemy 1877, 131, 132.)

(. . . in the great chamber in the tower, where Madame died . . . another chest, round and iron bound, which is called 'the jewels'.)

1427   Will of John Coventre.

'Volo eciam quod omnia vasa mea aurea, argentea et deaurata ac omnia iocalia mea . . . fuerint reponantur in quandam forti cista cum ferro bene ligata et quatuor seris diversis serata in illa cista . . . volo quod quilibet executorum meorum habeat unam clavem, . . .'

(Jacob 1937, 406.)

(I will also that all my gold, silver and silver-gilt plate and all my jewels . . . be placed in a certain strong chest well bound with iron, and with 4 different locks to the chest . . . I wish that each of my executors should have a key.)

1450   Will of Johan Bukland.

'. . . a flat pece gilt uncou'ed which is in a Standard at London at Seint Thomas of Acres.'

(Gibbons, 181.)

4.   Chests storing textiles

1200   See entry from *Curia Regis Rolls*, p. 121.

1334   Inventory of goods at Quatremares held by Robert d'Artois, after the arrest of his wife Jeanne de Valois.

'. . . ouvrismes et desseellames les huches . . . et en la première trouvasmes les choses qui ensuivent: Premièrement VIII grant pièces de biaux doubliers touz nuez, et une grant pièce de toille.
Item VI pièces de longues touailles à mettre sus table, . . .'

(Delisle, 111.)

(. . . on opening the chests . . . in the first was found the following things: firstly, 8 large pieces of beautiful *doubliers*, quite new, and a large piece of linen.
Item, 6 pieces of long cloth for putting on tables . . .)

1365   'It. une huche plate, et pardedans vint linssols de telle blanche et dix linssols de telle de Rains fine et deliée.'

(P. Marchegay, 'Inventaire des Meubles ayant appartenu à Madame de Royan, Mère de la Comtesse de Périgord', *Révue des Sociétés Savantes* 5 série, V, 1873, 482.)

(Item, a flat [lidded] chest, and within it 20 *linssols* of white cloth and 10 *linssols* of cloth of *Rennes* [fine sheeting] delicate and ?loosely woven.)

1371   From the Hostillar's rolls, Durham Abbey.
'1 archa ferro lig. pro pannis laneis et lineis imponend.'

(*Surtees Society*, 1898, 130.)

(1 iron bound chest for keeping woollen and linen cloth.)

1375   Duke of Burgundy's accounts.
'2371. . . . 20 fr. . . . pour 2 grans coffres à mettre partie des robes de Mgr, . . .'

(Prost, I, 449.)

(. . . 20 fr. . . . for 2 large chests for holding some of the Duke's clothes.)

1390   Duke of Burgundy's accounts.
'3597. Jehan Le Heron, coffrier, demourant à Paris, pour un grant coffre fermant à deux serrures, à mectre les robes de mons. le Comte de Nevers, 8 fr; . . .'

(Prost, II, 606.)

([To] Jehan Le Heron, coffrer, living in Paris, for a large chest, locked with 2 locks, for holding the Comte de Nevers's clothes,   8 fr; . . .)

1393   Will of Elizabeth la Warre.
'. . . j par Trussyngcofres in quibus solebam imponere sericum.'

(Gibbons, 85.)

(1 pr. trussing coffers in which I am accustomed to keep silk.)

1403   Purchase of a *layette* for the Comtesse de Rethel.

'27. A Robin Garnier, coffrier, demourant à Paris, pour deux coffres couvers de cuir, fermant à deux clefs, ung grant et ung moien, fermant à une clef seulement, prins et achettés de lui, c'est assavoir, le grant pour mettre et tenir les draps et couvertures devant dittes, et le moien pour tenir les drappeaulx et linges nécessaires pour la ditte gessine, pour ce 14 fr.'

(Garnier, 608.)

(To Robin Garnier, coffrer, living in Paris, for 2 leather covered chests, [the largest] locked with 2 keys, the chests being large and smaller [and the smaller] locked with 1 key only, taken and bought from the said Robin, the large chest to contain and store the above mentioned lengths of cloth coverings, and the smaller chest to contain the hangings and linens necessary for the said expected birth, for these [chests] 14 fr.)

1405   Inventory of the Duchess of Burgundy.

10 chests listed containing textiles, mostly linen:

'S'ensuivent plusieurs biens moebles, estans en plusieurs coffres en la salle au bout de la grant salle, la quelle ou l'en sauloit tenir conseil, les quelz coffres sont signé par lettres . . .'

(Dehaisnes, II, 887–900.)

(The following items, various goods which are personal property, stored in some chests in the hall at the end of the great hall, in the room where it was customary to hold council, which chests are marked with letters . . .)

1435   Inventory of the goods of Pierre Surreau.

'En la grant salle . . . une huche de quesne ouvrée, que l'en disoit estre la huche donnée en mariage à la femme dud. Jehan Surreau, avec les biens de dedans estans cy après déclairez . . .' [list of textiles including clothing.]

(Félix, 68, 71.)

(In the great hall . . . a carved oak chest, which one has been told is a chest given to the said Jehan Surreau's wife on her marriage, with the goods inside it which are listed below . . .)

1463   Will of John Baret of Bury.

'. . . a lityl grene coffre for kerchys, stondyng in my stodye, . . .'

(Tymms, 33.)

1496   Inventory of goods at the Château de Montbeton.

'31. Item plus en ladita granda cambra un grand coffre armat e cubert de cuer e de fer, loqual era clavat, e foc ubert e desbotat per forsa, e sans clau; en local a ung gran tros de folraduras de pels negras.'

(Forestié, 42.)

(Item, in addition, in the said great chamber, a large armorial chest, iron bound and covered with leather, which was locked and was opened by force, without keys; in which chest were a great number of black furs.)

1502   Privy Purse expenses of Queen Elizabeth of York.
'. . . for making a newe key to a grete standard being in the warderobe of the robys and for mending of boeth lokkes to the same, vj d.'
(Nicolas 1830, 68.)

1509   Inventory of the goods of Edmund Dudley.
'. . . a sprewis coffer, wherein is a carpet . . .'
(Kingsford 1921, 40.)

5.   Chests for Vestments and Chapel Ornaments
1246   Inventory of goods of the Abbey of Saint-Sernin de Toulouse.
'. . . 11e arche vel scrinia in quibus reponuntur panni, et IIIIᵒʳ candelabra et 1 turibulum de cupro.'
(Douais, 17.)
(. . . second chest or *scrinia* in which there is kept cloth, and 4 gold candelabra in 1 copper censer.)

1261   Henry III.
To Richard de Freitmantell, keeper of the manors of Cokham and Braye. '*Contrabreve* . . . to buy a chest (*coffrum*) to hold the vestments of the king's chapel; . . .'
(*Cal. Lib. R.*, v, 14.)

1351   Will of Johanna Cros.
'. . . a large Flemish chest for keeping books, vestments, and other ecclesiastical ornaments, . . .'
(Sharpe, 1, 665.)

1367   Goods of Guillaume de Cussigney, seized by the Duke of Burgundy.
'En la chapelle de la fort maison de Cussigney . . .
779. . . . une arche plate, en quoy sont li vestemans de l'autel; . . .'
(Prost, 1, 136.)
(In the chapel of the fortified house of Cussigney . . .
779. . . . a flat [lidded] chest, in which are the altar vestments.)

1379/80   Inventory of Charles V.
At St Germain-en-Laye:
'ITEM, EN LA CHAPELLE EMPRÈS L'ESTUDE DU ROY FUT TROUVÉ EN UNE HUCHE CE QUI S'ENSUIT . . .' [lists chapel plate and textiles.]

(Labarte, 234.)

(Item, in the chapel close to the king's study, were found the following items, in a chest . . .)

1384/5   Chapel of the infirmary, Durham Abbey.

'1 parve cista cum cruce deaurata et reliquiis.'

(*Surtees Society* 1898, 264.)

(1 small chest with a silver-gilt cross and other things.)

1416   Inventory of goods at the Château de Chailloué.

'Item, une huche où l'on met les vestemens de la chapelle et les oreilliers.'

(de Robillard de Beaurepaire, 19.)

(Item, a chest where one puts the chapel vestments and head cushions.)

1429   Will of Gerald Braybroke.

'. . . ij cofres bounden with yren oon to serve for vestimentes the other for bokes . . .'

(Jacob 1937, 411.)

1449   Will of William Bruges, Garter King of Arms.

'Item, I bequethe and ordeyne to the seyd chirch of St. George of Staunford a little coffre, standyng bounded wyth plate of yren, ful of vestments. (Nicolas, I, 1826, 269.)

1481   Will of Sir Thomas Lyttelton, Knight.

'. . . I wull, that a bigger cofer, and locke and key be provyded for the safe kepyng of these vestments and chales, within the Chapel of Frankley, and the Lord of Frankley for the time being have the keping of the said key by himself, . . .'

(Nicolas, 1826, 365.)

6.   Chests for Muniments

1259   Henry III.

Entry in the rolls concerning locks for the great chest (*cistam*) for the rolls for the Great Exchequer.

(*Calendar of the Liberate Rolls. VI 1267–1272*, H.M.S.O., 1964, 271 (2301B).)

1353   'Et quedam archa, in qua erant multi libri et cartularii, . . .'

(F. Vernet, 'Inventaires après décès des Biens de Pierre de Chalus, Evêque de Valence et de Die, Remis à la Chambre Apostolique d'Avignon', *Bulletin d'Histoire Écclesiastique et d'Archéologie Religieuse des Diocèses de Valence, Gap, Grenoble et Viviers*, IIe année, 1891, 201.)

(And a certain chest, in which were numerous books and registers, . . .)

1384/5   Duchess of Burgundy's accounts.

'i coffre à metre les escroes de l'ostel   xxs.'

(Canat de Chizy, 1898, 296.)

(1 chest to contain the entries concerning daily dispensations of food, etc., for the household,   20s.)

1407   Henry IV.

'. . . fuyt delivre en la T'szorie p Robt Fry Clerc une box contenant 1 alliance de Duc de Bretaign . . .'[296]

(Sir Francis Palgrave, *The Antient Kalendars and Inventories of the Treasury of His Majesty's Exchequer*, II, London, 1836, 76.)

(Delivery made to the treasury by Robert Fry, clerk, of a box containing 1 treaty of the Duc de Bretagne.)

1416   Inventory of goods in the Château de Chailloué.

'. . . une autre huche où l'en met des papiers.'

(de Robillard de Beaurepaire, 20.)

(. . . another chest where one puts papers.)

1418   Will of John Streche.

'. . . cistam meam apud Ayssh' pro evidenciis suis custodiendis.'

(Jacob 1937, 141.)

(. . . my chest at Ayssh' for storing her papers.)

1426   Inventory of the Château des Baux.

'3. Item, iii. grans arches vielles, plaines de vielles lettres et instrumens.'

(Barthélemy, 147.)

(Item, 3 old chests, full of old papers and instruments.)

1435   Inventory of Pierre Surreau.

'. . . plusieurs escriptures, . . . mis en ung grant coffre.'

(Félix, 6–7.)

(. . . various papers, placed in a large chest.)

7.   Chests for Books

1287   Statutes of Exeter Diocese.

'. . . cista ad libros et vestimenta.'

(F. M. Powicke/C. R. Cheney, *Councils and Synods*, II, Oxford, 1964, 1006.)

(. . . chests for books and vestments.)

---

[296] See the extant chests of the Treasury of Receipt, C. Jenning[s], *Early Chests in Wood and Iron*, H.M.S.O., 1974, I and II.

1321   Inventory of goods at the Château d'Hesdin.

'Item, en une autre huche, XIII romans que grans que petis.'

(Dehaisnes, I, 236.)

(Item, in another chest, 13 books of romance both large and small.)

1353   Books stored in an *archa*, see p. 126.

1379/80   Inventory of Charles V.

'LIVRES . . . EN UNG AUTRE ESCRIN . . . À DEUX COUVESCLES
EN L'UNE DES PARTIES DUQUEL COFFRE ESTOIENT LES
PARTIES QUI S'ENSUIVENT . . .' [follows list of chapel books.]

(Labarte, 336.)

(Books . . . in another *escrin* . . . with 2 lids, and in one of the divisions
of the said *coffre* are the following:)

1389   Duke of Burgundy's accounts.

'3235. Payé . . . à Jehan Le Heron, coffrier . . . pour . . . 1 autre coffre
à mectre ses rommans . . .'

(Prost, II, 503–4.)

(Paid . . . to Jehan Le Heron, coffrer . . . for . . . 1 other chest to contain
the duke's romances.)

1426   Inventory of goods at the Château des Baux.

'La chambre neve du parement . . .

59. Item, i. coffre rouge ferré en quoy a xx rommans.'

(Barthélemy, 137, 139.)

(The new state chamber . . . Item, i red iron bound chest in which are 20
books of romance.)

1429   Books stored in 'cofres bounden with yren', see p. 126.

1471   Inventory of goods in the Château d'Angers.

'S'ensuyvent les livres qui sont en ung des autres coffres de ladite gallerie.'

(Godard-Faultrier, 77.)

(The following are the books in one of the other chests in the said gallery.)

1480   Privy Purse expenses of Queen Elizabeth of York.

'. . . to Robert Boillett for blac papir and nailles for closyng and fastenyng
of divers cofyns of fyrre wherein the Kinges books were conveyed and
caried from the Kinges grete Warderobe in London unto Eltham . . .'

(Nicolas 1830, 125.)

8.   Chests for Arms and Armour

c. 1317   Will of Robert Blound.
             '. . . all his armour lying in a chest in his manse . . .'
             (Sharpe, I, 274.)

Duke of Burgundy's accounts:

1368   '914. . . . vente par Pierre Du Fou, coffrier, . . . 2 grans coffres, pour
             mettre le harnois de guerre de Mgr, . . .'
             (. . . purchased from Pierre Du Fou, coffrer, . . . 2 large chests for the Duke's
             battle armour, . . .)

1375   '2362. . . . une arche à mectre les arbelestres de Mgr., pour envoier
             en Bourgoingne, . . .'
             (. . . a chest for the Duke's cross-bows, for despatching to Burgundy, . . .)

1386   '1503. . . . a Pierre Du Fou . . . pour 2 grans coffres esquelz on a menez
             les bannieres, pannons et estandars par mer et par terre, 16 fr. . . .'
             (. . . to Pierre Du Fou [payment] for 2 large chests in which to carry the
             banners, pennants and standards by sea and by land, 16 francs. . .)

1388   '2553. . . . Guillaume Le Blonc, arbalestrier du roy . . . pour le portage
             de 240 arbalestres et l'achat de 15 coffres faconnez à mettre icelles,
             lesquelles furent menées en l'ostel d'Artois de Mgr. à Paris, . . .'
             (. . . Guillaume Le Blonc, bowmaker to the king [of France] . . . for trans-
             porting 240 bows and for the purchase of 15 chests made to hold the said
             bows, all brought to the Duke of Burgundy's hôtel d'Artois in Paris, . . .)

1390   '3597. Jehan Le Heron, coffrier, . . . pour . . . 1 autre coffre long et
             estroit pour mectre ses ars et fleches, 4 fr.'
             (Jehan Le Heron, coffrer, . . . for . . . another chest, long and narrow for
             holding the Duke's bows and arrows, 4 fr.)
             (Prost, I, 159–60; 447; Prost, II, 248; 387; 606.)

1393/4   Wardrobe account of Richard II.
             '. . . j paire de cofres emptis pro armuris . . .'
             (Baildon 1911, 512.)
             (. . . 1 pair of chests bought for holding arms. . .)

9.   Chests for lights

1284–6   Accounts of Bogo de Clare.
             'Item pro vna serrura empta ad vnam Cistam de Candelario   .iij.d.o.'
             (Giuseppi, 34.)
             (Item, for a lock bought for a chest of the office of lights   3*d*.)

1375   Duke of Burgundy's accounts.

'2244. ...a Pierre Du Fou, coffrier, et Michiel Travers, huchier, demeurans Paris ..., pour l'achat ... d'une huche à mettre torches et un coffre ferrez à porter chandoilles sur un sommier.'

(Prost, 1, 423–4.)

(...to Pierre Du Fou, coffrer, and Michiel Travers, *huchier*, living in Paris ..., for the purchase of ... a chest for torches and an iron bound chest for carrying candles on a sumpter-horse.)

1380   Inventory of goods at the Château de Cornillon.

'143. Item, una alia archa pro torticiis, longua et viridis.'

(Albanès, 209.)

(Item, another chest for torches, being long and green.)

1415   Will of Edward Cheyne.

'... a cofre to put yn wax y bounde with yren; ...'

(Jacob 1937, 47.)

10.   Chests for grain and bread

1227   Henry III.

'To the sheriff of Oxford. *Contrabreve* to cause to be made ... 1 garner (*granarium*) in the spense (*dispensa*) of his hall at Oxford to place his bread in, ...'

(*Cal. Lib. R. Henry III*, 1, 14.)

1367   Goods seized by the Duke of Burgundy, formerly belonging to the Seigneur de Cussigney, at Cussigney.

'En la sale:
791. Une arche plate, de chaaigne, ou il ai environ 10 *boisseaulx* de pois bis, à la mesure de Nuiz.'

(Prost, 1, 137.)

(A flat [lidded] chest of oak, where there is about 10 *boisseaulx* of dried peas, by the Nuiz standard of measure.)

1377   Will of Richard Groom.

'a chest called "Cornencheste".'

(Sharpe, 11, 199.)

1417   Will of Thomas Payn.

'... j cista ligata cum ferro continente ij busellos ...'

(Jacob 1937, 122.)

(... 1 iron bound chest containing 2 bushels...)

1435   Inventory of goods of Pierre Surreau.

            'En la despense . . . une petitte huchette on l'en met le pain . . .'

            (Félix, 50, 51.)

            (In the Spense, a little chest where one keeps bread.)

1468   Inventory of goods at the Château de Chateaudun.

            'Item, en l'eschansonnerie, . . . ung coffre à mettre le pain, . . .'[297]

            (Jarry, 125.)

            (Item, in the Buttery . . . a chest for keeping bread.)

1471   Inventory of goods in the Château d'Angers.

            'En la panneterie . . .

            Item deux huges à mectre pain dont lune a couvercle fermant à clef, et
            l'autre non, . . .'

            (Godard-Faultrier, 65.)

            (In the Pantry . . Item, 2 chests for bread, of which 1 has a lid lockable by
            key, and the other is without, . . .)

1485   Inventory of goods at the taking up of a lease on a house in Botolf Lane,
            London (inalienable goods).

            '. . . a grete bynn to leye in otes.'

            (Littlehales, 29.)

11.   Miscellaneous uses of chests

For spices

1361   Account of the executors of Jeanne de Bretagne.

            'La huche ou estoient les espices de cuisine fu aportée a Paris, . . .'

            (Dehaisnes, 1, 426.)

            (The chest in which were the kitchen spices taken to Paris, . . .)

As a coffin

1361   Will of Humphrey de Bohun, Earl of Hereford and Essex.

            '. . . ns . . . voiloms q'une huche soit faite auxi com' pur n're corps . . .'

            (Nichols, 45.)

            (. . . we . . . wish that a chest be also made for our body . . .)

---

[297] Normally, bread was kept in the Pantry (see 1471 entry, this page), wine in the Buttery (*Echansonnerie*), see
Canat de Chizy, 1898, 247.

For workshop tools

1372   Duke of Burgundy's accounts.

'Pour 2 coffres, achetez de Jehan l'archier, de Dijon, pour mettre les garnisons doud. Marville et ses instrumens à ouvrer,   25 s.'

(Prost, 1, 276.)

(For 2 chests, bought from Jehan the ark maker, of Dijon, for holding the decorative materials of the said Marville and his working tools, 25s.)

For salting meat

1372/3   Duke of Burgundy's accounts.

'1645. . . . pour 1 huis de bois . . . [qu'on] a fait mettre ou cellier de la tour de Villers, pour mettre et saler les venoisons de Mgr.'

(Prost, 1, 309.)

(. . . for a wooden chest for placing in the cellar of the tower of the Chateau of Villiers [-le-Duc], for placing the Duke's venison in, for it be to salted.)

For paints

1376   Duke of Burgundy's accounts.

'. . . à regnaut de Gray, serrurier, demorant à Dijon, pour ouvraiges de son mestier . . . c'est assavoir . . . serrures, . . . en 1 coffre pour garder l'ouvraige dud. paintre [Jehan de Beaumez] et les coleurs de Mgr.'

(Prost, 1, 525.)

(. . . to Regnaut de Gray, locksmith, living in Dijon, for works in his craft, that is to say . . . locks, . . . on a chest for the safe storage of the work of the said painter [Jehan de Beaumez] and the Duke of Burgundy's paints [which the said painter uses].)

For storing [glass] windows

1376   Inventory of the goods of Richard Lyons.

'2 standardes de fer pur 1 fenestre.'[298]

(Myers 1969, 318, fn. 98.)

(2 iron standard chests for 1 window.)

For saddles and harness

1384   Inventory of goods of Jeanne La Boiteuse, Duchesse de Bretagne.

'Item une grant huche plate où sont la belle selle de la haquenée de Madamme avec tout son hernois . . . En la dicte huche a esté mis le coffret long de bois où sont les reliquiaires coutenuz ci dessus . . .'

---

[298] Chests which are entirely of iron, rather than being of iron plates laid over wood, were rare in the Middle Ages; see Eames 1974, 4, fn. 14.

(La Borderie 1854, 206.)

(Item, a large flat [lidded] chest containing the fine saddle belonging to Madame's riding horse, together with all its harness . . . In the said chest is a long wooden coffer containing the remainder of the things belonging to the above . . .)

For storing alabaster

1385   Duke of Burgundy's accounts.

'1268. . . . Henry de Langres, serrurier demorant à Dijon, . . . pour la ferrure garnie de fraictiz et de serrures de fer par lui faites et mises en 5 arches, lesquelles sont en l'ovreur de Jehan de Marville, ouvrier et varlet de chambre de Mgr à Dijon, pour mectre et garder des pierres d'alabastre de la sepulture et besoingne qu'il fait pour Mgr . . .'

(Prost, II, 196.)

(. . . Henry de Langres, locksmith, living in Dijon, . . . for the ironwork bent round [the chests] and for the iron locks made by him and placed upon the 5 chests, which chests are in the workshop of Jehan de Marville, craftsman and 'Varlet de Chambre' to the Duke, at Dijon, for storing and preserving safely the alabaster stones of the tomb which he is making for the Duke . . .)

For storing gofering irons for wafers

1405   Inventory of the Duchess of Burgundy.

'Item, 1 grant coffre tout noef, estant en la paneterie, on quel ont esté trouvé III fers de gauffres et 1 petit fer a faire oublies . . .'

(Dehaisnes, II, 914.)

(Item, 1 large chest in the Pantry which is entirely new, in which one finds 3 gofering irons and 1 small iron for making the *oublies* . . .)

For medicines

c. 1471   Black Book of Edward IV.

'§45. Mastyr Surgeoune . . . And in this office a small cofer, with playsters and medycens for the king and his houshold, assigned by the countroller . . .'

(Myers 1959, 125.)

Chests as footstools/bedsteps

1471   Inventory of goods in the Château de La Menitré.

'. . . en la chambre du roy . . . deux coffres longs de boys servans de marchpié fermans a deux claveures chascun et ung marchepié par terre en la venelle dudict lit . . .'

(Godard-Faultrier, 90.)

'. . . in the king's chamber [René d'Anjou] 2 long wooden chests each closed with 2 locks and serving as footstools or steps to the ground [from the bed] placed in the passage beside the said bed. . .)

Apart from this evidence showing that chests fulfilled almost universal storage requirements, much other information may be gleaned from records to complement the evidence of extant chests. Dealing firstly with evidence effecting *form*, we hear of round chests;[299] of altar chests in continental sources to balance the English evidence provided by the extant altar chest at Newport, Essex (pls. 64B–65);[300] and of chests which served as counters, perhaps resembling the 'Fares' chest in the Victoria and Albert Museum.[301] A few chests with two or more lids, and with divisions inside, survive in England, e.g. at Winchester College,[302] and records show that this adaptable feature was also appreciated in France.[303] Let us now turn to evidence which might bear upon chests of many forms.

Locking arrangements for chests were obviously of the greatest importance and the attention given to them in records indicates that the *number* of locks involved was connected with custodianship, rather than with the value of the contents. We know that the surviving common chest of London's Guildhall, of *c.* 1427, had six locks with individual keys which were held by designated officers;[304] and a London merchant, in his will of 1427, left the four keys of his chest of plate individually to each of his executors.[305] Arrangements of this kind ensured that chests could only be opened when all those responsible for the contents were present. In certain cases, however important the contents, trust was much more narrowly confined than in these instances. Charles V of France, who himself supervised the compilation of the inventory of his movables in 1379, decided that only one other person beside himself should hold a key of the chest in the exchequer in which this document was stored;[306] and John of Gaunt held the single key of a certain small jewel chest.[307] Locked chests were frequently sealed, so that the persons who last checked their contents were readily identifiable; this procedure was particularly important and useful in cases involving a death or a seizure of goods.[308]

---

[299] Two round, iron bound chests were in the episcopal palace at Alet in 1354 (Guiraud 1904/5, 204); another two, also iron-bound, were used for Cardinal Arnaud Andrieu's plate in 1386 (Guiraud 1904/5, 334). See also the entry of 1426, p. 122.

[300] In 1388 in the Duke of Burgundy's accounts (Prost, II, 398, *2594*), and in the chapel of the Château des Baux in 1426 (Barthélemy, 129, *4*).

[301] For example, 1415: list of goods forfeited by Henry le Scrope. 'Item, vn Chest appell vn countour . . .' (Kingsford 1918–20, 89). Also 1477, will of Alice Colyn, '*a spruce desked cofer*' (Sharpe, II, 576).

[302] Three-lidded chest (box form) assembled *in situ* in the Audit Room and recorded in 1432/3; see Oakeshott, 8.

[303] For example, entry of 1379/80, p. 128; and 1420, in the Château de Vincennes (Douet d'Arcq, 459). Divided interiors are also mentioned, e.g. in 1380 (Albanès, 217); and 1429 (Le dr. Francus, 'Inventaire de la Commanderie des Antonins, à Aubenas en Vivarais', *Bulletin d'Histoire Ecclésiastique et d'Archéologie des Diocèses de Valance, Gap, Grenoble et Viviers*, 7e année, 1886/7, 149).

[304] See Eames 1974, 2.

[305] Will of John Coventre (Jacob 1937, 406).

[306] Labarte, III; the chest had 2 locks.

[307] We learn this from his will of 1398; see Armitage-Smith, 426.

[308] Wax for sealing a chest (*arche*) is referred to in 1220 (*Cal. Lib. R.*, VI, 240 (2157)); in a fourteenth-century context, the practice is referred to in Delisle, III; see also the entry of 1305 concerning the chest bearing the seal of J. de Wengrave (Thomas 1924, 200).

Frequently, keys were lost and locks forced,[309] and new locks had to be made[310] and the visual evidence of this kind of mishap exists on the majority of surviving chests.

Chests with iron rings at the ends are common, and an interesting sidelight on such fittings is given in the Chronicle of Jocelin of Brakelond where they are noted as being of Scandinavian origin.[311]

We have already seen much evidence for chests that were iron bound[312] and leather covered,[313] and although many leather covered chests were travelling articles (e.g. Cat. 47), the surviving cope chest at York Minster shows that not all leather covered chests were designed for this purpose. The type is early, as we know from the existence of a pre-1104 leather covered chest enclosing the body of St Cuthbert.[314] There were also basketry chests, though today we should probably describe such objects as hampers.[315]

Many late twelfth-century carved chests survive (e.g. Cat. 30), and again the evidence concerning St Cuthbert's chests provides an instance of this type of decoration at the beginning of our period;[316] surviving examples from the later Middle Ages are relatively common (e.g. Cat. 38 and 48).

Chests of several different kinds of wood survive. Apart from oak, whose position as the most valued wood for furniture in the Middle Ages is well recognized,[317] chests of walnut (e.g. Cat. 48), poplar (e.g. Hereford),[318] and pine (e.g. Cat. 42 and 43) survive. Records help to establish the pattern in the Middle Ages during the fourteenth and fifteenth centuries. For walnut, written evidence supports what is know from surviving chests: that walnut was a common wood for chests in France but not in England.[319] Poplar wood may have been included in the general term soft wood, to which many references are made: we may note 'blanc bois', 'sapino', 'sapo', etc., 'spruce', 'fyrre', and 'estriche bourdis'.[320] Exotic woods, such as cypress, are occasionally mentioned,[321] as are also chests made wholly of iron, like the extant Guildhall chest of c.1427.[322]

[309] See the evidence of 1496, pp. 124–5.
[310] The Duchess of Burgundy had 2 new locks made for chests in 1384/5 (Canat de Chizy 1859, 300).
[311] H. E. Butler, *The Chronicle of Jocelin of Brakelond*, London, 1949, 113. (See the slab-ended chest from Småland, Holmqvist, fig. 370.
[312] Evidence between 1371–1449, see pp. 118, 122, 123, 124, 130.
[313] The leather used on chests and cases was normally *cuir bouilli*, or hide treated with oil until it was malleable and highly impervious to water; the implication of the term is that the technique included boiling the leather. For example, 1337, inventory of the lord of Naste, 'Item, 1 autre coffre de cuir boulit . . .' (Dehaisnes, 1, 320).
[314] St Cuthbert's shrine was opened in 1104 and two accounts of what was found survive. There were 3 chests: the outermost, covered with leather and iron nails and clasps; the second chest of carved oak; and the innermost chest, which enclosed the body, which was studded all round with gold and jewels. See J. Raine, St Cuthbert, Durham, 1828, 185 ff.
[315] See the 1387 reference to 'coffres d'osier' (Prost, II, 295).
[316] See fn. 314.
[317] See p. 230.
[318] See B. H. Streeter, *The Chained Library*, London, 1931, 118.
[319] For example, 1338, 'arca de nuce ferrata' (Guiraud 1904/5, 50); also 1426, see p. 120; and 1435, 'ung grant coffre à deux serruses dont le couvescle est de deux pieces . . . de noyer' (Félix, 18).
[320] For example, 1403, see p. 96; 1372, 'Dua archas de sapino parvas' (Valous, 40); 1374, 'unam cayssiam de sapo' (E. Bondurand, 'Mobiliers du Vieux Temps', *Memoires et Comptes Rendus de la Societe Scientifique et Litteraire d'Alais*, XIV, 1883, 79; 1406, 'one chest of spruce well bound with iron' (Thomas 1943, 4); 1415, 'a chest of estriche bourdis' (Jacob 1937, 47); 1435, 'unam cistam de Spruse existentem apud Welton' (Raine 1834/5, 84). See also references dated 1480 and 1509 for 'fyrre' and 'sprewis', pp. 128 and 125.
[321] For example, 1377, Duke of Burgundy's accounts, '3089. . . . à un mercier de Paris . . . pour . . . un petit coffre de ciprès' (Prost, I, 580); also 1442, 'meam cistam de cipris' (Jacob 1937, 617).
[322] For the Guildhall chest, see Eames 1974. We may also note: 1376, see p. 132; 1384, 'Pixides . . . 199. Item in cista ferrea cum diuersis clauibus . . .' (Bond 1947, 68).

Traces of colour have been noted on a number of surviving carved chests, and rare examples such as the Newport altar chest (pls. 64B–65) and the Richard de Bury chest are painted with devices and images. References show that painted chests were common; red and green seem to have been the favourite colours, but references to white, yellow and black also occur.[323]

A number of interesting references describe ornate and precious chests. The majority of these entries refer to small boxes, as can be inferred from their contents (often holy relics and chapel appurtenances are involved).[324] There remain certain entries of this kind, however, which show that the chests in question were of substantial size. No doubt some of these ornate and expensive chests had religious connexions, like St Cuthbert's jewelled coffin,[325] but some appear to have been adjuncts of estate in a secular context. The four gilded chests which the Vicomtesse de Narbonne left to her daughters in 1377 appear to belong to this select group of furniture,[326] as does another gilded chest which held linen and stood in Charles V's sleeping chamber in 1378/80.[327] Another special chest, again from a royal French context, was of marquetry on all sides and stood in the king's sleeping chamber in the Château de Beauté in 1420;[328] it may possibly have resembled the chest Jan van Eyck painted as the seat for the Virgin in his *Madonna with Chancellor Rolin* of c.1435.[329] Whether the 'ivory chest' obtained for Queen Elizabeth of York in 1502 was small or full sized is uncertain;[330] although *small* ivory boxes were common enough, furniture itself was occasionally embellished with ivory plaques, as we know from the surviving chair in St Peter's, Rome.[331]

We seldom hear of the linings of chests, but an entry of 1388 informs us that the Duke of Burgundy's jewel chests were padded;[332] unfortunately, although we know the yardage of cloth involved we are not told how many chests were concerned, and therefore have no means of assessing the size of these chests. Since the term *joyaulx* embraced plate as well as personal jewellery, however, the chests might well have been full sized.

[323] Green: 1380, see p. 130; red: 1426, see p. 128; white: 1334, 'huche blance à 1111 piez' (Delisle, 113); yellow: 1384, 'Item une huche jaune de bois, . . .' (La Borderie 1854, 203); black: 1415, 'j alio standard nigro, sigillato et ligato cum ferro et firmato cum duplici serrura, . . .' (Kingsford 1918–20, 91).

[324] For example, 'coffras' of silver, and of wood plated with gilded copper at Windsor in 1384, holding relics (Bond 1947, 80); also the 'coffres' listed in 1402, J. Guiffrey, *Inventaires de Jean Duc de Berry*, II, Paris, 1896, 113–15 (*910–13; 917*)); also 2 'cixtes' of silver gilt and enamel listed among the chapel appurtenances in the Black Prince's will of 1376, Nichols, 72.

[325] See fn. 314.

[326] See J. Poux, 'Le Mobilier de Beatrix d'Arborée, Vicomtesse de Narbonne, en 1377', *Bulletin de la Commission Archéologique de Narbonne*, 1911, 401.

[327] See the heading in Charles V's inventory: 'AUTRE LINGE ESTANT EN BEAUTÉ. EN LA CHAMBRE OÙ LE ROY GIST, EN UNG COFFRE DORÉ' (Labarte, 351).

[328] 'En la tour de Beauté, appellée la chambre des Evvangelistes, où couchoit communément le roy Charles, a esté trouvé . . . Item, un coffre, marqueté de touz costez, sur lequel a eu un tablier' (Douet d'Arcq, 461).

[329] In the Louvre. See Faggin, pl. XLIII.

[330] 'Itm the same day to maistres Alianor Johns for money by hir geven in reward to a servaunt of the Lady Lovell for bringing a chest of iverey with the passion of oure Lord theron iij s. iiij d.' (Nicolas 1830, 15). We should note that the sum quoted is merely a present and does not represent the value of the chest.

[331] Ninth-century ivory plaques added to an earlier chair, see E. Hollstein, 'Jahrring chronologie der cathedra lignea von St Peter im Vatikan', *Trierer Zeitschrift*, XXXVII, 1974, 191–206.

[332] '2587. Jehanne du Val, teliere, demourant à Paris . . . 8 aunes et demie de toille de quoy on a fait 12 coussinez à mettre dessus les coffres des joyaulx de Mgr et aussi pour yceulx joyaux envelopper' (Prost, II, 396).

We occasionally learn of the precise location of chests, and at the foot of, or beside, the bed seems to have been a favourite position which illustrations confirm.[333] An interesting reference in Charles V's inventory to chests resting on crampons may refer to integral feet or to wall brackets, but the objects concerned here are clearly not full sized chests.[334]

There are many references to imported chests. The will of John de Coggeshale, a London corder, dated 1384, mentions a great chest of Gascony, which had belonged to the testator's father,[335] and King René of Anjou may have had chests described as Turkish in 1471.[336] By far the greatest number of references to imported chests, however, refer to those from Flanders: the 'coffres de Flandres' of French sources and the 'Flemish chests' of English wills and inventories. Many of these references are brief, merely referring to a Flemish chest,[337] but the will of John Somersham, dated 1368, mentions a long painted chest of Flemish work.[338] The brevity of most references implies that these Flemish chests were instantly recognizable, and several candidates may be suggested among extant chests which fulfil this requirement. Macquoid/Edwards thought they were light, panelled chests,[339] Havard believed they were iron bound,[340] and Hodges correlated them with the carved chests at Alnwick, Wath and Brancepeth.[341] If Flemish chests were only a single type, we can dismiss the suggestion that they were the light, panelled type as so many references are fourteenth century and too early for chests of this form.[342] It seems likely that we shall never satisfactorily identify the Flanders chests of written sources, though the fourteenth/fifteenth-century chests with narrative carving (e.g. York, Cat. 31) and the fifteenth-century iron bound standards, have strong claims on our consideration (though the case for the standards is weakened by the fact that surviving examples within our period of study appear to be predominantly, if not entirely, of fifteenth century date).

Let us now consider the varying forms of chests shown in Fig. 17. As we have already seen, we are unable to find medieval terms which may be meaningfully applied to each individual form of extant chest.[343] Some old terms such as hutch (*huche*) and standard[344] are part of modern usage and have been retained, but where no established habit exists,

[333] See the will of John Wodhous, 1445, [ed. J. Raine] *Testamenta Eboracensia*, I, Surtees Soc., 1834–6, 15; also the inventory of the hospital of St Antoine at Mâcon in 1482, Batault, 146. See also the Netherlandish illumination of the Birth of St John from the Turin Hours, Faggin, 87.

[334] 1379/80, at the Château de Vincennes, '3272. Item, ... ung petit coffre entaillé, assiz sur deux crampons de fer, en une fenestre dudit retrait, ...; 3278. Livres estans en la grant chambre dudit seigneur. En ung autre escrin assiz sur deux crampons, lequel est à la fenestre emprès la cheminée de ladite chambre, ...' (Labarte, 335, 336).

[335] See Sharpe, II, 250.

[336] 'deux arcz turquois ... quatre arcs turquois ...' (Godard-Faultrier, 55). Were these articles chests or bows?

[337] See example already quoted: 1351, p. 125; also references of 1349, 1352 and 1446, fn. 342.

[338] Sharpe, II, 146.

[339] 1954, Chests, 10.

[340] Havard, I, 910.

[341] C. C. Hodges, 'On Some Medieval Carved Chests', *Archaeologia Aeliana*, XV, 1892, 303.

[342] For example, the London registered wills of 1349 and 1352 of Roger Madour and Johanna Cros (Sharpe, I, 582–3; 665). Also the Prior of Durham's inventory of 1446: 'Garderobe ... Item una larga Cista de opere Flaundrensi' (Raine, 1834/5, 93).

[343] See pp. 110–11.

[344] Hutch is used throughout the Royal Commission volumes; standard is normally accepted as implying a chest of box form with a domed or canted lid, though not necessarily leather covered as Symonds implies, see Symonds 1941, 18.

L

new terms, based on simple visual qualities, have been adopted (slab-ended, box and plinth). Looking at the footed chests in Fig. 17, we see that there are four distinct types, with additional sub-divisions. Of these four, one uses the *sides* of the chest to produce the feet (slab-ended), and the other three all employ corner stiles for this purpose. Let us consider each form in turn in the Catalogue Raisonné.

SLAB-ENDED CHESTS (no Catalogue examples)

This form is inherently cruder than the other three forms of footed chests (see Fig. 17), for it depends upon weighty side boards which prohibit any attempt at extreme refinement in the design. Nevertheless, the form was used for important commissions associated with a degree of dignity, if we may judge from the armoire of *c*. 1441 made for the Spanish merchants of Bruges (Cat. 17) where the slab-ended principle of construction is employed. The form was evidently an extremely useful one; it is found throughtout the Middle Ages and can be noted in extant examples as early as the tenth century in Norway; in England, it continued in use into the seventeenth century.[345]

Slab-ended chests were sometimes iron bound. This strapping might be so thorough that the chest is virtaully iron plated, as in the crude example in Carlisle museum (stylistic date, fourteenth century); or it might be confined to a series of individual bands which reinforce the weakest areas, as in Richard de Bury's chest of 1334–5 in the Burrell Collection, Glasgow.[346] Once more we may note in passing that the Bruges armoire (Cat. 17), about one hundred years later in date, achieves greater delicacy in its strapping than the Richard de Bury chest and is the nearest example surviving which achieves some degree of refinement in this form of construction. As we have noted, in addition to banding with iron, slab-ended chests were also painted on occasion, and a number of flimsy late fifteenth-century examples have fronts carved with stylized tracery,[347] showing that the type was treated in a number of ways.

ARK CHESTS (no Catalogue examples)

This form is the crudest of the group of chests which have stiles elongated to form feet. The front and back boards are neatly joined by tenon and mortise, but the sides are normally dowelled through the front and back uprights, creating a primitive appearance. This character is enhanced by the pivot-hinged gable lid of several boards held within heavy end pieces; ark construction used riven timbers and is well illustrated by Macquoid/Edwards.[348] Although appearances suggest that the ark form is very early, there is insufficient evidence to show development satisfactorily and no securely dated examples have so far come to light in our field of interest. Late examples, stylistically

---

[345] Several oak chests of this form survive from the tenth-century Oseberg ship burial, two having spring locks and two being decorated with tin plated, round headed nails. See A. W. Brøgger/H. Shetelig, *Osebergfundet*, II, Oslo, 1928, figs. 65, 66, 68. For a seventeenth-century English example, see the chest in Great Canfield church, *Royal Commission on Historical Monuments Essex II (Central & S.W.)*, London, 1921, facing xxxiii.

[346] For an up-to-date account of this important chest, see W. Wells, 'The Richard de Bury Chest', *Scottish Art Review*, 10, no. 4, 14–18, 31–2; the chest was acquired for the Burrell Collection in 1942.

[347] For example, the chest at King's College, Cambridge, see *RCHM Cambridge*, I, 116b (chest 4).

[348] See 1927, Construction, fig. 1.

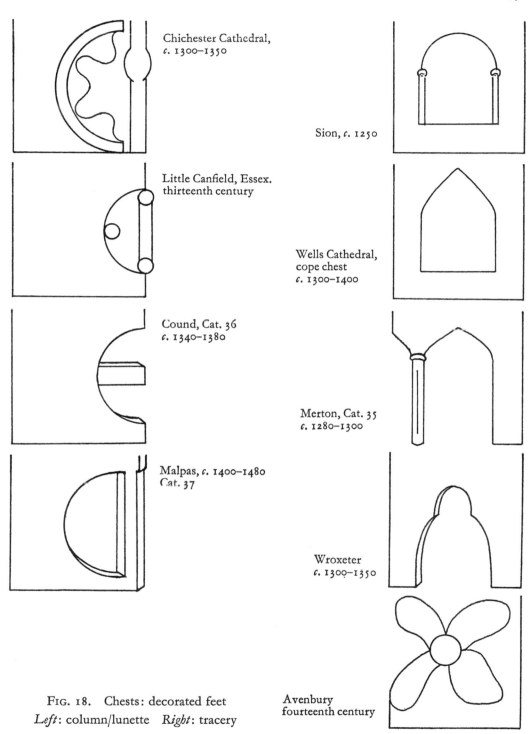

Chichester Cathedral,
c. 1300–1350

Sion, *c.* 1250

Little Canfield, Essex.
thirteenth century

Wells Cathedral,
cope chest
c. 1300–1400

Cound, Cat. 36
c. 1340–1380

Merton, Cat. 35
c. 1280–1300

Malpas, *c.* 1400–1480
Cat. 37

Wroxeter
c. 1300–1350

FIG. 18. Chests: decorated feet
Left: column/lunette *Right*: tracery

Avenbury
fourteenth century

dated fourteenth century, exist in the Victoria and Albert Museum and Townley Hall Museum,[349] both with feet carved with highly stylized forms of the lunette foot (see Fig. 18) resembling Cound, Cat. 36. Although German examples show that the type was both carved and painted, it is doubtful if the ark form was ever a vehicle for sophisticated decoration. It was essentially a utilitarian chest of strong and durable construction. Doubtless it had many uses, but it is unlikely to have been used to store articles of great value. Other forms of chest, more suitable to accommodate the necessary load of iron fittings than the ark, were available to serve as strong boxes.

HUTCH

Of the chest forms under consideration, the hutch is the most interesting, showing more variation in ornament and more adaptability in design than any other type. Hutches were of two main forms, those with framed sides (1), and those with plain boarded sides (2), see Fig. 17; pivot-hinged lids were sometimes present and both types existed side by side throughout our period. In type (2), the manner of framing the sides varied: we find a simple grid of timbers with hidden joints at Climping (Cat. 30) and Ypres;[350] a grid with visible dovetails at Westminster Abbey (Cat. 32); and sides fitted with rails only, at Brancepeth, Northumberland; (this feature is also present, though restored, at York, Cat. 31). Before discussing types of hutch in turn, let us look at an important feature which hutches and arks generally may share: the carved foot.

We see in Fig. 18, that the carved foot had two main streams of development: arcading (right column), and an obscure design characterized by a column with a lunette (left column). The arcaded foot is superbly illustrated in two Romanesque hutches at Sion;[351] these chests appear to be of similar date, and Hunt dates one to c. 1250.[352] We notice that the carving of the feet is architectural and the arches, though piercing the foot, have sills and are therefore *windows* rather than *doorways*. This tradition is found in England somewhat later at Wells, but in other English examples (Merton, Cat. 35 and Wroxeter) the voids have no sills, being pierced through at floor level and thus they resemble doorways rather than windows; the Merton foot is the most individual of the three in the diagram. We notice that only the Sion chest is wholeheartedly architectural in feeling; elsewhere the treatment becomes schematic.

The column/lunette foot may have originated in tracery, though at times its appearance suggests closer affinities with Roman pelta-shaped ornament;[353] the influence of Roman art generally upon architecture and sculpture in France, which began to fade in

[349] V. & A. chest, see H. Cescinsky/E. R. Gribble, *Early English Furniture and Woodwork*, II, London, 1922, fig. 9; Townley Hall Museum, Lancs., no. W21.1913.
[350] Chest carved with the legend of St George in St Martin's Cathedral.
[351] See A. de Wolff, 'The Romanesque Hutches of Valère at Sion in the Valais', *Conn.*, CLVIII, 1965, 39–42 (chests 2, ?3 and 4). (5 hutches seem to survive but the text is not altogether clear on this point: 4 are noted on p. 41 and 5 elsewhere.)
[352] J. Hunt, 'Byzantine and Early Medieval', ed. H. Hayward, *World Furniture*, London, 1965, fig. 46.
[353] Compare the feet of the Chichester and Little Canfield chests with the Roman stone sarcophagus at Westminster Abbey (*RCHM London*, I, pl. 181); also with F. H. Thompson, 'The Zoomorphic Pelta in Romano-British Art', *Antiquaries Journal*, XLVIII, 1968, pl. XXVb. I am indebted to my husband, J. V. H. Eames, for drawing my attention to Thompson's article.

the mid-twelfth century, lends support to this suggestion and it is pertinent to bear in mind the Roman origins of the chip carved ornament on medieval furniture.[354]

Figure 18 shows how abbreviated forms of ornament used on the feet of hutches and arks emanated from the two sides of the lunette/column design, drawing upon either the outer edge, as at Stoke d'Abernon[355] or using the inner, semi-circular form of the design, as at Cound and Malpas (Cat. 36 and 37). As Fig. 18 illustrates, versions of the arcaded or lunette foot are found throughout our period.

An unusual foot, which has no place in the sequences of ornament discussed above, exists on a chest formerly at the church of Avenbury where a bold, well carved four-petalled flower is associated with dovetails, bi-foliated straps and long articulated pole handles; the whole suggests a fourteenth-century context.[356] This chest, with its individuality of carving, serves to remind us that surviving hutches are a numerically inadequate sample for a full assessment of the richness and variety of design which was accomplished within our period. Although Avenbury now stands apart, it may represent the final, naturalistic expression of the rose or roundel, which, with other Romanesque architectural motifs such as the nail head, provided the strictly delineated patterns for the fronts of late thirteenth-century chests such as Climping (Cat. 30) and Hereford (Cathedral Library).[357]

Looking now at extant hutches with framed sides, see Fig. 17 (Hutch (1)), we find that carved fronts are common. In the earliest of these surviving examples, Sion (see p. 140) and Climping (Cat. 30) of c.1250 and c.1282–1300, the design of the fronts centres upon tracery and roundels. At a slightly later date the same ornament occurs in the early fourteenth-century Hereford chest in the Vicars Choral Library, though here it is used with greater richness and intensity. The Hereford chest resembles Climping in its unusual low relief work, though it is less delicate in feeling and execution. After the fourteenth century, however, the interest in roundels appears to have faded for a time, though the occupation with tracery continued undiminished. Two French chests with figures isolated by arcading[358] present a decorative scheme on the front which is paralleled in the underside of the lid of the Newport altar chest of c.1300, pl. 64B. This style of decorative treatment is most familiar in Romanesque and Gothic stone sculpture[359] and occurs on the painted retable of c.1300 at Thornham Parva, Suffolk.[360]

---

[354] See W. H. Forsyth, 'The Vermand Treasure', *Bull. M.M.A.*, IX, 1950/1, 236–40.

[355] See Macquoid/Edwards 1927, Chests and Coffers, fig. 4.

[356] See *RCHM Herefordshire II (East)*, London, 1932, pl. 45. Avenbury church is now destroyed and the present whereabouts of the chest is unknown to me.

[357] See Streeter, 4, 117.

[358] In the Musée Cluny and the Louvre, Paris. The Cluny chest, from the Gerente collection, is well known in print. It has faked ironwork and carvings and is thus a made-up piece. Though it has been suggested that parts of the chest are genuine (see A. Lambert, 'Le Coffre du pas Saladin, est-il Authentique?', *Revue Archéologique*, XXXIII, 1931, 275–306), comment should be suspended until such time as modern forms of analysis (ideally dendrochronology) have been applied to it. The enquiry will need to satisfy several questions: if any timbers are shown to be old, is the carving contemporary with them? And does it, in fact, come from a piece of furniture? Unfortunately, once objects are shown to have been constructed to deceive, no factor concerning them can be taken for granted.

[359] For example, the concentrated, typically twelfth-century arrangement of figures in an arcade at Saint-Denis (before 1151), and the more sophisticated disposition found later, exemplified in the superb tomb of Adelais of Champagne from Dilo abbey (c. 1260). (See W. Sauerländer, *Gothic Sculpture in France 1140–1270*, London, 1972 pls. 20 and 295.)

[360] See N. Pevsner, *Suffolk*, Harmondsworth, 1961, fig. 31a.

Whether these particular chests may be taken to represent genuine furniture carvings, however, is problematical, though the type of design was certainly used on French chests, as a record of 1367 shows.[361] The carved chests with roundels were sometimes painted, as is shown by traces of red remaining on a chest at Chichester Cathedral. A chest at Saltwood, Kent, dated c.1300 by Roe,[362] shows that grotesques, set in registers, might displace roundels on the stiles while tracery is retained in the central area, and the magnificently proportioned chest in St Mary Magdalen, Oxford, is another broadly similar example of the same date.[363] A chest at Alnwick, carved with remarkable vigour, has grotesques in registers on the stiles in the usual manner, and also on two of the three registers in the centre of the chest, and was believed to be early fourteenth century by Hodges.[364] This chest is important; not only do grotesques occupy the space which is filled with tracery elsewhere, but the uppermost register of the three at the centre front is carved with two hunting scenes, each orientated to face a central lock plate. This pair of narrative carvings provide a foretaste of the much more ambitious subjects which were to follow, as, for example, York.

But if the Alnwick chest is indicative of new decorative horizons, it does not mark the end of the tradition of grotesques carved on the stiles with tracery between. This earlier scheme continued, as is shown by several notable late fourteenth-century examples. The boldly carved chests at Wath, Yorkshire (traditionally from Jervaulx Abbey), Brancepeth, Northumberland, Derby,[365] and Chevington, Suffolk,[366] all follow this tradition and another chest at Haconby, Lincolnshire, is a similar if less precisely carved example.[367] The late fourteenth-century chest at Dersingham, however, is of a very different character.[368] The front carving symbolizes the four apostles of the New Testament while reticulated tracery occupies the stiles; it is an extraordinarily individual and powerful work.

The tradition and tracery and grotesques persisted into the fifteenth century as we see from the hutch at Coventry[369] and here we find a feature which is not present in any of the chests so far discussed, as far as this can be ascertained in view of the damage to lock plates:[370] a space for the lock plate accommodated in the design. The chest at York (Cat. 31) of c.1380 has this refinement, and it appears again on the Harty chest carved with knights and squires which may be dated early fifteenth century on the evidence of the clothes and armour.[371] In English work, carpenters or joiners making furniture did not generally take cognizance of the need for lock plates in their designs. Although

[361] 'Une huge, le plus grand entaillé d'ymages et de tabernacles, painturée de vermeille . . .'. Inventory of Ailleaume d'Auberchicourt, bourgeois de Douai (Dehaisnes, I, 474).
[362] Roe 1902, 34.
[363] See RCHM Oxford, 1939, 140. The front of this chest has been restored, but the manner in which this is done with areas left blank, indicating areas of uncertainty, shows that the work of restoration was accurate. The original lid, carved with exceptional delicacy, establishes the scale of the chest.
[364] See Hodges, 303 ff.; Hodges places this chest among the earliest under discussion in his paper.
[365] See Roe 1902, facing 39, 47.
[366] See Macquoid/Edwards 1927, Chests and Coffers, fig. 5.
[367] See Roe 1902, 38.
[368] See Macquoid/Edwards 1954, Chests, fig. 9.
[369] See Macquoid/Edwards 1954, Chests, fig. 11.
[370] Later lock plates mask the carving round the relevant areas of these chests.
[371] See Macquoid/Edwards 1954, Chests, fig. 12.

common enough in small objects,[372] the idea of the woodworker creating a reserve on a chest front for the smith to occupy seems to have been implemented in England at a relatively late date, and even when the idea was adopted it was never accomplished with the degree of precision and sympathy exhibited in French and Netherlandish work, if we may judge from surviving examples. (Compare the clumsy lock plate reserve at Neenton, Cat. 38, with the sophistication of the arrangments at Romsey and York, Cat. 48 and 31; and even the Gruuthuse chest, Cat. 41. While I would not suggest that the presence of so simple a feature as the integrated lock plate indicates an imported chest, its absence in a work as late as the fourteenth and fifteenth centuries does seem to imply that the object in question is English.

It seems probably that the fashion for narrative carvings on hutches continued throughout the fifteenth century. Surviving examples show that St George and the dragon, and knights in combat were popular subjects,[373] and a loose panel with lock plate reserve (showing that it belonged to a chest) is carved with scenes in the Virgin's life and indicates that other subjects were encompassed.[374] The carefully constructed, if dull, hutch of 1480 at Westminster Abbey (Cat. 32) shows that the hutch with framed sides was not always carved or ornamented in the fifteenth century; indeed, it is likely that plain hutches were once more numerous than ornamented ones but, having no decorative qualities to recommend them, relatively few survived.

CATALOGUE NO. 30 (PLATE 35B)

Chest (hutch type 1) in the church of St Mary, Climping, Sussex.

Oak. The wood is unusually pale, as if it had been cleaned with abrasives.

l. 6' 5"; h. 1' 7"; w. 1' 7½".

Description (August 1966; interior unseen)

The chest retains its original lid but has lost the lower part of its upright members, which in this category of chest are normally elongated to form feet. The lower edge of the chest is now encased in a modern plinth and raised from the floor on blocks. Although the chest is in ruined condition, it is included here because of its exceptional quality and early date.

The front is composed of three planks. The uprights are joined to the horizontal board by tenon and mortise joints, clearly visible on the left-hand side where the joint has sprung. Here, 4 pegs are driven into the joint as reinforcement; there are also nails which were presumably added when the joint developed weaknesses.

At the sides, the lowest rail is lost and is replaced by the modern plinth.

---

[372] The Franks casket (seventh or eighth-century A.D.) has a reserve for the lock plate and shows that the idea is much earlier than our period; see Mercer, pl. 18.

[373] For example, St George: at York (Cat. 31); Cathedral of St Martin, Ypres; and Gruuthuse Museum, Bruges, no. 556. Knights: Harty (see Macquoid/Edwards 1954, Chests, fig. 12); also chests listed by Roe 1902, 56, 64, 65.

[374] See Macquoid/Edwards 1927, Chests and Coffers, fig. 10.

The central board at the back of the chest is fitted with three vertical iron straps which commence at the top edge of the chest, run down the back and break off a short distance after turning beneath the chest. These straps have a single fixed ring attached to project at right angles, placed roughly half-way up the back, to which loose chains of three oval links (round section) were formerly attached; two of these chains survive. These terminate in a single link of flattened form which is attached to the chest lid and is broken at this point. Marks on the top of the lid indicate that originally the iron banding continued across the lid to the front.

The lid is fitted with an apron at the sides and is attached to the back of the chest by means of a wooden pivot hinge, fitted with an iron plate on its outer surface at the side of the chest.

The front of the chest is crudely patched with 3 rectangular insertions of wood. The marks of straps on the lid, continuing the line established at the back, show that these patches cover the positions of three original locking devices.

The chest is carved at the front, and along the apron of the lid, with great delicacy and refinement. The carving is worked in the solid and executed in low relief. The front stiles bear large, single chip-carved roundels. The central area is carved with an arcade comprising 10 pointed arches, and 2 small chip-carved roundels are set between the 2nd and 3rd and 8th and 9th arches respectively. The shafts of the columns disappear behind the modern plinth; the design of each roundel is unique.

The lower edge of the apron at the side of the lid is stop-chamfered, to form a finely worked, undulating pattern.

There are various crudely made slots in the lid.

Analysis

Although this remarkable chest has sustained severe mutilation through neglect, part of its lost grace can be appreciated by studying an engraving published in 1866 (see pl. 35B). Here we see that the lost feet were carved with rows of nail heads (5 horizontal and 6 vertical, total 30), set within a 3-sided border (top and sides) of similar, though distinct, ornament. As indicated in the engraving, the carving to the feet was the same as the roundels and arcading, i.e. in low relief. The ornament on the feet did not commence on a level with the edge of the bottom horizontal board but above it, level with the bases of the columns of the arcade. The engraving shows that in 1866 the right-hand foot was already in an advanced state of decay. Another fact gleaned from the engraving is the manner in which the column shafts were terminated: with delicate stepped bases which rested upon a border running the entire length of the central board. We also notice that part of each of the 3 straps on the lid were present in 1866, providing confirmation that the 3 straps on the back continued over the lid.

The stylistic features of the carving, which combines roundels with tracery, should be noted. Simpler, cruder chests, such as the example in Chichester Cathedral, have roundels alone.[375]

The Climping chest is so fine that an accurate date on stylistic grounds seems justified. Points of reference are provided in architecture by the blank arcading used in the ruined

---

[375] Several other examples survive, e.g. Stoke d'Abernon, and V. & A. chest no. W.30.1926.

chapter house at Thornton Abbey begun in 1282, and in woodwork by the lower arcading on St Edward's chair (Westminster Abbey) which was probably made in 1299.[376] These parallels suggest a date of *c*.1282–1300 for the Climping chest.

Select Bibliography

I. Nairn/N. Pevsner, *Sussex*, Harmondsworth, 1965, 191.

H. Shaw, *Specimens of Ancient Furniture*, London, 1866, pl. XXIX.

F. W. Steer, *Guide to the Church of St. Mary, Climping*, Sussex Historic Churches Trust, Chichester, [n.d.].

CATALOGUE No. 31 (PLATES 36–7)

Chest (hutch, type 1) in the chapter house, York Minster.

Oak, now black.

l.   6′ 3″
h.   without lid, 2′ 11¾″
w.   2′ 5½″
Thickness of lid, 2″; overhand at centre front, ¾″

Description (April 1970; interior unseen)

The chest has been altered and the mode of access revolutionized: the sides have been remade, possibly on the original pattern, and the centre front panel is now free on all sides and fitted with hinges underneath, thus becoming a drop front. In order to support this arrangement, and to keep the front level when it is lowered, hinged billets of wood have been attached on each side to form folding legs. The stiles on the front of the chest have been cut free at the point where they are normally elongated to form feet, and made into armoires, hinged by 2 hinge plates set on each side.

The back of the chest and the lid are original. The back is composed of a series of rails, worked with a delicate stop chamfering. The lid is panelled, having a single outer frame which contains a pair of horizontally joined boards; the frame is stop-chamfered and matches the work on the back of the chest. The corners of the lid are now strengthened with iron plates.

The front of the chest is carved in the solid in high relief, 2 carvings for each upright and a single long carving for the centre front. The border which surrounds each carving is extended at the top centre front to produce a rectangular reserve with 3 concave sides for a single lock plate. The left and right-hand uprights are carved with a queen and a king respectively, and the feet beneath with inward facing lions supporting shields. The central panel represents the legend of St George and the dragon. The story is told as three episodes which run into one another without any form of interruption, and the action takes place in open ground before a walled city. The carving is highly individual; the effect of portraying different episodes of the story as one scene gives a sense of almost

---

[376] See N. Pevsner/J. Harris, *Lincolnshire*, Harmondsworth, 1964, 18b, 403; also pp. 188, 191–2 (St Edward's chair).

hectic movement to the central area, and this impression is further enhanced by the convention of carving every void around the figures as an undulation to represent rocks, flora and occasionally fauna. The curves of the dragon's back and tail (which are represented twice), reinforce the sense of swirling motion.

The wood of the central reserve for the lock plate is very roughly finished and is imperfectly covered by the plate; nevertheless, the plate and hasp are original. The plate has a raised U-guard with a decorative leaf terminal on the right; the hasp falling beside the guard has a raised spine and ring terminal.

Analysis

Although the chest has been altered, there can be no doubt that its essential appearance when closed is unchanged, for the front, back and lid are original and have not been reduced in size. With regard to the carpentry, the panelled lid and the rhythmic stop chamfer applied to the back and lid are of particular interest, recalling the more delicate work at Climping (Cat. 30).

The York chest is one of a number of examples of complete chests, or chest fronts, carved with narrative scenes, surviving in England, France and the Netherlands. A chest front in the Victoria and Albert Museum,[377] also carved with St George and the dragon, resembles the York carving so closely that Roe believed both were the work of the same man.[378] In both these works we are dealing with masterpieces: works of art which may be favourably compared with carvings in more precious materials, such as ivory. Both works are characterized by a dramatic sense of movement and have mirror-images, such as the stance of the princess as she prepares to lead the dragon away. The equal mastery of both carvings mitigates against the suspicion that one is an apprentice's copy, as does the fact that they are not a pair but are variations upon a common theme. The disordered field present in the York and V. & A. carvings is pronounced as typically Flemish by Ffoulkes, who compares this characteristic with a narrative carving of the battle of Courtrai (1302) which, though Flemish, is *eccentric* in being arranged in registers.[379] Other Flemish details are present in the York chest, notably the stepped gables on the houses, noted by Roe.[380] The stepped gables (*corbie* or crow's foot) are characteristically Flemish; though they are also found in Scotland, political factors make this a less likely source of influence or provenance. Chamfering occurs in English work in an earlier context (it is found on the Climping chest, Cat. 30), but its use to create a running pattern on the rails at the back and on the lid at York is unusual, but also occurs on the lid of a chest at Ypres, in the Cathedral of St Martin. The York ironwork provides a further connexion with the Netherlands. Leaf terminals are certainly common in England (see Cat. 43), but the raised spine on the hasp of the York chest is not an English feature, though it can be paralleled in a chest at Bruges.[381] These factors,

[377] No. 82. 1893.
[378] Roe 1902, 51–2.
[379] The Courtrai panel is mutilated, and has been used as the front of a later chest; the carving is discussed by C. Ffoulkes, 'A Carved Flemish Chest at New College, Oxford', *Archaeologia*, LXV, 1914, 113–28.
[380] Roe 1902, 55, 63.
[381] Gruuthuse museum, no. 597.

although inconclusive in themselves, suggest a Flemish origin for the chest and here I disagree with Roe, who favoured an English source. There seems little to add to Roe's comments concerning the dating of the chest, which is established by the clothes and armour as *c.* 1380.[382] A number of other chests of the same form, decorated with narrative carvings, are loosely connected with York and some were believed by Roe to share a common, English provenance.[383] The chests carved with St George at Bruges and Ypres,[384] and chests with knights in combat at the Victoria and Albert Museum and Harty[385] are all inferior in imaginative compass as well as in execution. Much nearer in feeling, however, is the chest front carved with scenes from the life of the Virgin in the Victoria and Albert Museum which, like that at York, is probably of Flemish origin.[386]

After the mastery and individuality of technique exhibited in the carving of this chest, its chief interest centres upon the legend of St George and the manner in which it is portrayed, with different episodes of the story running into one another without any attempt at individual containment: the 'disordered field'. This convention was frequently used in tapestries, and when tales were familiar such a device presented no difficulty to the onlooker. It enabled complicated action to be portrayed without a consequent fragmentation of the design. Today, an interpretation of the scenes on the chest is less straightforward, but for clarification we can turn to William Caxton's printed English text of the Golden Legend[387] which establishes for us the particular form — one of several — which the story took in the area covered by this study. Caxton's work was compiled from a late thirteenth-century Latin text by Jacobus de Voragine, Archbishop of Genoa, and an early fourteenth-century French translation of this book by Jean Belet, plus material from the *Gesta Romanorum* and the Bible.[388] In the York chest and other carvings, in a woodcut in Caxton,[389] and even in so delicate an item as a jewel belonging to Henry VI,[390] we find certain essential elements of the legend portrayed: a castle with a king and queen; a princess; and St George and a dragon. In essence, the legend concerned a heathen city called Silene in Libya which was terrorized by a dragon. The dragon ate many of the city's inhabitants, and even the king's daughter could not be spared. When the sacrifice of the princess became inevitable she was led out of the city to meet the dragon by her distressed father, dressed as for her wedding day. While the princess awaited the dragon, St George, a knight born in Cappadocia, rode by. When the dragon appeared, St George made the sign of the cross about it and then wounded the beast with his sword; he instructed the princess to put her girdle round the dragon's neck and to be of good courage. The princess led the dragon into the city 'as it had been a meek beast and debonair'.[391] St George agreed to

---

[382] Roe 1902, 52; see also Macquoid/Edwards 1927, Chests and Coffers, fig. 9.
[383] Roe 1902, 52, 55, 56, 64.
[384] Gruuthuse Museum, no. 556 not included by Roe; Cathedral of St Martin, Ypres.
[385] V. & A. no. 738.1895; Harty church, Isle of Sheppey.
[386] No. W.15.1920.
[387] F. S. Ellis, *The Golden Legend by William Caxton*, III, London, 1900, 126–9.
[388] William Caxton, *The Golden Legend*, London, 1878, 35–6.
[389] In the first edition of the Golden Legend to be printed in Dutch (Delft, 1489).
[390] In the inventory of the regalia etc., see Palgrave, II, 256–7 (102).
[391] Ellis, 128.

kill the dragon after the people were converted to Christianity; the king and his subjects were immediately baptized and the dragon was slain. After the king had built a church of 'our Lady and of St George'[392] the saint departed.

If we now look at the carving, we see that the story is told in a sequence which starts at the top left of the centre panel and continues on in the form of a U laid on its side, thus ⊃. We see:

(1)   The city of Silene with the heads of the king and queen visible among the battlements and gables.

(2)   A symbolic lion (courage).

(3)   A princess or a queen, who may or may not be kneeling but has hands in the the position of supplication, faces St George who has dismounted.

(4)   St George, now mounted and identified by his shield which he holds before him, attacks the dragon; the royal lady seen in (3) is kneeling and still prays.

(5)   St George, with shield now slung from his shoulder, follows the dragon which is leashed round the neck and is subservient to the princess who stands ready to lead it into the city.

Although the broad outlines of the tale are clear, certain details remain obscure. The royal figure in (3) and (4) has dagged sleeves; yet the figure in (5), who must be the princess since she is preparing to lead the dragon, has plain sleeve draperies. If (3), (4) and (5) are the princess, then in removing her girdle she also removed a garment with dagged sleeves. Alternatively, (3) and (4) are not the princess at all but are the queen, who according to Harris symbolized prayer for the whole community,[393] though there is nothing of this in Caxton.

The carving of the left and right-hand uprights may possibly refer to the establishment of Christianity and the building of churches at Silene. On the left, a queen holds ?a bible, and on the right a king (with crown broken off) holds ?a lamb. The architectural details above each figure may refer to the church or churches built at the instigation of St George.

Select Bibliography

H. Cescinsky/E. R. Gribble, *Early English Furniture and Woodwork*, II, London, 1922 figs. 13, 14.

Macquoid/Edwards 1927, Chests and Coffers, fig. 9.

F. Roe, *Ancient Coffers and Cupboards*, London, 1902, 51 ff.

[392] Ellis, 128.
[393] H. A. Harris, 'Medieval Mural Paintings', *Proceeds of the Suffolk Institute of Archaeology and Natural History*, XIX, 1927, 301.

CATALOGUE No. 32 (PLATE 38)

Chest (hutch type 1) in the Chapel of the Pyx, Westminster Abbey.

Oak, now polished

l. 7′ 4½″; h. without lid, 3′ 4″; w. 3′ 6¾″.

Description (January 1974)

The chest is very plain, and is now of box form without feet. It has 2 wide uprights, in the manner of chests of hutch form, with 4 horizontal boards set between at front and back. Three iron straps (a 4th, right-hand strap is now missing) are visible at front and back at the bottom of the chest and these run beneath it and strengthen the attachment of the bottom board.

The side construction is a highly individual form of the framed construction, with a series of rails and stiles with dovetailed joints, see Fig. 19.

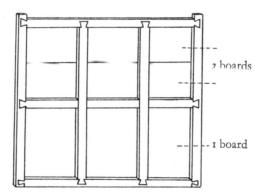

2 boards

1 board

FIG. 19.   Framing at sides of chest

The chest has 3 simple rectangular lock plates fitted with U-shaped guards for the hasps only. The plates are set askew in relation to one another. The original hasps survive and are hinged to straps on the lid; the hasps are handsome, being worked with circles and triangles and fitted with a nail on a stem to serve as a handle, see Fig. 20.

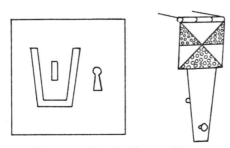

FIG. 20.   Lock plate and hasp

Analysis

The chest is dated *c*.1480 by dendrochronology;[394] thus we may use the few interesting details it possesses — dovetail rails and stiles and bold hasps — as an aid in stylistic dating elsewhere.

Although the underneath of the chest was not examined, it is assumed that the chest was once hutch (1) form, and that the feet became rotten and were removed; at this time the 3 (once 4) iron bands, running beneath the bottom board and extending a short distance up the front and back, were added.

It will be noticed that the chest is exceptionally high.

Select Bibliography

A. W. G. Lowther, 'The date of Timbers from the Spire of Chilcomb Church and from the Wreck in the River Hamble', *Hants Field Club*, XVII, Part 2, 1951, 132.

Let us now turn to hutches of the second type, that is with plain boarded sides (see Fig. 17) described as hutch (2). This form gave a clear field for decoration on the three sides of a chest that were normally visible, whereas the framing on hutches of type (1) meant that only the front was available for decoration. The possibilities of a continous band of ornament running from the back of one side round to the back of the other side of a chest was fully exploited by smiths in France and England, as is shown by three spectacular chests decorated with wrought iron (Cat. 33, 34 and 37). The earliest surviving hutch of this type of *c*.1200–50 is probably the example in the Musée des Arts Décoratifs (Cat. 33), where a design of simple, regular scrolls is placed vertically and horizontally on three sides of the chest. The slightly later chest in the Carnavalet Museum (Cat. 34) of *c*.1250–70, is the finest hutch of type (2) which has survived (if we exclude the Newport altar chest, now unforgivably mutilated pls. 64B, 65), and is indeed one of the finest extant chests of any group. The scrollwork on the Carnavalet chest covers three sides, though the lid is unornamented. In both these early French examples, the scrolls, however simple, are part of a connecting pattern and this characteristic of an *interrelationship* in the elements applied to the whole unit is a feature of early work; we have already seen it expressed with distinction in the Chester armoire of *c*.1300 (Cat. 22). The exceptional altar chest at Newport, whose raised lid painted with figures forms an altar retable (pl. 65A) is now denuded of its inlaid lead ornament,[395] but it shows that in *c*.1300 interesting variations upon the theme of a three-sided design in metalwork were employed. The chest at Wroxeter, with ironwork on the lid which resembles Richard de Bury's slab-ended chest of 1334–45, also uses strapping decoratively, though is restrained by comparison with the thirteenth-century French examples, and a fourteenth-century hutch at Bruges[396] is entirely utilitarian, being laced with iron bands which form a grid, like the chest of box form at Winchester of 1396/7 (Cat. 40). Exuberance in applied wrought iron returns again with the English chest at Malpas of *c*.1400–80 (Cat. 37). But here, for all its decorative richness in which the lid is included

[394] Lowther, 132.

[395] As recorded by Macquoid/Edwards 1954, Chests, 7. The lead inlay is preserved in the Victoria & Albert Museum, Department of Metalwork, no. 7437.1860.

[396] Gruuthuse museum no. 513; 7 original locking arrangements equip this hutch. The dating is stylistic.

as well as the front and sides, we are immediately aware of the angularity of the iron-work and of the fragmentation of the design; these factors, contrasting with the flowing curves and interrelated designs of earlier work, proclaim the revivalist move-ment of the fifteenth century.

Simpler hutches were doubtless once common, and the early example at Merton of *c*.1280–1300 (Cat. 35), which is innocent of ornament save for bi-foliated terminals to its iron strapping and carved feet, together with the chest at Cound of *c*.1340–80 (Cat. 36) show how satisfactory to the eye such plain workmanship can be; we notice that both these chests, and also the Malpas example, contribute something to our knowledge of the carved foot (see Fig. 18), and in fourteenth and fifteenth-century examples dovetails often replace the mortise and tenon joint between stiles and front board.

The Neenton chest of *c*.1500–25 (Cat. 38) stands apart from other examples of hutch (2) type, being carved on the front only with architectural motifs. Neenton is also eccentric in other ways, for the whole front is treated as a single, uninterrupted field of ornament, and the normal division in the carving of the stiles and front (which re-inforces the principles of construction) is abandoned. It is an important example of a changed attitude to design, familiar in late fifteenth-century slab-ended chests, but its inherent possibilities and its power to arouse our admiration are seriously weakened by the flimsy quality of the timbers used and the coarseness and inadequacy of the construc-tion with a *single* dovetail linking front and stiles. Neenton carries the hutch (2) form forward into the sixteenth century, and we are aware that the appearance as well as the durability of the type is impaired when thin boards are employed.

An elaboration of the hutch form was created by linking the feet with a band of carving, see Fig. 17, hutch (2a). The fifteenth-century chest carved with the name N. Fares in the Victoria and Albert Museum is a remarkable example of this develop-ment and shows that carving, in common with other forms of decoration, might embellish sides and front.[397] The carving of the Fares chest, however, is even continued round the back of the chest as well, showing that it was designed to stand away from the wall and was probably used as a kind of counter.

Finally, the hutch was responsible for the creation of an entirely new chest form — the plinth (see Fig. 17), which will be discussed below among unfooted chests.

CATALOGUE No. 33 (PLATE 39)
Chest (hutch type 2) in the Musée des Arts Décoratifs, Paris. Peyre collection, no. 982.
Oak and applied wrought iron
l. 5′; h. 2′ 10¼″; w. 2′ 5½″.

Description (September 1973)
The chest is covered at sides and front with wrought iron scrollwork of B section rod. The single original lock is missing (its central position is marked by a wooden insertion) and the lid is modern.

[397] See Macquoid/Edwards 1927, Chests and Coffers, figs. 11, 12.

The front and sides between the uprights are each of 2 boards. The uprights, elongated to form feet, are cut away on the inner edges at the front in an arc, but are straight at the back.

The 3 decorated surfaces are covered with the same design: a simple stem set either vertically or horizontally with opposing symmetrical spirals with terminals impressed with trefoils and rosettes. The centre front of the chest has 3 vertical stems with spirals, the central one being shorter than the other two to leave space for a lock plate. The centre of each side is decorated with a single vertical stem with spirals. The corners are bound with 3 horizontal stems, but the uppermost, resting just below the lid, is unique in having spirals on one side only (pendant). The spirals on the horizontal corner stems change direction, so that they always turn downwards from the termination of the stem on the same plane. In this manner, the simple design stated by the vertical stems is sustained.

The spirals are formed by laying additional rods beside the main stem as required, never by stacking rods one above another, as happens, for instance, in the St Quentin armoire (Cat. 23). The clumsiness of the junctions is alleviated by collars placed below the joins which are embellished with cross hatching.

Analysis

The chest has frequently been compared with that in the hôtel Carnavalet (Cat. 34). There are important differences between the chests, however, in technique, manipulative skill and artistry of design. Except that the present chest employs collars to mask joints (which offers a more sophisticated solution to the problem of integrating varying thicknesses of rod than a plain, welded joint), it is inferior to the Carnavalet chest in all other respects. The ironwork here is relatively crude and the design is intellectually unexciting, though it is clear from the easy lines of the scrolls that the chest is early.

The arch of the front feet preserves one of the outlines of the traceried foot, but the column, indicated by the point of the spring of the arch, is here unrealized (see Fig. 18). At Merton (Cat. 35) and at Chichester Cathedral, however, the column is intact. The present chest is important in demonstrating that at a relatively *early* date the design of the column/lunette foot might be compromised.

We know that the collared joint is not a particularly helpful feature in stylistic dating for ironwork in the twelfth and thirteenth centuries,[398] and the simplicity of the design, together with its relatively crude execution, are other features which make close dating unrealistic; for these reasons a time scale of *c.*1200–50 seems appropriate. A chest with similar wrought iron scrolls and feet exists in the Victoria and Albert Museum.[399]

Select Bibliography

M. Faré, 'Les Caractères de Raison du Mobilier Gothique', *Art et Industrie*, 1946, no. 2, 56.

J. Viaux, *Le Meuble en France*, Paris, 1962, 35–6.

J. Viaux, 'French Domestic Furniture of the Middle Ages', *Conn.*, cxxxiii, 1954, 252.

[398] See p. 154.
[399] No. 735.1895.

Catalogue No. 34 (plate 40)

Chest (hutch type 2) in the Musée Municipal de la Ville de Paris (hôtel Carnavalet). Traditionally from the Abbaye Royale de Saint-Denis.

Oak and wrought iron

l. 5′ 6¼″; h. without lid, 2′ 5¾″; thickness of lid, 1¼″; w. 2′ 2½″.

Description (October 1973; inside unseen)

The chest is decorated at front and sides with elaborate wrought iron scrolls. The front and sides between the uprights are each of two boards. The lid is original and is also of two boards. Most of the iron rod is of B section attached with large nails with carefully finished heads; some of the smaller forms in the design are D section rod. The nails attaching the iron rods are also used to strengthen the attachment of the bottom board of the chest and as a decorative studding elsewhere, e.g. along the edge of the lid.

The design of the ironwork at the centre front is based upon a central, vertical stem from either side of which spring a pair of large, inward turning spirals. The outermost strap of these two spirals is widened to produce a short straight stem running horizontally, and also a second large spiral which lies above the first and is also inward turning. The central stem is carried a short way above the top of the lower spirals to finish in two short stalks and one central taller one. The rest of the ironwork on the chest forms a single symmetrical design on either side of the four central spirals and matches them in running clockwise or anti-clockwise. The design is carried right through from the back edge of each side of the chest to the front, being bent as is necessary at the corners but otherwise remaining unchanged. This main design consists of two horizontal straps with spirals on one side and short, curved bands on the other separated by a single plain strap. The spirals are attached to the lower edge of the upper band and to the upper edge of the lower band. There are thus three bands (two with appendages and a central one without) and these run right across the back of the chest as reinforcement straps. The die stamped finials are of various forms: rosettes, trefoils and multilobed oval forms resembling fruits. The strapping is entirely of single rod, additions being set alongside the main stem and never laid over it; at the junctions, the iron has been flattened and stamped with a die cut with cross hatching.

The lid is original and has a slight projection over the chest at the front and sides. At the sides, there is a nosing which is bound with iron.

The original lock at the centre front has been replaced. The left-hand upper spiral is incomplete and was probably broken when the lock plate was changed.

There are seven large loops for chains fixed to the back of the chest.

Analysis

The chest is very fine, with ironwork which is more vigorous and sophisticated in design, if not in technique, than the somewhat similar example in the Musée des Arts Décoratifs (Cat. 33). In the Carnavalet chest, the design is oblique, with large spirals running *out of each other* at the centre front, rather than springing from a common stem.

M

This arrangement creates the usual counterbalance of spirals running clockwise and anti-clockwise, but has the added attraction of ensuring that the directional differences are not only on either side of one another, but also *above* one another, giving a certain fascination to the design and a greater sense of upward movement than is possible in an arrangement of coils springing from a common stem. This basic rhythm, boldly stated at the centre front of the chest, is sustained throughout the subsidiary coils by confining them to a single side of individual horizontal rods and by allowing a generous spacing between the registers; thus the eye remains unconfused and the full visual potential of the design is realized.

With regard to dating, our sole evidence is stylistic. In the Carnavalet chest, the junctions of the rods are uncovered, whereas the junctions on the Musée des Arts Décoratifs chest are collared. The collared junction is clearly a more sophisticated technique since it masks points of visual weakness, but we find it was already in use in *c*.1125,[400] and many surviving church doors with decorative ironwork in England and Sweden illustrate that the two techniques were used concurrently in the twelfth and thirteenth centuries.[401] Indeed, it is evident that as early as the twelfth century, the presence or absence of collars had more to do with the practice of individual smiths than with date or locality. The magnificent doors of Henry III's chapel at Windsor, in which black iron scrolls are flaunted on a field of scarlet gesso, were made before 1270[402] yet ignore the principle of collars used at St Albans in the twelfth century.[403] The welded joints at Windsor, in conjunction with the arrangement of spirals and tendrils which is so similar to the Carnavalet chest, prompts me to suggest a comparable date of *c*.1250–70 for this chest, somewhat later than the date suggested by Jacqueline Viaux.[404]

Select Bibliography

P. Ansart, 'Le Bahut, Meuble Essentiel du Moyen Age', *La Vie à La Campagne*, 1911, 243, 244.

J. Viaux, *Le Meuble en France*, Paris, 1962, 35–6.

[400] See the illumination in Cottonian MS Nero C IV, Turner, 10 ff.

[401] The following examples may also be noted, twelfth century: without collars, Höjby, Sweden, with collars St Albans. Thirteenth century: without collars, Appuna, Sweden, Näsby, Sweden, and Faringdon; with collars, Wheatenhurst. (For Swedish examples, see W. Holmqvist, *Sveriges Forntid och Medeltid*, Malmö, 1949, figs. 359, 360, 361; for English examples, see Ayrton/Silcock, figs. 20, 29, 32.)

[402] St John Hope believed that Gilbertus was the smith responsible because his stamp is found upon the scrolls and also upon some crampons of Henry's tomb at Westminster (St John Hope 1913, 409). Lethaby, however, believed the smith was Henry of Lewes (Lethaby, 305).

[403] Formerly the Slype door, S. transept; now in the V. & A. From that part of the Abbey completed before 1195.

[404] Early thirteench century (Viaux 1962, 35).

Catalogue No. 35 (plate 41)

Chest (hutch type 2) in the Library, Merton College, Oxford.

Oak; very pale, possibly due to cleaning with abrasives

l. 5′ 5″; h. without lid, 2′ 7¾″; w. 1′ 10½″.

Description (June 1967)

The front, back and sides of the chest are of single boards; the original lid has been replaced.

The 4 uprights of the chest, which are extended to form feet, were originally identically treated with an octagonally faceted column on the inside surface and a pointed arch above; the most perfectly preserved is the right front foot.

All the joints of the chest at the back, front and sides are strengthened with rows of substantial nails, symmetrically arranged. The chest is surrounded with iron strapping. The sides and corners are bound with an original horizontal strap which extends beyond the joint with the uprights at front and back and is finished with bi-foliated terminals at each end; beneath it is a second, shorter horizontal strap without decorative terminals which may be secondary. The front of the chest has a pair of original vertical straps with bi-foliated terminals which run beneath and appear at the back to finish a short way above the bottom board with matching terminals. In addition, there are 3 other vertical straps on the front which are probably secondary. The 3 original straps for the lid, which extend down the back of the chest and lie beneath the corner horizontal strapping, have been re-used for a later lid.

The 3 lock plates and hasps are secondary.

The interior of the chest has grooves at each side for a small shelf, now missing.

Analysis

Visually, the interest of the chest centres about the well-formed Early English traceried foot and the bi-foliated terminals to the iron strapping which recall the mid-thirteenth-century Bayeux armoire (Cat. 11).

The earliest building at Merton is the hall of *c.*1274 and the chest is unlikely to pre-date this structure. We know that the College had two loan chests in the Middle Ages, one for pledges put into it by borrowers of books from the library, and another for money given by William Rede in the late fourteenth century. Only one chest survives at Merton and it is not known when the second disappeared.[405]

The stylistic evidence of the arcaded foot (see Fig. 18) rules out the possibility that this chest was made in the late fourteenth century for William Rede's gift. Therefore it is presumably the chest used in respect of borrowers of books from the library. A date of 1280–1300 satisfies the stylistic evidence and agrees with the early history of the College, and is near the date advanced by the Royal Commission.[406]

Select Bibliography

RCHM *Oxford*, 1939, 83.

[405] I am much indebted to Dr R. Highfield for this information.
[406] RCHM *Oxford* gives a late thirteenth/early fourteenth-century date.

CATALOGUE No. 36 (PLATE 42)

Chest (hutch type 2) at St Peter's church, Cound, Shropshire.

Oak

l. 6′ 1¼″; h. 1′ 9¼″ without lid; w. 1′ 5¼″.

Description (June 1967; inside unseen)

    The chest is heavy and well made. The front and back are single timbers neatly dovetailed into the uprights which are extended to form feet. The feet are carved with distinctive but graceless elements which give a somewhat hieratic appearance to the chest; the left front foot is the most complete. The sides of the chest are single boards and rest upon rebates in the uprights, an unusual feature in a chest of this form. The bottom board of the chest, and the joints between front, back and sides with uprights, are reinforced with large round nails which are carefully arranged to form pleasing structural delineations. The original lid survives and is a single piece of timber of gable form; it was designed to fit without overhanging.

    The chest has lost all original lock fittings and now bears 2 large and 1 small lock plate on the front. The lid is strengthed with 3 heavy iron bands which are secondary, but the 3 original hinge straps still support the lid; the right-hand strap is broken but the centre and left straps are complete and follow the curve of the gable lid to finish a short distance from the front edge with bi-foliated terminals. The sides of the chest have large ring handles attached to a free double link which falls from a loop fixed to the chest with 2 rectangular iron plates. The handles and links are sufficiently long to extend above the chest lid when raised. The joints of the chest have sprung in places, but otherwise its condition is excellent.

Analysis

    The Cound chest has a number of features which are paralleled elsewhere: a gable lid of precisely the same form as Malpas and Neenton (Cat. 37, 38); dovetails as at Malpas and Avenbury; substantial bi-foliated iron straps common in early contexts (e.g. Bayeux, Cat. 11) but continuing in use over a considerable period and present at Avenbury and on the Richard de Bury chest made between 1334–45; and large, circular handles attached to long links which are designed to be raised free of the lid to enable the chest to be swung by a pole, again present on the Avenbury and Richard de Bury chests. The strong links with the Avenbury and Richard de Bury chests suggest a fourteenth-century date for Cound, but its simplicity and utilitarian character makes close stylistic dating impossible; 1340–80 is therefore suggested.

Select Bibliography

N. Pevsner, *Shropshire*, Harmondsworth, 1958, 114.

CATALOGUE No. 37 (PLATE 43)

Chest (hutch type 2) in St Oswald's church, Malpas, Cheshire.

Probably oak

l. 7' 1½"
h. without lid 2' 6½", minimum thickness of lid, 2"
w. 1' 8"

Description (September 1967)

The front of the chest is a single board; the sides cannot be examined for joins owing to a coating of plaster which has been liberally applied on all sides of the chest. All 4 feet of the chest are pierced with a lunette, with the front edges chamfered. The front and back boards of the chest are attached to their respective uprights with two large dovetails. The lid fits the chest without an overhang and is of gable form.

The central lock plate and hasp are secondary and post-medieval but lie in the original position, as can be seen from scars on the lid showing where the original hasp was removed and the iron scrollwork carefully prised up to allow the alteration to be made.

The chest is covered at front, sides and lid with decorative ironwork in which a single design is repeated many times upon the field. The design comprises a single upright stem with sharply curving branches springing from it on either side; each element is fitted next to its neighbour in such a way that the branches from one fill the voids of its companion. Thus each element is entirely separate from its neighbour, yet the field is well covered. The iron rod is of B section, attached with substantial nails, and is broadened and flattened at the ends of stems and branches to produce irregular finials of leaf and fleurette forms.

Analysis

This chest creates an impression of richness, born of the texture of iron on wood and the massed nature of the design with a multitude of cranked branches with leaf finials decorating all visible surfaces. (Ayrton and Silcock state that the stamped finials are created with the hammer only, without the aid of dies or punches.[407] In spite of richness, however, admiration fades as we analyse the design and note the fragmentation of the elements and the staccato nature of their treatment. This work fails to produce either the spiky vigour of the unsophisticated work of the twelfth and early thirteenth centuries in England or the superb and felicitous scrolls of the same period found at their more exquisite at Notre Dame de Paris (pl. 59) and on Henry III's doors at Windsor (see p. 154). The latter works are indeed of an accomplishment which is beyond our expectations for furniture, yet a number of surviving examples of furniture with early decorative ironwork ably demonstrate the shortcomings of the Malpas design (Cat. 22, 23, 33, 34). Stylistically, Malpas belongs to the revival of interest in curvilinear wrought iron in the late fourteenth and fifteenth centuries, rather than to the greatest years of achievement of the Middle Ages.[408] If we compare Malpas with the ironwork for a pair of concertina

---

[407] Ayrton/Silcock, 27.
[408] Here I must disagree with Ayrton/Silcock, who appear to suggest a thirteenth-century date for Malpas (see Ayrton/Silcock, 27–8).

doors removed from an armoire and stylistically dated *c*.1450 by Macquoid/Edwards,[409] we find the same lack of unity coupled with an inability to create a single, graceful curve in the design. These two factors are characteristic of late wrought iron and they survived in unsophisticated contexts into the seventeenth century, as we see from a door at Dartmouth which is medieval in feeling, yet is dated 1631.[410]

Regarding details of carpentry, the gable lid, dovetails and lunette feet are the most striking features and though none serve to date the chest as convincingly as the ironwork, the treatment of the feet reinforces the evidence for a late date. It may be noted in passing that all three features are present in the extraordinarily primitive chest at Bitterley.[411] The lunette piercing/carving at Malpas and Bitterley is recognizable as the column/lunette foot in decadence, see Fig. 18. In the Malpas foot, the architectural connotations are lost and the column with lunette has become schematic.

To sum up, it must be said that although the Malpas ironwork has been treated critically above, its deficiencies are a relative matter. As a late and derivative work, it cannot fail to compare unfavourably with the work of the period which inspired it. It is a country chest, decorated in accordance with an early tradition at a time when sophisticated design was implemented in terms of the hard brilliance of bench work, rather than wrought iron. Thus, in fashionable terms, the Malpas chest is anachronistic. Yet it has certain valid qualities which we may wholeheartedly admire: strength, individuality and confidence. As a country piece, it defies close dating on stylistic grounds and belongs within the period 1400–80.

Select Bibliography

M. Ayrton/A. Silcock, *Wrought Iron and its Decorative Use*, London, 1929, 27.

CATALOGUE No. 38 (PLATE 44)

Chest (hutch type 2) in All Saints church, Neenton, Shropshire.

Oak, now polished

l. 5′ 10¼″; h. 2′ 3½″ without lid; minimum thickness of lid, 1″; w. 1′ 5½″.

Description (March 1968; inside unseen)

The construction is poor; the carving vigorous.

The front of the chest is a single board, attached to the uprights by means of a single dovetail. The uprights are elongated to form feet and are cut away in a curve on their inner edges and chamfered. The whole front above the bottom board is carved as if it were a single unit, the joint between the main front board and the uprights being ignored in terms of the design. Part of the field has a horizontal division and the remainder is carved with lozenges. The area within the division is carved in 3 sections: on the left, quatrefoils (4 complete and 1 half quatrefoil); in the centre, 3 fleurettes, all different, with a reserve above for a lock plate; and on the right, 3 circles of flamboyant

[409] 1954, Aumbry, fig. 3 (V. & A.).
[410] See Ayrton/Silcock, fig. 54.
[411] See N. Pevsner, *Shropshire*, Harmondsworth, 1958, pl. 25b.

tracery. All the carving is worked in the solid. The sides of the chest are plain (left side missing), the right side being nailed to the front. The lid is original, of gable form and now split; it was designed to fit without overhang.

The chest has 3 lock plates which are crudely fitted and encroach upon the carving; all are secondary. The carving indicates that the chest was designed for a single, central lock. Of the 3 fittings present, the left hand survives only as a lock plate; the central fitting has part of the strap on the lid which once fitted hinge and hasp — the finial of this strap is of pointed, leaf form, Fig. 21.

Fig. 21.   Leaf-shaped finial

The third, right-hand fitting is complete with hasp and strap as well as lock plate.

The lid is still held by 2 original straps which reach half-way across its surface and terminate in pointed leaf finials, as shown Fig. 21.

Analysis

The Neenton chest is an intermediate work, lying somewhere between the high sophistication and painstaking carpentry of many decorated chests of the second half of the fifteenth century and the unoriginal and clumsy productions of Tudor date stylistically orientated towards Gothic rather than Renaissance art.[412] The carpentry at Neenton is poor, the coarse dovetailed front comparing unfavourably with Cound and Malpas (Cat. 36, 37). The carved design, ignoring structure, unlike e.g. York (Cat. 31), uses the front as a single decorative field. We cannot fail to recognize this approach as decadent, since it ignores architectural principles, though equally we may appreciate that such an approach, given different historical circumstances, *might* have fathered a new, vigorous phase of Gothic art. Neenton bears no evidence of that uncomfortable marriage of Gothic/Renaissance which infected design in the Netherlands and England in the sixteenth century, for it is entirely Gothic in character. Not only the tracery of the front, but also the carving of the feet reflects Gothic forms: here, on the inner face, is a vestigial lunette surviving as a chamfered curve (see Fig. 18) which is at variance with the Renaissance treatment of furniture supports.

The flamboyant tracery, allied to the rebellious treatment of the chest front, suggests a date somewhere between 1500–25. The pointed leaf terminal on the hinge straps can be widely dated in sophisticated work between the second half of the fifteenth century and the mid-sixteenth century, so provides less precise evidence for dating.[413]

Select Bibliography

N. Pevsner, *Shropshire*, Harmondsworth, 1958, 216.

[412] For example, the large number of carved or pierced oak armoires ('dole cupboards') at Haddon Hall, Derbyshire.
[413] See the hinge straps on the seat of a bench painted in the mid-fifteenth century by Friedrich Herlin; see Evans 1966, pl. 32; also the Wrangelschrank in the Landesmuseum für Kunst und Kulturgeschichte, Münster, of 1556, see Mercer, figs. 134–5.

PANELLED CHESTS

The development of panelled construction is discussed in Appendix IX, where it is noted that the medieval technique of *applying* a framework to boards, which gives an appearance of panelled construction, makes it difficult for us to know when true panelling originated. However, the peculiar needs of the Middle Ages were best served by solidity and durability in furniture, rather than by lightness and economy in the use of timber, and for this reason the principle of panelled construction was largely ignored until the fifteenth century.[414]

Numerous fifteenth-century illuminations of Netherlandish and French origin, as well as panel paintings by the Master of Flémalle, Jan van Eyck and others, suggest that panelled furniture was common on the Continent at this date; though panelled construction is generally applied to seating or to buffets in these works, a panelled chest is occasionally portrayed.[415] Unfortunately, the inherent fragility and elegance of the type has meant that very few pieces of furniture surviving now furnish the kind of evidence we require. Large quantities of panelled chests probably perished as a result of hard treatment and neglect, and what survived was enthusiastically collected and restored. Few fifteenth-century panelled chests survive in original condition and possessed of a secure provenance. A rare exception may be noted standing in the nave of the church of St Catherine at Honfleur, Normandy, which is stylistically dated *c.* 1450; this chest is of relatively heavy construction and the panels are carved in the solid with a rudimentary kind of linen fold. In an English context, it is difficult to know whether the panelled chest was as common in the fifteenth century as it appears to have been on the Continent. If surviving chests present an accurate picture, *light* panelled furniture was not in use in any quantity in England before the second quarter of the sixteenth century, though *heavy* panelling is used throughout in the chest of *c.* 1500 at Brasenose College, Oxford (Cat. 39).

CATALOGUE NO. 39 (PLATES 45–46A)

Chest (panelled) in the treasury at Brasenose College, Oxford

Oak

l. 6′ 6½″; h. 1′ 10″ without lid; thickness of lid, 2¼″; w. 1′ 10½″.

Description (June 1967)

The chest is very plain but extremely solid and well made. It is of panelled construction throughout, with a single panel set in a heavy frame at front, back and lid, and with 3 panels for each side. On the lid but nowhere else, the corners of the frame are mitred. The framework has a simple, flat chamfer. At front and back, the uprights are extended to form 4 short feet and the upper and lower rails join the uprights in the usual manner;

---

[414] See Appendix IX.
[415] See, for example, the copy of a painting of the Virgin and Child, believed to be from an original by Jan van Eyck, at Burgos (see Faggin, 99, cat. no. 38).

at the sides, however, this construction is varied with rails and stiles cutting into adjacent framing in the manner of dovetails, pegged in position, but here the wedge form, normal for dovetails, is not employed.

The lid is designed to fit the chest without overhang. The corners of the lid, and of the chest below the lid are bound with iron; these corner pieces are probably later than the chest itself.

The interior of the chest is fitted with 2 original narrow lockers at either end.

The chest has 3 hasps and lock plates which have been numbered 1–3 in white paint. The outer pair, nos. 2 and 3, are secondary. Hasps 2 and 3 are attached to hinge plates which lie beneath the lid; the position of plates and hasps has necessitated clumsy cutting of the upper rail of the chest. The two fittings are very similar, the plates being roughly shaped rectangles with projecting moulded nibs at each side; keyhole and hasp guards are present with tabs beneath. The hasps have protruding nails to serve as handles. The central lock plate and hasp no. 1 are original, and were the only locking arrangements when the chest was made. The hasp is unique in being attached to the front edge of the lid, and is stepped to ride in front of the frame. The lock plate is rectangular and more elaborate than the other two. It is fretted with ogee lobes and has a projecting nib on the right. The hasp has a protruding nail at its free end to serve as a handle.

The sides of the chest have long, heavy drop handles, cranked to avoid pinching the hand when raised. They are held in collars set in quatrefoil ogee traceried plates.

On the centre front of the lid is a rounded drop handle which is secondary.

Analysis

This chest is referred to in the Old Plate Book which was used for records concerning College silver and also for entries regarding money in the College chest, and its first entry is dated 1519/20. The original statutes of Brasenose College stipulate that the College should use a chest with 3 locks, and since locks 2 and 3 on the chest are secondary but are not later than the sixteenth century, it has been assumed that they were added in 1516 to satisfy this requirement.[416]

The evidence of the locks shows that the chest was not specially commissioned after the formulation of the College Statutes, for it was made with a single lock. The two designs of lock plate, nos. 2 and 3 and the earlier no. 1, are broadly similar and do not suggest many years difference in date. Other evidence reaffirms an early sixteenth-century horizon. The handles at the side are common in fourteenth and fifteenth-century contexts but their quatrefoil plates, echoing the lobed edges of lock plate no. 1, have closer parallels. Plates of this shape occur at Windsor (Cat. 19) and secure the handle to the door of Bishop Fox's chantry in Winchester Cathedral of 1528. Since we find that the chest existed well before 1528, we must rely upon the evidence of the locks and the College Statutes to provide the closest dating evidence, and this material indicates a date of 1500–15 for the chest.

The Brasenose chest is important in establishing the kind of panelled furniture which was being made at the close of the fifteenth century; although it is not carved, it shares

---

[416] See Ed. F. Madan, A. J. Butler, E. W. Allfrey, 'The College Plate', BNC *Quatercentenary Monographs*, no. v, *Oxford Historical Society*, LII, 1909, 5, 11.

the same heavy quality with the chest at Honfleur (see p. 160). Panelling, used in both these chests, is employed in a manner which retains all the strength associated with earlier forms of construction. The Brasenose chest is entirely utilitarian, yet is individual in character as is shown by the carpentry of the sides; it has none of the weaknesses of style and technique which were becoming common at this period (see Neenton, Cat. 38).

Select Bibliography

Ed. F. Madan, A. J. Butler, E. W. Allfrey 'The College Plate', *BNC Quatercentenary Monographs,* No. v, *Oxford Hist. Soc.,* LII, 1909, 5, 11.

RCHM Oxford, 1939, 25a.

Let us now examine the second group of chests in Fig. 17, those which have no feet and rest directly upon the ground.

DUG-OUT CHESTS (no Catalogue examples)

This is unquestionably the most primitive form of chest, being in essence a log, flattened along one side to enable it to lie firmly on the ground, with an area hollowed out of the uppermost surface closed with a lid which seems to have been generally hipped or curved. The sides and back were normally flattened, so that the log presented a rectangular appearance. Chests of this kind survive at Wimborne Minster, Dorset, and in the church at Lower Peover, Cheshire. They were useful as collection boxes, as Macquoid/Edwards have shown;[417] their great weight made them difficult to move and only a small hollowed out space was necessary to render them eminently suitable for this purpose. Collection boxes of this type were still favoured in the later Middle Ages, as the sophisticated fourteenth-century example illustrated by Viollet-le-Duc shows.[418]

BOX CHESTS

This form of chest was the ideal for practical storage, in cases where security and convenience were more important than appearance. The box form is less graceful than a footed chest, but it was more readily transportable and any problems arising out of contact with the floor could be simply overcome by using blocks underneath. Indeed, continental furniture such as the chest at Bruges (Cat. 41) was equipped with its own runners which raised it off the ground and added some grace to the appearance of such furniture. The side and front boards of box chests were normally nailed or dowelled together and the joints made rigid and durable by horizontally placed iron clamps extending round the corners. (If *broad* stiles and mortise and tenon joints at the front are

---

[417] See Macquoid/Edwards 1954, Chests, 2, citing the reference to such chests in the Chronicle of Jocelin of Brakelond.
[418] Viollet-le-Duc 1858, 280, fig. 1.

present in a box chest, it generally means that the object in question is a mutilated hutch, as in the case of Climping Cat. 30.)

The box form was probably the commonest for the numerous small, practical containers, generally called *coffrets*, which were stored within armoires or chests. The few that survive, that were not jewel *coffrets* and are in no way intrinsically precious objects themselves, are similar to box chests in form and decoration. A finely made example in the Public Record Office with four separately lidded compartments of *c*. 1255 is bound with thin vertical bands of iron rod round its whole circumference as well as at the corners, and has trefoil terminals; and a smaller pair of boxes of *c*. 1360 without iron strapping are painted with heraldic ornament.[419] The boxes at Durham have sliding lids and fifteenth-century horn covered labels, and the elaborately worked iron fittings on an example at Ghent bear a close resemblance to the fittings on the York armoires (Cat. 3–7).[420] These oak *coffrets* of box form fall outside our survey of furniture, but they are mentioned here as they provide valuable evidence in the present context, being dated either by dendrochronology (in the case of the Public Record Office examples) or stylistically by sophisticated ironwork (in the case of the Ghent example).

The appearance of the majority of surviving box chests indicates that the form generally served strictly utilitarian purposes in which display played no part, for we cannot trace a tradition of elaborate carving and ironwork in this form of chest, as we can with hutches and plinth chests; though highly decorative box chests survive, they are exceptional. One of the earliest of the utilitarian box chests is at Cradley church, Herefordshire, and is over 9′ long. The front is a single oak board which was originally bound with twelve iron straps with bi-foliated terminals which turn underneath to grip the bottom board. The sides are bound with two long straps which turn the corners at front and back, as at Merton (*c*. 1280–1300, Cat. 35), and the lid is gently hipped, covered with iron strapping and divided into two sections. As the chest is unsophisticated work and lacks its original locking arrangments which could aid stylistic dating, a wide dating range must be allowed to include the Bayeux armoire of *c*. 1240 (Cat. 11) and the Richard de Bury chest of 1334–45 (see p. 138), both of which have similar strapping. The chest of poplar wood at Hereford discussed by Streeter[421] is interesting in showing how a very plain form can become distinguised by the use of regular, carefully positioned iron strapping with matching terminals — in this case fleur-de-lis. The chest bears one long, articulated handle at each end for pole suspension and although the lid is modern, its restoration as a flat rather than a domed cover must be correct, as is shown by the length of the carrying handles.[422] The concave sided, centrally placed lock plate is original and is restrained in its treatment, lacking the exuberant leaf ornament common in mid-fifteenth-century work of this kind (e.g. All Souls chest, Cat. 43) and the shortening of the iron strap binding the chest at the centre front makes careful allowance for

[419] See Jenning[s], nos. IV, I and II respectively.
[420] 'Locellus' boxes at Durham were kindly described for me by Mr A. J. Piper, Department of Palaeography and Diplomatic, University of Durham, under whose care they rest. The archive box at Ghent is from St Peter's Abbey and is now preserved in the Bijloke museum, no. 60.6.3.
[421] In the chained library of the Cathedral, see Streeter, 118–19.
[422] The length of these handles indicate that the chest was of box form and was not a standard with a domed lid.

the position of the lock plate above. The Hereford chest is sophisticated in its arrangements of iron on wood and may be Flemish rather than English; a stylistic date of *c.* 1350–1400 is suggested through comparisons with the Richard de Bury chest (1334–45), Wroxeter, York (Cat. 31) and All Souls of *c.* 1440 (Cat. 43).

The chest at Icklingham, Suffolk, pronounced *c.* 1400 by Macquoid/Edwards,[423] is quite exceptional among box chests, being covered with wrought iron scrolls in the manner of the earlier French hutch (Cat. 33). Icklingham has the long drop handles, cranked to prevent hand injury when in use, which are associated with fourteenth and fifteenth-century box and standard chests. Although a critical appraisal will find fault with the design and execution of the Icklingham ironwork when placed alongside twelfth and thirteenth-century wrought iron, it nevertheless presents a magnificently rich, encrusted appearance and is probably more aesthetically successful than Malpas (Cat. 37).

The practical nature of the box form is once again manifested in the chest at Bury St Edmunds, where iron plating and strapping almost obliterate the wooden core and arrangments for multiple padlocks and iron bars indicate that this chest was a strong box or safe; the ironwork is too crude to permit close dating but suggests the fourteenth century.[424] The Winchester College chest of 1396/7 (Cat. 40) has massive iron strapping which fails to conceal the wood beneath and establishes the kind of workmanship and design which might be expected of country craftsmen in England at this date. The Bruges box chest of 1400–25 (Cat. 41), unusual in being carved, is raised on runners which can be paralleled in Flemish paintings supporting seating,[425] and upon an extant fifteenth-century Flemish armoire,[426] and its elegance and sophistication provide a considerable contrast with most of the chests discussed above. Another example at Bruges, however, is more characteristic,[427] being plain except for the usual strapping at corners and elsewhere; here the considered placing and design of straps and terminals recalls both the Hereford example (see pp. 163–4) and the carved Bruges chest (Cat. 41), and its date should therefore conform with these examples and lie within the period *c.* 1400–25.

The All Souls chests of *c.* 1440 (Cat. 42, 43) are important examples of English work using soft wood, and show how chests of very plain, rough character might carry relatively elaborate and decorative lock plates, as has already been noted in Netherlandish contexts.

The Ghent chest of *c.* 1480 (Cat. 44) may have been originally leather covered. It carries the possibilities of refinement in the placing and finish of iron strapping to their ultimate conclusion, perfecting a tendency already established at Hereford, and reinforces the impression that in the Netherlands the unornamented, utilitarian chest was sometimes furnished with ironwork created by a master craftsman, as has already been shown in the Malines armoire (Cat. 13).

---

[423] Macquoid/Edwards 1927, Chests and Coffers, fig. 6.
[424] In Moyse's Hall Museum, Bury St Edmunds.
[425] For example, the Master of Flémalle, see Caullet 111–13.
[426] At Courtrai, see Caullet 111–13.
[427] Gruuthuse museum no. 560; the chest has secondary painting.

CATALOGUE No. 40 (PLATES: 46B, see also 47A)

Chest (box form) at Winchester College. In the Muniment Room; this is the left-hand chest beneath the window on the E. wall.

Oak, iron bound

l. *c.* 6′; h. without lid, *c.* 1′ 8″; w. *c.* 2′.

Description (July 1973)

The chest is raised off the floor on modern blocks.

The back, front and sides of the chest appear to be of single planks of oak. The lid is made of two planks. The chest is strapped with wide iron bands attached with heavy nails. The bands are not interwoven (verticals tend to lie over horizontals), and do not entirely cover the wood; the eleven vertical bands appear to surround the chest, passing down the front, underneath and up the back where some are hinged to the lid. Six of the bands on the lid are hinged for hasps at the front. The hasps are set in pairs:

1 2   3 4   5 6

and each pair is designed for a padlock or bar fitting and for an integral lock, so that 1, 4 and 6 are for bar or padlock fittings and 2, 3 and 5 for integral locks. The hinges of the padlock hasps (1, 4 and 6) are attached at one side of hasp plates which are about one and a half times wider than the straps themselves. These plates are cut back on the hinge side a short way below the thickness of the lid, so that they become the correct size required for a hasp but now fall in a manner which is no longer coincidental with the line of the vertical straps to which they are attached. This enables the special plates fitted with padlock or bar loops to be attached to the wood of the chest rather than to the iron strapping. Hasps 2, 3 and 5 are stepped in equally on either side below the hinge, however, and thus fall straight from their respective straps, but the lock plates into which

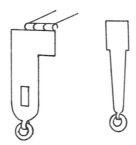

Fig. 22.   Hasps

they engage, although they may cover the iron strapping at their edges, do not lie over strapping entirely. Thus lock plates, as well as padlock or bar plates, lie on the chest in a similar manner and all hasps engage evenly; the distance required for these plates from the chest face is dictated by the position of the lid *vis-à-vis* the chest. The lock plates have simple, squared off U-shaped guards set in roughly rectangular plates. Each hasp has a small loop at its end for a ring handle, Fig. 22.

The sides of the chest are fitted with substantial handles, one at each side, which are formed with an unusual lug, see A Fig. 23, designed to hold the handle at the correct distance from the chest when in use, a requirement more usually effected by cranking the handle.

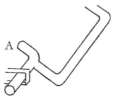

FIG. 23.   Type of handle at sides of chest

The workmanship of the chest is crude yet serviceable; its condition is excellent.

Analysis

For all its crudeness, this chest is important, for it has been correlated by J. H. Harvey with an account of 1396/7 in the Winchester College records[428] and dated by dendro-chronology to *c.* 1370.[429] The entry of 1396/7 in the *Custus Operum* account (WCM 74), which Harvey believes refers to this chest and to its neighbour[430] in the muniment room, is as follows:

> 'Et in sol' pro ligatione ij cistarum pro Thesauro et ferramento fenestre euisdem et clavis et serruris cum totidem clavibus ad easdem cistas . . .'[431]

> (And finally, for binding [with iron] two chests for the Treasury and for ironwork to the window of the same room and for nails and locks with all necessary keys for the same chests . . .)

We see that there is a certain conflict in the evidence, since dendrochronology produces a date some twenty-six years earlier than the account cited by Harvey. We cannot look to stylistic analysis as a means of resolving this problem, since such a modest object will not allow close dating on visual grounds. Since dendrochronology is established as an accurate dating technique, we must believe that the oak from which the chest is made was felled in *c.* 1370. Believing this, we are left with the following alternatives in respect of the record of 1396/7.

(1).   It does not refer to the present chest and its companion
(2).   It refers to ironwork which was secondary, being a replacement of the original locks and hinges which were fitted to the chest when it was made in *c.* 1370.
(3).   The smith, and the carpenter before him, worked on wood which had been stored for some twenty-six years before it was used.

---

[428] Harvey, 1961/2, 203 and fn. 6.
[429] Lowther, 132.
[430] The second chest stands to the right of the present chest in the muniment room (August 1973). Although the chests are not a pair, they are very similar, being of comparable form and size and bound in exactly the same manner, see pl. 47A.
[431] I am much indebted to Mr Peter Gwyn, formerly Archivist of Winchester College, for supplying me with a copy of this entry.

Regarding point (1), the survival of two similarly bound chests of medieval date seems too great a coincidence for us to ignore and argues for a rejection of this explanation. Moving on to point (2), the rigidity of the chest depends upon its iron strapping, so that it seems most improbably that this work can be secondary. Furthermore, the chest would have always needed hinges and locks of some kind and there is no evidence that the present fittings are replacements. We are therefore left with point (3) as the most satisfactory explanation of the disparity between the evidence of dendrochronology (*c.* 1370) and of the *Custus Operum* account of 1396/7, and must conclude that the chest was made from mature timber.

Although this discussion has only been concerned with the chest which was analysed dendrochronologically, it is quite clear by looking at it and its companion in the muniment room that both were made at the same time. The second box chest is almost identical with Cat. 40 but differs from it in having only three locks which are all integral with the chest and there are no arrangments for padlocks or locking bars, as there are on the chest which has been studied above. The six locks on the first chest (Cat. 40) and the three on the second are numerically compatible with Harvey's findings that the provision and distribution of keys to the door of the muniment room and to the chests ensured that three Fellows had to be present at the opening of a chest.[432]

Select Bibliography

J. H. Harvey, 'Winchester College Muniments', *Archives,* v, 1961/2, 203 and fn. 6.

A. W. G. Lowther, 'The Date of the Timbers from the Spire of Chilcomb Church: Some Evidence from Dendrochronology', *Papers and Proceedings of the Hants Field Club and Archaeological Society,* XVII, Part 2, 1951, 132.

CATALOGUE No. 41 (PLATE 47B)

Chest (Box type) in the Gruuthuse museum, Bruges, no. 597.

Oak, now polished

l. 3′ 7½″; h. including lid and runners, 1′ 9¾″; w. 1′ 9″.

Description (August 1970)

The chest has its original lid, lock and hasp and battens or runners along the bottom at the sides. It is carved in the solid at the front only.

The front is crisply carved in high relief with an unmoulded border. The design incorporates a central vertical band which allows ample blank space for a lock plate above and has trefoils and stylized rosettes below. On either side, the upper register is filled with 4 large individual roses of flamboyant tracery with arcading below. The plain lid, now askew, fits without overhang.

The chest is raised off the ground with battens which run along the sides and are carved with stylized animal paws at the front.

---

[432] Harvey, 1961/2, 203.

The sides of the chest are plain, but all corners are braced with 3 iron plates, their ends plain at the sides and fretted at the front, Fig. 24.

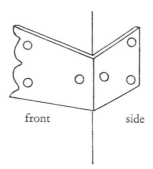

front   side

FIG. 24.   Iron corner plates

Each side has a single, long drop handle. The lock plate is rectangular with simple fretted edges, raised nibs at each side with diagonal scoring and raised U-shaped guard. The hasp is attached to the front edge of the lid; above it, on top of the lid, is a small octofid rosette or iron, scored to represent petals, which is presumably the head of a rivet which holds the hasp hinge in position. The hasp is stepped and tapered and has a raised spine, scored and curled at the top, ?representing a snake or salamander. A drop handle of some form was once attached to the end of the hasp.

Analysis

This chest shows that the box form might be decoratively treated. It retains the iron corner clamps or straps found necessary with this form of assembly, and confines their elaboration to the front only, which is consistent with the emphasis of the carving, also confined to the front.

The use of battens is an interesting feature of continental origin which occurs in an important carved armoire of the hospital of Notre-Dame at Courtrai, published by Caullet. Caullet shows that such battens were in use from 1400 and notes that they are found in interiors painted by the Master of Flémalle.[433] The paw feet which decorate the front of the battens are a classical habit on seating and are ultimately derived from Egypt; they are familiar in the Middle Ages on X-chairs.

Although the chest is modest in size and appearance, the quality of the carving and ironwork is high. The hasp is reminiscent of York (Cat. 31) with its raised spine and attachment to the front edge of the lid, and at York the ring handle is still present. The character of the flamboyant tracery is not yet extreme in form, and the graceful flow of line on the decorated edges of the corner clamps which have none of the sharpness characteristic of the end of the fifteenth century (e.g. Cat. 44) suggests a date of *c.*1400–25.

[433] Caullet, 111–13.

Select Bibliography

Catalogue Musée Gruuthuse, Bruges, 1970, 597.

G. Caullet, 'Les Œuvres d'Art de l'Hôpital Notre Dame à Courtrai', *Bulletin du Cercle Historique et Archéologique de Courtrai*, XI, 1913/14, 111–13.

CATALOGUE NOS. 42 AND 43 (PLATE 48)

Chests (Box type) in the gateway tower of All Souls College, Oxford.

Soft wood, now stained reddish brown

No. 42	No. 43
l. 7′ 10½″	l. *c.* 8′ 6″
h. with lid 2′	h. with lid 2′ 1″
w. 2′ 3″	w. 2′ 4″

Description (June 1967; sides, backs, lids and interiors unseen)

These chests formed part of the equipment of a full storeroom and had books stacked around and upon them; although a proper examination was therefore impossible, the evidence these chests offer makes it important to include them here.

The chests are not a pair, differing in measurements and in the design and execution of their lock plates, but their similarities and the lack of detailed information makes joint treatment desirable.

The chests are similar in form and appearance showing that they were made by the same carpenter and smith, at one and the same time. The front of no. 42 is of a single, heavy board pegged to the sides; it is strapped with iron bands. The finish of the carpenter's work on both chests is extremely rough, though the weight of the timbers employed, and the iron strapping, make them very strong. Both chests have 3 locks.

Chest Cat. 42.   The outer two lock plates have slightly concave sides and are furnished with bold and simple single raised U-guards, protecting the hasp but not the keyhole. The centre lock plate is rectangular. All plates are crudely formed. The right-hand hasp is missing, but the other two remain, hinged to bands on the lid. The centre hasp has a substantial nail on a projecting stem at its free end, which serves as a handle when the hasp is engaged and lying flush within the U-guard.

Chest Cat. 43.   Here, although the strapping resembles Cat. 42, the lock plates are finer and more elaborate. Of the three present, one with original hasp was examined, see pl. 48 This lock plate has concave sides and two elaborate raised guards, the hasp guard of the usual squared-off tapered U-form and the keyhole guard which is rectangular rather than tapered. Each guard has toothed side edges and traceried tabs below. The keyhole guard has a fleur-de-lis surmounting its rectangular frame. At the edges of the guards, four tendrils extend to the corners of the plate. The hasp is nipped in to fit snugly within its guard, and has a four-sided nail on a stem fitted at its free end to serve as a handle. The hasp is hinged to a strap on top of the lid.

N

Analysis

These chests were made *in situ*, providing unassailable evidence that they were made for All Souls, for they are too large to have been introduced into the small tower room where they lie. The documentary evidence for the building of the front quadrangle of the College, including the gateway tower where the chests lie, shows that the area was completed by 1440.[434] The accounts of the building operations are concerned with fabric, so that furniture is not mentioned; therefore there is no evidence that the chests were not made for the room where they lie, at a later date. However, the highly individual toothed guards to the hasp and lock of chest no. 43 are almost exactly paralleled at Wells Cathedral, in the iron lock plate on the entrance to the chantry chapel of Thomas Bekynton, Bishop of Bath and Wells (1443–65) built some thirteen years before his death and therefore of *c.*1452, see pl. 66A. This correlation provides a satisfactory reason for accepting the chests as part of the original furnishing of the gateway tower undertaken shortly after completion, sometime between 1440–5. The room was originally used for muniments and *jocalia*.[435]

The marked difference in the quality of the lock plates on chests 42 and 43, accompanied by strapping which is similarly straightforward on both chests, suggests that the smith responsible for the ironwork fashioned the bands on both chests and the locks on chest 42, but for some reason which we cannot explain obtained the lock plate and hasp on chest 43 shown in the plate from elsewhere.

The chests are examples of simple, utilitarian furniture. They are of particular interest and significance, however, in providing dating evidence from an impeccable context, and in indicating that soft wood furniture was made in England and not necessarily introduced ready made from abroad in the fifteenth century.

Select Bibliography

E. F. Jacob, 'The Building of All Souls College, 1438–1443', ed. J. G. Edwards/V. H. Galbraith/E. F. Jacob, *Historical Essays in Honour of James Tait*, Manchester, 1933, 121–35.

CATALOGUE No. 44 (PLATE 49)

Chest (Box type) in the Bijloke museum, Ghent.

Oak, ironbound

l. 3′ 8⅛″; h. without lid, 2′ 1″; thickness of lid, 1¾″; w. 1′ 11⅝″.

Description (August 1970; inside and back unseen)

The chest is raised off the floor on modern blocks. In its present state it is a simple, strong oak box fashioned from heavy timbers but is given exceptional refinement by the quality of its iron fittings.

---

[434] E. F. Jacob, 'The Building of All Souls College, 1438–1443', ed. J. G. Edwards/V. H. Galbraith/E. F. Jacob, *Historical Essays in Honour of James Tait*, Manchester, 1933, 132.

[435] The late Professor E. F. Jacob gave me this information in 1967, and there can be no doubt that it was based on his intimate knowledge of the College muniments.

Two groups of iron straps bind the chest: a series of 3 interrupted bands which cross over the lid, run vertically down the front and turn underneath, and 8 short horizontal straps which brace the corners. The vertically placed group run right to the front edge of the lid and, at the front, finish just below it, except for the central strap on the front which stops short to allow room for a lock plate. These straps are finished with pierced traceried terminals, Fig. 25.

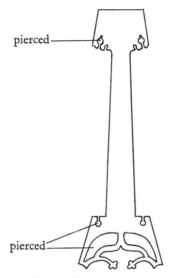

FIG. 25.   Type of strap placed vertically on the chest

The corner straps have simpler terminals, Fig 26. All the terminals have a leather foil showing through the pierced areas.

Each side of the chest is fitted with a long drop handle held in two sex-foil rose mounts; the handles are of round section rod which widens at the centre, Fig. 26.

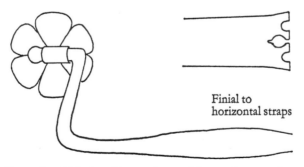

Finial to
horizontal straps

FIG. 26.   Side handle on chest with attachment plate

The chest retains its original, centrally positioned lock plate; it is rectangular, with edges fretted with tracery. The 2 lock plates on either side of the centre are secondary.

Analysis

The quality of the ironwork of this chest contrasts with the simplicity of the wood-work. Such a juxtaposition is in keeping with late twelfth/early thirteenth-century work (see Cat. 33 and 34) but is less characteristic of the fifteenth century, to which this iron strapping clearly belongs. Simplicity in woodwork and extreme refinement in ironwork can occur in a fifteenth-century context, however, as the Malines armoire has shown (Cat. 13). In the case of the present chest, the presence of leather behind the tracery suggests that the wood may not have been exposed originally, but covered with hide; if this was the case, the leather must have been glued to the wood, for the iron bands are insufficiently numerous to hold leather closely without additional aid.

The iron strapping and central lock are stylistically late fifteenth century. The terminals to the corner straps (Fig. 26), flared and cut with ogival tracery, may be compared with the Malines armoire (Cat. 13) of *c.* 1470, and the sex-foil rose handle plate (Fig. 26) is present on the late fifteenth-century York armoires (Cat. 3–7) and upon the state cradle of 1478/9 (Cat. 28) made for one of the children of Marie of Burgundy. The more elaborate and beautiful terminals to the vertical straps on this chest (Fig. 25), with their pendant trefoiled fleurettes, are almost precisely matched in the gesso gilt tracery of the late fifteenth-century chancel screen at Southwold, Suffolk.[436] (Though earlier examples of the pendant fleurette can be cited, the exaggerated form used in the Bijloke terminals does not seem to occur before the late fifteenth century.)

Less easy to place in this context, however, are the long drop handles of round section which are swollen at the centre to render them easy to the hand, found on the sides of the Bijloke chest (Fig. 26). A similar handle with swollen centre is found on the lid of a small box at Antwerp dated 1587, though in all other respects the ironwork on this box is dissimilar for it is not, like the Bijloke chest, purely Gothic in form.[437] If the side handles on the Bijloke chest are not sixteenth-century additions (and their rose mounts suggest they are original rather than secondary) the quality of the work throughout allows us to accept the premise that the smith responsible was able to draw on very up-to-date models. If we take this view, we may accept a stylistic date of *c.* 1480–1500 for the chest, in agreement with the main burden of evidence.

STANDARD CHESTS

The term 'standard' has been discussed, and we have seen that it was used in English sources to describe a large travelling chest (see Fig. 17; also p. 112); it is here iden-tified following accepted usage, with a form of chest with a domed or gabled lid rendering it particularly suitable for travel since the lid threw off water and a flange fitted round the rim of the box at the point of closure helped to keep the interior dry. Apart from usefulness in travel, the domed lid was probably convenient in preventing the use of such chests as seats or tables; the Guildhall iron chest of this form shows that standards were not invariably fashioned as travelling equipment.

[436] See Cescinsky/Gribble, I, fig. 122.
[437] Van den Burgh museum no. 826. Leather covered box, inscribed: 'FRANCHOIS VAN DUCK ANNO 1587'.

A number of large fifteenth-century standards have survived in England and the Netherlands (Cat. 45–46). Another kind of standard chest, which has survived in England, is smaller sized and slighter on construction; it may have a gabled or a domed lid and be wholly or partially leather covered; this group is represented by the Westminster Abbey chest (Cat. 47).

If we consider the large standards first, we find that the Hereford example of *c.* 1440 (Cat. 45) is one of a number of similar chests which have wide iron bands leaving the wooden box clearly visible. Poplar wood seems to have been favoured for these chests.[438] and lock plates often exhibit exaggeratedly concave sides. Handles are generally at the sides and are sometimes for ropes rather than for manual use, as in the Hereford example. Wooden lids are exposed at the ends and are cut without join, following the curve of the tree trunk. The chest at Little Waldingfield, Essex[439] is an example which is closely akin to the Hereford standard (Cat. 45) and other fifteenth-century chests at Bruges[440] and Malines.[441] belong to the same class.

Another group within the large standard class is represented by the Bruges example of *c.* 1450–1500 (Cat. 46). Here, iron plating virtually conceals the wooden chest beneath and wheels are attached at the sides. These iron-plated standards tend to have multiple locking arrangements. St John's College, Cambridge, has such a wheeled standard and here wheels and wheel attachments are of the same pattern as the Bruges chest (Cat. 46), and another Bruges example,[442] without wheels, provides a third example of the type. Sidney Sussex College, Cambridge has the most elaborate surviving standard of this iron-plated group, unhappily much deteriorated through oxidation. It is important in showing that slotted hasps were designed for bars (here intact) and not necessarily for individual padlocks, and in providing an instance of a highly decorated chest of this utilitarian form. The chest has wheels, multiple ornament, traceried terminals on the corner bands like those of the Malines armoire of *c.* 1470 (Cat. 13) and many of the graceful Gothic details exhibited on the St Ursula shrine painted by Hans Memling (1433–1494),[443] without any of the angularity of ornament associated with early sixteenth-century work. Although the Sidney Sussex chest was brought from the Netherlands in the seventeenth century, it has long been recognized as of fifteenth-century date;[444] the comparisons suggested here indicate a date of *c.* 1460–90.

A chest which belongs to this sturdy group, yet stands somewhat apart from it, is the remarkable iron standard of *c.* 1427 which was a common chest of London's Guildhall; its material has dictated its structural details, which are of necessity unlike any wooden chest. The Guildhall chest appears to be a unique survivor of a type made wholly of iron which was always rare.[445] Before moving on to the smaller standards, we should

[438] See the Suffolk examples at Chelsworth and Groton (Cescinsky/Gribble, figs. 3 and 4), Little Waldingfield (H. M. Cautley, *Suffolk Churches and their Treasures*, London, 1937, 311); and also the Hereford box chest (pp. 163–4), of poplar wood.
[439] See Cautley, 311.
[440] Gruuthuse museum no. 557.
[441] In the Busleydon museum. This standard is painted red and bears the arms of Malines on the lid.
[442] Gruuthuse museum no. 559.
[443] At St John's Hospital, Bruges.
[444] Brought by the Master, Samuel Ward (1610–1643) for the College Treasury, see M. Grant, *Cambridge*, London, 1966, fig. 25, 180.
[445] See Eames, 1974.

note in conclusion that there is a Flemish bias in the evidence concerning these large standards. We see them deployed by the Duke of Burgundy's campaigning soldiers in a drawing,[446] we note how many survive in the Netherlands or are known to come thence, we observe that a group of survivors in England come from Suffolk which had convenient ports for trade with the Low Countries, and we see also in the survivors in England characteristics which seem foreign to the English tradition. It is true that many of the lock plates of these standards, in particular the Hereford group, closely resemble a fitting on the English All Souls chest (Cat. 43) but in other ways the comparison fails, for the All Souls chest has iron strapping which is devoid of that precise, pattern making approach which is so characteristic of Netherlandish work. The evidence suggests that all the large wooden standards discussed above are Flemish. For the one excluded from this conclusion, however, the iron Guildhall 'common chest', the lack of comparable examples elsewhere and the plain nature of the hasps and handles makes conclusions based on comparisons impossible. However, the most cogent evidence to help us here is the ownership and use of the chest, and it seems highly unlikely that the masters of English guilds, ever mindful of individual commercial interests, would consider employing the skills of foreigners in a circumstance of this kind.

To turn now to the smaller, slighter standards, illustrated by the Westminster Abbey example (Cat. 47), it is likely that we see in this group examples of the trussing coffers or sumpter chests of written sources, which are generally listed in pairs and were designed to be carried on horseback rather than in carts.

CATALOGUE No. 45 (PLATE 50)
Chest (standard type) at Hereford Cathedral, Vicars Choral Library.
Soft wood
l. 4′ 2¾″; h. without lid, 1′ 9½″; w. 1′ 11″; Thickness of lid at apex, 4¼″.

Description (April 1968; inside unseen)
The chest, without lid, is formed of 4 single boards of nearly equal height (front and back are tapered to stand slightly higher than the sides); an additional board is joined at each end and is curved at the top to accommodate the lid.

The lid is domed and utilizes the natural curve of the tree trunk; it is shaped to give a heavy overhang at the sides and a narrow flange at front and back. The flange, which is thin and vulnerable, has broken away in places.

The chest is strapped with wide bands of thin gauge iron, nailed in position. Five vertical bands bind the lid; the inner 3 are repeated on the front (though the central band is interrupted by a lock plate). The vertical straps on the front originally turned underneath; this can be seen in the left-hand band (the lower edge of the centre and right bands are hidden by a secondary horizontal iron strap).

Each of the sides of the chest have 2 vertical straps which turn beneath the chest and are fitted with 2 small ring handles. The corners are strengthened with 3 horizontal

---

[446] By Master 'W.A.' See Deuchler, fig. 354; the chest that lies open contains armour.

bands which extend to meet the vertical bands at front and sides. The side and corner bands are original but the 3 other bands are replacements, lying in original positions.

The 3 hasps hinged to the 3 inner bands on the lid were for padlocks or bars (outer pair) and a lock plate (centre). All hasps are secondary but their number, position and type are unchanged. The central lock plate is original with concave sides, 2 raised linked U-guards and 2 decorative leaf terminals. The right-hand terminal originally extended beyond the plate, but this portion of the leaf has been broken off. A small catch for releasing the lock without the aid of a key, fitted on the plate to the right of the hasp, presumably belongs to the repair work undertaken when a new hasp was fitted.

Analysis

This chest is a serviceable luggage article and is entirely utilitarian in character. The terminals on the lock plate are of stereotyped appearance and indifferent finish. Three very similar chests are recorded in Suffolk churches and are almost certainly also of soft wood in every case; other examples survive in the Netherlands.[447]

There is no evidence to suggest that the Hereford chest was ever leather covered.

The Hereford lock plate is very similar in character to the All Souls chest fitting (Cat. 43), although it is less elaborate and of inferior workmanship; nevertheless, the comparison is close enough to suggest parallel dating for both chests and *c.* 1440 is therefore a likely date for the Hereford standard.

CATALOGUE No. 46 (PLATE 51)

Chest (standard type) in the Gruuthuse museum, Bruges, no. 558.

Wood, iron plated

Without lid: l.   4' 3"; w. 1' 7"
Lid: l. 4' 5½"
      Max. h. including wheels, 2' 5 "
      Max. h., lid at side 3½"; w. 1' 8"
      Diam. wheels, 4½"

Description (August 1970; inside unseen)

The chest is entirely covered with wide iron bands, no wood being visible. The lid is curved, following the shape of a tree trunk which is, no doubt, utilized beneath the iron cladding; it now lies askew on the chest. Most of the outermost iron bands are laid vertically, but horizontal bands lie uppermost at the corners. There are 2 cranked drop handles of square section iron rod placed one at each side of the chest.

The chest has 3 original locking arrangements at the front: 2 hasps which have rectangular slots and engage heavy loops for padlocks or a bar, and a central hasp which fits a lock plate. Above each hasp hinge on the lid are 3 iron clamps gripping the iron bands; these clamps appear to be original, since the rivets on the bands involved take cognizance of the band attachments. The padlock or bar hasps are boldly formed and

[447] See pp. 172–4.

were both finished with substantial pear-shaped or cusped drop handles; the right hand only survives.

The lock plate is of simple, rectangular form with raised U-guard and tab beneath. The central hasp fitting the lock plate is stepped and is furnished with a long, raised handle which has an exceptionally delicate shell above and a stylized quatrefoil tab below.

The chest is raised on 4 iron wheels which have 3 spokes on each side. The wheels are connected in pairs by means of iron rods placed across the width of the chest, and each wheel is attached to the chest by a heavy iron strap. The chest has no secondary fittings; except for the distortion of the lid due to broken hinges, its condition is excellent.

Analysis

This chest is an efficiently produced strong box, like others that have survived,[448] but it possesses one feature which is unusual in such a context. The central hasp of this chest is undoubtedly one of the most beautifully worked accessories of its period to have survived; in quality of design and in execution it suggests that the chest belonged to a great seigneurial lord, accustomed to employ men of exceptional talents. The presence of the shell motif upon the central hasp probably indicates a connexion with St James of Compostello and shows that the chest was commissioned by a person who claimed this saint as his, or her, particular patron. The commonest reasons for the choice of a patron saint by individuals was either that they bore the saint's name (see pl. 72c) or were born on the saint's festival day.[449] As James was such a common name, it is not surprising that other objects bearing shells upon the lock have survived.[450]

Leaving aside the revelation of the work on the central hasp, there are other extant wheeled standards for comparison. The Sidney Sussex College chest is a standard of exceptional elaboration, but of entirely different design, but the St John's College, Cambridge, chest is very similar to the present example. The St John's chest has the same form of padlock or bar hasps (one with pendant, cusped handle surviving), and the same wheels and wheel attachments as the present chest, and these striking similarities surely indicate that the two must be of comparable date.[451]

In spite of the sophisticated hasp on the present chest, stylistic dating is difficult, for this feature seems to be unique. The raised spine on the hasp of the York chest of *c*. 1380 comes to mind (Cat. 31), and the side handle cranked to protect the hand in use is found in many late fifteenth-century contexts (e.g. Cat. 47), as well as on the Guildhall iron chest of *c*. 1427.[452] But I am chiefly guided by the stylistic qualities of the *coquille de*

---

[448] For example, another standard chest in the Gruuthuse museum, no. 559.

[449] Charles V of France was born on St Agnes's day and therefore chose her as his patron saint; his son, Charles VI was presented in 1391 with a gold cup enamelled with scenes from her life which was probably made for his father and is preserved in the British Museum, see O. M. Dalton, 10.

[450] See the *cuir bouilli* coffer no. 2885 in the Musée d'Art et d'Histoire, Brussels; believed to be Spanish of *c*.1500, the coffer has shells upon the lock and as terminals to the iron strapping.

[451] See Ffoulkes, 1913, fig. 79.

[452] See Eames 1974, pl. 1.

Saint Jacques upon the hasp and the sharply nicked in padlock or bar hasps, in suggesting a date of *c.* 1450–1500.

Select Bibliography

Catalogue Musée Gruuthuse, Bruges, 1970, 558.

Catalogue No. 47 (plate 52)

Chest (standard type) at Westminster Abbey, in the Library.

Wood, covered throughout with leather and bound with iron

l. 4′ 2¼″; Max. h. including lid, 2′; w. 1′ 7½″.

Description (February 1971)

The leather covering of the chest is securely held by widely spaced flat iron straps running vertically and horizontally, interwoven around the chest. The spacing of the straps on box and lid coincide and, except for the locks and hasps on the front, back and front match. The lid is domed. The front has two original lock plates and hasps, with a padlocked fitting between in the centre of the chest. The hasps are stepped and fitted with loose ring handles at their ends. The outer locks have plates which are ornamented with raised S-guards, handed so that the left-hand is a true S-form while the right-hand side is reversed. The sides of the chest are fitted with cranked handles of thick, square section rod which curl round their attachments.

Two coverings exist on the inside of the chest: an earlier covering, which appears to be of thick painted paper, and a later canvas. The interior has modern plates and bolts.

Analysis

This chest, together with another in the Abbey Museum and a third in the Public Record Office,[453] is traditionally associated with Lady Margaret Beaufort who died in the Abbot's house in 1509. The evidence for this attribution is circumstantial, but stylistic evidence accords with a late fifteenth-century date. The S-guards on the lock plates almost certainly derive from flamboyant tracery. Linked S-forms are used on Flemish jewellery and are found on the Flemish chest in Sidney Sussex College of *c.* 1460–90. In the present context, the restrained, non-angular ornament of the plates and hasps suggests *c.* 1480–1500.

The chest is an example of a type of small standard which was probably taken on horseback, see pp. 172, 174.

Select Bibliography

RCHM London, 1, 51, chest no. (5).

L. E. Tanner, *The Library and Muniment Room*, Westminster Papers, no. 1, London, 1935, 15.

---

[453] The PRO chest is no. III of Jenning[s]' booklet and is the pair to the Westminster Abbey Museum chest.

PLINTH CHESTS

The plinth form of chest was the most sophisticated and ornate type in the later Middle Ages. Favoured in the fifteenth century in France for essays in brilliantly carved walnut, like the examples in the Victoria and Albert Museum[454] and Romsey Abbey (Cat. 48), the plinth form lent itself to an overall scheme of decoration on three sides, as did the closely allied hutch (2) type (see Fig. 17). Indeed, as Fig. 17 indicates, the plinth form is derived from the hutch (2) with the feet masked by a plinth. The plinth itself, largely in direct contact with the ground even in fretted examples, suggests the certainty of a location upon tiled or wooden floors free from litter.[455]

Mid-fifteenth-century French plinth chests are normally equipped with a single, central lock plate which is scrupulously fitted within the design and is itself a masterpiece of bench work or cold cut iron, as we see at Romsey (Cat. 48). The degree of elaboration and the quality of the carving accorded to these chests indicates that they were adjuncts of estate; armorial bearings are frequently used, though they occupy a subordinate role in the general scheme of decoration which, in the most successful examples, is flamboyant tracery. Carving is generally carried out in the solid, in individual panels separated by applied buttresses.

The plinth form is much older than surviving furniture suggests. It is the form used for the wooden tomb chest of William Longespée, Earl of Salisbury, who died in 1226 and is buried in Westminster Abbey; here, applied arcading decorates the chest. Late fourteenth-century English storage chests at Huttoft[456] and Faversham[457] are also decorated with applied tracery, but these chests are homely examples compared with the diamond-hard quality of the French fifteenth-century work. (The Huttoft carving is wholly applied, like the Longespée tomb, but the Faversham chest is closer to later French examples in its combination of solid and applied carved detail.) The remarkable chest of Prior Thomas Silksted, dated 1512, carved with the letters T S in an early Renaissance manner,[458] carries interest in plinth chests forward to a time when Gothic art ceased to be dominant; comparisons with Italian *cassone* come to mind as we note the complete absence of buttresses or arcading on the front.

CATALOGUE No. 48 (PLATE 53)

Chest (plinth type) at Romsey Abbey, Hampshire.

Walnut

l. 6' $11\frac{1}{4}$"; h. including plinth, excluding modern blocks and lid, 2' $11\frac{1}{2}$"; w. 2' $5\frac{1}{2}$".

Description (July 1969)

The chest stands upon modern blocks and has a modern lid.

---

[454] No. W.17.1914.

[455] (The covering of grasses and similar matter distributed over earth and other floors in medieval times, and later.)

[456] See Roe, facing 43.

[457] See Macquoid/Edwards 1954, Chests, fig. 8.

[458] In Shanklin church, Isle of Wight; see Roe, facing 111. This important chest is in line with metropolitan developments, for the best known early example of Renaissance ornament in England is provided by Pietro Torrigiano's commission for Henry VII's chapel in Westminster Abbey, *c*.1519 (see *RCHM London*, I, pl. 8).

The front is composed of 2 horizontally joined boards; the back has 2 original boards with a third lower down which is a repair. At the back, the horizontal boards are dovetailed into the uprights. The back is rough and was clearly not meant to be seen.

The chest is elaborately and expertly carved at the front and sides; except for the corner buttresses, which are separately worked, all the carving is in high relief in the solid. The carving on the front is divided by a vertical panel at the centre which accommodates lock plate and shield and the main design on either side consists of three different flamboyant tracery panels which repeat symmetrically on either side, making 6 panels in all. These main panels provide the only varied tracery, for above them is a repetitive band of tracery serving as a frieze. The carving is worked within a plain, unmoulded border which is interrupted on its upper side by the central lock plate. The lock plate precisely fits the space reserved for it. Immediately below it is a shield surmounted by a coronet and a mask with arms on either side below. The shield is carved with a field *chevronée*.

The carving of the sides of the chest retains the strong horizontal lines created at the front; there is a single panel in the centre (similar to the first and sixth panels on the front), which is supported on either side by roses of flamboyant tracery with tendrils flowing from them upwards and outwards to contain and balance the design. The front corners are each finished with two applied buttresses with crocketted finials and there is a single buttress at each side at the back. The buttresses rest on the plinth and stop just short of the top of the box.

The chest has a moulded edge beneath the carving at front and sides; immediately beneath is the plinth which may be a restoration.

The only ironwork on the chest is the central lock plate and hasp, both original and of fine workmanship. The plate is bench work and is elaborate, with pierced tracery foiled with scarlet ?leather. The hasp has a Christ figure applied to it, and fits so neatly within its guard and within the design as a whole that it reads as a figure in a design of tracery rather than as a decorated hasp.

Analysis

The chest is a work of the very highest quality and is representative of a number of similar surviving examples of French origin. It may be compared with no. W.17.1914 (V. & A.), also of walnut and carved on three sides and having dovetailed joints and a single lock plate. Another example, in the Musée de Bourg, is dated by heraldry 1487–1520 and resembles Romsey in its arrangement of tracery with three different panels on the front which are repeated symmetrically.[459] Parallels in the ironwork may be found in the Plougrescant buffet (Cat. 27), stylistically dated *c.* 1495–1502, and in the plate of the door knocker of the palace of Jacques Cœur at Bourges, built 1443–54, pl. 66B.

The Romsey chest is a rare example of a piece of furniture which is equal in quality to anything found within a strictly architectural context, e.g. screen or stallwork. Particularly noteworthy in French work of this kind is the perfectionism with which

[459] See J. Tricou, 'Trois Meubles Armoriés Lyonnais', *Nouvelle Revue Heraldique*, 1946, 13–14, pl. III.

woodwork and ironwork are integrated in the design. In most furniture of the Middle Ages, we are very much aware that the woodwork was completed before a smith was asked to fit ironwork; an interaction of the two crafts at the design stage does not become common until the fifteenth century, and even then is more usual in France than in England or the Netherlands.

Stylistically, the Romsey chest should be dated *c.* 1480–1500; it is entirely a late Gothic work.

SECTION D
SEATING

The symbolic role of the seat has long been appreciated, for it survives in modern ceremonial in the seat of privilege occupied by a sovereign, a judge or a bishop; and we acknowledge the implications of the distinctive seat in many walks of life when we refer to an individual in control as a 'Chairman'. Thus we have no difficulty in accepting that in earlier times, as now, authority *as recognized on a particular occasion*, was expressed by a special seat which symbolized the power of one individual, whether spiritual or temporal, while the inferior seating (or the absence of any form of seating) accorded to all others present expressed the subservient nature of their *relative* positions. But, as we have seen in other contexts, all symbolic expressions of lordship in the Middle Ages were subject to rules of precedence, and the failure to give due weight to this fundamental characteristic of social organization has frequently led to a distortion of the evidence.[460] The use of important seats was not the sole prerogative of rank, but was conditioned by the social make-up at a particular occasion and individuals, including peasants, in their own homes might occupy a distinctive seat which they could not aspire to in their feudal lord's hall.[461] The evidence of illuminations and other works of art, biased in favour of recording events which familiarize us with ceremonial usages but largely ignore private situations, have fostered the mistaken view that the distinctive seat or chair was a rare object in the Middle Ages, instead of *an object in general ownership whose use was subject to social restraints*.

The important or distinctive seat in the Middle Ages was normally termed *cathedra*, *trosne*, *chaiere*, *chaeze* etc., chayer, chair etc. but *described a seat which was not necessarily equipped with a back*. For clarity in this analysis, however, I shall adhere to more modern usages:

chair: single seat with back
bench: seat for two plus persons, with back
stool: single, backless seat
form: seat for two plus persons, backless

SEATS OF AUTHORITY

It is evident that several ancient traditions influenced the form of seats of authority, and there is one constant factor present in all these traditions which may be instantly

[460] Mercer's comment '. . . only the very great could aspire to a chair' misses the point (Mercer, captions, figs. 11, 12).
[461] Written records show the ownership of chairs at all levels. In 1302, a bourgeois of Paris had 4 chairs (*cathedre*) as well as 4 forms (*forme*) in the hall (Stein, 169); and in England, middle-class men such as John Olyver, a London draper, owned at least 2 chairs in 1406 (Thomas, 1943, 3). Evidence concerning the peasantry is rare, but we find that Thomas atte Frythe used 1 *chayere* in his dwelling in 1409 (R. K. Field, 'Worcestershire Peasant Buildings, Household Goods and Farming Equipment in the Later Middle Ages', *Medieval Archaeology*, XIX, 1965, 138 (Appendix B, Table I, no. 3); and a record of 1529 shows that one peasant owned 4 chairs (W. G. Hoskins, *The Midland Peasant*, London, 1957, 295), while Barley has drawn attention to the use of an elaborate chair by a peasant, as seen in a fourteenth-century misericord at Screveton, Nottinghamshire (Barley, pl. 10).

recognized, though it does not necessarily form an integral part of the seat itself: a footstool/cushion/step or steps/dais placed before and/or beneath the seat. Thus the essential ingredient in the creation of a chair or stool of authority was generally concerned with the elevation of the seated figure, enabling that figure to dominate and be seen by less privileged persons, whether seated or standing. The preoccupation with height in seats of authority is ancient, and Wormald has compared the description of Solomon's throne in the Second Book of Chronicles with medieval records and with St Edward's Chair in Westminster Abbey.[462] He shows that although the important elements of Solomon's throne were not always reproduced in their entirety in medieval examples, its influence upon medieval symbolism was profound. Solomon's throne was equipped with a gold footstool attached to the throne and was approached by six steps. (There were also fourteen lions associated with it, twelve on the steps and two by the arms or stays of the throne.) The importance of the elevated seated figure is made abundantly clear in many descriptions and paintings of coronations or occasions of high ceremony;[463] and in less majestic contexts it can be more subtly implied, as we find in the surviving row of three seats from a French seigneurial chapel of *c.* 1500–25,[464] where, the seats are attached, with tall backs which form a continuous unbroken line, but *the central seat is higher than those on either side of it.*

Turning now to the actual shape or form of seats of authority, we shall discover that many forms were used concurrently throughout our period which will be discussed in groups under X-, Post and Boarded seats. We shall notice that some of these forms were not, in themselves, imposing though they were potent symbols to medieval eyes through ancient associations. All could be rendered imposing, however, by easily regulated means: an adjustment to their height and a judicious use of rich drapery.

X-SEATS

One of the most ancient of such forms was the X-stool or chair, familiar in the twentieth century through the magnificent fixed as well as folding examples found by Howard Carter in the Egyptian tomb of the pharaoh Tutankhamun who died in 1349 B.C.[465] In the contexts which concern us, however, the inseparable associations of the X-form with authority were forged and disseminated through the influence of Roman bureaucracy by the use of the conveniently portable, folding X-stool as the seat of office, the *sella curulis*, known in medieval times as *faldistorium, faudesteuil, faulxdesteuil,* etc. faldstool, as well as *cathedra.* The role played by Roman tradition in the use and development of the X-form in secular and ecclesiastical contexts in medieval times and

---

[462] F. Wormald, 'The Throne of Solomon and St. Edward's Chair', ed. M. Meiss, *De Artibus Opuscula XL. Essays in Honour of E. Panofsky*, New York, 1961, 532–9.

[463] For example, the illustration of the crowning of Henry IV in 1399 (Harley MS) where the King is enthroned on a dais approached by four steps; the seat itself is of indeterminate form, being fully draped (J. L. Kirby, *Henry IV of England*, London, 1970, pl. facing p. 85.) Note also 'L'Ordre Observé aux Estats Généraux de France à Tours', 1467, quoted by Havard: 'Audit premier parquet estoil assis le Roy en une haute chaire en laquelle falloit monter par trois haults degréz' (Havard, 1, 641).

[464] From the church of Palluau, Indre; Musée des Arts Décoratifs, Peyre collection 1058.

[465] For an illustration of the fixed form of X-chair, less familiar than the folding stool, see Penelope Fox, *Tutankhamun's Treasure*, Oxford, 1951, pl. 60; the significance of the interdependence of royal seat plus footstool here, as in other Egyptian contexts, may also be appreciated.

later has been fully appreciated in published accounts, and Wanscher's recent survey is particularly useful in its wealth of illustrative material.[466] Ancient X-stools can be studied in examples from Pompeii[467] and elsewhere; the precise date and context of these extant metal stools are often debatable[468] and rarely concern us, but one example — the Chair of Dagobert — crystallizes their significance in terms of the present study. This pre-twelfth-century bronze folding stool, to which various dates have been assigned,[469] was altered by Suger, Abbot of St Denis, in the second quarter of the twelfth century. Suger gave it a back and arms and believed it to be the seat used by Frankish kings to receive the first homage of their nobles. (Its historical associations and its veneration over the centuries attracted the attention of Napoleon, who used it as his coronation throne.) Weinberger has convincingly correlated the design of the twelfth-century back of the Chair of Dagobert with St Peter's Throne in Rome. This alignment is interesting at a technical level, since it demonstrates the adoption of an element of the four-post chair (the *back* of St Peter's Throne) with the folding X-stool which is thus rendered a fixed X-chair. Although we now know from Tutankhamun's tomb furniture that fixed X-chairs were very ancient, the common *Roman* form, which must have been the most familiar in the twelfth century, was the folding stool. But Weinberger's comparison has a much more important intellectual aspect which has remained unrecognized. The X-seat, associated in Suger's mind with terrestial authority, is altered by him to resemble the supreme seat of the church in Rome, becoming at a stroke a symbol of ecclesiastical as well as secular and judicial authority. This duality of roles continued throughout the Middle Ages; indeed, Dagobert's Chair provides the most eminent of many illustrations to demonstrate that secular and ecclesiastical forms for furniture were comparable rather than distinct. (In this matter, I am unable to accept Wanscher's view that there are *separate* ecclesiastical and secular lines to be traced from the Roman *sella curulis*.)[470]

The use of the X-seat as an expression of supreme majesty throughout the Middle Ages has already been traced. Dervieu shows the form used by Philippe I for his seal of 1082, and notes that it was favoured by French kings for this purpose up to the time of Charles VII.[471] Viollet-le-Duc published a free adaptation taken from the seal of Charles V which clearly shows the traditional, free-standing X-stool associated with two lions upon the steps of approach (see the reference to Solomon's throne, above) and standing against a high, traceried screen which forms an imposing tester and celour.[472] Wanscher reproduces an illustration of 1371 showing the Emperor Charles IV with crown and orb seated upon an X-stool,[473] and another showing its use by Pope

[466] Wanscher, 18 ff.

[467] See G. M. A. Richter, *The Furniture of the Greeks, Etruscans & Romans*, London, 1966, 103–4, fig. 527.

[468] The problems, in one particular instance, are illustrated by D. M. Wilson, 'An Inlaid Iron Folding Stool in the British Museum', *Medieval Archaeology*, I, 1957, 39 ff.

[469] Thought to be Roman by Sir W. Martin Conway, 'The Abbey of Saint-Denis and its Ancient Treasures', *Archaeologia*, Second series, XVI, 1915, 121; M. Weinberger, however, in the most recent authoritative account, dates it to a time 'when Merovingian tradition was still in its early youth', see his paper 'The Chair of Dagobert', ed. L. F. Sandler, *Essays in Memory of Karl Lehmann*, New York, 1964, 378.

[470] Wanscher, 87.

[471] Lt.-Col. Dervieu, 'Les Chaises et les Sièges au Moyen Age', *Bulletin Monumentales*, 1910, 217.

[472] Viollet-le-Duc, 1858, Fauteuil, 112.

[473] Wanscher, pl. 105; MS in the Belgian royal library, Brussels.

Boniface IX for his coronation in 1389;[474] in the latter illustration, as in Charles V's seal, the stool is supported by an intrusive tester and celour. (The significance of the tester and canopy as adjuncts of estate has already been discussed with regard to beds, and need not detain us further.)

We have looked at the use of the X-form in the most important ceremonial contexts; other evidence shows that it expressed authority at many levels. It was often used as a comfortable chair on occasions which were not overburdened with royal ceremony (see the miniature of 1372 showing Charles V receiving an illuminated bible, pl. 67), and Dervieu believed that this form was adapted as the special toilet chair, whose uses included hair dressing.[475]

Written sources show that elaborate examples were sometimes decorated with, or made of, precious materials; the animal or human heads found on these seats were a favourite vehicle for valuable materials. The folding potentiality of the X-form made it the ideal choice for the seat which accompanied the medieval lord when soldiering[476] or committed to other itinerant pursuits. (We are probably right in assuming that most references to *iron* seats refer to X-stools or chairs.)

c. 1241   In St. Paul's Cathedral, London, were 5 iron chairs, 2 of which were given by G. de Lucy, Dean of St. Paul's, who died in 1241. One of these seats was elaborate:

'Item, una [cathedra] ferrea deargentata cum capitibus humanis et deauratis, quam episcopus F. habet.'

(Simpson, 474.)

(Item, a Bishop's seat of silvered iron, with gilded human heads, which Bishop F. had.)

Early   Inventory of John Fitz Marmaduke, lord of Horden; at the time of death
fourteenth   he was Governor of St. John's Town, Perth, under Edward II.
century:
               'j cathedra ferrea ijs.'

(Raine 1834/5, 17.)

An early fourteenth-century illumination highlights the humbler uses of the X-stool. We see a man of modest appearance sitting on an X-stool and having his wounds dressed.[477] This particular stool is composed of four wooden struts on each side which cross their opposite numbers and interlock, in the manner familiar in Renaissance furniture. The following evidence concerns precious faldstools once more. Dervieu quotes a reference to a *faudesteuil* listed in 1353 which was of silver and 'cristal', enriched with pearls and other stones and enamelled work.[478]

---

[474] Wansher, pl. 104; from Froissart, B.M. Chronicle.
[475] The 'chayere à peigner le chef du Roy, notre sire'. Dervieu 1910, 220.
[476] See the late fourteenth-century illumination of an attack upon a city with a king seated on an X-stool in a tent; B.M. MS., Sloane 2433 (11), fol. 113.
[477] Bodleian MS. 264, fol. 152 V.
[478] Dervieu 1910, 218, fn. 3.

1379/80   Inventory of Charles V.

'3891. Item, une chayère de fust, très richement ouvrée en manière de fauldestueil, garnye de drap d'or à quatre pommeaulx de fueillages reneversez.'

(Labarte, 393.)

(Item, a chair of faldstool type of very richly worked wood, embellished with cloth of gold and with 4 knops of leafage turned under.)

1388   At Westminster Abbey.

'De Cathedris et pannis cathedralibus . . . Cathedre sunt tres pontificales quarum una est deargentea. Secunda et tercia fereeᵈ et tres panni eisdem Cathedris . . .'

(J. W. Legg, 'An Inventory of the Vestry in Westminster Abbey, taken in 1388', *Archaeologia*, LII, 1890, 240.)

(Seats and seat cloths . . .
3 bishop's seats, one being silvered, the second and third iron, and 3 cloths [for laying upon] the said seats.)

Dervieu quotes references to two other elaborate X seats. One, 1388, *faulxdesteuil* was painted red and decorated with flowers, and another in 1396 (*faus d'esteuil*) was painted red and upholstered in *velours*, the cloth being attached with small latten nails.[479]

1405   Inventory of the Duchess of Burgundy.

'Item, trois veilles chayeres a faulx esteux, l'une noire l'autre vermeille a P et M et l'autre verde a brebis et feulles d'aubespin . . .'

(Dehaisnes, II, 902.)

(Item, 3 old chairs of faldstool type, one black, another red with P and M (Philippe/Marguerite) and the other green with? . . . and hawthorn leaves . . .)

1420   Château de Vincennes.

'En la chapelle . . . une vieille chaeze de laiton à 1111 testles de lieppars . . .

Château de Beauté . . .

En la tour . . . appellée la chambre des Evvangelistes, où couchoit communément le roy Charles, à esté trouvé . . .
Item, deux autres chaezes ployans, l'une de fer bien ouvrée, et l'autre de boys.'

(Douet d'Arcq, 458, 461.)

(Château de Vincennes. In the chapel . . . an old latten seat with 4 leopard heads upon it . . .

---

[479] Dervieu 1910, 218, fn. 3.

O

Château de Beauté . . . In the tower . . .

in the chamber called the room of the Evangelists where King Charles was accustomed to lie were found . . .

Item, 2 other folding seats, one of iron finely worked and the other of wood.)

The variations in design, worked upon the X-form, may be studied from a few surviving examples and from representational art. The management of the X-frame allows a frontal or a lateral emphasis. Wanscher believed the lateral arrangement to be the earlier,[480] and certainly it is found in the ancient Egyptian context referred to above. However, the lateral form was not abandoned in favour of the frontally orientated X but continued to be used as an alternative form, as we shall see below.

Dagobert's Chair and the thirteenth-century X-stool in Vienna[481] are both examples of frontally orientated seats. They employ animal heads as upper finials, and the latter example uses ducks' heads for feet, a feature found in Tutankhamun's furniture. Stools other than X-form were also ornamented with animal heads at seat level, as a number of examples depicted in the Bayeux tapestry show,[482] and the quality which was sometimes lavished upon such fittings may be judged from two particularly fine survivors.[483] These leopard head finials in crystal and whale bone ivory respectively probably belonged to stools made of precious materials, such as the examples referred to above (see entries for c. 1241, and 1420). Some X-seats were surmounted by knops in place of figurative carvings, and the surviving frontally orientated wrought iron stool at Bayeux Cathedral is a fine example of this less exuberant approach.[484] The Bayeux X-stool has a leather seat slung between two bars, rounded ?latten knops and the indication of an animal's paw for the feet; it has delicately worked narrow iron panels pierced with quatrefoils linking back and front X-frames above the seat, and is listed in an inventory of 1476. It is certainly one of the seats of the bishops of Bayeux and its character suggests a fourteenth-century date.[485]

The frontally orientated X-frame, when rendered fixed, became the basis for a comfortable chair; we see it with open arms and a modest back in the miniature of 1372 of Charles V referred to above, pl. 67A. The occasion portrayed appears to be one of dignified ease rather than stilted ceremony, and the importance of the King's presence is indicated here by the conical tester, or sparver, above him rather than by a raised position for his chair. Similar chairs with higher backs occur in miniatures, and sometimes the sides are closed with a material (?leather) which is attached on the inner face of the arms of the chair to form a kind of hammock for the sitter.[486] Another,

[480] Wanscher, 88.
[481] From Admond, Steiermark (Kungstgewerbemuseum, Vienna); see Wanscher, pl. 101.
[482] For example, ed. F. Stenton, *Bayeux Tapestry*, London, 1965, figs. 11, 14.
[483] Rock crystal from the borders of the Rhine, Musée Cluny; and whale bone, believed to be English or S. German and dated c.1150 by Kreisel, see Kreisel, 1, fig. 7.
[484] See also the iron X-stool, inlaid with copper and silver, with copper knops (formerly gilt); ?twelfth-century Byzantine, V. & A. 696.1904.
[485] See Janneau, pl. 7; also Vallery-Radot, 55. The leather seat is a replacement; the stool is in the Cathedral treasury.
[486] See the illumination from *La Bible Historiale*, Macquoid/Edwards 1927, Introduction, fig. 5.

similar form, noted by Mercer,[487] includes a cunningly contrived cloth canopy stretched over brackets on the chair itself. These ample, comfortable chairs are the immediate ancestors of the somewhat cumbersome examples like those at York Minster and London.[488] Of very different character, however, are the examples of frontally orientated X-seats made from interlocking slats of wood which interleave from either side. A miniature depicting one of these stools has already been mentioned, 'wound dressing', and comes from an early fourteenth-century context (see p. 184), while another representation occurs in a bas relief in Amiens Cathedral and is of early sixteenth-century date.[489]

Incidences of the laterally orientated X-seat are less easy to discover than frontally orientated forms, but an interesting late fourteenth-century example is shown in a miniature. We see John of Gaunt seated upon a fixed stool which has its X-members linked by rails at floor and seat levels, with an attractive curled over leaf ornament on the upper side rails.[490] Another miniature, of fifteenth-century date, shows the lateral X-form as a high backed folding chair composed of a series of interlocking wooden slats;[491] this chair is particularly interesting in demonstrating the varied approach of the designers of such seating, for it reproduces all the advantages of lightness and mobility found in the similar, *frontally orientated* seats noted above but turns the design about *in order to retain the folding characteristic while at the same time achieving a back to the seat*. In passing, it may be noted that this interesting chair is depicted in a bed chamber.

Before turning to the visual evidence for seats of the post and boarded types, let us examine documentary and literary sources which throw light on seats of authority. Several kinds of seat will be represented in this evidence, for only the X-form was singled out for an exclusive term, faldstool, in the Middle Ages. Here, we shall find important evidence concerning the use of height and textiles to create an imposing arrangement, the costly elaboration of the actual seats which might involve the services of important artists, and the mobility often required of seats of estate which is demonstrated by the common provision of individual cases to protect them in transit.

First half of twelfth century	Theophilus, writing at this time, speaks of copper sheets fitted round painted chairs, stools and beds (*cathedrae pictae et sedilia atque lecti*). (Dodwell, 130.)
1238	For the chapel at Winchester. To the sheriff of Southampton. '*Contravreve* to . . . cause a seat for the queen's use to be made . . . and to cause it to be painted; . . .' (*Cal. Lib. R.*, 1, 319.)

---

[487] See Mercer, fig. 83; (Royal MSS, 15 D 111 f. 245v B.M.; French, fifteenth century).
[488] The York chair has finials paralleled in a portrait of Lady Scudamore of 1614 (Nat. Portrait Gallery, London) which serves to date it. The London chair (V. & A., W12, W13.1928) which has a matching footstool, was made for William Juxon, Archbishop of Canterbury 1660–3, yet is largely uninfluenced by Renaissance ideas.
[489] See Viollet-le-Duc 1858, 31.
[490] B.M. MS, Nero D.vi.
[491] See Furnivall 1868, pl. XIV, 'bedroom chair' from the fifteenth-century MS 'Comte d'Artois'.

1267–9   For the great hall at Westminster.

We learn that the king ordered a throne embellished with 2 small lions, 2 turrets, 2 plates and 3 cups of gilded copper.

(H. M. Colvin, *Building Accounts of Henry III*, Oxford, 1971, 422–3.)

1250   Hall at Windsor Castle.

To Godfrey de Lyston. '*Contabreve* to make a royal seat in the middle of the table in the hall of the castle of Windersores, and paint on it an image of the king holding a sceptre in his hand, taking care that it be suitably adorned with painting in gold, . . .'

(*Calendar of Liberate Rolls 1245–51*, III, H.M.S.O., 1937, 296.)

1252   Hall at Silverstone.

To the sheriff of Northampton.
'*Contrabreve* to . . . make a new stone bench . . . with a chair in the middle for the king . . .'[492]

(*Cal. Lib.* R. IV, 23.)

1252   Hall at Woodstock.

To the keepers of the king's works at Woodstock.
'*Contrabreve* to make . . . a canopy (*tabernaculum*) above the king's seat in the hall with a royal chair; . . .'

(*Cal. Lib.* R. IV, 24.)

1299   Walter of Durham, King's Sergeant Painter since 1270, was paid 100 s. for a chair for Edward I; the Wardrobe Accounts for 1300 give the details that 13/4 was paid for carving and painting 2 small wooden leopards and £1. 19. 7 for making and painting a footboard and case for the chair.[493]

(W. Palmer, *The Coronation Chair*, H.M.S.O., 1953, 5.)

1300   At the Château of Hesdin of the Comtesse d'Artois et de Bourgogne; here Guissin, one of the group of *imagiers* most frequently employed by Mahaut, Comtesse d'Artois, worked upon 'sieges et chaieres cloans de la chambre monsgr.'[494]

(Richard 1887, 308.)

(. . . seating and nailed chairs for the Count's chamber.)

---

[492] Stone was commonly used for seating in the Middle Ages. Such seating frequently survives in the form of window seats. Stone was favoured for bishops' thrones and several examples, most of which are mutilated, survive, e.g. Norwich Cathedral (*c.* eighth century A.D.); Welsh Newton church, Herefordshire (thirteenth century), etc.; and Professor Jacques Thirion has kindly drawn my attention to continental survivors at Aachen, Avignon and Toul.

[493] This account has been correlated with the extant St Edward's Chair.

[494] As Richard has pointed out, the *imagiers* were highly paid sculptors who gave artistry to the basic forms undertaken by carpenters (Richard 1887, 306).

1304   Accounts of Mahaut, Comtesse d'Artois.

           'Le XI jour de juing, por II chaires por le chambre madame, achatées a
           Paris a Renaut l'imagier,   c s.'

           (Dehaisnes, I, 160.)

           (11th June, for 2 chairs for the Countess's chamber, purchased in Paris
           from the sculptor Renaut, 100s.)

1306   For the Queen's visit to the bishop's castle at Wolvesey, a painted throne
           joined with gilded and silvered nails was made by Master Michael of
           Canterbury and a master carpenter named Reginald; these men travelled
           from London to fit up chambers for the Quuen and her suite.

           (Brown/Colvin/Taylor, II, 862–3.)

1307   Great hall at Westminster.

           At the time of Edward II's coronation a goldsmith . . . made 2 copper
           knobs for the king's seat in the great hall, and a copper gilt image of a
           king was made to stand in 'a certain arch of the royal seat on the feast of
           the coronation'.

           (See Brown/Colvin/Taylor, I, 506.)

1352   The accounts of Etienne de la Fontaine, silversmith to King Jean,
           mention gilded and painted chairs for the King, the Dauphin, the Duc
           d'Orléans, the Comte d'Anjou and others.

           (Havard, I, 643–4.)

1357   Inventory, Edward III.

           '84. Itm i . . . catheder de ebore in i coffin coreo . . .'

           (Sir F. Palgrave, *The Antient Kalendars and Inventories of the Treasury of His
           Majesty's Exchequer III*, London, 1836, 239.)

           (Item, 1 . . . ebony chair with a leather case thereto . . .)

1385   Duke of Burgundy's accounts.

           '1220. . . . à Martin Covet, brodeur, . . . pour un estuy de cuir à mettre
           une chaiere.'

           (Prost, II, 188.)

           (. . . to Martin Covet, embroiderer . . . for a leather case for enclosing a
           chair.)

1379/80   Inventory of Charles V.
           'CHAIÈRES PREMIÈREMENT:
           3887. Une chayze à testes de lyon et d'aigles, et le siège de veluiau azuré à
           fleurs de lys.
           3888. Item, une grant chayère, haulte, painte à fleurs de liz, et le siège
           et le dossier de veluiau azuré, brodez à fleurs de liz.

3889. Item, une chayère de cyprès.

3890. Item, une chayère que donna au Roy maistre Nicole de Vaires.'

(Labarte, 393.)

(CHAIRS: FIRSTLY,

3887. A chair with the heads of a lion and of eagles, the seat of blue velvet with fleur-de-lis.

3888. Item, a large, high chair, painted with fleurs-de-lis, with seat and back of blue velvet embroidered with fleurs-de-lis.

3889. Item, a chair of cypress wood.

3890. Item, a chair which Master Nicole de Vaires gave to the King.)

It may be noted here that as item 3891 (quoted above, p. 185) is listed as a faldstool, the chairs which precede it in the inventory and are not so described are certainly of post or boarded form.

1388   Duke of Burgundy's accounts.

'2594. a Pierre Du Fou, coffrier, demourant à Paris . . . pour . . . une grande bouge pour y porter une chaere . . .'

(Prost, II, 398.)

(To Pierre Du Fou, coffrer, living in Paris . . . for . . . a large case for carrying a chair.)

1461   Marble seat in Westminster Hall.

At the accesssion of Edward IV and Richard III, the chroniclers speak of the 'marble seat' in Westminster Hall. This was the seat at the southern end of the Hall which was raised upon a dais. The furniture placed there (seating, table(s)) was used by the Courts of Chancery and King's Bench, so that both the chancellors and the king used the accommodation when their respective courts were in session. The seat played an important part in coronation ceremonies and was also used by the king for dining in state.

(Brown/Colvin/Taylor, 543 f., 102.)

1466   Inventory of the Duchess of Suffolk.

'. . . a chaire of tymbre of astate covered wt blue cloth of gold and panells of copper' and 'a case of lether thereto'.

(Macquoid/Edwards 1954, Chairs, 224.)

1474   Olivier de la Marche, *Mémoires*, regarding Charles the Bold, Duke of Burgundy.

'*Du Conseil, et de la Justice* . . . le duc . . . tient audience publique pour ouyr et depescher toutes requestes qui luy sont apportées, . . . et le duc . . . va en la salle où l'audience est preparee, et est accompaigné de la noblesse de son hostel . . . Le duc se sied en sa chaire, richement parée de palle de

drap d'or, et le marchepied, qui est large et de trois pas de montée, est
tout couvert de tapisserie richement; . . .'

(Petitot, x, 481–2.)

(Of [the Duke of Burgundy's] Council and Court . . . the Duke . . . held
public audience to hear and dispatch [justice] concerning all the cases
brought to him . . . and the Duke . . . entered the hall prepared for the
audience accompanied by the nobility of his court . . . The Duke sat in his
chair which was richly hung with cloth of gold and had a large foot board
3 steps in height and all covered with costly tapestry; . . .)

1484   For Anne of Brittany.

Joannes de Bourdichon, 'paintre du roy, demourant à Tours' made for
the Queen 2 large 'chaires par lui painctes et toutes dorées de fin or'.
(Havard, I, 644.)

(Joannes de Bourdichon, King's Painter living at Tours, made for the
Queen 2 large chairs which he painted and gilded overall with fine gold.)

1513   John de Veer.

'Itm v tapetts of tapistry damaske werke paly [striped] Redde and yelowe
wt cheyres of estate . . .
Itm A cheir couerid wt old crymsyn velvet.'

(W. H. St John Hope, 'Last Testament and Inventory of John de Veer,
13th Earl of Oxford', *Archaeologia*, 2nd series xvi, 1915, 328, 347.)

POST AND BOARDED SEATS OF AUTHORITY

In turning to these forms of construction, we encounter types which gave greater
freedom to designers than was possible with the X-form, and the variety which was
created is truly remarkable and has remained largely unrecognized, through the rarity
of surviving examples and the difficulty of examining illuminated MSS which are the
richest source of evidence. The use of post and boarded forms as supreme symbols of
authority — thrones — can be quickly established for there is a wealth of evidence
available, but it must be emphasized once more that, as with the X-form, it was the
accessories assembled with the seat on a particular occasion which were often the chief
ingredient in the creation of a throne, rather than a particular form for the seat itself, so
that when we discuss seat forms *out of context* we are dealing with seats which expressed
authority at many levels of society. Some modification of this view is clearly
necessary, however, in the case of seats which were specially decorated or embellished
as part of their fabric. We have seen that precious materials were often used; seats of this
character may have been imbued with a symbolic significance, quite apart from creating
an aura of power through the display of wealth. What is certain, however, is that the
seats painted with the image of a king were permanently designated thrones, irrespective
of any additional accessories which might be introduced in use. We find such seats
referred to in 1250 and 1307 above, and recall that St Edward's chair in Westminster

Abbey was given such an image, painted on the inside face of the back, as a secondary decoration in *c.* 1330–50. This secondary decoration, which covered the whole chair, modified the stark architectural quality of the original design but was a work of the highest quality carried out in glass mosaics and gold leaf; it may now only be studied in drawings and tracings, owing to the appalling misuse of the chair over the centuries.[495] To return briefly to the importance of the king's image upon a throne, suggesting, among other things, an ever watchful regal presence, it is pertinent to note a possible ancestor of the type in the extraordinary ?tenth/eleventh-century stone throne with back *shaped* like a figure, shown in Fig. 29.

Note establishing post and boarded seat types as thrones.

Stool	Edward the Confessor's throne, Bayeux tapestry, *c.* 1066–77, see ed. Stenton, pl. V.
Chair without arms	St Peter's throne, Vatican (extant). *c.* 843 A.D.
	Harold's coronation throne, Bayeux tapestry, see ed. Stenton, fig. 35.
Chair with arms	St Edward's Chair, Westminster Abbey, almost certainly made for Edward I in 1299.
	Throne of Edward III on his first seal (see Palmer, pl. 3).
	Richard II's throne, *c.* 1395, on extant panel painting, see pl. 68.

This short note is misleading in that it suggests that date (and fashion) dictated the choice of form for thrones. As has been demonstrated above regarding X-seats, however, the choice was chiefly influenced by tradition.

Let us now examine the post and boarded forms individually.

POST SEATS OF AUTHORITY

Some indication of the varied and imaginative designs which fall within this group is shown in the sketches on Figs. 27–28 below. It is not suggested that the survey is in any way comprehensive, for it must largely rely upon illuminations which present particular problems for research.[496] But the most important problem regarding illuminations is the question of their reliability: do they reflect real furniture forms familiar to the illuminator of the manuscript? Looking at the surviving examples of seats of post form, we find good reasons for believing that illuminations were generally realistic in the present context. St Peter's throne, thought by Weinberger to be after 1010[497] has been shown as *c.* 843 A.D.[498] Its character, with the superb ivory plaques added at a later date, is comparable with what we know of precious seating from documentary sources and art. The Hereford chair (Cat. 49), together with other extant examples of medieval turned furniture, shows that pictures of this form of seating are in no way out of context. And at a later date, the extant bishop's throne at Exeter cathedral, which was

---

[495] See Palmer, pls. 5, 6, 9 showing the engraving made in 1808 and tracings made in 1953, when vestiges of the decoration still remained.
[496] These precious and delicate objects are often unavailable for the kind of research needed.
[497] Weinberger, 381.
[498] See Hollstein, 206.

Eighth to tenth-century
Byzantine ivory relief
see Schmitz, 22.

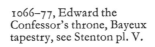

1066–77, Edward the
Confessor's throne, Bayeux
tapestry, see Stenton pl. V.

1066–77, Harold's throne,
Bayeux tapestry, see Stenton
fig. 35.

Twelfth-century MS, Herrade
de Landesberg, Strasbourg.
See Viollet-le-Duc 1858,
Trône, 283.

Late thirteenth century. Metal.
From a bible, BM VII, see
Viollet-le-Duc 1858,
Trône 288.

Extant silver chair, 'Throne of
Martin of Aragon', Barcelona
Cathedral.

Richard II's throne, c. 1395;
see pl. 68.

FIG. 27   Seating: Type Post (1).

probably designed by Thomas of Witney and made *c.*1312–17[499] provides an example of woodwork which is so fantastical in its soaring, pinnacled forms that it outstrips imagination, making the traceried thrones of panel paintings and illuminated MSS seem pedestrian affairs; (confronted with the Exeter throne, we have no difficulty in accepting the panel painting of Richard II of *c.*1395 as portraying a real chair, see pl. 68.) We should not leave the Exeter throne without noting that Pevsner considered it the 'most exquisite piece of woodwork of its date in England and perhaps in Europe'.[500]

BOARDED SEATS OF AUTHORITY

An indication of the varied forms of boarded seats is shown in Fig. 29; for reasons set out above, the survey is not intended to be comprehensive.

The most important extant example of this form of chair is St Edward's chair in Westminster Abbey which has been correlated with an entry in the wardrobe accounts of 1300 and discussed by Wormald in the context of Solomon's throne. Its grand, architectural proportions prove the accuracy with which illuminators portrayed thrones (see the Corpus Christi Cambridge MS)[501] and the exquisite decoration in gold leaf and glass mosaics, now hardly discernible, provides a valuable insight into the true appearance of the many precious chairs familiar from written sources. As with the painting upon the state cradle made for Philip the Fair or Margaret of Austria in 1478/9 (Cat. 28), we recognize that the secondary decoration to St Edward's chair is the work of a great artist or team of artists in an important workshop, though no written evidence concerning this phase of the chair's history survives.

KEY TO FIG. 28

1   Ivory relief, sixth to tenth century. See Schmitz, 23.
2   MS Douce 180, Bodleian. See Turner 1, 16. A similar seat, supported on recumbent lions from French MS Bib. Imp. Anc. f.S- no. 37 is shown by Viollet-le-Duc, 1858, 46.
3   MS Douce 180, see 2.
4   Bas-relief from Auxerre Cathedral, thirteenth century; see Viollet-le-Duc, 1858, 48, 49.
5   Bas-relief, from the right-hand door of the church of St Lazare of Avallon; twelfth century. See Viollet-le-Duc, 1858, 44.
6   Wooden polychrome figure of the Virgin; French, mid-twelfth century. Statens Historiska Museet, Stockholm; see Holmqvist, fig. 391.
7   Extant chair from Vallstena church, Gotland; twelfth century. Statens Historiska Museet; see Holmqvist fig. 368.
8   Extant chair, Hereford Cathedral, Cat. 49.
9   Bas-relief, church of St. Croix à la Charité (Nièvre); see Dervieu 1910, fig. 7.
10   From a painting of St Jerome attributed to Jan van Eyck; fifteenth century, Naples Museum. See Dervieu, 1910, fig. 13.
11   Thirteenth century, hexagonal plan. MS Douce 180, Bodleian; (See Turner, 16); MS Bib. imp. Anc. f.S-G., no. 37, Paris. (See Viollet-le-Duc, 1858, 46.)
12   Fourteenth century. MS Royal Coll. of the St Grail, British Museum. (See Gloag, 48.) Gloag notes that the infill appears to be basketry.
13   Mid-fourteenth century. MS 264, fol. 123v, Bodleian; (see Gloag, pl. 12 upper). Gloag notes that this chair anticipates eighteenth-century spindle backed chairs.
14   Twelfth-century bas relief, Chartres. See Gloag, pl.10.

---

[499] The accepted view, stated by Pevsner (*South Devon*, Harmondsworth, 1952, 142) and reiterated in the most recent comment, see J. H. Harvey, *The Medieval Architect*, London, 1972, 135.
[500] Pevsner, *South Devon*, 142.
[501] See Palmer, pl. 1. The throne depicted is not precisely the same as St Edward's chair but represents its *haracter* most faithfully.

FIG. 28.   Post seats type (2) (turned)

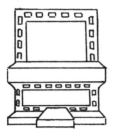

Ninth-century MS, Psalter of
Charles le Chauve, See Dervieu
1910, fig. 1.

Muchelney, Cat. 51

Tenth to eleventh-century,
stone extant chair, back shaped
as seated figure, see Schmitz 25.

Tenth to eleventh-century,
extant stone chair on
elephants, see Schmitz 25.

Coronation Ed. II, Corpus
Christi Cambridge MS, 20
fol. 682. See Palmer, pl. 1.

1290, Bible, MS, Corps,
legisl., Paris, see Viollet-le-
Duc 1858, 92.

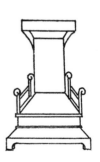

Fourteenth century,
Romance of Alexander,
Bodley 360. See [Parker], II, 93.

Fourteenth century,
Romance of Alexander,
Bodley 360. Posts set corner-
wise. See [Parker], II, 52.

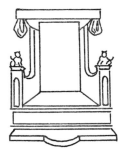

1423, 'MS Bib. imp. 6731';
see Viollet-le-Duc 1858, 93.

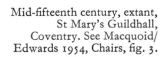

Mid-fifteenth century, extant,
St Mary's Guildhall,
Coventry. See Macquoid/
Edwards 1954, Chairs, fig. 3.

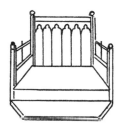

c. 1459 or 1480, panel ?by
Simon Marmion; see Evans
1966, fig. 45.

FIG. 29.   Seating, boarded type

The boarded chair from Stanford Bishop (Cat. 50) is probably a unique survivor of the type at its most primitive, but sophisticated fifteenth-century examples exist in many continental museums, though most are restored and lack provenances. The Muchelney bench, with integral chairs, is a valuable example of the type which has remained *in situ* (Cat. 51).

A second type of boarded seat was tub-shaped. The sumptuous sixth-century ivory 'throne of Maximian' in Ravenna springs first to mind when considering this form. More relevant in the present context, however, is the stone throne at Hexham Abbey, *c.*680, and the similar example at Beverley Minster. These stone thrones have low backs swinging round to form arms of the same height. This handsome outline is repeated in wood in a chair shown beside a bed in a French MS of 1447–60.[502] Dervieu shows a different version of the type taken from a work attributed to Jan van Eyck which is of basketry held between bobbin turned uprights, see Fig. 28 (10).[503]

It has been noted that it was often the *accessories* rather than the form of furniture which proclaimed a situation of high estate and that *precedence* controlled use. We know that a footboard was a fundamental requirement, for it is present in all representations of thrones from earliest times. We also observe that in the Middle Ages additional height provided by a dais and steps was a potent symbol (see Olivier de la Marche's description of Charles the Bold's court of justice, pp. 190–1). The other important ingredient in the assemblage of parts making up the chair of state was the tester and canopy; but

[502] Bib. Nat. MS, Fr. 989 f. 3., Paris; see *Bull. M.M.A.*, 1965/6, 289.
[503] Dervieu 1910, fig. 13.

whereas the footboard was always present, the canopy appears as an *essential* ingredient at a relatively late date and is not, for instance, shown above the enthroned figures in the Bayeux tapestry (1066–77). The importance of the canopy has been discussed elsewhere and its significance with regard to seating has been recognized.[504] We cannot be certain at what point in time the canopy became indispensable for chairs of state, but we can note with interest that Henry III ordered one above a particular chair in 1252, see p. 188. It remains only to demonstrate here how this emphasis upon accessories, controlled by rules of precedence, proclaimed lordship at many levels of society. If we look at a miniature from the *Livre des proprietez des choses* produced in Flanders in 1482,[505] we see a seated figure in ermine robes placed on a small dais. The seat, tester and canopy (which has curtains looped up like a hung bed) is entirely covered with rich cloth (so that we cannot define the precise form of the seat) and the figure appears before us as one enthroned. (We may compare this equipment with a state seat shown in a miniature of Philip the Good, Duke of Burgundy, attributed to Roger van der Weyden and find it no whit inferior.)[506] Yet the man in the *Livre des proprietez des choses* is not a great seigneurial lord but a master tradesman, acting as overseer of the mason and carpenter who work before him in the foreground of the painting. His position of authority (and superiority) is fully justified *in the context in which he is depicted*; if such a man were received by the Duke of Burgundy, however, the seating accorded to him — if seating there was — would be utterly different.

The examination of seats of authority has been largely confined to contexts involving a high degree of state or ceremony, and many of the seats discussed belonged to the hall or chapel where the seigneurial lord displayed his power and influence to large groups of people. Chairs were also used in chambers in more select company, however, and here the atmosphere might be less formal though the forms employed for furniture remained the same and rules of precedence obtained here, as elsewhere. Alexander Neckam (1157–1217) stated that a chair was placed beside the bed in the chamber ('Juxta lectum cathedra...')[507] and there is much later evidence to indicate that the practice was common. The Flemish masters of the later Middle Ages, who have familiarized us with the material comforts of the rich bourgeois society of their time, often show a high backed chair beside the hung bed; for instance, such a chair is shown in this position by Jan van Eyck in the Arnolfini wedding of 1434 in the National Gallery.

Documentary sources indicate that chamber chairs were of several kinds and show that while most chair coverings were loose, *upholstered* chairs were also produced.

1251   King's Chamber, Nottingham Castle.

            To the sheriff of Nottingham. '*Contrabreve* to . . . wainscot the chamber and
            make wooden stalls and chairs therein round about; to make a spike

[504] See Macquoid/Edwards 1954, State, 164 f.
[505] MS ROY 15. E.II, fol. 265r, British Museum; see D. King, 'Currents of Trade', ed. Evans 1966, 266, fig. 64.
[506] See Faggin, 84.
[507] Ed. Scheler, 90.

(*esporum*) in front of the doorway, and iron candlesticks fixed in the wall; . . .'

(*Cal. Lib.* R. iv, 11.)

1304   For the chamber of Mahaut, Comtesse d'Artois, 2 chairs were purchased from a Parisian *imagier*, see p. 189.

1307/8   Accounts of Mahaut, Comtesse d'Artois.

'Por iii chaieres por la chambre madame et por le drap à couvrir lesdites chaieres fait par la main maistre Pierre le talleur et Perrin de Salins, vi l. v.s.'

(For 3 chairs for Madame's chamber and for the cloth for upholstering the said chairs, made by the hand of master Pierre the tailor and Perrin de Salins . . .)

1310   'Pour i banc, une chaiere . . . mis en la chambre madame à Arras acaté à Guillaume le huchier de Gant, x l.'

(For 1 bench, a chair, . . . for placing in Madame's chamber at Arras, bought from Guillaume the *huchier* of Ghent . . .)

1324/5   'Pour ii caieres aaisiées ploiches à couverchiaus cloans et ouvrans' (Given to the convent of Thieulloye.)

(For 2 folding chairs of ease with nailed on coverings; opening.)

(Richard 1887: 1304, 1307/8, 1310: 365, fn. 1; 1324/5: 369, fn. 2.)

1368   Thomas Kynebell, rector of St. Martin Pomeroy.
'In the Hall: . . . 12 chairs, . . . In the Chamber: . . . one long *chayer* . . .'

(Thomas 1929, 91–2.)

Duke of Burgundy's Accounts.

1366/7   '605. . . . à Oudot l'archer, de Dijon, pour une chaiere pertusie, pour la chambre de Mgr.' (Required for Talent castle.)

(. . . to Oudot, chest maker of Dijon, for a sluice chair [w.c.] for the Duke's chamber.)

1381   '550. . . . à Jehan de Sainte Menaor, seillier, demorant à Dijon . . . pour covrir de cuir et clouher une chiere pour la chambre de Mme . . . pour rubans, filz vert et autre fil pour lad. Chaiere . . .'

(. . . to Jehan de Saint Menehould, saddler of Dijon . . . for covering with leather and nailing a chair for Madame's chamber . . . for ribbons, of green thread and other thread for the said chair . . .)

1383   '769. . . . à Thomas de Sombreffe, maistre des menues euvres de Mgr, pour le bois et façon de 2 chaieres qu'il a faites . . . du commandement de

Mme pour madamoiselle Marguerite, c'est assavoir l'une à tourner et l'autre à laver.'

(... to Thomas de Sombreffe, master of minor works to the Duke, for the wood and for the making by him of 2 chairs ... by order of the Duchess for Mlle Marguerite, namely, one chair *à tourner* and the other for washing.)

1388

'2576. ...à Jehan de Troyes, sellier, demourant à Paris ... pour avoir recouvert de drap vermeil et doublé de toile tainte deux chayeres de retrait pour elle et pour ycelles avoir garnies de cloux dorez ... pour avoir couvert de drap vermeil pour mons. le conte de Nevers une chayere de retrait ...'

(... to Jehan de Troyes, saddler of Paris, for having recovered with red cloth lined with *toille tainte* 2 chairs for the Duchess's inner chamber and for fitting upon the same chairs gilded nails ... for having covered with red cloth a chair for the inner chamber of the Comte de Nevers ...)

(1366/7, Prost, I, 96; 1381, Prost, II, 94; 1383, Prost, II, 127–8; 1388, Prost, II, 394.)

1390

Duke of Burgundy's Accounts.

'3522. ...à Jehan Poireau, sellier' of Paris 'pour ... une chaiere de retrait de bois garnye de drap et fourrée de duvet pour mons. le conte de Nevers et pour une bourse de cuir à mectre ycelle chaiere.'

(... to Jehan Poireau, saddler, for ... a chair, for the Comte de Nevers's inner chamber, of wood garnished with cloth and padded with down and for a leather case into which the chair may be placed.)

(Prost, II, 588.)

1399

French royal accounts.

'Perrin Balloches, paintre, demourant à Paris ... pour Mgr messire Loys de France, deux chaieres, c'est assavoir l'une de salle l'autre de retrait, celle de salle painte de finnes couleurs, couverte de cuir vermeil escorchié, frangiée de franges de soye et garni ainsi comme il appartient, et celle de rettrait couverte de drap vermeil.'

(Havard, I, 644.)

(Pierrin Balloches, painter of Paris ... for Mgr Louis of France 2 chairs, namely, one a hall chair the other for an inner chamber, the hall chair painted with fine colours, covered with red leather (?cut to a fine thickness), fringed with silk and equipped as is fitting, and the chair for an inner chamber covered with red cloth.)

1404

Durham Abbey accounts.

'Item in Camera et in solario sub camera sunt ... 5 cathedra, 5 nyght chares, ...'

('Extracts from the Account Rolls of the Abbey of Durham', Vol. II, *Surtees Society*, C, 1899, 398.)

(Item, in the Chamber and in the solar beneath the chamber are . . . 5 chairs and 5 night chairs, i.e. chairs of ease.)

1420   Château de Beauté, King's Chamber.

'Item, deux chaezes de boys, à dos, ouvrées de menu ouvrage.
Item, deux autres chaezes ployans, l'une de fer bien ouvrée, et l'autre de boys.'

(Douet d'Arcq, 461.)

(. . . Item, 2 wooden chairs with backs, of minor workmanship.
Item, 2 other chairs, folding, one of iron finely made and the other of wood.)

1440   In the inventory of the Old Deanery, Salisbury, 'a chair of Sarum make' was noted as present in the Principal Chamber, the Chamber Adjoining the Principal Chamber, and the Chamber at the end of the Hall.

(Drinkwater, 57.)

1454   In the most sumptuous guest chamber at Durham Abbey called the King's Chamber.

'Item 1 cathedra
1 scamnum voc. langsedile
3 formule.'

('Extract from the Account Rolls of the Abbey of Durham, I,' *Surtees Society*, XCIX, 1898, 147.)

(Item 1 chair, 1 bench called long seat, 3 forms.)

*c.*1459   Sir John Fastolf's furniture at Caister Castle.

'Schipdam, is chambre . . . Item, j chayre . . . My Maister is Chambre . . . Item, j long Chayre. Item, j grene Chayre . . . The Chambure there Margaret Hodessone laye . . . Item, j Chayre withe j pece of palle white and grene. The utmost Chambur nexte Winter halle . . . Item, j rede Chayre.'

(Aymot, 266, 268–9.)

1485   Reparations to Coldharbour (London), against the coming of Lady Margaret Beaufort, mother of Henry VII.

Joiners' account:

'A close chayre for my lady, . . .'
(Kingsford 1920/1, 44 (fn. 9).)

The evidence quoted highlights the two types of seat furniture equipping chambers at an important level. We find the seating intended for keeping company, for the

P

chamber of a seigneurial lord was a place where persons might be received and meals taken, and the seating connected with more private occasions. In French and Burgundian contexts, we find the more private quarters designated *chambre de retrait*, which described the room approached via the chamber. We notice that in both the chamber and the *chambre de retrait*, or inner chamber, upholstered chairs were used (entries 1307/8, 1381, 1388, 1390, 1399) and we also see with interest that one entry (1399) shows that a hall chair might also be fitted up in this way. The upholstery was in leather and cloth and the use of padding (1390) and gilt nails (1388) shows these comfortable chairs were the forerunners of the library or study chairs familiar in eighteenth-century contexts. One example had its own leather case (1390). A chair covered in red velvet occurs in Henry V's inventory of 1423, which was presumably a chamber rather than a hall chair.[508] It should also be noted that the craftsmen concerned in the making of these chairs were tailors (1307/8) as well as saddlers. We see that chairs of ease occur (1324/5, 1366/7, and 1404 and find the 1366/7 entry suggests a form of water closet. The chairs 'à tourner' and 'à laver' (1383) were concerned with the toilet of important persons. The latter was almost certainly for hair washing, and the chair 'à tourner' may have been on a swivel base, as the description suggests. The 'close chair' (1485) is a frequent term in English sources and probably described the high backed armed chair of the type found in the Muchelney group (Cat. 51).

BENCHES, FORMS AND STOOLS

These were the commonest forms of seating in the Middle Ages, and the bench was considered superior to the form or stool. On occasion, rules of precedence forced great lords to occupy the humblest of these seats, as Havard has shown in the following evidence. Philippe de Comines describes how the Comte de Charolais (heir to the Duke of Burgundy), dined with the Duc de Berry and the Duc de Bretagne; he gave them the honour of the bench (*banc*) while he and the Duc de Calabre sat facing them on stools (*escabeaux*).[509] Benches were frequently used by great lords for dining, precedence being accorded by the use of canopies fixed above the position of the persons concerned, as illuminations and paintings show.[510] As with chairs, the provision of a footboard (normally attached to the bench) was important in contexts of this kind. There is a wealth of written evidence concerning benches, forms of stools, though most references lack any kind of description. Much of this furniture was associated with tables, as we notice in the 1253 entry below, and belongs more properly in Section E (Tables). The thirteenth-century Liberate Rolls contain many references to the kind of seating under discussion, and some typical examples are given below. (We have noticed that in England at this date, a separate chair for the king seems to have been preferred, see 1252, p. 188, and 1252, p. 203) rather than a seat upon the bench which was the arrangement favoured in the later Middle Ages.[511]

---

[508] 'Item, 1 Cheir' covert de velvet rouge, pris XXVI s. VIII d.' *Rot. Parl.*, IV, 238.
[509] Havard, I, 237.
[510] See Eames 1971, pl. 21.
[511] Le Fèvre de Saint-Remy's description of the meeting between Charles V and Henry V in the king's hall at Saint-Pol to hear the complaint concerning the assassination of Jean-sans-Peur notes that both lords 'estoient assis sur le mesme bancq' (Havard, I, 237).

Benches, forms and stools were used in halls and chambers alike, and chamber benches were often fitted around the walls like church stalls. Hall seating was occasionally fixed, but movable furniture was more convenient for it allowed scope for a variety of activities within the hall. Window seats, which caused no interference in this respect, were fitted in halls and chambers.[512] Some light is thrown on early evidence regarding benches and stalls in halls and chambers by looking at the evidence of ecclesiastical work.

Pre–1100   The choir stalls in the church of St.-Denis (consecrated 775), which were destroyed by Abbot Suger, were decorated with copper plaques.

(Weinberger, 377.)

Early twelfth   See p. 187 regarding the evidence of Theophilus concerning the use of
century   copper sheets round painted chairs, stools and beds.

1240   'The Chancels of St. Mary and St. Peter in the church of St. Peter within the bailey of the Tower of London, . . . the stalls made for the king and queen, are to be well and suitably wainscotted (*lambruscari*) and the stalls painted, and the small figure of St. Mary with her tabernacle, the images of St. Peter, St. Nicholas, and St. Katherine, the beam above the altar of St. Peter, and the small cross with its images are to be repainted and refreshed with good colours.'

(*Cal. Lib.* R., II, 14.)

1251   The King's Chamber at Nottingham Castle given wooden panelling and wooden stalls and chairs round about.

(See pp. 198–9.)

1252   'To the sheriff of Northampton. *Contrabreve* to remove the great bench in the hall [at Silverstone] and to make a new stone bench in its place with a chair in the middle for the king; . . . and forms and tables in the chamber of Edward the king's son; . . .'

(*Cal. Lib.* R., IV, 23; see also above, p. 188.)

1252   'To the sheriff of Wiltshire. *Contrabreve* to make . . . a window for the king's wardrobe to be glazed with white glass, with a column and seat and a bench to put the king's clothes on when he takes them off.'

(*Cal. Lib.* R., IV, 90.)

1253   'To the bailiff of Havering. *Contrabreve* . . . to make a screen well carved and a table with its stools in the queen's chamber . . .'

(*Cal. Lib.* R., IV, 119.)

[512] Such stone seats survive at Alnwick and Belsay, Northumberland, and at Meare, Somerset; see [Parker] 1853, facing 37, 94.

1313   Accounts of Mahaut, Comtesse d'Artois.

'un banc de fust à 11 roes ès 11 bous, entaillé à 1111 bestelettes as bous, mis en la sale à Paris, acheté en la presence madame.'

(A wooden bench, with 2 wheels fitted on 2 legs [i.e. ?both at the same end] and carved with 4 small beasts on the top, to be placed in the hall at Paris, purchased in Madame's presence.)

(The full entry concerning this interesting bench shows that the Comtesse went herself to the workshop to purchase the seat and had it immediately transported to her hôtel by 8 men who received 4 sous for their trouble.)

1314   Entry regarding the purchase of stone from Pronville 'pour faire les V fourmes de la sale' of the Château de Bapaume.

(stone for making the 5 forms of the hall.)

1320   Another entry notes that a mason was paid for making 'toutes les fourmes de pierre' in the hall at Conflans.
(all the stone forms.)

(Richard 1887: 1313, 320; 1314, 269; 1320, 295.)

The works undertaken by Mahaut, Comtesse d'Artois between 1302–9 were extensive. Richard notes that forms for the chapels at Paris and Conflans are entered on a number of occasions; these forms, he states, were in the nature of works of art.[513]

1338   Château de Rouen.

45 forms are listed here; the following entry is typical.

'En la chambre dessous la salle au bailly, . . .
item trois fourmes, 11 de vuicts et l'autre de VII piés de lonc, séant chascune seur 1111 piés au tarelle; item, une fourme séant seur 111 piés, et y a 1111 papeillons, de XX piés de lonc . . .'

(Roman, 545.)

(In the chamber beneath the hall in the bailey, item, 3 forms, 2 of 8' and the other of 7' long, each supported upon 4 feet of turret (round) form; item, a form supported on 3 feet and 4 butterfly supports of 20' long . . .)

This form may have resembled Fig. 30, which combines 'turret' and 'butterfly' supports

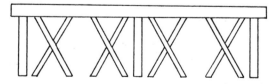

FIG. 30.   Form resting on supports of post and X-form

[513] Richard 1887, 321.

1373 Concerning the Château de Montbard, held by the Duke of Burgundy.

'1672. Ban en sale, 1; buffet, 1. table pour Mgr., 1; trestaulx, 3; aultres tables, 3; granz fourmes, 3; pié de bois à mettre bacin pour lave, 1.'

(Prost, I, 312.)

(Benches in hall, 1; buffet, 1; table for the Duke, 1; trestles, 3; other tables, 3; large forms, 3; wooden stand for holding a basin for [hand] washing, 1.)

1378/9 Concerning the Château de Montbard, held by the Duke of Burgundy.

'388. Wooden boards used for the following: 'sièges de 11 fenestres croisiés de la chambre rouge ... pour cause de la pierre qui estoit trop froide, et Mme se seoit sus.'

(Seats [of wood] made across the 2 windows of the red room [the Duke's chamber] because the stone [of the window seats] is too cold, and Madame [the Duchess] sits upon them.)

(Prost, II, 63–4.)

1382 Concerning the Château de Rouvre, held by the Duke of Burgundy.

'741. Thomas de Sambreffe, maistre des euvres de Mgr, recoit 6 fr. à lui dus pour le bois et façon d'un grand banc qu'il a fait ..., pour la chambre de Jehan mons. à Rouvre, et de une chayere pour led. Jehan mons.'

(Prost, II, 122.)

(Thomas de Sambreffe, master of works to the Duke, received 6 fr. due to him for wood and for making a large bench made by him ... for M. Jean's chamber at Rouvre, and for a chair for the said M. Jean.)

1409 Concerning the hôtel of the Comte de Hainaut, Paris.

'Item, plusieurs bancs, tables, chayères et tresteaulz estans en plusieurs lieux et estages dudit hostel, donnez avecques icellui hostel à mondit seigneur.'

(Devillers, 416.)

(Item, several benches, tables, chairs, and trestles are located in various places on the different floors of the said house, given with the house to my lord.)

1415 Goods of Richard Gurmyn.

'Item, Joynid Stole, pris iij d ...
Item, vn Chaiere, pris vj d.'

(Kingsford 1918/20, 99.)

1416 1 little bench was used by John Haukes, a Worcestershire peasant.

(Field, 142 (Appendix B, Table III, no. 5).)

1420   Goods in the Château de Vincennes.

                 'Ou donjon, en la chambre de dessus le logis du capitaine . . .
                 Item, ung banc, sans perche, de v piez de long ou environ . . .
                 Ou Retrait [de la chambre de la Cage, estant en la grosse tour] un banc
                 à perche et à marche, de six piez ou environ.'

                 (Douet d'Arcq, 456–7, 460.)

                 (In the keep, in the chamber above the captain's dwelling . . .
                 Item, a bench without a back rail, of about 5' long . . .
                 In the inner chamber of the chamber of the *Cage*, in the great tower, a
                 bench with rail forming a back and with a footboard, of about 6' [long].)

1440   Inventory of goods in the Old Deanery, Salisbury.

                 'The old parlour is benched around.'

                 (Drinkwater, 57.)

The entries quoted give substance to a number of points which have been raised, as well as providing evidence concerning unusual seating. We find references to fitted benches and stalls in chapel and chamber (1240, 1251 and 1440); to stone forms and benches in England and France (1252, 1314 and 1320); to window seats for the king of England and the duke of Burgundy (1252 and 1378/9); and to an elaborate bench made in Paris fitted with two wheels (1313). This bench, purchased by Mahaut, Comtesse d'Artois must have been about 20' long, for it required eight men to transport it through the streets of Paris; presumably four boards were passed underneath it, the men carrying it in pairs, four on each side. We note that it was for the hall, and also that it could be moved out of the way whenever necessary. It seems probable that the wheels were fitted to the back and front legs at one end only; had wheels been fitted to all the feet of the bench, it would have tended to move in use.

Some indication of the variety of forms produced for stools, forms and benches is shown in Fig. 31. Much of the information gathered is drawn from MS sources and the survey is not intended to be comprehensive. We notice that slab-ended as well as post stools with animal heads existed in the eleventh century (Bayeux tapestry). We also observe that benches 'à perche' often had a *swinging* back rail in place of a fixed bar (see St Barbara by the Master of Flémalle and the MS *Le Romuléon*), so that the sitters could choose which way to face without moving the bench; paintings suggest that it was customary to sit towards the fireplace in winter and with back to the fire facing into the room in summer.[514]

Some of the forms shown in Fig. 31, can be studied in extant furniture. Stools or forms with a decorative underframe which sometimes pierces the slab ends, as in the Hans Memling St Barbara, are well represented and there is a particularly fine example in the Victoria and Albert Museum from Barningham Hall, Norfolk, which was built by a member of the Paston family in the reign of James I.[515] Stools of the slab-ended

---

[514] Dervieu states that some benches *à perche* survive on the Continent. (Dervieu 1910, 234.)
[515] See Macquoid/Edwards 1927, Benches, fig. 4.

1

2

3

4

5

6

7

8

(See KEY on page 209)

FIG. 31.   Forms found in benches and stools

shape had both straight and canted supports, as examples in the Metropolitan Museum of Art show, see pl. 63B. An altar retable carved with the Last Supper by Jean de Molder of Antwerp 1513 is an important source for different forms of stool.[516] The familiar slab-ended and triangular turned stools are present, and also a highly ornate 4-post type with traceried underframe which swings outward and inward between the posts. The carving is in such high relief that the furniture is almost shown in the round.

Surviving benches are much rarer than forms and stools. Winchester Cathedral has an example which is over 12' long. The back, which is framed and closed with riven boards, is surmounted by rudimentary poppy heads carved with stars in relief. This carving is unlike the chip-carved roundels on early chests which are incised. It may be compared with the late eleventh-century stone carving on the doorway of the exchequer building at Caen Castle, which has the same raised star pattern. The correlation suggests a date of 1100–1200 for the bench, making it one of the earliest pieces of furniture in the country.

A number of bench fragments may be compared with the complete example at Muchelney (Cat. 51). The closest parallel comes from a French context, see pl. 69; another example was recorded by Macquoid/Edwards and by Margaret Wood following Parker.[517] All that survives of this bench, which was in use in the Dragon Inn, Coombe St Nicholas, in the early nineteenth century, is the back, return and high corner post, all crisply carved with linen fold panels and rope mouldings. The mutilated corner post which rises above the top of the bench back was apparently one of the hammer beams of a roof, for Parker recorded it complete with carved angel in the engraving published by him. This evidence indicates that the bench was created *as part of the structure of a building*, but nothing about its original context is known.

KEY

1   Count Guy's throne, Bayeux Tapestry, see Stenton fig. 11. 1066–77.
2   William's throne, Bayeux Tapestry, see Stenton fig. 18.
3   Edward's throne, Bayeux Tapestry, see Stenton pl. V.
4   Twelfth century. See Dervieu 1910, fig. 3.
5   Jan van Eyck, Ince Hall Madonna, 1433, see Faggin, pl. XXXIV.
6   Miniature, Death of Godefroi de Bouillon, *c.* 1475, see Macquoid/Edwards 1927, Introduction, fig. 4.
7   Jan van Eyck, Annunciation, 1435, see Faggin, pl. XXXV.
8   From Bib. imp. fond La Vallière, 92, see Viollet-le-Duc, 1858, 106.
9   Flemish MS, *Liber de Proprietatibus*, BM; see Macquoid/Edwards 1927, Cupboards, fig. 1.
10 Master of Flémalle, St Barbara (Prado); 1438.
11 Master of Flémalle, Mérode altar piece, New York.
12 MS, *Le Romuléon*, Bib. imp. 6984, see Viollet-le-Duc, 1858, 105.
13 MS Bodleian 283; fifteenth century.
14 Panel, St Barbara by Hans Memling, *c.* 1433–94.
15 MS, fifteenth-century French, BM; see Macquoid/Edwards 1927, chandeliers, fig. 1.
16 MS, *Le Romuléon*, Bib. imp. 6984, see Viollet-le-Duc, 1858, 117; fifteenth century.

[516] Musée Cluny, Paris. The retable is dated by a document, see Mme. Ciepka's *Cat. des Bois Sculptés des Anciens Pays-Bas 1480–1530 au Musée Cluny* (typescript, Musée Cluny), 110.
[517] Macquoid/Edwards 1927, Settles, fig. 11; M. Wood, *The English Mediaeval House*, London, 1965, pl. 32b shows the engraving of a drawing made in the early nineteenth century when the bench was in use in the Green Dragon Inn.

CATALOGUE No. 49 (PLATES 54–5)

Arm-chair (Post type 2), in Hereford Cathedral.

Measurements: see *Royal Commission on Historical Monuments Herefordshire I (South-West)*, London, 1931, 107, for scale drawings.

Description (April 1968)

With the exception of the seat, the entire chair is composed of turned members. Four heavy posts with turned knops are linked by rails and stiles of smaller section. The majority of the turned posts are simple rods decorated at regular intervals with pairs of incised rings; the spaces at the front below the seat, and at the sides, however, are filled with moulded shafts. At the front, these shafts once formed pairs of Romanesque arches set in 2 bays; the right-hand pair survive. Apart from the main uprights, the posts which formed the back of the chair are largely missing, but enough remains above the seat to establish the design as a series of rectangles set one within the other and therefore diminishing in size. At the sides of the chair, the shafts are arranged in 2 registers without arcading; the number of shafts on each side is different, an original arrangement; below the seat there are 4 shafts on the right side, 3 on the left. The seat of the chair is made of two boards joined from front to back and held in grooves in the front and back rails but free at the sides. The lowest front rail of the chair has a groove running its whole length.

Analysis

The scale drawings published by the Royal Commission give front and side elevations of the chair together with sections of mouldings; this excellent analysis renders verbal comment concerning the precise form of the chair superfluous. The published drawing, however, should be corrected in one particular: the lowest rail at the front of the chair has a groove and the incised circles upon this rail pass across the groove but otherwise ignore it, they are not cut *within it* as is indicated. As the groove was certainly made to link the chair with a *matching footboard*, now lost, its inner face would have been invisible in use. The point seems trivial but becomes significant when we consider the purpose of the groove, for it establishes that the chair was designed to serve as a seat of estate.

The chair is now venerated as the throne of Stephen (1135–1154), and is placed in a position of importance below the steps of the sanctuary. This position, however, is relatively new, for in 1827 the chair stood in the Lady Chapel, having been removed from the Bishop's Palace, and in 1840 it was to be found in the Cathedral Library.[518] The Royal Commission report dated the chair late twelfth/early thirteenth-century, finding that the *arcading* was distinctive in this period, although the posts and rails were of a type which may be found as late as the sixteenth century.[519] The Commissioners compared the Hereford chair with a similar survivor from Rusby, Sweden.

The Hereford chair may be compared with the French twelfth-century carved wooden figure of a seated Madonna now in Stockholm; the chair in this carving has turned

---

[518] See F. T. Havergal, *Fasti Herefordenses and other Antiquarian Memorials of Hereford*, Edinburgh, 1869, 123 for the 1827 account; also Oakeshott, pl. IIa for a sketch showing the chair standing in the library.
[519] *RCHM Herefordshire*, I, xli, 106.

posts which are incised at regular intervals, the incisisions providing the divisions between the colours red and blue-green with which the chair is painted. Not only does the Hereford chair resemble the form of this figure closely, but according to Havergal the Hereford example still displayed vestiges of original vermilion and gold paint in 'several of the narrow bands', in the nineteenth century.[520] Another important comparison is provided by the surviving group of furniture from Vallstena church, Gotland, with Romanesque arcading, which is stylistically dated twelfth century. This group includes an arm chair and an armed bench, the backs of which are entirely closed with turned members arranged in rectangles.[521]

The Hereford chair is in good condition, apart from the missing members and the footboard. A late twelfth/early thirteenth-century date is convincing, in view of the evidence of the moulded shafts and the close correlations with other twelfth-century work noted above. The chair is one of the most important pieces of medieval furniture in Britain, representing a group which was once common, as is established by written records as well as by pictorial evidence, e.g. the round chair *with columns* provided by Stephen 'le Joignur' for Edward I (1272–1307),[522] the turned chair worth 8*d.* mentioned in an action for debt against Richard Bye in 1440,[523] and 'j cathedra turnyd' in the Durham Abbey accounts for 1488.[524]

Select Bibliography

F. T. Havergal, *Fasti Herefordenses & other Antiquarian Memorials of Hereford*, Edinburgh, 1869, 123–8, pl. VI.

W. Oakeshott, 'Winchester College Library before 1750', *Trans. Bibliographical Society*, 5th series, IX, 1954, pl. IIa.

RCHM *Herefordshire*, I, 1931, xli, 106, pl. 127, fig. p. 107.

CATALOGUE NO. 50 (PLATE 56)

Chair (boarded type) in St James's church, Stanford Bishop, Herefordshire.

Oak, now polished

l. 2′ 5¾″; h. right front upright, 2′ 6½″; Max. d. of seat, 1′ 2½″.

Description (April 1968)

The construction is simple with 4 uprights grooved or slotted to receive boards which form the back, sides, front and seat of the chair. The back uprights are cut on the inner face near the back with a long groove designed to receive a series of boards; one only remains. These back uprights are also cut with a slot on the edge which faces the front which is suitably positioned to receive the board which forms the side of the chair. The front uprights are cut along their narrow back face in sympathy to receive the

---

[520] The French figure is shown by Holmqvist, fig. 391; see also Havergal, 123.
[521] Statens Historiska Museet, Stockholm; see Holmqvist, fig. 368.
[522] Brown/Colvin/Taylor, I, 224.
[523] See P. E. Jones, *Cal. Plea & Memoranda Rolls 1437–1457*, Cambridge, 1954, 31.
[524] See *Surtees Society*, 1898, 99.

other end of the side boards of the chair. The front uprights are also slotted on their side and inner faces, lower down, to hold the horizontal board which forms the front of the chair below the seat.

The seat is a single, loose board cut with integral, roughly circular dowels which engage in holes pierced through the back uprights, forming a pivot hinge and enabling the area below the seat to be used for storage. The seat is thus supported by the dowels at the back, piercing the back uprights, and by the horizontal board at the front of the chair. Except for this front horizontal board, all the boards which once formed the chest (of which the seat is the lid) are missing. Dowel holes low down on the uprights indicate points of attachment for the boards which formed the chest and they also mark the position of a missing footstool.

The uprights are mutilated, having been cut down at the feet as well as at the top; the indication of gable shaped working on the inner face of the back uprights suggests that these posts were only slightly taller at the top.

The chair is entirely of wood; no nails or iron fittings of any kind are present.

Analysis

This chair is much more interesting than its crude appearance suggests. In the first place, it is conceived as a knockdown chair, an example of a piece of furniture designed for travelling, in which a group of boards are slotted and grooved into 4 uprights. The choice of boards for uprights rather than rectangular or round posts keeps all the elements relatively flat and simple for packing.

The practicability of the construction rests upon a certain tightness between boards and slots or grooves and upon the weight of the user, who produces a downward thrust and stabilizes all the elements. It is, in a way, a clever design, producing an object which is quickly taken apart, packed without the need for an expensive and bulky case, and reassembled in a very short time. An occasional application of beeswax or gum would retain the necessary tightness in grooves and slots.

The second point which excites interest in the chair is the fact that it appears to have had an integral foot board and this, as we have seen, is an accessory which is always present when seigneurial power is displayed. The absent foot board indicates that this chair was an adjunct of estate; its construction shows that it accompanied its owner when he, or she, travelled. The crudeness of the boards presents little problem with regard to this important role, for the chair could have been entirely draped with cloth or furs when in use.

There is considerable difficulty in dating the chair. Tradition relates that this is St Augustine's chair, used by him at a conference in 603.[525] We cannot compare it with *fixed* seating, like the Hereford chair, for its use as a knockdown unit precludes much that was sophisticated in design, and the only relevant comparisons we can make are with folding X-chairs. The construction bears some resemblance to ark chests; the pivot hinge is found on a few early hutch chests, e.g. Climping (Cat. 30). The general characteristics of the chair suggest that it is twelfth century, or earlier.

---

[525] See N. Pevsner, *Herefordshire*, Harmondsworth, 1963, 290; also J. Johnstone, *The Finding of St. Augustine's Chair*, Birmingham, 1898.

Select Bibliography

J. Johnstone, *The Finding of St. Augustine's Chair*, Birmingham, 1898.

N. Pevsner, *Herefordshire*, Harmondsworth, 1963, 290.

Transactions of the Woolhope Naturalists' Field Club, 1942, lvi, lxxv–lxxx, 179–86.

CATALOGUE NO. 51 (PLATES 57–8)

Bench (boarded type) at Muchelney Abbey, Somerset.
In the Abbot's Parlour. The bench is fitted along the S. wall, with short returns along the E. and W. walls.

Oak, now polished

l. (S. wall), 17′ 9¾″; h. seat from floor, 2′ 1″; Max. h. from seat to top of back, 3′ 6½″; w. seat, 1′ 3½″.

Description (December 1969)

The bench is fixed in its original position and occupies the whole S. wall of the first floor Parlour of the Abbot's lodging. The bench has returns on the W. and E. walls respectively, providing a single seat beside the fireplace on the W. wall and a double seat opposite on the E. wall. Both these seats are terminated with arms. The back of the bench is high for its entire length, except where its position coincides with the two windows in the S. wall, and here the back is reduced in height to accommodate the height of the windows. The bench is boarded in beneath the seat and panelled both here and on the seat back. The lower panels are each carved in the solid with a single linen fold design; the upper panels forming the back of the bench have more intricate convolutions of linen fold design, carved in the solid. The uppermost rail of the bench is surmounted by a carved, pierced frieze in those areas which are of full height, and above this frieze is a series of finials which, in all but the central example, coincide with the stiles beneath. Beneath the seat, the uppermost rail bears scars made by the removal of 2 lock plates situated on either side of the central area. The seat of the bench is restored and ignores the evidence of lockers beneath.

Analysis

The Muchelney bench is of the greatest importance since it survives *in situ* and has preserved its complete form, thus enabling us to appreciate permanent seating arrangements, which records suggest were once common, in their proper context; we see here the type of seating appropriate to the chamber rather than the hall. The interest of the seating is enhanced by the completeness of this area of the room, with its windows and carved stone fireplace intact, which Pevsner has described as 'one of the most sumptuous pre-Reformation fireplaces in the country'.[526] We notice that ?2 chests were originally provided within the seating, showing that the Muchelney bench may be correlated with the 'banc à coffre' of French sources. The position of the storage area can be partly

[526] N. Pevsner, *South and West Somerset*, Harmondsworth, 1958, 249.

judged by the scars of the missing lock plates and by examining the photograph published by Macquoid/Edwards in 1927 (though we cannot now say whether one long locker with 2 locks, or two smaller separate lockers, were involved). It is regrettable that the Ministry of Works obliterated the lift-up areas of the seat when the bench was removed from the room and restored in the 1960s.

The bench may be compared with a pair of seats in the Musée des Arts Décoratifs in Paris (Peyre, 1049) which are carved with the mutilated arms of Rigaud d'Aurelhe, sénéchal d'Agenais et de Gascogne, and reputedly from the Château de Villeneuve, Auvergne (pl. 69). This French seating is a 'banc à coffre' with the same broad linen fold panels beneath the seats as at Muchelney, but the seat backs are differently treated with a diaper pattern; the pair were probably originally fitted in a chamber and the unfinished side of one indicates that they were part of a larger group. The Rigaud d'Aurelhe seats share with the Muchelney bench a pierced frieze with finials above; although restored, the French seats appear to present their original characteristics, and are dated by heraldry to the last quarter of the fifteenth century.

The external architectural characterstics of the Abbot's lodging at Muchelney are of early sixteenth-century style, but no records of this phase of abbey building survive. Very little is known about the monastery during the fifteenth century. Thirteen monks were present at the election ot Thomas Pipe in 1463 and the number had risen to fifteen at the election of Wiliam Wyke as abbot in 1489; the last abbot was John Shirborne who resigned in 1532. The Abbey was surrendered in 1538.[527]

The stylistic evidence ot the architecture as well as of the bench itself is in harmony with the dating of the seating of Rigaud d'Aurelhe; the Muchelney bench may, therefore, be dated with confidence to c.1500. It is amusing to note that, with the addition of a modestly proportioned movable bench facing the present fitting, all the monks in the Abbey could have been accommodated round the abbot's fire, if required.

Select Bibliobraphy

P. Macquoid/R. Edwards, *Dictionary of English Furniture*, London, 1927, Benches, fig. 12.

N. Pevsner, *South and West Somerset*, Harmondsworth, 1958, 249.

A History of Somerset II (The Victoria History of the Counties of England), London, 1911, 103–7.

---

[527] *A History of Somerset II* (The Victoria History of the Counties of England), London, 1911, 105–6.

SECTION E
TABLES

This section will discuss the ordinary tables which served many different uses, and will omit the various specialized items such as counters, gaming boards and altar retables which shared the same terms in medieval sources: *tabula*, table etc.[528] As surviving medieval tables are so rare, the evidence provided by paintings and by documents is crucial to our appreciation of the many forms that once existed. In using documentary evidence, the lack of precise terms to differentiate between these different articles occasionally poses problems, but generally the matter is resolved by the context of a particular reference or by the accessories noted with an object, such as pieces in the case of gaming boards.

Tables were made of various materials: soft wood and oak were the commonest but stone and marble were also used. Some indication of the variety of materials found is given below.

Beech

1240   Windsor Castle.

'. . . et quandam fagum ad faciendas mensas in coquina Regis.'

(St John Hope 1913, 45.)

(. . . and a certain beech for making tables for the King's kitchen.)

Soft wood

1253   'To the Sheriffs of London. *Contrabreve* to buy 3,000 Norway boards and half a hundred of great boards in their bailiwick to make tables, and carry them without delay to Windesores for delivery to the keeper of the king's works there to use as the king has enjoined.'

(*Cal. Lib.* R., IV, 99.)

1373   Château d'Argilly.

'1834 . . . à Huguenot l'archier, demorrant à Chalon, pour 2 tables de sapin, de environ 40 piez de lonc et 3 piez de large et de 3 doies d'espaux, randue ancournées aux deux bout et esparées en 3 lieux, ou moitant, garnies chascune de 3 tresteaulx, bien faiz selonc les tables, achetées de luy à Chalon . . . pour mectre en la sale du chastel d'Argilli.'

(Prost, I, 341.)

(. . . to Huguenot, chest maker, living at Chalon, for 2 soft wood tables of about 40' long and 3' wide and of 3 fingers thickness, made horn-

---

[528] For example, for accounts: 1350, 'tabulam plicabilem ad desuper computandum' (Sharpe, I, 639); for gaming: 1397, 'table de ij foyles de cokyle [shell] ovesq la meyne [pieces]' (Viscount Dillon/W. H. St John Hope, 'Inventory of the Goods and Chattels belonging to Thomas, Duke of Gloucester, and Seized in his Castle at Pleshy', *Archaeological Journal*, LIV, 1897, 308); painted or carved panels for retables, etc.: 1361, Hugh Peyntour left his wife 'unum tabulam de VI. peces de Lumbardy' (Sharpe, II, 107).

shaped at each end, ?joined in 3 places or in the middle, each complete with 3 trestles, well made in accordance with the tables, bought from him at Chalon . . . to put in the hall of Argilly castle.)

Walnut

1400   Château de Sainte-Galle.

'Item unam tabulam nucis et duos gastors.'

(L. Royer, 'Le Mobilier des Châteaux Dauphinois en 1400 d'après un inventaire des biens de la Maison de Sassenage', *Bulletin de la Société Dauphinoise d'Ethnologie et d'Anthropologie*, 1923, 61.)

(Item a walnut table and 2 trestles.)

Oak

1420   Château de Beauté.

'Item, une autre table de chesne, de diz piez ou environ, avec deux meschans treteaux.'

(Douet d'Arcq, 461.)

(Item, another table of oak of about 10′ [long], with 2 broken trestles.)

Cypress

The use of cypress for furniture seems to have been very rare. Dervieu notes an entry concerning a table in a French context dated 1439.[529]

Ash

1485   Coldharbour, London.

'An asshyn table set in the Eaury in Coldherber for the wexchaundellers, . . .'

(Kingsford 1920/1, 44 (f. 14).).

Marble or stone

The most noteworthy English reference to such a table concerns arrangements in the great hall at Westminster where there was a marble seat and table (see 330). The date at which these objects were installed is unknown, but they were there in 1377, for the official account of the coronation of Richard II says that he went up to the marble table on the dais and demanded wine.[530] In a French context, Alienor de Poitiers states that Charles VIII used a marble table for dining in 1484:

'. . . & au soir quand le Roy soupa a la Table de marbre au Palais . . .'[531]

Tables fall into two main categories, movable and fixed, which will be discussed in turn.

---

[529] Lt.-Col. Dervieu, 'La Table et le Couvert du Repas au Moyen Age', *Bulletin Monumentales*, 1922, 392.
[530] See Brown/Colvin/Taylor, 543 f.
[531] Alienor de Poitiers, 'Les Honneurs de la Cour', La Curne de Sainte-Palaye, *Mémoires sur l'Ancienne Chevalerie*, II, Paris, 1781, 206.

MOVABLE TABLES

We have seen that the strong inclination towards movable furnishings and away from fixed arrangements in a great household had three main justifications: to facilitate the movement of the household from one dwelling to another; to enable valuable or delicate furnishings to be stored when not under surveillance; and to render floor space available for a variety of pursuits. This general tendency towards adaptability in furnishings was strongly in evidence with regard to tables. The number of persons who might be seated for meals in halls or chambers in a great household was very large, and tables to accommodate the numbers required were often enormous (see the reference to a pair of tables 40′ long, 1373, pp. 215–16). Thus knockdown tables were an essential requirement in great households, and in those of lesser standing the maximum utilization of limited space was still best served by removing tables after meals. The normal arrangment in halls was for a dais table for the lord (and more important members of his household and guests), with a number of tables placed at right angles to it ranged down the length of the hall. This plan is familiar from Oxford and Cambridge colleges, but whereas the tables are now fixed, in the Middle Ages they were generally knock-down, made up of heavy boards which rested upon trestles and remained in place by virtue of their weight alone. These tables were easily removed after meals by a number of persons lifting the boards and standing them against the walls of the hall, and taking up the trestles and stowing them in corners or outside the hall. This procedure in the management of hall space has long been understood, and Macquoid quotes a reference from Froissart (1350) stating that the tables were raised if the king of England or ladies remained in the hall;[532] their lingering after a meal indicated the use of the space for dancing or other entertainment. Olivier de la Marche, writing of the feast of the Toison d'Or at Ghent in 1445, noted that after the tables had been raised spices and wine were served in the hall, before the princes and knights returned to their chambers.[533] But whereas this aspect of household management has been fully recognized in so far as the hall was concerned, it has been less well understood with regard to chambers in great households. In fact, both hall and chambers were subject to the same procedures, so the trestle tables were needed equally in both contexts. Olivier de la Marche's treatize enables us to sympathize with the lot of the officer of the Duke of Burgundy's household in charge of the arrangement of appropriate furnishings, the *Fourrier*. We note that his task was one of unending responsibility since every setting he created was transient, and we see that the lord's chamber, as much as his hall, was organized on the removal system. We also note that boards and their trestles receive special attention for they, more than any other type of furniture with the possible exception of beds, occupied most space and inhibited the free movement of persons within a room.

> 'Le fourrier . . . quand le prince vient, . . . doit mettre le bancq, les tresceaux et la
> table; il doit reculer, remettre et oster à icelle table les tresceaux, et à toutes autres

---

[532] Macquoid 1938, 90 f.
[533] '. . . et, tables levees, furent les espices aportées, et furent les princes et les chevaliers servis d'espices et de vins; et puis se retrairent les chevaliers en leurs chambres, . . .' (Petitot, IX, 436).

Q

dont le prince est servy; il doit faire son banc, chaieres, et toutes autres ouvraiges de bois; il doit livrer les linceux et estrain pour les licts, et pour paillaces de l'hostel du prince; et livre bois de livrée et bois de despense, . . . et en iceluy office sont douze personnaiges et aides pour aider le fourrier, . . . et y a varlets de fourrier qui portent le bois en la chambre du prince, et besongnent aux feux et aux lumieres comme il appartient, et doivent tenir l'hostel du prince net et honneste.'

(Petitot, x, 544.)

(The Quartermaster . . . at the prince's coming, . . . must place the bench, the trestles and the table; he must pull back from, put together again, and remove from these tables their trestles, and do the same regarding all the others used for the service of the prince; he must make [i.e. place in position, accompanied by the right accessories] the prince's bench, chairs and all other furnishings; he must take up sheets and pewter [vessels for night time bread and drink], for the beds and for the [straw] mattresses of the prince's house; and take up wooden furniture and wooden vessels issued [with food and drink to individuals] . . . and in this office are 12 persons to aid the Quartermaster, . . . and there are valets of the Quartermaster who carry the wooden [furniture] of the prince's chamber, and attend to requirements regarding fires and lights, and these persons must keep the prince's house tidy and clean.)

The nature of the arrangements which might be temporarily required within the chamber are well illustrated in the account of Bluemantle Pursuivant describing the banquet given by Queen Elizabeth Woodville in her chambers at Windsor for the ambassador of the Duke of Burgundy in 1472, the lord Gruuthuse.

'The quene dyd order a grete banket in her owne chambre. At the wch banket were the Kinge, the quene, my lady Elizabeth the Kinges eldest doughter, the Duches of Excester, my lady Ryuers, and the lorde Gruthuse, settinge at oone messe, and at the same table sat the Duke of Bokingham, My lady his wyff, wt diuers other Ladyes, whose names I have not, My Lorde Hastinges, Chamberleyn to the Kinge, My lorde Barnes, chamberleyn to the quene, John Grutehuse son to ye forsaid lorde, Mr. George Bart, secretory to the Duc of Burgoine, Loys Stacy, asher to the Duke of Burgoine, [and] George Mytteney: also certeyn nobles of the kinges owne courte. Item, there was a syde table, at the wch sat a grete vewe of ladyes, all on ye one syde. Also in the vtter chamber sat the quenes gentlewomen all on one syde. And at the other syde of the table agenest them sat as many of the lorde Gruthuse servauntes: as touchinge to ye abondant welfare, lyke as hyt ys accordinge to soche a banket. And when they had sopt, my lady Elizabeth, the Kinges eldest doughter, daunsed wt the Duke of Bokingham: and dyuers other ladyes also.'

(Kingsford 1913, 387.)

The general ownership and use of trestle tables, particularly for halls, has been demonstrated by Dervieu and others,[534] and the amount of documentary evidence for

[534] Dervieu 1922, 388–93.

the later Middle Ages is considerable. Dervieu notes that the *numbers* of such tables in any one context was small, and certainly the total of 14 tables for the Château d'Aisey, quoted below, seems modest at first sight; however, it must be remembered that ideas of size were greatly different from those of today and the 12 average-sized tables listed were almost certainly large by our standards, as the requirement of 51 trestles to a total of 14 tables shows; furthermore, the larger the tables, the fewer that would be needed. The following evidence serves to highlight the widespread use of trestle tables in England, France and Burgundy.

1302   Guillaume As Feives, bourgeois of Paris.

'Item, in aula . . . quatour tabule, cum totidem tretellis, . . .'

Elsewhere were

'quinque tabule tam magne quam parve, cum septem tretellis . . .'

(Stein, 169, 171.)

(Item, in the hall, 4 tables with the same number of trestles . . .
Elsewhere: 5 tables both large and small with 7 trestles.)

1377   Château d'Aisey-le-Duc.

'2851. En tout le chastel: deux grans tables et douze autres, moiennes et petites; cinquante et un treteaulx.'

(Prost, 1, 545.)

(Throughout the whole castle: 2 large tables and 12 others, of average size and small size; 51 trestles.)

1377   Duke of Burgundy's accounts.

'. . . à Jehannin de Fontaines et à Estienne de Beaune, oivriers des menues euvres . . . pour deux tables et quatre tresteaux pour les chambres de Jehan monsr et de mad. damoiselle aud. Rouvre.'

(Prost, 1, 581–2.)

(. . . to Jehannin de Fontaines and to Estienne de Beaune, craftsmen of minor works [to the Duke] for 2 tables and 4 trestles for the chambers of M. Jehan and Mlle at Rouvre.)

Note: these tables were, in effect, nursery tables; John the Fearless was only five years-old in 1377.

1393   Richard Toky, grocer of London.

'*Hall* . . . one table with trestles, 2s. 6d.'

(Thomas 1932, 209.)

1412   Roger Kyrkby, vicar of Gainford.

In the hall, 'ij mensae cum tristillis   xijs.'

(Raine 1834/5, 56.)

(2 tables with trestles, 12s.)

Viollet-le-Duc has shown that ninth/tenth-century trestle tables were sometimes semicircular, with a gallery round the edge which supported drapery on rings.[535] It seems likely that this draped cloth, which was short, served as a napkin for the diners; it appears to have been displaced by the table cloth. The semicircular type without a gallery is depicted in the Bayeaux tapestry (1066–77) when William is shown dining with Odo,[536] and the type seems to be indicated in the reference of 1373 where the table ends are required to be horn-shaped (see p. 215). Dervieu shows that round boards on trestles were in use in the twelfth century,[537] and it is clear that the democratic connotations of the form made it attractive in important contexts throughout the Middle Ages, but documentary evidence shows that it was popular at many levels.

1335   Manoir de Quatremares.

              '. . . une table ronde et 11 tretiauz à viz, . . .'
              (Delisle, 119.)

              (. . . a round table and 2 trestles of screw type [?spiral turned pedestals].)

1405   A round trestle table was included among the *principalia* used by Roger Beodul, a Worcestershire peasant.

              (Field 139 (Appendix B, Table II, 1).)

The remarkable circular table top surviving in Winchester Castle suggests how the type was decorated at the highest level. The Winchester table has lost its supports, but as it measures 18' in diameter it is inconceivable that it was ever of fixed form. The table surface is painted with radiating divisions (which roughly match the boards of which it is made) from a central Tudor rose and bears a portrait of King Arthur and the names of twenty-four knights. Unfortunately, the indifferent quality of the restorations to the Tudor painting makes it impossible to assess its original quality. The early history of the table is unknown, but it was recorded as an antiquity by John Hardyng (born 1378) in his *Chronicles*.[538]

The most usual form for the trestle table in the later Middle Ages was the plain rectangle, which was the easiest to make and the most convenient to store when not required. At all times it was usual for diners to utilize one side of the table, leaving the other free for service (see the account of 1472, p. 218); this meant the table could be relatively narrow but needed to be exceptionally long to accommodate a large number of persons.

Trestles were of two main forms: those with separate, splayed legs and the tower or column type which rose from a heavy, spreading base. The type with splayed legs seems to have been the commonest form, for it is the most usual one portrayed in illumina-

---

[535] Viollet-le-Duc 1858, 253–6.
[536] See Stenton, fig. 49.
[537] Dervieu 1922, 389.
[538] See M. Portal, *The Great Hall of Winchester Castle*, Winchester/London, 1899, 87–93. This table has recently been taken down from the wall where it hung in Winchester Castle and examined by a team of experts, under the direction of Mr Martin Biddle. The team's tentative conclusions, announced in December 1976 on BBC Television prior to a full analysis of wood and paint samples, were as follows: carpentry, 1250–1350; dendrochronology, 1336; and painting of Arthur and knights, 1518–1522 (with later restorations).

tions;[539] the tower or column form is probably a later invention and it may be studied in two surviving tables at Penshurst Place, Kent.[540] Each table has three massive trestles to support a rectangular board over 27′ long; the boards are unattached, resting firm by virtue of their weight alone. The trestles are cruciform, wide at the top and at the foot, with a waisted centre; they have substantial mouldings and are massively handsome. These tables are stylistically dated late fifteenth century on the evidence of the heavy, confidently handled trestle mouldings. With one possible exception,[541] they are the only recorded complete trestle tables surviving *in situ* within our field of interest.

Viollet-le-Duc cites evidence concerning the existence of precious tables made of silver and gold which were sometimes set with jewels.[542] The evidence comes from Éginhard, in the will of Charlemagne,[543] from a twelfth-century representation in a Strasbourg MS,[544] and from a fourteenth-century account which speaks of a solid gold table from Spain.[545] Viollet-le-Duc suggests that these tables were sometimes more like trays than tables, but an entry in the exchequer inventories of Henry IV shows that they might, on occasion, be susbstantial enough to qualify as furniture, for one particular example needed three trestles for its support.

1399   '43. Itm un table . . . in trois pties ove III . . . trestes de arbre enplatez
            dehors d arg. endorrez ovre et enaymellez de diverses ymagerie del
            overeigne de Spayne .   ’

            (Palgrave, III, 320–1.)

            (Item, a table . . . in 3 sections with 3 . . . trestles, of wood plated with
            silver gilt, worked and enamelled with various figures, of Spanish work . . .)

It will be recalled that a solid silver chair survives in Spain[546] and the tradition of making large objects such as tables and chairs in metal is possibly Moorish, as well as classical.

Although tables of precious metal appear to have been very rare, there are a number of references to tables which were painted, or were fine in some way which is unexplained, making them special and distinct from those generally used. We cannot always be sure that these tables were, in fact, movable, but their precious nature makes it probably that this was the case.

1252   'To the keepers of the king's manor at Woodstock.
            Contrabreve . . . to buy a fair table to keep in the queen's chamber, . . .'
1260   Hall at Winchester. To the sheriff of Hampshire.
            '*Contrabreve* to renew the painting of . . . the queen's hall and table, . . .'

            (*Cal. Lib. R.*, IV, 67, 526.)

---

[539] See Bodleian MS Arch A 154 (thirteenth century); also Furnivall 1868, pl. IV.
[540] See Macquoid/Edwards 1927, Tables — Dining, fig. 3.
[541] Maffei states that a heavy trestle table of 1424 survives in Bruges, but gives few details (Maffei, 37).
[542] Viollet-le-Duc 1858, 257–60.
[543] See L. Halphen, *Éginhard, vie de Charlemagne*, Paris, 1938, 98–101.
[544] Viollet-le-Duc 1858, 260, fig. 5.
[545] Viollet-le-Duc 1858, 258–9.
[546] See Fig. 27, p. 193.

1394/5   Payment in account of the Receiver General of the Duke of Lancaster.
                'For making [a] great gold table for the Duke's chamber £10.'
                (Armitage-Smith, 449.)

In this entry, we are uncertain as to the material of John of Gaunt's table; as it was to
be large, it is likely that it was covered with gold leaf rather than made of metal. The
references to special, painted tables may be compared with the Winchester table
mentioned above, and with two others which are not strictly speaking within our
sphere of interest; they are noted here, however, since they indicate that elaborately
painted tables had widespread uses and continued to be made throughout the Middle
Ages.[547]
     Some movable tables were arranged to fold, perhaps to render the units smaller for
transportation. The entries of 1304 and 1420 are particularly interesting, for they
suggest that these particular tables were raised and lowered by some unusual and
ingenious means.

1304   Payment to carpenters for work at Hesdin (held by Mahaut, Comtesse
                d'Artois).
                'Pour faire un hestaus à haucier et à abaissier le table madame   VIIIs.'
                (Richard 1887, 368.)
                (For making a ?jack for raising and lowering Madame's table   8s.)

1373   Goods in the house of Emma Hatfeld.
                '. . . 3 folding tables (tables pliants) and 4 plain tables with trestles, . . .'
                (Thomas 1929, 159.)

1420   Château de Beauté. King's Chamber ('Chambre des Evvangelistes').
                'Item, une table de deux pièces, où il y a III charnières, de VIII piez ou
                environ, avec II tréteaulx, lesquels on avale et monte quant on veult.'
                (Douet d'Arcq, 461.)
                (Item, a table of 2 parts, having 3 hinges, of about 8' [long], with 2
                trestles, which can be let down and lifted up at pleasure.)

1433   Will of John, Bishop of Dromore.
                '. . . unum faldyngbord', . . .'
                (Jacob 1937, 483.)

1446   Prior of Durham's inventory.
                'Item una Mensa de Prusia cum foliis.'
                (Raine 1834/5, 93.)
                (1 soft wood table with leaves.)

___

[547] A long, folding 3-leaf table painted with secular subjects and resting on modern trestles (c.1400, ?N.
German), Musée Cluny; and a table in Zurich which Dervieu notes as painted by Holbein (Dervieu 1922, 400).

*c.*1459   Caister Castle, Sir John Fastolfe's chamber.

'Item, j foldyng Table. Item, j long Chayre. Item, j grene Chayre . . .'

(Amyot, 269.)

An extant table in the Musée Cluny which is designed to knockdown[548] should probably be included as a folding table. It is one of the most precious examples of fifteenth-century furniture surviving in France and is probably unique of its type. Its importance is enhanced by virtue of its condition, for although it lacks a provenance the oak of which it is made had reached such an advanced state of disintegration before it was restored that every restoration to the various parts is as clearly defined as if it were accomplished in a different material; restorations to medieval furniture in continental collections are rarely so eloquently identified for us. The Cluny table has an elaborately carved and pierced frame; the logic of its design rests upon two separate boards slotted to accommodate each other so that they form a cruciform shape and thus a stable base. This arrangement of the underframe is confirmed and temporarily fixed by the addition of the table top, and as long as this remains in place the underframing cannot be separated. The whole comes apart when the table top is removed to form a series of loose members which can be easily transported. Such a table was almost certainly a chamber piece which accompanied its owner from place to place as part of the baggage equipment. The tracery and other details date the table to *c.*1480–1500.

FIXED TABLES

As has been noted in Section D, tables were often intimately linked with seating.

1253   To the bailiff of Havering.

'*Contrabreve* to . . . make . . . *a table with its stools* in the queen's chamber; . . .'
                                                                              [*my itals.*]

(*Cal. Lib.* R., IV, 119.)

While many of the associations between tables and seating concerned movable tables, it is possible that certain fixed tables accommodated the stools used with them upon the underframing, when they were not in use.

Fixed tables were exceedingly common throughout the Middle Ages; they were frequently described as *dormiens, dormant, dormaunt,* etc. to distinguish them from boards on trestles. Dervieu cites French sources containing references to fixed tables of 1313, 1338, 1348, 1460.[549] The following evidence complementing Dervieu's survey comes from English and Burgundian sources.

twelfth   Manor of Ardleigh, Essex, leased by the Chapter of St Paul's, London.
century
'In aula [manerii de Ardleigh] fuerunt duo bancha tornatilia, et una mensa dormiens, et unum buffeth; . . .'

(Lehmann-Brockhaus, 34 (113).)

[548] Musée Cluny, no. 22795.
[549] Dervieu 1922, 395, 396, 397.

(In the hall of Ardleigh manor, were 2 turned benches, 1 fixed table and 1 buffet . . .)

1192   Fittings of canons' houses in Chichester.

'. . . scamna inmobilia et mensas inmobiles, . . .'

(H. Mayr-Harting, *The Acta of the Bishops of Chichester 1075–1207*, Torquay, 1964, 144.)

(. . . fixed benches and tables.)

1252   To the sheriff of Northampton.

'*Contrabreve* . . . to make a permanent (*dormientem*) table in the great hall . . .'

(*Cal. Lib.* R., IV, 19.)

1384/5   Ducal palace, Dijon.

At this date, the kitchen was a vaulted room with 8 columns and 3 vast chimneys; in the centre of the room stood a great table fixed to the ground.

(Canat de Chizy 1859, 117–18.)

1485   Reparations to Coldharbour, London.

'vj dormaunt tables,   xxiijs. iiijd.'

(Kingsford 1920/1, 48 (f. 27).)

As the evidence of 1384/5 shows, fixed tables were sometimes fixed in more senses than one: their frames and boards were fixed one to another, and the whole table was fixed to the ground or floor. The group of tables in the hall at Winchester College, which are of medieval form even if they are not of medieval date, are fixed in this double sense, pl. 70.

As Dervieu has shown, fixed tables were constructed in a number of ways, 4-post, slab-ended and pedestal;[550] these forms will be discussed in turn.

4-Post Tables

1390   Priory of St. Eloy de Paris.

'en une chambre lambroissiée, un petit banc tourneis viez, une table à quatre piez, un petit pupitre et une petite couche de boys . . .'

(Pannier, 362.)

(in a panelled chamber, a small turned bench which is old, a 4-footed table, a small desk and a small wooden couch . . .)

The context suggests that this 4-post table was small.

[550] Dervieu 1922, 393–404.

1066–77   The Bayeux tapestry shows food being taken to William and Odo from
a fixed table,[551] Fig. 32.

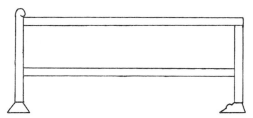

FIG. 32.   Fixed table of 4-post or slab-ended type

An extraordinary table survives at Haddon Hall, which shows the 4-post type at its
most primitive, Fig. 33.

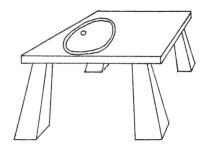

FIG. 33.   Table at Haddon Hall for joints of meat

The table was designed to take a large joint of meat directly upon its surface and has a
channel and a hole to draw off liquid which presumably fell into a bowl placed under
the table; the table may be fifteenth century. A table in New York with a deep apron
which accommodates drawers is published as fifteenth century.[552] If this table is genuine,
the evidence it provides is particulary interesting.

Slab-ended Tables

Like the slab-ended chests discussed in Section C, this form in a table is likely to be
very early. (It is possibly the type depicted in the Bayeux tapestry, see Fig. 32.) Turner
published a drawing of a thirteenth-century slab-ended table in the kitchen of the
Strangers' Hall, Winchester, with carved ends and quatrefoils.[553] The slab-ended type
reached a pinnacle of sophistication in fifteenth-century Germany, which lies outside
the scope of this enquiry.[554] Within our field of interest, the slab-ended type was used
with great delicacy and refinement in the later Middle Ages for tables which were small

[551] See Stenton, pl. IX.
[552] See *Bull. MMA*, 1947/8, 256.
[553] See Turner, facing 96.
[554] See the 1445 example, Kreisel, fig. 97.

and fragile by medieval standards. Although the evidence for this type of table is drawn from paintings and illuminations,[555] the surviving knockdown table in the Cluny shows[556] that the refinement indicated was well within existing practices.

The form of the slab-ended table is akin to, and sometimes merges with the pedestal form, discussed below.

Pedestal Tables

Dervieu shows that this type of table was in use in the later Middle Ages, and cites a number of examples including the fourteenth-century stone table in the garden of the Château de Rouvres which was round and had benches, so that meals could be taken out of doors.[557] Dervieu illustrates a hexagonal example supported on a cruciform base which has a screw at the top of the pedestal, allowing the table to be raised and lowered.[558] (Screw pedestals for library tables, usually designed for individual use, were evidently common though their specialized nature precludes their inclusion here.) A circular board with column resting upon a circular base is shown in a French Book of Hours of *c.* 1500, Fig. 34.

FIG. 34.   Pedestal table from a French Book of Hours, *c.*1500
Sold at Sotheby's in 1966, see *Illustrated London News*, 29.x.66, 27

A group of five extant tables at Winchester College[559] have pedestal supports which are fixed to the wooden floor boards, pl. 70. This type of pedestal is medieval, as we see from a leaf in a polyptych painted by Pietro Lorenzetti in 1341.[560] As well as the pedestals, the Winchester tables have another feature which suggests a medieval date, for pedestals and table boards are linked by heavy, arched braces which are also present on an extant table in France, stylistically dated late fifteenth century by Brunhammer and de Fayet.[561] In spite of their ancient appearance, however, records in Winchester College concerning the employment of craftsmen upon tables for the hall in the years 1565/6, 1637 and

---

[555] See the examples from the fourteenth-century Bodleian MS 264, the Romance of Alexander, illustrated in Parker 1853, 92.
[556] See discussion on p. 223.
[557] Dervieu 1922, 394.
[558] Dervieu 1922, 395.
[559] Each table is accompanied by a fixed form matching it in length. The forms, unlike the tables, are regular in appearance and appear to have all been made at the same time, perhaps 1660–1750.
[560] Uffizi, Florence. See Evans 1966, fig. 27.
[561] Y. Brunhammer/M. de Fayet, *Meubles et Ensembles Époques Moyen Age et Renaissance*, Paris, 1966, fig. 22.

1674/5 make it unlikely that any of the surviving examples are wholly medieval.[562] It would appear, however, that the character of the medieval tables provided when the college hall was first equipped (Winchester College was founded in 1382) was never abandoned, probably because repair work was undertaken throughout the centuries, so that when new tables were needed they were invariably made to match exiting ones, irrespective of current fashion. This conclusion is supported by the records (nowhere is the provision of five new tables recorded at any one time) and by a study of the tables themselves which bear eloquent witness of adjustment, alteration and repair.[563]

[562] The first record of hall tables appears to be the inventory of 1421/2 where 4 are listed (WCM 21865); in 1565/6, 3 new tables were made for the boys (WCM 22215); in 1637, 2 × 2 tables were made (WCM 22219); and in 1674/5, 600′ of wood was used for hall tables for the boys and for another table in the kitchen.

[563] The most obvious changes may be quickly noted. The table boards are of matching widths; 3 tables use broad single boards and the other 2 tables use 2 boards laid side by side to make up the required width. The single boarded tables have been re-edged on both sides; the double boarded tables have had the crevice between the boards filled. Two different shapes of cradle support the boards. One table, which has a join in its length, lacks a curved brace in the appropriate place; as there are no scars indicating that the brace has been lost, it is clear that the table never had one in this position because it was made up from the more central parts of 2 other tables. The pedestals are very varied; this is partly due to wear and partly, no doubt, due to the different dates at which they were made. The forms contrast sharply with the appearance of the tables, for they are even and regular in all respects.

I am especially indebted to Mr Peter Gwyn, former Archivist of Winchester College, who gave up much time in showing me the hall furniture and in supplying me with copies of the relevant records concerning it. Without the evidence of the records and Mr Gwyn's assistance, I should certainly have dated the hall tables to the medieval period on stylistic grounds.

Part 2

STYLE AND TECHNIQUE

The structural characteristics of medieval furniture are solidity, weight and durability. These qualities reflected priorities which existed throughout our period, although signs of the erosion of established practices are apparent in the later Middle Ages in the appearance of a few fragile objects which were practicable for the first time because of a new combination of social factors: wealth allied to greater privacy in settled circumstances. To believe that the solidity of medieval furniture was an unconscious expression of primitive technology is absurd when we remember architectural achievements. Indeed, we observe that a knowledge of sophisticated methods of woodworking, e.g. the dovetail joint, was known and largely ignored in furniture making for centuries, because the requirements of strength, weight and durability favoured other methods of construction.[564] To understand why medieval furniture design largely ignored the delicacy which was expressed in the other applied arts, it is necessary to reopen briefly the question of its function.

We have already noted that seigneurial lords needed to support extravagant display within their households, as a means of retaining and strengthening their power and influence. The objects they used were potent symbols, for they expressed power over individuals and over events, and their ownership and use had little or nothing to do with personal pleasure in the contemplation of works of craftsmanship or art; if these sentiments were felt, they were the by-products of the situation, rather than the active ingredients. *The whole scheme of priorities in furnishings in medieval times centres around the necessity of creating significant display.* In circumstances where problems of security can be readily overcome, and where mobility for furnishings is not a serious consideration, it is possible for furniture to take its place with easily transportable goods such as textiles and plate as a vehicle for extravagant display. Such a situation existed in the French royal apartments in the eighteenth century, when the most elaborate, ingenious and costly furniture ever created was assembled. The situation was very different in the Middle Ages, however, for the necessary ingredients of security and permanence were lacking. If influence was to be adequately felt, great households needed to be open in the Middle Ages in a manner rarely paralleled in later times, so that even strangers might gain access to the king's chamber where he slept.[565] The hazards of interference by unauthorized persons within the household were combatted by relying largely upon

---

[564] Dovetails, though relatively uncommon in medieval furniture, are found on a number of chests in the Catalogue, and the following earlier evidence may be noted. Pre-1104: one of the chests containing the body of St Cuthbert, seen when the burial was opened in 1104, was described by the monk Reginald as follows: 'joined and united by the toothed tenons of the boards which come from this side and from that to meet one another, and by long iron nails'; *c.*1200: 'Bare-faced lap-dovetail with entrant shoulder' used on the tying joint of the Barley Barn, Cressing Temple, Essex (see C. A. Hewett, *The Development of Carpentry 1200–1700. An Essex Study*, Newton Abbot, 1969, 57).

[565] The Black Book of Edward IV expressly states that the king's bedding must be returned to the Wardrobe of Beds each morning for safety 'that no stranger shall touche hit', see Myers 1959, § 40, 119.

easily transportable goods when lavish display was required, which could be safely locked away in wardrobes and other offices when not in use. Areas were quickly transformed by hanging walls and covering bare woodwork with tapestries and silks, and by displaying quantities of gold and silver plate on buffets and tables.[566] The importance of movable furnishings was reinforced by another consideration, that of the movement of households from place to place and the habit of *adapting* space within dwellings to several uses. Thus, a number of practical considerations produced a situation in which it was both inconvenient and imprudent to encourage the use of techniques and materials in furniture making which would render that furniture valuable, except in a few important instances where considerations of display outweighed convenience. These exceptional circumstances operated when the actual surface of items of furniture required for ceremonial purposes was displayed, instead of being shrouded in loose textiles; these significant pieces of furniture are best described as furniture of estate.

This short analysis of the situation stresses the problems at the highest levels but lower down the social scale, where persons might have less need for mobility in furnishings,[567] the priorities remained unchanged since they were *a recognized means by which social realities were expressed*. Thus at all levels textiles and plate occupied positions of supreme importance among furnishings and upon them was lavished much artistry and technical skill, as well as enormous sums of money. They were treated as investments and were sold in times of emergency. By contrast, furniture in general was of small account and items such as armoires, benches, tables and bed frames were often treated as fixtures.[568] They might remain behind when the household moved on, ready to be used again when occupation was resumed;[569] they filled the essential, if modest, role of supporting all activities and providing a framework upon which valuable movables could be deployed as occasion demanded. The relative unimportance of furniture in social terms meant that it was largely exempt from pressures to conform with changing taste, and craftsmen making furniture were probably only concerned with expressing nuances of fashion when special commissions for furniture of estate were involved. Furniture fulfilled its function best if it survived the effects of casual and even rough treatment without the necessity of replacement; since no man was judged by the quality of his furniture (though his plate, household textiles, clothing and jewels were the cynosure of all eyes) no advantage accrued from changing it or *acquiring more of it than could conveniently be used*, as was the case with textiles and plate.[570]

[566] See the discussion on open households and the use of furnishings, Eames 1971, 47 ff.

[567] Middle-class persons were generally less influential and wealthy than the nobility and their houses were more private; in addition, if land holding was modest, household movements were fewer.

[568] See the evidence quoted in Group B inventories, Eames 1973, 34–6, 38–9. See also the French evidence of 1409, p. 205.

[569] Richard notes this with regard to the different dwellings used by Mahaut, Comtesse d'Artois, in the early fourteenth century (Richard 1887, 364).

[570] Inventories of quantities of textiles of enormous value are not difficult to discover, e.g. the Duke of Gloucester's textiles listed at Pleshy Castle in 1397 (see Dillon/Hope 1897, 275–308). And the total of more than 92 copes in Scrope of Masham's possession at the time of his execution in 1415 is an indication of the kind of stockpiling which was practised, see Kingsford 1918–20, 77. Regarding plate, the treasury of the exchequer inventories transcribed by Palgrave are a rich source of material to illustrate what English kings possessed; and Olivier de la Marche tells us that Philip the Good left his son over 60,000 marks of table plate made into vessels and ready for use (see Petitot, IX, 314). See also pp. 6, 57–8.

The prevailing attitude to furniture profoundly affected its character and established the lines of its development. The value placed upon strength and endurance meant that among native woods *oak was at all times the first choice* and oak set the standard against which other woods were judged; its properties dictated the direction of ornament and design. Riven oak, even when immature, is remarkably stable, and working with riven timbers was practised throughout our period; it has been identified by Prost as the 'bois d'Illand', 'bois d'ollande' etc. of inventories and accounts.[571] (In employing the riven technique, in which wood is reduced to workable components by splitting down the medullary rays, makers of furniture were following a practice employed in those areas where strength and stability were of even greater consequence — in the construction of buildings and of ships.)[572]

Significant display was achieved by designing furnishings in two ways: by choosing forms and ornament which were meaningful and symbolic (e.g. heraldic decoration, and the number of stages on a buffet) and by using precious materials which were the prerogative of wealth. Practical considerations meant that most furniture could only comply with the first requirement; furniture of estate, however, might also comply with the second. (As we have seen, furniture of estate could be precious indeed, employing such materials as silver, gold and glass mosaics, and marquetry or inlay was also employed within this special group.)[573]

It is fascinating to observe how art, when it is *not* free to follow individual fancy but is locked into the exigencies of function, seems to create the most satisfying and powerful forms and images; in one sense it is subservient to function yet, through imaginative power, it transcends it. The use of riven oak, which was trimmed to shape with adze, saw and plane, suggested forms of ornament which did not weaken the robustness and durability of the wood: applied wrought iron, carving in the solid, applied carving and painting and, rarest of all, inlay or marquetry. Some of these techniques are represented in surviving pieces of furniture which happen to have been worked on by great artists, rather than by merely competent craftsmen. Such furniture is very rare and is underrated; it should be treasured and take its place with other exceptional works of its age. The Carnavalet chest (Cat. 34) is such an example, using the technique of applied wrought iron to reinforce the qualities of strength, weight and durability of the structure. Its scrollwork is sufficiently coarse to achieve harmony with the rugged quality of the chest yet the intellectual concept of the design is subtle and refined. The Chester and St Quentin armoires (Cat. 22, 23), also decorated and strengthened with wrought iron,

---

[571] See entries pp. 92, 96 (28); the term evidently referred to a *technique* and the wood came from local sources; it was not an exotic import, see Prost, I, 369–70.

[572] See Van de Walle in Taylor, III, 1969, 152–5.

[573] See Cat. 28, St Edward's Chair and the silver plated trestle table of 1399 (p. 221). With regard to marquetry and inlay, although the techniques are distinct (inlay being a material set into *sunken* areas of a carcase and marquetry being cut out shapes laid *upon* a carcase), records and paintings make it impossible for us to distinguish between them, though inlay seems the most likely technique to have been employed. The following evidence may be noted. 1401–16: '30. Item, un autre tableau de bois ou il a un ymaige fait de marqueteure, et entour garni d'argent a ouvraige de Damas . . .' (J. Guiffrey, *Inventaires de Jean Duc de Berry*, I, Paris, 1894, 22). Guiffrey notes that the use of marquetry was widespread in Italy and well known in France at this date (Guiffrey, I, 22, fn. 2). 1434 Jan van Eyck, Madonna with Chancellor Rolin (see Faggin, pls. XLIII–XLVI). The end of the Madonna's seat, which may be a chest, is panelled, with part of a panel visible, worked with a geometric design in inlay or marquetry, apparently using different coloured woods.

are only less impressive because they have lost much of their original woodwork. The Climping, York and Romsey chests (Cat. 30, 31, 48) demonstrate the artistry devoted to carving in the solid. In all three examples the decoration respects and enhances the massive qualities of each piece of furniture, yet each tackles the problem from a different standpoint. The Climping chest is carved in low relief with architectural motifs; the execution is as delicate as is possible in a coarse grained wood such as oak but the design is so simple and spare that there is no conflict between the heavy form of the chest and the refinement of the carving. The York and Romsey chests confidently match vigorous, heavy shapes with vigorous carving in high relief which casts deep shadows and divides the surfaces into a series of carefully related episodes and designs. The York chest, carved with the legend of St George, is a vital work full of individual mannerisms and carved with impressive skill. The Romsey chest is less exciting, for the design is wholly based upon tracery, but it demonstrates that in the later Middle Ages it was possible for carpenter or joiner, carver and smith to produce a piece of furniture in which the contribution of each craft was subordinated to the whole. In much medieval furniture it is evident that the smith attached his locks without much concern for the appearance of the object as a whole, and a certain lack of finish is, therefore, characteristic; indeed, it provides an insoucient quality which to the eyes of those living in an age dominated by machine-made objects is particularly engaging. The Romsey chest has a lock which is immaculately and sympathetically designed and set; the result is an object of extreme sophistication with carving which is so superb that the great quality of almost all medieval furniture — vitality — is not destroyed. We may confidently infer from the character of both the York and Romsey chests that they were finished by sculptors or *imagiers*, those special craftsmen who, as Richard has shown, sometimes created elaborate and important furniture for the nobility in the later Middle Ages.[574]

Painted furniture falls into two groups: the group in which painting gives colour to wrought iron or carved ornament, and the group in which the painting itself provides the design. Much furniture in the Middle Ages belonged to the first category, to judge from the specks of colour clinging to the interstices of carvings which escaped the zeal of nineteenth-century improvers. The second type, in which the painting itself furnished the ornament, must also have been common, even if the most frequent images were heraldic, like those on the Richard de Bury chest. The Richard de Bury chest is an important but not a skilful work, and though it seems likely that able painters sometimes ornamented ordinary furniture as well as furniture of estate, no exceptional work of this kind seems to have survived. The only beautifully painted pieces of furniture extant are a few mutilated examples of furniture of estate; their original qualities have been established by close scrutiny, but at normal distances they show little or nothing of their former splendour. We know that special chairs or thrones were often made and might have individual cases for safe storage and transportation. Walter of Durham, king's Sergeant Painter, made such a chair and case for Edward I in

---

[574] Richard discusses the work of these important men at the end of the thirteenth century; they occasionally finished furniture prepared by less well paid woodworkers and worked on statues and decorations for the chapel of Mahaut, Comtesse d'Artois (see Richard 1887, 306–8).

1299 and it is generally accepted that this chair has survived and is St Edward's Chair in Westminster Abbey. Modern restoration work upon this chair has shown that it was given a secondary decoration of glass mosaics and gold leaf worked with various designs, including the figure of a seated king, and the most exquisite panels of birds and foliage. The cradle made for the birth of one of the children of Marie of Burgundy and Maximilian of Austria (Cat. 28) is another example of masterly painting in colours and gold leaf; and the famous armoire at Bayeux (Cat. 11) was similarly decorated. The Bayeux armoire differs from the other two examples in being a fixture. We have seen that valuable fixtures created practical problems, but the Bayeux armoire was erected in the cathedral treasury which, by its very nature, must have been a secure place. The Bayeux armoire held relics which were probably only viewed with considerable ceremony; its gorgeous surfaces, painted with religious subjects, expressed not only the veneration due to saints but also the temporal and spiritual power of the bishops of Bayeux.

We have discussed the analogy between the function of furniture (which required strength to be the primary quality) and design. It remains to be noted that the open nature of the medieval household necessitated the provision of strong wood or iron locks for doors and storage furniture.[575] The importance of the smith's contribution to furniture (he was paid separately to equip furniture after it had been made by a carpenter, joiner or leather worker)[576] is obvious in cases like the Carnavalet chest (Cat. 34) when elaborate wrought iron scrollwork was fashionable; it is, perhaps, less well appreciated when confined to hinges, bolts and locks. Nevertheless, the necessity for strength and durability in furniture affected the smith's work as much as it did the wood or leather worker's, and created a tradition in which technical skill was allied to lively design. In some cases, the iron fittings are grander than the actual piece of furniture, as the Malines armoire and two Netherlandish chests show (Cat. 13, 44, 46). In certain cases, particularly when cold cut ironwork ousted wrought iron in sophisticated work in the later Middle Ages, a perfect alliance between smith and woodworker was achieved, as we have noticed in the case of the Romsey chest (Cat. 48).

A full investigation into the divisions of the skills involved in furniture making will be omitted in this study, for two main reasons. Firstly, considerable space would be needed and secondly the results gained from such an exercise are unlikely to prove helpful. The following brief note concerning carpenters and joiners shows that the medieval situation does not readily resolve itself into precise lines of activity and interest.

There is considerable confusion concerning the distinction between joiners and carpenters in England, and between *huchiers* and *charpentiers* in France and Burgundy, and although much evidence can be cited regarding the activities of these craftsmen from the mid-thirteenth century in England, and earlier in France,[577] we cannot distin-

---

[575] Wooden locks have rarely survived, unlike their iron counterparts, but are occasionally noted in records: e.g. 1367 'une arche plate, fermant a une serreure de bois' (Prost, I, 139, *808*).

[576] As entries such as the following in the Duke of Burgundy's accounts show: 1375 '. . . à Baranville, gainnier, demeurant à Troies . . . pour la façon de 3 petis coffres de cuir . . . à Thomas le serrurier, pour ferrer lesdiz coffres . . .' (Prost, I, 452). See also entry for 1379 (Prost, II, 56–7, *351*).

[577] See Brown/Colvin/Taylor, 175–6; also R. E. Swartwout, *The Monastic Craftsman*, Cambridge, 1932, 133–4.

guish between the work of either group — if distinct groups there were — *in terms of the categories of objects made*.[578] The following evidence illustrates the position.

Carpenters

1307/8   *carpentarii junctores* joined boards, panels for gates and made doors, screens and windows.

               (Brown/Colvin/Taylor, 224–5.)

1485   John Davy, carpenter, and Robert Westwode, smith, worked upon windows and forms at the mansion of Coldharbour, London (a royal palace), being also specifically responsible for two tables as well.

               (Kingsford 1920/1, 43, 44.)

Charpentiers

1307   made altars which were later elaborated by *imagiers*.

1318, 1323   wainscotted chambers (*lambrisser*).

1328   made hall dais, kitchen dressers (*drechoirs*).
               (Richard 1887, 266, 293, 297, 271.)

1361   made an *huche*.
               (Dehaisnes, I, 432.)

1388   made a *coffre*.
               (Prost, II, 385, 2543.)

Joiners

1253   made bed panels of the king's bed at Westminster. Made tables.

*c.*1272   made tables for the great hall, Westminster; made chairs, 1 square, 1 round with columns.

1414   made a chest.

               (Brown/Colvin/Taylor, 224–5.)

1446   made chests, doors, windows and lattices, see fn. 70.

Huchiers

1329   made tables, seating and undertook wainscotting (*lambrisser*); also did window woodwork at Arras.

               (Richard 1887, 312.)

---

[578] See E. B. Jupp/W. W. Pocock, *An Historic Account of the Worshipful Company of Carpenters of the City of London*, London, 1887, which shows that in England the appropriate work of carpenters and joiners was a matter for debate as late as the seventeenth century.

R

In the light of this evidence, it would perhaps be truer to say that there existed *overlapping interests* between joiners and carpenters (and their continental counterparts), rather than a *confusion* between rigidly separate crafts. Indeed, we find this situation clearly illustrated when we look at what craftsmen did at the highest level; Walter of Durham, King's Painter, executed a painting for Queen Eleanor's tomb in 1294 and carved a chair in 1299,[579] and the *imagiers* and painters employed by the French and Burgundian nobility worked on a wide range of objects which might include joke machinery, bridges, elaborate woodwork for secular and ecclesiastical uses including articles of furniture, and the painting of walls, banners and panels.[580] The adaptability which we see operating in the evidence concerning joiners and carpenters is at a relatively humble level, but it is undoubtedly part of a general pattern in which great artists and craftsmen were able to take creative responsibility over a wide range. We remember that in *c.*1174, when William de Sens came to control work at Canterbury, he was described as a 'most curious workman in wood and stone';[581] that in the thirteenth century, Villard de Honnecourt designed works of architecture, statuary, furniture and devices for industry and war;[582] and that Walter of Durham, designated Painter, executed a painting in 1294 and carved a chair in 1299, as has been noted above.

[579] See Palmer, 5.
[580] See pp. 243–4.
[581] The total separateness of the man who carved in stone and the man who carved in wood, suggested by Symonds, does not seem justified by the evidence; see R. W. Symonds, 'Furniture: Post Roman', ed. C. Singer, *History of Technology*, ii, Oxford, 1957, 245.
[582] See Canat de Chizy 1898, 249.

Part 3

CONCLUSION

The aim of this study has been to enlarge our understanding regarding the use and appearance of medieval furniture within a certain political and geographical framework and within a defined period, through the systematic use of different kinds of evidence. This approach to the subject has proved to be rewarding, for earlier correlations have been less thorough and have been largely unconcerned in taking cognizance of the bias which every form of evidence reflects; without this appreciation of the scope and limitations of evidence, no convincing conclusions upon a wide basis are possible. The results which have accrued from the rigorous methods of analysis are discussed throughout the text, within the narrow limits of individual fields of enquiry; it is the purpose of this chapter to assess our findings in a wider context and to emphasize the most important and far-reaching implications.

The interest of the subject develops naturally from a knowledge of the medieval furniture that has survived, and the detailed treatment of examples in the Catalogue Raisonné provides a basis for appreciation. The selection of furniture discussed has depended, as far as possible, upon items with a secure provenance in order to provide a much needed comparative framework for future work upon less historically important pieces. The form chosen, in which descriptions and analyses are distinct, allows a clear statement of the sources upon which comment is based and provides, for the first time, a reasoned justification for stylistic dating, where applicable. The insistence upon a secure provenance for items in the Catalogue, wherever possible, cuts across former studies (which have tended to draw solely on readily available objects), and has resulted in a widening of our understanding concerning extant furniture through opening up a number of uninvestigated channels of enquiry. In the first place, the Catalogue Raisonné offers a reasonably balanced survey of extant furniture which includes basic, utilitarian objects,[583] as well as the more familiar, decoratively treated pieces whose visual qualities have formerly provided the primary basis of selection elsewhere.[584] It also brings into focus types of furniture whose very existence has remained un-recognized in print within the confines of furniture studies, for example, the armoires fitted with drawers for records,[585] and the fitted armoires which were part of the partitioning of buildings.[586] The Catalogue has also produced valuable evidence in matters relating to style and technique (discussed in Part 2), and one of its most important contributions has been to enable us to consider and form a balance between objects of similar function but of widely different technical and artistic merit.[587] Through this process, we have been able to note that a function which might be seen to reflect upon

---

[583] See, for example, the armoire at Winchester College, Cat. 12.
[584] See, for example, the Carnavalet chest, Cat. 34.
[585] Cat. 17, 18–21.
[586] Cat. 9, 24.
[587] See, for example, Cat. 12, 13.

the lustre of an individual, a household, or an institution, was served by more elaborate furniture than was the case when purely utilitarian considerations were involved. This becomes obvious when we are dealing with sections such as seating, where the significance of special items such as thrones is fully understood, but the fact that this attitude affected all types of furniture to some degree has remained unrecognized. If we take armoires as an example, we see that the prestige of the relics of Bayeux, and the dignity of the cities of Malines and Ghent, is reflected in the richness or quality of the armoires which were once connected with these matters.[588] These finely made objects, which are best described as *furniture of estate*, contrast sharply with the careless finish characteristic of armoires at Wells, Windsor and Winchester College where the provision of adequate storage for accounts and other records connected with day to day administration was more casually treated. We learn from these and other examples that persons or institutions capable of lavish patronage might be expected to promote the production of elaborate or well finished furniture only when degrees of dignity or estate were involved. In medieval times, we see that the *usage* of individual items of furniture, rather than the ability to pay highly for the services of skilful artisans or artists, dictated the quality of furniture. We can use this observation to arrive at a better understanding of individual examples of extant furniture in other sections; let us take as examples the Richard de Bury chest, the buffet of Marguerite of York and the cradle made for the birth of either Philip the Fair or Margaret of Austria.[589]

The Richard de Bury chest and the buffet of Marguerite of York bear devices connecting each with persons of power and wealth: a bishop of Durham on the one hand and an English princess married to the Duke of Burgundy on the other. But although these objects bear august symbols they are merely serviceable items and have little artistic merit beyond a bold, uninhibited approach to ornament. By contrast, the cradle made for the birth of Philip the Fair or Margaret of Austria, also distinguished by devices which connect it with a powerful household (in this case with Marie of Burgundy and Maximilian of Austria, parents of Philip the Fair and Margaret), was once a work of art, though it is now sadly mutilated. We can, I believe, infer from the brief observations regarding armoires (and from the evidence in other sections which may be found in the text) that the chest and buffet, both modest items in a technical sense, were used within the households of the persons identified upon them by officers of Richard de Bury and Marguerite of York respectively, and were never used personally by either of these important personages. The cradle, on the other hand, with its superb artistry, was beyond doubt designed and made for a royal occupant (we are aided in this conclusion in this particular case, not only by the cradle's quality, provenance and restricted use, but also by the evidence of documents concerning elaborate cradles which have been investigated in the appropriate section).[590] To sum up, it seems fair to suggest that a connexion of a piece of furniture with an important individual, through heraldry or other means, does not suggest an important use unless quality of execution is

---

[588] The Bayeux armoire held relics (Cat. 11); and the armoires of Malines and Ghent (Cat. 13, 15) traditionally contained the privileges of these cities.
[589] Richard de Bury chest, see above p. 138; buffet of Marguerite of York, Cat. 26; cradle, Cat. 28.
[590] See above pp. 99–100.

evident. Before moving on, it must be recognized, in any discussion of the relative qualities of different items of furniture (and in the identification of furniture of estate), that although we can observe that objects which reflected dignity were more elaborate or distinguished in some way than items which were devoid of these connotations, the degree, character and incidence of the elaboration was controlled by the circumstances and fashions of the time. Thus, in forming conclusions regarding furniture of estate, every example has to be considered on its own merits; in the examples quoted above, the Malines armoire is less expensively elaborate than that of Bayeux.[591] And when we consider the incidence of elaboration in surviving furniture, although we are to some extent inhibited by the uneven pattern of survival (the earlier, the rarer), the impression that elaboration in furniture became more widespread in the later Middle Ages is almost certainly correct, since elaboration is a likely result of the greatly increased wealth and influence of the middle classes at that time.

If wealth created the opportunity for elaboration in furniture, fashion harnessed to practicability controlled the form it should take. It has been shown that the need for robust, durable furniture made oak the most favoured and admired wood and in-fluenced the techniques which were most commonly employed, so that elaboration was achieved chiefly through painting, carving and applied ironwork.[592] Interest in painting and carving extended over our entire period, but the use of wrought iron as a decorative technique was less consistent. The Bayeux armoire and the cradle made for the birth of Philip the Fair or Margaret of Austria[593] are examples in the Catalogue which provide an early and a late example of elaborately painted furniture, and in the same way carving is represented, in applied form, by the freestanding armoire at Obazine and the Romsey chest.[594] Many examples of carving in the solid survive, and the Catalogue highlights this wealth of material with examples ranging from the Climping chest of $c.1282-1300$ to the Romsey and Neenton chests of $c.1480-1525$.[595]

To turn now to wrought iron, the apogee of this decorative technique is exemplified in the Carnavalet chest of $c.1250-70$ and by the Chester and St Quentin armoires of $c.1294-1320$;[596] thereafter, interest in elaborate wrought iron waned until a revival in the later Middle Ages produced examples such as the Malpas chest.[597] The wrought iron revival does not seem to have been inspired by contemporary work at the highest level, and its inadequacies may be explained by this lack of vital inspiration. The Malpas chest is an important and impressive work, but it lacks both the technical skill and the cohesive brilliance of design characteristic of the earlier examples covered in the Catalogue. The wrought iron technique had become anachronistic in the fifteenth century, metropolitan work being carried out in the cold cut technique which could produce the hard and precise architectural forms found in miniature in the Romsey chest lock plate[598] and the door knocker at Bourges, pl. 66B.

---

[591] Cat. 13, 11.
[592] See pp. 230 ff.
[593] Bayeux $c.1250$; cradle of 1478/9; (Cat. 11, 28).
[594] Obazine, $c.1176$ Cat. 10; Romsey chest $c.1480-1500$, Cat. 48.
[595] Cat. 30, 48, 38.
[596] Cat. 34, 22, 23.
[597] Cat. 37.
[598] Cat. 48.

The furniture surveyed in the Catalogue Raisonné demonstrates the richness of invention and the high degree of individuality characteristic of medieval work; the types of furniture may have been limited, but the manner of solving problems within a narrow scope was extraordinarily varied. If we look at chests, we see examples in the Catalogue of a whole range of forms which are separately identified and analysed for the first time (Fig. 17). This range is in itself indicative of the freedom of medieval work, and if we look within each form we find that differences of detail, rather than close similarities, are what strikes the eye; indeed, when close parallels occur, as with the panel carved with St George and the dragon and the York chest carved with the same subject,[599] we find this remarkable. The unique nature of almost every example of medieval furniture makes every object important; there are no parallels to the manner of opening of the Selby armoires, now alas destroyed,[600] no low relief carving of similar quality and date to compare with the Climping chest,[601] no tinned iron fittings comparable with those on the Malines armoire,[602] and nothing which corresponds to the iron Guildhall chest[603] — indeed, the list is almost as long as the number of pieces of furniture that have survived. Although it is clear that surviving furniture is a wholly inadequate sample of all sections of what once existed[604] it is clear that the existing variety cannot be explained by inadequate representation alone but must represent the way in which labour was organized in the Middle Ages, with small groups of men who were free to produce individual solutions to different problems. Not only are the similarities which shop working produces largely absent in medieval work, but we can see that managerial skills, generally evident when centralization occurs, were rarely brought into play.[605] There is a typically uneven balance in the contribution of the woodworker and the locksmith in the All Souls chest;[606] here, the smith's work is finer, though this situation is often reversed. The characteristic lack of sympathy between the work of different craftsmen often manifests itself in the haphazard placing of iron fittings upon a carved chest front;[607] it results in a lack of regularity which is extremely attractive to an age in which the conformity imposed by the use of machinery so often means monotony.

The visual evidence provided by surviving furniture answers some of our questions regarding the style and quality of the types of furniture in use in the Middle Ages, but in order to go beyond the scope of these matters in a significant manner the present study has drawn upon documentary and literary material, and to a lesser extent, upon works of art. The use of this evidence has furthered these wider lines of enquiry, and it has also produced a reciprocal, cross-fertilization of ideas and explanations with regard to individual examples of extant furniture. It has been shown that written evidence allows us to judge the quantity of wooden furniture owned by the nobility and

---

[599] Panel, V. & A. no. 82.1893; chest, Cat. 31.
[600] See above p. 20.
[601] Cat. 30.
[602] Cat. 13.
[603] See Eames 1974.
[604] See above p. xxii.
[605] A notable exception is the Romsey chest, see above p. 231.
[606] Cat. 43.
[607] For example, York chest, Cat. 31.

middle classes and by important institutions in the later Middle Ages and to understand how it was used and where it was located. It would be difficult to overstress the importance of this evidence (which is quoted extensively in individual sections of the study). In the first place, written evidence highlights the arbitrary factors which have determined the survival of medieval furniture. The implications of this arbitrary pattern have long been recognized for certain objects such as beds; only a handful of examples survive and no one questions that thousands once existed. In the case of armoires and chairs, however, the rarity of surviving examples has sometimes been taken as an accurate reflection of the medieval situation.[608] Written evidence acts as a control upon such assumptions, and shows in these particular instances that armoires were common items of storage furniture and that chairs, though rarely needed in more than ones and twos in halls and audience chambers, were common in private quarters such as bed chambers.[609] Inventories provide one of the most valuable sources for assessment regarding quantity and situation, but need to be used in groups since those that survive are often orientated towards legal requirements which separated movables and fixtures one from another; as medieval furniture fell within both categories, isolated inventories may be of limited use.[610] Wills occasionally notice furniture, and accounts are very valuable in showing how furniture was acquired, the craftsmen involved and the cost incurred. For instance, we learn from the Duke of Burgundy's accounts that the ducal records at the castle of Talent were stored in large, specially constructed armoires, and we can compare this provision with the surviving furniture, built for similar purposes in many locations, for example Westminster, Malines and Ghent.[611] But if wills, inventories and accounts tell us how much, where, when and by whom furniture was used, literary sources answer some of the most interesting of all questions, those we pose by asking *why*? Literature provides the key to much which otherwise seems unaccountable, and allows the evidence from every other source to slot into place and produce a convincing overall picture. An analysis of Alienor de Poitiers's treatise, and of many passages in the works of Olivier de la Marche and others, has enabled this study to demonstrate for the first time that, apart from the need for mobility in furniture, the greatest single factor which controlled its character and use centred upon the needs of display, in which precedence as a first consideration and rank as a second were advertised and acknowledged through the use of recognized and carefully graded forms and materials in furniture.[612]

All kinds of furniture discussed in the study were sometimes used as furniture of estate, and the use of armoires in this way has been noted above, but certain groups were particularly associated with displaying privilege or power. We may point to the raised chair, or throne, which is well recognized in such a context, but other furniture, such as the buffet or cup board for displaying plate have received less attention. The study has traced the development of the stepped buffet with its series of open boards for

[608] See fn. 75.
[609] See pp. 181 ff., 198 ff.
[610] See Eames 1973.
[611] Cat. 14, 13, 15.
[612] See pp. xviii–xx, 228–9.

plate and has been able to show from the evidence of Alienor de Poitiers's treatise how precise numbers of shelves expressed the degrees of precedence accorded to individuals.[613] Although we might feel that these matters were of small importance, it is clear that they were not regarded in this light in the later Middle Ages. The surprise, bordering on disapproval, which Alienor de Poitiers expresses in commenting on the adoption of a buffet of five stages by Marie of Burgundy, who thus placed herself on a level with the queen of France, reflects a situation which was far more explosive than the mere breaking of a rule of etiquette might suggest. In this tiny instance, we see the inevitable outcome of the policies of aggrandizement pursued by the Valois dukes of Burgundy brought to a logical conclusion, for we see a statement, made in visual terms, that the subservience due to the French crown in respect of certain lands held by the house of Valois was no longer relevant.

The study has demonstrated the interrelationship between the high, stepped buffet and the narrow buffet of more accommodating proportions, which developed in parallel.[614] We see how this piece of furniture, with its novel combination of enclosed storage space (armoires) and display boards, outstripped the ability of language to change sufficiently fast to identify it in a single term, thus producing considerable confusion when the exact identification of an object was necessary, and varied descriptions such as 'buffet a serrure', 'drecheur a deux aumaries fermans à clef', 'dressouers fermans' etc. are found.[615] Because the woodwork of the narrow buffet, unlike the stepped buffet, was chiefly exposed it was often elaborate (for it was an adjunct of estate) and the magnificently carved buffet at Plougrescant[616] provides an eminent example of the type, here made especially significant by the inclusion of a canopy. The Plougrescant buffet also shows that the display board of the narrow buffet was sometimes designed *solely* for display, a factor which has not yet been demonstrated by any other evidence.

The importance of the buffet as an object of prestige outlasted the Middle Ages, and it is suggested that it was precisely because the word cupboard carried such strong connotations of gentle manners that it remained attached to the piece of furniture in England, even after the display of plate ceased to be a recognized means of conveying social distinction and the object in question had become entirely enclosed — an armoire. (In France, the true distinction between the terms buffet and armoire was retained.)

The buffet, in use, conveyed its message of privilege in two ways: by its form and by the value of the plate which was exposed upon its open boards. In a similar way, the bed was used in the later Middle Ages to measure degrees of privilege by its form and by the value of the textiles exposed upon it. But the study has demonstrated that the process of expressing power symbolically was carried to more extravagant lengths with beds than with any other type of furniture,[617] and some forms were deemed only suitable for servants.[618] The bed with a whole canopy (a canopy extending over the

[613] See Fig. 36, p. 272.
[614] See pp. 56 ff.
[615] See p. 62.
[616] Cat. 27.
[617] See pp. 75 ff.
[618] See pp. 77 ff.

entire couch) signified rank, but this simple statement was insufficiently subtle to express the intricate and highly stylized etiquette in the fifteenth-century courts of France, Burgundy and England. The suites of rooms set aside for noble ladies against the birth of children, which Alienor de Poitiers discusses,[619] were equipped with beds which by their number, form, and position within the room, as well as by the type, colour and decoration of their hangings, signified degrees of privilege. The elaboration of the idea of the bed as a significant symbol had become so overwrought that beds which were never intended for use were included in these suites of rooms (and were also ceremonially used in other contexts)[620] and stood in the positions ordained for them, displaying textiles of enormous value and signifying to all who were versed in courtly manners the degree of precedence accorded to the individual concerned. Although we can only visualize these structures through miniatures and panel paintings, the importance of display in this area of family life is brought home to us by the survival of the cradle of Philip the Fair or Margaret of Austria.[621] This cradle has been correlated with passages in Alienor de Poitiers's treatise and with a number of important documentary references,[622] and we are able to state that it is a unique survivor of a type of cradle — the cradle of state — which extended the symbolic expression of privilege (manifest in the adult beds in the suite of rooms occupied for the birth of infants) through its form, decoration and the arrangement, type and decoration of the textiles and furs with which it was covered.[623] It has been shown that this type of cradle was reserved for display, the infant being nursed and rocked on private occasions in a night cradle which carried no overtones of privilege but was designed for practical use, low enough for the occupant to be tended by a seated nurse.[624] The identification of the extant Newland cradle[625] as belonging to this category provides an interesting juxtaposition with the cradle of state made for the birth of Philip the Fair or Margaret of Austria which is of similar date.

The variety found in the form and ornamentation of chests has been noted above. Some of the forms chosen may be directly attributed to use: at its simplest level, this meant that travelling chests were of box form, without feet, like the extant examples at Hereford and Westminster.[626] Documentary evidence shows that the way in which custodianship of the contents of chests and other furniture was arranged controlled the number of locks which were provided.[627] Large numbers of chests were clearly intended to be nothing more than strong storage receptacles, whether they were designed specifically for travelling or not, and examples in the Catalogue of this hardy type are at Winchester and Westminster.[628] But we are also aware that chests were often needed in important rooms — Charles V had a gilded chest in his sleeping chamber in 1420,[629]

[619] See Appendix VIII (b), (c).
[620] See pp. 85 ff.
[621] Cat. 28.
[622] See pp. 93 ff., 99 ff.
[623] See Appendix VIII, Fig. 36.
[624] See pp. 94 ff.
[625] Cat. 29.
[626] Cat. 45, 47.
[627] See pp. 134–5.
[628] Cat. 40, 32.
[629] See p. 136.

and we may infer from the many elaborately decorated examples which survive, and the Carnavalet and York chests spring immediately to mind,[630] that these and others like them belonged in places where they might be seen to reflect upon the dignity of individuals or institutions.

Turning now to seating, we find that the important, finely carved fixed seating at Muchelney[631] provides tangible evidence for the documenatry material[632] which shows that fitted seating was once common but has almost entirely disappeared, along with the rooms that contained it. The survey of seat types shows a richness of invention which has already been noted in respect of other types of furniture, and the tenacity of the important X-form, with its connotations of lordship inherited from antiquity,[633] is yet another example of the power of symbolism to control design.

It has been noted above that the importance of the seat as a symbol of privilege has never been in doubt, but the frequent confusion between rank and precedence has gained acceptance for the theory that only the great could use chairs. The study shows that in this, as in every other context, estate was marked by precedence which is mutable, before rank which is fixed, so that when, to take one example, the king of England's steward presided at court in the absence of his royal master, he represented the king and, regardless of his own personal rank, took precedence over all other persons including those of royal blood. We see clearly how the rules of precedence could affect seating in the description of a meeting between the Comte de Charolais, heir to the Duke of Burgundy, and a group of nobles which included a royal French duke; the Comte de Charolais sat on a stool on this occasion and gave his companions the honour of the bench.[634] This emphasis on precedence meant that the more private the occasion, the greater was the opportunity for those of modest social standing to use important seating, and the study shows that we can see this principle in operation in the case of chairs which were an established item of furniture in the room most likely to be private, the bed chamber.[635] (We see this location for the chair brought vibrantly to life in Jan van Eyck's Arnolfini Wedding in the National Gallery, painted in 1434.)

It has been shown that when seating was intended to be particularly significant, height was a necessary requirement. On occasions of great ceremony, the seat was raised high and approached by steps, but even when the occasion was more casual an important seat, whether a chair or a bench, was always provided with a footboard, footstool, or cushion for the feet.[636] The marks of attachment for a footboard, identified on the extant turned chair at Hereford[637] show that this seat signified privilege. Another important accessory with similar implications was the canopy, used to denote estate for seating as well as for beds and buffets.[638]

[630] Cat. 34, 31.
[631] Cat. 51.
[632] For example, entries of 1251 and 1440, pp. 198–9, 206.
[633] See pp. 182–7.
[634] See p. 202.
[635] See pp. 198 ff.
[636] See pp. 181 ff.
[637] Cat. 49.
[638] Seating, see p. 198; beds, see pp. 75 ff.; buffets, see p. 59.

With regard to tables, the study shows that movable and fixed forms existed throughout the period. Although tables were occasionally designed as adjuncts of estate, like the Spanish example with silver-plated trestles owned by Henry IV,[639] the commonest tables which were used for dining were massive and simple, though the pair surviving at Penshurst show that they could achieve a certain grandeur.[640] Small tables were clearly important in the later Middle Ages and could be extremely delicate, as the ingeniously designed knockdown example in the Musée Cluny shows.[641]

Finally, a significant aspect of the study has been to show from documentary evidence how great artists, who were both painters and carvers (and occasionally architects like Villard de Honnecourt)[642] designed, made or finished furniture for important patrons in the Middle Ages. The evidence is extensive, and shows that these men were versatile and highly valued masters whose talents were recognized, not only by generous financial remuneration[643] but also by social preferment. The entries in the wardrobe accounts of Edward I concerning payments to Walter of Durham, styled King's Painter, for painting and carving a chair are well known,[644] and from France Richard has drawn attention to the frequent employment of *imagiers* by Mahaut, Comtesse d'Artois, in the early fourteenth century. In 1313 Evrart Orleans of Paris, 'imagier et peintre', supplied the Comtesse with forms, chairs, a lectern and a mannequin used in the toilet of great ladies,[645] and at the Château d'Hesdin the *imagiers* this lady employed were responsible for such diverse works as a bridge, joke machinery, a crucifix, altar retables, a statue of St Louis, the walls of the hall and an armoire for the chapel ornaments.[646]

It is not surprising that the Burgundian dukes, committed to extravagant display as a means of furthering political power, used the greatest artists to glorify their courts. They commissioned important furniture, either using artists attached to the French court, as in the case of the cradle of state made for the birth of John the Fearless by Jehan d'Orleans in 1438,[647] or employing those they had succeeded in attaching to their own sphere of power; these men were often given privileged titles such as 'varlet de chambre', after the custom of France.[648] The important artists who were drawn within the net of Burgundian ducal power to undertake tasks ranging from the sublime to the trivial were an impressive group and included among their number Melchior Broederlam, judged by Panofsky to be the greatest of all panel painters, prior to Jan van Eyck, whose work has survived.[649] Broederlam was styled 'varlet de chambre' to Philip the Bold and also 'peintre monseigneur', and he carried out all the usual assignments including furniture. It has been shown that these masters were regularly called

---

[639] See p. 221.
[640] See p. 221.
[641] See p. 223.
[642] See p. 234.
[643] See Richard 1887, 306–7.
[644] See p. 188.
[645] Richard 1887, 288.
[646] See p. 10.
[647] Peintre and varlet de chambre to the king of France, see fn. 69.
[648] The greatest in the land did not disdain to hold this honorific title, see Canat de Chizy 1859, 156.
[649] Panofsky, I, 86.

upon to provide cradles of state, and there can be no doubt that the surviving cradle in Brussels is an example of the work of one of these artists.[650]

Having regard to the wide framework which existed over hundreds of years in which those of the greatest skills, whether goldsmiths, painters, sculptors or other specialists[651] were valued by great patrons and suitably rewarded for their services, I believe we should infer that outstanding excellence in extant furniture is the *calculated* result of employing men whose talents were recognized, and is unlikely to be the result of the *chance* employment of an unusually gifted artist working among the general mass of craftsmen of average ability. We can point to a select number of surviving examples of furniture which are clearly the work of masters[652] but such furniture has not received the recognition it deserves. While carved and painted altar retables, statues and painted panels have excited widespread attention, furniture bearing the qualities of decoration found, for instance, on St Edward's chair in England and on the cradle of state in Brussels,[653] though evidently made by the same versatile artists or craftsmen, has been largely ignored. There is no doubt that the failure to include such furniture in wide discussions is largely due to its mutilated conditions. This study has shown that medieval furniture, whether armoires, beds, chests, seating or tables, included not only utilitarian types but also furniture of estate which cannot be easily separated from the other works of art of its time. The traditions of creating elaborate furniture which were developed in antiquity did not disappear in Northern Europe after the decline of Roman power, to be reintroduced with the ideas of the Italian Renaissance in the early sixteenth century; they survived the Dark Ages and continued to be felt through the limited but recognized activities of the greatest artists and craftsmen of the Middle Ages.

---

[650] Cat. 28.
[651] A counterpoint maker was styled 'varlet de chambre' to the Duke of Burgundy in 1371; p. 84.
[652] For example, Cat. 8, 11, 22, 23, 27, 28, 30, 31, 34, 48.
[653] I refer to the secondary decoration on St Edward's chair of *c.*1330–50, see pp. 191–2; cradle, Cat. 28.

APPENDIX I

THE OBAZINE ARMOIRES (Cat. 1, 2, 10, Pls. 1–3) IN THE
CONTEXT OF THE HISTORY OF THE ABBEY CHURCH OF ST ETIENNE

The freestanding armoire at Obazine (Corrèze) is one of the earliest extant armoires in Europe and has survived *in situ*, in the church of St Etienne (Cat. 10);[654] thus, there is no question of its authenticity. It has delicate carving in the form of Romanesque arcading and elaborate iron fittings, and is therefore an object of some sophistication in the context of the time in which it was made. So important a piece has obviously attracted much attention in print, since no study which purported to include French twelfth- or thirteenth-century furniture could fail to discuss it. Fortunately for the serious student, the bulk of this comment can be ignored.

In 1858 Viollet-le-Duc discussed the armoire as an isolated object, outside the context of its provenance, dating it stylistically to the first years of the thirteenth century;[655] he described it in some detail but inaccurately in certain respects for, it seems, he never saw it. The report published in 1890 by the Marquis de Fayolle was of a different kind.[656] De Fayolle visited Obazine and considered the armoire in the context of the church of St Etienne, drawing attention to the survival of a series of armoires of locker type (Cat. 1, 2), some of which were equipped with original doors and iron fittings. De Fayolle believed that the ironwork of the lockers and of the freestanding armoire were contemporary. He suggested that the church must have been built at least to the height of these lockers in 1176, at which date an altar was dedicated to St Etienne.[657] De Fayolle gave the freestanding armoire a stylistic date of 1150–1200 which was reinforced by the correlation with the lockers, themselves part of the *fabric* of the church and for this reason securely dated to a period not later than 1176.

Since 1890, no new evidence has been published. The most recent serious discussion of the subject reiterates de Fayolle's findings.[658]

After so long a period in which, it appears, no historian has visited Obazine, a review of the evidence at the site is desirable. De Fayolle's case, although entirely convincing, leaves a number of questions unanswered. The lockers, a vital link in the evidence, have remained unpublished. This appendix seeks to fill this gap in the published record by examining all the armoires in the context of the church itself. A factual account of the furniture is given in the appropriate places in the Catalogue Raisonné (see Cat. 1, 2, 10), together with a recent photographic record.

The date of the completion of the church of St Etienne is unknown; the foundation stone was laid by the bishop of Limoges in 1156 and an altar was dedicated in 1176, as we have seen. The church was part of an abbey founded by St Etienne in 1135. The abbey buildings are much altered, mutilated and, in parts, destroyed, but there is still a visual connexion between the church and the abbey through a fine staircase in the north transept which once led to the monks' dorter. The plan of the abbey (Cistercian) was carried out on an impressive scale and it is clear that Obazine was the primary place of pilgrimage of the saint. This importance had dwindled to insignificance by the eighteenth century and in 1757 the facade of the church and over a third of the nave were destroyed, in order to reduce the financial problems of maintenance. In 1789 the few remaining monks dispersed and the abbey became private property. The

---

[654] St Etienne lived *c*. 1085–1159.
[655] Viollet-le-Duc 1858, 5.
[656] de Fayolle, 'Armoire du XIIe Siècle et Tombeau de St. Etienne à Obazine', *57th Congrès Archeologique de France*, 1890, 223–36.
[657] The dedicatory inscription survives in one of the chapels of the church.
[658] Viaux 1962, 33–4.

mutilated church remained in use, serving a tiny village community; it has retained this function to the present day.

The church and abbey were evidently well equipped with armoires of locker type by the twelfth-century designers. The refectory (N. wall) and the small library in the cloister (S. wall), both now in ruin, have pairs of lockers with grooves for shelves and rebates for wooden doors and stonework which corresponds with the pair of lockers in the north transept of the church (Cat. 1). However, our main interest concerns those armoires which retain their doors and iron fittings and these are found only in the church.

Three lockers in the church claim attention: a pair in the north transept of traditional form (Cat. 1), and another armoire in the W. end, on the N. side of the main door (Cat. 2). The latter armoire is of curious form, being a projecting stone armoire with sides and front free of the wall, fitted with flush wooden doors in the usual manner.

The pair of armoires in the north transept (Cat. 1) are sited between two doors, the left of which leads to what is now the vestry. (The stairs to the dorter rise immediately to the left of the vestry door.) Both of these doors, flanking the pair of armoires, have simple straight hinge straps, simpler in character than those upon all the armoires in the church. The vestry door has a singular, toothed lock plate which may be stylistically dated fourteenth century, but it accommodates an original twelfth-century bolt which has a knop, now much worn, in the form of a head, resembling the bolt finial on the freestanding armoire (Cat. 10). In appearance, the doors are crude and are untouched twelfth-century woodwork and hinge work. Turning now to the locker armoires (Cat. 1), the bolt, which serves the pair of lockers, is a replacement and there are clear signs in the wood of the position of the original fitting. The iron straps, however, three to each door (upper and lower hinge straps, and centre decorative) are primary and are fitted to the original wooden doors. As Pl. 2B shows, the ironwork is countersunk to lie flush with the wood as far as the fleur-de-lis finials where, although still countersunk, the character of the straps changes from flat to raised or humped. This refinement, together with the widening of the straps in an arc which occurs at intervals in each strap, is found on the freestanding armoire (Cat. 10). Both woodwork and ironwork upon these lockers are coarser than on the freestanding armoire but are entirely in character with the doors of the church between which the pair of lockers are sited.

The armoire at the W. end of the church (Cat. 2) poses somewhat different problems. De Fayolle believed it to be twelfth century, rebuilt out of old materials,[659] and I am in agreement with his conclusion. Dealing first with the stonework, it is, in appearance, a twelfth-century work with a round arch and a characteristic moulding in lieu of a capital. However, there can be no doubt whatever that the whole structure is not in its original position, for it is built against the eighteenth-century wall which closes off the truncated nave, see above. The fitting is unusual in form and no parallels come to mind, for it stands away from the wall on three sides and is not buried within it, in the usual locker manner. That this is a primary characteristic, and not a feature of the rebuilt phase of the armoire's history, is shown by the continuation of the moulding along the sides, which is surely not an eighteenth-century creation. Turning now to the doors, we find a character which is precisely the same as that encountered in the pair of lockers in the north transept (Cat. 1). Here, at the W. end, the doors are simple riven timbers of about the same thickness as those in the north transept, and the iron straps in each case are so similar that they must have been made by the same smith. We find a strap design which echoes that used for the freestanding armoire, though in both

[659] De Fayolle, 227.

woodworking and ironworking the freestanding armoire shows considerably greater refinement.

Let us now consider the freestanding armoire (Cat. 10) in the present context. In the first place, it is finer in all respects than any of the woodwork and ironwork so far discussed. But, like the other work, it is unmistakably twelfth century in character and the parallel features between the various fixtures and the freestanding piece suggest that the same group of craftsmen were involved, and that everything was made at one and the same time, as the church was being built. The common features may be summarized as follows:

(1) The iron strapwork upon both the lockers and the freestanding armoire is of the same design and is attached to the woodwork in the same manner: flat straps, widened in an arc at intervals, with fleur-de-lis finials which are raised or humped; countersunk.

(2) The locking bar on the freestanding armoire has a knop at each end worked in the form of a grotesque head. A similar bolt with a head for its knop is still in position on the door of the present vestry, see above.

(3) The arcading on the sides of the freestanding armoire has an inward kick at the spring of the arch, a feature which is found in the stone arches of the nave.

The burden of evidence supports de Fayolle's thesis for a date of *c.* 1176 for all the furniture in the church, both movable and fixed. The remarkable survival of such a group is clearly due to the peculiar history of the church in which, apart from the building of an important tomb over St Etienne's grave in the thirteenth century, no unnecessary expenditure seems to have been incurred after the initial building period.[660] After the thirteenth century, a period of inactivity, or decline, ensued which culminated in a calamitous economic situation in the eighteenth century. The destruction of part of the nave in 1757 highlights an obscurity which had probably existed over a considerable period. This obscurity no doubt saved the furniture from the zeal in restoration which was so prevalent in France in the nineteenth century, and it has remained unchanged to the present day.

APPENDIX II

THE 'ZOUCHE CHAPEL' AT YORK MINSTER (Cat. 3–7, Pls. 4–6)

The so-called Zouche Chapel at York Minster, which contains a series of five locker armoires, accommodated within the thickness of the walls is at present a chapel, though in 1819 it was used as a vestry.[661] The accepted view concerning the dating of the Zouche chapel is as follows: a chantry chapel, founded in accordance with the terms of the will of Archbishop William La Zouche (1342–52), built against Archbishop Roger's choir (1154–81) and later altered to accommodate the new choir of 1361–72.[662] This Appendix seeks to demonstrate that this view is incorrect, and that the building itself, as well as the lockers within it, is a unity, the whole designed and erected in the late fifteenth/early sixteenth century and having no connexion with William La Zouche.

---

[660] A new lock for the vestry door, utilizing the old bolt, was provided in the fourteenth century, doubtless of necessity; and a fifteenth-century freestanding armoire, Cat. 16, now in the vestry, was acquired, presumably at that time.

[661] See I. Britton, *The History and Antiquities of the Metropolitan Church of York*, London, 1819, 32.

[662] *V.C.H. City of York*, 338. See also G. H. Cook, *Medieval Chantries and Chantry Chapels*, London, 1963, 154. A glance at the leaflet which includes a plan of the Minster, published in 1957 and signed W.J.G. (*A Plan of York Minster Shewing the Architectural Styles*), shows clearly by differential marking the accepted view concerning the dating of the 'Zouche' chapel.

Visually, the Zouche Chapel *is* a unity, having many sophisticated details which, although restrained, are of unmistakably late Gothic form. The north wall forms a late fifteenth-century 'skin' which is grafted upon the earlier outer wall of the 1361–72 choir and the armoires, in this wall, are set in finely executed flat voussoirs; thus they have no arch and no lintel, but are dependent for the security of their ceilings upon two straight courses of radially set stones. These armoires are accommodated in bays between cluster columns which are engaged to the wall and which continue to rise above their capitals in an uninterrupted flow, before branching into a series of ribs to form the vault. Columns which are similarly conceived, though more advanced in that they dispense with capitals altogether, are found in the Orange-Nassau family chapel of St George at Brussels, completed in *c.* 1516.[663] At York, the arrangement of columns on the N. wall is complemented on the S. wall, but here there are no lockers. The sense of free flowing upward thrust, held in a balanced symmetry, is disturbed by the clumsy setting of the E. window which is off centre and is thus at variance with the position of the vault. Although this can be explained by reference to the plan (an external buttress supporting the choir would block a centrally placed window in the Zouche Chapel) one cannot help feeling that such an unsatisfactory arrangement must have been due to lack of forethought. The Zouche chapel has a door in the outside S. wall and this door, with its Tudor arch, as well as the whole exterior range of chapel and adjoining vestries, are late fifteenth/early sixteenth century in character.

If the architectural evidence is clear on stylistic grounds, what is the basis for the accepted view of the dating of the building? It is clear that the source for the established view concerning the history of this part of the Minster comes from the writings of James Torre (1649–99), who compiled a great MS volume in around 1690 which provides an elaborate index to the cathedral muniments and a commentary upon them.[664] Torre's work has never been superseded, and it is his conclusions concerning the Zouche chapel which are found in Drake's *Eboracum*[665] and elsewhere. We find that Torre, knowing that William La Zouche's will of 1349 provided 300 marks for the foundation of a chantry and discovering documentary evidence for a license to build that chantry in June 1352 (and small payments to workmen before that time), assumed that the chantry had been built although, in fact, *no further documentary evidence concerning the chantry existed.*[666] Now, although there are notable gaps in the documents with regard to the building of certain parts of the Minster,[667] the lack of further evidence for a chantry is particularly significant. In every other case at York where chantries are concerned there are references both to the enrolment of priests and to the dissolution of the chantries themselves. However, at least one modern scholar believes that the Zouche chapel was demolished:

> '. . . the chantry chapel, if completed, was swept away when Archbishop Thoresby [1352–1373] a few years later rebuilt the choir on the existing lines.'

This source also draws attention to the difficulties over La Zouche's will, and the disregard by his executors and kinsfolk concerning the directions contained therein.[668] It should also be remembered that the Archbishop was not buried in his chantry, but was interred in a grave without a monument before the altar of St Edward. It would seem that the quality of Torre's work commanded such respect that his conclusions were generally accepted without critical

---

[663] See Comte J. de Borchgrave d'Altena, 'Note au sujet de la Chapelle S.-Georges à Bruxelles', *Bulletins des Musées d'Art et d'Histoire à Bruxelles*, January 1955, 2–17.
[664] Housed in York Minster Library.
[665] F. Drake, *Eboracum*, London, 1736, 482.
[666] Torre's comments concerning the Zouche chantry are found on p. 112 of his manuscript volume.
[667] For example, there are no records for the building of the Chapter House.
[668] Ed. Sir Leslie Stephen/Sir Sidney Lee, *Dictionary of National Biography*, XXI, Oxford, 1967–8, 1337b.

analysis.[669] Once it was accepted that the chantry was completed around 1352, the theory of subsequent alterations to the building had to follow since, in 1352, Archbishop Roger's choir still stood and the S. wall of the existing, later choir (a party wall with the Zouche Chapel) is wider than the earlier one.

If we accept that the Zouche Chapel had nothing to do with Archbishop La Zouche, but was erected in *c.* 1500 together with the two vestries which lie to the W. of it, what are we to believe concerning its purpose and the use for which its fitted lockers were designed? We should briefly consider the range of three rooms as a whole, for they belong to one building period and interconnect internally, showing an intimate functional relationship. The plan suggests not ceremonial, but service or office use, and indeed it appears that the rooms to the W. of the Zouche chapel were the old Treasury and the Consistory Court.[670] The Zouche Chapel itself has a well in the SW. corner which seems to rule out any suggestion that the room was built for ceremonial use; (the presence of the restored piscina in the E. wall, even if original, does not necessarily infer chapel usage, as evidence at Wells shows, see pl. 72B). It would seem almost certain that the Zouche Chapel was either a muniment room, a store for service books, or a library; with its external south door, it is too vulnerable to have been designed as a treasury.

APPENDIX III

DATING EVIDENCE CONCERNING THE SCREEN AND ARMOIRE (Cat. 14, Pl. 16) IN THE MUNIMENT ROOM, WESTMINSTER ABBEY

A fixed screen in the muniment room, composed of wood and plaster, is painted with a white hart and with star, or sun, devices. Against the centre of one side of the screen is a free-standing armoire which is also painted with the star or sun device. This evidence has been used to show that the armoire was in place in Richard II's reign.[671] Yet the armoire is of unmistakably fifteenth-century character and therefore this Appendix examines the question of the painting of the screen and seeks to show that the evidence for a fourteenth-century date for the armoire is unconvincing.

Certain facts are not disputed.

(1) The white hart, as the badge of Richard II, indicates that the portion of the screen which is decorated with this creature was painted in Richard II's reign.

(2) The connexion between the painting of the stars or suns upon the screen and upon the armoire *is* relevant in considering the date of the armoire, for the style of painting and the colouring (in so far as this can now be judged) are the same. It follows that both the part of the screen which bears this device, and the armoire, were painted at one and the same time and that the armoire was sited in the same room as the screen, though not necessarily in its present position.

The divergence of opinion comes with the connexion between the painting of the white hart and the painting of the star or sun device. The published view assumes that the screen exhibits a single decorative scheme. My view is that there are two periods of painting involved, one

---

[669] Mr C. B. L. Barr, Sub-Librarian-in-charge of York Minster Library informed me in April 1970 that this particular instance was the only occasion known to him where Torre had resorted to speculation. I would like to express my thanks to Mr Barr who patiently and expeditiously answered all my enquiries over this matter and showed me Torre's great work.

[670] I have not seen these rooms which are now private vestries.

[671] *RCHM London I (Westminster Abbey)*, 51b and pl. 96. This view is upheld by Lethaby, 289.

S

fourteenth century and one of the late fifteenth century. The diagram in Fig. 35 shows how each side of the screen is made, and decorated.

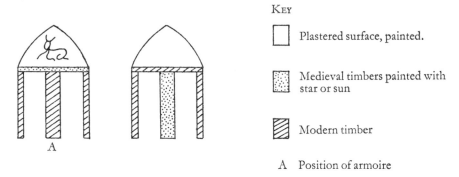

KEY

☐ Plastered surface, painted.

▦ Medieval timbers painted with star or sun

▨ Modern timber

A Position of armoire

FIG. 35.   Diagram of each face of the screen in the Muniment Room

As the diagram indicates, very little medieval woodwork survives, and the early painting on plaster is confined to one face. There is no decorative link between the painting on the plaster and the painting on the wood. The plaster panel shows the white hart in a flowery meadow; no star or sun device is used in this panel and there is nothing to suggest a single decorative scheme. Quite the reverse. Scale, subject matter and character of painting are equally at variance in the upper and lower parts of the screen. Unless it can be demonstrated that the star or sun device is connected with Richard II, there is no impediment to treating the painting of the upper and lower portions of the screen as of different periods.

Taken as a whole, the evidence suggests that the upper (plaster) part of the screen was decorated in the time of Richard II. And that in the fifteenth century, probably in the reign of Edward IV, an armoire was made for the room and was painted in accordance with decorations carried out at the same time to the lower portions of the walls.[672]

APPENDIX IV

THE SUITE OF ADMINISTRATIVE OFFICES OF
THE VICARS CHORAL, WELLS CATHEDRAL

The Vicars Choral of Wells Cathedral, which developed from an endowment for chantry priests in 1334, were refounded as a College by Bishop Ralph of Shrewsbury in the mid-fourteenth century. A street of houses known as Vicars' Close was built for the priests by Bishop Ralph and further additions to the College were made by Bishop Bekynton (1443–65) during his lifetime and this work was continued by his executors after his death. Although the College has ceased to function, the street of houses and the communal buildings of the fourteenth and fifteenth centuries survive, forming an entity which is probably unique of its kind.

On the west side of the gateway to Vicars' Close is the Hall or Refectory, giving access to a suite of administrative offices, and it is with these rooms that we are concerned since they are equipped with some of their original furniture. The offices are part of Bishop Bekynton's

---

[672] The original uses of the muniment room, and its alterations, as well as the muniments preserved within it, are discussed by Tanner, 13–15.

work, dating from 1457, and they have remained virtually unchanged since that time.[673] These rooms provide us with evidence of the kind of facilities which must have been common enough in large households in the fifteenth century, as well as in institutions such as the Vicars Choral.

A door in the Refectory gives onto a narrow, spiral staircase leading to the Exchequer with Muniment Room off it and Treasury beneath. The Exchequer is entered through a wooden screen which incorporates an armoire (Cat. 9, Pl. 9), and the room was obviously comfortable, having a large, glazed window, fireplace and handsome laver (pl. 72B). Leading off the Exchequer is a tiny Muniment Room equipped with a substantial multi-drawer armoire for records, now sadly mutilated (Cat. 18, Pl. 22), and another fitment in ruinous condition. In the corner of the Muniment Room a narrow staircase descends to a tiny Treasury beneath which has a crude yet practical armoire of sixteenth-century date[674] with ironwork in an advanced state of oxidation due to the close proximity of an unglazed, unshuttered window. The Treasury can be reached only through the Muniment Room; the door to it has no lock but it may be effectively barred by passing a long pole through a special hole in the floor above.

Select Bibliography

W. H. Godfrey, 'Vicars' Close', *Archaeological Journal*, CVII, 1950, 112–13.

H. C. Maxwell-Lyte/M. C. B. Dawes, 'Register of Thomas Bekynton', *Som. Rec. Soc.* XLIX, 1934, xii, xxxii–xxxiii.

J. H. Parker, *Architectural Antiquities of Wells*, Oxford/London, 1866, 27–38.

[H. T. Riley], *Hist. Mss. Comm.* 1st Report, 1870, 93; 3rd Report, 1872, 364.

V C H Somerset, II, London, 1911, 167.

A. Watkin, 'Dean Cosyn and Wells Cathedral Miscellanea', *Som Rec. Soc.,* LVI, 1941, 139–49.

APPENDIX V

BONNOR'S PERSPECTIVE ITINERARY, London 1798

Caption to Pl. XI, fig. 3:
'The Cradle of Prince Henry afterward King Henry V born at Monmouth Castle 1388. Drawn from the original 1773 by permission of the Rev. Mr. Ball, Rector of Newland, Gloucestershire.'

Text, p. 34:
'For a mile in length, the surface of Copped-Wood Hill is nearly level, exceeding pleasant, and perfectly safe for travellers, either on foot or horseback.

---

[673] In December 1969 the rooms were unused. No form of modern heating had been installed and the Treasury window was barred but unglazed. Apart from the deterioration of the furniture, the rooms looked much as they must have done at the time they were built.
[674] Stylistic date, based on the ironwork. Both handles and hinges are original; round handles attached to round plates and hinge straps thus:

The pointed, leaf-shaped terminal is associated with sixteenth-century work in England and earlier on the continent, see p. 159.

Proceeding along the path, you have a view of the old mansion, venerable woods, and hanging gardens of Court Field,[675] the residence of the late William Vaughan, Esq. For the benefit of this salubrious air, Henry Prince of Wales, born 1388, at Monmouth Castle, and therefore called Harry of Monmouth, was nursed here. Fig. 3, pl. XI represents the CURIOUS CRADLE in which he was rocked. It became an honorary perquisite of one of the rockers, who was an ancestor of the Rev. Mr. Ball, Rector of Newland (which is in this vicinity). And in 1773, when this drawing was made with his permission it was in his possession, who related that it had continued in his family from that time: it is given as a real curiosity of the fourteenth century. Since the death of that gentleman, his son has presented it to — — — — — Whitehead, Esq., of Hambrook, French-Hay, near Bristol.'

Footnote, pp. 34–5:

'A drawing of it was presented to the publisher of the London Magazine the same year, but the inaccuracy of the engraving from it, which appears in that work for March 1774; and a very material error in the history which accompanies it, renders its introduction here necessary to their correction; as will be obvious from a comparison with the representation here offered.

The mis-statement of its history was occasioned in the following manner: To the drawing was annexed a written description of the Cradle only. When it was put into the editor's hand, he was informed that it was the Cradle of Prince Harry of Monmouth, afterwards King Henry V, who was born at Monmouth Castle. In preparing the article for the press sometime after, he erred in his recollection of the account that was given him, and not aware of the mistake, he stated it to have belonged to the first Prince of Wales, who was born at Caernarvon Castle. The error was pointed out by Mr. Bonnor, but was never corrected. The editor was unwilling perhaps to proclaim his own mistake, at so material an injury to the story as it would have sustained by losing an hundred years of its antiquity, yet is it sufficiently respectable on that account, it being 410 years since it was really in use.

The body of the Cradle, which is wider at one end than the other, is suspended by staples, and a ring at each end, from two pillars joined by frame work; a carved bird perches at the top of each, with foliage at the feet; it has six long holes at the upper edge for the rockers (three on each side), and twelve round holes at the bottom, for cordage to pass through; which formerly was for supporting a rush mattress, upon which beds of the best fashion in this country were used to be laid. A full inclination is shown to add all the ornament the workman's planes would afford upon the sides, which are covered with variety of irregular mouldings, struck from end to end; although it is remarkable that his Cambrian artist seems to have been unacquainted either with dovetailing or mitreing; the ends being plain boards, to keep out and fasten the sides to, which is done simply with nails; and yet the carving of the birds, and foliage to the pillars, between which it swings, are specimens of better execution. Old wainscotting, of excellent impannelling, carved in this style, has frequently no better joinings. Whence it appears, that those who executed the nicer parts, were not employed to put the work together.

Its dimensions are, 3 feet two inches long; 1 foot 8 inches wide at the head; 1 foot 5¾ inches at the foot; and 1 foot 5 inches deep. It is made of oak, inch and half thick; and the pillars are 2 feet 1 inches, from the ground to the top of the birds.'

---

[675] Courtfield is about 6 miles NE. of Monmouth, but the great house seems to have disappeared; Newland is some 5 miles S. of Courtfield.

APPENDIX VI

PART OF AN ACCOUNT BY GEORGES CHASTELLAIN OF A FEAST OF THE KNIGHTS OF THE ORDER OF THE GOLDEN FLEECE HELD AT THE HAGUE ON 2 MAY 1456[676]

1 'Je ne fait devise des tables droit-là assises ne du haut riche dais ou	I do not speak of the tables justly set there nor of the high and sumptuous dais where
estoit assis le duc au	was seated the duke [Philip the Good] in
5 milieu de ses frères, dont	the midst of his brothers, of whom
nul plus magnifique, mais	none was more magnificent, wherefore
en icelle salle avoit trois	in this hall were 3
dressoirs couvers et en grant	buffets, draped and far
distance l'un de l'autre,	apart one from another
10 dont l'un sy estoit de	one of which was a buffet of
parement et tout de	state entirely garnished with
vaisselle d'or enrichie	vessels of gold set
de pierreries, à cinc ou	with precious stones, of 5 or
six estages de haut pour	6 stages in height, providing
15 faire admirer gens, le	as was intended a cynosure for men, the
second dont se servoient les	second buffet for the use of the
chevaliers de l'ordre estoit	knights of the order was
plein de vaisselle dorée	full of gilt vessels,
autretant chargié de riches	or garnished with sumptuous goods
20 meubles et en multitude	set on numerous
d'estages que nulle chose	stages of which nothing was
plus riche, et le tiers	more sumptuous, and the third
dressoir dont se servoient	buffet which was for the use
les autres tables des assis	of those seated at the other tables
25 estoit tout de vaisselle	was garnished entirely with
blanche, et en telle	ungilded silver vessels, and in such
multitude et hauteur que	numbers laid out and at such a height
peu a esté vu de pareil . . .'	that little of the like has [ever] been seen [before] . . .

APPENDIX VII

(a) PART OF THE ACCOUNT BY OLIVIER DE LA MARCHE OF A FEAST CELEBRATING THE MARRIAGE OF CHARLES THE BOLD AND MARGUERITE OF YORK IN 1468[677]

1 '. . . En celle salle avoit trois tables drecees dont l'une fut au bout de dessus, traversant	In that hall were 3 laid tables of which 1 was at the end and above, placed crossways:

[676] Text, Lettenhove, III, 90–1.
[677] Text, Petitot, II, 313–14.

5	à potence: et estoit	and this was
	la table pour l'honneur.	the table of honour or High Table.
	Celle table estoit plus-	This table was
	haute que les autres,	higher than the others,
	et y montoit on à	and was approached
10	marches de degrés: et	by steps: and
	tout du long d'icelle	extending its whole length
	table avoit un riche	was a sumptuous
	ciel, et dossier si-	canopy, and seat back so
	grand qu'il faisoit	large that it made
15	tapis au banc, tout de	a covering for the seat itself as well, all of
	tresriche drap d'or.	the richest cloth of gold.
	Aux deux costés de	At the 2 sides of
	ladicte salle, tirant	the hall, set
	du long, furent les	lengthwise, were the
20	autres deux tables	other 2 tables
	drecees, moult-belles	set or laid, exceedingly fine
	et moult-longues; et	and exceedingly long; and
	au milieu de ladicte	in the middle of the
	salle avoit un haut et	hall was a high and
25	riche buffet, faict à	sumptuous buffet, made in
	manière d'une losange.	the form of a lozenge.
	Le dessus dudict buffet	The upper part of the buffet
	estoit clos à manière	was closed
	d'une lice, et tout	with a barrier, and the whole
30	tapicé et tendu des	was covered with tapestry and hung
	armes de monsieur le	with the arms of the
	duc: et de là en-avant	duke: and in front
	commençoyent marches et	began steps and
	degrés chargés de	risers furnished with
35	vaisselle, dont par les	vessels, whereof about the
	plus-bas estoit la plus	lowest part [of the buffet] were
	grosse, et par le plus-	the largest vessels, and about the
	haut estoit la plus riche	highest part were the most sumptuous
	et la plus-mignote:	and the most delicate:
40	c'estasçavoir par le bas	be it understood, about the lower part
	la grosse vaisselle	the large vessels
	d'argent dorée, et par	of silver-gilt, and about
	l'amont estoit la	the highest were the
	vaiselle d'or, garnie	vessels of gold, set
45	de pierrerie: dont il	with precious stones: of which
	y avoit à tresgrand	vessels there were a very great
	nombre. Au-dessus	number. Uppermost
	dudict buffet avoit une	on this buffet was a
	riche couppe garnie de	sumptuous cup set with
50	pierrerie, et par les	precious stones, and about the
	quarres dudict buffet	angles of the buffet
	avoit grandes cornes de	were large and complete

licorne toutes entières / unicorns' horns, very
moult-grandes et moult- / large and very
55 belles: et de toute la / fine: and of all the
vaisselle de la pareure / vessels with which the
dudict buffet ne fut / buffet was garnished, none
servi pour ce jour, / were used that day,
mais avoyent autre / but there were other
60 vaisselle d'argent, / silver vessels,
de pots et de tasses, / pots and cups and it
dont la salle et les / was with these that the hall and
chambres furent servies / chambers were served
ce jour; et à la / that day; and in
65 verité monsieur de / truth the Duke of
Bourgongne pouvoit / Burgundy [Charles the Bold] was able to
bien servir sa feste / serve his feast well
largement en vaisselle / and generously with vessels
d'argent: car le duc / of silver: because the duke
70 Philippe (dont Dieu / Philip [the Good] (whose soul
ait l'ame) luy en / may God receive) left to
laissa pour provis- / him provision of
ion plus de soixante / over 60,000 marks
mille marcs, ouvrés et / of plate, worked and
75 prests pour servir.' / ready for use.

(b) EXTRACT OF AN ACCOUNT OF A FEAST AT BRUGES IN JULY 1468, IN CELEBRATION OF THE MARRIAGE OF MARGUERITE OF YORK AND CHARLES THE BOLD, DUKE OF BURGUNDY

(See Sir Thomas Phillips, 'Account of the Ceremonial of the Marriage of the Princess Margaret, sister of King Edward the Fourth, to Charles, Duke of Burgundy, in 1468', *Archaeologia*, XXXI, 1846, 333–4.)

1 'The hall that my Ladie kept in hir estat was iii^{xx}v.
paas of lenght and xxxii^{ta} of bred: an hight table,
the first daye, nat all thing conteyninge the bredithe
of the hall, and over that table, conteyninge the
5 lenght of the table, and more, a clothe of golde of
tyshu, right riche riche, and w^t in that clothe,
another clothe of astat royall, of richer clothe of
golde, of viii. bredis, of the Ducke's coullers, of
purple and blacke, the vallaunce of the said clothe
10 richely frengid. On bothe the sides the hall, tables
on stages, the costeris of the said hall of rich
arrase. Marvelous in my mind, the curyous makinge that
is in the forsaide arras, and is of auncient historie of
the Byble, of famous Gedeon, that by the Angell of God was
15 commandid the flees and displaie it in ban^r, and he
answherid the Angill, and said, Thou maist be a sprit
of the . . . [blank in orig.] and not an angill, and
maist cause me to offend God: yf it be so, that this
flees that thou hast takine to me wilt not receve water

20 in tyme of raine I will beleve that thou art ane angel
    of God. And it fortunid, that in short tym after,
    ther fell gret rayne, and the flees recevid no watter;
    but in great droughtis it was moyste, wher thorrow,
    the said Gedeon trustid that it was the will of God,
25 that he shold rulle the people, as more opinlye is
    shewid in the Byble. In the said hall was hanginge
    two candelstikes gevinge lyght egally. Unto me
    nothinge so obscure as the crafte of the makinge of
    the Rocke, the whiche a castell stood uppon, everiche of
30 the said candylstickes; the said Roke semynge to be a
    Roke of precious stonis, marvelously wrought,
    envyronyd abowt w^t wallis of golde. And the nethermost
    part of the said candelstikes, in eche of them seven
    gret glassis curiouslye sett ther in, and in such wise
35 as the abowndance of the people and countenaunce
    aperid in the said glassis, and one every of the saide
    candelstickes viii lyghtis, and over that, to encrese
    the lumer of the said hall, one every side vii other
    candelstickes, one eche iiii lyghtis. The Roffe of
40 the said Hall, paly whitte and blew clothe. And
    in the myddis a copeborde, in triangle of IX stagis
    hight, richelye inramplysshid w^t couppis one the
    lowest stage, and the second stage covered couppis,
    and so environginge the said coopp borde in triangle,
45 what in cooppis, flagins, and pottis, right richely
    to the IX stage; and apone the rund a coup conteyninge
    the cercuyte of the triangle above and over the thre
    corners of the said triangle beneth, thought it were
    not above, but after the brddithe of the coope before
50 rehersid, were of a great cercuyte. On every corner
    unnycorns' horns, the poyntes garsysshid, and othe
    thre in other places, accomplessinge the coopborde.'

APPENDIX VIII

(a) ALIENOR DE POITIERS: LES HONNEURS DE LA COUR
INTRODUCTION

In *Les Honneurs de la Cour*, Alienor de Poitiers demonstrates for us more fully than in any other single text, the elaboration with which degrees of estate were expressed. We know that the rules she describes were French and that they had much bearing upon the English court in the fifteenth century, as well as upon that of Burgundy.[678] The account of the correct furnishings for the chambers of the ladies of the nobility for childbirth seems worth giving here in English, rearranged and loosely translated (Appendix VIII (c)) together with the original French text (Appendix VIII (b)), as a means of grasping the extraordinary, and to us alien,

---

[678] See pp. xv–xvii, and footnotes 4, 6, 7 and 8.

importance attached to the correct *form* and *character* in furnishings. We see that these matters are imbued with an almost mystical significance, and although most of Alienor de Poitiers's points concern textiles, she is as much involved with form as with quality, and since textiles are often formed by an underframe the implications for furniture are clear.

Alienor de Poitiers is chiefly concerned with describing the magnificence of the arrangements for the birth of the baby daughter of Isabelle of Bourbon and Charles, Count of Charolais, heir to the dukedom of Burgundy, in 1456; this baby, Marie, became the heiress of the Duke Burgundy and married the Emperor Maximilian of Austria. She thus became one of the greatest ladies in Europe. After discussing the arrangements for Marie of Burgundy's birth, Alienor de Poitiers goes on to discuss the arrangements for the birth of Marie of Burgundy's first child, Philip the Fair, born at Bruges in 1478. There follows a short discussion which gives us some comparative material regarding the furnishings permitted for ladies of the nobility ranking second and third below the degree of princess (both Isabelle of Bourbon and Marie of Burgundy were of this rank). A table, fig. 36, shows at a glance the way in which the estate of these ladies was immediately apparent to any visitor to their rooms. As the summary and text show, however, the visual expression of rank was detailed as well as elaborate, whereas the comparative table is very simple. Alienor de Poitiers naturally speaks less concerning less important persons, so that we are only able to project the differences which were observed in the simplest terms.

(b) AN EXTRACT OF THE TEXT OF ALIENOR DE POICTIERS: LES HONNEURS DE LA COUR, written between 1484–91[679] as set out in La Curne de Sainte-Palaye: *Memoires sur l'Ancienne Chevalerie*, II, Paris, 1759, 216–53. (The lines, numbered here, are unnumbered in the printed version; the translation is also added.)

Alienor de Poictiers was the daughter of Jean de Poictiers, Seigneur d'Arcies, and of Isabeau de Souse, a lady descended from the Portuguese royal line who came to Burgundy in 1429 in the train of Isabelle of Portugal. Alienor lived with her mother at the Court of Burgundy until she was 7 years old. She married Guillaume, Vicomte de Furnes (Flanders) in 1474 and died in 1506 or 1508.

Nativité de Madamoiselle Marie de Bourgongne.

1 Du temps que Monsieur le Dauphin estoit par deça deschassé du
Roy Charles son pere, Madame
Isabelle de Bourbon femme de
5 Monsieur le Comte de Charrolois,
seul fils de Monsieur le Ducq Philippe de Bourgogne & de Madame
Isabelle fille du Roy de Portugal,
accoucha de Mademoiselle Marie,
10 depuis Duchesse d'Austriche, & a
esté seule fille, car Monsieur de
Charrolois (qui a esté depuis Ducq
de Bourgogne, après le trépas de
Monsieur le Ducq Philippe son

15 pere) n'eust jamais enfant masle,
& fut laditte Marie mere du Ducq
Philippe à present, & de Madame
Margaritte Royne de France à
present, & eust ces deux enfans
20 de Monsieur le Ducq d'Austriche
son mari, seul fils de l'Empereur.
Et c'est à sçavoir que maditte
Dame de Charrolois accoucha à
Bruxelles, & n'estoit pour celle
25 heure le Duc Philippe audit Bruxelles.
La Chambre de maditte Dame
estoit grande & y avoit deux grands
licts l'un emprez l'autre d'un rang,
30 & au milieu des deux licts y avoit

---

[679] The text is dated by internal evidence. We hear of the accession of Charles VIII in 1484; and the authoress calls Marguerite of Austria Queen of France, unaware that this title was relinquished in 1491.

une allée, bien de quatre ou cinq
pieds de large.

    Item au bout de l'allée emprez
le chevet des deux licts estoit une
35 grande chaire à hault dos par derriere, comme ces grandes chaises
du temps passé.

    Item il y avoit une couchette
devant le feu, & estoit ceste cou-
40 chette basse à roullets, comme
celles que l'on boutte dessoubs les
licts.

    Item il y avoit un grand ciel
de drap de damas verd, lequel ciel
45 comprenoit tous les deux grands
licts, & y avoit courtines de demy
satin verd tout autour ceste entrée des deux licts, & lesdictes
courtines estoient cousues au ciel,
50 & ne couvroient point celles des
pieds, & n'approchoient point l'une
l'autre d'aussi large que l'allée estoit
entre les deux licts; les franges qui
estoient autour des gouttieres du
55 ciel estoient de soye verde.

    Aux pieds des deux grands licts
estoient deux autres Courtines de
demy satin verd comme les aultres,
& estoient lesdictes courtines à
60 annelets pour courre touttes deux,
joindans ensembles, quand on
vouloit; & estoient ces dictes courtines tendues aussy hault que le
ciel; & à deux ou trois pieds loing
65 des autres courtines, & quand on
vouloit on les clooit tout prez,
que l'on ne voyoit point l'allée entre les deux licts, mais de jour elles
estoient ouvertes, autant que l'al-
70 lée entre les deux licts portoit.

    Au milieu des deux grands licts,
il y avoit une pareille courtine, laquelle estoit troussée tout hault,
comme l'on trousse courtines, &
75 estoit toutte ferrée au bout dessus
la chaire, & ceste-là n'estoit jamais
tendue.

    Ces trois courtines dont j'ay icy

parlé on les appelle traversaines;
80 & ay ouy dire que quand la Royne
de France gist, elle en a une plus,
& est au travers de la chambre:
mais Madame la Duchesse de Bourgongne ne Madame de Charrolois
85 sa belle-fille n'en avoient que trois,
comme cy dessus est escript.

    La couchette estoit tendue d'un
pavillon quarré aussy grand que la
couche estoit, aigu à mont & avoit
90 audit pavillon tout entour courtines de satin verd, lesquelles estoient cousues audict pavillon,
mais aux deux costez les courtines estoient fendues pour les lever
95 de quelque costé que l'on vouloit,
& estoit le dessus dudit pavillon
de damas verd, comme le ciel
des licts.

    La chambre autour n'estoit ten-
100 due que de soye verde; & au bas
toutte tapissée de tapis velus jusques à l'huis, & entre les deux
grands licts & tout par tout.

    Les deux grands licts & la cou-
105 chette estoient couverts d'ermines
arminées, & dedans desdicts
couvertois estoit de fin drap violet;
& passoit le drap violet bien trois
quartiers la panne; & quand ils
110 estoient sur les licts, la panne &
le drap pendoient bien à terre
aulne & demie, & est à sçavoir que
l'on mect toujours la panne dehors.

    Dessus ces couvertoirs il y avoit
115 deux beaux draps de fin couvre-chief
de crespe empresé, qui traînoient plus
long que les couvertoirs, & la couchette estoit couverte comme les
grands licts, & estoient touts les
120 licts rebrassez, comme pour s'y cou-
cher: mais les couvertoirs d'ermines
estoient si hault que l'on ne voyoit
point les draps; sinon au chevet, &
estoit ledit chevet couvert de drap
125 de crespe: sur chaque grand lit avoit
sur le chevet un carreau; & estoient

lesdits quarreaux de trois quartiers
de long & de deux de large ou environ. La chaire qui estoit entre les
130 deux grands licts estoit couverte
depuis le haut jusques au plus bas
de drap d'or cramoisy; & un carreau de même dans laditte chaire.

En laditte Chambre il y avoit ung
135 grand dressoir, sur lequel y avoit
quatre beaux degrez, aussi longs
que le dressoir estoit large, & tout
couvert de nappes, ledit dressoir
& les degrez estoient touts char-
140 gez de vaisselles de cristalle garnies
d'or & de pierreries & sy en y avoit
de fin or; car toute la plus riche
vaisselle du Ducq Philippe y estoit,
tant de pots de tasses, comme de
145 couppes de fin or. Autres vaisselles
& bassins, lesquels on y met jamais
qu'en tel cas. Entre autre vaisselle,
il y avoit sur ledit dressoir trois
drageoirs d'or & des pierreries, dont
150 l'un estoit estimé à quarente mil
escus, & l'autre à trente mil.

Sur ledit dressoir estoit tendu un
dorsset de drap d'or cramoisy bordé de velour noir, & sur le velour
155 noir estoit bordée de fin or la devise de Monseigneur le Ducq Philippe, qui estoit le fusil.

Pour déclarer de quelle façon est
un dorseret, pour ce que beaucoup
160 de gens ne sçavent que c'est; un
dorseret est de largeur de trois draps
d'or ou d'un autre drap de soye, &
tout ainsi fait que le ciel que l'on
tend sur un lict, mais ce qu'est des-
165 sus le dressoir ne le passe point plus
d'un quartier ou d'une demie aulne,
& est à gouttieres & à franges comme le ciel d'un lict, & ce qui est
derriere le dressoir, depuis en hault
170 jusques en bas est à deux costez,
bordé de quelque chose autre que
le dorseret n'est; & doit estre la
bordure d'un quartier de large ou
environ, aussy bien au ciel que

175 derriere.

Item, sur le dressoir qu'estoit en
la chambre de maditte Dame,
avoit tousjours deux chandeliers
d'argent, que l'on appelle à la Cour
180 mestiers, là où il y avoit tousjours
deux grands flambeaux ardens, tant
qu'elle fut bien quinze jours avant
que l'on commençât à ouvrir les
verrieres de sa chambre.

185 Auprès du dressoir à un coing, il
y avoit une petite tablette basse, là
où l'on mettoit les pots & tasses
pour donner à boire à ceux qui
venoient veoir Madame, après
190 qu'on leur avoit donné de la dra-
gée; mais le drageoir estoit sur le
dressoir.

Item, en laditte chambre y avoit
tousjours grand feu, mais cela se
195 fait selon le temps, car ce n'est
point d'état.

La chambre de l'enfant (qui estoit Madamoiselle Marie de Bourgongne, depuis Duchesse d'Aus-
200 triche) estoit pareillement à deux
grands licts, & le bers où elle couchoit estoit devant le feu, & n'y
avoit point de couchette; & estoient les deux grands licts tendus
205 de drap de damas verd & violet,
& les courtines de pareil couleur,
& estoient de samyt: & estoit
le ciel si long, qu'il couvroit les
deux licts: mais il n'y avoit nulles
210 traversaines, & estoient les licts
couverts de pareil de la chambre,
qui estoit tendue de sayette verde
& vermeille.

Il y avoit dessus le bers un pa-
215 villon de damas verd & violet,
comme le ciel de grands licts, &
les courtines de mesme, à sçavoir
de samyt.

Le bers estoit couvert d'ermines
220 arminées traînantes à terre, & un
fin drap de crespe dessus, & tout au
tour tapis velus; & entre les deux

grands licts une chaire couverte de
mesme.

225   Item, devant laditte chambre de
madite Dame, avoit une grande
chambre, de laquelle on entroit
dans la chambre de Madame, &
estoit ceste chambre appellée la
230   chambre de parement, laquelle estoit parée, comme s'ensuit.

En ladicte chambre avoit seulement un grand lict, lequel estoit
tendu de satin cramoisy tout au
235   tour, & le couvertoir de mesme, &
avoit au ciel un autre couvertoir,
en chacun piece un grand soleil
aussy grand que le tapis brodé de
fin or moult riche, & estoit appel-
240   lée cette tapisserie, la Chambre
d'Utrecht, & crois que ceux d'U-
trecht la donnerent au Ducq Philippe. Les tapis d'autour la chambre estoient de soye rouge, à ce
245   que j'ai retenu, les courtines de
samyt cramoisy, & estoient trous-
sées, & le lict fait & couvert du
couvertoir, comme un lict où nully
ne couche : à un bout du chevet
250   il y avoit un grand carreau de drap
d'or cramoisy, item autour du lict,
tant aux pieds, qu'au chevet, un
fort grand tapis velus.

Au bout de la chambre loing du
255   lict y avoit un grand dressoir à trois
dégrez, fort hault & large, tout
chargé de grands flacons & pots
& autres vaisselles d'argent doré &
tasses & drageoirs ; ledit dressoir
260   couvert de nappe sur les degrez &
autour, comme il appartient.

Au chevet y avoit une petite
chaise couverte de velours, comme
sont celles où Princesses s'assis-
265   sent souvent, & un carreau de
drap d'or dedans ; mais il n'y avoit
en cette chambre qu'un seul lict,
comme dessus est dict.

268a Baptesme de Mademoiselle Marie

268b   de Bourgongne.

Madame de Charrolois sa
270   mere accoucha d'elle en la ville de
Bruxelles la nuit de S. Valent l'an
M. CD. LVI. estant adonc le Ducq
Philippe en une autre ville ; mais
Madame la Duchesse Isabelle &
275   Monsieur de Charrolois, pere de
madite Damoiselle Marie, estoient
tous deux pour l'heure à Bruxelles,
& s'y y estoit Monsieur le Dauphin, comme j'ay dit ci-devant.

280   Est à sçavoir qu'au jour de la
nativité l'on fit audit Bruxelles
grandes festes de feu, & de sonner
les cloches & autres grands signes
de joye, & ainsy fit-on ès autres
285   pays subjets à mondit Seigneur,
quand ils furent advertis de ladicte
nativité.

Ceux de la ville de Bruxelles
baillerent quatre cent torches ;
290   Monsieur de Charrolois en fit faire
deux cent, ainsy furent DC. en
tout, & pesoit chacune quatre ou
cinq livres.

Item, ledit baptesme se fit à Co-
295   berghe, pour ce que S. Goulde
est trop loing de l'hostel de mondit Seigneur, & y avoit des bailles
faictes depuis la moitié des grez
de la salle à deux costez jusques à
300   l'huis de l'Eglise de Coberghe, &
estoient si larges, qu'il y pouvoit
bien aller entre deux six ou sept
personnes de front.

Item, les torches que ceux de
305   Bruxelles avoient baillé, furent
portées par leurs gens, tous ha-
billés d'une livrée, & estoient mis
à deux costez des bailles, & estoient
arrangez tant que les derniers ve-
310   noient à l'huis de l'Eglise, & ne
se bougeoeint lesdittes torches,
car le chemin est trop court de
l'hostel de Monsieur jusques à Coberghe. Dedans l'Eglise y en avoit

315 cent que Monsieur avoit faict faire,
& estoient arangées en la nef de
l'Eglise, & les portoient les offi-
ciers de l'hostel qui pareillement
ne se bougeoient.

320 Item, les autres cent torches que
mondit Seigneur avoit fait faire
porterent tous gentilhommes de
l'hostel, chacun bien en point, &
allerent tousjours devant l'enfant,

325 par le milieu des bailles, tant au
aller qu'au revenir, & pareillement
dedans l'Eglise.

Item, toute l'Eglise estoit tendue, & par especial la nef, de ta-

330 pisserie fort riche: & droit devant
le grand Autel estoit fait un font,
& y avoit un bassin d'argent mis
sur un bois aussy hault qu'un font,
& rond & gros comme en façon

335 d'une tour.

Lequel font estoit tout autour
couvert & environné de drap d'or
cramoisy & dessus un pavillon rond
de samyt verd, & estoit ledit pa-

340 villon rollé à mont tout autour,
bien trois ou quatre pieds plus hault
que la teste des gens: dessus les
bords des fonds avoit un bien fin
doublier, afin que l'on ne vit point

345 le bois.

Item, ledit font estoit clos à une
clef, jusques à tant que Monsieur
l'Evêque de Cambray vînt, à qui
la clef fut baillée, & celuy qui en

350 avoit eu la charge au paravant, en
fit l'essay, en baillant la clef à Monseigneur de Cambray qui baptisa
maditte Damoiselle.

En la chapelle auprès du choeur

355 de l'Eglise estoit fait un lict de carreaux de drap d'or, & est à sçavoir
que c'estoit une table quarrée sur
deux tretteaux haults comme un lict.
Dessus cette table avoit un beau

360 fin drap de toillette de Hollande, &
dessus ce drap avoit un couvertoir
de drap violet fourré d'ermines

arminées, & passoit le drap violet
une demie aulne la pane, & estoit

365 ledit couvertoir mis sur ladicte table
tout estendu, & traînoit tout autour bien une aulne, & estoit mise
la panne dehors, comme aux licts,
& par-dessus un beau fin drap de

370 crespe empesé, & dessus tout avoit
deux carreaux de drap d'or cramoisy, l'un au chevet & l'autre plus
bas, comme on fait un lict.

Item, dessus ledit lict estoit ten-

375 du un pavillon verd quarré aussy
grand que la table, & estoient les
courtines roullées devant: & estoit
le dessus du pavillon de satin verd
& les courtines de samyt.

380 Item, tout autour estoient tapis
velus, & la Chapelle estoit toute
tendue autour comme l'Eglise.

Madame la Duchesse de Bourgongne, grand-mere de l'enfant,

385 l'apporta aux fonts, & l'addrextra
Monsieur le Dauphin luy seul, &
ouy lors dire à ceux qui s'y cognois-
soient que Monsieur le Dauphin
addrextroit seul l'enfant, pour ce

390 qu'on n'eust sceu trouver son pareil pour l'addrextrer à l'un des costez de Madame, lequel honneur
estoit fort grand, comme j'ouys
dire.

395 Madame la Duchesse avoit pour
ce jour vestu une robbe toutte
ronde, car dez lors elle ne portoit ne queue de drap de soye, aussy
je n'ay pas retenu que nul luy porta

400 sa queue.

Madame de Ravestein (niepce
de Madame la Duchesse & fille du
Duc de Coimbre, laquelle avoit
espousé M. Adolphe de Cleves,

405 nepveu de Monsieur le Ducq Philippe) porta la queue de manteau
où l'enfant estoit enveloppé, &
l'addrextroit Monsieur le bastard de
Bourgongne, & la queue de la

410 robbe de maditte Dame de Raves-

tein estoit troussée & nulluy ne
la portoit, & estoit maditte Dame
de Ravestein vestue de drap d'or
bleu fourré d'ermines arminées.

415   Monsieur d'Estampes, frere de
Monsieur de Nevers, cousin ger-
main du Ducq Philippe, porta le
cierge devant l'enfant, & Monsieur de Ravestein, fils du Ducq

420   de Cleves, & neveu du Ducq Philippe, porta le sel en une couppe
couverte, & Monsieur de Geldres,
fils seul du Duc de Geldres, porta
les bassins couverts, comme il est

425   de coustume. J'ouys lors dire qu'on
luy faisoit tort, qu'il n'alloit devant Monsieur de Ravestein, mais
parce que Monsieur de Ravestein
éstoit son oncle, & qu'il estoit

430   beaucoup plus ancien, on le fit
ainsy. Et est à sçavoir que le cierge
& puis le sel, sont les plus hon-
norables à porter.

       En cest estat fut porté & rap-
435   porté l'enfant, lequel fut prins en
la chambre de parement & fut
rapporté en la chambre de Madame
de Charrolois couchée en son grand
lict, lequel estoit à la droite main,

440   paré comme cy-dessus s'est dit: &
touttes les Dames & Damoiselles
Seigneurs & Gentilhommes y en-
trerent, jusques la chambre fut
plaine.

445   Et là, quand Madame la Duchesse fut deschargée de l'enfant
(lequel fut baillé a la nourrice par
Madame de Berzé qui en avoit le
gouvernement), Madame la Du-

450   chesse vint dehors les courtines,
là où elle & Monsieur le Dauphin
avoient présenté à Madame de
Charrolois son enfant. Et lors elle
allat au dressoir, là où celle qui

455   le gardoit luy bailla le drageoir
garny d'espices, comme il appartient, & quand Madame l'eust en
la main, elle leva la serviette, dont

il estoit couvert, & en bailla l'es-
460   say à celle qui estoit au dressoir.

       Et lors Madame vint àtout le
drageoir devers Monsieur le Dauphin, & s'agenouilla & fit l'essay,
& présenta les espices à Monsieur

465   le Dauphin, lequel fit grande dif-
ficulté de les prendre d'elle, touttes
fois il le fit; & Madame de Ravestein le servit du goublet, comme il appartient: & lors l'on servit

470   tous les Seigneurs & Dames & Damoiselles, comme il appartient.

       Mais bien est à sçavoir que quand
Madame la Duchesse eust servy
Monsieur le Dauphin d'espices,

475   l'une des Dames print le drageoir
des mains de Madame, & en servit Monseigneur d'Estampes & aultres Princes qui estoient-là, & puis
l'une des plus grandes Damoiselles

480   print le drageoir & en servit touttes les autres Dames & Damoiselles, qui estoient là venues au
mandement de Monsieur & de
Madame.

485   Le mois durant tous ceux & celles
qui venoient vers Madame, quand
ils avoient prins congé d'elle, &
qu'ils estoient esloignez du lict où
elle couchoit, on leur bailloit de

490   la dragerie & de l'hypocras, & ser-
voit-on aux Seigneurs, Dames &
Damoiselles, selon qu'ils estoient
grands personnages.

Baptesme de Monsieur Philippe
495   d'Austriche Archiducq.

Le Baptesme de Monsieur Philippe à présent fils de Monseigneur
le Ducq d'Austriche & de Madame Marie Duchesse de Bourgon-

500   gne, fut assez tel que celuy de
Madame sa mere, sinon que depuis la maison de Monsieur à Bruges jusques dedans l'Eglise S. Donas on alloit tous sur hourts faits

505 selon la rue & au travers du marché : lesdits hourts estoient de la haulteur d'un homme & clos de drapperie & bois tout du long ; & y

510 montoit-on à degrez qui estoient à l'entrée de la porte de la Cour & si estoit toute la Cour tendue de tapisseries. Les rues par où on portoit l'enfant jusques à S. Donas estoient tendues & fort jolloyées ;

515 car chacun s'estoit mis en peine de faire son debvoir devant sa maison.

Il y avoit un grand & large hourt sur lequel les fonts estoient faits, afin que le peuple le vist, & le

520 hourt sur lequel on venoit en apportant l'enfant joindoit à cestuy-là, & du surplus en fut fait comme cy-devant est escript du baptesme de Madame sa mere.

525 Item, la chambre de maditte Dame estoit tendue autour de samyt verd, & celle de Madame de Charrolois sa mere n'estoit tendue que de saye verde autour, mais les

530 licts estoient tout un de toutte chose, excepté que ceux de Madame dessus les ermines estoient couverts de draps de crespe fort fin empesé, & ceux de Madame sa fille

535 l'estoient de violet de soye ; mais au regard de cela il n'y a point d'estat, ce qu'on y met n'est que plaisir, car il faut tousjours qu'il y en ait ou d'un ou d'autre.

540 Madame de Charrolois n'avoit que quatre degrez sur son dressoir, & Madame la Duchesse sa fille en avoit cinq. Touttes fois Madame de Charrolois fit tout tel estat dans

545 sa gesine, que fit Madame la Duchesse de Bourgongne sa belle-mere du Ducq Charles son fils, pere de Madame d'Austriche : & touttes fois j'ay maintes fois ouy dire à

550 Madame la Duchesse Isabelle, & à plusieurs autres qui sçavoient des honneurs de France, que nulles

Princesses ne debvoient avoir cinq degrez, fors seulement la Royne

555 de France. Depuis les choses sont changées en plusieurs lieux, comme l'on voit journellement ; mais cela ne peut déroger, ny abolir les anciens honneurs & estats que

560 sont faits & ordonnez par bonne raison & délibération.

J'ay ou dire à Madame la Duchesse Isabelle du temps que Madame de Charrolois accoucha de

565 Madame d'Autriche, que nulles Princesses ne debvoient avoir la chambre de soye verde autour, fors la Royne seulement ; & est à croire que Madame la Duchesse Isabelle

570 avoit fait faire à Madame sa fille comme il appartenoit : car elle & Monsieur le Ducq Philippe avoient courage & biens assez pour ce faire, comme chacun sçayt, mais elle

575 vouloit que Madame sa fille fit comme elle avoit fait ez gesines de Messieurs ses enfans selon les estats de France, & ay maintes fois ouy racompter que toutte la tenture

580 du lict doict estre de damas, & les courtines de samyt, comme cy-devant est escript.

J'ay ouy dire à Madame ma mere que Madame de Namur disoit à la

585 Duchesse Isabelle que les Roynes de France souloient gesir tout en blancq ; mais que la mere du Roy Charles, grand-pere de cestuy à présent, print à gésir en verd, &

590 depuis toutes l'ont fait. Maditte Dame de Namur, comme plusieurs fois j'ay ouy dire, avoit un grand livre en quoy estoit escripts tous les estats de France, & tousjours

595 par son advis la Duchesse Isabelle faisoit touchant ces choses. Car les estats de Portugal & ceux de France ne sont pas tout un.

Comme les Comtesses & autres grandes

600　　　　　Dames doivent gesir.

Plusieurs Comtesses peuvent
gesir à deux grands licts, mais ils
ne doivent estre couverts que de
menu vair, & sy peut avoir cou-
605　chette devant le feu, mais elles ne
doivent point avoir la chambre
verte, comme la Royne & grandes Princesses ont.

J'ay veu gesir plusieurs grandes
610　Dames à la Cour, comme Madame
la Vicedamesse d'Amiens & aultres,
mais elles n'avoient qu'un grand
lict, & deux couchettes, dont
l'une estoit à un cornet de la cham-
615　bre, & l'autre devant le feu, &
pavillon de soye, & le grand lict
& la chambre tendue d'herbages ou
de personnages, comme les tapisseries estoient, mais tousjours les
620　courtines estoient de soye, quand
on le pouvoit avoir, & le grand
lict & les couchettes estoient tous
couverts de menu vair, & dessus
fin drap de crespe empesé, & traî-
625　noient le couvertoir & les draps
bien une aulne autour; & est à sçavoir que les couvertoirs sont de drap
violet fourré dessus de menu vair,
& la panne passe le drap bien demy
630　aulne tout autour, & quand on
couvre le lict, il faut tousjours que
la panne soit dehors, & si fault que
le menu vair soit du long du couvertoir le poil allant envers les pieds,
635　& fault que quand le couvertoir est
mis sur le lict, que le menu vair
traîne avecq le drap bien demie
aulne autour du lict, & sy faut-il
que le drap de dessus soit aussy
640　long.

Item, le dressoir doit estre de trois
degrez, & chargé de vaisselles,
comme de pots, flaccons, & gros-
ses couppes, & sur le large du dres-
645　soir doit aussy avoir pots, couppes,
drageoirs & aussy deux chandeliers

d'argent, où il doit avoir deux
grands flambeaux de cire pour faire
ardoir, quand quelqu'un vient à la
650　chambre, & y doit tousjours avoir
deux torches devant le dressoir,
pour pareillement faire ardoir,
quand il est mestier.

Item, la chambre doit estre toutte
655　tapissée embas de tapis velus, aussy
plaine qu'on la peut mettre jusques
à l'entrée de l'huys.

Item, sur le grand lict & sur les
couchettes doit avoir sur le chevet
660　petits quarreaux de drap de soye
ou de velour, ou de brodure; à
sçavoir, sur le grand lict deux, à
l'un des bouts du chevet l'un, &
à l'autre bout l'autre, & sur le che-
665　vet des couchettes à chacun un,
au milieu du chevet, & susfit d'autant pour les couchettes.

Item, sur le dressoir doit avoir
un dosseret de velour, comme le
670　ciel d'un lict, ainsy que devant est
mis par escript; & fault que ledit
dosseret soit de velour, ou d'autre
soye; & sy est à sçavoir que celles
qui ont les deux couchettes peu-
675　vent bien avoir le dosseret de velour sur velour.

Item, j'ay ouy dire que nulles ne
doivent avoir le dosseret bordé d'autre couleur, n'est que ce sont grandes
680　Princesses.

Item, en la chambre des Dames
susdittes doit avoir une chaire à
doz emprez le chevet du lict, couverte de velours ou d'autre drap de
685　soye, ne chault de quelle couleur
il soit; mais le velour est le plus
honorable qui le peut recouvrer.
Et au plus prez de la chaire y aurat
place où l'on peut mettre un petit
690　banc sans appois, couvert d'un
banquier, & des quarreaux de soye
ou autres pour s'asseoir quand on
vient veoir l'accouchée.

Item, les deux drageoirs, qui

695 sont sur le dressoir doivent estre
plains de dragerie, & couverts de
deux serviettes fines, & faut qu'ils
soient l'un à un bout du dressoir,
& l'autre à l'autre.

700   Item, les Dames de bannieres
grandes ont en leur gesine le grand
lict, & une couchette à un coing
de la chambre, & tout ainsy tendus & ordonnez, comme cy-des-
705 sus est escript; & n'y a rien de dif-
férent, sinon qu'elles n'ont point
de couchette devant le feu.

    Touttes fois depuis dix ans ença,
aucunes Dames du pays de Flan-
710 dres ont mis la couche devant le
feu, dequoy l'on s'est bien mocqué,
car du temps de Madame Isabelle
de Portugal, nulles du pays de
Flandres ne le faisoient: mais un
715 chacun fait à cette heure à sa guise:
par quoy est à doubter que tout irat
mal, car les estats sont trop grants,
comme chacun scayt & dit.

    Item, en la chambre d'une gi-
720 sante (quelque grande Dame ou
Princesse que ce soit) nuls ne doivent servir d'espices, ne du vin,
que femmes, quand le plus grand
maistre du monde les viendroit
725 veoir, & pareillement en touttes
autres gesines de Dames ou Damoiselles.

    Mais si quelque Princesse vient
voir une gisante, l'on doit tous-
730 jours présenter à sa premiere femme, soit Dame ou Damoiselle, de
porter le drageoir à sa Maistresse;
au cas toutte fois que la gisante
n'ayt nulle de meilleur lieu, que
735 celle qui suit la grande Dame ou
Princesse qu'est venue veoir la gisante, car si elle en avoit une de
meilleur lieu, elle le pourroit faire
sans reprinse.

740   Item, à touttes Dames qui gisent
doibt tousjours avoir une petite
tablette du costé du dressoir là où

les pots, où est l'hypocras & le vin,
& les tasses de quoy l'on donne à
745 boire, sans les prendre du grand
dressoir, & s'y doibt estre couverte
ladicte table d'une belle nappe.

La Chambre des Enfans de telles
Dames pour le jour du Baptesme.

750   L'enfant doibt estre apporté en
une chambre, & doibt estre le
bers tendu d'un pavillon quarré ou
rond comme le pavillon que l'on
mect sur la couchette & doibt estre
755 de soye ou saye: mais la soye est
plus honnorable & plus riche;
touttes fois l'on en a bien veu de
toille blanche, pour monstrer l'estat de celles qui n'avoient point
760 puissance de l'avoir de soye ne de
saye.

    Il fault que le bers soit couvert
de menu vair comme sont les licts,
mais ne le fault point plus grand
765 que le bers n'est, & si il passe les
bords du bers de chacun costé
quartier & demy, il suffit, car il
ne fault point qu'il pende jusques
à terre.

770   Item, il fault que ce soit un
hault bers, pendant à anneaux de
fers entre deux bois, comme l'on
fait de coustume.

    Item, il faut que devant le bers
775 soit estendu un tapis velu, & ne
fault point de drap sur le bers, sinon
le couvertoir de menu vair, de quoy
l'enfant est couvert: mais l'on mect
bien un beau fin couvre-chef devant
780 la bouche de l'enfant, qui vient
sur le couvertoir une paulme ou
un quartier.

    Item, en la chambre de l'enfant
doibt avoir un grand lict tendu
785 de ce qu'on fait des tapisseries ou
saye: & le jour du baptesme on
doibt mettre l'enfant sur le lict,
& ne doibt estre le lict couvert si-

T

790 non du couvertoir tel qu'à la tapisserie de la chambre : là le prend
celle qui le doibt porter au baptesme, mais le bers doibt estre
paré comme cy-dessus est escript.

795 Si il y a une chambre devant la
chambre de la gisante qui soit tendue, comme il appartient, l'on
peut là mettre l'enfant sur le lict :
& puis après revenu de baptesme
le porter en celle où le bers est,
800 mais tousjours faut-il que quand
on le rapporte du baptesme on le
porte à la gisante, & delà on le
porte en sa chambre.

805 Comment le Baptesme des Enfans de
telles Dames, ou Damoiselles
de tel estat se doit faire.

L'enfant doit estre enveloppé
en un manteau de velour de quelque couleur qu'on veut, & faut
810 qu'il aye du moins trois aulnes de
long, mais la largeur de velour y
suffit, & faut qu'il soit tout fourré
de menu vair, & quand l'enfant est
enveloppé dans le velour, il fault
815 mettre par dessus l'enfant (quand
celle qui le doibt porter l'a sur les
bras) un long couvre-chef de soye
violet, qui voise de la teste de l'enfant jusques à la terre, & du costé
820 des pieds aussy long que le manteau ou plus.
Item, celle qui le porte doibt
estre addextrée des Chevaliers ou
Gentilhommes de bon lieu, &
825 doibt avoir une Damoiselle qui
porte la queue du manteau de l'enfant.
A la Cour nulles ne faisoient
porter la queue du manteau des
830 enfans par femmes que les Princesses ; mais les Dames Baronnesses
en leur maison le peuvent faire,
comme j'aye veu : & celles qui
demeuroient à la Cour les faisoient

835 porter par l'un de ceux qui les
addextroient, & mettoient la queue
sur leur bras.
Item, il faut avoir trois Gentilhommes pour porter le cierge,
840 le seel & les bassins devant l'enfant.
Le plus noble doit porter le cierge,
& doit avoir une piece d'or dedans, & cestuy-là vat le plus prez
de l'enfant : droit devant luy vat
845 celuy qui porte le seel, & doibt
estre mis le sel en une couppe, où
est un goblet couvert ; & droit
avant cestuy-là, doibt aller cestuy
qui porte les bassins d'argent, dont
850 cestuy de dessoubz doibt avoir un
bibeton, comme un aiguiere & y
doibt avoir de l'eau de roses, &
de l'autre bassin l'on couvre cestuy-
là : & quand l'on baille à laver aux
855 fonts, on verse du bassin qui at le
bibeton en l'autre, & n'y at point
d'autres aiguieres.
Item, il faut que ces Gentilhommes qui portent ce que dessus
860 est dit, ayent chacun une longue
serviette au col toutte ployée,
comme d'une paulme de large, &
faut que les deux bouts de la serviette pendent devant, & que de
865 l'un des bouts, ils tiennent ce qu'ils
portent.
Item, telles Dames en leur mesnage peuvent avoir au baptesme
de leurs enfants quarante ou cin-
870 quante torces : mais à la cour des
Dames Baronnesses n'en avoient
que trente-six du tems de la Duchesse Isabelle.
Item, il faut que ceux qui por-
875 tent les torces, voissent deux à
deux devant l'enfant.

Comment les Fonts & les Eglises
doivent estre ordonnées pour les
Enfans de telles Dames

880 Le Portail, où l'on commence

l'office du baptesme, doit estre
tendu de tapisserie; & sy le font
est en une chapelle, elle doit estre
tendue tout autour, & s'il ny at
885 chapelle, sy doibt-on mettre tapisserie là où sont les fonts.

Item, la pierre des fonts, jusques à terre tout autour doibt
estre couverte de velour, & des-
890 sus les bords du font tout autour
un beau doublier, & dessus les
fonts il ne doit rien avoir de tendu, car cela est pour les Princesses.

Item, il y doibt avoir une cha-
895 pelle toutte tendue, & là doibt
avoir une table carrée, comme un
lict, & dessus un couvertoir de
menu vair, & par dessus le menu
vair un drap de crespe, & la-dessus
900 des oreillers ou quarreaux de drap
de soye pour desmaillotter & ren-
velopper l'enfant.

Item, la Sage-femme & la Ma-
rainne doibvent venir à l'Eglise
905 avec la Damoiselle servante de
Dame, & doibt la Sage-femme
porter le cresmeau, & le bailler
quand le Prebstre le demande aussy, s'il y at quelque Prélat qui
910 veuille faire cet honneur à l'enfant
que de le baptiser, bien le peut
faire sans reprinse, mais qu'il ne
soit compere, car autrement ce se-
roit trop grand estat.

915 A la relevée de touttes Princesses,
Dames d'Estat, & Banneresses, ne
doit avoir guaires de gens, & se
doibt faire bien matin selon les
lieux là où on est, & selond la cous-
920 tume des Eveschez, & se doibt
faire dans l'hostel sans aller à l'E-
glise.

Les Princesses le font selon la
coustume de la Cour, qui est toutte
925 telle que les autres, excepté qu'à
l'offrande l'accouchée offre une
chandelle & une piece d'or ou
d'argent dedans, & un pain enve-

930 loppé dans une serviette, & un pot
plain de vin, & ces trois offrandes,
portent trois femmes après elle: &
quand l'accouchée est à genouil
devant le Prestre pour offrir, chas-
935 cune des trois femmes lui baille ce
qu'elle a apporté, & à chascune
fois l'accouchée baise la paix que
le Prestre tient: & aux Princesses
l'on baise ce qu'on leur baille, &
aux aultres point.

940 Du temps passé les Princesses
estoient assises sur le lict, fort pa-
rées & ornées richement, & delà les prenoient Princes ou Chevaliers, & Trompettes & Menes-
945 triers les menoient en la Chapelle
relever, comme si ce fussent esté
espousées: & le fit la Duchesse
Isabelle de son premier enfant,
comme j'ay ouy dire; mais depuis
950 point: & aussy il me semble que le
moins de feste, & le plus simple-
ment est le plus honest pour ce
jour: quand le lendemain on en
debvroit plus faire; touttes fois
955 c'est une joye pour ceux à qui il
touche, & peut-on faire chere
raisonable selon l'estat de chacun.

Des Dames de plus petit estat pour
leur Gesine & Baptesine
960 de l'Enfant.

Un Banneret qui a trois ou quatre fils, ils ne peuvent tous estre
Bannerets: ainsy un maisné peut
faire avoir à sa femme en sa gésine
965 deux degrez sur son dressoir, ou un,
selon les lieux dont ils sont.

Aussy un quy est fort noble de
tous cotez le peut faire pareillement & avoir la chambre tapissée
970 & les licts, comme des autres
Dames, mais l'Eglise point tendue,
sinon le poriet & les fonts.

Aultres nobles Dames ont un
degré sur le dressoir, & le lict cou-

975 vert de menu vair, & leur couchette à un coing de la chambre, sans
rien avoir tendu, ny autour, &
leur chambre tapissée à demy.
    Aultres femmes qui sont de quel-
980 que estat, nobles femmes de bon
lieu, peuvent avoir le dressoir chargé de vaisselle, & leur lict & couchette du menu vair; aucunes
n'ont point de couchettes couver-
985 tes, & n'ont qu'un tapis devant le
lict, sans plus.
    Et les fonts pour celles-là ne
sont de rien tendus, sinon d'une
nappe autour pour le bord des fonts;
990 mais pour les autres Dames dessus
nommez, peuvent estre tendus de
tapisseries ou de satin, ou de damas, selon qu'on les cognoit, &
toujours un fin doublier sur le bord
995 des fonts tout autour.
    Des torces, on les fait selon
l'estat de la chambre, à sçavoir

l'une XL, l'autre XXX, XX, XII, VIII,
VI, chacune selon son degré.
1000   Nulles debvoient avoir chambre ne bers paré pour l'enfant, que
celles qui ont trois dégrez sur le
dressoir: & celles de deux, à grande
paine; & de plus bas, rien, sinon
1005 que l'enfant peut estre mis pour ce
jour en lict en une chambre; &
de celles de plus petit estat qui
est icy escript, l'enfant doibt estre
en leur chambre sur la couche, &
1010 là le doit-on rapporter du baptesme sans le porter autre part, &
tousjours la Nourrice emprez.
    Item, touttes Dames & Da-
moiselles qui tiennent ces enfans,
1015 & pareillement celles qui sont au
baptesme, & par especial les mar-
rines doivent faire donner par leur
premiere femme à la nourrice une
piece d'or, les unes plus, les autres
1020 moings, selon que les gens sont.

(c) FREE TRANSLATION AND REARRANGEMENT OF PART OF ALIENOR DE POITIERS'S TREATISE, LES HONNEURS DE LA COUR

lines in text
(Appendix VIII (b))

Isabelle of Bourbon, wife of the Count of   4–8
Charolais was delivered of her daughter Marie at Brussels [in 1456].   22–4
The Duke and Duchess of Burgundy [Philip the Good and Isabelle of
Portugal] wished that everything should be done for the birth of the child of
their son and daughter-in-law according to the rules of estate of France.   571–8
The French rules and those of Portugal were not the same,   597–8
so Isabelle of Portugal consulted a large book belonging to the Countess of
Namur in which were set out all the rules of the French court regarding
matters of estate. In matters of this kind, Isabelle of Portugal was always
guided by this book.[680]   590–6

For the birth, the furnishings of three chambers are described:

the *Chambre de Parement*, the *Chambre de Madame*   230, 27
and the *Chambre de l'enfant*.   197

---

[680] It appears that the Duke and Duchess of Burgundy normally took charge of arrangements for the birth of grandchildren. Margaret of Flanders, wife of Philip the Bold, did so for her daughter-in-law, the Countess de Rethel, in 1403. The total cost of the lavishly conceived furnishings (4,923 *frs*. 15*s*. 10*d*.), which had been ordered by the Duchess, was borne by the Duke and not by the child's parents. (See an extract of the account, pp. 96–8.) The Countess concerned was Jeanne of Luxembourg; she married Anthony, second son of the Duke and Duchess of Burgundy, b. 1381, died at Agincourt.

The *Chambre de Parement* was connected with the *Chambre de Madame*, [and
the latter could not be entered without first passing through the former.]   225–30
[The *Chambre de Parement*, or *Chambre de Parade* later became the State
Bedchamber.]
The *Chambre de Madame* was where Isabelle of Bourbon lay,   434–9
and the Infant's Chamber contained the cradle of estate.[681]   197–201

Chambre de Parement
This chamber was large, with hangings   225–30
round the walls of red silk, and with a   243–4
single large bed   232–3
whose bedclothes and hangings were ordered as was customary for beds
which were not used for sleeping upon.   247–9
The bed had curtains all round and a coverlet, all of matching satin.   234–5
Above the bed was a canopy [colour], made of fine and   236
exceedingly rich embroidery, and each piece [curtains, coverlet and celour]
was worked overall with a great sun. These hangings were called the
Chambre d'Utrecht, and I think that they were given to Duke Philip by the
people of that town.   239–43
Upon the bed, at the head end, was a large cushion of cloth of gold,   249–51
and about the bed, at the foot and at the head, was a very large carpet.   251–3
Standing beside the head of the bed was a small chair covered with *veloux*,
like the chairs which are often used by princesses, and upon it was a cushion
covered with cloth of gold.   262–6
At the end of the chamber, far from the bed, stood a very large, high,
buffet. It had 3 stages and each stage,   254–6
as well as the whole buffet, was covered with linen.   259–61
Upon the stages were ranged many large pieces of precious plate, including
spice plates (*drageoirs*).   257–9
The *Chambre de Madame* (Isabelle of Bourbon's Chamber).
This was a large room; there was always a large fire [lighted], according to
the weather, & having nothing to do with degrees of estate; the walls were
hung around   27–8, 193–6
with nothing but green silk and the floor was completely covered with a
carpet right up to the door.   99–103
There were 2 large beds standing near one another with an alley between
them about 4 or 5 feet wide.   27–32
The beds were arranged to be used for sleeping.   119–21
Above the beds was a single great canopy of green *damas* which covered
both beds entirely, as well as the alley between them, and its pelmet was
fringed with green silk.   43–6, 55
Around the two beds hung curtains of green half satin which were
suspended from the canopy but did not reach the floor; they stopped short
of the alley both at the head end and at the foot of the beds.   46–53
For the alley between the beds, three separate curtains of matching cloth
were provided called *traversaines*.   58, 78–9

---

[681] In contexts of this kind, 2 cradles were required, as has been shown. The description given by Alienor
de Poitiers for the single cradle which she mentions (canopy over cradle, and cover of ermine) indicates that she
is concerned only with the state cradle. See discussion of cradles, pp. 93 ff.

The queen of France had a fourth curtain of this kind which hung across the chamber, but neither Isabelle of Portugal nor Isabelle of Bourbon, her daughter-in-law, had more than three.[682]   80–5

The two *traversaine* curtains at the foot of the beds were longer than the other bed curtains, and were hung from the canopy upon rings, enabling them to be drawn back and forth at will, so that the alley was open or closed. In the day time, it was kept open.   56–70

The third *traversaine* curtain closing the alley at the head end of the beds was permanently caught up and never fell straight.   71–7

In the alley at the head of the beds stood a large chair with a high back, like the large chairs of earlier times, and   33–7

the third *traversaine* curtain was draped above its high back.   74–6

The chair itself was covered with cloth of gold from top to bottom and had a cushion of the same cloth.   129–33

On both beds were covers of ermine skins lying on a fine violet cloth, and both the ermine and the violet cloth reached fully to the ground and trailed along it for a yard and a half.   104–13

Beneath these covers was a beautifully fine gauzy sheet completely covered by the ermine and violet coverlets on the beds themselves, but showing on the floor, for the sheet was longer than the coverlets and trailed on the floor beyond the violet and ermine.   114–17, 119–23

The head of each bed was covered with *crespe*   124–5

and each had a large bolster.   125–9

In front of the fire stood a low couch on castors, like the couches which are stowed beneath other beds.   38–42

It was arranged to be used for sleeping.   117–21

The couch was equipped with covers of ermine and violet and with sheets matching those of the large beds.   104–6, 117–19

Over the couch was a square canopy (*pavillon*) of green *damas* which was as large as the couch itself [whole celour] and hanging from the canopy were curtains of green satin which could be raised on either side.   87–98

There was a large buffet (*dressoir*) with 4 stages [stepped shelves] stretching the full length of the buffet. The stages were covered with linen and bore quantities of precious plate, including vessels of solid gold, vessels set with jewels and all the richest vessels owned by Duke Philip. There were three spice plates of gold set with jewels; one was valued at 40,000 *écus* and another at 30,000 *écus*.   134–51

The buffet had a *dorseret*. A *dorseret* was like the canopy over a bed, except that it did not extend over the buffet for more than $\frac{1}{4}$–$\frac{1}{2}$ a yard's depth; it hung behind the buffet from top to bottom. Both the canopy part and the

---

[682] Clearly, Alienor de Poitiers considered this was a matter of estate. However, in 1403, the daughter-in-law of the Duke and Duchess of Burgundy, Jeanne of Luxembourg, married to Anthony, their second son, had a *traversaine* dividing the chamber itself: '... la courtine ... au travers de la chambre ...' see Garnier, 606. The question of the curtain across the chamber, associated with the bed (we are told it was one of the bedcurtains called *traversaines*) is one of considerable significance in view of later developments. I suggest that this curtain was the forerunner of the balustrade used to define the bed area in seventeenth-century (and later) French palaces. Like the curtain across the room, the balustrade was a royal privilege reserved for princes of the blood and dukes. See H. Murray Baillie, 'Etiquette and the Planning of the State Apartments in Baroque Palaces', *Archaeologia*, CI, 1967, 186–7.

back had borders on each side of different cloth, which had to be about ¼ of
the width. The whole *dorseret* was of cloth of gold and had a fringed pelmet;
the border was of black *velour* embroidered in gold with the gun (*fusil*), the
heraldic device of Duke Philip.   152–75

Upon the buffet were two silver candlesticks which were permanently lit,
for a full fifteen days had to elapse [after the birth] before the shutters were
opened.   176–84

In a corner of the room, near the buffet, was a little low table. Here were
placed the jugs and drinking cups for serving those who visited the Countess,
after they had first partaken of the delicacies in the spice plates kept on the
buffet.   185–92

The Infant's Chamber. (*Chambre de l'enfant*)
The walls were hung with green and vermilion *sayette*, and there was a fire
in the room.   212–13, 202
There were no couches in the room but there   203
were two large beds, having a single canopy large enough to extend fully
over both. The canopy was of green and violet *damas*, the curtains of
matching samite and the bed covers were of green and vermilion *sayette*, to
match the wall hangings. The beds had curtains, as has been stated, but no
travorsaines   197–213
Between the beds was a chair covered to match.   222–4
The cradle, where the baby lay, was in front of the fire.   201–2
Above it was a canopy like that above large beds, of green and violet *damas*,
with curtains of samite, and the cradle had a covering   214–18
of fine *crespe*   220–21
and one of ermine which reached the ground and trailed upon it.   219–20
A carpet lay all round the cradle.   221–2

SHORT NOTE COMPARING THE ARRANGEMENTS MADE FOR MARIE OF BURGUNDY AT THE TIME OF THE BIRTH OF PHILIP THE FAIR AT BRUGES (1478) WITH THOSE OF HER MOTHER, ISABELLE OF BOURBON

The chamber of Marie of Burgundy was hung all round with green samite,
whereas her mother's was hung with green *saye*. However, the beds were the
same in all particulars, except that Marie of Burgundy's bed had violet silk
below the ermine cover whereas her mother's had fine *crespe*; but as to this
difference, no point of estate was involved for it was a matter of personal
choice, both materials being equally honourable.   525–39

Yet, in the matter of the number of stages to the buffet, Marie of Burgundy
had five stages whereas her mother had only four, and many times it has been
said in the past that only the queen of France could have five stages to the
buffet. These old rules have been changed in several instances, but that
cannot degrade nor abolish such ancient honours and estates, which were
made and formed after much thought and for good reasons.   540–3, 550–61

Madame de Namur told Isabelle of Portugal that the queens of France
always had white hangings to their rooms at the time of childbirth, until the
mother of Charles VII chose to have green; after this, all followed her
example.   583–90

	Marie of Burgundy	Isabelle of Bourbon	Countesses (rank as the Countess of Amiens) (609–11)	'Bannieres Grandes' (700–701)	'Bannerets' (961)	'Autres Nobles Dames' (973)
STAGES OF BUFFET	5 (540–3)	4 (134–6)	3 (641–2)	3 (700–5)	2 (961–6)	1 (974)
'CHAMBRE DE MADAME': COLOUR OF HANGINGS	Green (605–8)	Green (43–7, 55, 58, 91, 97, 100, 605–8)	Never green (605–8)	Never green (605–8)	Never green (605–8)	Never green (605–8)
LARGE BEDS	2 (525–31)	2 (27–32)	1 (609–15)	1 (700–5)	[1]	1 (974–5)
COUCHES	[1]	1	2	1	[1]	1
Position	[by fire]	by fire (38–42)	1 corner 1 by fire (609–15)	corner room (700–5)	[corner room]	corner room (975–6)
FUR COVERING OF BEDS AND/OR COUCHES	Both: ermine (529–31)	Both: ermine (104–6)	All: miniver (622–40)	Both: miniver (700–7)	Both: miniver (982–3)	Bed: miniver Couch none (974–5, 983–5)

INFANT'S CHAMBER: HANGINGS FOR BED & CHAMBER

Presumably 2 beds, as Isabelle of Bourbon	2 beds canopy over both (197–213)	1 hung tapestry or *saye* (783–6)	No hangings room or cradle (1000–3)

FUR CRADLE COVERING

Presumably *as* Isabelle of Bourbon	Ermine, trailing (219–20)	Miniver, never touching ground (762–5)	None (1000–3)

FIG. 36.   Table indicating types of furnishings permitted for different degrees of estate, as set out by Alienor de Poitiers. Lines to text given in brackets

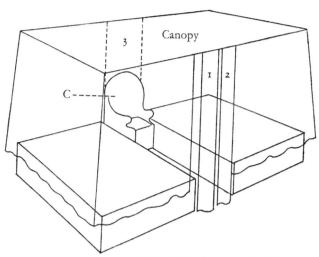

1, 2, 3: '*traversaines*'. 3 at back of alley between beds is permanently looped up. 1 and 2 are on rings and are kept open in the
day time.

Canopy covers both beds.

C   Chair with high back.

Curtains right round beds except at alley front and back which
is occupied by the *traversaines*.

FIG. 37.   Form of beds used in 1403 for the Comtesse de Rethel, in 1456 for Isabelle of
Bourbon, and in 1478 for Marie of Burgundy. (See Appendix VIII (c), 475, 478.)

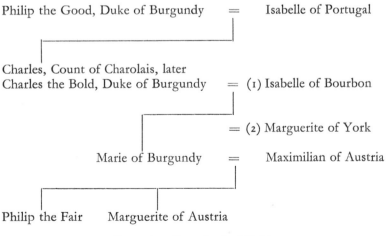

FIG. 38.   Genealogical Table

APPENDIX IX

PANELLED CONSTRUCTION

It has generally been held that panelled construction was introduced in France and the Netherlands at the end of the fourteenth century; this is stated by both Havard and Maffei.[683] There is some slight evidence to suggest that panelled construction was occasionally used earlier, but the situation is obscured by the medieval habit of *applying* framing to boards which gives the *appearance* of panelling; St Edward's chair in Westminster Abbey is an example of this technique. Sometimes, as in the case of a chair, all the sides of the object can be checked to ascertain the techniques used but sometimes verification is more difficult. The following examples await verification.

1296	Lid of the wooden tomb chest of William de Valence, Westminster Abbey; this construction was originally covered with copper. See *RCHM London*, 1, pl. 186.
c. 1300	Lid of the chest in the church of St Mary Magdalen, Oxford. The lid is original and unrestored; the chest, much restored, is carved with tracery and monsters.
1325–30	Chest lid of a reliquary in Winchester Cathedral; wood painted with figures. (See N. Pevsner/D. Lloyd, *Hampshire*, Harmondsworth, 1967, 680.)

The idea of panelled construction is implicit in the Aylesbury armoire (Cat. 24), and simple, heavy panelling is used on the Wells armoire of *c.* 1457 (Cat. 9), on the sides of the Malines armoire of *c.* 1470 (Cat. 13) and on the Brasenose chest of *c.* 1500–15 (Cat. 39). The commonest form of medieval panelled furniture surviving, however, is carved in the solid with linen fold (see below).

The framework of medieval panelling was often moulded on three sides only, with the lower edge left plain; the framing on the door of the Audley Chapel of 1492–1502 in Hereford Cathedral, however, has mouldings on all sides (see below).

Panelled Construction, *linen fold*

Cat. 15, 16, 26, 51

In medieval times, these carved panels were worked in the solid in a symmetrical pattern which represented folds of cloth; they were used to decorate doors (pl. 72A), window shutters (pl. 71) and walls as well as furniture and have often been discussed in print, although their early history has yet to be traced. The regular draping of cloth round dining tables[684] is regarded as a possible origin for the idea of linen fold panels, and wall hangings, and simulations of them, may equally well have contributed something to the invention of linen fold.[685] But if the inspiration behind linen fold was, indeed, drapery of some kind, rather than folds of cloth laid flat, then the original idea was soon forgotten for linen fold panels were placed horizontally as well as vertically, as we see in a number of pieces of furniture (for example the Vleehuis narrow buffet shown on pl. 61).

Much evidence of the use of linen fold belongs to the sixteenth century; it is found on the pulpit of Henry VII's chapel, Westminster Abbey,[686] and is much at home in architectural

---

[683] Havard, I, 154; Maffei, 32.

[684] See the page from the psalter of Robert de Lisle of *c.* 1295, J. Evans, *English Art, 1307–1461*, Oxford, 1949, pl. 5.

[685] See, for example, the regular simulated drapery carved beneath the statues on the W. porch at Rheims; also, painted drapery favoured by Henry III and recorded at Westminster, Woodstock and Clarendon (Brown/Colvin/Taylor, I, 129).

[686] First half of the sixteenth century, see *RCHM London*, I, 69, pl. 22.

contexts which may be loosely described as early Tudor.[687] Much of this early sixteenth century
linen fold panelling is elaborate and technically accomplished, carved to appear as if several
distinct layers of cloth were rolled over one another in symmetrical undulations; English work
can be as fine as anything surviving in a continental context.[688]

The early history of linen fold belongs to the fifteenth century, and the following securely
dated objects provide a framework for less well substantiated works.

1467–81	Linen fold panels on the head board of the bed in the painting of the Death of the Virgin by Hugo van der Goes (d. 1481). Panofsky believes this to be a late work, see p. 91.
Probably 1483 and not later than 1536	Linen fold panels on the extant armoire bearing the arms of Choul and Paterin. Tricou has shown that the armoire was made for Guichard Choul and Jeanne Paterin who married in 1483; Guichard Choul died in 1505, Jeanne in 1536. The most likely date for the armoire is the date of the marriage. (See Tricou, 9–13.)
1492–1502	Linen fold panels on the door of the Audley Chapel, Hereford Cathedral. Four linen fold panels are carved with the Audley badge upon the door of the chantry chapel built by Bishop Audley between 1492–1502. (See *RCHM Herefordshire*, 1, 103, 107.)
1498–1524	Linen fold panels, with early Renaissance cresting, on a wall in the S. transept of Winchester Cathedral; the panels bear Prior Silkstede's initials (1498–1524).
c. 1520	Linen fold panels in the upper left part of a retable, La Legende de S. Jean-Baptiste. Other ornament in this work is entirely flamboyant Gothic without Renaissance elements. The retable is dated by the presence of a bust of the Emperor Charles V. (See Casier/Bergmans, pls. XLIII, XLIV.)
1522–8	Linen fold wall panelling in the Long Gallery of The Vyne, Hampshire. The panelling bears devices of Bishop Tunstall of London, d. 1522, and of Cardinal Wolsey, disgraced 1528.

We see from this list that linen fold occurs in England in Hereford Cathedral only slightly
later than in the Netherlands; but two additional pieces of evidence suggest that the form was,
in fact, in use considerably earlier in the Netherlands, though the evidence for this remains
uncertain until further facts are brought to light. In the first place, we find linen fold portrayed
in a miniature from the Turin Hours depicting the Birth of St John. The date and authorship
of the remarkable group of paintings in this MS are uncertain, and the miniatures have been
assigned to various artists by different scholars.[689] Investigation has remained oriented within
the first half of the fifteenth century by virtue of the acceptance of suggestions that arms on a
banner in the Prayer on the Shore miniature are those of either Count William IV (d. 1417) or
his successor John (d. 1435), of the House of Holland-Bavaria. It is noted on art historical
grounds that either date is extraordinarily early for the works. The difficulty surrounding the
whole question of attribution for the miniatures — and it is not even certain that all are by the

[687] For example, the Jericho Parlour, Abbot's Lodging, Westminster Abbey, see *RCHM London*, 1, pl. 177.
[688] For example, the panels from a door in Suffolk, V. & A.; see Wanscher, pl. 120.
[689] See Faggin, 85–6.

same hand — is aggravated by the uniqueness of the group, and Faggin quotes Hulin de Loo's remark that 'nothing like them was to be seen again until the 17th century'. Mercer states that the Birth of St John is by Hubert van Eyck (*d.* 1426), and is thus apparently the earliest evidence of linen fold;[690] but, as we have seen, this attribution is but one of several hypotheses regarding the authorship of the paintings. It can, however, be stated with certainty that elements in the miniatures (including the Birth of St John) exhibit a familiarity with the works or thought processes of Jan van Eyck; it follows, therefore, that the miniatures in the Turin Hours were either by Jan or an artist working with him, or by a master drawing upon his work, after 1434.[691] The attribution of the miniatures to Jan or Herbert van Eyck is rendered somewhat doubtful, to my mind, by the absence of linen fold in all the works which are incontrovertibly by Jan van Eyck; as for Hubert van Eyck's work, no surviving painting can be attributed to him with certainty.[692]

The second piece of evidence suggesting an earlier date for linen fold in the Netherlands is furnished by two doors in the Hotel de Ville, Damme, which appear to date from the 1464 phase of the building's history, see pl. 72A. One door, in good condition, is in the NE. corner of the hall and the other, which is smaller but otherwise identical on one face, is beyond the hall and gives onto the exterior and is now much decayed.[693] Both doors are carved with panels of simple linen fold, resembling the folds on the lower part of the Muchelney bench (Cat. 51). The hall door retains its original hinge straps which are highly individual, having a raised spine on either side of a central rosette.

The hinge straps on the Damme door cannot be precisely paralleled in another dated context for the raised spine appears to make them unique, but the flared terminals cut with an ogee recall the Malines armoire (Cat. 13) and the rose, here placed centrally on the strap, is a common late fifteenth-century form found, e.g. on the cradle of 1478/9 (Cat. 28); on the armoire in Westminster Abbey (see Fig. 8, p. 31) and York (Cat. 3–7); and on the Bijloke chest (Cat. 44), (see Fig. 26, p. 171). These comparisons furnish dates ranging from *c.* 1470–1500. A further comparison is suggested by the hinge strap in the painting of St Jerome in Detroit, dated 1442.[694] Here, a long hinge strap has a flared traceried terminal and is interrupted by a central rose pierced with tracery. Although the St Jerome hinge strap is given an openwork roundel (like that upon the Bijloke armoire, Cat. 15) where the Damme ironwork has a solid, petalled flower, the idea of a strap with a central roundel is common to both and suggests broadly similar dating. The St Jerome comparison thus places an earlier horizon for work comparable with the Damme hinges, suggesting a date between 1442–1500, indicating that 1464 (the date of the building of the hall at Damme) is a possible date for the doors and thus for the linen fold panel decoration.

---

[690] Mercer, 167, fn. 14.
[691] Jan van Eyck signed the Arnolfini Wedding (National Gallery) in that year and the work has a little dog in the foreground; the same idea is incorporated in the Birth of St John miniature.
[692] See Faggin, 5.
[693] Seen August 1970.
[694] See Faggin 98–9, Cat. 33.

BIBLIOGRAPHY

ALBANÈS, L'ABBÉ J-H. 'Inventaire du Château de Cornillon en 1380', *Révue des Sociétés Savantes*, 7e série, I, 1879, 182–232.

D'ALTENA, J. DE BORCHGRAVE. 'Note au sujet de la chapelle S.-Georges à Bruxelles', *Bulletins des Musées d'Art et d'Histoire à Bruxelles*, Jan. 1955, 2–17.

AMYOT, T. 'Transcript of two rolls containing an inventory of effects formerly belonging to Sir John Fastolfe', *Archaeologia*, XXI, 1827, 232–80.

ANSART, P. 'Le Bahut, Meuble Essentiel du Moyen Age', *La Vie à la Campagne*, 1911, 243–5.

D'ARCQ, D. 'Inventaires des châteaux de Vincennes et de Beauté', *Révue Archéologique*, XI, 1854, 456–62.

ARMITAGE-SMITH, Sir S. *John of Gaunt*, London, 1904.

AYRTON, M./SILCOCK, A. *Wrought Iron and its decorative use*, London, 1929.

BAILDON, W. P. 'Three inventories: (1) The Earl of Huntingdon, 1377; (2) Brother John Randolf, 1419; (3) Sir John de Boys, 1426', *Archaeologia*, Second Series, XI, 1908, 163–76.

—— 'A Wardrobe Account of 16–17 Richard II, 1393–4', *Archaeologia*, Second Series, XII, 1911, 497–514.

BAILLIE, H. M. 'Etiquette and the Planning of the State Apartments in Baroque Palaces', *Archaeologia*, CI, 1967, 169–99.

BARLEY, M. W. *The House and Home*, London, 1963.

BARRETT, E. E. 'Cradles of the Past', *Connoisseur*, XXXIII, 1912, 91–101.

BARTHÉLEMY, A. DE. 'Inventaire du Château des Baux en 1426', *Révue des Sociétés Savantes*, 6e série, 1877, 129–58.

BATAULT, H. 'Inventaire du Mobilier de l'Hopital Saint-Antoine à Mâcon', *Mémoires de la Société d'Histoire et d'Archéologie de Chalon sur Saône*, VII, 1883–8, 140–50.

DE BEAUREPAIRE, C. DE ROBILLARD. *Inventaire du Mobilier du Château de Chailloué*, Rouen, 1866.

BLAIR, C. 'The Emperor Maximilian's Gift of Armour to King Henry VIII', *Archaeologia*, XCIX, 1965, 1–52.

BLOND, V. LE. *Testament et Inventaires des biens d'Eudes de Mareuil, Chapelain de la Cathédrale de Beauvais; Inventaire du Mobilier de Maitre Thomas, Macon de Voisinlieu-lès-Beauvais*, Beauvais, 1913.

BOND, M. F. *The Inventories of St. George's Chapel, Windsor Castle 1384–1667*, Windsor, 1947.

—— 'The Windsor Aerary', *Archives* I no. 4, 1950, 2–6.

BONDURAND, E. 'Mobiliers du Vieux Temps', *Mémoires et Comptes Rendus de la Société Scientifique et Littéraire d'Alais*, XIV, 1883, 78–82.

BONNOR. *Bonnor's Copper Plate Perspective Itinerary or Pocket Portfolio*, London, 1798.

BORDERIE, A. DE LA. 'Inventaire des meubles de Jeanne La Boiteuse, Duchesse de Bretagne', *Révue des Provinces de l'Ouest*, I, 1854, 202–11.

—— 'Inventaire des meubles et bijoux de Marguerite de Bretagne, première femme du duc de Bretagne François II', *Bulletin de la Société archéologique de Nantes et de la Loire-Inférieure*, IV, 1864, 45–60.

BOULAY, F. R. H. DU. *An Age of Ambition*, London, 1970.

BRABANT, F. 'Étude sur les Conseils des Ducs de Bourgogne', *Bull. Com. Roy. Hist.* (5), i, 1891, 90–101.

BRASSARD, F. 'Inventaire, après décès, de Jean Haut-de-Coeur', *Memoires de la Société impériale d'Agriculture, Sciences et Arts, séant à Douai, centrale du département du Nord*, 2e série II, 1852/3, 273–81.

BRITTON, I. *The History & Antiquities of the Metropolitan Church of York*, London, 1819.

BROCHE, L. 'Inventaire du mobilier du palais Episcopal de Laon, au décès de l'Evêque Geoffroy le Meingre (1370–1371)', *Bulletin Archéologique du Comité des Travaux Historiques et Scientifiques*, 1903, 244–9.

BRØGGER, A. W./SHETELIG, H. *Oseberg fundet*, II, Oslo, 1928.

BROOKE, C. 'The Structure of medieval society', Ed. J. Evans, *The Flowering of the Middle Ages*, London, 1966, 12–40.

BROWN, R. A./COLVIN, H. M./TAYLOR, A. J. *History of the King's Works*, I–II, London, 1963.

BRUNHAMMER, Y./FAYET, M. DE. *Meubles et Ensembles Époques Moyen Age et Renaissance*, Paris, 1966.

BUTLER, A. J. 'The College Plate', Ed. Madan, F./Butler, A. J./Allfrey, E. W. *Brasenose College Quartercentenary Monographs no. V, Oxford Historical Society*, LII, 1909.

BUTLER, H. E., Ed. *The Chronicle of Jocelin of Brakelond*, London, 1949.

CAIN, J. *Le Siècle d'Or de la Miniature Flamande* [Catalogue of an exhibition held at Brussels, Amsterdam and Paris in 1959].

Calendar of the Liberate Rolls, Henry III, I, 1226–40 [Ed. Stevenson, W. H.], London, 1916.

—— II, 1240–5 [Ed. Chapman, J. B. W.], H.M.S.O., 1930.

—— III, 1245–51 [Ed. Chapman, J. B. W.], H.M.S.O., 1937.

—— IV, 1251–60 [Ed. Chapman, J. B. W.], H.M.S.O., 1959.

—— V, 1260–7 [Ed. Chapman, J. B. W.], H.M.S.O., 1961.

—— VI, 1267–72 [Ed. Chapman, J. B. W., revised by Latham, R. E.], H.M.S.O., 1964.

CARTELLIERI, O. *The Court of Burgundy*, London, 1929.

CASIER, J./BERGMANS, P. *L'Art Ancien dans les Flandres. Mémorial de l'Exposition retrospective organisée à Gand en 1913*, Brussels/Paris, 1914.

Catalogue Musée Gruuthuse, Bruges, 1970.

CAULLET, G. 'Les Oeuvres d'Art de l'Hopital Notre Dame à Courtrai', *Bulletin du Cercle Historique et Archéologique de Courtrai*, XI, 1913/14, 109–13, and pl. VII.

CAUTLEY, H. M. *Suffolk Churches and their Treasures*, London, 1937.

CAXTON, W. *The Golden Legend*, London, 1878.

CESCINSKY, H./GRIBBLE, E. R. *Early English Furniture and Woodwork*, I–II, London, 1922.

CHEW, H. M./KELLAWAY, W. Ed. *London Assize of Nuisance 1301–1431*, London Record Society, 1973.

CHIZY, M. CANAT DE. 'Marguerite de Flandre, Duchesse de Bourgogne; sa vie intime et l'etat de sa maison', *Mémoires de l'Academie Impériale des Sciences, Arts et Belles-Lettres de Dijon*, VII, 1859.

—— 'Étude sur la Service des Travaux Publics et specialement sur la charge de Maitre des Oeuvres en Bourgogne', *Bulletins Monumentales*, LXIII, 1898.

CIEPKA, MME. *Catalogue des Bois Sculptés des Anciens Pays-Bas, 1480–1530 au Musée de Cluny*, Musée de Cluny. [Typescript.]

COLVIN, H. M. *The Building Accounts of King Henry III*, Oxford, 1971.

CONWAY, SIR W. M. 'The Abbey of Saint-Denis and its ancient treasures', *Archaeologia*, Second Series, XVI, 1915, 103–58.

COOK, G. H. *Medieval Chantries & Chantry Chapels*. London, 1963.

Curia Regis Rolls of the Reigns of Richard I & John, I, 1196–1201 [Ed. Flower, C. T.], H.M.S.O., 1922.

—— VI 1210–12 [Ed. Flower, C. T.], H.M.S.O., 1932.

DALTON, J. N. *MSS of St. George's Chapel, Windsor*, Windsor, 1957.

DALTON, O. M. *The Royal Gold Cup in the British Museum*, London, 1924.

DALY, C. 'Armoire Peinte du XIIIe Siècle', *Révue Générale de l'Architecture et des Travaux Publics*, X, 1852, 130–4.

DEHAISNES, C. C. A. *Documents et Extraits divers concernant l'Histoire de l'Art dans la Flandre, l'Artois, et le Hainaut avant le 15e Siècle*, I–II, Lille, 1886.

DELISLE, L. *Actes Normands de la Chambre des Comptes sous Philippe de Valois*, Rouen, 1871.

DERVIEU, LT COL. 'Les Chaises et les Sièges au Moyen Age', *Bulletins Monumentales*, 1910, 207–41.

—— 'Le Lit et le Berceau au Moyen Age', *Bulletins Monumentales*, 1912, 387–415.

—— 'Serrures, Cadenas et Clefs du Moyen Age', *Bulletins Monumentales*, 1914, 199–231.

—— 'La Table et le Couvert du Repas', *Bulletins Monumentales*, 1922, 387–414.

DESTRÉE, J. 'Berceau dit de Charles Quint', Destrée, J./Kymeulen, A. J./Hannotiau, A., *Les Musées Royaux du Parc du Cinquantenaire et de la Porte de Hal à Bruxelles*, Brussels [n.d.], no. 20.

DEUCHLER, F. *Die Burgunderbeute*, Bern, 1963.

DEVILLERS, L. *Cartulaire des Comtes de Hainaut de 1337 à 1436*, III, 1886.

DILLON, VISCOUNT/HOPE, ST JOHN. 'Inventory of the Goods and Chattels belonging to Thomas, Duke of Gloucester and seized in his castle at Pleshy, Co. Essex, 21 Richard II (1397); with their values, as shown in the Escheator's Accounts', *Archaeological Journal*, LIV, 1897, 275–308.

DODWELL, C. R. *Theophilus De Diuersis Artibus*, London, 1961.

DOUAIS, M. J. C. *Inventaire des biens, meubles et immeubles, de l'Abbaye de Saint-Sernin de Toulouse*, Paris, 1886.

DRAKE, F. *Eboracum*, London, 1736.

DRINKWATER, N. 'The Old Deanery, Salisbury', *Antiquaries Journal*, XLIV, 1964, 41–59.

EAMES, P. *Medieval Domestic Furnishings*, M.A. Thesis, Liverpool University. 1969.

—— 'Documentary Evidence concerning the character and use of Domestic Furnishings in England in the 14th and 15th centuries', *Furniture History*, VII, 1971, 41–60, and pls. 20, 21.

—— 'Inventories as sources of evidence for domestic furnishings in the 14th and 15th centuries', *Furniture History*, IX, 1973, 33–40.

—— 'An Iron chest at Guildhall of about 1427', *Furniture History*, X, 1974, 1–4, and pl. 1.

ELLIS, F. S. *The Golden Legend by William Caxton*, III, London, 1900.

EVANS, J. *English Art, 1307–1461*, Oxford, 1949.

—— Ed. *The Flowering of the Middle Ages*, London, 1966.

Extracts from the Account Rolls of the Abbey of Durham, I, Surtees Society, XCIX, 1898.

FAGGIN, G. T. *The Van Eycks*, London, 1970.

FARÉ, M. 'Les caractères de raison du mobilier gothique', *Art et Industrie*, 1946, no. 2, 50–6.

FAYOLLE, LE MARQUIS DE. 'Armoire du XIIe Siècle et Tombeau de Saint Étienne à Obasine (Corrèze)', *57th Congrès Archéologique de France* (Société Française Archéologique), 1890, 223–36.

FELIX, J. *Inventaire de Pierre Surreau*, Paris, 1892.

FFOULKES, C. J. *Decorative Ironwork from the 11th–18th century*, London, 1913.

—— 'A carved Flemish chest at New College, Oxford', *Archaeologia*, LXV, 1914, 113–28.

FIELD, R. K. 'Worcestershire Peasant Buildings, Household Goods and Farming Equipment in the Later Middle Ages', *Medieval Archaeology*, IX, 1965, 105–45.

FILLET, L'ABBE. 'Le mobilier au Moyen Age dans le Sud-Est de la France', *Bulletin Archéologique du Comité des Travaux Historiques et Scientifiques*, 1896, 55–100.

FORESTIÉ, E. 'Un mobilier seigneurial du XVe siècle. Le château de Montbeton en 1496.', *Bulletin Archéologique et Historique de la Société Archéologique de Tarn-et-Garonne*, XXIII, 1895, 17–51.

FORSYTH, W. H. 'The Vermand Treasure', *Bulletin of the Metropolitan Museum of Art*, IX, 1950/1, 236–40.

FOX, P. *Tutankhamun's Treasure*, Oxford, 1951.

FOX-DAVIES, A. C. *Public Arms*, London, 1915.

FRANCUS, LE DR. 'Inventaire de la Commanderie des Antonins, à Aubenas en Vivarais', *Bulletin d'Histoire Écclesiastique et d'Archéologie des Diocèses de Valence, Gap, Grenoble et Viviers*, 7e année, 1886–7, 148–50.

Furness Abbey, H.M.S.O., 1966.

FURGEOT, H. 'Inventaire du mobilier du Château de Berzé', *Cabinet Historique*, XXV, 1879, 150–7.

FURNIVALL, F. J. *The Babees Book*, Early English Text Society, 1868.

—— *The Fifty Earliest English Wills in the Court of Probate, London*, Early English Text Society, 1882.

GARNIER, J. 'État des objets d'habillement, de literie, d'ameublement et de vaisselle, achetés à Paris par ordre de Marguerite de Flandres, Duchesse de Bourgogne, pour les couches de la comtesse de Rethel, sa belle-fille (Janvier 1403)', *Révue des Sociétés Savantes*, 6e série, I, 1875, 604–11.

GHEYN, J. VAN DEN. 'Contributions à l'iconographie de Charles-le-Téméraire et de Marguerite d'York', *Annales de l'Academie Royal d'Archéologie Belgique*, LVI, 1904, 384–405.

—— 'Encore l'iconographie de Charles-le-Téméraire et de Marguerite d'York', *Annales de l'Academie Royal d'Archéologie Belgique*, LIX, 1907, 275–94.

GIBBONS, A. *Early Lincoln Wills*, Lincoln, 1888.

GIUSEPPI, M. S. 'The Wardrobe and Household Accounts of Bogo de Clare, 1284–6', *Archaeologia*, LXX, 1918–20 [1920], 1–56.

GLOAG, J. *The Englishman's Chair*, London, 1964.

GODARD-FAULTRIER, V. 'Le Château d'Angers au temps de Roi René', *Mémoires de la Société d'Agriculture, Sciences et Arts d'Angers*, IX, 1866, 49–90.

GODFREY, W. H. 'The Vicars' Close', *Archaeological Journal*, CVII, 1950, 112–13.

GRAND, L. LE. 'Les Quinze-Vingts depuis leur fondation jusqu'à leur translation au Faubourg Saint-Antoine (XIIIe–XVIIIe Siècles)', *Mémoires de la Société de l'Histoire de Paris et de l'Ile-de-France*, XIII, 1886.

GRANT, M. *Cambridge*, London, 1966.

GRIMME, E. G. *Der Aachener Domschatz*, Dusseldorf, 1972.

GUIFFREY, J. *Inventaires de Jean Duc de Berry*, I–II, Paris, 1894–6.

GUIRAUD, J. 'Inventaires Narbonnais du XIVe Siècle', *Bulletin de la Commission Archéologique de Narbonne*, VII, 1902/3, 215–67, 375–413.

—— 'Inventaires Narbonnais du XIVe Siècle', *Bulletin de la Commission Archéologique de Narbonne*, VIII, 1904/5.

HALE, W. H. Ed. *The Domesday of St. Paul's of the Year MCCXXII*, Camden Society, 1858.

HALPHEN, L. *Éginhard, Vie de Charlemagne*, Paris, 1938.

HARRIS, H. A. 'Mediaeval Mural Paintings', *Proceedings of the Suffolk Institute of Archaeology & Natural History*, XIX, 1927, 286–303.

HART, C. J. 'Old Chests', *Trans. Birmingham and Midland Inst.*, XX, 1894, 60–94.

HARVEY, J. H. 'Winchester College Muniments. An Introduction with a Summary Index', *Archives*, V, 1961/2, 201–16.

—— *The Mediaeval Architect*, London, 1972.

HAVARD, H. *La Serrurerie*, Paris [n.d.].

—— *Dictionnaire d'Ameublement et de la Décoration depuis le XIIIe Siècle jusqu'à nos jours*, I–IV Paris [1887].

HAVERGAL, F. T. *Fasti Herefordenses and other Antiquarian Memorials of Hereford*, Edinburgh, 1869.

HAYWARD, H. Ed. *World Furniture*, London, 1965.

HEWETT, C. A. *The Development of Carpentry 1200–1700. An Essex Study*, Newton Abbot, 1969.

Historical Manuscripts Commission, Appendix to the 8th Report, 1881.

HODGES, C. C. 'On some medieval carved chests', *Archaeologia Aeliana*, XV, 1892, 295–309.

HOHLER, C. 'Kings and Castles: Court life in peace and war', Ed. J. Evans, *The Flowering of the Middle Ages*, London, 1966, 134–78.

HOLLSTEIN, E. 'Jahrringchronologie der Cathedra lignea von St Peter im Vatikan', *Trierer Zeitschrift*, XXXVII. 1974, 191–206.

HOLMQVIST, W. *Sveriges Forntid och Medeltid*, Malmö, 1949.

HOMMEL, L. *Marguerite d'York où la Duchesse Junon*, Paris, 1959.

HOPE, W. H. ST. JOHN. 'Inventories of the goods of Henry of Eastry (1331), Richard of Oxenden (1334), and Robert Hathbrand (1339), successively priors of the monastery of Christchurch, Canterbury', *Archaeological Journal*, LIII, 1896, 258–83.

—— 'Of the great almery for relics in the abbey church of Selby, with some notes on some other receptacles for relics', *Archaeologia*, LX, 1907, 411–22.

—— *Windsor Castle*, London, 1913.

—— 'Last Testament and Inventory of John de Veer, Thirteenth Earl of Oxford', *Archaeologia*, 2nd series XVI, 1915, 275–348.

HOSKINS, W. G. *The Midland Peasant*, London, 1957.

HUIZINGA, J. *The Waning of the Middle Ages*, London, 1952.

HUNT, J. 'Byzantine and Early Medieval', Ed. Hayward, H. *World Furniture*, London, 1965, 19–24.

HUNT, R. 'The Sum of Knowledge', Ed. Evans, J. *The Flowering of the Middle Ages*, London, 1966, 179–202.

JACOB, E. F. 'The Building of All Souls College 1438–1443', Ed. Edwards, J. G./Galbraith, V. H./Jacob, E. F., *Historical Essays in honour of James Tait*, Manchester, 1933, 121–35.

—— *The Register of Henry Chichele, Archbishop of Canterbury 1414–1443*, II, Oxford, 1937.

JANNEAU, G. *Les Meubles*, I, Paris, 1929.

JARRY, L. 'Inventaire de la bibliothèque et du mobilier de Jean, bâtard d'Orleans, Comte de Dunois, au Château de Châteaudun', *Mémoires de la Société Archéologique et Historique de l'Orleanais*, XXIII, 1892, 117–45.

JENNING[S], C. *Early Chests in Wood and Iron*, H.M.S.O., 1974.

JOHNSTONE, J. *The Finding of St. Augustine's Chair*, Birmingham, 1898.

JONES, P. E. *Calendar of Plea and Memoranda Rolls, 1437–1457*, Cambridge, 1954.

JUPP, E. B./POCOCK, W. W. *An Historical Account of the Worshipful Company of Carpenters of the City of London*, London, 1887.

KING, D. 'The currents of trade', Ed. Evans, J. *The Flowering of the Middle Ages*, London, 1966, 245–80.

KINGSFORD, C. L. *English Historical Literature in the 15th century*, Oxford, 1913.

—— 'Two Forfeitures in the year of Agincourt', *Archaeologia*, LXX, 1918–20 [1920], 71–100.

—— 'On some London houses of the early Tudor period', *Archaeologia*, LXXI, 1920–1 [1921], 17–54.

KIRBY, J. L. *Henry IV of England*, London, 1970.

KREISEL, H. *Die Kunst des Deutschen Mobels*, I, Munich, 1968.

LABARTE, J. *Inventaire du mobilier de Charles V*, Paris, 1879.

LAMBERT, A. 'Le Coffre du Pas Saladin, est-il authentique?', *Révue Archéologique*, XXXIII, 1931, 275–306.

LARKING, L. B. 'Inventory of the effects of Roger de Mortimer, at Wigmore Castle and Abbey, Herefordshire', *Archaeological Journal*, XV, 1858, 354–62.

LEGG, J. W. 'An inventory of the vestry in Westminster Abbey, taken in 1388', *Archaeologia*, LII, 1890, 195–286.

LEHMANN-BROCKHAUS, O. *Lateinische Schriftquellen zur Kunst in England, Wales & Schottland, I, 901–1307*, Munich, 1955.

LETHABY, W. R. *Westminster Abbey Re-examined*, London, 1925.

LETTENHOVE, LE BARON K. DE. Ed. *Oeuvres de Georges Chastellain, III, Chronique 1454–1458*, Brussels, 1864.

LETTS, M. *The Travels of Leo of Rozmital*, Cambridge, 1957.

LEX, L. 'Inventaire estimatif, après décès, des meubles de Jean Lemaigre, curé de Pont-Sainte-Marie, près de Troyes', *Révue de Champagne et de Brie*, XI, 1881, 212–25, 313–23.

LITTLEHALES, H. *The Medieval Records of a London City Church*, Part I, Early English Text Society, 1904, 28–9.

LOWTHER, A. W. G. 'The date of the timbers from the spire of Chilcomb church . . . some evidence from Dendrochronology', *Papers & Proceedings of the Hampshire Field Club & Archaeological Society*, XVII, part 2, 1951, 130–3.

MACQUOID, P. *A History of English Furniture — The Age of Oak*, London, 1938.

MACQUOID, P./EDWARDS, R. *Dictionary of English Furniture*, London, 1927.

—— *Dictionary of English Furniture*, London, 1954.

MAES, L. TH. *Le Parlement et le Grand Conseil à Malines*, Malines, 1949.

MAFFEI, E. *Le Mobilier Civil en Belgique au Moyen Age*, Namur [n.d.].

MARCHE, OLIVIER DE LA. See Petitot, C-B.

MARCHEGAY, P. 'Inventaire des meubles ayant appartenu à Madame de Royan, mère de la Comtesse de Périgord', *Révue des Sociétés Savantes*, 5 série, V, 1873, 481–3.

MARECHAL, J. 'L'armoire aux privileges et titres du consulat de Castille-Leon à Bruges en 1441', *Handlingen Société d'Emulation Bruges*, 1961, 105–9.

MAXWELL-LYTE, H. C./DAWES, M. C. B. 'The Register of Thomas Bekynton', *Somerset Record Society*, XLIX, 1934.

MAYR-HARTING, H. *The Acta of the Bishops of Chichester 1075–1207*, Torquay, 1964.

Medieval Catalogue. London Museum Catalogues, no. 7, H.M.S.O. 1954.

MERCER, E. *Furniture 700–1700*, London, 1969.

METZDORF, L. 'Le Berceau de Charles Quint', *Bulletin Mensuel de Numismatique et d'Archéologie*, II, no. 2 and 3, 1882, 29–31, and pls. II, III.

MYERS, A. R. *The Household of Edward IV*, Manchester, 1959.

—— 'The Wealth of Richard Lyons', Ed. Sandquist, T. A./Powicke, M. R., *Essays in Medieval History presented to Bertie Wilkinson*, Toronto, 1969, 301–29.

—— *London in the age of Chaucer*, Norman, Oklahoma, 1972.

NAIRN, I./PEVSNER, N. *Sussex*, Harmondsworth, 1965.

NECKHAM, A. *De Naturis Rerum*, Ed. Scheler, A. *Lexicographie Latine du XII et du XIII siècle. Trois traités de Jean de Garlande, Alexandre Neckam et Adam du Petit-Pont*, Leipzig, 1867.

NICHOLS, J. *A collection of all the wills. . . . of the kings and queens of England . . . and every branch of the blood royal*, London, 1780.

NICOLAS, N. H. *Testamenta Vetusta*, I, London, 1826.

—— *Privy Purse expenses of Elizabeth of York*, London, 1830.

NYEVELT, A. VAN ZUYLEN VAN. *Episodes de la Vie des Ducs de Bourgogne à Bruges*, Bruges [n.d.].

OAKESHOTT, W. 'Winchester College Library before 1750', *Transactions of the Bibliographical Society*, 5th series, IX, 1954, 1–16.

PALGRAVE, SIR F. *The Antient Kalendars and Inventories of the Treasury of His Majesty's Exchequer*, II, London, 1836.

PALMER, W. *The Coronation Chair*, H.M.S.O., 1953.

PALSGRAVE, J. *L'esclarissement de la langue Francoyse*, London, 1530.

PANNIER, L. 'Inventaire des meubles contenus dans la maison de la rue des Murs', *Bibliothèque de l'École des Chartes*, XXXIII, 1872, 361–2.

PANOFSKY, E. *Early Netherlandish Painting*, Cambridge, Massachusetts, 1964.

PARKER, J. H. *Architectural Antiquities of Wells*, Oxford/London, 1866.

[PARKER, J. H.] *Some Account of Domestic Architecture in England from Edward I to Richard II*, Oxford, 1853 [vol. II] (See also Turner).

—— *Some Account of Domestic Architecture in England from Richard II to Henry VIII*, Oxford, 1854 [vol. III in 2 pts.] (See also Turner).

PAUWELS, H. 'De Begijnenkast vorm en oorsprong', *Bulletin des Musées Royaux d'Art et d'Histoire*, 1960, 48–62.

PETITOT, C-B. *Collection Complète des Mémoires Relatifs à l'histoire de France. T. IX–X. Les Mémoires de Messire Olivier de la Marche*, Paris, 1825.

PEVSNER, N. *South Devon*, Harmondsworth, 1952.

—— *Shropshire*, Harmondsworth, 1958.

—— *S. & W. Somerset*, Harmondsworth, 1958.

—— *Buckinghamshire*, Harmondsworth, 1960.

—— *Suffolk*, Harmondsworth, 1961.

—— *Herefordshire*, Harmondsworth, 1963.

PEVSNER, N./HARRIS, J. *Lincolnshire*, Harmondsworth, 1964.

PEVSNER, N./LLOYD, D. *Hampshire*, Harmondsworth, 1967.

PEVSNER, N, see also Nairn.

PHILLIPS, SIR T. 'Account of the ceremonial of the marriage of the Princess Margaret, sister of King Edward the Fourth, to Charles, Duke of Burgundy, in 1468', *Archaeologia*, XXXI, 1846, 326–38.

DE POICTIERS, A. See Sainte-Palaye, La Curne de.

PORTAL, M. *The great hall of Winchester Castle*, Winchester/London, 1899.

POUX, J. 'Le mobilier de Beatrix d'Arborée, Vicomtesse de Narbonne en 1377', *Bulletin de la Commision Archéologique de Narbonne*, 1911, 385–403.

POWICKE, F. M./CHENEY, C. R. *Councils and Synods*, II, Oxford, 1964.

PROST, B. *Inventaires mobiliers et extraits des comptes des ducs de Bourgogne. I. Philippe le Hardi 1366–1377*, Paris, 1902/4.

PROST, B. & H. *Inventaires mobiliers et extraits des comptes des duc des Bourgogne de la Maison de Valois 1363–1477. II. Philippe le Hardi, 1378–1390*, Paris, 1908–13 [4 fascs.].

RAINE, J. *St. Cuthbert*, Durham, 1828.

—— [Ed.] Wills and Inventories, I, *Surtees Society*, 1834–5.

—— [Ed.] *Testamenta Eboracensia*, I, *Surtees Society*, 1834–6.

RICHARD, J-M. *Mahaut, Comtesse d'Artois et de Bourgogne (1302–1329): étude sur la vie privée, les arts et l'industrie, en Artois et à Paris au commencement du XIVe siècle*, Paris, 1887.

—— 'Vente après décès des meubles de Jehan Le Caron dit Caronchel, bâtard et usurier à Arras', *Bulletin de la Commission des Antiquités départmentales du Pas-de-Calais* (Arras), IV, 1875[–1878], 90–8.

—— 'Inventaire du mobilier des maisons épiscopales d'Arras et de Mareuil-lez-Arras en 1322', *Révue des Sociétés Savantes*, 7e série, V, 1882, 252–9.

RICHTER, G. M. A. *The Furniture of the Greeks, Etruscans and Romans*, London, 1966.

RILEY, H. T. *Memorials of London and London Life 1276–1419*, London, 1868.

[RILEY, H. T.] *Historical Manuscripts Commission: 1st report*, 1870; *3rd report*, 1872.

ROBERTS, A. K. B. *St. George's Chapel, Windsor Castle, 1348–1416*, Windsor, 1947.

ROE, F. *Ancient Coffers and Cupboards*, London, 1902.

ROMAN, J. 'Inventaire des meubles du chateau de Rouen', *Bulletin Archéologique*, 1885, 545–8.

RORIMER, J. J. 'The Treasury at the Cloisters and two Ingolstadt beakers', *Bulletin of the Metropolitan Museum of Art, New York*, IX, 1950/1, 249–59.

Rotuli Parliamentorum, IV.

ROYAL COMMISSION ON HISTORICAL MONUMENTS. *Cambridge I–II*, London, 1959.

—— *Essex, II. Central and South-West London*, London, 1921.

—— *Herefordshire I, South-West; II, East*, London, 1931 and 1932.

—— *London, I (Westminster Abbey)*, London, 1924.

—— *Oxford*, London, 1939.

ROYER, L. 'Le mobilier des châteaux dauphinois, en 1400, d'après un inventaire des biens de la Maison de Sassenage', *Bulletins de la Société dauphinoise d'ethnologie et d'anthropologie*, 1923, 33–72.

SAINTE-PALAYE, LA CURNE DE. *Mémoires sur l'Ancienne Chevalerie*, II, Paris, 1759; incorporating de Poictiers. A., 'Les Honneurs de la Cour', 183–267.

SANDLER, L. F. Ed. *Essays in memory of Karl Lehmann*, New York, 1964.

SAUERLÄNDER, W. *Gothic Sculpture in France 1140–1270*, London, 1972.

SCHELER, A. Ed. *Lexicographie Latine du XII et du XIII siècle. Trois Traités de Jean de Garlande, Alexandre Neckam et Adam du Petit-Pont*, Leipzig, 1867.

SCHMITZ, H. *The Encyclopaedia of Furniture*, London, 1956.

SHARPE, R. R. Ed. *Calendar of Wills, proved and enrolled in the Court of Husting, London, I, 1258–1358*, London, 1889.

—— *Calendar of wills, proved and enrolled in the Court of Husting, London, II, 1358–1688*, London, 1890.

SHAW, H. *Specimens of Ancient Furniture*, London, 1866.

SIMPSON, W. S. 'Two inventories in the cathedral church of St. Paul, London, dated respectively 1245 and 1402', *Archaeologia*, L, 1887, 439–524.

SINGER, C. Ed. *A History of Technology, II*, Oxford, 1957.

SQUILBECK, J. *Marguerite d'York et son temps*, Brussels, 1967.

STALINS, BARON A. *Origine et histoire de la famille Stalins de Flandre, depuis le XIIe siècle, et du briquet heraldique dit de Bourgogne, ou fusil de la Toison d'Or*, Paris/Gand/Macon, 1939.

STEER, F. W. *Guide to the Church of St. Mary, Climping*, Chichester [n.d.].

STEIN, H. 'Inventaire du mobilier de Mᵉ Guillaume as Feives', *Bulletin de la Société de l'histoire de Paris*, 1883, 165–74.

STENTON, SIR F. Ed. *The Bayeux Tapestry*, London, 1965.

STEPHEN, SIR L./LEE, SIR S. Eds. *Dictionary of National Biography*, XXI, Oxford, 1967–8.

STREETER, B. H. *The chained library*, London, 1931.

Surtees Society, XCIX, 1898. Extract from the Account Rolls of the Abbey of Durham. I.

—— C, 1899. Extract from the Account Rolls of the Abbey of Durham. II.

—— CVII, 1902. The Rites of Durham.

SWARTWOUT, R. E. *The Monastic Craftsman*, Cambridge, 1932.

SYMONDS, R. W. 'The chest and the coffer: their difference in function and design', *Connoisseur*, CVII, 1941, 15–21.

—— 'The evolution of the cupboard', *Connoisseur*, CXII, 1943, 91–9.

—— 'Furniture: Post Roman', Ed. C. Singer, *A history of technology II*, Oxford, 1957.

TANNER, L. E. *The library and muniment room*, Westminster Papers, no. 1, London, 1935.

TAYLOR, A. J. Ed. *Château Gaillard III*, London, 1969.

THOMAS, A. H. Ed. *Calendar of Early Mayors' Court Rolls*, London, 1924.

—— *Calendar of Plea and Memoranda Rolls, 1364–1381*, Cambridge, 1929.

—— *Calendar of Plea and Memoranda Rolls, 1381–1412*, Cambridge, 1932.

—— *Calendar of Plea and Memoranda Rolls, 1413–1437*, Cambridge, 1943.

THOMPSON, F. H. 'The zoomorphic pelta in Romano-British Art', *Antiquaries Journal*, XLVIII, 1968, 47–58.

TIMBRELL, W. F. 'The medieval bedposts in Broughton church', *Transactions of the Historical Society of Lancashire and Cheshire*, LXVI, 1914, 228–44.

TOUT, T. F. *The place of the reign of Edward II in English history*, Manchester, 1914.

TRÉMOILLE, L. DE LA. *Archives d'un serviteur de Louis XI*, Nantes, 1888.

[TRÉMOILLE, L. DE LA] *Les La Trémoille pendant cinq siècles. I. Guy et Georges 1343–1346*, Nantes, 1890.

TRICOU, J. 'Trois meubles armoriés Lyonnais', *Nouvelle Révue Heraldique*, 1946, 8–15, and pls. II, III.

TURNER, T. H. *Some Account of Domestic Architecture in England from the Conquest to the end of the 13th century*, Oxford, 1852, vol. 1 (See also Parker).

TWINING, LORD. *European Regalia*, London, 1967.

TYMMS, S. 'Wills and inventories from the registers of the Commissary of Bury St. Edmund's and the Archdeacon of Sudbury', *Camden Society*, XLIX, 1850.

VALLANCE, A. *English Church Screens*, London, 1936.

VALLERY-RADOT, J. *La cathédrale de Bayeux*, Paris, 1958.

VALOUS, V. DE. 'Inventaire des biens de Jean de Bellora, curé de Vaise, dressé le 10 Juillet 1374', *Révue Lyonnaise*, 4e série, VIII, 1879, 246–52.

—— 'Inventaire des biens d'un serrurier de Lyon', *Mémoires de la Société litteraire, historique et archéologique de Lyon*, XIII, 1879–81 [Lyon, 1882].

VAUGHAN, R. *Philip the Bold*, London, 1962.

—— *John the Fearless*, London, 1966.

—— *Philip the Good*, London, 1970.

—— *Charles the Bold*, London, 1975.

VERHAEGEN, BARON A. 'Armoire de refectoire à l'usage des béguines', *Révue de l'Art Chrétien*, I, 1883, 225–6.

VERNET, F. 'Inventaires après décès des biens de Pierre de Chalus, évêque de Valence et de Die, remis à la chambre apostolique d'Avignon', *Bulletin d'histoire écclesiastique et d'archéologie religieuse des diocèses de Valence, Gap, Grenoble et Viviers*, IIe année, 1891, 160–6; 199–207.

VERNIER, J-J. 'Philippe Le Hardi, Duc de Bourgogne. Sa vie intime pendant sa jeunesse. Ses qualités et ses défauts; ses goûts et ses habitudes', *Mémoires de la Société Academique du Département de l'Aube*, LXIII, 1899, 29–63.

VIAUX, J. 'French domestic furniture of the Middle Ages', *Connoisseur*, CXXXIII, 1954, 252–5.
—— *Le meuble en France*, Paris, 1962.
THE VICTORIA HISTORY OF THE COUNTIES OF ENGLAND, *A History of Somerset II*, London, 1911.
—— *The City of York*, London, 1961.
VIOLLET-LE-DUC, E. E. *Dictionnaire Raisonné du Mobilier Francais*, I, Paris, 1858.
—— *Dictionnaire Raisonné de l' Architecture Francais*, I–II, Paris, 1867.
WALLE, A. L. J. VAN DE. 'Some technical analogies between building and other crafts in the use
     of split wood during the Middle Ages', Ed. Taylor, A. J. *Château Gaillard III*, London,
     1969, 152–5.
WANSCHER, O. *The art of furniture*, London, 1966.
WATERER, J. W. 'Leather', Ed. Singer, C. *History of Technology*, II, Oxford, 1957.
WATKIN, A. 'Dean Cosyn and Wells Cathedral Miscellanea', *Somerset Record Society*, LVI, 1941,
     139–49.
WATTEVILLE, BARON DE. 'Un interieur de grand seigneur Francais', *Révue France Moderne*,
     1890, 31–61.
WEAVER, F. W. Ed. 'Somerset Medieval Wills, 1383–1500'. *Somerset Record Society*, XVI, 1901.
WEINBERGER, M. 'The chair of Dagobert', Ed. Sandler, L. F., *Essays in memory of Karl Lehmann*,
     New York, 1964, 375–82.
WELLS, W. 'The Richard de Bury chest', *Scottish Art Review*, vol. 10, no. 4, 14–18, 31–2.
WILSON, D. M. 'An inlaid iron folding stool in the British Museum', *Medieval Archaeology*, I,
     1957, 39–56.
Winchester College, its history, buildings and customs, Winchester College Archaeological Society,
     1926.
WOLFF, A. DE. 'Romanesque hutches of Valère at Sion in the Valais', *Connoisseur*, CLVIII,
     1965, 39–42.
WOOD, M. *The English Mediaeval House*, London, 1965.
WORMALD, F. 'The throne of Solomon and St. Edward's chair', Ed. M. Meiss, *De Artibus
     Opuscula XL. Essays in honour of E. Panofsky*, New York, 1961, 532–9.

U

ERRATA

p. 43   The Museum of Leathercraft has now moved from Walsall to Northampton

p. 91 and
fn. 241   *For* Hugo van Goes *read* Hugo van der Goes

p. 176   *For* Compostello *read* Compostella

p. 186   *For* Kungstgewerbemuseum *read* Kunstgewerbemuseum

p. 241   *For* Charles V *read* Charles VI

INDEX

Note: Cat. Raisonné nos. and catalogue pagination are given in italics

Aachen, 67
adze, 230
Aisey-le-Duc, Château d', 61, 219
Albanès, J.-H., 116, 130, fns. 280, 303
ale, 60
Alet, Guillaume, Bishop of, 3, 77, 90
Allmand, C. T., xiii
Altena, J. de Borchgrave d', fn. 663
Amiens, Cathedral of, bas relief in 187, fn. 489
Amyot, T., 87, 201, 223
Andrieu, Arnaud, 91, 116, fn. 299
Angers, Château d', 59, 71, 89, 92–3, 128, 131
Anjou, King René of, 59, 89, 92–3, 133–4
Ansart, P., 154, fn. 292
architecture, xv, xvii, xix, 15, 23, 25, fn. 18
Arcq, Douet d', 92, 185, 201, 206, 216, 222, fns. 303, 328
Ardleigh, manor of, 60, 223, fn. 137
Argilly, Château d', 215
Armitage-Smith, Sir S., 88, 222, fn. 307
armoires, see furniture
armorial decoration, xxiv, 11, 32, 37, 69, 76, 78–9, 95, 97, 98–9, 100, 116–17, 124, 125, 136, 163, 178, 179, 231, 236–7, 254, fns. 58, 91, 249, 441, see also *Cat. 26, 28, 48* and Appendix III
   as evidence of ownership, 69, fns. 184–5
armour, 6, 7, see also furniture, armoires, contents; chests, contents
Arras, 7, 96, 199, fn. 285, see also textiles, tapestry
Artois, Mahaut, Comtesse d', 49, 88, 91, 114, 204, 206, fn. 569; special folding table of, 222; post/canopy beds of, 75, 91, fn. 202; *imagiers* employed by, 10, 106, 188, 189, 199, 243, fns. 494, 574; rank of, fn. 258; *taillerie* of, 7, fn. 128
Artois, Robert d', 122
Arundel Castle, 16
Arundel, Richard, Earl of, 80
Aubazine, see Obazine
Augustine, St, chair of, 212, fn. 525
Aurelhe, Rigault d', see furniture, beds, type, post; also seating, type, benches
Austria, Marguerite of, 101, 103; see also Fig. 38, p. 273
Auxerre Cathedral, seat at, see Fig. 28 (4), pp. 194–5
Ayrton, M., 46, 157, 158, fns. 117, 401, 407–8, 410

Bafcop, Dr M., xiii,
Baildon, W. P., 115, 122, 129

Baillie, H. M., fn. 682
Ball, Peregrine, 105, 106
Bandol, Jean, 83, see also Pl. 67
banners, 129
Bapaume, Château de, 204
Barcelona Cathedral, silver throne at, see furniture, seating, function, estate, precious materials
Baret, John, of Bury, 124
Baring Foundation, The, v
Barley, M. W., fns. 16, 461
Barr, C. B. L., fn. 669
Barrett, E. E., 106, 107, fn. 275
Barthélemy, A. de, 4, 120, 122, 127, 128, fns. 42, 300
Bataille, Colin, 80–1
Batault, H., 8, 88
bath, 83, 85, 96–7
Baux, Château des, 4, 82, 120, 122, 127, 128, fns. 42, 300
Bavaria, Margaret of, 100
Bayeux Cathedral, 232, 236; tapestry of, 48, fn. 19; seating depicted in, 186, 192, 206, 225, fn. 482, Fig. 32, p. 255 tables, 220; see also furniture, armoires, type, Freestanding (a), and seating, type, X-form
Beaufort, dukes of, 106, 121
   Lady Margaret, 90, 177, 201; see also furniture, chests, type, standard, *Cat. 47*
Beaurepaire, C. de Robillard de, 98, 126, 127
Beauté, Château de, 92, 136, 201, 222 fns. 327–8
beds, see furniture
Bekynton, Bishop, 40, 250; ironwork on chapel of 170, Pl. 66A; see also Appendix IV
Belin, Maître (d'Anchenoncourt), 5, fn. 44
benches, see furniture
Bergmans, P., see Casier
Berry, Duc de, 48–9, 202, fn. 324
Berzé, Château de, fn. 284
Besan, Christofle, 97, fn. 277
Bethune, Robert de, Comte de Flandres, 119; fn. 281
Beverley Minster, throne at, 197
Blair, C., fn. 93
Blond, V. le, 2–3, 6, 63, 120
Blound, Robert, 129
Bluemantle Pursuivant, 218
Bohun, Humphrey de, 131
Bond, M. F., 42, 43, fns. 94, 111, 322, 324
Bondurand, E., fn. 320
Bonnor, 105, 106, 107, fn. 275, see also Appendix V
Borderie, A. de la, 99, 122, fn. 323
Boulay, F. R. H. du, fns. 5, 30

Bourbon, Isabel of, 87, 257, see also Figs 36–8, pp. 272–3; Appendix VIII (b–c)
Bourdichon, Joannes de, 191
Bourges, see Coeur, Jacques
Bouts, Dieric, 60, 64, see also Pl. 63
Boynton, L. O. J., xiii
box, at Antwerp, 172, fn. 437
boxes, small, 38, 108, 136, fns. 107, 324, see also documents, cases for
Brabant, F., fn. 181
Brakelond, Jocelin of, 135, fns. 311, 417
Brassard, F., 120
Braybroke, Gerald, 126
Bretagne, Anne of, 191
    Duc de, 202
    Jeanne La Boiteuse, Duchesse de, 122, 131, 132
    Marguerite de, 98–9
Britton, I., fn. 661
Broche, L., fn. 124
Broederlam, Melchior, 243
Brøgger, A. W., fn. 345
Brooke, C. N. L., xiii, fn. 39, 194
Broughton, Chester, 92, fn. 249
Brown, R. A./Colvin, H. M./Taylor, A. J., 75, 189, 190, 233, fns. 70, 201, 522, 530, 577, 685
Bruges, xvi, xviii, 10–11, 19, 35, 36, 66, 67, 72, 85, 103, 257, fn. 140, 185, 541
Bruges, William, 126
Brunhammer, Y., 226, fn. 561
Brussels, 6, 103
buffets, see funiture
Bukland, Johan, 122
Burgos, 37
Burgundy, Valois dukes of, Fig. 38, p. 273
    campaign chest of, 174
    courts of, etiquette, 241, 256, fn. 17; magnificence, xvi, xvii, 57–8, fn. 140, see also Appendices VI–VIII; precedence and ceremony, xvi–xvii
    household of, Fourrier arranges furnishings, 217–18; furniture for, 115, 116–17, fn. 321; important furniture for, 2, 37, 80–1, 84, fn. 105
    initials and devices as ornament, 69, 185, 254, fns. 184, 185
    patronage of artists for furniture, 243–4
    policy of aggrandizement, 240
    Charles the Bold, xvi, xx, 66, 100, 218, 257, chair of Conseil et Justice, 190–1, 197; marriage to Marguerite of York, 58, 85, 255–6, fn. 141, see also Appendix VII (a–b)
    John the Fearless, xvi, 61, 84, 96, 100, 219, fn. 511
    Philip the Bold, xvi, 5, 100, fn. 184; furniture for, 199–200, 205, 224, 239, 243–4, fn. 576; trestle tables, 219

Philip the Bold/Margaret of Flanders, 5, 8, 61, 84, 114–15, 116–17, 119, 123, 127, 128, 129, 130, 132, 133, 190, fns. 3, 35, 44, 70, 300, 310; Margaret's inventory of 1405, 62, 124, 133, 185, fns. 37, 184, 280; her clothes, fn. 128; her household, fn. 285; purchases for birth of heirs, 96–8, 100, 124, fns. 70, 277, 680
Philip the Good, xvi, xx, 57–8, 66, 85, fns. 140, 170; seat of, 198; treasure of, 6, 57–8, 255, fn. 570
Burgundy, Marie of, 67, 100, 102, 103, 236, 257, fns. 185, 229, Figs. 36–8, pp. 272–3; see also Appendix VIII (b–c); assumes equality with queen of France, 57, 77, 100, 240, fn. 212; tomb chest of, 72, 92
Burrell Collection, 69, 138, fn. 346
Bury, Richard de, see furniture, chests, type, Slab-ended
Busleydon, Dr Francis, 67–8
Butler, A. J., 162, fn. 416
Butler, H. E., fn. 311

Caen, exchequer doorway at Castle of, 209
Caernarvon Castle, 105, fn. 275
Cain, J., 70, fn. 173
Cailleux, J., xiii
Caister Castle, 87, 201, 223
Calabria, Duc de, 89, 202
Calais, 81
Calendar of Liberate Rolls, I, 113, 120, 130, 187; II, 114, 203; III, 188; IV, 6, 7, 8, 188, 199, 203, 215, 221, 223, 224; V, 64, 125; VI, 126; fn. 308
Cambridge, King's College, xiii, see also furniture, armoires, type, Uncertain
    Saint John's College, see furniture, chests, type, standard
    Sidney Sussex College, as above
canopy, significance of, 59, 77, 186, 198, 240–1, 242, 254, 255, fns. 13, 152, see also furniture, esp. beds, buffets and seating; Appendix VIII (b–c)
Canterbury, 234, Christchurch, monastery of, fn. 34; shrine of St Thomas at, 121
carpet, 125, from wall to wall, 94, 95, 101, 269
Cartellieri, O., fn. 145
Casier, J., 275, fns. 67, 185
casket, at Bruges, Gruuthuse mus. (no. 1281), 43; at Walsall, dated 1532, Mus. Leathercraft, 43
Catherine of France, 98
Caullet, G., 168, 169, fns. 185, 425–6, 433
Cautley, H. M., fns. 438–9
Caxton, William, 147, 148, fn. 387
cedar, see wood
ceremony, for mourning, fn. 138; great lords serving meals, 60, fn. 160; religious, as part

of everyday life, xx, xxiii, fn. 30; used to reinforce social and political power, xvi–xvii, xx–xxii, 57, 59, 77, 85, 86–7, 228–9, 239–40, see also Appendices VI–VIII; furniture, of estate; precedence

Cescinsky, H., 148, fns. 349, 436

Chailloué, Château de, 126, 127

chairs, see furniture

Chalons, Thomas de, 84

chapels, within households, xx, xxiii, 8, 10, 13, 108, 113, 116, 119, 125–6, 128, 136, 182, 187, 198, 204, 206, fns. 28, 29, 279, 324, 570, 574

Charlemagne, tables of, see furniture, tables, technique

Charles V of France, 48, 83, 91, 183, 184, 186, fns. 449, 511, Pl. 67; 1379 inventories of, 1, 61, 84, 125–6, 128, 134, 136, 137, 185, fns. 306, 327, 334

Charles V of Hapsburg, 43, 101, 102–3

Charles VI of France, 1420 inventory of, 136, 185, 241, fns. 328, 449

Charles VII of France, 96, 271

Charles VIII of France, 216, fn. 679

Chartres, 73, 74, 75, 194–5 (14)

Chastellain, Georges, xvii, xx; his account of feast of 1456, 57, 253, fn. 139, see also Appendix VI

Châteaudun, Château de, 4, 8, 9, 84, 87, 90, 98, 131

Cheney, C. R., see Powicke

Chepstow Castle, 106, fn. 275

chests, see furniture

Chew, H. M., fn. 39

Cheyne, Edward, 78, 119, 130

Chichester, fittings in canons' houses at, 224

Chizy, M. Canat de, 8, 64, 127, 224, fns. 30, 31, 128, 165, 285, 297, 310, 582, 648

Choul, Guichard, 275

Christus, Petrus, 34

Ciepka, Mme, fn. 516

Cirasse, Philippe, 61

Clare, Bogo de, 7, 129

Clark, John, fn. 273

Coeur, Jacques, 91, 179, Pl. 66B

Coggeshale, John de, 137

Coldhabour, mansion of, 90, 201, 224, 233

Colvin, H. M., 188, see also Brown, R. A.

Colyn, Alice, fn. 301

Comines, Philippe de, 202

Confédération Internationale des Negociants en Oeuvres d'Art (CINOA), v, vi, xiii

Conflans, Château de, 204

Conway, Sir W. M., fn. 469

Cook, G. H., fn. 662

Corbeil, 64

Cornillon, Château de, 116, 130, fn. 280

coronation throne, the, see furniture, seating, function, estate, 'St. Edward's chair'

Cortenay, Margaret, 118

Cosset, Jehan, 116–17

Cournanel, Château de, 90

Courtfield, manor of, 106, fn. 275

Courtrai, church of, fn. 281; hospital of Nôtre Dame at, fn. 185

Courts, of Chancery and King's Bench, 190

Coventre, John, 122, 134, fn. 305

Coventry, chair from, 197

Cox's History of Monmouthshire, fn. 276

craftsmen

by craft

arbalestrier, 129

archier, makes chair, 199; tables, 215; sells chests 132

brodeur, makes leather case for chair, 189

carpenter, 198; makes armoire, 28; buffet, 61; cradle, 96–8, fn. 277; folding table, 222; master, makes throne, 189

charpentier, fn. 31; maître, fn. 44; makes buffet, 61; cradle, 100, 104; fittings for armoire, 38; litter, fn. 70; sells armoire, 7; cradles, cases etc., 96

coffrier, makes case for chair, 190; supplies coffres, 123, 128, 129; iron-bound, 118, 190; leather covered, 124; with bahuts and travelling equipment, 114, 116, 117

courtepointier, 84, fn. 651

escrinner, 38

gainnier, makes leather coffres, fn. 576

goldsmith, 189

huchier, supplies chair and bench, 199; huche, 130

imagier, 10–11, 106, 188, 189, 199, 231, 233, fns. 494, 574; scope of undertakings, 234, 243, fn. 580

joiner, makes bed panels, 90; chair, 201; with columns, 211; chest, 119; King's, makes doors, windows, fn. 70

locksmith, 121–3, 132, 133; importance of, 232; master, 164

mason, 198, 204

ouvrier, 133; des menues euvres of Duke of Burgundy, makes tables, 219; maître, makes seating, 199–200, 205

painter, King's Serjeant, 188, 231; Walter of Durham, see furniture, seating, function, estate, 'St Edward's chair'

peintre, 132; du roy, makes cradle of estate, 96, 100, 104, fn. 70; chairs, 191

sellier, supplies cover, 115; upholsters chairs, 199, 200, 202.

serreurier, 38, 121, 132, 133, see also metal, ironwork

silversmith, 189

tailleur, covers chair, 199

organization of,

carpenters and joiners, huchiers and charpentiers, respective responsibilities of, 232–4,

fn. 578; Cofferer's' Ordinance, 113; combinations of crafts working on individual objects, 10, 38–9, 96–8, 107, 121–2, 143, 179–80, 231, 232, 233, 238, fns. 277, 494. divisions within crafts, 113, fns. 292–3; employment of, 238, 239, fn. 70; secular and ecclesiastical, 10–11, 234, fn. 31; incidence of managerial skills in, 238
recognition and preferment of, 5, 96, 100, 104, 243–4, fns. 44, 100
travelling, 189
Craon, le Seigneur de, 89
crédence, fn. 133
Cros, Johanna, 125, fn. 342
Croydon, John, 62
Croyland Abbey, fn, 281
cupboard, court, 59, fn. 154, see also furniture, buffets
Curia Regis Rolls, I, 121; VI, 6
curtains, 73, see also textiles
Cussigney, Guillaume de, 125, 130
Cuthbert, St, coffins of, 135, fns. 314, 564

Dachet, Johanna, 79
Dalton, J. N., 43
Dalton, O. M., fns. 36, 449
Daly, C., 27, fn. 85
Damme, xvi; doors at, 17, 35, 274, 276, Pl. 72A
Dangle, Richard, 115
Dawes, M. C. B., see Maxwell-Lyte
Dehaisnes, C. A. A., 7, 10, 62, 80, 81, 95, 114, 117, 119, 121, 124, 128, 131, 133, 185, 189, 233, fns. 35, 280, 281, 295, 313, 361
Delisle, L., 4, 79, 114, 123, 220, fns. 308, 323
dendrochronology, 150, 163, 166, 167
Dervieu, Lt. Col., 30, 73, 101, 107, 183, 184, 194–5 (9–10), 196, 197, 216, 218, 219, 220, 223, 224, 226, fns. 90, 191–3, 195, 215, 262, 263, 266, 278, 471, 475, 478–9, 503, 514, 529, 534, 537, 547, 549, 550, 557–8, Fig. 31, pp. 207–9
Destrée, J., 102, 103, 104, fn. 267
Detroit, Institute of Arts, fn. 96
Deuchler, F., 66, 69, fns. 170, 172, 446
Devillers, L., 81, 205, fn. 232
Dijon, 115, 117, 132, 133, 199, 224
Dillon, Viscount, see Hope, St John
dining, privately, 21, 65, 202, fns. 74, 161
documents, cases for, 3, 38 127, 163, fns. 107, 296, 419–20
Dodwell, C. R., 187, fns. 196–8
Douais, M. J. C., 4, 125
Drake, F., 248, fn. 665
dressers, see furniture, buffets and dressoirs
Drinkwater, N., 63, 201, 206
Dromore, John, Bishop of, 222
Dudley, Edmund, 85, 89, 119, 125
Dunois, Jean, Comte de, 62, 84, 87, 90, 98

Durham Abbey, 5, 83, 118, 123, 126, 211, 222, fn. 342
Durham, Walter of, 188, 231, 234, see also furniture, seating, function, estate, 'St. Edward's chair'

Eames, P., fns. 14, 20–1, 23, 25, 41, 70, 76, 153, 186, 200. 206, 209, 232, 240, 282, 298, 304, 322, 445, 452, 510, 566, 568, 610
ecclesiastical foundations, xxiii; as repositories for furniture, xxii, 1, 4, 5, 26–7, 110–11, 126, fns. 26, 281
Edward, St, the Confessor, 113, 192; see also furniture, seating, function, estate
Edward I, 188, 231, 243
Edward II, coronation chair of, 196
Edward III, throne of, 192
Edward IV, xvi, xix, 85, 86, fns. 4, 8, 128, 130, 156, 160, 285; the 'Black Book' of, 65, 118, 121, 133, fn. 565
Edward, the Black Prince, fns. 33, 324
Edward VII, 106
Edwards, R., see Macquoid, P.
Éginhard, 221
Egypt, her influence on furniture design, 168, 182, 186
Eleanor, Queen, see Westminster Abbey
Elizabeth of York, Queen, 5, 16, 119, 125, 128
Ellis, F. S., 148, fns. 387, 391–2
Eltham Palace, fn. 70
enamels, Limoges, 74, see also metal
England
   court of Edward IV, modelled on that of Burgundy, xvii, fn. 17; opulence of, fn. 8
   courts of, etiquette of, 241, 256, fn. 9
Etienne, St, see *Cat. 1, 2, 10, 16,* Appendix I
Evans, Joan, 197, fns. 38, 505, 560, 684
Exeter Cathedral, bishop's throne at, 194; Diocese of, 127
Eyck,
   Hubert van, 276, fn. 692
   Jan van, xvii, 34, 76, 136, 194–5 (10), 197, 198, 242, 243, 276, fns. 204, 208, 329, 415, 573, 691, Fig. 31, pp. 207–9

Faggin, G. T., 209, 276, fns. 204, 329, 333, 506, 689, 692, 694
Faré, M., 49, 152, fn. 242
Fastolf, Sir John, 87, 201, 223
Fayet, M. de, see Brunhammer
Fayolle, le Marquis de, 14, 24, 25, 245, 246, 247, fns. 60, 63, 64, 77, 79, 656, 659
feasts, xxi, 57, 59, fn. 140, see also Appendices VI and VII
Feives, Guillaume As, 90, 219, fn. 416
Félix, J., 5, 30, 62, 89, 124, 127, 131, fns. 132, 319
feudal concepts, xviii; great lords as servants, fn. 160

Fevre, Jean le, 66

Ffoulkes, C. J., 146, fns. 116, 379, 451

Field, R. K., 205, 220, fn. 461

Fillet, L'Abbé, fn. 213

Flanders, Margaret of, see Burgundy, Valois Dukes of, Philip the Bold

Flémalle, Master of, xvii, 33, 84, 168, 206, fns. 81, 92, 425

floors, covering of, 178, fn. 455, see also carpet

Forestié, E., 87, 93, 124, fn. 73

Forsyth, W. H., fn. 354

Fou, Pierre Du, 114, 116, 117, 129, 130

Fox, Bishop, ironwork to his chantry chapel, 161

Fox-Davies, A. C., fn. 216

France,
    courts of, etiquette at, 241; influence of, xv, 243; rules of, a model for Burgundy and England, xvii, 99, 256, 268, fn. 7
    kings of, craftsmen to the, 96, 100, 129, 243, fn. 70; special furniture for the, 136; see also furniture, French

Francus, le Dr, fn. 303

Froissart, 217

fur, 77, 87, 94, 95, 96, 100, 123; ermine, 76, 79, 81, 84, 87, 94, 95, 96, 98, 99, 100, 198, fn. 258; miniver, 76, 94, 95, 96; see also Appendix VIII (b–c)

Furgeot, H., fn. 284

Furness Abbey, fn. 39

furniture,
    acquired second-hand, fn. 182
    armoires, xxii, 1–54, 229, 239, 244, fn. 75; in convents, 9; ventilated, 9, 35, fn. 51; with chains, 8; drawers, 2, 35 ff., see also Freestanding (b); pigeon holes, 2, fn. 42
    contents, armour, 7, 93, fn. 87; books and records, 4–5, 13, 16, 17, 28, 29, 32, 37–44, 239, fns. 58, 68, 249; chapel equipment, 8, 10, fn. 58; clothing and textiles, 6–8, 49–52, see also Cat. 24, Pls. 30, 60A; food, utensils, etc., 8–9, see also dressoirs; jewels (including plate), 6
    documentation,
        12th–13th cent., 1, 2, 4, 6, 7, 8, 10, 49, fn. 39; 14th cent., 2, 3, 4, 5, 6, 7, 8, 9, 10–11, 16, 38, 49, 50, fn. 40; 15th cent., 3, 4, 5, 6, 7, 8, 9, 16, 18, 36–7, 38, 42, 50, 93, fns. 41, 42, 62
    function,
        estate, 10–11; marriage, with armorials Choul/Paterin, 275, fn. 459
    technique,
        panelled, see type, Locker (ii), Cat. 9, Freestanding (a), Cat. 13–16, Uncertain, Cat. 24–5, also Appendix IX
    type,
        as part of bed, 93; drop-front, fn. 43; fixed, 1–2, 4, 5, fn. 39

Freestanding (a)
    at Antwerp, Vleehuis mus., 9; at Bayeux Cathedral, Treasury, Cat. 11, 24, 25–7, 30, 32, 155, 232, 236, 237, fns. 588, 591, 593, 652, Pls. 12–13A, Fig. 6, p. 25; at Courtrai, 168, fn. 185; at Ghent, Bijloke mus., Cat. 15, 17, 33–4, 236, 239, 276, fns. 588, 611, Pl. 17, Fig. 9, p. 34; at Malines, Busleydon mus., Cat. 13, 24, 28, 29–30, 34, 43, 54, 164, 172, 173, 232, 236, 237, 238, 239, 274, 276, fns. 587–8, 591, 611, Pls. 14–15; at Obazine, (12th cent.), Cat. 10, 12, 13, 14, 21–5, 27, 30, 34, 54, 237, fn. 594, Pls. 10–11, see also Appendix I (15th cent.), Cat. 16, 24, 35, fn. 660, Pl. 18; at Wells Cathedral, Vicars Choral Treasury, 251, fn. 674, see also Appendix IV; at Westminster Abbey, Muniment Room, Cat. 14, 16, 30–3, 239, 276, fn. 611, Pl. 16, Fig. 8, p. 31, see also Appendix III; at Winchester College, Exchequer, Cat. 12, 27–8, fns. 583, 587, Pl. 13B, Fig. 7, p. 27; at York Minster, fn. 65

Freestanding (b)
    at Bruges, Gruuthuse mus., of Spanish merchants, Cat. 17, 19, 30, 35–7, 38, 44, 138, fn. 585, Pls. 19–21, Fig. 10, p. 36

Freestanding (c)
    at Wells Cathedral, Vicars Choral Muniment Room, Cat. 18, 38, 40–1, fn. 585, Pl. 22, see also Appendix IV; at Winchester College, Muniment Room, Cat. 20–1, 38, 40, 43–4, fn. 585, Pl. 26; at Windsor, St George's Chapel, Aerary, Cat. 19, 30, 38, 40, 41–3, 44, 161, fn. 585, Pls. 23–5, Fig. 11, p. 41; see also contents, books and records

Locker (i)
    at Obazine, Cat. 2, 13–14, 22, fn. 39, Pl. 3, see also Appendix I; N. transept, Cat. 1, 12–13, 22, 24, fn. 39, Pls. 1–2, see also Appendix I; at York Minster, Cat. 3–7, 1, 12, 15–17, 33, 163, 172, 276, Pls. 4–6, Fig. 1, p. 15, see also Appendix II

Locker (ii)
    at St Alban's Cathedral, 'The Watching Loft', Cat. 8, 1, 17–20, 32, 33, 34, fn. 652, Pls. 7–8, Figs. 2, 3, pp. 17, 18; at Wells Cathedral, Vicars Choral Exchequer, Cat. 9, 1, 20–1, 30, 40, 274, fn. 586, Pl. 9, Fig. 4, p. 20, see also Appendix IV

stone, 1, 12–14, fn. 39, see also Locker (i)

Uncertain
at Aylesbury, *Cat. 24, 50–2*, 54, 274, fn. 586, Pl. 30, see also Pl. 60A; at Cambridge, King's College, *Cat. 25, 52–4*, Pl. 31, Fig. 15, p. 53; at Chester Cathedral, *Cat. 22, 44–6*, 150, 157, 230, 237, fns. 596, 652, Pl. 27, Figs. 12–13, pp. 44, 45; at London, V & A mus., with iron scrollwork, 157–8, fn. 409 formerly at Noyon, 24, fn. 80; at Paris, Mus. Arts Déc. (St Quentin), *Cat. 23, 46–9*, 54, 152, 157, 230, 237, fns. 596, 652, Pls. 28–9, Fig. 14, p. 47; formerly at Selby, 20, 238, fns. 69, 72; see also buffets, dressoirs

beds, xxi, 73–93, 108, 217, 244
for servants, 77–8, 87, 240; frames for, 83, 90–1, 229, fn. 237, see also furniture, fixed and inalienable; in churches, fn. 229; king's bedding removed daily, 228, fn. 565; surviving examples, 92, 239, fns. 246–7, 249, 250; textiles for, 7, 78 ff., see also Appendix VIII (b–c); textiles
documentation,
12th-13th cent., 74, 75, 76, 90, 91, 233, fn. 215; 14th cent., 77, 78, 79, 80, 84, 88, 89, 90, 91, 224; 15th cent., 78–9, 81–3, 84–5, 87–8, 89, 90, 91, 92–3, 218, fn. 215, see also Fig. 37, p. 273; Appendix VIII (b–c)
function,
estate, 75–87, 240–1, 242, fns. 13, 70; not for sleeping in, 77, 85, 86, 241, fns. 220, 229; see also Appendix VIII (b–c); type, hung, sparver
technique,
boarded or panelled, 91, 92–3, 233, fn. 250, see also type, post, at Saffron Walden
type,
folding, 87–9, fn. 236
bedstead, 89–91
box, 92, fn. 250
canopied, 73, 74 ff.; in wood, 91–3; with half celour, 77, 79, 81, 91; whole celour, 77, 78, 81, 82, 91, 92, Fig. 37, p. 273; see also type, post
couchette, 87 ff., 224; see also Appendix VIII (b–c)
hung, 75 ff., 198, fn. 13, Fig. 37, p. 273; advantages of, 86–7, fn. 13; components of, 74; fn. 200, Fig. 16, p. 74, Fig. 37, p. 273; ornament of hangings, 75–7, 78–9, 80, 81, fn. 184
post, 73, 75, 91, 92, fn. 202; at Broughton, Chester, 92, fn. 249; at Paris, Mus. Arts Déc., of Rigault d'Aurelhe, 92, fn. 246; at Saffron Walden, 92
sparver, 83 ff., 98, fn. 216
wheeled, see type, *couchette*

buffets, 2, 55–72, 242; confusion with armoire, dressoir and cupboard, 55–6, 58, 59, 62, 71, 240, fns. 132, 134, 135, 163
type,
narrow, 58–62, 240, fn. 132, see also Pl. 60B; at Antwerp, Vleehuis mus. (no. 31.E.23), 58, 66, 274, Pl. 61; (no. 31.E.24), 58, Pl. 62; at Malines, Busleydon mus., of Marguerite of York, *Cat. 26, 65–70*, 236, fn. 589, Pl. 32; at Plougrescant, *Cat. 27*, 34, 58, 59, *70–2*, 179, 240, fns. 616, 652, Pl. 33
stepped, 55, 56, 57, 58, 59, 60, 238–40, 254–5, 256; stages of, signifying degrees of precedence, 57, 59, 240; see also Appendix VIII (b–c), Fig. 36, p. 272
buffets/dressoirs, 55–72; documentation, 12th-13th cent., 60, 223, fn. 137; 14th cent., 60, 61, 62, 63, 64, 65, 205, 233, fn. 141; 15th cent., 58, 59–60, 61, 62, 63, 64, 65, 71, 254–5, fns. 140, 141, 156, see also dressoirs

bureaux, fn. 43

chests, xxii, 108–80, 238, 244; closed with paper and nails, 128; forms reflecting use, 108–10, 120, 140, 172, 178, 241, Fig. 17, p. 109; sealing of, see metal, ironwork; terminology, 110–11, 128 (1379), 137–8, fns. 283–4, 286–7, 292–4.
contents,
armour and weapons, 129, fns. 70, 446; books, 5, 126, 127–8, fn. 334; chapel goods, 116, 118, 119, 125–6; coin, 118, 120–1; grain and bread, 130–1; jewels (including plate), 115, 116, 117, 119, 121–2, see also *Cat. 42, 43*; lights, 116, 118, 129–30; miscellaneous articles, 131–2; muniments, 126–7, see also *Cat. 42, 43*, documents, cases for; papers, 119, 120; textiles, 116, 117, 122–5;
documentation, 12th cent., fns. 311, 314; 13th cent., 113–14, 120–2, 125–7, 129–30, fn. 308; 14th cent., 114–23, 125–33, 137, 233, fns. 70, 299, 300, 303, 306–8, 310, 313, 315, 319–24, 327, 332, 334, 338, 342, 361, 575–6; 15th cent., 30, 96–7, 118–22, 124, 126–8, 130–1, 133, 137, fns. 70, 300–3, 305, 309, 319–21, 323–4, 328, 333, 342; 16th cent., 85, 119, 125, fns. 320, 330
function,
as bed steps, 133–4
case, 114
coffin, 135, fns. 314, 564
marriage, 124
travelling, 108; *bahuts*, of tapestry, fn. 295; with other kinds of baggage, 111–

20, 241; 'trussing coffers', 115, 116, 118,
123, 174, 177, see also type, standard
technique,
   carved, 124, 135, 138, 140, 141-3, 164,
     178, fns. 316, 347, see also *Cat. 30-2,
     38, 41, 48*; of St Cuthbert, fn. 314
   dove-tailed, fn. 564, see also *Cat. 32, 37,
     38, 39*
   iron, 132, 134, 135; fns. 76, 322; at Mus.,
     London, from Guildhall, 134, 135,
     173, 174, 176, 238, fns. 76, 304, 322;
     -bound, 30, 118, 122, 123, 124, 126,
     128, 130, 133, 135, 137, 138, 163-4,
     4, fns. 299, 312, 320, 323, see also
     Cat. 35, 40, 42, 43, 44, 45, 47
   leather, 113, 114, 115, fn. 576; -covered,
     30, 122, 124, 135, 164, 172, fns. 313,
     314, 344, see also *Cat. 47*; of St
     Cuthbert (pre-1104), 135, fn. 314;
     'cuirbouilli', fns. 313, 450; -healed, 117
   lined/padded, 136, fn. 332
   marked with letters, 124
   of precious materials, 136, 241-2, fns.
     314, 324-30, 334
   on crampons, 137, fn. 334
   painted, 124, 128, 130, 136, 138, 140,
     fns. 323, 361, 441, see also Pls. 64B, 65;
     for identification, 116-17, fn. 285
   wicker, 115, 135, fn. 315
   with interior divisions, 134, fn. 303;
     multiple lids, 85, 128, 134, 163, fns.
     302, 319
type,
   altar, 134, 136, 141, 150, fns. 300, 395,
     see also Pls. 64B, 65
   Ark, 6, 138-40, 212; at Burnley, Town-
     ley Hall mus., 140, fn. 349; London,
     V & A mus., 140, fn. 349
   Box, 112, 138; at Bruges, Gruuthuse
     mus. (no. 560), 164, fn. 427; (no. 597),
     Cat. 41, 143, 146, 164, *167-9*, fn. 381,
     Pl. 47B; Bury St Edmunds, 164, fn.
     424; Cradley, 163; Ghent, Bijloke
     mus., *Cat. 44*, 164, 168, *172-7*, 232,
     276; Hereford Cathedral, 163-4; Ick-
     lingham, 54, 164, fns. 131, 423;
     Oxford, All Souls College, *Cat. 42,
     43*, 163, 164, *169-70*, 175, 238, fn. 606,
     Pl. 48; Winchester College, *Cat. 40*,
     150, 164, *165-7*, fn. 628, Pl. 46B,
     Figs. 22 and 23, pp. 165, 166; (Audit
     Room), fn. 302
   cope 108; at Wells Cathedral, 140, Fig.
     18, p. 139; York Minster, 135; see
     also type, round
   counter, 134, 151, fn. 301; desk, fn. 301
   Dug-out, at Lower Peover, 162; Wim-
     bourne Minster, 162

Hutch, 137, fn. 344; at Alnwick, 137,
   142, fn. 364; Avenbury, 141, 156,
   fn. 356, Fig. 18, p. 139; Bitterley, 158;
   Brancepeth, 137, 140, 142; Bruges,
   Gruuthuse mus. (no. 513), 150,
   fn. 396; Chevington, 142, fn. 366;
   Chichester Cathedral, 142, 144, 152,
   fn. 353, Fig. 18, p. 139; Climping,
   Cat. 30, 140, 141, *143-5*, 146, 163, 212,
   231, 237, 238, fns. 595, 601, 652,
   Pl. 35B; Cound, *Cat. 36*, 140, 141, 151,
   156, Pl. 42, Fig. 18, p. 139; Coventry,
   142, fn. 369; Derby, 142, fn. 365;
   Dersingham, 142, fn. 368; Haconby,
   142, fn. 367; Harty, 142, 147, fns.
   371, 373, 385; Hereford Cathedral
   (Library), 141, fn. 357; Little Canfield,
   fn. 353, Fig. 18, p. 139; London,
   V & A mus., 'Fares' chest, 134, 151,
   fn. 301; (no. 735, 1895), 152, fn. 399;
   (no. W.30.1926), fn. 375; Malpas,
   Cat. 37, 141, 150-1, 156, *157-8*, 164,
   237, fn. 597, Pl. 43, Fig. 18, p. 139;
   Neenton, *Cat. 38*, 143, 151, 156,
   158-9, 237, fn. 595, Pl. 44; Oxford,
   Merton College, *Cat. 35*, 140, 151,
   152, *155*, 163, Pl. 41, Fig. 18, p. 139;
   St Mary Magdalen, 142, 274, fn. 363;
   Paris, Carnavalet mus., *Cat. 34*, 150,
   152, *153-4*, 157, 230, 232, 237, 242,
   fns. 584, 596, 630, 652, Pl. 40; Cluny
   mus. (Gerente Coll.), 141, fn. 358;
   Mus. Arts Déc., *Cat. 33*, 150, *151-2*,
   153, 154, 157, 164, Pl. 39; Saltwood,
   142, fn. 362; Sion (Switzerland), 140,
   141, fn. 351, Fig. 18, p. 139; Stoke
   d'Abernon, 141, fns. 355, 375; Wath,
   137, 142; Westminster Abbey, *Cat. 32*,
   140, 143, *149-50*, fn. 628, Pl. 38,
   Figs. 19, 20, p. 149; Wroxeter, 140,
   150, 164, Fig. 18, p. 139; York Minster,
   Cat. 31, 140, 142, *145-8*, 164, 176, 231,
   238, 242, fns. 373, 599, 607, 652, Pls.
   36-7; Ypres Cathedral, 140, 146, 147,
   fns. 350, 373, 384; with decorated
   supports, 140-1, 151, 152, 158, *Cat. 30,
   31, 35, 36, 37*, Fig. 18, p. 139
Panelled, 137, 160; at Honfleur, 160, 162;
   Oxford, Brasenose College, *Cat. 39,
   160-1*, 274, Pls. 45-46A
Plinth, 151; at Bourg mus., 179, fn. 459;
   Faversham, 178, fn. 457; Huttoft, 178,
   fn. 456; London, V & A mus. (no.
   W.17.1914), 178, 179, fn. 454; Romsey,
   Cat. 48, 143, *178-80*, 231, 232, 237,
   fns. 594-5, 598, 605, 652, Pl. 53
round, 122, 134, fn. 299; see also type,
   cope
'ships chests', 119-20

Slab-ended, 36, 138, fn. 311; at Carlisle, Tullie House mus., 138; of Richard de Bury, 69, 136, 138, 150, 156, 163, 164, 231, 236, fns. 346, 589

Standard, 112, 117, 118, 122, 125, 132, 137, 164, fns. 323, 344, 422; at Bruges, Gruuthuse mus., *Cat. 46*, 35, 173, 175–7, 232, fn. 442, Pl. 51 (no. 557), 173, fn. 440; (no., 559), 173, 176, fns. 442, 448; Cambridge, St John's College, 173, 176, fn. 451; Sidney Sussex College, 173, 176, 177, fn. 444; Hereford Cathedral, *Cat. 45*, 173, *174–5*, 241, fn. 626, Pl. 50; Little Waldingfield, 173, fn. 439; London, P.R.O., 177, fn. 453; Malines, Busleydon mus., 173, fn. 441; Westminster Abbey, *Cat. 47*, 176, *177*, 241, fn. 626, Pl. 52; resembling Cat. 47, 177

various, at Ghent, Bijloke mus., bearing *briquet de Bourgogne*, fn. 185; London, V & A mus. (no. 738.1895), carved with knights in combat, 147, fn. 385; V & A mus. (no. 82.1893), chest front, 146, 238, fn. 377; V & A mus. (no. W.15.1920), chest front, 143, 147, fns. 374, 386; Tournai mus., of *Corporation de Chaudronniers*, fn. 185; of Thomas Silksted, 178, fn. 458; reliquary at Winchester Cathedral, 274; with wheels, 173, see also *Cat. 46*

types, Fig. 17, p. 109

cradles, 93–101; cases for, 96–7, 100; documentation, 94–5, 96–9

function,
estate, 94, 95–6, 98–9, 100, 103, 106, 107, 241, 271, fns. 256, 277, Fig. 36, p. 272; at Brussels, Mus. Roy. Art Hist., of Marie of Burgundy, 1478/9 ('Cradle of Charles V'), *Cat. 28*, 26, 33, 68, 93, 100, *101–4*, 172, 232, 236, 237, 241, 244, 276, fns. 573, 589, 593, 621, 650, 652, 653, Pl. 34; significance of textiles and furs, 94, 241, fn. 258; night cradles, 94, 95–6, 99, 103, 106, 107, 241, fns. 256, 277; at London, Mus. of, from Newland ('Cradle of Henry V'), *Cat. 29*, 93, 99, 100, 101, *104–7*, 241, fns. 625, Pl. 35A; see also Appendix V

made by court artists, 96–7, 243
of Beaufort family, 106

technique,
turned, 101, fn. 264

type,
sparver, 94, 96–7

court cupboards, see buffets

decorated with personal initials and devices, see armorial; Burgundy, Valois dukes of

decoration of, 237–8; differing at front and sides, 24–5, 34

delicacy of largely impracticable, 229–30

display cabinets, fn. 72

dressoirs, 2, 62–5; as food counters and hatches, 56, 60, 62–5, see also buffets

ecclesiastical, xi, xxiii, see also chapels, within households

elaboration of, controlled by fashion, 237

English, 143, 232; in Cat. Raissoné, *Cat. 3–7, 8–9, 12, 14, 18–22, 24–5, 29–30, 32, 35–40, 42–3, 47, 49–51*; see also esp. craftsmen

evidence for; bias of types of, xxi–xxii, 60, 68, 73, 93, 110, 235, 238–9; documentary, xix, xxi, xxii, 239, fn. 14; literary, xix, xx–xxi, xxii, 239, Appendices VI–VIII; art, 56, 58, 73, 74, 93, 220, 225, fns. 482, 536; Fig. 32, p. 225; drawings and illuminations, xxi–xxii, 17, 66–7, 68, 73, 75, 83, 91, 101, 137, 160, 174, 183–4, 186–7, 206, 221, 226, 241, 275–6, fns. 68, 138–9, 152, 173, 194, 208, 235, 242, 244, 333, 400, 463, 473, 476–7, 486, 490–1, 684, Pls. 64A, 67, Figs. 27, pp. 193–4; 28, p. 195; 29, pp. 196–7; 31, pp. 207–9; 34, p. 226; paintings, xvii, xxi–xxii, 64, 75–6, 83–4, 91, 160, 168, 173, 206, 241, 242, fns. 139, 208, 241, 329, 415, 425, Pl. 63A; sculpture, 73, 210–11, fn. 520

fixed and inalienable, xviii, 1, 2, 4, 5, 76, 86, 91, 131, 203, 223–7, 229, 239, fns. 11, 41, 214, 232, 240, 569

French, 143, 178, 183, 240, 274; in Cat. Raisonné, *Cat. 1, 2, 10, 11, 16, 23, 27, 33, 34, 48*; of 18th century, 228; see also esp. craftsmen

German, 35, 74, 140, 225, fns. 2, 43, 97, 104, 143, 554

given personal names, 88, 90

imported into England, 125, 137

in Cat. Raisonné, 12th–13th cent., *Cat. 1, 2, 10, 11, 22, 23, 30, 33, 34, 35, 49, 50*; 14th cent., *Cat. 31, 36, 40*; 15th cent., *Cat. 3–9, 12–18, 24–9, 32, 37–9, 41–8, 51*; 16th cent., *Cat. 19–21*

in chambers, 3, 4, 6, 60, 61, 62, 63, 82, 83, 85, 91, 122, 124–5, 128, 133, 136, 137, 185, 188, 199, 200, 201, 202, 203, 204, 205, 206, 217–18, 219, 223, 239, fn. 334

in ecclesiastical foundations, xxii

in garderobes, 6, 7, 8, 50, 82, 114, 115, 118, 125, 128, fns. 37, 127, 128, 342

in halls, 60, 61, 63, 65, 124, 130, 188, 198, 199, 200, 202, 203, 204, 205, 206, 215, 217, 219, 223, 224, 239, fn. 511

in private libraries, 226, 249

in service quarters, 8, 9, 63, 64, 130, 131, 133, 215, 216, 224, 233

influence of social organization on design of, xv, xviii–xix, xx, 217–18, 220, 228–30, 237, fn. 5

inherited with property, 205

medieval ideas expressed in later periods, xv, xviii, 9, 63–4, 75, 86, 138, 184, 240, fns. 13, 345

movable, xviii, xx, xxii, 76, 203, 206, 217–23, 229, 239, fn. 40

Netherlandish, 125, 137, 143, 146–7, 164, 173, 174, 177, 274; in Cat. Raisonné, *Cat. 13, 15, 17, 26, 28, 31, 41, 44–6*, fns. 335–342, see also esp. Burgundy, Valois dukes of; craftsmen

of estate, xvii, 10–11, 229, 230, 236–7, 243–4; see also esp. beds, buffets, cradles, seating; precedence

of peasantry, xix, xxii, 205, 220, fns. 16, 250, 461

quantity surviving, xi, xix, xxii, 1, 2, 21, 57, 73, 108–10, 143, 209, 235, 238, 239, fn. 75

response to changing fashions, 229, 237

restorations to, 223

Scandinavian, xv, 101, 135, fns. 236, 264, 311

seating, xx, 10, 21, 77, 181–214, 244; cases for, 189, 190, 200, 231; decorated with animals, 182, 183, 185, 186, 188, 189–90, 204, fn. 483, Figs. 27, p. 193; 28 (2), p. 194; leafage, 185; masks, 184

documentation for benches, forms and stools, 12th cent., 223, 224; pre-13th cent., 203; 13th cent., 203; 14th cent., 204, 205, 224; 15th cent., 205, 206, 217–18, 224, 233, 254; for chairs and X-stools, 12th cent., 187; 13th cent., 184, 187, 188, 198–9, 211, 233, fn. 522; 14th cent., 184, 185, 188, 189, 190, 199, 200; 15th cent., 185, 190, 191, 200–1, 211, 218, fns. 508, 523–4; 16th cent., 191

evidence from art, 191, 192, 194, 197, 198, 206, Figs. 28, pp. 194–5; 29, pp. 196–7; 31, pp. 207–8

function,
chamber chairs, 188, 189, 198–202, 239, 242

estate, xii, xxiii, 181–4, 185, 186, 187, 188, 189, 191, 202, 231, 236, 239, 242, 243, fn. 32; assumed by master craftsman, 198; at coronations of kings and popes, 182, 183–4, 189, 196, fns. 462–3; 'Chair of Dagobert', 183, 186, fn. 469; created by accessories, 191, 197–8; created through use of textiles, 182, 187, 189, 190–1, 212, 254, 255; presence of foot support, 182, 191, 197–8, 242, fn. 465; for bishops, 184, 185, 186, 192–3; importance of height, 182, 197, 242, 254, fns. 463–4; precious materials used for, 189–91, 192; 'St Edward's chair', 26, 145, 182, 188, 191–2, 231–2, 234, 243, 244, 274, fns. 462, 493, 495, 573, 653; 'St Peter's

Throne', 136, 183, 192, fns. 331, 497, 498, silver chair in Barcelona, 221, Fig. 27, p. 193; Solomon's throne, 182, 183, fn. 462; throne on Edward III's seal, 192; throne of Maximian at Ravenna, 197; throne of Richard II, 192, 193; Pl. 68; use of benches with footboards, 202, 242; forms and stools, 204, 242, 243, fn. 513; X-form, 182–4, 242; with king's image, 188, 189, 191–2; tester and celour, 183, 184, 198, 242, 254, 255, fn. 472

for bed chambers, 187, 269, fn. 491, see also Fig. 37, p. 273

hair dressing etc., chairs for, 184, 200, 202, fn. 475

technique,
copper, gilded, 188, 189; image, 189; panels and plaques, 190, 203; tinned, 74, fn. 196

cypress, 190

ebony, 189

glass mosaics, see function, estate, 'St Edward's Chair'

iron, silvered and gilded, 184; (X-form), 185; metal, 183, 184; see also function, estate, precious materials

nailed, 185, 188, 189, 199, 200; see also upholstered

painted, 74, 189, 200, 211, 223; and gilded, 189, 191, 192; joined with silvered and gilded nails, 189; with figures, 203

panelled, with linen fold, 209; see also type, bench, fitted at Muchelney, *Cat. 51*; Appendix IX

silvered, 185

silver, enamel and precious stones, 184, fn. 478; see also function, estate, silver

stone and marble, 188, 190, 196, 197, 203, 204, fn. 492

turned, 209, 223, 224, fn. 137; at Hereford Cathedral, *Cat, 49,* 192, 194–5, *210–11,* 242, fns. 265, 637, Pls. 54–5; see also Fig. 28, p. 195

upholstered, 185, 188, 198, 199, 202, fn. 479;
in leather, 199, 202; silk-fringed, with painted frame, 200; red velvet, 202, fn. 508; with down, 200; with gilded nails, 200, 202

using precious materials, 184, 185, 186, 187, 188, 189, 190, 191, 194; see also function, estate

terminology, 181, 182, 187

type, xix
benches, 7, 199, 201, 202–9, 224, 229, fn. 137; at Winchester Cathedral, carved with stars, 209; fitted at Coombe St

Nicholas, 209, fn. 517; at Muchelney, *Cat. 51*, 196, 197, 202, 209, *213–14*, 242, 276, fn. 631; at Paris, Mus. Arts Déc. (no. Peyre 1049), with arms of Rigaud d'Aurelhe, 209, 214, Pl. 69; Salisbury, the Old Deanery, 206; for Henry III, 198; integral with hammer beam, 209; stone, in hall, 203, 206; with swinging back rail, 206, fn. 514; see also Fig. 31 (10, 12), p. 208

boarded, 191, 194–7, Fig. 29, pp. 196–7

chairs, xix, xxi, xxiii, 181–202, 203, 223, 239, 243; beside beds, 198, 242, Fig. 37, p. 273, see also function, chamber chairs; boarded, at Stanford Bishop, *Cat. 50, 211–13*, Pl. 56; figure-shaped, 192, Fig. 29, p. 196; of ease, 199, 200, 202; 'of Sarum make', 201; swivel, 200, 202; tub-shaped, 197, 233, Fig. 28 (10), p. 195; used universally, 198, fn. 461

folding (? X-form), 185, 199

forms, 201, 202, 203, 204, 206, 224, 233; in London, V & A mus., from Barningham, 206, fn. 515; with butterfly and turret supports, 204, Fig. 30, p 204

incorporating lockers, see esp. bench, fitted, at Muchelney

knock down, see chairs, boarded, at Stanford Bishop

post, 191–4; (1), Fig. 27, p. 193; (2), turned, Fig. 28, pp. 194–5

slab-ended, 206–7

stalls, xxiii–xxiv, 179, 198, 203, fn. 32; at Paris–Mus. Arts Déc. (no. Peyre 1058) from Palluau, 182, fns. 32, 464; in private chapels, 203, 206

stools, xix, 202, 203, 205–9; in New York, Metropolitan Mus., 209, Pl. 63B; 'joined', 205; triangular, 209; see also X-form; tables associated with own stools

window, 203, 205, 206, fn. 512

with canopies/sparvers, 186, 187, 188

with casters, 205, 206; traceried frame, 209

X-form, 168, 182–7, 191, 192, 212, 242, fn. 184; at Bayeux Cathedral, 186; London, V & A mus. (no. 696.1904), fn. 484; (no. W.12.W.13.1928), 187, fn. 488; Vienna, Kunstgewerbe mus., from Admond, 186; York Minster, 187, fn. 488; for travelling, 184, fn. 476; frontal and lateral designs, 186–7; in general use, 184–6

Spanish, 37, 221, 243, fns. 43, 450

tables, xxii, 21, 60, 64, 65, 108, 215–27, 229, 244, 274, fn. 229; arranged for meals, xix, 57, 217; associated with own stools, 203; with seating, 202, 203, 223–4, 226

documentation,
12th–13th cent., 215, 221, 223–4, 233; 14th cent., 205, 215, 219, 220, 221, 222, 224, fn. 528; 15th cent., 42, 216, 217–18, 219, 220, 222, 223, 224, 233, fns. 111, 533, 562, Appendices VI–VII

dormant, see type, fixed

function,
dining, 217–18, 220, 226, 243, 253–4, 255; estate, see type, trestle, silver-gilt; travelling, see type, knockdown; gaming, 4, 215

of ash, 216; cypress, 216, fn. 529; marble, 216, fns. 530–1, see also type, round, stone

technique,
carved, 223, see also type, fixed, slab-ended, at Winchester, Strangers' Hall; gold, 221; of John of Gaunt, 222

inlaid, fn. 528

jewelled, 221, fn. 542

painted, 221–2; at Paris, Cluny mus., fn. 547; Winchester, see type, trestle, round; Zurich, fn. 547

raising and lowering mechanisms, 222, 226

silver, 221, 243, fn. 542; of Charlemagne, 221

terminology, 215

type,
counters, 215; fixed, 223–7, 243, Figs. 32–3, p. 225; at Winchester College, 224, 226–7; fns. 559, 562–3, Pl. 70; in Bayeux tapestry, 225, Fig. 32, p. 225

pedestal, 226

slab-ended, 225–6; at Winchester, Strangers' Hall, 225, fn. 553

folding, 222–3, fns. 528, 547

four-post, 224–5; at Haddon Hall, 225, Fig. 33, p. 225

knockdown, at Paris, Cluny mus. (no. 22795), 223, 243

round, stone, 226, fn. 557; see also trestle, round

trestle, 217–222; at Penshurst Place, 221, 243, fn. 540; horn-shaped, 215–16; of softwood, 215–16; walnut, 216; number owned, 219; round, 220, fn. 537; at Winchester Castle ('Arthur's table'), 220, fn. 538; semi-circular, 215, 220; shape of supports, 220–1; silver-gilt, plated, table of Henry IV, 221, fn. 573

with drawers, 225, fn. 552

types few, designs numerous and individual, 21, 238, 242

value of, 19, 100–1, 229, 239, fns. 14, 70, 214

furniture and furnishings, priorities in, xix–xxi, 228 ff., 235–6, 241, fn. 570

special provision of, for birth of heirs, 61, 84,

93–4, 96–8, 100–1, 103, 241, 256–7, fn. 680, Fig. 36, p. 372, see also cradles, Appendix VIII (b-c)

secular and religious types and ornament intermingled, xxiii, xxiv, 9, 49–50, 71, 84, 93, 97, 108, 255–6, fns. 33–6, 279, see also *Cat. 11, 27, 31, 48*, Pl. 61

with drawers, see armoires Freestanding (b-c); Buffets, narrow; tables, type, Fig. 10, p. 36

see also armorial, craftsmen, metal, wood

Furnivall, F. J., 78, 81, 117, fns. 9, 133, 158, 159, 161, 235, 491

Garnier, J., 124, fns. 252, 255, 260
Garnier, Robin, 118
Gaunt, John of, 88, 134, 187, fns. 397, 490, see also furniture tables, technique, gold
George, St, legend of, 147–8; see also furniture, chests, type, Hutch, *Cat. 31*
Germoles, Château de, fn. 222
gesso, 154
Ghent, xviii, 9, 102, 103, 115, 199, 217, fn. 241
St. Peter's Abbey, fn. 420
Ghent, Joos van, fn. 227
Gheyn, van den, 69, 70
Gibbons, A., 122, 123, fns. 26, 182, 281
gifts, from seigneurial lords, 68, 76, 81, 88, 89, 115, fn. 183
Gilbert, C., v, xiii
Gillingham (Dorset), 64
Giuseppi, M. S., 7, 129
glass, 256, mosaics of, 230; see also furniture, seating, function, estate, 'St Edward's chair'
Gloag, J., 194–5 (12–14)
Gloucester, Humphrey, Duke of, fn. 9
Godard-Faultrier, V., 64, 89, 93, 128, 131, 133–4, fns. 155, 187, 336
Godfrey, W. H., 251
Goes, Hugo van der, 91, 275, fn. 241
Gothic art, xi, xv, fn. 1
Grand, L. le, 38–9
Grand Conseil, 68, fns. 180, 181
Grant, M., fn. 444
Gribble, E. R., see Cescinsky
Grimme, E. G., 70
Groom, Richard, 130
Grosseteste, Bishop, fn. 27
Gruuthuse, Lord, 85, 86, 218, fn. 156
Guiffrey, J. fns. 324, 573
Guildhall, London, iron chest of, see furniture, chests, technique, iron
Guiraud, J., 3, 60, 77, 91, 116, fns. 125, 299, 319
Gurmyn, Richard, 205
Gwyn, P., fns. 431, 563

Haddon Hall, 'dole' cupboards at, fn. 412; table at, see furniture, table, type, four-post

Hainaut, le Comte de, 81, 205, fn. 232; Marguerite de, 76
Hale, W. H., fn. 137
Halphen, L., fn. 543
Hardyng, John, 220
Hart, C. J., fn. 284
Harris, H. A., 148, fn. 393
Harvey, J. H., 28, 166, 167, fns. 115, 429, 432
Hatfeld, Emma, 222
Haut-de-Coeur, Jean, 120
Havard, H., 111, 137, 189, 191, 200, 202, 274, fns. 118, 286, 340, 463, 509, 511, 683
Havergal, F. T., 211, fns. 518, 520
Havering, 203
Haynin, Jean de, fn. 175
heirlooms, 76
Henry I, 74, fn. 194
III, 113, 126; chair with canopy of, 188, 198; chapel goods of, 125; favours painted drapery, fn. 685; gilded seat for, at Windsor, 188; panels for bed of, 90; seat canopy for, 188; state bed of, 75, 91, fn. 201; stone bench for, 188; throne of, at Westminster, 188; treasure of, 114, 120
IV, 127, 243, fn. 463
V, xv, 84, 98, 105, 106, 118, 202, fns. 35, 275, 508, 511
VI, 83, 147
VII, 59, 85, 92, fn. 458
VIII, 33, fn. 163
Hereford Cathedral, xiii; Audley chapel in, panelled door of, 274, 275; see also furniture, chest, type, Box, Hutch, Standard; seating, technique, turned, *Cat. 49*
Herlin, Friedrich, fn. 413
Heron, Jehan Le, 117, 123, 128, 129
Hesdin, Château d', 7, 121, 128, 188, 222, 243
Hewett, C. A., fn. 564
Hexham Abbey, throne at, 197
Highfield, R., fn. 405
Historical MSS. Commission, 118
Hodges, C. C., 137, 142, fns. 341, 364
Hohler, C., fn. 38
Hollstein, E., fns. 331, 498
Holmqvist, W., fns. 311, 401, 520–1; see also Fig. 28 (6), pp. 194–5
Hommel, L., 68, 70, fns. 176–80
Honnecourt, Villard de, 234, 243
Honyboorn, William, 61
Hope, W. H. St John, 18–19, 20, 43, 191, 215, fns. 34, 69, 72, 120, 167, 169, 402, 528, 570
horn, 163
horses, ridden within doors, 57; see also households, travelling equipment for
Hoskins, W. G., fn. 461
Hoste, Put, 121, 122
households,
food and drink rations in, 69; importance of,

xx–xxi; movements of furniture within, xx, 217–18, 228–9, fn. 158; Offices of, Ewery, 60, fn. 161; Kitchen, 63; Ordinances of, 65, fn. 285; travelling equipment for, 111–20, fn. 285; see also esp. Burgundy, Valois Dukes of; Edward IV, 'Black Book' of
Hugham, William, 119
Huizinga, J., fns. 4, 22
Hunt, J., 140, fns. 193, 352
Hunt, R., fn. 68

inlay, see wood
iron, see metal
ivory, boxes of 136
on chairs, see furniture, seating, function, estate, 'St Peter's throne' and throne of Maximian

Jacob, E. F., 78, 81, 88, 119, 122, 126, 127, 130, 170, 222, fns. 305, 320–1, 434–5
James, the Joiner, 90
James, St, of Compostella, 176–7
Janneau, G., fns. 80, 485
Jarry, L., 4, 8, 9, 84, 87–8, 90–1, 98, 131, fn. 234
Jenning[s], C., fns. 296, 419, 453
John II, of France, xvi, 84, 189
Johnstone, J., 213, fn. 525
Jones, P. E., fn. 523
Jonville, Château de, 13
Jupp, E. B., fn. 578
Juxon, William, see furniture, seating, type, X-form, at London, V & A mus. (no. W.12.W.13.1928)

Kelderman, Antoine, 68
Kellaway, W., see Chew
King, D., fn. 505
Kingsford, C. L., 64, 85, 89, 90, 119, 125, 201, 205, 216, 218, 224, 233, fns. 29, 156, 160, 225–6, 279, 301, 323, 570
Kirby, J. L., fns. 463
Kreisel, H., fns. 2, 43, 97, 104, 143
Kynebell, Thomas, 199
Kyrkby, Roger, 78, 219

Labarte, J., 61, 84, 126, 128, 185, 190, fns. 306, 327, 334
Lambert, A., fn. 358
Lambrechts-Douillez, J., xiii
Langres, Henry de, 133
Larking, L. B., 114
Lavenham, early panelling at, 105
laver, 15th cent. at Wells, 21, 249, Pl. 72B
leather, 89, 111, 115, 116, 171, 179; barehides, 119; cases for chairs, 189, 190, 200, see also furniture, chests, function, travelling;

chests, technique; chests, type, standard, at Westminster Abbey, Cat. 47; seating, technique, upholstered
Lee, Sir S., see Stephen, Sir L.
Legg, J. W., 185
Leghtone, Thomas de, 46
Lehmann-Brockhaus, O., 60, 223
Lethaby, W. R., 33, fns. 91, 402, 671
Lettenhove, le Baron K. de, fns, 6, 676
Letts, M., 6, fn. 8
Leverhulme Trust, the, xiii
Lex, L., 3
library or study, 202; see also furniture, armoires, contents; chests, contents
Liège, armoire at, 48
Liège, Jehan Du, 96–7, fn. 277
Lincoln, fn. 58
linen fold, see Appendix IX
Littlehales, H., 4, 91, 131, fn. 41
Liverpool, University of, v, xiii
locks, see craftsmen; metal; wood
London; Botolf Lane inventory, see Littlehales; Guildhall chest, see furniture, chests, technique, iron; Public Record Office, chests and boxes at, 163, 177, fns. 296, 419, 453; St. Paul's Cathedral, 50, 121, 184, 223, fns. 30, 126, 137; see also, museums; Westminster Abbey
Longespée, William, tomb chest of, 178
Loo, Hulin de, 276
Louis XI, fn. 149
Louvain, 67
Lowther, A. W. G., 150, 167, fns. 394, 429
Luxembourg, Jeanne de, fn. 680
Lyons, Richard, 89, 115, 132
Lyttelton, Sir Thomas, 126

Macon, hospital of St Antoine, 87–8, fn. 333
Macquoid, P., 43, 217, fns. 114, 532
Macquoid, P./Edwards, R., 46, 71, 137, 138, 148, 158, 162, 190, 197, 209, 214, fns. 75, 108, 131, 157, 166, 216–17, 247, 256, 274, 339, 348, 355, 366, 368–9, 371, 374, 382, 395, 409, 417, 423, 457, 486, 504, 515, 540, see also Fig. 31, pp. 207–9
Madonna, wooden figure of the, in turned chair, 210–11, fn. 520
Madour, Roger, fn. 342
Maes, L., fn. 181
Maffei, E., 48, 49, 274, fns. 119, 135, 152, 541, 683
Malines, 29, 30; connexion with Marguerite of York, 67–9; see also furniture, armoires, type, Freestanding (a), Cat. 13; buffets, narrow, Cat. 26; chests, type, Standard; museums
mannequin, used in toilet of great ladies, 243
Manney, Sir Walter, 88
Marc Fitch Fund, The, xiii

Marche, Olivier de la, xvii, 58, 190–1, 197, 217–
18, 239, fns. 4, 30, 570; his account of the
marriage of Charles the Bold and Marguerite
of York, 253–5, fn. 139; see also Appen-
dix VII
Marchegay, P., 123
Maréchal, J., 36, 37, fns. 99, 100–103
Mareuil, Eudes de, 2–3, 6, 63, 120, fn. 284
Marmaduke, John Fitz, 184
marquetry, see woodworking
Marville, Jean de, 132, 133
masons, see craftsmen
Mathey, Dr F., xiii
Maximilian of Austria, 67, 102, 236, 257, fns.
180, 185, 257, Fig. 38, p. 273
Maxwell-Lyte, H. C., 251
Mayr-Harting, H.M.R.E., xiii, 224
Meingre, Geoffroy le, 49, 50, fn. 124
Mellon, Paul, Centre for Studies in British Art,
Memling, Hans; St Barbara, 206, Fig. 31, pp.
207–9; shrine of St Ursula, 173
Menitré, Château de La, 133
Mercer, E., 187, 276, fns. 2, 75, 243, 372, 413,
460, 487, 690
Mérode triptych, see Flémalle, Master of
metals,
 brass, 8, 39, 185
 copper, 8, 63–4, 74, 98–9, 125, 274, fn. 324;
 gilded, 189
 enamelled, silver-gilt table, see furniture,
 tables, type, trestle
 ironwork,
  attachment ignoring/acknowledging woodworker's design, 231, 238
  by master craftsmen, 48, 164, 172, 178, 231,
  232, 237
  decorative, in Cat. Raissoné, 12th–13th
  cent., *Cat. 10, 22, 23*; 15th cent., *Cat. 13,
  15, 27, 44, 46, 48*, see also Figs. 25–6, p.
  171; 16th cent., *Cat. 20, 21*; bench work,
  158, 232, 237, fn. 130, *Cat. 27, 48*, Pl.
  66B
  decoratively wrought, 150–1, 164, 237,
  Cat. 22, 23, 33, 34, 37
  technique,
   tinned; see furniture, armoires, type,
   Freestanding (a), at Malines, *Cat. 13*
  type,
   bolts, 12th–13th cent., 22, 24, 26, 245,
   246; 14th–15th cent., 18, 24, 35
   chains, 144, 153
   handles and handle plates, 12th–13th cent.,
   245; 14th cent., 33, 163–4, *Cat. 40*;
   15th cent., 16, 29, 32, 33, 35, 41, 54,
   see also *Cat. 28, 45, 47*, Figs. 8, p. 31;
   11, p. 41, see also Bekynton, Bishop
   hinges and straps, 12th–13th cent., 12–13,
   14, 22, 23–4, 25–6, 163, 245 ff., Fig. 12,
   p. 44, see also *Cat. 22*; 14th cent., 141,

   163; Pls. 46B, 47A, see also *Cat. 40*;
   15th cent., 16–17, 18, 19, 28, 29, 30, 32,
   33, 34, 35, 36, 37, 38–9, 276, fn. 413,
   Figs. 1, p. 15; 3, p. 18; 8, p. 31; 21, p.
   159; 24, p. 168, see also *Cat. 26, 38, 41*;
   16th cent., fn. 674
   knocker, at Bourges, 237, Pl. 66B
   locks and lock-plates, 10th cent., fn. 345;
   12th–13th cent., 12–13, 22, 26; 15th
   cent., 16, 24, 29, 36, 38–9, 59, 142,
   164, 237, see also *Cat. 39, 42–3, 48*;
   broken and renewed, 135, fns. 309,
   310; iron, 22, 24, 28, 232; number
   indicating type of custodianship, 24,
   30, 36–7, 122, 126, 134–5, 167, 241,
   fns. 76, 100, 304–10; sealing of, 134,
   fns. 308, 323
   nails, 155, 165, 188, fn. 314; gilded and
   silvered, 189; tin-plated, fn. 345; see
   also furniture, seating, technique
   rings, 135, 156, 163, 168, 173; fn. 311
   see also furniture, chests, technique
 lead, inlay, 150, fn. 395
 pewter, 8, 63–4
 silver, 230, see also furniture, seating, estate,
 precious materials, tables, technique,
 type, trestle
 gold, 230, see also furniture, chests, technique
 of precious materials, also tables, technique
 tin, 74, fn. 345
 Theophilus on, 74, 187, 203
Metzdorf, L., 102, 103, 104, fn. 267
Moissac Abbey, fn. 192
Molder, Jean de, Last Supper by, 209, fn. 516
Monmouth Castle, 105, 106, fn. 275
Montbard, Château de, 61, 205, fn. 58
Montbeton, Château de, 93, 124, fn. 73
Mortimer, Roger de, 114
Muchelney Abbey, 214; bench at, see furniture,
 seating, type, benches, fitted
Museums
 Antwerp, Vleehuis, xiii, see also furniture,
 armoires, type, Freestanding (a); buffets,
 type, narrow
 Bourg, see furniture, armoires, function,
 marriage; chests, type, Plinth
 Bruges, Musée Gruuthuse, see Casket;
 furniture, armoires, type, Freestanding
 (b); chests, type, Box, Hutch, and
 Standard
 Brussels, Musées Royaux D'Art et d'Histoire,
 see furniture, cradles, function, estate
 Burnley, Townley Hall Museum, 140, fn. 349
 Carlisle, Tullie House Museum, see furniture,
 chests, type, Slab-ended
 Ghent, Musée Bijloke, see furniture, armoires,
 type, Freestanding (a); chests, type, Box,
 Various; Shutters

London, British Museum, 83, see also plate; Museum of London, see furniture, chests, technique, iron; cradles, function, night c.; Victoria & Albert Museum, see furniture, armoires, type, uncertain; chests, type, Hutch, Plinth and Various; seating, type, forms & X-forms

Malines, Musée Busleydon, history of, 67 ff., see also furniture, armoires, type, Freestanding (a); buffets, type, narrow; chests, type, Standard

New York, Metropolitan Museum of Art, vi, 19, 20, fns. 71, 92, 139, 208, see also furniture, seating, type, stools

Paris, Musée Cluny, altar retable by Jean de Molder at, 209, fn. 516; rock crystal finial at, 186, fn. 483, see also furniture, chests, type, Hutch; tables, technique, painted; tables, type, knockdown; Musée des Arts Décoratifs, vi; see also furniture, armoires, type, uncertain; beds, type, Post; chests, type, Hutch; seating, type, stalls; Musee du Louvre, 83, fn. 208; Musée Municipal de la ville de Paris (Carnavalet), see furniture, chests, type, Hutch

Stockholm, Nordiska Museet, fn. 236

Saffron Walden Museum, see furniture, beds, type, post

Tournai, Musée de, see furniture, chests, type, various

Vienna, Kunstgewerbemuseum, see furniture, seating, type, X-form

Walsall, Museum of Leathercraft, see casket

Myers, A. R., xiii, 63, 65, 89, 115, 118, 121, 132, 133, fns. 17, 30, 74, 134, 285, 565

Nairn, I., 145

Nancy, battle of, 66, 68, see also textiles

Naste, the lord of, 114, fn. 313

Neckham, A., 49, 198, fns. 24, 507

Netherlands, The, influence on England of, xvi, see also furniture, Netherlandish

Nichols, J., 80, 90, 121, 131, fns. 33, 324

Nicholas, N. H., 5, 88, 119, 125, 126, 128, fns. 35, 128, 163, 207, 330

Normandy, dukedom of, xv

Northburgh, Michael de, 121

Northerne, Stephen le, 90

Nottingham Castle, 198, 203

Nyevelt, A. van Zuylen van, fns, 140, 171, 175, 223-4

oak, see wood

Oakeshott, W. 211, fns. 58, 302, 518

Obazine, see furniture, armoires, type, Free-standing (a), and Locker (i); also Appendix I

Old Soar (Kent), fn. 58

Orange-Nassau, chapel of, at Brussels, 248

Orléans, Jehan d', 96, fn. 70
  Louis, duc d', fn. 127

Olyver, John, fn. 461

Oseberg, ship burial from, fn. 345

Oxford, All Souls College, xiii, see also furniture, chests, type, Box; Brasenose College, xiii, see also furniture, chests, type, Panelled; Merton College, vi; see also furniture, chests, type, Hutch; Queen's College, 121

Padua, 67

Palgrave, Sir F., 127, 189, 221, fn. 390

Palmer, W., 188, 192, 196, fn. 579

Palsgrave, J., fn. 163

panelled rooms, 198, 203, 224, 233, 274; walls, see Lavenham

Pannier, L., 64, 224

Panofsky, E., 243, 275, fns. 10, 81, 96, 218, 227, 241, 244, 649

Paris, 61, 80, 81, 90, 96, 97, 115, 116, 123, 124, 189, 190, 199; Abbey of St-Denis, 153, 203; Nôtre Dame de, gate of St Anne, 48, 157, Pl. 59; Priory of St Eloy-de-, 64, 224; St Germain-en-Laye, 125

Parker, J. H., 196, 209, 251, fns. 58, 73, 139, 512, 555; see also Turner, T. H.

Parr, Queen Katherine, 43

Paterin, Jeanne, 275

Pauwels, H., 9

Payn, Thomas, 130

Penshurst Place, see furniture, tables, type, trestle

Petitot, C-B., 191, 218, fns. 6, 149, 533, 570, 677

Pevsner, N., 156, 159, 213, 214, 274, fns. 360, 376, 411, 499-500, 525-6

Philip I of France, seal of, 183
  VI, of France, 84

Philip 'the Fair', 67, 68, 101, 103, 257, fn. 270, Fig. 38, p. 273; see also Appendix VIII (b-c)

Phillips, Sir T., see Appendix VII (b)

Pierrefonds, Chateau de, garderobes at, 50, fns. 127, 128, Pl. 60A

Piper, A. J., fn. 420

plane, 230

plate, (silver and gold), xv, xix-xx, xxiii, xxiv, 6, 8, 229, fns. 19, 21, 36, 570; gold cup in British Museum, xxiv, fns. 16, 36, 449; on buffets, 57-8, 59-60, 61-2, 229, 240, 254-5, 256, fns. 140, 158

Pocock, W. W., see Jupp

Poitiers, Alienor de, xvii, 56, 57, 61, 77, 85, 87, 93, 94, 95, 96, 99, 100, 103, 216, 239, 240, 241, fns. 6, 138, 229, 233, 235, 238, 253-4, 258-9, 269-70, 531, Appendix VIII

Pontoise, 114

poplar, see wood

Portal, M., fn. 538

Portugal, Isabelle of, 57, 66, 85, fn. 140, Fig. 38, p. 273; see also Appendix VIII (b-c)

Poux, J., fn. 326
Powicke, F. M., 127
precedence, rules of, xvii, 100, 198, 202, 240, 241, 257, fns. 9, 258; oblige a great lord to use a stool, 202, 242, fn. 509; kings to use bench, fn. 511; and rank, distinction between, xix, 77, 181, 239, 242, fn. 17; see also ceremony, Fig. 36, p. 272, Appendix VIII (b-c)
Prost, B and H., 3, 7, 61, 62, 115, 116, 117, 119, 121, 123, 125, 128, 129, 130, 132, 133, 189, 190, 200, 205, 215, 219, 233, fns. 18, 44, 70, 184, 219, 222, 295, 300, 315, 321, 332, 571, 575-6

Quatremares, Château de, 78, 122-3

Raine, J., 5, 78, 118, 184, 219, 222, fns. 314, 320, 333, 342
records, storage of, 6
Renaissance, influence of the, xi, xvi, 34, 159, 178, 184, fn. 458
Rethel, Comtesse de, confinement of, 96-7, 107, 124, fns. 252, 680
Richard II, 81, 129, 216, 249, 250, Pl. 68; see also furniture, seating, function, estate
Richard, J-M., 7, 10, 88, 188, 199, 204, 222, 231, 233, 243, fns. 123, 202, 205, 494, 513, 569, 574, 643, 645
Richmond Palace, 59
Richter, G. M. A., fn. 467
Riley, H. T., 90, 251
Roberts, A. K. B., 43, fn. 109
Roe, F., 27, 142, 146, 147, 148, fns. 362, 365, 367, 373, 378, 380, 382-4, 456, 458
Rolin, Chancellor, 136
Roman traditions, influence of, 140-1, 182-3, 244, fn. 353
Roman, J., 63, 204
Romance of the Rose, 80
Romanesque art, xi, xv, 141, 210, 211, 245
Roo, Dr R. de, xiii
Rorimer, J. J., 20, fn. 71
Rose, Cecilia, 90
Rotuli Parliamentorum, IV, 84, 118, fn. 508
Rouen, Château de, 63, 204
Roussel, Guillaume, voiturier, 117, 118
Rouvre, Château de, 115, 205, 219, 226, fn. 557
Royal Commission on Historical Monuments, vi, 33, 53, 54, 155, 162, 177, 210, 211, 274, 275, fns. 58, 129, 248, 345, 353, 356, 363, 519, 671, 686-7
Royan, Mme de, 123
Royer, L. 216
Rozmital, Leo of, xvii, 6
Rupplemonde, Château de, 119
Rusby, turned chair from, 210
Russell, John, fns. 9, 133, 159

St Alban's Abbey, see furniture, armoires, type Locker (ii)
Remy, Jean le Fevre de, fn. 140
Severin, Master of, fn. 139
-Galle, Château de, 216
-Palaye, La Curne de, fn. 6
saints, patron, 176
Salisbury Cathedral, tomb of William Longespée in, fn. 81; 'the Old Deanery' at, 63
Sandler, L. F., see Weinberger, M.
Schayes, M., 102, 103
Sauerländer, W., fn. 359
saw, 230
Scandinavia, see furniture, Scandinavian; museums; Oseberg; Rusby; Vallstena
Scheler, A., fn. 24, 507
Schmitz, H., 193, 196, 197, fn. 243
Schryver, Dr A. de, xiii
screens, 19, 21, 32, 89, 172, 179, fns. 73, 91; see also Appendix III
Scrope, Henry le, fns. 29, 279, 301
Sens, William de, 234
servants, for infants, 94, 99, 106, 241, fns. 252, 255, 268
Sharpe, R. R., 2, 62, 79, 90, 116, 120, 121, 125, 129, 130, fns. 40, 301, 335, 338, 342, 528
Shaw, H., 145, Pl. 35B
shells, as decorative devices, 176-7, Pl. 72C
shutters, 38-9, 51-2; window, at Ghent, Bijloke mus., 274, Pl. 71
Silcock, A., see Ayrton, M.
Silksted, Thomas, chest of, 178, fn. 458; panelling of, 275
Silverstone, 188
Simpson, W. S., 184, fn. 126
Singer, C., fns. 287, 581
Somersham, John, 137
Southwold Cathedral, screen at, 172
Spain, 19
Squilbeck, J., 70
Stafford, Edmund, 81; Humphrey, 88
Stalins, Baron A., 70
Stanford Bishop, chair at, see furniture, seating, type, chairs, boarded
state apartments, 68-9, 85-6, see also furniture, of estate; Appendix VII (b)
Staunford, St George's church, 126
Steer, F. W., 145
Stein, H., 90, 219, fn. 461
Stenton, Sir F., 192, 193, 198, fns. 482, 536, Fig. 31, pp. 207-9
Stephen, Sir L., fn. 668
Stokesay castle, fn. 58
stools, see furniture, seating
Stratford-upon-Avon, armoire of, 38, fn. 108
Streche, John, 127
Streeter, B. H., 163; fns. 318, 357, 421
Sudbury's Hutch, 69
Suffolk, Duchess of, 118; chair of estate of, 190

Surreau, Pierre, 5, 62, 83, 89, 124, 127, 131, fn. 132
Surtees Society, 83, 123, 126, 201, fn. 524
Swartwout, R. E., fn. 577
Symonds, R. W., 113, 292, 293, fns. 344, 581

tables, see furniture
tailors' workshops, 7
Talent, Château de, 5, 16, 37
Tanner, L. E., 33, 177, fns. 95, 672
Taylor, A. J., fns. 106, 572
techniques in furniture making, see furniture; ironwork; woodworking
textiles, xxi, xv, xvi, xix–xx, xxi, 7, 56, 58, 100, 241, fns. 14, 161, 214
    for boards (i.e. tables, etc.), 123; chamber hangings, 80, 81, 83, 94–5, 101, 229; re-use of, 101
    quantities collected, fn. 570
    standards, captured at Nancy, 66
    type,
        canvas, 7, 113, 120, 177, waxed, 111, 112, 113; cendal, 76, 79, 82, 84, 94; cloth of gold, 79, 81, 86, 95, 96–7, 98, 99, 185, 190–1, 255–6; cloth of 'Rennes', 84, 123; estamine, 93; linen, 24, 123, 124, 136, see also Appendix IX; sarge, 81, 82, 90, 98; sarsenet, 85; satin, 80; saye, 87, 94; silk, 80, 81, 94, 123, 200, of Arras, 80; taffeta, 84, 99; tapestry, 80, 81, 191; velvet, 79, 85, 97, 99, 189, fn. 207; wool, 7–8, 79, 81, 123
        used for luggage, see furniture, chests, function, travelling, bahuts; for upholstery, 185, fn. 479
    see also esp. furniture, beds, cradles, also Appendix VIII (b-c)
Theophilus, see Dodwell; metals
Thieulloye, convent of, 199
Thirion, J., xiii, fn. 492
Thomas, A. H., 3–4, 6, 8, 9, 117, 118, 199, 219, 222, fns. 308, 320, 461
Thompson, F. H., fn. 353
Thornham Parva, painted retable at, 141
Thornton Abbey, 145
Thornton, P., xiii
Timbrell, W. F., fn. 249
Toison d'Or, Order of the, 57, 67, 253, fn. 140
Toky, Richard, 117, 219
Torre, James, 248, fns. 664–6
Torrigiano, Pietro, fn. 458
Toulouse, Abbey of St Sernin de, 125
Tournai, 119
Tours, 191
Tout, T. F., 65
Trémoille, Guy de La, 117
    L. de La, 87, 89, 118
Tricou, J., 275, fn. 459
truffles, 48–9

Tunstall, Bishop, 275
Turin Hours, the, evidence from for dating linen fold, 275–6
Turner, T. H., 225, fns. 28, 39, 58, 400; see also Parker, J. H.
Tvoky, Thomas, 81
Twenty-Seven Foundation, The, xiii
Twining, Lord, 70; fn. 174
Tymms, S., 61, 124

unicorns' horns, 58, 255
Upholsters' Company, fn. 216
upholstery, see furniture, seating, technique, also textiles, type

Vaernewyck, Marcus van, 103, fn. 268
Valence, William de, tomb of, 74, 274
Vallance, A., fn. 81
Vallery-Radot, J., 27, fn. 485
Vallstena (Gotland), 12th cent. furniture from, 211, fn. 521
Valois, Jeanne de, 78, 122
Valous, V. de, 3, fn. 320
Vaughan, R., fn. 3
Veer, John de, 191
Verhaegen, Baron A., 9
Vernet, F., 126
Vernier, J-J, 5
vestments, xxiii, 8, fn. 29; see also chapels, private; textiles
Vézelay, Abbey church of, fn. 58
Viaux, J., 27, 49, 152, 154, fns. 283, 658
Victoria County History, 214, 251, fns. 527, 662
Vieupont, Yves de, 98
Villeneuve-Lembron, Château de, 92
Villiers-le-Duc, Château de, 132
Vincennes, Château de, 1, 48, 61, 206, fns. 303, 334
Viollet-le-Duc, E. E., 24, 27, 50, 52, 73, 75, 85, 86, 101, 111, 162, 183, 193, 194–5 (2–5, 11), 196, 197, 220, 221, 245, fns. 58, 75, 77, 78, 80, 82, 83, 84, 127, 128, 133, 189–90, 195, 203, 220, 229, 262, 283, 418, 472, 489, 535, 542, 544–5, 655, Pl. 60A, Fig. 31, pp. 207–9
Vyne, the (Hants), 275

Walle, A. L. J. van de, fns. 106, 572
walnut, see wood
Walpole, Horace, 110
Wanscher, O., 183, 186, fns. 43, 466, 470, 473–4, 480–1, 688
Warre, Elizabeth la, 123
Waterer, J. W., fn. 287
Watkin, A., 251
Watteville, Baron de, fn. 121
Weaver, F. W., 118
Weinberger, M., 183, 192, 203, fns. 469, 497

Welby, Richard, fn. 281

Wells Cathedral, xiii; Vicars Choral, 20, 40, fn. 74; laver in Exchequer, 249, Pl. 72B; see also furniture, armoires, type, Freestanding (a), (b), Locker (ii); Appendix IV

Wells, W., fn. 346

West, Lady Alice, 77, 117

Westminster Abbey, 185, fns. 58, 199
    Henry VII's Chapel in, 92, 274
    Queen Eleanor's tomb of 1294 in, 46, 234, fn. 579
    Muniment Room of, xiii, 32, fn. 91; partition in, 32, fn. 91, see also furniture, armoires, type, Freestanding (a); Appendix III
    see also furniture, chests, type, Hutch and Standard

Westminster, Palace of, 233
    hall of; marble seat and table in, 190, 216; throne in, 188, 189; tables for, 233

Weyden, Roger van der, xvii, 198, fn. 208

wicker, see furniture, chests, technique

William, 'the Conqueror', xv, 220, fn. 12

Wilson, D. M., fn. 468

Winchester, Castle, 6, 114; round table at, see furniture, tables, type, trestle, round
    Cathedral, 209, fn. 58;
        Bishop Fox's Chantry in, 43; Prior Silksted's panelling in, 275
    College, xii, see also furniture, armoires, Freestanding (a), (c); chests, type, Box; tables, type, fixed
    Strangers' Hall, see furniture, tables, type, slab-ended

Wolvesey, palace of, 189

Windsor Castle, 6, 8, 65, 85, 86, 215, 218, fns. 156, 167; hall of, 13th cent. royal seat in, 188; St George's Chapel, xiii, 38, 154, 157, fn. 130, see also furniture, armoires, type, Freestanding (c); door of Aerary, 33, fn. 94

wine, 60

Wodhous, John, fn. 333

Wolff, A. de, fn. 351

Wolsey, Cardinal, 275

wood, 1
    locks of, 232, fn. 575
    sawn, 37, 41
    type,
        beech, 215
        bois d'ollande (riven oak), 230, fn. 571

cedar, 70

cypress, 135, 190, fn. 321

ebony, 189

elm, 64

'estrich borde', 91, 135, fn. 320, see also softwood

oak, 5, 124, 130, 135, 215, 216, 230; *Cat. 1–22, 24–6, 28–41, 44, 50–1*; pre-eminence of, 230, 237; properties of controlling design, 230 ff.; riven, 37, 44, 92, 96–7, 138, 209, 230, fns. 106, 317; see also type, *bois d'ollande*; used in house and shipbuilding, 230, fn. 572

poplar, 135, 173, fns. 318, 320, 438

softwood, 3, 96–7, 125, 128, 135, 164, 175, 215–16, 222, fn. 320, see also *Cat. 42, 43, 45*,

walnut, 5, 120, 135, 178, 216, fn. 319, see also *Cat. 48*

woodworking techniques, 91, 138, 140, 151, 228, Fig. 19, p. 149; early reference to dovetail, fn. 564; inlay and marquetry, 4, 73, 74, 86, 136, 230, fn. 573; in Jan van Eyck's painting of 1434, fn. 573; panelling, 43, 90, 92, 160, Fig. 9, p. 34, see also *Cat. 9, 13, 15, 16, 24, 25, 26, 27, 28, 39*, Appendix IX; turnery, 73, 101, 209, 223, 224, fn. 137, see also *Cat. 49*

Wood, M., 209

Woodstock, 221

Woodville, Queen Elizabeth, her banquet for the lord Gruuthuse, 218

Worcester, John of, fn. 194

Wormald, F., 182, fn. 462

Wrangelschrank, the, fn. 413

York,
    Marguerite of, xvi, 236; crown of, 67; household of, 68–9, see also Burgundy, Valois dukes of, Charles the Bold; *Cat. 26*; Fig. 38, p. 273
    Minster, xiii; X-chair at, fn. 488; Zouche Chapel in, see *Cat. 3–7*, Appendix II; see also furniture, armoires, type, Freestanding (a); chests, type, Hutch

Ypres, xviii

Zouche, William La, 247, 248, 249, fn. 668

Zurich, see furniture, tables, technique, painted

PLATE I. Cat. 1. Pair of armoires, of locker type, in the church of St Etienne at Obazine (N. transept), c. 1176. The armoires are part of the wall pierced by the entrance to the present vestry (left door) flanked by the stairs to the monks' dorter

PLATE 2A.   Cat. 1. Pair of armoires at Obazine (N. transept), *c.* 1176

PLATE 2B.   Cat. 1. Detail of centre of left door

PLATE 3.   Cat. 2. Armoire (locker type) at Obazine (W. end), *c.* 1176

(facing page)

PLATE 4. Cat. 3. Armoire of locker type
at York Minster, *c.* 1500

PLATE 5A.   Cat. 4. Armoire at York
Minster, *c.* 1500

PLATE 5B.   Cat. 4. Detail of the iron
fittings to the two upper doors

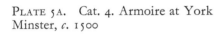

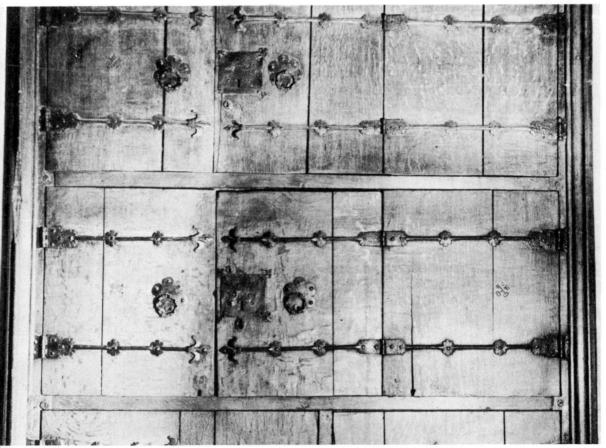

PLATE 6A.   Cat. 5. Armoire at York Minster, *c.* 1500.
Note concertina hinges, upper right

PLATE 6B.   Cat. nos. 4–6. Armoires in the 'Zouche chapel', York Minster;
room with fittings, *c.* 1500

PLATE 7. Cat. 8. The 'Watching Loft', St Alban's Abbey,
incorporating four armoires of locker type, 1413–29

PLATE 8A.   Cat. 8. Armoire no. 4 of the
'Watching Loft', St Albans, 1413–29;
left door

PLATE 8B.   Cat. 8. Left door, lower bolt
and countersunk, traceried hinge strap

PLATE 9A. Cat. 9. Armoire of locker type
at the entrance to the Exchequer,
Vicars Choral, Wells, *c.* 1457

PLATE 9B. Cat. 9. Detail of interior and
panelled construction

PLATE 10.   Cat. 10. Armoire in the abbey church o
St Etienne, Obazine, *c.* 1176. Note the counterbalance achieve
through relief and linear designs on each fac

(facing page

PLATE 11A.   Cat. 10. Detail of upper hinge strap on left doo

PLATE 11B.   Cat. 10. Detail of lock fittings on right door
note single bar serving both door

(*facing page*)

PLATE 12. Cat. 11. Right-hand side of armoire in the Treasury, Bayeux Cathedral, *c.* 1230–40; flat surfaces provided a field for painted decoration (Photograph about 1912)

PLATE 13A. Cat. 11. Detail of painted decoration and iron fittings on armoire at Bayeux Cathedral (Photograph about 1912)

PLATE 13B. Cat. 12. Armoire in the Exchequer, Winchester College, fifteenth century; lower view of bays 1–3

PLATE 14. Cat. 13. Armoire in the Busleydon Museum, Malines, *c.* 1470
from the house of the city aldermer

(facing page)

PLATE 15A. Cat. 13. Detail of the upper locks; two hasp bars
are lodged in a single, central housing

PLATE 15B. Cat. 13. Another view showing the superb quality
of design and execution

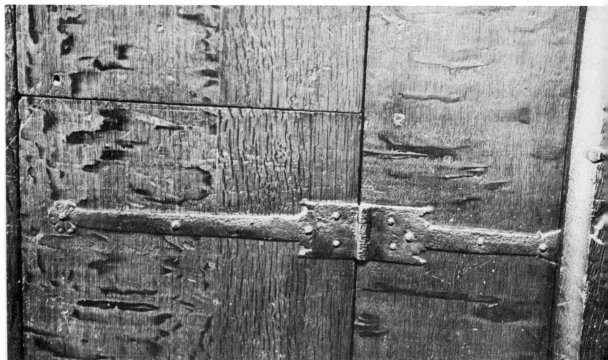

ATE 17.   Cat. 15. Armoire in the Bijloke Museum, *c.* 1490–1510;
ɔm the Town Hall, Ghent

ucing page)

ATE 16A.   Cat. 14. Armoire in the Muniment Room, Westminster
ɔbey, *c.* 1500

ATE 16B.   Cat. 14. Detail of left bay

PLATE 18A.   Cat. 16. Armoire in the Vestry, church of St Etienne,
Obazine, *c*. 1450–90

PLATE 18B.   Cat. 16. Detail of lower ironwork.   PLATE 18C.   Cat. 16. Side
view, with linenfold panels contrasting with front treatment

PLATE 19A. Cat. 17. Armoire of the Spanish merchants of Bruges (Gruuthuse Museum), *c.* 1441

PLATE 19B. Cat. 17. Detail of interior showing the two surviving drawers

PLATE 20A. Cat. 17. Armoire of the Spanish merchants of Bruges,
c. 1441; shield of Castille–Leon (top)

PLATE 20B. Cat. 17. Detail of the arms of Burgos and
traceried iron strap (left door)

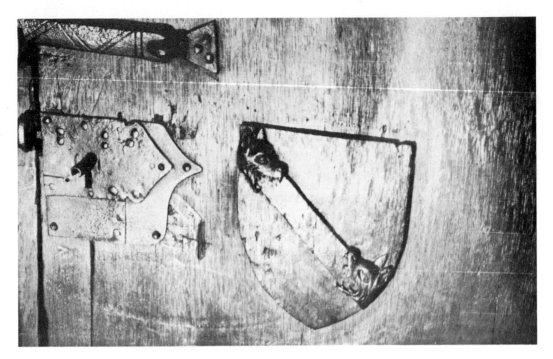

PLATE 21A. Cat. 17. Shield with Spanish device (right door)

PLATE 21B. Cat. 17. Detail of lock fitted in 1547

PLATE 22A. Cat. 18. Multi-drawer armoire in the Muniment Room, Vicars Choral, Wells, 1458–70

PLATE 22B. Cat. 18. Detail of drawers showing finger tabs

(*facing page*)

PLATE 23. Cat. 19. Multi-drawer armoire (far wall) containing rolls in the Aerary, St George's Chapel, Windsor, *c.* 1500–30

PLATE 25. Cat. 19. Detail showing differently constructed drawers; both
re nailed, and assembled without refinements

facing page)

LATE 24A. Cat. 19. Armoire at Windsor; detail of handle type B

LATE 24B. Cat. 19. Detail of handle type A

PLATE 27.   Cat. 22. Armoire in Chester Cathedral; original doors of *c.* 1294
later framework

(facing page)

PLATE 26A.   Cat. 20. Multi-drawer armoire in the Muniment Room,
Winchester College, *c.* 1510–30

PLATE 26B.   Cat. 20. Detail of 4th drawer from top, 2nd bay

PLATE 29A.   Cat. 23. Left detail with border of pigs amid oak leaves

PLATE 29B.   Cat. 23. Right detail with mythical beasts as tree roots

facing page)

PLATE 28.   Cat. 23. Armoire in the Musée des Arts Décoratifs, traditionally
from the church of St Quentin; doors *c.* 1290–1320

PLATE 30A. Cat. 24. Armoire in
St Mary's Church, Aylesbury,
c. 1480–1500

PLATE 30B. Cat. 24. Detail of the swinging
supports for clothing

(facing page)

PLATE 31A. Cat. 25. Armoire at King's College, Cambridge, c. 1450–80

PLATE 31B. Cat. 25. Massive countersunk hinge strap, and handle
(centre, right door)

PLATE 31C. Cat. 25. Detail of panelled interior

(facing page)

PLATE 32A.   Cat. 26. Buffet of Marguerite of York's household
(Busleydon Museum), *c.* 1478–97

PLATE 32B.   Cat. 26. Left door; Burgundian ducal devices with
marguerites

PLATE 32C.   Cat. 26. Right door incorporating C M (Charles and
Marguerite)

(this page)

PLATE 33A.   Cat. 27. Buffet at Plougrescant, *c.* 1495–1502

PLATE 33B.   Cat. 27. Detail of centre lower door

PLATE 34A. Cat. 28. State cradle of
Philip the Fair or Marguerite of
Austria, 1478–9

PLATE 34B. Cat. 28. Foot panel painted
with double M for Mary of Burgundy and
Maximilian of Austria

(*facing page*)

PLATE 35A. Cat. 29. Cradle from Newland
(*H.M. the Queen*), *c.* 1500

PLATE 35B. Cat. 30. Chest at St Mary's
Church, Climping, *c.* 1282–1300
(From Shaw, pl. XXIX)

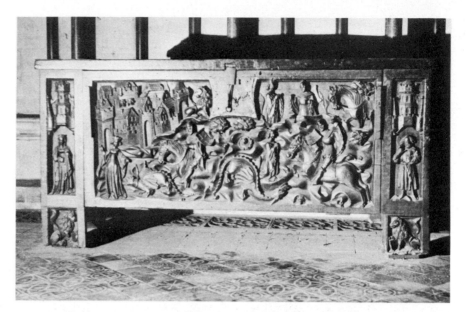

PLATE 36A. Cat. 31. Chest at York Minster, *c.* 1380

PLATE 36B. Cat. 31. Carved front (St George and the Dragon)
and plain sides

(*facing page*)

PLATE 37A. Cat. 31. Detail of lock plate reserve

PLATE 37B. Cat. 31. Left stile

PLATE 37C. Cat. 31. Right stile

PLATE 38. Cat. 32. Chest in the Chapel of the Pyx, Westminster Abbey, *c.* 1480. The chest (of hutch type 1, with truncated stiles) has sides with an individual form of framed construction using dovetailing. The plain front is enlivened by handsome iron hasps patterned with circles and triangles, fitted with a grip of nail type projecting at right angles from the tab

(*facing page*)

PLATE 39A.   Cat. 33. Chest in the Musée des Arts Décoratifs, *c.* 1200–50

PLATE 39B.   Cat. 33. Detail of scrollwork on front, upper left

PLATE 41A.   Cat. 35. Chest at Merton
College, Oxford, *c.* 1280–1300

PLATE 41B.   Cat. 35. Back view

(*facing page*)

PLATE 40A.   Cat. 34. The Carnavalet
chest, traditionally from Saint-Denis,
c. 1250–70

PLATE 40B.   Cat. 34. Detail of scrollwork,
front upper right

PLATE 42A.   Cat. 36. Chest in St Peter's Church, Cound, *c.* 1340–80

PLATE 42B.   Cat. 36. *View showing side pole handles and gabled lid*

PLATE 42C.   Cat. 36. *Detail of dovetailing and stylized traceried foot*

(*facing page*)

PLATE 43A.   Cat. 37. Chest in St Oswald's Church, Malpas, *c.* 1400–80

PLATE 43B.   Cat. 37. *View showing ironwork decorating three sides and lid*

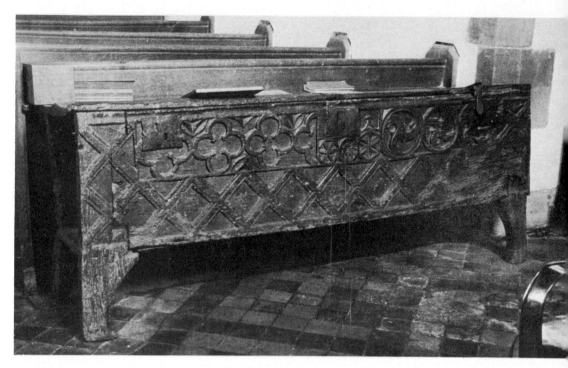

PLATE 44A. Cat. 38. Chest in All Saints' Church, Neenton, *c.* 1500–25

PLATE 44B. Cat. 38. Detail showing gabled lid

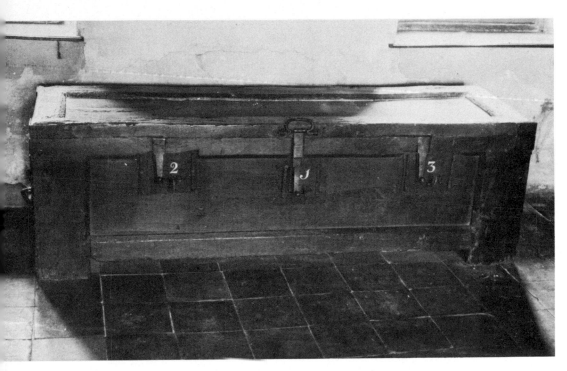

PLATE 45A.   Cat. 39. Chest at Brasenose College, Oxford, *c.* 1500–15

PLATE 45B.   Cat. 39. Detail of original lock (1) with secondary lock (3)

PLATE 46A. Cat. 39. Chest at Brasenose; detail of unusual side panelled construction

PLATE 46B. Cat. 40. Chest at Winchester College, 1396–7

(facing page)

PLATE 47A. Chest at Winchester College (companion to Cat. 40), showing fittings for hasp and bar locks

PLATE 47B. Cat. 41. Chest in the Gruuthuse Museum, *c.* 1400–25; note animal paw terminals

PLATE 48A.   Cat. 42. Chest at All Souls College, Oxford, *c.* 1440–5

PLATE 48B.   Cat. 43. Companion chest at All Souls showing
original hasp and lock plate

PLATE 49A. Cat. 44. Chest in the Bijloke Museum, c. 1480–1500

PLATE 49B. Cat. 44. Note original lock plate (centre) with secondary
fittings at sides

PLATE 50A.   Cat. 45. Chest of the Vicars Choral Library,
Hereford Cathedral, *c.* 1440

PLATE 50B.   Cat. 45. Note natural curve
of lid, and handles for ropes

PLATE 50C.   Cat. 45. Original centre
front lock plate with secondary hasp

PLATE 51A.   Cat. 46. Iron-plated chest in the Gruuthuse Museum,
c. 1450–1500

PLATE 51B.   Cat. 46. Hasp with strap handle and shell terminal

PLATE 52.   Cat. 47. Leather-covered chest in Westminster Abbey
library, traditionally associated with Lady Margaret Beaufort
c. 1480–1500

(facing page)

PLATE 53A.   Cat. 48. Walnut chest at Romsey Abbey, *c.* 1480–1500

PLATE 53B.   Cat. 48. Side view

PLATE 53C.   Cat. 48. Single central lock plate with owner's
shield beneath

(*facing page*)

PLATE 54. Cat. 49. Turned chair at Hereford Cathedral with Romanesque arcading and grooved rail for footstool, *c.* 1200

(*this page*)

PLATE 55A. Cat. 49. Back view of Hereford chair

PLATE 55B. Cat. 49. Seat area; note contrasting turnery

PLATE 57A. Cat. 51. Bench *in situ* along
the S. wall of the Abbot's Parlour,
Muchelney Abbey, *c.* 1500

PLATE 57B.   Cat. 51. Detail of single seat
on W. wall, adjacent to fireplace

(*facing page*)

PLATE 56.   Cat. 50. Chair in St James's
Church, Stanford Bishop; twelfth century
or earlier

PLATE 58A. Cat. 51. Bench at Muchelney;
detail of double seat on E. wall

PLATE 58B. Cat. 51. Seat locker on S.
wall showing position of lock

PLATE 59. Wrought ironwork on the S. door of the W. end of Nôtre
Dame de Paris (the Portal of St Anne)

(*facing page*)

PLATE 60A.   Reconstruction of a fifteenth-
century wardrobe (see Cat. 24)
(From Viollet-le-Duc 1858, pl. XVI)

PLATE 60B.   Narrow buffets in fifteenth-
century illuminations
(From Shaw, pl. XXV)

(*this page*)

PLATE 61A.   Narrow buffet in the
Vleehuis Museum, Antwerp, no. 31.E.23
(restored)

PLATE 61B.   Detail shows use of religious
ornament in secular furniture

PLATE 62A. Transitional furniture: armoire and narrow buffet combined, Vleehuis Museum, Antwerp, no. 31.E.24 (restored)

PLATE 62B. Detail of upper section with niche, anticipating later cabinet fittings

(*facing page*)

PLATE 63A. Detail of *The Last Supper* by Dieric Bouts, *c.* 1468 (Louvain)

PLATE 63B. Stools in the Metropolitan Museum of Art, Cloisters Collection

PLATE 64A. Illumination from the title-page of the second book of the Toison d'Or, *c.* 1473, with margins decorated with Burgundian ducal devices, C and M and marguerites

PLATE 64B. Altar chest at Newport, Essex

PLATE 65A. Altar chest at Newport; painted, raised lid forms
altar retable

PLATE 65B. Centre front showing lock plate, shields, and band
(formerly inlaid)

PLATE 66A. Lock plate on the entrance screen of Thomas Bekynton's chantry chapel, Wells Cathedral (Bekynton was Bishop of Bath and Wells 1443–65)

PLATE 66B. Door knocker of the palace of Jacques Cœur, Bourges, built 1443–54; plate original, knocker restored

(*facing page*)

PLATE 67. Charles V receiving an illuminated bible. Miniature by Jean Bandol, 1372 (MS. 10B 23, Rijksmuseum, The Hague)

PLATE 68.   Richard II. Panel painting of *c.* 1395, Westminster Abbey

(facing page)

PLATE 69.   Mutilated bench, Musée des Arts Décoratifs, bearing defaced
arms of Rigaud d'Aurelhe (no. 1049). Seats designed with lockers.
Attachment points of adjacent seat now missing, visible on right

PLATE 70A.   Fixed table of medieval type in the hall of
Winchester College

PLATE 70B.   Detail of chamfered support, cradle, and curved brace

PLATE 71A. Oak window shutters from a fifteenth-century house in the Brandstraat, Ghent (Bijloke Museum)

PLATE 71B. Concertina hinges permit two open positions revealing linenfold carving

PLATE 72A. Door of hall, Town Hall, Damme (N.E. corner), with original hinge straps and linenfold panels; this door apparently belongs to the building work of 1464

PLATE 72B. Stone laver with concealed drain in the Exchequer, Vicars Choral, Wells

PLATE 72C. Original carved oak panel incorporating hearts and shells on the chapel door, palace of Jacques Cœur, Bourges